AMERICAN

HOOPS

American Hoops

U.S. MEN'S OLYMPIC BASKETBALL
FROM BERLIN TO BEIJING

Carson Cunningham

UNIVERSITY OF NEBRASKA PRESS
LINCOLN

An earlier version of chapter 4 appeared as
"The Russell Model: Melbourne 1956 and
Bill Russell's New Basketball Standard" in
Olympika 15 (December 2006): 59–85.

An earlier version of chapter 12 appeared
as "Basketball Bedlam in Barcelona:
The Dream Team, a Reflection of the
Globe's 'New Order'" in *Journal of
Olympic History* 15, no. 3 (2007): 39–53.

Library of Congress Cataloging-
in-Publication Data
Cunningham, Carson.
American hoops : U.S. men's
olympic basketball from Berlin to
Beijing / Carson Cunningham.
p. cm.
Includes bibliographical
references and index.
ISBN 978-0-8032-2293-9
(cloth : alk. paper)
1. Basketball — History.
2. Olympics — History. I. Title.
GV883.C86 2009
796.3230973—dc22
2009027920

Set in Arno by Bob Reitz.
Designed by Nathan Putens.

CONTENTS

List of Illustrations *vii*

List of Tables *ix*

Acknowledgments *xi*

Introduction *xiii*

1. American Hoops Help
   Establish the International
   Standard in Berlin *1*

2. U.S. Basketball Advances the
   Game in Postwar London *29*

3. Cold War Basketball's Opening
   Salvo in Helsinki *61*

4. The Russell Model Revolutionizes
   the International Game
   in Melbourne *89*

5. Basketball Accelerates as
   Robertson, Lucas, and West
   Run through Rome *119*

6. In Liberal, Postwar Tokyo,
   Teamwork, Television, and a
   Cold War Tilt for Gold *150*

7. Haywood Shines as Satellites,
   Cable, and Shoes Mature
   in Mexico City *174*

8. Mayhem in Munich *202*

9. Trademark Speed Returns
   in Montreal, Then Politics
   Intrude in Moscow *233*

10. Air Jordan Arrives and
    The General Delivers
    in Los Angeles *257*

11. Oddities in Seoul Open the
    Lane for the Dream Team *288*

12. Basketball Bedlam in
    Barcelona *318*

13. From Underrated Greatness
    in Atlanta to the Gap
    Closed in Athens *350*

14. Reclamation in Beijing *385*

Notes *417*

Index *483*

ILLUSTRATIONS

1. An outdoor court in
   Berlin, 1936 3

2. Don Barksdale 44

3. The 1948 Olympic team 49

4. Robert "Jackie" Robinson 52

5. The 1948 team celebrates
   its gold medal 57

6. Bob Kurland and
   Marcus Freiberger 79

7. Vrais Akhtaev 92

8. Australia's Exhibition
   Building 108

9. Bill Russell and
   Chuck Darling 110

10. Oscar Robertson 147

11. Spencer Haywood 196

12. Premature U.S. victory
    celebration 225

13. Alexander Belov 227

14. Yugoslavia vs. the
    United States 250

15. Michael "Air" Jordan *282*

16. The Soviet Union gold
    medal team *314*

17. Magic, Pippen, Ewing,
    Jordan, and Barkley *329*

18. Charles Barkley and
    Vlade Divac *360*

19. Kevin Garnett *370*

20. The United States
    finishes third *380*

21. Team USA reclaims gold *412*

TABLES

All tables are courtesy of USA Basketball.

1. 1936 U.S. Men's Olympic Basketball cumulative stats *26*

2. 1948 U.S. Men's Olympic Basketball cumulative stats *59*

3. 1952 U.S. Men's Olympic Basketball cumulative stats *88*

4. 1956 U.S. Men's Olympic Basketball cumulative stats *117*

5. 1960 U.S. Men's Olympic Basketball cumulative stats *149*

6. 1964 U.S. Men's Olympic Basketball cumulative stats *172*

7. 1968 U.S. Men's Olympic Basketball cumulative stats *200*

8. 1972 U.S. Men's Olympic Basketball cumulative stats *232*

9. 1976 U.S. Men's Olympic Basketball cumulative stats *255*

10. 1980 U.S. Men's Olympic Basketball cumulative stats *256*

11. 1984 U.S. Men's Olympic
    Basketball cumulative stats *286*

12. 1988 U.S. Men's Olympic
    Basketball cumulative stats *316*

13. 1992 U.S. Men's Olympic
    Basketball cumulative stats *348*

14. 1996 U.S. Men's Olympic
    Basketball cumulative stats *382*

15. 2000 U.S. Men's Olympic
    Basketball cumulative stats *383*

16. 2004 U.S. Men's Olympic
    Basketball cumulative stats *384*

17. 2008 U.S. Men's Olympic
    Basketball cumulative stats *415*

ACKNOWLEDGMENTS

My love for basketball began in one of the places in which it is most celebrated: the great state of Indiana. And I have fellow Indianans, my parents, and my siblings to thank for that. *American Hoops* is an extension of that love and was first recommended as a dissertation project by Purdue professor and fine mentor, Dr. Randy Roberts. Thank you.

So many former Olympic players and coaches, as well as other major basketball figures, helped bring this book to fruition: Pete Newell, Larry Brown, Gene Keady, Robert "Jackie" Robinson, Vincent Boryla, Clyde Lovellette, William Hougland, Robert Kenney, Burdette Haldorson, Ron Tomsic, Terry Dischinger, Bill Hosket, Adrian Dantley, Tiit Sokk, Russ Granik, and John Wooden, to name several. Thank you all.

Thanks are due to the historians Patrick Hearden, Raymond Dumett, David Welky, Barbara Keys, and Aram Goudsouzian, among others, who helped tremendously. The LA 84 Foundation Sports Library (Los Angeles CA), the Naismith Memorial Basketball Hall of Fame's Edward J. and Gena G. Hickox Library (Springfield MA), the National Library of Estonia (Tallinn, Estonia), the United States Olympic Committee's archives (Colorado Springs CO), and the Amateur Athletic Union National Headquarters' archives (Orlando FL), are filled with helpful librarians and great information. My gratitude goes out to a host of collegiate libraries, including those at Purdue University, the University of Notre Dame, DePaul University, the University of Chicago, the University of Illinois, and the University of California, Los Angeles. Thank you to USA Basketball and the International Basketball Federation (FIBA), to IOC member Richard Pound and basketball guru Dan Dakich, to the keen eyes of Justin Smith and Eric Furman, and of course to the professional and astute folks who worked on this project for the University of Nebraska Press.

Most of all, thank you to my wife, Christy, and my children, Caroline and Case. As the late Al McGuire might have said, you are my seashells and balloons.

Over the past eighty years, basketball's sweeping international growth has come about because of the creativity and acumen of individuals on and off the court. The history of the U.S. men's basketball team at the Olympic Games shows this in striking fashion.

The U.S. team's history makes for a dynamic tale as it takes us from Olympic basketball's humble beginnings as a full-medal sport at the 1936 Games in Berlin, where the tournament took place outdoors in the rain, to Bill Russell's marvelous play in Melbourne, to the controversial 1972 U.S. versus Soviet Union gold medal matchup in Munich, where the final seconds of the game were replayed three times. It takes us to Michael Jordan's wondrous performances in Los Angeles and Barcelona, and it takes us to Beijing, where in a basketball-loving nation of over one billion, the 2008 U.S. men's Olympic basketball team made a valiant effort to return the United States to the pinnacle of the basketball world.

Drama packs this tale. So too do victory, loss, and redemption. Major issues arise, such as the impact of basketball and its superstars on popular culture in a world where free, socialist, and authoritarian countries compete for people's hearts and minds. The tale resonates on personal levels as well. Take U.S. Olympic basketball players Joe Fortenberry and Sam Balter at the original 1936 tournament. Not too long after coming back from those Games, Fortenberry would serve in the U.S. military in its effort to turn back Hitler. And Balter, a Jewish American basketball player, would decide that because of Hitler's horrificness he should not have even attended those Games.

Tracing the story of U.S. Olympic men's basketball reveals how hard the players work, the simple joy to be found in playing, coaching, or watching the sport, and much as well about the dynamic relationship basketball fosters between individuality and teamwork. The tale highlights the pride players have felt in representing the United States but also the racism that some of those very same players have had to confront in their home country.

Despite their modest start in Berlin, the Olympics and basketball have made a successful partnership. Both enjoy striking popularity in the new millennium. In 2008 the Olympic movement boasted 205 member nations, which was greater than the United Nations' membership. For the Beijing Games, television viewership numbered 4.7 billion people, about 70 percent of the world's population.[1] Meanwhile, the International Basketball Federation (FIBA), which sanctions Olympic basketball, partners with more than 210 different nations.[2] Billions of people play and watch basketball worldwide, and the sport's stars are known from the Himalayas to the American plains. And the Olympic basketball tournament stands as one of the Olympic festival's most popular events, while the U.S. squad counts as the tournament's marquee team. Therefore, it makes sense to examine basketball in the global age through the U.S. men's basketball team at the Games.

Even the most basic components of the squad's history, which features a diverse cast of characters, a merit-based selection process, high-scoring, and an innovative style of play, help explain basketball's emergence. From a broader perspective, its history relates to nearly all of the world's major issues, from race relations to liberalism to globalization to the behavior of multinational corporations. Olympic basketball has also tested many of America's favorite ideals.

Among U.S. Olympic basketball's colorful cast of past players are the aforementioned Balter, who went on to post-Olympic fame as a sports announcer, radio commentator, and movie actor; Russell, who in Melbourne showed that he was the consummate teammate; and, of course, the artful Jordan.[3] There is also Don Barksdale, the first African American basketball Olympian; Oscar "The Big O" Robertson, a thoroughly dominant force; Jerry Lucas, a middle-America marketer's dream with an elephantine memory and eccentric persona; Larry Bird, a former sanitation worker from Indiana; Earvin "Magic" Johnson, who helped put a human face on HIV/AIDS and has built a remarkable business empire in the wake of his international basketball success; and Dwyane Wade, initially the least heralded of the newest batch of American stars. Among those who have coached the U.S. team are Jimmy Needles, Pete Newell, Hank Iba, Dean Smith, Bob Knight, John Thompson, Chuck Daly, Lenny Wilkens, Rudy Tomjanovich, Larry Brown, and Mike Krzyzewski.

As for the team's worldwide impact, a poignant example of that took place at the 1992 Olympic Games in Barcelona when three forces—liberal capitalism, technological innovation, and basketball—blossomed with exquisite timing. This flowering led to the phenomenon that was the "Dream Team."

With the Berlin wall down and the iron curtain lifted, the *New York Times* dubbed the 1992 Barcelona Games, which a record 172 countries attended, the "New Order Olympics."[4] It was also a "New Order Olympics" for basketball, as these Games marked the first appearance of full-fledged professionals participating on behalf of the United States, resulting in the greatest basketball team of all time. International reaction to the Dream Team, from fans across the globe to multinational corporations, was astonishingly positive. Deputy Secretary General of the USOC and marketing legend John Krimsky said: "There are young people out there who think the Olympics are one big basketball tournament."[5]

Basketball's attractiveness as a game of action, aided by the deft marketing efforts of multinational corporations and America's position as a global leader in capital and innovation, helped turn the Dream Team stars into some of the most recognizable faces on the planet—particularly Jordan, whose effect on culture transcended sport.[6] The historian Walter LaFeber puts Jordan's popularity into perspective by noting that at the end of the twentieth century, Chinese schoolchildren selected Jordan as one of the two greatest figures in twentieth-century history; the other was the Communist revolutionary Zhou Enlai.[7] The Dream Team's imprint on international basketball will last well into the new millennium.

It was just before the turn of the nineteenth century in Massachusetts that a young Canadian immigrant named James Naismith invented basketball. Soon the sport was played on a global level. In an interview with the author, the Naismith Hall of Fame coach and player John Wooden summed up basketball's appeal well, saying, "It's played with the largest object, more or less in the smallest area, and it is, when played properly, a game of action."[8]

The skills needed to handle its easy-to-see ball, the footwork it demands within relatively tight boundaries, and its calls for bursts of controlled athleticism help create a form of play that is alluring to the human mind.

Just four years after Naismith conjured basketball, Pierre de Coubertin officially started the modern Olympic movement, the charter of which presently calls for "respect for universal fundamental ethical principles" and maintains that "any form of discrimination with regard to a country or person on grounds of race, religion, politics, gender or otherwise is incompatible with belonging to the Olympic Movement." By the time basketball became an official part of the Games in 1936, the liberal, capitalist-leaning Olympic movement had evolved into a massive international festival.[9] By 2008 the International Olympic Committee (IOC) was using market-style methods to generate massive revenues and to give a striking level of visibility to its value-infused product.[10] In the meantime, basketball became a major part of the Olympic program.

The first few Olympic basketball tournaments, from 1936 to 1952, were marked by the codifying of its rules, the arrival of the Soviets, and the establishment of the traditional big man as a dominant force—even as scoring and the speed of play increased.

Nearly all of the important rule changes that took place during that time emanated from the United States, where a faster and more creative brand of basketball resided than that in most other parts of the world. At the time, America's representative body for Olympic basketball was the Amateur Athletic Union (AAU), and the AAU played the lead role in getting the new Olympic basketball rules adopted. Driven largely by commercial considerations, these rule changes sped up the sport and gave its players more opportunities to innovate. Considering the AAU's and the Olympic movement's emphasis on amateurism, it was ironic that AAU basketball's commercial thrust helped bring about these rule changes.[11] It was also fortuitous—because the changes spurred by commercial considerations attracted more fans to the sport.

The Soviet Union's appearance on the Olympic stage occurred at the end of this early period of Olympic basketball, in 1952 under Joseph Stalin. Despite its decades-long aversion to western-styled sporting federations, the Soviet Union chose to participate because it could not deny the Olympics' significance, and because it wanted to use the Games to showcase its culture. From the outset, the Soviets made a point to emphasize Olympic basketball, which led to the greatest team-sport rivalry in Olympic history. It also led Soviet officials to exhaustively search for tall talent to combat the "American Gullivers." That search resulted in the appearance of a veritable Soviet giant at the 1956 Games in Melbourne, where the seven-feet-four-inch Ivan Krumminch, a former woodcutter, suited up against Bill Russell and the Americans.[12]

In addition to the appearance of a slew of Soviet Gullivers, the Olympiads from 1956 to 1964 were marked by increased scoring and further rule changes, as well as by a diverse group of American players, especially Russell and Robertson, who capitalized on the changed rules to create new models of play. Both brought versatility to their positions, and Russell, as the author was told by the 1960 Olympic coach Pete Newell, quixotically affected the game in another major way at the Olympics. Newell pointed to the six-feet-eleven-inch Russell as the reason behind FIBA's decision to make the lane trapezoid-shaped, a change intended to limit the impact of big men. The rule came into effect after Russell had dominated at the 1956 Melbourne Games (before him, American big men Bob Kurland, Clyde Lovellette, and Joe Fortenberry had dominated too).[13] In addition to new styles, models of players, and rules, from 1956 to 1964 the emergence of television and the beginnings of satellite and cable technology enhanced the diffusion of sports.

Subsequently, during the 1970s and 1980s, ever-improving play worldwide, cold war rivalry, and breathtaking advances in an array of technologies and products highlighted the Olympic basketball tournaments. The technological and product innovations took place on a number of fronts, from the shoe industry to the computer industry to fiber optics. And in combination with creative players, these advances propelled the sport forward, leading to the Dream Team and contributing greatly to basketball's cultural currency.[14]

Of course, the story does not end with the Dream Team. Soon after the Berlin wall crumbled and the emotions associated with the cold war melted away, the Olympic basketball tournament entered a new phase. In a more free and economically open world, that phase, rather than reflecting American cultural and economic dominance, which many had predicted would be the Dream Team's legacy, was instead a striking reflection of how the world had flattened.

The Dream Team itself helped forge this new phase, because in 1992 it created a standard that, by 2002, a number of international teams had demonstrated an ability to approach more effectively than the United States. As the long-time journalist and author Thomas Friedman has suggested, the success of international players and the teams they played on forced the United States to rethink its own game. A lack of teamwork became the prime source of American woes. In fact, Friedman used the 2004 U.S. Olympic team in Athens as a symbol of how excessive individualism can hurt America on a global stage that features increasingly open economic models and intense competition.[15] By 2005, U.S. basketball had found itself in a new position within the very international sporting community it had helped forge: either adapt or continue to face defeats.

In addition to accentuating more teamwork, U.S. struggles in international competition brought a reemphasis, ironically enough, on speed. Spurred by the effective styles of teams like Argentina and players like Manu Ginobli, Dirk Nowitzki and Steve Nash, as well as the tactics of coaches such as Mike D'Antoni, who was groomed as a professional player and coach in Europe, America has begun adapting its game to meet the challenge.

While teamwork has regained prominence of late, the importance of standout individual play has remained. This relationship between the team and the individual is an important part of basketball. With five easily identifiable players on each side operating in relatively tight boundaries, basketball can showcase individual stars while also promoting teamwork. Historically, balancing the seeming divide between the individual and the community has been a staple component of American popular culture.[16] Basketball can allow its star players to balance these two basic precepts in appealing fashion.

In fact, Scott Bedbury, the head of Nike advertising from 1987 to 1994, has suggested that Nike found success by capitalizing on people's "near-universal desire for greater personal freedom" as well as their need to be part of a group.[17] And basketball helped Nike tap into those emotions well, especially through its association with Jordan. At the Barcelona Games, Jordan showed that a celebration of the individual and the team could happen simultaneously in a way that changed the game on a global level. In the process, and with the help of the marketing efforts of transnational firms like Nike, he proved that basketball can have, just as the film historian Robert Ray asserts movies do, an effect on "the way we live now."[18]

Of course, the story of basketball's rise to global prominence is not a seamless tale. At various points and to varying degrees, basketball has been associated with a number of problems of the modern global era. As you will see, among these are racial issues, the exploitation of cheap labor in countries controlled by authoritarian regimes, super-nationalism, and, as Friedman has noted, overwrought individuality.

Nonetheless, evidence of basketball's worldliness is all around. As an example, for the 2008 Games, Beijing officials agreed to stage many events, including swimming and gymnastics, at times favorable to NBC (in other words, quite early in the day in China)—but not basketball.[19] NBC pushed for basketball time changes, but the sport was too popular in China and elsewhere for the U.S. network to get special consideration in scheduling it. Other examples of basketball's internationalism abound. In 2008, the NBA featured seventy-six players from thirty-one countries, a development sometimes referred to as the Dream Team effect. For the NBA Finals that year, which aired in 205 countries and in over forty different languages, seven international players suited up. With NBC Universal and other firms delivering Olympic basketball to millions around the globe, international players like Ginobli, Nowitzki, and Nash have contributed stylistic advances to basketball, while enhancing the sport's global popularity.[20]

Basketball's internationalism suggests a more dynamic relationship with the world than single-dimension American domination. In turn, then, nationalism has been forced to give ground to a shared global basketball language. It may not be a true language in the traditional sense, but it can be expressed through a sweet pass, a wicked crossover, or an awe-inspiring slam. And its terms fit well with the open, competitive, and universalistic framework of the international sporting community. The history of U.S. Olympic basketball helps explain the nature of this language.

1

AMERICAN HOOPS HELP ESTABLISH THE
INTERNATIONAL STANDARD IN BERLIN

On August 14, 1936, in Hitler's Berlin, the United States beat Canada 19–8 to win the world's first Olympic basketball gold medal. The game was played outdoors in a downpour and on a dirt and clay court described by the *New York Times* as a "sea of mud."[1] Hindered by the adverse conditions, players found simple passes and close shots difficult; dribbling was nearly impossible. Summing it up, the *Washington Post* asserted that the game "might have been better had it been played under water polo rules."[2] Even with the lack of flow, the low score, and the inclement weather, however, the contest was a seminal event. This humble beginning marked an important step in basketball's rise in the global age.

At its inception, the Olympic basketball competition was far behind the standards maintained by basketball's leading nations. From a performance standpoint, many of the Olympic players lacked basic skills, and the Olympians played under outdated rules compared to those in nations like the United States. Time-outs were disallowed, only one unpaid referee per game officiated, no three-seconds-in-the-lane rule existed, and no rule limiting a team to ten seconds for advancing the ball past half-court was enforced. Only seven of the players on a roster were allowed to suit up for any given contest, and just two substitutions were permitted per game. In contrast to the rules enforced at the Berlin Games, for its 1934–35 basketball season, the Amateur Athletic Union (AAU) limited players to three seconds in the lane and forced them to advance the ball across half-court in less than ten seconds. That same year, the AAU reduced the size of its basketballs from thirty-two inches in circumference to thirty inches in order to make dribbling easier (the center-jump was not eliminated until 1937, but it too ultimately gave way to the appeal of faster play). The collegiate game had sped up considerably by 1936, too, partly on account of rule changes passed before the 1934–35 season. Like the AAU's rules, those changes relieved congestion around the basket. Commenting on the new rules after the 1934–35 season, Nat Holman, coach of the College of the City of New York, said they "were necessary and basketball profited immensely because of them."[3]

In addition to outdated rules, an outdoor venue, and shortcomings in players' skills, the 1936 Olympic tournament was plagued by inadequate equipment (the Berg ball players used in Berlin was lopsided, stitched, and ungrained). So although the first tournament drew solidly—an estimated 10,000 fans filtered in and out of the Olympic basketball venue on the opening day of action—it became obvious by tournament's end that the faster brand of basketball played by the likes of the United States represented the sport's future.[4] Sam Balter, the U.S. team's only Jewish player and later a sports journalist and play-by-play man for the Cincinnati Reds, described the tournament as "a comedy of errors and unfortunate circumstances."[5] Yet this is what made 1936 Olympic basketball so important. Its logistical shortcomings, inadequate equipment, and outdated rules forced action on the part of representatives from the International Basketball Federation (FIBA) to standardize the international game. Consequently, the new standards called for a faster and more open style—the style that has attracted so many fans in the second half of the twentieth century and beyond.

Ironically, most of the new rules FIBA adopted in the wake of the 1936 Olympic basketball tournament had been implemented by the AAU largely on account of commercial considerations. Elite AAU teams functioned

1. One of the outdoor courts in Berlin during a game between Mexico and the Philippines. Olympic Museum Collections. Copyright © IOC.

essentially as commercial entities, partly because corporations sponsored them, and both the AAU brass and its corporate sponsors realized that fans tended to find fast, creative basketball attractive. In fact, before the rule changes, basketball's comparably slower pace and lack of inventiveness had caused signs of disinterest. In 1932 the *New York Herald Tribune*'s Red Smith highlighted the threat this posed to organizations such as the AAU when he wrote: "It will be remembered that the manly art of stalling, the slow break and the sleepy, center-feed style of play which came into general use during the last few years so slowed up the game that last season the customers stayed away very briskly."[6] His sentiments indicated that the market called for speedier play and more innovative action. Ultimately, basketball leaders responded. The AAU's and college game's mid-1930s rule changes demonstrated that they had received the message. And thanks to the Olympics, FIBA did too.

To be sure, even with these rule changes, the international rise of basketball did not take place overnight. In 1936, a number of developments that would dramatically change the world had yet to happen: the Second World War, the postwar emergence of the United States as the eminent economic superpower, the lengthy cold war, and the marvelous technological advances from the 1970s on. As these things unfolded, basketball's reach expanded dramatically. Still, in 1936 the initial seeds of a major international basketball tournament that would enable the sport's international language to take root needed planting. And on the dirt and clay courts of Hitler's Berlin, they were.

By 1936 the sport had generated noteworthy interest around the globe, particularly in the United States, many parts of South America, and parts of Asia—especially China, where crowds at basketball games routinely numbered over 10,000 (China's 1936 National Basketball Tournament in Beijing drew an average of 23,000 spectators per game).[7] But basketball did not have a signature international event to build upon until the 1936 Olympics.

It is ironic that the first Olympic tournament for basketball took place in Nazi Germany, not only because Germany was slow to catch on to basketball, but also because Hitler and his henchmen did not, theoretically, support modern sports. Nazi leaders detested that modern sports had originated in England, and that modern sports functioned as equalizers, insomuch as a core tenet of modern sport was that race, religion, and ideology should not matter on the field. Sports received scant mention in Hitler's *Mein Kampf* and in the party's newspaper *Der volkische Beobachter*.[8] In many respects, this aversion to modern sports made sense for Nazis, because the merit-based nature of sports works well with the values associated with open markets and democracy. But in the end, the cultural attractiveness of modern sports proved too powerful for the Nazis to ignore—even though sport took on an increasingly liberal capitalist character in the 1930s.[9]

The IOC had actually awarded the 1936 Olympics to Germany's Weimar Republic in 1931: Hitler simply inherited them when the Nazis came to power in 1933. The IOC responded to Hitler's emergence with a meeting in Vienna to review Berlin as a site. Initially, many Nazi leaders thought Hitler would not accommodate the IOC, given his distaste for modern sports, Germany's contentious relationship with the Olympic movement over the years, and its tradition of *Turnen* athletics, which emphasized "synchronized calisthenics to foster collective discipline." However, the propaganda maestro Josef Goebbels persuaded Hitler that the Games could serve as a showpiece for the Nazi government, so Hitler guaranteed the IOC that his Nazi regime would respect the Olympic movement's ideals. As part of that guarantee, the Nazis agreed to a number of conditions, including allowing Jewish participation on its teams, even though at the time Jews were banned from the private clubs that served as the center of German athletics. Armed with Hitler's assurances, the IOC decided to move forward with the Berlin Games.[10] In hindsight, it is clear that some IOC members did not sufficiently challenge the Nazis for disrespecting Olympic ideals, and Hitler's ultimate use of the Games to promote German nationalism remains a stark reminder of how the Olympics can be manipulated in a sinister fashion.[11] Yet, on balance, this has not ruined the Games' ability to carry out the goals of facilitating peaceful exchange and promoting ethical principles. As the historian Barbara Keys has noted, the Nazis displayed organizational efficiency in putting on the Games, but "at the price of allowing other messages—about the virtues of internationalism and the achievements of other races—a prominent place in the narrative of the Berlin Games."[12]

In the United States, AAU president Avery Brundage, considered by many to hold anti-Semitic and other prejudiced views, agreed with the

IOC's decision to support Germany as host.[13] Brundage, who after the Berlin Games went on to have a long career as head of what is now called the U.S. Olympic Committee (USOC) and then as president of the IOC, even went to Germany to review the situation himself. He reported back that all was well. This verdict came as no surprise to his critics, who, as would subsequent biographers, accused him of sympathizing with Nazi Germany.[14] But regardless of Brundage's motives, his decision to support Berlin as the host city was quite important for U.S. basketball, because the AAU was America's representative in FIBA, which regulated the Olympic basketball tournament.[15] In fact, given the AAU's considerable influence in the 1930s, Brundage's support of Hitler's Berlin played an important role in quelling support for a U.S. boycott of the Olympics in general.

Still, some did challenge Brundage's position on the issue.[16] A final objection occurred in December 1935 when AAU members met to vote on whether or not to participate in the Games. Not without its fair share of controversy, this meeting ultimately recommitted the U.S. Olympic basketball committee to Berlin. Patrick J. Walsh, a Brundage crony, scored a political victory by opening the proceedings with a motion to stop discussion on the prospect of a boycott. The motion passed by a 61–55 margin, cutting short the much-anticipated debate. The AAU president, Judge Jeremiah T. Mahoney, who supported a boycott, was then defeated in a second vote, this one regarding whether Mahoney could go on an official fact-finding mission to Germany. As a result, he resigned, paving the way for Avery Brundage to retake the AAU's top job.[17] Any boycotts from then on would be the result of individual action. Indeed, some did choose to boycott. In fact, the entire 1935–36 Long Island University squad, coached by the legendary Clair Bee and winner of the previous year's unofficial NCAA championship, boycotted the Olympic trials, citing distaste for the Nazis' treatment of Jews to explain its decision.[18] The absence of Long Island University was no small matter. For part of the 1935–36 season, the team was in the midst of a record forty-three-game winning streak.

As it turned out, only one Jewish player, Balter, a former starter at UCLA and a star on the AAU's 1936 Universal Pictures team, actually qualified for the Olympic squad. Urged to boycott by the likes of the *California Jewish Voice*, among others, his qualification caused an "awful dilemma" for him. As his teammate Art Mollner recalled, "He [Balter] got a lot of telegrams from people who did want him to compete."[19] Despite the concerns, Balter chose to play, explaining that he wanted to "see for himself" the situation in Germany. His wife weighed in as well, saying that she neither feared for his safety nor questioned the ethics of his decision. She did, however, predict that Hitler would not "show his hand" at the games.[20] After the Berlin Games, however, Balter said it had been a mistake to participate. He spoke out about the issue as host of a radio program in Philadelphia by criticizing the American Olympic Committee's "whitewashing," as the historian David Clay Large puts it, of the Nazis' racial practices. In turn, the AOC secretary Frederick Rubien wrote to Avery Brundage that it was "highly desirable" to develop a plan to "exclude individuals of Balter's type from future Olympic teams regardless of athletic ability."[21]

Balter may have chosen to participate, but the sponsor of his AAU team, Universal Pictures, chose not to. Founded by Carl Laemmle, a Jewish immigrant from Eastern Europe, Universal Pictures supported the boycott movement and in turn did not support its team's efforts to play in the Games. As Mollner remembered, Laemmle and his son "wanted nothing to do with it [the Olympics]."[22] This left the team's players with the responsibility of finding their own way to New York City for the April 1936 Olympic qualifying tournament in Madison Square Garden. They financed the trip by playing a series of exhibition games en route.[23]

The Universal Pictures team, out of Hollywood, California, played its regular season in an "industrial league" that the AAU recognized as amateur—these leagues functioned as the leading adult leagues in the United States and as commercial enterprises. The leagues' top teams had corporate partners such as Universal Pictures. In the case of the AAU's McPherson Globe Refiners (also known as the Oilers), out of McPherson, Kansas, the team received sponsorship from the Globe Oil & Refining Co. The Globe Refiners played their regular season in the Missouri Valley (Industrial) League. In addition to demonstrating support for sports, these corporations sponsored teams in the AAU as a way to increase visibility. As *Time* magazine explained in 1936, the Globe Oilers' players "should be employed by a central Kansas oil concern in a town of 5,000 and that their basketball ramblings should be paid for by the company is less mysterious than it seems. Like Universal Pictures' five, and thousands of similar groups in the U.S., they are a company promotion scheme."[24] Competition among the various sponsors to procure players and win games was fierce. A common inducement offered to elite players was a job working for a particular team's title sponsor.

The AAU's Globe Oilers and Universal team qualified for the trials in Madison Square Garden by reaching the AAU's championship game. This seems odd by modern standards, because the method utilized to select the 1936 Olympic squad stands in marked contrast to recent ones. In fact, the selection process has changed rather consistently throughout the history of U.S. Olympic basketball. For 1936, the basketball committee, which comprised six AAU officials, four NCAA representatives, two American Olympic Association (AOA, now called the USOC) members, and honorary member Dr. James Naismith, reserved five slots in its eight-team qualifying tournament at Madison Square Garden for the NCAA, two for the AAU, and one for a YMCA squad. Seven players from the Olympic-qualifying tournament champion, six players from the tourney's runner-up, and an alternate from the remaining teams in the field, rather than a collection of all-stars, were ultimately sent to Berlin.

On the surface, it looked like the structure favored the NCAA, since five NCAA teams were eligible for the quarterfinal field, but the process really favored the AAU. For example, to determine which five NCAA teams had the right to attend the Olympic qualifying tournament, the committee forced NCAA member institutions to endure a series of regional contests apart from the NCAA's regular season.[25] Meanwhile, the committee determined that the two AAU teams for the Olympic qualifying tournament would simply be the two finalists from the AAU's annual national tournament, which came to Denver, Colorado, in 1935 and remained there until 1968. Likewise, the YMCA representative would be the champion of its annual tournament held in Peoria, Illinois.[26] This meant that in preparation for the qualifying tournament, neither the AAU nor the YMCA had to alter their usual schedules or pay extra expenses. In fact, both could keep any extra money generated as a result of their tournaments, because none of the proceeds from them were earmarked for the committee's coffers. Sure, the NCAA technically got the most berths in the qualifying tournament, but the process required to land one of those berths seems to have dissuaded a number of teams from participating.

As an indication of this, Mr. A. A. Schabinger, who was hired to run the NCAA's complicated portion of the trials process, encountered difficulties in recruiting NCAA teams. Ultimately, the majority of colleges and universities in the NCAA, most of whom had supported the movement to get basketball on the Olympic program, chose not to play. Presidents and athletic directors offered a number of reasons for their absences; among the most commonly cited were the expense of traveling to regional contests, fatigue from the regular season schedule, a desire to protect team records, opposition to the United States' participation in Hitler's Games, and the fear that participation would take too much time away from studies.[27] Early on, Purdue and Notre Dame, both considered among the nation's top teams, cited time-commitment issues when announcing their decisions not to participate. Then in March, as noted, Bee's Long Island Blackbirds announced that they "had decided not to compete because the university would not, under any circumstances, be represented in the Olympic Games held in Germany."[28]

Largely as a result of the NCAA's reluctance to participate in it, the qualifying process failed miserably. The secretary of the U.S. Olympic Basketball Committee, J. Lyman Bingham, wrote in his official post-Olympic report that the committee had initially planned to make $100,000 to $200,000 from the NCAA qualifying games. Instead, it barely broke even. Secretary Bingham stated that no one had predicted that "America's most popular sport, which attracted 80 million spectators during the year of 1935, would not be able to adequately finance its own squad to the Olympic Games."[29]

Indeed, Bingham's and the rest of the committee's initial projections were understandable. During the 1935–36 basketball season, college games across the country sold out. In January 1936 *Newsweek*, citing the fact that New York University (NYU) basketball attendance had eclipsed football attendance, declared that NYU basketball had surpassed football in popularity.[30] Undoubtedly, the presence of more prominent college teams at the Olympic qualifying tournament would have enabled the committee to at least come closer to meeting its goals. But the absence of so many leading college teams, coupled with the fact that the two AAU teams making it to the finals in Madison Square Garden came from Kansas and California, proved too much to overcome. So even though basketball's popularity was growing wildly in 1936, the qualifying tournament at Madison Square Garden was unable to capitalize on this success.

The watered-down Olympic qualifying field saw the Universals and the Globe Oilers advance to the finals with relative ease. Both companies had gone to great lengths to tap top talent to play and work for them. Universal featured a number of former collegiate stars, mostly from UCLA, as did the Globe Oilers, though its players came more predominantly from the Midwest and were particularly tall—a characteristic of basketball teams that was not yet entirely common at this point in time. That the Globe team's height was unusual was indicated by *Time* magazine's characterization of the squad as a "collection of athletic freaks." The magazine also noted that when the team traveled, its taller players slept "on hotel bedroom floors."[31] Ironically, like Universal Pictures, Globe Oil also refused to support its team's efforts to represent the United States in the Olympics, but while the objections of Universal Pictures were political in nature, the Globe Company simply thought its players would miss too much time from work if they went to Berlin.[32] The lack of interest expressed by Globe Oil management indicated that the Olympic basketball tournament, at this time, was not yet considered a major event. However, in the case of both Universal and Globe, the players decided to play in the Olympics anyway.

In the qualifying tournament final, Universal, which the *Los Angeles Times* maintained came to the trials "still disregarded by the hoop know-alls," managed to win a tight affair 44–43. The squad had lost two games to the Oilers earlier that year, one of them occurring just two weeks beforehand at the AAU championship, making the victory in the trials that much sweeter.[33] Though they were shorter, the Universals played more deliberately, while the Oilers were known for their "fire-department" style of play. Oilers coach Gene Johnson, considered among the early innovators of fast-break tactics, explained his team's style by stating, "We like to turn the game into a wild, helter-skelter, all-over-the-court scuffle . . . because we play bad basketball better than the other fellow."[34]

To combat this at Madison Square Garden, the Universals hoped to limit miscues by implementing a "slow breaking offense" against the Oilers' aggressive zone defense with "man-to-man principles." On defense, the Universal squad played an active man-to-man defense with zone principles—in other words, with much "switching."[35] These strategies ultimately helped Universal win, although from an international standpoint, its offensive attack was hardly methodical, considering it resulted in forty-four points. That this was considered slow in America reflected how in 1936, by global standards, even some of the more deliberate American teams scored abundantly. Furthermore, the Universal method of play did not mean the team was inactive on the court. In fact, the player Frank Lubin recalled that his Universal team benefited from running the Oilers around: "I think we tired the McPherson Globe Oilers by running them so fast," he remembered, and added, "Because we played them before, we utilized our experience against them and learned how to attack their zone defense, their big men." Universal did this by "running around in the corners and getting shots that they never expected us to take."[36] (Exploiting the corners against zones remains a common practice.)

All told, the Universal team sent seven players to Berlin. Lubin, along with Balter, not only played lead roles amongst those seven but represent how the U.S. Olympic team managed a measure of diversity in Berlin, even though the team did not include any African Americans.

At the turn of the century, before Frank Lubin was born, his parents came to the United States from Lithuania. "They were forced out of Lithuania by Russia, which occupied their country," Lubin explained late in life. Young Frank did not pick up basketball until high school, and he did so then mainly because his pole-vaulting efforts had sputtered. At first, given his long frame, which was listed at anywhere from six feet four to six feet seven, he was used mainly to win the center jump. And even at UCLA, where he became the first of the Lubin clan to attend college, he was not known as a scorer. This made Lubin a fairly unlikely candidate to have the effect that he ultimately had on basketball, both at home and abroad. But his hardwood exploits eventually earned him the nickname "Frankenstein Lubin" in America, and then the reputation as the "Godfather of Lithuanian basketball."[37]

Both his nickname and his "Godfather" standing were earned in an odd fashion, and both indicated basketball's commercialism and diffusion. After college, Lubin initially studied law at Berkeley, but a short stint working for a law firm disinclined him toward a tort career. This, coupled with lean times back at his parents' home in Southern California, motivated him to return to Los Angeles. There, Frank Pierce, a Hollywood makeup artist, of all things, who loved basketball, recruited Lubin to play for the AAU's Universal team. In turn, Pierce found Lubin work at the studio, as he did for many of his players.

On the AAU circuit, Lubin's game started to mature. By the mid-1930s he had started to master offensive moves from the pivot position and to shoot effectively with both hands, becoming one of the team's standout players. In 1935 the Universal team took a basketball road trip through the heartland while Universal Picture's *Bride of Frankenstein*, for which Pierce served as the makeup man, was in release. To publicize the film, Pierce asked if he could "make me [Lubin] up as Frankenstein" before the games. Lubin agreed. So, before the pregame warm-ups, Lubin, with makeup on his face, little metal things jutting out the side of his neck, a ragged coat, and shoes raised six inches, would "come out and stimulate the crowd, walk in front of them and they'd get excited." Soon, Lubin explained, "All around the Midwest, and I don't know how far east . . . I was 'Frankenstein Lubin,' that's where I got my nickname." This tale sheds light on the relationship between corporations, basketball, and the AAU, and by extension, the Olympic Games, even at this early period. As Lubin recalled, "Here in Southern California, and I think all over the United States, organizations, clubs and studios in Hollywood were organizing teams for publicity purposes, and perhaps write-offs."[38] Although technically he never directly received "a penny" for playing basketball from Universal or later with Twentieth Century Fox, Lubin did admit that in return for playing on AAU teams, "most of the players did get jobs, which was very nice." Regarding the Phillips Oilers, a perennially dominant AAU team, Lubin said, "They traveled around so much that I wonder whether any of them did any work."[39]

While Lubin's American nickname hinted at the commercial forces behind AAU basketball, the reputation he earned as the "Godfather" of Lithuanian basketball hinted at how the first Olympic basketball tournament, in addition to crystallizing the sport's international standards, affected the advancement of the international game. It was in Berlin, soon after the United States won the gold medal, that a member of the Lithuanian government invited Lubin and his family to Lithuania. Once there, Lubin, his father, his wife, and his sister-in-law "met the President of Lithuania . . . went to banquet after banquet and for a week and a half we just had a beautiful time." But near the scheduled end of the trip, while the family was traveling to visit Lubin's father's sister-in-law in the countryside, Lubin's wife broke her leg when their wagon tipped over. This forced the Lubins to stay in Lithuania for a few extra months as she convalesced. It just happened to be basketball season there, and as a result, Frank was asked to train Lithuanian athletes.

By the end of the Lubins' already extended stay, officials pleaded with them to remain in Lithuania even longer. When Frank said they could not, officials asked him to consider returning in a year to help train athletes for the 1938 all-Lithuanian Olympics and the subsequent 1939 European basketball championship to be hosted by Lithuania. The Lubins did return, and Frank, in a stadium filled with 12,000 seated spectators and 14,000 more standing in specially built aisles, led his Lithuanian team as a player-coach to the European championship. The pivotal win in that championship run came against Latvia, the winner of the inaugural 1935 European championship, which had sent a few of its players to New York and Philadelphia to learn the American style of play. Recalling the victory decades later, Lubin said, "I think they carried us around the floor for ten minutes there. They couldn't get the second game going, they were so excited."[40]

In subsequent decades the Soviet Union competed against the United States with basketball rosters that included many Lithuanians. And as Lubin said, "It was found out that they had taken up a lot of the young athletes that I had coached." In the 1980s, with the versatile Lithuanian Aryvidas Sabonis causing fits for the United States in international competition, Lubin noted, "I didn't coach him, naturally; I don't think he was born when I was in Lithuania. But he has been trained by individuals I trained and has been taught methods I introduced in Lithuania over fifty years ago." That the Soviets co-opted the Lithuanian basketball tradition and used numerous Lithuanian players during the cold war caused Lubin to opine, "I don't know whether I'm famous, or infamous, for having helped the Russian team by teaching the young Lithuanians how to play the American style of basketball."[41] Of course, the story did not end with the Soviet Union. At the 1992 Olympic Games Lithuania fielded its own team, one that served as a symbol of the nation's resilience. It beat the Russia-backed Unified Team in those Games, and then at the 2004 Olympics, Lithuania toppled the Americans.

Before he would make his trip to Lithuania, Lubin, and his fellow Universal Olympians, needed to get to New York again—this time by mid-July to catch the ship to Europe for the Olympics. Compounding the difficulty of that task was the fact that by that time, Universal Pictures had already taken "their name off of our back and said they could not sponsor us to go to Nazi Germany." Therefore, when makeup-man Pierce received the telegram stipulating that his players needed to make it on their own accord to New York by July 12, Lubin recalled, "We were in a bad way."[42]

To raise the necessary funds for travel, the Universal Olympians scheduled exhibition action again. Before leaving for New York, they played games at Los Angeles's Olympic Auditorium thanks to the help of the sports editor of the *Los Angeles Times*, Baven Dyer Sr., who arranged the opposing squads, which were composed of collegians from USC, UCLA, and Loyola. He organized one of those teams a little too effectively, as they beat the future Olympians 22–20, prompting speculation that the Olympians "weren't strong enough."[43] In addition to the exhibitions in LA, the Universal Olympians played games as they traveled to New York City in places like Kansas City, Topeka, Tulsa, and Denver.[44] Also helping finance the squad were Hollywood stars associated with Universal Pictures, such as Boris Karloff, a horror film icon and Pierce's actual Frankenstein. Along with Karloff, John Boles, who played the lead in *Bride of Frankenstein*, donated money to the team.[45]

Even with these efforts, it was not certain that the Universal players would actually make it to Berlin. In 1939, Forrest "Phog" Allen recalled, "I talked with the manager of the McPherson Oilers. He stated to me that the boys on both the Universal Picture Company of Hollywood and the McPherson Oilers actually had to put up their jewelry and borrow money to make the trip to Berlin. It was a sorry mess."[46] Late in life, Lubin, laughing at the recollection, said that during this second trip to New York, "I telegraphed my wife and my dad and my wife's sister, who were in New York, and I said: 'Don't get on the boat to go to Berlin until you see us there.'"[47]

As runners-up at the trials, the McPherson Globe Oilers secured six Olympic roster spots, and the University of Washington's Ralph Bishop rounded out the team. Originally, the committee intended to send fifteen players, but the limited funds generated by the qualifying tournament led them to choose only fourteen. Furthermore, initially, the committee had reserved eight spots for the qualifying tournament winner and five for the second-place team. But when Universal's Lloyd Goldstein ended up not participating in the trials, even though he had traveled with the Universal squad from the West Coast, the committee decided to take six players from the second-place Globe Oilers. Lubin claimed Goldstein did not play because the committee accused him of having played semiprofessional baseball, but during the trials, the *Los Angeles Times* said Goldstein chose not to play in Berlin on account of business commitments. However, Art Mollner has maintained that the "studio convinced him [Goldstein] not to go."[48]

Among the U.S. Olympic basketball players, Jack Ragland, who was thirty, was the oldest, and Ralph Bishop, who was twenty-one, was the youngest. Five-feet-ten-inch Sam Balter was the shortest, while Willard Schmidt stood tallest. Joe Fortenberry, a former West Texas State star who had powered the Globe Oilers at the trials, along with Francis Johnson, Balter, and Lubin, ultimately proved the Olympic team's top players.

Of them all, in Berlin the six-feet-eight-inch Joe Fortenberry emerged as the U.S. team's best player. He not only led the squad in scoring but also played terrific defense. Born on the outskirts of Amarillo, Texas, Fortenberry grew up on a farm. Only his length and leanness set him apart from the other young boys in rural Texas. After graduating from Happy High School, he set out for West Texas State Teachers College. Playing at West Texas in an era before goaltending was outlawed, Fortenberry's ability to stand under the goal and swat the ball away frustrated opposing players and fans. He soon developed into one of the country's first dominant big men and an All-American center.[49]

Despite the attention his basketball exploits generated throughout his life, Fortenberry remained a soft-spoken farm boy at heart. Unless prodded by family members, rarely did he bring up his basketball career in later life. In an interview years after the Olympics, Fortenberry did, however, recall meeting Hitler: "When I saw him, I thought, 'How could a little guy like that have so much control over these people?' It was a comedy to us Americans. We laughed about it. They treated him like he was their god." Little did Fortenberry know when he met Hitler in 1936 that just a few years later, he would don the uniform of the U.S. military and join the effort to turn back Hitler's Nazi regime.

After serving in World War II, Fortenberry retired from basketball and returned to Amarillo, Texas, where he raised a family and worked mostly as a land-man for the Phillips oil company, whose AAU team Fortenberry had played for. (The Phillips team excelled on the hardwood, winning eight national AAU championships between 1940 and 1950. Basketball historian Adolph H. Grundman has noted that "by the end of the 1940s Phillips justly deserved its nickname as the New York Yankees of basketball."[50])

Somewhat surprisingly, evidence points to Fortenberry and his Globe teammate and fellow Olympian Willard Schmidt as among the earliest to popularize the slam dunk. One might expect that this would have been done earlier by the members of teams such as the Harlem Rens or the original Celtics, but the longtime Rens player John Isaacs, in an interview years after his playing days had ended, said, "We all could jump high enough. But we never envisioned doing anything like dunking the ball. All we wanted was the basket."[51] Not until the 1936 Olympic qualifying tournament did headlines in major publications run about the new dunk shot. The *New York Times*, obviously baffled by the maneuver, led its March 10, 1936, story during the qualifying tournament with the banner line: "Awesome Kansas Giants Reverse Basketball Lay-Up Shot Process." The *Times*'s Arthur J. Daley attempted to describe the feat that left crowds in awe by writing: "The McPherson [Globe Oilers] version of a lay-up shot left observers simply flabbergasted. Joe Fortenberry, a six-feet-eight-inch center, and Willard Schmidt, six-feet-nine-inch forward, did not use an ordinary curling toss. Not those giants. They left the floor, reached up and pitched the ball downward into the hoop, much like a cafeteria customer dunking a roll in coffee."[52]

Daley's description gave birth to the moniker "dunk." In short order, the maneuver caught on. For instance, within a month, *Amateur Athlete* magazine highlighted the dunk shot with a comic that featured Schmidt and Fortenberry, along with a cartoon figure that hovered over a basketball rim easily stuffing a basketball through. The caption read, "I'll dunk it to make sure."[53] No single shot deserves more credit for giving basketball its cultural currency in the modern era than the slam dunk.

The Universals' victory at the trials made their coach, Jim Needles, the head Olympic coach, while the Globe Oilers' Gene Johnson took on assistant duties.[54] Needles's distinction as America's first Olympic basketball coach came about in rather unlikely fashion. Like the story about the nickname "Frankenstein Lubin," this tale also involves Pierce's *Bride of Frankenstein* movie. In the spring of 1936, after the Universals had won their Southern Californian section of the AAU tournament to qualify for the national AAU championships, Pierce realized that commitments for the Frankenstein movie would keep him from continuing as the manager/coach. As a result, Baven Dyer recommended Needles to Pierce as a replacement. Needles happened to be relocating to Los Angeles after having built his basketball reputation in the Bay Area as the coach of San Francisco's St. Ignatius High School and then Santa Clara University. Pierce took the advice, thereby paving the path that ultimately led to Needles becoming America's first Olympic head coach.[55]

Oddly enough, Needles's time with Universal did not go smoothly. Before he arrived, the players had mostly coached themselves, as Pierce had served more as a manager than a coach. So when a new coach suddenly showed up, some friction ensued. As Mollner, a defensive specialist on the 1936 U.S. Olympic squad, put it, "You know, don't fix it if it's not broke. Anyway, he didn't get along too well with the ballplayers." Problems continued even after the Olympic team formed, when the newly named Universal component of the Olympic team played a couple of exhibition games without Needles. "He thought we were trying to cut him out and he was a little mad," Mollner explained. This did not seem to adversely affect the team on the court in Berlin, however. According to Mollner, that was because "the American team was so much more superior to all of the other teams, you couldn't lose if you wanted to."[56] Still, that the 1936 U.S. Olympic team was far ahead of the competition in Berlin and Needles clashed with some of the Universal players should not obscure his basketball savvy. Needles knew the game.

Needles boasted a colorful, feisty personality, which surely contributed to the tensions between him and the wary Universal players. Bruce Jenkins has described him as an "energetic, street-wise man who sold liquor on the side and loved a good shot of whiskey come sundown," but Jenkins also notes that Needles became "one of the finest basketball minds on the West Coast." Legendary coach Pete Newell, who played for Needles in college and manned the sideline for the 1960 U.S. Olympic team, considered Needles "the most important influence on his coaching career" and characterized him as "the most ingenious man I ever ran into."[57]

An offensive innovator, Needles employed methods that influenced the sport greatly. For instance, in the 1960s numerous teams adopted components of what many considered Pete Newell's reverse-action offense, but, as Newell has pointed out, "I was given all the credit for it because so many teams used it after 1960. . . . But hell, Jimmy Needles taught us that. I just added some things that we never did." As late as the 1990s, the Michael Jordan–led, six-time NBA champion Chicago Bulls under coach Phil Jackson used a form of the reverse-action with its triangle set, according to Newell. By that time Newell still considered Needles's offense the best, stating, "Of all the offensive sets, reverse action was the best the game has known. I truly believe this."[58]

Needles also influenced the false-motion offense that Newell implemented in the 1950s and 1960s as the coach of California—it was rooted in Needles's operational-zone offense. Later, Newell's false-motion influenced the better-known four-corner offense that longtime North Carolina coach and 1976 U.S. Olympic coach Dean Smith utilized. "He [Needles] was a stickler for operational zones—what they call 'spacing' today. He wanted to make sure that you were spread apart, so if they double-teamed somebody, one of your men would be open," Newell explained.[59] Clearly, Needles's methods resonated.

With the United States Olympic basketball contingency set, the most conspicuous absence was that of Dr. Forrest C. "Phog" Allen, the legendary basketball coach of the Kansas Jayhawks. He had toiled for years to get basketball on the official Olympic program. In fact, as early as 1930 it looked as if his labors would be successful. That year, the IOC, with nudging by the AOC, adopted basketball as part of the 1932 Los Angeles Games. But the Los Angeles Olympic Committee counted as the final arbiter, and it opted for an exhibition football game between Northern and Southern Californian players rather than basketball. Disappointing as that was, Allen went to the LA Games anyway. There he met Sohaku Ri, lead official of the Japanese Olympic contingency and an ardent basketball supporter. Ri told Allen of his intention to include basketball on the Olympic program if Japan hosted the Games in 1940. A couple of years later, in late October 1934, Ri surprised Allen with a telegram informing him that a week earlier, Berlin's Organizing Committee had resolved to adopt basketball as an official medal sport for the Berlin Games. And so it was through the efforts of international champions of the sport that basketball made the Olympic program.[60]

At first it seemed that Dr. Allen would play an important role with the 1936 team, if not as coach, then as the team's director of basketball. But his hopes of coaching the squad ended in Olympic qualifying regional action when Utah State upset his Kansas Jayhawks team, which had gone 18-0 during that year's collegiate basketball season. Shortly afterward, Allen's reign as director of basketball ended in controversial fashion. To serve in that capacity, Allen had gained the support of the NCAA, the National Basketball Coaches Association, and the National Basketball Rules Committee. However, he did not get along with the ultrapowerful AAU brass. Subsequent squabbles between Dr. Allen and the AAU ultimately led Brundage to decide not to include him in the Olympic basketball team's travel contingency—although Brundage claimed that he did not include Dr. Allen because eighteen people were simply too many to send to Berlin for basketball.[61]

When Brundage announced that Dr. Allen would not travel with the team, "Phog" publicly rescinded his effort to serve as director of the U.S. Olympic basketball team in order to "give the AAU a good blast and refuse to have anything to do with the outfit."[62] In his letter of resignation, Allen characterized the leadership of the AAU as "oceanic hitchhikers [who] chisel their way across [the Atlantic] on the other fellow's money."[63] He also argued that his three-game regional series with Utah State, which earned the Olympic Basketball Committee $8,000, compared with the $700 earned by the Missouri Valley AAU on three nights of action, showed "the difference in public favor between college and independent basketball." A short time later, Dr. Allen referred to AAU players as "technical amateurs but actual semi-professionals."[64]

The AAU men Dr. Joseph A. Reilly and Avery Brundage responded to Dr. Allen's characterization of the AAU as being made up of "oceanic hitch-hikers" by charging him with "talking out of his hat" and accusing him of being the real "hitch-hiker" for pursuing a position as "an extra and unnecessary official."[65] Brundage said of Dr. Allen, "He quit a job the American Olympic Committee never has given its approval, and might never have approved."[66] The unfortunate spat and public relations fiasco exemplified the tension between the AAU and the NCAA. That tension has lasted, to varying degrees, ever since.

The U.S. Olympic basketball team set sail for Europe on July 15, aboard the SS *Manhattan*, a state-of-the-art ship that offered high-end accommodations for spectators heading to Berlin, as well as to the American Olympic athletes. Describing the journey, Mollner beamed, "Oh, it was great! It was beautiful . . . We had beautiful staterooms and the food was just the best." The Olympians could even watch movies on "A" deck. Occasionally, when it was not windy, the team would work out on the top deck. "We'd pass the basketball—we threw a couple of them over the side," Mollner said, laughing.[67]

Shortly after stepping off of the ss *Manhattan*, the team received some surprising news. Two years earlier, a FIBA meeting, dubbed the Congress of Lyon and dominated by France and Italy, had taken place at the insistence of R. William Jones, a British man who went on to have a remarkably long career as a FIBA leader—the same R. William Jones who, thirty-eight years later, inexplicably meandered onto the court at the 1972 Olympic final between the United States and Soviet Union, demanding that three seconds be put back on the clock. Although no U.S. representatives were in attendance at the 1934 Congress of Lyon, FIBA made important decisions there, including applying French basketball rules to the Berlin Games. These rules limited teams to seven players per game, only two substitutions, and zero time-outs. If a player was substituted for, he could not return to the action. Furthermore, as the *Los Angeles Times* reported, French rules called "for a foul when two players touch each other—even when they collide accidentally."[68] As noted, the rules also did not recognize the three-seconds-in-the-lane rule or the ten-second rule. It was also in Lyon that FIBA deemed outdoor courts the official venue for the 1936 Games.[69] These conditions were applied to the Olympic Games in Berlin even though, as the *Los Angeles Times* mentioned, "most of the countries who will participate this summer desired American rules."[70] The absence of U.S. influence at the Congress of Lyon suggested the direction basketball could have taken without American influence.

As if the unforeseen rule changes were not enough, shortly after stepping off the ss *Manhattan*, the U.S. team faced the prospect of competing without its big men, because Fortenberry and Schmidt's height aroused fear among opposing coaches. Many of these coaches attempted to jam a resolution through FIBA that restricted "future contestants to five feet eight." It did not succeed, but FIBA did pass a rule limiting contestants to a height of "about six feet one." Facing strong U.S. opposition, however, the resolution was revoked "at the last minute."[71]

As the U.S. basketball team readied to deal with the unexpected rules and conditions, the Berlin Olympics opened on August 1, 1936, in front of some 105,000 fans. Germany built upon the spectacular advances that the 1932 Los Angeles Games had brought to the Olympic movement in the way of venue construction, media attention, and commercialism.[72] More than 4,500 athletes from fifty nations were on hand as Adolf Hitler, "attired in a brown uniform and smiling genially," presided over the affair.[73] Media members filled the Olympic stadium press stand, signaling the Olympics' ability to attract massive attention. By the Games' end, an estimated 1,500 reporters had observed Olympic action from the press stand, which amounted to "hundreds more than customarily report League of Nations doings at Geneva," as *Time* magazine noted.[74] And commercialism abounded as corporations such as Coca-Cola continued to associate with sports to help sell products.[75] Television, though still more than a decade away from becoming widely accessible, brought the ceremonies to even more people in Berlin, Potsdam, and Leipzig. To do this, officials that spring had stationed public viewing tents in these cities. An estimated 160,000 people caught some part of the 138 hours of action transmitted, though a weak signal made the images "fuzzy."[76] Television signals were beamed into the Olympic Village too. "The first time I ever saw television was in our Olympic Village in the office there," Mollner recalled.[77]

Within a week of the opening ceremonies, the first Olympic basketball tournament commenced, with players representing nearly every corner of the globe competing under the Berlin sky.[78] But the U.S. players were not among them. Their first-round opponent, Spain, embroiled in a Civil War that pitted Leftists versus Fascist uprisers led by Francisco Franco, were unable to attend the Games; therefore, the United States won rather anticlimactically, 2–0, by forfeit.

There were some first-day highlights, however, including a Canadian victory against Brazil in a tight contest, and a sound win by Japan over China, 35–19. Japanese and Chinese fans helped pack the stands for the partisan affair, and Japan impressed onlookers with its skillful ballhandling, which was considered well ahead of that of most European teams. China tried to contain Japan's "tall" six-feet-three-inch center by implementing a zone defense, but it was Japan's superior ball skill, as Coach Needles reported, that helped propel them to victory. The contest created great interest from

American observers, who were pleasantly surprised to see the quality of play emanating from the Japanese and Chinese squads. Needles characterized the two teams' "skillful display of ballhandling" as "markedly different from the exhibition of European teams."[79] In some ways, though, their performances should not have surprised. In the early 1900s, as the YMCA played a lead role in introducing the sport worldwide, many parts of Asia took to basketball immediately. As noted earlier, by the 1920s thousands of fans were attending championship basketball contests in cities like Beijing and Shanghai.

Other Asian teams impressed, too, such as the Philippines, with a 39–22 win over Estonia, the 1935 European champion. The Philippines, utilizing a nifty fast break and led by some spectacular individual play by Johnny Worrel, an American youth who resided in the Philippines, also beat Mexico in early-round action.[80]

Some European teams showed promise as well, like Czechoslovakia and France, but their old-school methods hurt their ability to advance. For example, as Balter reported, "their passing was all overhead instead of from the chest, and they could not manage their feet to get set for shots."[81] This factored into Needles's assertion directly after the Games that, despite the solid play from some teams, "Bluntly it seemed evident that any good Midwestern high school team could defeat any team in the tournament, with the exception of the United States, Canada, Japan, Mexico, and the Philippines."[82]

As for the United States, its first live game ended in a relatively easy victory over Estonia, 52–28. The Americans' superior passing, height, and fast break enabled them to tally the highest point total of the tournament at that juncture. After the game, the Estonian coach said he had never seen such play in Europe.[83] The United States was also helped by Estonia's implementation of the old "sleeper play" strategy, in which one of the team's five players remained on the offensive end, under his own basket, while his teammates played defense. Once the Estonians gained possession, they would then attempt to heave it down the court to their basket for a lay-up by the "sleeper." Using this strategy, Estonian forward Georg Vinogradov, the "sleeper," scored twenty-one of his team's twenty-eight points. However, the method left the Estonians shorthanded on defense, which enabled the United States to score "practically at will."[84]

In the third round, the United States received a bye, which allowed them to reach the one-and-done final-eight medal round despite having played only one game. In the opening game of the final-eight medal round, the Americans beat the Philippines handily, 56–23, moving them into the semifinals with little exertion.

Joining Needles and company in the final four were Mexico, Canada, and Poland. With three of the final four teams hailing from North America, it was clear that basketball supremacy still resided there. However, that domination was short-lived. Since the Berlin Games, Canada has won only one other basketball medal, a bronze, and Mexico has yet to win another.

In its semifinal matchup, the United States met its neighbor to the south, while Canada played Poland. Plagued by poor outdoor conditions created by precipitation that mixed with the dirt and gravel court, Lubin and Balter led the United States over a speedy Mexican squad, 25–10. Mexico came into the game known for its fast play offensively (like most Central and South American teams), but it surprised the United States with what the *Chicago Tribune* characterized as "stout" defense. It did not hurt the Mexicans that Fortenberry, because of the player limit and substitution restrictions, did not suit up for the game. At the same time, the United States played well defensively, as evidenced by a 13–2 halftime score. Of course, both defenses were abetted by the adverse weather conditions.[85]

In the other semifinal, Canada managed the conditions well on the way to a 42–15 victory over Poland.[86] To win, Canada utilized a fairly sophisticated offense for the time. Dubbed the "figure-eight," it called for deft ballhandling and perpetual motion from all five players in a pattern that resembled a figure eight. As for Poland, just qualifying for the bronze medal game was remarkable, considering its relatively late start with basketball. Barney Ain, a member of the New York City Board of Education and a longtime basketball player, coach, and referee, is counted as among the first to have helped introduce the game to large numbers of Poles in 1929.[87] In a mere seven years, Poland had won a European championship and made the Olympic semifinal. And after the team's loss to Canada, Poland nearly took the bronze from Mexico. Unfortunately, that bronze medal game, which saw the Poles come up just short, was marred by horrible weather conditions, too. Describing it, Balter wrote that because of the mud and water, "none of the players were recognizable," and "every attempt at a dribble wound up in a ten-foot skid."[88]

After watching the Mexicans and Poles compete in mud-soaked uniforms among puddles, German Olympic officials, whom the Americans had beseeched to move the final indoors, decided that the gold medal game would be played on Platze Number Four, a court that had yet to be played on and was supposedly better drained. But since the rain continued, the new venue did not change matters significantly.[89] And nothing changed about the inferior Berg basketball that was used in Berlin, which exacerbated the already difficult conditions. That official Olympic basketball, made by a German company, was selected for use by German officials even though more sophisticated basketballs existed, such as the American-based company Converse's 1935 "stitchless" basketball.[90] In contrast to Converse's ball, the Berg ball was the maximum size allowable under FIBA rules and yet rather light, lopsided, and, most troubling, ungrained, which made it particularly difficult to handle in wet conditions. The Berg ball, coupled with the weather conditions, meant that, as Balter explained, in the gold medal game, "holding a pass proved a rarity; accurate shooting, an impossibility."[91]

One important piece of equipment the Americans sported that must have aided them, at least a little, were their rubber-soled shoes made by Converse, the "Chuck Taylor All-Stars." Though the basketball high-top was far from the days of featuring innovations like the air pocket, in the 1930s the basketball shoe business was robust, and the shoes themselves were technologically inventive, especially the mid-1930s Chuck Taylor model, with its durable design and its signature Toe Smile—the leather trim over the toe of the shoe. Starting in 1923, Converse had made a string of decisions, in addition to design improvements, that helped the company position itself as the dominant player in the U.S. athletic footwear market for the next fifty years. One of those was adding Chuck Taylor's actual signature to the Converse All-Star shoes; another was sending Taylor on what became a thirty-five-year "evangelist" tour promoting basketball across the nation while hawking his signature line. In addition to capitalizing on having an individual endorse a shoe, in 1923 Converse allied itself with the New York Renaissance Rens, marking an early example of a shoe company associating with a particular team. Through its relationships with Taylor and the Rens, Converse allied itself with basketball champions of creativity, speed, competitiveness, and teamwork.[92] Subsequently, Converse grew significantly.

By 1927, its Malden, Massachusetts, plant ran at capacity as the company manufactured 17,000 shoes daily.[93] As early as 1931, Sol Metzger observed that "rubber-soled basketball shoes, incidentally, because of their comfort and durability, remain perhaps the most popular footwear among the rural youth of America."[94] This success enabled Converse to become the footwear supplier of the 1936 team, and it would outfit U.S. basketball teams for the next forty years. During that time, the basketball shoe, like the Olympics, transcended sport and became increasingly packed with cultural meaning. It also underwent remarkable technical changes. On the rain-soaked and muddy courts of Berlin, however, even Chuck Taylors could only help so much.

At around 6:00 p.m. the starters for the American and Canadian squads took off their raincoats and readied for the tip-off. Meanwhile, roughly "two thousand spectators emerged from hiding behind trees and under sheds."[95] Those spectators witnessed a championship game that lacked any flow and featured numerous scrums as players grappled for the elusive ball. Of one such struggle, Balter, likely exaggerating, claimed that it took two full minutes and numerous kicks, squirts, and fumbles before the American Jack Ragland finally fell on it.[96]

Against the U.S. zone defense, Canada scored only one field goal the entire first half. Needles chose to implement the zone even though his team was known more for man-to-man defense, because of the weather and Canada's ballhandling-oriented "figure-eight" offense. The strategy worked in conjunction with the weather, as Canada struggled throughout to penetrate. It also helped that when Canada did make it past the front line, the zone was anchored by Fortenberry, Johnson, and Carl Knowles. Fortenberry in particular took advantage of there being no rule outlawing goaltending by "twice leaping up and catching balls headed for the net," wowing the crowd in the process.[97] He played well offensively, too, and by halftime, the U.S. team enjoyed a 15–4 advantage.[98] In the second half, the action got even uglier as the teams' combined score was a paltry eight points. With both teams scoring four apiece, the United States ultimately won, 19–8. Throughout the game, but particularly in the second half, America's trademark speed, complemented by handy ball work, took a back seat to simple passes and close shots with the heavy, wet ball.

In some respects, with the conditions on the court mitigating much of

TABLE 1. 1936 U.S. Men's Olympic Basketball cumulative stats

NAME	G	FGM*	FTM	PTS/AVG
Joe Fortenberry	2	13	3	29/14.5
Frank Lubin	2	10	2	22/11.0
Francis Johnson	2	10	0	20/10.0
Sam Balter	2	8	1	17/8.5
Willard Schmidt	1	4	0	8/8.0
John Gibbons	1	3	0	6/6.0
Carl Shy	2	5	0	10/5.0
William Wheatley	2	4	1	9/4.5
Jack Ragland	2	3	1	7/3.5
Carl Knowles	2	2	2	6/3.0
Art Mollner	2	3	0	6/3.0
Ralph Bishop	2	2	0	4/2.0
Don Piper	2	2	0	4/2.0
Duane Swanson	2	2	0	4/2.0
USA TOTALS	4	71	10	152/38.0
OPP. TOTALS	4	29	11	69/17.3

* Figures for field goals and free throws attempted are not available.
Note: The USA played five games; however, statistical totals reflect four game totals because the USA was declared a 2–0 winner over Spain by a forfeit.

America's advantage in speed and skill, the 1936 gold medal win was even more impressive than it might have been. Really, given the tournament's rules, it can be said that throughout, U.S. strengths were minimized. After the final, the *New York Times*'s Daley recognized as much and credited the U.S. basketball team for overcoming adverse conditions and "odd" rules to take the gold in convincing fashion.[99]

Even after having won the gold medal, upon returning to Hollywood, the Universal players did not receive a warm reception from Universal Pictures. As Lubin recalled, "They [Universal] had fired all the players for having gone to the Olympic Games against their request that we do not attend."[100] Nor did the gold medal win resolve the tensions between the Universal players and Needles. In fact, Mollner claimed that Needles had specifically directed the American unit that was not composed predominantly of Universal players to stand up on the podium to receive the gold medal, rather than the whole team, because "of the friction between us." Furthermore, Mollner said that several weeks later, Universal players found out, through reading telegrams on Needles's desk, that numerous countries had asked the U.S. team to visit them at the host nation's expense. "They were dying to see what the American basketball team was like because they were getting interested in basketball. But he wanted to go back home to make money, so he never told us about those things," Mollner claimed. Mollner thought Needles should have let the players visit the nations on their own if they pleased.

The team did play an exhibition game upon making it back to the States, against the Phillips Oilers in New York's Hippodrome. That game materialized when a tugboat came out to pull the *Manhattan* into harbor and Ned Irish, a groundbreaking basketball promoter in the New York area, came aboard and asked the players, as Mollner recalled, "How would you guys all like to make some money?" Such an arrangement would not have sat well with the Olympic committee, or Brundage for that matter, but Mollner intimated that they did not know of it.[101]

In hindsight, those who had opposed participation in Hitler's Games were proven correct in that the IOC's decision to allow Berlin to remain as the host city, despite Hitler's rise to power, has left a scar on the legacy of the modern Olympics. But the Berlin Games also managed to add to the Olympic legacy. Athletes like Sam Balter and Jesse Owens serve as examples of the fallacy of Aryan superiority, and a record number of countries sent a record number of athletes to Berlin. And though they were not adopted by Hitler, the basic, key Olympic ideals—to use sports to bring about goodwill and to represent "respect for universal fundamental ethical principles"—survived intact.[102] In the end, as Keys has argued, while the Games did not change the Third Reich's character, "the Third Reich did little to alter the character of the Olympics."[103]

For basketball, the legacy of the 1936 Olympics became clear when the tournament ended and FIBA quickly convened meetings to enact important rule changes. These changes pushed the international game toward a faster, more open brand of basketball.[104] And the AAU, with its essentially commercial model for its top men's league having already pushed the sport in that direction, played a lead role in bringing about these changes internationally.

At the post-Games FIBA meetings, the U.S. Olympic Basketball Committee led a successful movement to abolish the center-jump after each basket. In addition, FIBA adopted a ten-second rule to discourage "freezing" of the ball and enacted rules stipulating that the next tournament would take place indoors on "board" floors. In many instances, FIBA had simply adopted U.S. rules straight from the AAU's 1934–35 rule book, word for word.[105]

Of all the rule changes, abolishing the center-jump ranks as the most important. Pete Newell said that before the center-jump was abolished, basketball "was a slow game." Getting rid of it made basketball better for the spectator and brought the sport more attention from the press. "The greatest single change, the greatest, was that rule right there. Because it brought in the fast break, it brought in a quick game," Newell explained.[106]

Though no progress took place on a proposed "three-seconds-in-the-lane" rule, many aficionados voiced their opinion that opening the lane would enhance the speed and acrobatic flow of the game.[107] Meanwhile, FIBA members voted down a proposal to limit players at the 1940 Olympics, slated to take place in Tokyo, to a height of five feet eight, although it did adopt a ban on players over six feet three.[108] However, by the time the next Olympiad actually took place, which was not until 1948 because of World War II, FIBA had lifted that height restriction. Overall, these rule changes positioned basketball to emerge as the globe's fastest growing sport after World War II. The action they brought about created additional opportunities for creative play, attracted more followers, and allowed basketball's cultural language to mature.

2

U.S. BASKETBALL ADVANCES THE
GAME IN POSTWAR LONDON

It was 1948 and high tea in London's Buckingham Palace, where the U.S. Olympic basketball player Robert "Jackie" Robinson was meeting King George VI and Queen Elizabeth. Shortly after the tea, Robinson (not to be confused with the Robinson of Brooklyn Dodgers fame) regaled radio listeners in America with a recap. Decades later, he explained, "They told me that he [the King] stuttered, and he did. And they told me he had big ears and I caught myself looking as I talked to him . . . I remember thinking, 'You dope, look away,' and I did." Before meeting the king, Robinson had been encouraged to bow, but he felt foolish while practicing, so instead "I shook his hand" and said "delighted to know you, sir."[1]

At Buckingham palace that afternoon stood a monarchy that was still adjusting to the new world wrought by World War II. And along with them stood a young man from Fort Worth, Texas, whose brother had helped take back Europe, while he had helped lead Paschal High School to the Texas AA State Basketball Championship. Later, Robinson took Baylor from an

0-22 record in 1945 to a place among the nation's elite in a sport that Britons in the 1940s still associated with "net ball" (a hybrid of basketball played in England mainly by females). The changes that Robinson lived to see—in basketball, the Olympics, and the world—would prove remarkable.

It was on account of World War II that London had, given the torment it had undergone during the war at the hands of the Nazis, become the sentimental choice of the IOC to host the 1948 Olympiad. And it was a consequence of that deadly conflict that the 1948 Games marked just the second Olympic basketball tournament in history. Still, the tournament played to crowds that reveled in the advances the sport had made since Berlin—the tournament not only featured higher scoring than in 1936 but also led to further rule changes that opened basketball's action even more. At the same time, it solidified the role of the big man in the international game and helped convince the Soviets that basketball was a coveted sphere of influence. All told, the 1948 tournament provided a bridge between the 1936 Games and the second half of the twentieth century.

Highlighted by its increased speed and scoring, the U.S. hoops team pointed the way forward in London. It averaged 65.5 points per contest there, compared to 43 per game in Berlin. "Of the USA team the salient features were the enormous height of their players and their speed. Normally, men of 6ft 9in to 7ft tall are not fast, but these players had all the agility of bantams!"[2] wrote William Browning, the honorary secretary of Britain's Amateur Basketball Association.

Overall, the tournament, with its improved play, and the Olympics, with its display of technological advances in transportation and communications, hinted at magnificent developments on the horizon—both for sports like basketball and for the global economy in the postwar world. Consequently, as the world awoke from the horrors of World War II, the dynamic relationship between sports, television, and the marketplace budded at the London Games.

This should not, however, make one think that the 1948 Olympics resonated internationally in the same way the Games do in the twenty-first century. As 1948 Olympic basketball player Vince Boryla put it, "To be truthful with you, I didn't even know what the hell the Olympics were. I'm serious." (Boryla had been only nine years old when the last Olympics, in Berlin, had taken place.) He explained that when he says that to people, they look at him as if he has a hole in his head, but he noted that, compared to later times, 1948 Olympic hoops simply did not get much space in the newspaper.[3]

In addition to the rules changes, between the Berlin and London Games important basketball advances had taken place in America, such as Hank Luisetti's one-handed jump shot in the late 1930s. Pete Newell said Luisetti "was the greatest any of us had ever seen play," and he credited Luisetti with bringing the modern, fast, jump-shooting style of ball from the American West to the East shortly after the Berlin Games.[4] And basketball had advanced during the twelve-year Olympic hiatus in many other parts of the world too. This was apparent when France and Japan turned in noteworthy performances in London, partly on account of the influence of U.S. soldiers stationed there during and after the war, as well as when Argentina and Mexico solidified South America's strong basketball tradition. In addition, Britain's Browning noted that the Far East teams of Korea, Philippines, and China were "a joy to watch. Though small in stature, their speed and ball-manipulation were an education. How the crowd loved them, and how well they earned the admiration and respect of basketball enthusiasts."[5]

Still, FIBA, which named the AAU's Willard N. Greim as president in 1948, implemented important new rules shortly after the London Olympics. At the outset of the London tournament, there was still no rule limiting a player to three seconds in the lane, no restrictions on defensive goaltending, and no shot clock. Within a decade of the tournament, however, all of these rules would apply to FIBA play. In fact, FIBA adopted the three-seconds-in-the-lane rule at meetings in London because it became clear there that "centre-pivot play had slowed the game."[6] Furthermore, in 1948 FIBA's court dimensions were slightly smaller than the U.S. courts, both in length and width. And even more important, FIBA rules called for only two feet from underneath the basket to the baseline, rather than the United States' four feet (adopted by the AAU in 1938). This meant that players in the international game had less room to operate on forays to the basket.

Other notable differences applied in London. Four personal fouls led to disqualification, rather than five, as in AAU play, and players could re-enter a game only twice rather than unlimited times. In one of its oddest departures from AAU rules, FIBA stipulated that after the ball crossed half-court, "the first player of that team who touches it after a throw for goal, jump ball, throw-in from out of bounds, or recovery from possession of opponents, may cause the ball to go backcourt" (those were the four exceptions allowed in the United States when the ten-second rule was first passed the previous decade). Basically, this meant there was not a complete over-and-back rule in London. Finally, in one of the few rule differences that encouraged faster play in FIBA games, players in London were allowed to take the ball back in-bounds after it went out-of-bounds without having to hand it to the referee first, as long as there was no confusion regarding possession.[7]

Most of FIBA's new rules in the aftermath of the London Games more closely approximated American guidelines, and all of the important changes that took place encouraged swifter, less-congested action. So, though the 1948 Olympic basketball tournament only hinted at basketball's global potential, the rule changes made in its wake proved crucial. This fine-tuning of the international game positioned basketball well for the second half of the twentieth century.

Following World War II, the United States stood alone as the eminent economic power in the world. Propelled by America's enhanced industrial might, Western Europe, parts of Asia, and the United States geared up for a postwar period of mass consumption and general economic recovery. In addition, technological advances, many emanating from the United States, soon configured a truly global age. The emergence of a more connected globe made America's timing in taking a clear lead as the world's economic superpower fortuitous. Its newfound economic muscle enhanced the value of its cultural currency, helping it lead the way in defining global culture as globalization took root. In time, basketball both complemented and charged this popular international culture.

Technological advances in the wake of World War II allowed more time for leisure activities and spurred economic growth. In turn, after the war, Americans spent more than 20 percent of the nation's total consumer budget on play, travel, and sports. Among the advances were improvements to automobiles, planes, and home appliances. Passenger airlines transformed logistical issues for athletic events, both at home and abroad, and the use of powerful electric lights for outdoor games gave athletes more opportunities to play. Americans and Europeans alike chose to spend much of their free time engaged in sports, either as participants or spectators.[8]

In addition, though it was still nascent, television took off soon after V-J Day, serving as a symbol of postwar consumerism.[9] Within the host city, the London Games offered limited television feeds of the Games. In America in 1947, CBS had broadcast, from Madison Square Garden, fifty collegiate and professional basketball programs to New Yorkers with "highly gratifying" results. James Kane of CBS predicted more to come, noting that the American Telephone and Telegraph Company (AT&T) planned to lay 6,500 miles of coaxial cable by the end of that year. It took some time, but Kane presciently reckoned that with television, "the total hoop audience will soar to stratospheric heights."[10] While television, more than any other technological advancement, deserves credit for basketball's subsequent growth, other technological innovations also strengthened the game, such as the manufacturing of more advanced basketballs by the likes of Spalding and Converse, which utilized "better air-retaining qualities of a synthetic rubber called Butyl," developed during the war.[11] The basketball shoe, led by Converse, continued to evolve too, though not as rapidly as it would in the 1960s and 1970s.

Just as important as the technological advances spreading around the globe, following World War II, American culture swept across much of Europe. The sports historian Allen Guttmann has noted that during this time, America passed England "as the primary agent in the diffusion of modern sports" and that basketball, reflecting America's newfound status, saw "markedly more rapid growth in participation."[12] Already booming at home, America's extended influence helped make basketball the world's fastest-growing sport in the second half of the twentieth century.[13] Increasing numbers of people became attracted to basketball's fast-paced action and the dynamic mix of athleticism and skill it demanded.

In addition to providing a bridge from Berlin to the second half of the twentieth century, the 1948 Olympic basketball tournament likely influenced the Soviets to count basketball as a coveted sphere of influence. Though tenuous allies during World War II, directly afterward, the opposing economic and political philosophies of the United States and Russia led to the decades-long cold war.[14] Rather quickly, the East versus West battle for supremacy raged in nearly every facet of life, including the playing field. As the historian William J. Baker has put it, "No less than the Berlin Blockade, the Korean War, and the Cuban Missile Crisis, East-West athletic contests represented tests of will as well as strength of skill."[15] The Soviet versus U.S. basketball rivalry that emerged after the London Games indicated this. Given that in the ensuing decades, the attendant culture, associated products, and dissemination of both basketball and the Olympics came mainly from liberal capitalist nations, on balance, the rivalry worked in the United States' favor.

In many ways, the visibility of basketball during the cold war was a surprising development. First of all, the London Games marked just the second time basketball was part of the Olympic program. It still counted as a young sport. And, as mentioned, before World War II, the Soviets maintained an aversion to Western-dominated "bourgeois" sports, much like Hitler had before getting the opportunity to host the Olympics. In a way, from Stalin's perspective, this aversion made sense, considering "bourgeois" sports and festivals like the Olympics were generally driven by democratic-based countries with market-oriented economies. But following World War II, the Soviet Union's aversion to "bourgeois" sports started to change, largely because of the seemingly ubiquitous attractiveness of sports. As a result, the Soviets flirted with entering the 1948 Games. Ultimately, they decided to send only observers, but their interest signaled the growing importance of sports. Indeed, in London, Stalin's observers, keen to win the ideological battle for people's hearts and minds throughout the world, came away convinced that to achieve their goal of cultural supremacy, they had to compete directly with the Western world at the Olympics. Therefore, as they were doing with other sports, the Soviets intensified their efforts to improve in basketball.

In London, Soviet observers saw a U.S. basketball team stacked with tall men. The U.S. Olympic Basketball Committee, chaired by Lou Wilke, had worked for several years to determine who would be on that team. Wilke, a native of Chicago and former captain of Northwestern Oklahoma State's basketball team (known as the "sixty-five-inchers" for its lack of height), and a former coach of Phillips University's hoops squad, possessed seemingly natural administrative and organizational skills. After successfully chairing the U.S. basketball committee for the London Games, Wilke went on to play important roles in FIBA, and in 1961 he mediated a dispute between the AAU and NCAA about which one of the organizations should represent the United States in international basketball competition. Thanks largely to his guidance, the committee's success in preparing for London helped mollify its 1936 failures.

In addition to Wilke, J. L. Bingham was chosen by the committee to direct the 1948 qualifying tournament, despite the debacle he'd overseen twelve years earlier. He too deserves credit for the committee's success. One crucial adjustment the committee made in 1948 was in treating the NCAA more equitably. Now, colleges did not have to play a string of regional games at their own expense to make it to the eight-team qualifying tournament. Instead, the winners of the biggest collegiate tournaments of the year, the NCAA championship and the National Invitation Tournament (NIT) championship, simply had to make their way to Madison Square Garden, all expenses paid. In addition, from the outset, seniors were deemed eligible for play. As a result, instead of having to plead for NCAA teams to participate, the schools lined up at Bingham's door, public interest was piqued, and ticket sales increased dramatically.

In another departure from the 1936 system, the basketball committee decided that an equal number of collegiate players and AAU or YMCA players should represent the United States in the Olympics. To achieve this end, the brackets for the eight teams in the Olympic qualifying tournament were organized so that a collegiate team would encounter an AAU or YMCA squad in the championship. From the two qualifying tournament finalists, the committee picked five players apiece and then rounded out the fourteen-player squad by choosing four more players among the six other teams that made it to Madison Square Garden. The forging of a mixed Olympic team made up of collegiate and AAU or YMCA stars had the secondary consequence of further enlivening public interest in the Olympic qualifying tournament, since there was a good chance the nation's top AAU team and top NCAA team would compete against one another in the final. This interest, coupled with the committee's inclusion of contribution stubs on qualifying game tickets and its hosting of exhibition games across the United States after the Olympic team was selected, enabled basketball to become a sizable moneymaker for the United States Olympic Association (USOA).

One of the qualifying tournament's two brackets comprised the finalists from both the AAU and YMCA national tournaments. The AAU's Phillips 66ers/Oilers emerged as the class of this group. With the support of company founder Frank Phillips, Phillips Company had financed its basketball team for nearly two decades. In 1929 it had taken the name "66ers," and in short order, the team made news in the sports pages, thereby advertising the company name. And it continued to do so for decades. Ultimately, the Phillips squad came to compile a record of 1,543 wins and just 271 losses; it also won two Olympic trials championships and produced fourteen Olympic basketball players. As Bill Martin, a star with Phillips in the early 1940s, explained, "Basketball became quite important to Phillips. We thought that we were gaining advertising we couldn't buy any other way and we were getting a lot of goodwill as a result [for playing benefit games in small towns]."[16]

The two finalists from the NCAA tournament, the NIT champion, and the champion of the National Association of International Basketball (NAIB), the forerunner of the National Association of Intercollegiate Athletics (NAIA), made up the other bracket. The teams on the college side of the bracket were NCAA runner-up Baylor University and NCAA champion University of Kentucky, NAIB champion University of Louisville, and NIT runner-up New York University. (St. Louis University had actually won the NIT, but the squad opted not to go to the Olympic trials because of a couple of pending marriages for players on the team. As the Hall of Famer Ed Macauley explained it, "We weren't going without them." The Bilikens' absence, as explained to the press by St. Louis officials at the time, however, was attributed to concern about spending too much time away from school).[17]

For the trial's four sets of games, roughly 50,000 fans descended upon Madison Square Garden. Both the AAU's elite teams and college basketball were attracting quite a following at that time, and people wanted to be associated with the action. So, too, it seems, did gamblers. Jackie Robinson recalled that on the morning of his Baylor squad's opening trials game, against New York University, he'd gone down to the lobby of his team's New York City hotel, when this guy "saddles up to me and wants to buy me a paper . . . and we're talking and he's friendly." Then the man asked, "'Well, how you think ya'll will do?'" It did not take Jackie too long to figure out the man's intentions. "It scared me to death. They had warned us. So I got out of there like my shirt tail was on fire," Robinson recalled.[18]

As it happened, just a year after the London Games, two U.S. Olympic basketball players—guard Ralph Beard and center Alex Groza, who from 1945–47 served in the U.S. Army by working at a hospital and playing on a basketball team out of Fort Hood, Texas—tarnished the exploits of the 1948 Kentucky squad when news broke of their possible indictment in a gambling probe that would shake the NCAA basketball community to its core. In the course of the investigation, Beard and Groza admitted that, while at Kentucky, they had been showered with gifts by alumni and boosters and had schemed with gamblers to fix games.[19] The ordeal led to banishment from the NBA for both Beard and Groza, who had starred together on the NBA's Indianapolis Olympians, a franchise built around its gold medalists. (Beard tried to turn to professional baseball but got banned from it as well.) Later, Beard said, "If taking $700 was wrong, then I was guilty. But I was totally innocent of influencing games. I never had two dimes to rub together. My mother cleaned six apartments so we could have one to live in. I took the money, and that was it." And he told his Olympic teammate Robinson that "he would cut off his right arm to play one more game." Robinson explained, "He was just a young kid, that kind of money, $500 I guess . . . he was supposed to throw it; he didn't throw it, he just shaved points."[20] Both Beard and Groza paid a heavy price for it.

In the buildup to the 1948 Olympic trials, the *Washington Post* had noted that usually the AAU champ would be "automatically installed the favorite," but most thought the University of Kentucky's "fabulous five" could provide a stiff challenge.[21] Coach Adolph Rupp's Kentucky squad had garnered its nickname because of the spectacular play of its starters: the quick ball-whiz Beard, the agile Groza, Cliff Barker, Kenny Rollins, and Wallace "Wah Wah" Jones. They had helped Kentucky post a 36-3 record during the 1947–48 collegiate season, capped by its NCAA championship. And sure enough, in the Olympic qualifying tournament final in Madison Square Garden, a record crowd of 18,475 witnessed the AAU champion Phillips 66ers of Bartlesville, Oklahoma, play Kentucky in a hotly contested affair. With professional leagues in the United States only beginning to gain a foothold in the postwar climate, many considered Phillips and Kentucky the two best teams in the United States and, for that matter, the world. The game received front-page treatment in the *New York Times*, and many touted it as the "most exciting game in basketball history."[22]

Not to be outdone by the "fabulous five," the 66ers also boasted a formidable lineup. Bob Kurland, a near-seven-footer widely considered, along with George Mikan, the best center in the world, was complimented by a bevy of former collegiate stars from all over the country. By the time Phillips met Kentucky in the Garden, it had won the AAU's previous six national titles.[23]

Kurland, nicknamed "Foothills" as a collegiate star under coach Henry "Hank" Iba at Oklahoma A&M (now Oklahoma State), is quite possibly the most underrated basketball player of all time. His name should be summoned with the likes of Mikan, Chamberlain, and Russell, but because he played in the AAU's "industrial leagues" rather than the NBA, Kurland often gets overlooked. He was not overlooked during his time, though. En route to winning back-to-back national championships with Oklahoma A&M in 1945 and 1946, he also won the first ever back-to-back NCAA tournament MVP awards. Furthermore, the Kurland-led Oklahoma A&M championship teams helped enhance the national prominence of the NCAA tournament, which had played a distant second to the NIT beforehand.

After his All-American college career, Kurland powered Phillips to a remarkable 369-26 record over six seasons, which included three national AAU titles, and anchored both the 1948 and 1952 U.S. Olympic basketball gold medal teams, becoming the first two-time gold medalist in Olympic basketball history.[24] Among the many contributions he made to the sport, both he and Mikan are credited with forcing the NCAA to make goaltending illegal after the 1943–44 season. And Kurland is credited with mastering the dunk shot and tip-in around the basket.[25] Unfortunately, his decision to turn down NBA offers to play and work for the 66ers diminished his legacy later on.

Kurland amassed all of these accolades despite being bypassed by most colleges in high school. In addition to not recruiting him, some collegiate coaches even lampooned him for his height. Before Kurland stepped foot on a college basketball court, the revered Dr. "Phog" Allen referred to him as a "glandular goon."[26] Kurland used Allen's derogatory comments as motivation throughout his career. "If you take pride in anything, it's not the physical, it's not the mechanics of learning how to play—it's in having the guts to stay in there and prove that you could play when Phog Allen called you a glandular goon," he said later in life.[27] Dr. Allen, who nicknamed the center-dominated pattern offense of his rival Iba the "barnacle of basketball" because he thought it slowed down the game, predicted that Kurland would ruin basketball.[28] Instead, Kurland helped revolutionize it. Even Allen could not deny this as he soon found himself scouring the countryside for big men.

With coaches like Dr. Allen staying away, Iba was able to lure the scholastic Kurland to Stillwater, Oklahoma, with a steak dinner and a bus ticket from Saint Louis, Missouri.[29] And as it happened, as soon as 1945, Kurland and his Oklahoma A&M teammates, fresh from winning that year's NCAA title, played a game in Madison Square Garden that served as a hallmark demonstration of how the big man had changed basketball. The much-anticipated matchup pitted Iba's NCAA championship team versus the NIT champion DePaul, and it became known as the "Clash of the Titans" because it featured Kurland against Mikan. Scheduled as a special Red Cross war benefit game, it technically counted as an exhibition, but lots of folks considered it the true national championship. As Kurland remembered years later, there was "a lot of hullabaloo for the mythical national championship." In that mythical national championship, Kurland emerged as the dominant titan, leading Oklahoma A&M to a 52–44 victory.[30] According to Kurland, his most effective weapon during the matchup was a "shot we called a 'scoop sucker shot,' where I spun and came in low." Puzzled by the maneuver, Mikan fouled out in the first half. "After that, it was anticlimactic," Kurland remembered.[31] A&M's victory enhanced the NCAA tournament's prestige. It also reflected how the big man, lampooned just a few years earlier, had become a staple component of basketball. Within a few years—thanks, it seems, in large part to the giant American team in London—the emphasis on tall centers spread across the oceans as well, namely, to the Soviet Union.

In the championship game of the 1948 Olympic qualifying tournament, Kurland proved the difference again as he outplayed Kentucky's center Groza in Phillips's 53–49 victory.[32] The win gave the AAU its second straight qualifying tournament title, but Kentucky had fared better than many prognosticators had expected. As the Los Angeles Times reported, "the Oilers [Phillips] were picked to win easily" beforehand, despite the "flashy, dashing style" that Kentucky had displayed in a semifinal win over Baylor.[33] Yet winning the game took all that Kurland and the rest of the Oilers had.

Along with Kurland, from Phillips the committee selected Jesse Renick, Gordon Carpenter, R. C. Pitts, and Olympic captain Lew Beck, who in July 1944 had injured his leg so severely in a World War II training exercise that he was hospitalized for three months and told his playing days were over. However, before getting asked to suit up for Phillips and then for his country, he had returned to Oregon State as an All-American guard on its speedy "Thrill Kids" squad of 1946–47. Tex Winter said of Beck in 2005, "It's a shame people don't know how good he was. He was like a John Stockton, but Lew was a better scorer."[34]

From Kentucky, the committee simply chose the "fabulous five." And from the previously eliminated teams at the trials, the committee tabbed Don Barksdale, an African American from the AAU's Oakland Bittners, Ray Lumpp, from New York University; Vince Boryla of the AAU's Denver Nuggets; and Jackie Robinson, the white guard from Baylor who studied ministry and got to meet the King and Queen of England. News of Robinson's selection came the morning after the Phillips versus Kentucky final. As he told the author, "I get up to go get a paper, it's Sunday . . . and look down at my feet. And back then when you rode the elevator, the elevator man would sell you the morning paper . . . I look down at the stack of papers and it says Robinson, Lumpp picked for the Olympic team . . . That's the way I found out."[35]

Boryla, a six-feet-five-inch center with a "patented hook shot" who grew up in East Chicago, Indiana, and whose parents both came to America from Poland, had taken a peculiar route to the Games. For the 1944–45 season he attended Notre Dame, but then the armed services called, and, rather than get shipped overseas, he agreed to take a spot at Annapolis to get trained as a naval officer. At first, things went well. The upperclassmen were away on a cruise, and "I said, 'Maybe this isn't too bad.' We were eating great . . . they [Annapolis] had everything." Boryla even got some ingrown toenails fixed. "Then the upper class came back and all hell broke loose," he maintained. "I was eating in the middle of the table and eating underneath the table and all this bullshit. And they had more hazing." He called his parents and said, "I gotta get outta here."

Boryla had studied premed at Notre Dame and used that as a way to get a discharge. He played two more semesters on the varsity level at Notre Dame, turning in a fine season that included a high-scoring performance at the Garden. But since he had not put in enough time in the service, he joined again and got stationed at Fort Sheridan in Illinois. While there, he got a call from military folks at Lowry Field in Denver, Colorado, to see if he wanted to be stationed there and also play for the Denver Nuggets of the AAU. Boryla liked the idea. Asked if in 1947 he had expected to find himself on the Olympic team a year later, Boryla said, "Oh, hell no. Oh God, that was the furthest thing."[36]

Nonetheless, at the trials he helped his Olympic cause with a stellar performance when his team beat the Oakland Bittners by two in its first game. In that win, Boryla scored twenty-one points and impressed the crowd with his "southpaw hooks." His squad did lose next to the Oilers by twenty-nine points.[37] As he had years earlier when he played at the Garden for Notre Dame, Boryla said he felt great in New York City. "The buckets at the Garden were like a sieve to me," he explained. "[To] most of the guys who played basketball at the Garden the basket looked like a little pee hole. Somehow I always had great games there."[38] (During the 1948 49 college basketball season, in which Boryla finished fourth in the nation in scoring for the University of Denver, he got voted as the outstanding collegiate player to have played in Madison Square Garden.[39]) Following that stellar year, Boryla averaged double figures for four of his five seasons with the New York Knicks. Then, in the late 1950s, he took up the coaching reins with the Knicks, followed by front-office work in the ABA and NBA, where in 1984, while with the Denver Nuggets, he won Executive of the Year. In addition, the devout Catholic built a successful real-estate investment portfolio based in Colorado.[40]

As head coach of the qualifying tournament champion, Omar "Bud" Browning would lead the 1948 U.S. Olympic team, while Adolph Rupp was designated associate head coach. In the end, by choosing four players from squads that were not in the qualifying tournament final, as opposed to one in 1936, the committee enhanced roster quality from top to bottom. It also helped that FIBA, a month before the Olympic trials, had announced its decision to allow "unlimited" heights for players.[41]

Upon selection, Don Barksdale of the Oakland Bittners became the first African American to play on an Olympic basketball team. It "was never publicized too much," according to Barksdale (there was a smattering of coverage by dailies such as the *Chicago Defender* and weeklies such as *Parade* magazine, but overall very little press). In a February 18, 1948, op-ed piece entitled "On Second Thought," the *Oakland Tribune*'s Alan Ward did take a look at Barksdale the "private citizen." Ward noted Barksdale's desire to make the Olympic squad, to go into business for himself, and to uplift his race. Barksdale told Ward he thought his basketball skills could put him in a position to do just that. "There will be many of my race taking part in the Olympics this year and I know they'll make this country proud of them. I would like to be with them and if I fail it won't be for lack of try-ing," Barksdale told Ward.

Although there was not much press coverage of his being on the team, Barksdale did recall that some Los Angelinos in the movie business "picked up on" the *Parade* story and "became interested in making a movie, a thing called *Big Don and the Baron*, and baron naturally was Rupp." But the movie never got made. The attention Barksdale did generate from the media focused on the pre-Olympic exhibition games he played in segregated Oklahoma and Kentucky more than it did on his play in London.[42]

Some members of the U.S. Olympic basketball committee were opposed to including Barksdale on the final roster, but committee member and Oakland politician Fred Maggiora backed Barksdale, helping matters.[43]

Though Barksdale's direct path to the Olympics went through the AAU's Bittners, in college he had played for UCLA—first in the early 1940s and then again, following a stint in the armed services, during the 1946–47 basketball season. In 1948, with his NCAA eligibility exhausted, Barksdale had "fully expected that the NBA would open its doors, but they did not," which is why he ended up in the AAU.[44]

Even though Barksdale did get a chance to play at UCLA, such preju-dice plagued the collegiate game, too, especially the NCAA. Many NCAA southern schools did not integrate until the late 1960s: this was one way in which the NCAA was behind the NAIB. Granted, it took the NAIB until 1948 to open its intercollegiate postseason tournament to African Americans. And even then, as the *Chicago Defender* noted, its primary reason for doing so was a desire to compete more effectively for Olympic representation; also influencing the decision was the impact of previous boycotts of its national tournament by member schools such as John Wooden's Indiana State Teachers' College (now Indiana State) and Manhattan College, whose student body led a successful movement to reject its tournament bid on the grounds that the NAIB's "Jim Crow clause" conflicted with the school's "Catholic principles."[45] Still, the NAIB did blaze a trail, and in 1953 it also became the only intercollegiate association to allow predominantly African American institutions to participate in its national tournament.[46] A similar process occurred among NCAA institutions, but it took much longer for such developments in parts of the South.

As for the AAU, in the 1940s it was more receptive to African Americans, at least comparably. For instance, a year after joining the AAU, Barksdale turned down an NBA overture because his AAU team had treated him so well. (Still, the AAU basketball historian Adolph Grundman has maintained that "black players were never numerous" at the AAU championship, until the 1960s.[47])

As noted, originally Barksdale's AAU team was called the Oakland Bittners, but by the time Ned Irish of the NBA's New York Knickerbockers came calling for him to come to the NBA in 1949 and 1950, Blue and Gold Beer had picked up the sponsorship of Barksdale's team. Blue and Gold had also given Barksdale a beer distributorship in Oakland—a business arrangement that critics would point to when attacking a system that continued to classify the AAU's NIBL players as amateurs. Other perks had come Barksdale's way, too, so when Irish's offer to become the NBA's first black player emerged, Barksdale said he "was not that interested, because the money they offered was less than I was making."[48] As Doug Harris, producer of a biographical film on the life of Don Barksdale, explained, "At the time, Don was making more money than the league's highest paid player, George Mikan."[49]

Despite turning down Irish's offers to become the first African American in the NBA, Barksdale, as evidenced by his appearance on the 1948 Olympic team, did have a penchant for being "the first ever." Following his 1946–47 season at UCLA, he became the NCAA's first black consensus All-American basketball player, a feat all the more remarkable considering that he never even made the basketball team as a prep at Berkeley High School, despite trying out three times. (He played football and participated in track and field at Berkeley, but the basketball coach, Jack Edy, "didn't allow blacks to play on his team often," Barksdale explained.[50]) Another first came just after the 1948 Olympics, when Barksdale landed a job as a disc jockey on Oakland's KLX, a station owned by the *Oakland Tribune*. Then, two years

2. Don Barksdale, the first African American U.S. Olympic basketball player. The Statue of Liberty is in the background. Unfortunately, Barksdale had to overcome much racism during his life and career. From the author's collection, courtesy of R. J. Robinson.

later, he became the first African American to host a television show in the Bay Area. Shortly thereafter, in 1952, the multitalented Barksdale finally suited up for the NBA's Baltimore franchise, having signed a three-year $60,000 contract, which was "huge money at that time." Still, even with his prominence and hefty salary, when Barksdale played in Baltimore, he could not "go to the restaurants and eat . . . I could not go to the hotel and racism was a little rough."[51]

Coincidentally, had the Olympic basketball roster not been decided before that of track and field, Barksdale might have missed out on becoming the first African American basketball Olympian. That is because he posted marks in the high jump and long jump as well as times in a couple of running events that put him in contention to make the Olympic team in track and field (in 1944 he had also won the AAU triple jump championship).[52] At the time, athletes could compete only on one Olympic team, however, and when basketball chose him first, Barksdale accepted.

Ironically, when Barksdale did decide to play on the Olympic basketball team, his associate head coach would be Adolph Rupp, a man who would not have allowed Barksdale on his University of Kentucky team. At first, this understandably created tension between the two. Barksdale noted years later, "I started with a very stormy relationship with Adolph Rupp." But after the Games, Barksdale said that Rupp waited for him as they disembarked from the ss *America* and told him it had been a pleasure to coach him. "More importantly," Barksdale continued, "he suggested that if he could find a black player for the University of Kentucky, he would."[53]

But of all the NCAA schools, Rupp's Kentucky was one of the last to integrate. He did not welcome a black player on his team until the 1969 signing of a seven-foot-tall scholastic standout fittingly named Tom Payne. To be fair, Rupp did recruit some black athletes earlier than that, such as Wes Unseld in 1964, and in the 1950s he did play against integrated teams when many southern schools would not. But a source that wishes to remain anonymous on the subject told the author that during the 1948 pre-Olympic training, Rupp once refused to play a split-squad exhibition game in Lexington, Kentucky, if Barksdale were present; he relented on the issue only after Barksdale's split-squad teammates said they would not attend if Barksdale was not welcomed (tickets had already been sold for the affair, which ultimately did take place outdoors on Kentucky's football field and with Barksdale).

It would be nice to be able to say that the SEC and Rupp ultimately recognized the blatant unfairness of segregation in the late 1960s, but the timing of their decision to integrate is too suspicious. The begrudging acceptance of black players by the old vanguard of SEC coaches at that time is more likely explained by the exploits of their less-heralded colleges, particularly Texas Western University, which won the NCAA basketball championship in 1966 with an all-black starting five.

After the 1948 Olympic team was named, it promptly divided into two groups for training and then set out on an exhibition tour. One of the groups included the Phillips players, along with Robinson and Barksdale, while the other had the fabulous five and Boryla and Lumpp—both groups were augmented with a few alternates. For their period of training at the Phillips basketball facility in Bartlesville, Oklahoma, Robinson roomed with Barksdale. The 66ers were a big deal, Robinson remembered: "We practice at four o'clock in the afternoon. And the stands are full, just to watch them workout. They're crazy about this team." But Bartlesville was still segregated, and for Barksdale, "that wasn't easy," Robinson recalled. Once, the two went to catch a show, and a sign at the theater read "'colored in the balcony.'" So Robinson marched right up there with Barksdale and they watched the show together.[54]

With Coach Browning leading the predominantly AAU team and Coach Rupp manning the team made up mainly of collegiate players, the first matchup in the three-game exhibition series took place in Tulsa, Oklahoma. There, the AAU-heavy team, using experienced "ball-control tactics" down the stretch, beat the collegiate stars 60–52. It was an especially difficult road trip for Barksdale, who remembered it being filled with "extreme prejudice, extreme segregation. There were white and colored water fountains, different hotels, and different travel arrangements."[55] At the same time, the game marked another 1948 milestone in the integration of basketball for the state of Oklahoma. (As it happened, just months earlier, Barksdale had figured prominently in that state's first integrated game, too, when his Bittners squad played Phillips. At that standing-room-only affair, Barksdale scored seventeen and held Kurland to five in leading his team to victory.[56])

A few days later, in Kansas City, Missouri, the collegiate players responded with a double-overtime victory, 70–69. The second game saw many moments of high drama, not the least of which occurred in the closing seconds when a fan set off a firecracker just as one of the collegiate players pulled up for a shot. Despite the distraction, the shot went through the hoop, and Rupp and his boys had their revenge.[57]

In the rubber match, the older AAU players reasserted their superiority with a 56–50 victory in Lexington, Kentucky—the land of Rupp. Coach Browning's team came back from twelve points behind in the final ten minutes to pull out the victory in front of the partisan crowd. Aware of the attendant racial issues, Jackie Robinson and other Phillips players made it a point to feed Barksdale the ball, and Barksdale's performance proved pivotal in leading his team to the win. Afterward, Barksdale thanked Robinson for looking out for him. Robinson acted as if it was nothing, but Barksdale and he knew what Barksdale's teammates had done. And they both felt good about it.[58]

As had been the exhibition game in Oklahoma, the outdoor game in Kentucky was a milestone for integrated hoops in the Bluegrass state. The crowd included roughly 1,000 African Americans, who were seated on the ends behind the baselines. But, as with the Oklahoma game, tension arose because of the racially mixed crowd and integrated game. As an indication of this, the night before the contest, Barksdale, who was staying with a local black family in town, received an anonymous call from someone who threatened: "I'd advise you not to go out on that court tomorrow night. If you do you are going to get shot, bang." Barksdale played, but early on, the tension in the atmosphere seemed palpable. It remained that way among the restless crowd until a break in the action with about three minutes to go in the first half. That was when the trainer came out onto the court with a water bottle. Cab Renick took a swig of it and passed it on to the next guy, who did the same. Then Barksdale's turn came. Barksdale recalled thinking to himself, "Oh shit, what do I do?" Like the others, he decided to pick up the bottle and take a drink. When he did, "the whole audience got quiet." Then he passed it to Gordon "Shorty" Carpenter, who was actually six feet seven and 250 pounds, and Barksdale thought, "What's he ["Shorty"] going to do with it? If he turns down the bottle . . ." What "Shorty" Carpenter did do, after holding it in his hand for a half-second, was take a swig, just like Barksdale had. And "all of a sudden it broke the whole tension. Had he not drank after me, I do not know how things would have proceeded," Barksdale recalled.[59]

All told, the exhibition games generated marked interest throughout the nation, especially in the basketball-hungry cities where they took place. This indicated the tour's popularity and suggested its money-making potential. Sure enough, Wilke and Bingham reported that, after paying all expenses, the basketball committee handed the USOA a check for $75,000 from the exhibition games alone. In turn, Wilke rightfully declared that basketball had become "an integral part of the Olympic program." He added, "The procedures established in 1948 have set a precedent that should be followed for future Olympic Games."[60]

Despite the economic success of the exhibitions, not everyone agreed that the committee had found the model system for team selection. Pointing to the AAU teams' affiliations with corporations, critics questioned whether AAU players should count as amateurs. Barksdale's and Kurland's willingness to turn down professional basketball suggests that the argument contained some validity.[61] In a June 1948 article in Readers Digest, Stanley Frank, striking a pessimistic tone, weighed in on the issue. He declared that the "Olympic ideal of sportsmanship is a visionary theory that simply does not work in practice." The remedy he proscribed could be found in the article's title: "Let's Ditch the Olympics."[62] A couple of weeks before the 1948 qualifying tournament, John Lardner wrote an op-ed piece for *Newsweek* that also touched on the dilemma Americans faced: a desire to embrace amateurism mixed with a desire for victory. In his piece, Lardner predicted that overall at the Olympics, the United States would "make a dreadful showing" since it used "purely amateurs." Continuing, he argued that people like Brundage held on to idealistic, anachronistic ideas of amateurism that hurt American chances. These ideals, Lardner reasonably argued, were based more on British nineteenth-century social elitism than Greek history, and he pointed out that the ancient Greek Olympic stars did not perform under the contemporary amateur code.

Lardner actually highlighted the case of the U.S. basketball team to show how some Olympic sports circumvented the idealism of Brundage. He questioned the premise that five members of the team, all near or around seven feet tall, "worked" for the Phillips Company, and he asserted that if Phillips did not pay its players for *playing*, then finding what Phillips did pay its players for is "a question that would have Scotland Yard scurrying to the doorstep of Sherlock Holmes for help." Sarcastically, he mused that since they were Oilers, "perhaps they oil," though no evidence of oiling from the roster had surfaced. His point, of course, was that practically speaking, the players were employed at least partly to represent Phillips in the AAU and, if they qualified, in the Olympics.[63]

Adolph Grundman has noted that Phillips responded to criticism of its basketball operation by legitimately pointing out that "80 percent of its basketball players remained with the company, many in positions of responsibility." Yet Grundman did also report that before the London Games, Coach Browning of Phillips suggested that some "key" players on the team would not get to go because they could not "be spared that long from work." But instead, Phillips sent to London not only the five Phillips players selected for the Games, but also the squad's seven other players as "guests of the company."[64]

In July 1948, however, such weighty issues were not the U.S. team's immediate concern. Its focus was on winning the Olympic basketball tournament. And in New York on July 14, 1948, the team readied to board

3. The 1948 U.S. men's Olympic basketball team aboard the SS *America* en route to London. From the author's collection, courtesy of R. J. Robinson.

the Europe-bound SS *America* to do just that. Throngs turned out to see the athletes off, and the SS *America* powered away at 4:25 p.m., with the Olympic flag "fluttering bravely from its foremast." Among the athletes also traveling to the Games that day was the American oarsman John B. Kelly, whose sister had come to see him off. The basketball players certainly noticed her. As U.S. center Bob Kurland remembered, "She was quite the prettiest thing that anyone had ever seen." The sister was none other than Grace Kelly.[65] On board the SS *America* the squad did virtually no training, but as Robinson recalled, "We did watch the women, and men too, but mostly the women swimmers . . . [as] they tied ropes around their waist" to practice in the ship's swimming pool.

The SS *America* powered across the Atlantic toward a Europe that was enjoying a period of economic rebound and increased consumerism similar to that in the United States. To bolster Western Europe against the Soviet threat and to provide markets for American products, the United States had implemented the Marshall Plan, the world's most ambitious rebuilding campaign ever—and it was paying dividends. In the years to come, the spectacularly successful Marshall Plan not only enabled Europe to emerge from the war as a prosperous, relatively unified entity but also greatly enhanced America's position as the world's undisputed economic superpower. America's economy, diverse inhabitants, open society, and emphasis on individuality made its culture one that youth across the globe wanted to emulate. With American popular culture spreading across the European continent, fast-paced basketball gained traction in places where previously it had largely been shunned.[66]

Postwar American aid also paved the way for Japan to prosper as a peaceful, democratic nation. Rebuilding efforts in Japan left a lasting legacy that transformed the country into a prosperous, liberal, and economically open one that came to embrace American popular culture. Within a few decades, in fact, Japan became an important outpost for the production and sale of U.S. products by such transnational corporations as Nike. During the postwar occupation of Japan, General MacArthur encouraged both baseball and basketball, and since basketball already boasted a strong tradition, it was indeed embraced enthusiastically in the new Japan.[67] Aided by the tutelage of American soldiers stationed on the homeland, Japanese players made vast improvements on their already respected play. But because of the difficulty of reconstruction, these skills were not displayed at the Olympics until 1952.

In other parts of Asia, problems for the United States loomed. For example, though during the 1948 Olympic Games General MacArthur attended the inauguration in Seoul of the new Korean Republic president Syngman Rhee, the moment was tempered by the impending communist overthrow in China.[68] Soon war raged in Korea, too. In the coming decades, battles over security, access to markets, and ways of life, between China and Russia in the East and the United States and Europe in the West, occurred throughout Asia. One of America's greatest weapons, its culture, played an increasingly important role in this long, drawn-out battle. And sports, either as a diplomatic tool or a gateway through which American culture could be brought to Asian youth, eventually moved to the frontlines of this extended East-West competition.[69] So the re-establishment of the Olympics and the growth of basketball in the immediate postwar world were important.[70]

Upon making it to Europe, the U.S. team toured Scotland. There, the squad put on clinics and played exhibition games. Wilke, the team manager and its unofficial spokesman, provided entertaining play-by-play commentary of the exhibition games for Scottish fans and hosted civic receptions detailing the finer points of the game. These efforts reflected one of the main goals put forth by the U.S. Olympic Basketball Committee beforehand: to facilitate the spread of basketball internationally.[71] Scottish fans turned out in droves.

The *Washington Post* noted that three thousand showed up on July 23, 1948, to watch Kurland lead his "white" team over Groza and Beard's "blue" team, 45–44.[72] However, Neil Harris of Albright College, who coached the Egyptian basketball team at the 1948 Games, maintained that at an exhibition tilt in Paisley, Scotland, the fans "sat in utter silence, waiting for the second half of the program—a soccer game."[73] The team's final game in Scotland took place outdoors in Edinburgh on Princes Street in front of a huge crowd. "The damn boards didn't fit on the floor . . . Try to dribble the ball, the floor wasn't even," Boryla recalled.[74]

In addition to drawing notable crowds, the tour provided coaches Browning and Rupp with an opportunity to fine-tune strategy. They determined that the squad was most effective when a majority of the Phillips teammates played with each other and when a majority of the Kentucky cagers played together. And because 1948 FIBA rules stipulated that only ten players were eligible for each single contest, the two coaches devised a unit method of substitution in which, in each half, a Phillips-laden five played for ten minutes, followed by a predominantly Kentuckian lineup.[75] The tour of Scotland also gave the U.S. squad an opportunity to adapt to other FIBA rules. Better prepared for the Games, the team then traveled to London.

Few Americans knew what to expect of London. As noted, the city had endured severe damage from air raids by Germany during World War II. Given that punishment, American critics and some English ones voiced concerns that Britain was not up to hosting the Olympics. For instance, Stanley Frank, writing in the *Readers Digest* in June 1948, asserted that Britain was unprepared from a housing and food standpoint and that Britons were not anxious to divert much-needed funds to the "meat-and-muscle show." To support his claim, Frank pointed to opinions expressed in London's *Evening Standard*. The paper had noted that even in good times, British enthusiasm for the Olympics lagged and that many Brits feared a "bad show" since the country was still recovering from the havoc wreaked by

4. Robert "Jackie" Robinson at the London Games Opening Ceremony. From the author's collection, courtesy of R. J. Robinson.

Germany. In addition, the *Standard*'s Hylton Cleaver wrote, "The Larder is bare, and most of us are broke," making it difficult to "show hospitality to distant cousins who have the money."[76] The *Sunday Pictorial* of London stated, "If well-fed American competitors were to run their ration-hungry opponents into the track, the general reaction would be: 'Well, what do you expect? It's not a fair contest.'" The *Pictorial* also maintained that if the British were able to pull off some victories, the cry would be, "Why, [the Americans] can't even win with all their steaks, butter and cream."[77]

In the end, though, these concerns could not damper enthusiasm for the Games. The U.S. basketball players and their fellow Olympians found a London that, though not completely rebuilt, still wanted to celebrate, and forty-eight countries and more than 4,500 athletes, both records, along with tens of thousands of fans, joined that celebration.[78]

Ultimately, Englanders displayed the kind of resilience they had summoned to turn back the German Luftwaffe during the Battle of Britain. After the Games, Bill Henry, the secretary of the U.S. Olympic Committee, raved about London's ability to overcome tremendous obstacles in logistics, venue preparation, transportation, and financing.[79] Thousands of other American visitors, many of whom years earlier had listened to Edward R. Murrow begin his dramatic reports of the Battle of Britain with "London is burning," shared Henry's sentiments. It was quite a turnaround. The success of the 1948 Games set the stage for the phenomenal growth of the Olympic movement in the coming decades. Nearly every Olympiad since has built upon the record number of countries and athletes that participated in London.

This is not to say that the Games were unaffected by the war. William J. Baker has noted that they still had a makeshift feel, similar to that of the Antwerp Games after World War I. Athletes felt the effects of London's battered condition firsthand: they bunked in decrepit school buildings and military camps on the outskirts of the city and had to run on a hastily put-together track, which contributed to slower-than-usual times.[80] Robinson remembered that in London the players ate "horse meat in the city and the bombed-out places were still there." (Food brought over from the United States on the SS *America* was stored at the RS Barracks in Uxbridge, where the U.S. hoops squad resided during the Games.) Signs of the changing times were all around, though. For instance, the U.S. basketball team was in London when the rations on sweets were lifted. "We gave gum and candy bars to the little children and watched them eat candy for the first time in their lives," Robinson recalled.[81]

Fortunately, the venue where the basketball tournament was played posed no notable concerns for the players. They played their contests in the quaint but relatively new Harringay Arena. Built in 1936, it had emerged from the bombing of London unscathed. The 10,000-seat-plus capacity arena "wasn't filled all the time," but it had "a good floor . . . everything was good," Robinson remembered.[82]

The United States opened Olympic pool play at Harringay Arena by soundly beating Switzerland, 86–21. (A total of twenty-three teams were divided into four pools, with seeding based on that of the 1936 Olympic tournament.) After defeating Switzerland, the U.S. beat the 1946 European champion Czechoslovakia 53–28.[83] Most figured the United States, with its height, agility, and skill, would wallop the remaining teams in its pool, including its next opponent, Argentina, but the Argentines had other plans. Utilizing superb ball movement, they stayed close in the early going against the U.S. starting five: Groza, Jones, and Rollins of Kentucky, along with NYU's Lumpp and the Denver Nuggets' Boryla. Approximately midway through the first half, with the score 14–9 in favor of the United States, Browning's second unit, which included Carpenter, Pitts, and Beck of Phillips, along with Barksdale of the Oakland Bittners and Robinson of Baylor, took the floor, but Argentina remained a threat as the first half ended with the United States ahead by only seven, 33–26. By most any standard of the time, it was a high-scoring affair.

The United States' original starting five returned to the floor after intermission and soon got into foul trouble. This created problems in the substitution pattern the rest of the way and helped keep the score close. With three minutes remaining, the teams were tied at fifty-five, but then the United States tallied four straight points on a basket by Robinson and a free throw apiece by Rollins and Carpenter. From there, the United States staved off the Argentineans for a 59–57 win.[84] Thus, Robinson, who in 2008 still kept the game ball from that contest on his desk, tallied the crucial go-ahead basket in what proved to be an amazing few weeks for the Texan. In addition to receiving the gold medal, making the go-ahead basket, and meeting the King and Queen, during the Games he took the team to hear the renowned preacher James S. Stewart. Stewart spoke with Robinson after the service and asked about getting tickets for his family to watch the U.S. squad. Robinson left him four. The following Sunday, Robinson attended services again and asked Stewart about the prospect of attending his famed New College in order to study the ministry there. Sure enough, within a year Robinson, out of basketball by then on account of a patellar injury he suffered in the build-up to the Games, studied in Edinburgh under the man that *Preaching Magazine* chose as the best preacher of the twentieth century.[85]

As for the near loss to Argentina, the *Louisville Journal-Courier's* Earl Ruby, who traveled with the U.S. squad to the Games, attributed part of the team's struggles to the "unit" system of substitution. Of the four players that Browning and Rupp deemed ineligible that night, two came from Phillips and two from Kentucky. Thus, in the first half, Phillips and Kentucky tried to run their main offenses with only three of their original team members on the floor at any one time. But Ruby did admit that Argentina deserved much credit for its spirited play—an early indicator of that nation's rich basketball tradition. The closeness of the game reflected an increased quality of basketball internationally, especially in South America, where fast, well-coordinated attacks have defined the stylistic tendency into the twenty-first century (even though Argentina did use a measure of deliberateness against the United States in London).

Following its narrow escape from Argentina, the United States encountered Egypt, which, coached by Albright College's Harris, was one of eight teams coached by an American (the others were England, France, Uruguay, Chile, Italy, Peru, and, of course, the United States).[86] In front of a crowd of some 2,500 at Harringay, the Americans handled the Egyptians with ease, 66–28. Yet during the game, Kurland incurred the wrath of British fans, who thought his size made the game too easy for him. Both times Kurland entered the game, he was "roundly booed," though, as the *Los Angeles Times* reported, "Big Bob just takes their boos with a wide grin." Later, in the finals, the crowd did applaud Kurland "lustily."[87]

It seems that fans were not the only ones to begin to react negatively to U.S. basketball supremacy, because after the U.S. team's convincing win over Egypt, murmurings started to emerge among Olympic officials that the United States played too aggressively. An unnamed "high Olympic official" charged the United States with using bad language and chattering too much from the bench, and said they "played too hard against Egypt when far ahead." Coach Browning denied the charges and claimed that officials had called fouls against Americans more frequently than against their opponents. In the meantime, Browning and Rupp instructed their players to "lean over backward in courtesy against Peru," their next opponent. Utilizing a faster game plan against Peru, described by the *Chicago Daily Tribune* as one that depended on "deception and sharpshooting," the United States won 61–33. The team also committed just thirteen fouls compared to twenty against Egypt.[88]

The victory over Peru advanced the United States to the one-and-done quarterfinals with the top seed in its bracket. Uruguay, another South American country with a strong basketball tradition, met Browning and his boys in the medal round opener. A notable episode occurred midway through the second half of the game, when the Uruguayan player Héctor Ruiz and Kurland became tangled, resulting in Ruiz being sent to the floor. As Ruby reported, rather than getting up quickly and jumping to his feet, as a college player would have done, Ruiz "rolled over and played dead." Stretcher-bearers then appeared to carry Ruiz off the court, but in rather short order, Ruiz "recovered miraculously and returned to the game."[89] These antics seemed to resemble those in soccer, a sport whose players are well known for their tendency to overdramatize injuries and who are commonly carted off the field on stretchers. Regardless of the drama of Ruiz's injury, the United States' size, speed, and skill gave them a convincing 63–28 win.

Next, in the semifinals, the United States encountered Mexico, considered by many the biggest hurdle en route to the gold. Known for its speed, too, Mexico came into the game undefeated. But in the game's early going, its hopes were dashed. Browning's Kentucky-laden starting unit opened the action so effectively that Kurland did not appear until well into the second half. Yet it was still a hotly contested affair, evidenced by Kurland's ejection, which occurred under the basket after his legs became entangled with those of the Mexican player Gudina Goya, sending Goya sprawling to the floor. According to Rubin, Goya then "flipped over twice and collapsed dramatically on his face." Though Rubin thought Kurland's infraction would have garnered no more than a personal foul in the States, Kurland was immediately ejected. Nonetheless, the United States won 71–40.[90]

5. The 1948 U.S. men's Olympic basketball team celebrates its gold medal. Photo by Popperfoto. Popperfoto Collection/Getty Images.

Surprising many, France awaited in the final. Thousands of spectators in Harringay watched the two finalists as they readied for the tip-off. To start the game, the predominantly Oiler-laden unit, anchored by Kurland and then Barksdale, raced to an early lead; Kentucky's fabulous five built on the early advantage the Phillips men made for a 28–9 U.S. lead at intermission.[91] Ultimately, U.S. size, skill, and speed delivered a 65–21 win. Though French basketball had improved since World War II, its national team was not yet a match for that of the United States. As the *Los Angeles Times* reported, "The slickest basketball team ever seen in England, possibly anywhere, bewildered France's Cinderella kids tonight."[92]

Before the final horn sounded, all fourteen of Browning's men had played. They could do so because Coach Browning, who had recently announced his intention to retire after the Games, and the French coach Robert Busmel had successfully "begged the officials" to waive the rule limiting each team to ten players per game so that "the players can tell their grandchildren they played in the final."[93] For the Americans, Alex Groza and Raymond Lumpp led the way with eleven points apiece.[94] For the tournament, Groza, Kurland, and Barksdale finished as the team's three high scorers.

Following the win, the team spent several days in Paris basking in the glow of its gold-medal showing and being entertained by Phillips company executives. "Strictly billed as [a] 'Thank you for raising all that money for other teams,'" Robinson said of the Paris jaunt, "it really was, I'm sure, funded by Phillips 66."[95] Boryla said of the trip to France, "We went to the Folies-Bergère [the famed Parisian music hall] and all that stuff and just had a hell of a time."[96]

Despite France's lopsided loss, the appearance of a European team in the final, along with Argentina's near-upset of the United States and Brazil's surprising 52–47 victory over Mexico for the bronze medal, showed that the level of basketball had improved outside North America in the twelve years since the last Olympiad. Ruby noted as much in his report on the tournament, asserting that the overall level of play at the 1948 tournament "was keener" than it had been in 1936. With an increase in the number of international basketball exchanges on the horizon, exemplified by a trip Barksdale's Oakland Bittners made to Asia a couple of months later, subsequent international play would become even sharper.[97]

With hindsight, one can see that on display in London was the flowering of the political, economic, technological, and cultural climate that has emerged across so much of the globe since World War II, a climate that has complemented a sport like basketball and an event like the Olympics. The limited local television feeds marked one example.[98] With market-oriented economies and democratic-based political models taking root in Japan and throughout Europe, with America positioned as the world's economic superpower, and with an increasingly open-market economy becoming more connected globally, it makes sense that basketball enjoyed phenomenal growth as this new world order matured. Basketball works well in urban and rural areas and puts a premium on innovation, scoring, agility, ballhandling skill, and athleticism in a relatively confined space, all of which came to complement television.

In America, basketball's dynamic growth was becoming evident in newspapers and magazines like the *Amateur Athlete*, Converse's annual basketball report, and the *Basketball Bulletin*, which carried ads by companies such as the electronics-maker Emerson that featured basketball players who touted new state-of-the-art televisions. In one particular ad, Emerson showed basketball players rising for jump shots and making other moves inside

TABLE 2. 1948 U.S. Men's Olympic Basketball cumulative stats

NAME	G	FGM*	FTM-FTA	(%)	PF	PTS/AVG
Alex Groza	7	35	8-14	.571	19	78/11.1
Robert Kurland	7	27	11-15	.733	17	65/9.3
Don Barksdale	6	20	14-19	.737	16	54/9.0
R. C. Pitts	4	13	5-6	.833	3	31/7.8
Raymond Lumpp	5	14	8-10	.800	11	36/7.2
Wallace Jones	6	19	5-9	.556	11	43/7.2
Gordon Carpenter	5	13	9-12	.750	6	35/7.0
Vincent Boryla	5	11	6-10	.600	11	28/5.6
Jesse Renick	7	17	5-7	.714	13	39/5.6
Lewis Beck	7	13	7-11	.636	3	33/4.7
Kenneth Rollins	6	10	4-5	.800	5	24/4.0
Clifford Barker	5	7	5-12	.417	13	19/3.8
Ralph Beard	7	10	6-12	.500	7	26/3.7
Robert Robinson	5	6	1-3	.333	6	13/2.6
USA TOTALS	8	215	94-145	.648	141	524/65.5
OPP. TOTALS	8	81	94-166	.566	132	256/32.0

* Figures for field goals attempted are not available.

a printed television screen with the caption: "So real, so clear-cut, you're in there yourself."[99] Meanwhile, sporting goods companies like Spalding, Wilson, Converse, and Keds, among others, were enjoying robust sales and increasing advertising for their various basketball-related products. These ads invariably touted the allure of basketball's speed, innovative action, and high scores. Converse, which in addition to supplying the U.S. team with Chuck Taylors in London, outfitted the Philippines, Cuba, and Egypt at the Games—while also partially equipping five other squads—tried to capitalize on the U.S. Olympic team's performance by advertising its relationship with the squad.[100] The tone of basketball's cultural language was getting reflected and formed in such ads.

As noted, immediately after the London Games, basketball received a boost internationally when FIBA passed another round of rules that established an even faster, higher-scoring brand of basketball. U.S. leagues already enforced most of the new rules. For instance, FIBA voted to double the width of the lane and adopted America's three-second rule, keeping offensive players out of the newly widened lane for more than three seconds.[101] Both rules provided more space for players to operate around the basket, thereby encouraging wing and guard action. In addition to increasing the sport's speed, this increased the opportunity for in-the-air innovation during drives to the basket, a crucial component of basketball's attractiveness.

With France's strong showing symbolizing basketball's increasing popularity in Europe, and with Japan set to buttress basketball's already strong presence in Asia by fielding a team in 1952, the Olympic basketball tournament was poised for growth. Those prospects for growth increased even further when, near the end of the London Games, the Soviet Union announced its intention to participate in the 1952 Olympics. A primary element of their Olympic efforts became basketball, leading to the greatest team-sport rivalry in the history of the Olympic Games.

3

COLD WAR BASKETBALL'S OPENING
SALVO IN HELSINKI

Even though Stalin's paranoia about the West continued and McCarthyism raged in the United States, in 1952 the Soviets, drawn by the Olympics' popularity and influence, officially made the Games a front in the cold war struggle. And the Soviets' arrival generated considerable interest. As the *New York Times*'s Arthur Daley put it, "There will be 71 nations in the Olympics at Helsinki. The United States would like to beat all of them, but the only one that counts is Soviet Russia.[1]"

At its base, the cold war pitted two divergent ways of life against each other. For some forty years, the two leading nations of that war stood toe-to-toe in an epic struggle for supremacy that touched nearly every facet of life. The ideological conflict led both countries to engage in economic rivalry, a weapons race, a race to space, and fierce competition in the sports arena as well. Summing up the ever-growing role of sports in the cold war, the historian William J. Baker has written, "No less than the Berlin Blockade, the Korean War, and the Cuban Missile Crisis, East-West athletic contests represented tests of will as well as strength and skill."[2]

For basketball, it was at the Helsinki Games that the United States, led by centers Bob Kurland and Clyde Lovellette, a native Hoosier who remains the only men's player in NCAA history to lead in the nation in scoring and win the NCAA championship in the same season, first engaged the Soviets in Olympic basketball. It would prove to be only the beginning of what would become a decades-long rivalry that symbolized the cold war. During the breadth of that competition, the Soviet Union challenged the United States in a sport in which the bulk of the rules and the stars, along with many of its associated products, emanated from America. In Helsinki, the two foes played each other twice: the first was a high-scoring rout, the second a slow-moving affair that the *New York Times* described as so boring it "took on the character of a truce meeting in Korea."[3] Both contests created electric atmospheres in Helsinki's jam-packed Messuhalli II arena.

As noted, the Soviets wanted to utilize the Olympics to assert the supremacy of their way of life. But this had not always been the case. In the 1920s, rather than embrace competitive "bourgeois" sports, communist Russia emphasized mass-sport activities founded on the old gymnastics-based athletic system that had originated in Germany in the mid-nineteenth century.[4] The Russian government sanctioned massive sports festivals like May Day and the Trade Union Games, which were held every four years and functioned as Russia's answer to the Olympics. These festivals were part of a plan to promote physical fitness programs designed to produce robust, athletic youth capable of handling the rigors of war, industry, and farming. Each year, millions of "citizen-athletes" earned the "Ready for Labor and Defense" insignia for meeting certain requirements in gymnastics, obstacle-course running, track-and-field events, skiing, rifle shooting, and more.[5] During this time, the Bolshevik idea that sports were to play an integral role in a world revolution discouraged contact with western-driven international sports federations, especially the IOC. Western-led international competitions were seen as "instruments of chauvinism, expressing the spirit of rivalry, individualism and the obsession with breaking records."[6]

Finding themselves in a more connected world after World War II, however, the Soviets concluded that isolation from western-based sports was no longer viable. They had begun to reach this conclusion in the 1930s, but a post–World War II directive to participate in the Olympic Games signified an important, thorough shift in Soviet policy. Yuri Rastvorov, a former Soviet secret agent, explained, "The government realized the tremendous propaganda possibilities that international athletics offered."[7] The Soviet decision remains a watershed development in the history of international sport. As the historian Barbara Keys has noted, that the Soviet Union (and earlier Nazi Germany) "came to embrace a world so deeply embedded in the structures of liberal capitalism is perhaps one of the most surprising outcomes in the history of cultural internationalism."[8]

To compete in this international sporting community, the Soviets embarked on an ambitious sports program and joined virtually every major international sports federation.[9] As an indication of this renewed emphasis on sports, the Soviet government bestowed cabinet-level status on the All-Union Ministry of Physical Culture and Sports, which was in charge of managing the country's sports system.[10] Suddenly, the international sporting stakes behind the iron curtain were amplified. Signs hung from stadiums throughout the country reading, "All World Must Be Taken by Soviet Athletes."[11] Evidence of increased pressure on sporting officials surfaced at an event in Volga, where Russian sports officials doctored results in an effort to make a good showing.[12] These officials had received the message all too clearly: The Communist party expected results.[13]

In the months leading up to the 1952 Games, American magazines and newspapers carried articles analyzing every facet of Soviet participation. Theories abounded. Some expressed surprise that the Soviets chose to participate; others questioned the ethics of the Soviet sports system. Some warned that the Soviets would fare well; still others predicted a poor showing. Allison Danzig, writing for the New York Times, summed up the one thing pundits could agree on: that the Soviet Union's presence "added enormously to the world-wide interest in the Games."[14]

The New York Times's Harry Schwartz counts among the pundits who predicted a strong showing by the Soviets. He noted that up to that point, the Soviets had generally sneered at the Olympic Games as merely another form of "degenerate bourgeois" activity unfit for Russian participation.[15] Now that Stalin had chosen to participate, he warned Americans not to doubt the Soviet Union's preparedness. According to Schwartz, Stalin and his cohorts knew a poor showing would cause "disastrous consequences" for their propaganda machine. Schwartz has also pointed out that the party apparatus, working with a population of over 200 million people, had doggedly cultivated athletic talent ever since the Communist Party had directed Soviet athletes to position themselves to win top international honors in their field of sport a few years earlier.[16]

Basketball was on the front lines of the Communist Party's ambitious plan. The Soviet Union figured that beating the United States in basketball would return huge dividends on the cultural front. Unfortunately for the Soviet officials, they did not enjoy a strong basketball tradition. However, all was not bleak. The Soviet Union benefited from some advantages that aided its effort. For starters, its long winters worked well with basketball, a sport invented to occupy athletes in the cold months. In addition, Russia alone boasted more than 200 million people. Finally, and most important, many of the eastern European nations under the iron curtain, especially those in the Baltics, already enjoyed excellent basketball traditions. This had already helped reap quick success for the Soviet Union, which won the 1947 European championship thanks largely to the contributions of players who hailed from the Baltics. The Baltic presence on Soviet teams would prove to be a trend throughout the cold war.

Considering the relative youth of its basketball program, the Soviet Union continued to make remarkable progress following its 1947 European championship. In 1951 and 1952, it won two more. After the 1952 European title at Paris's Palais des Sports, which gave the Soviets an automatic berth in the Olympic basketball tournament, the Soviet coach declared, "Basketball in Russia begins with Stalin." In between games, team captain Ivan Lissov told *Time* that "from Vladivostok to Leningrad, everybody plays." Unfortunately, that was about the extent of the quotes *Time* could muster from the Soviet players before they were whisked away to the Soviet Embassy. Even when the team was accessible, a "hollow-cheeked cultural attaché" constantly surrounded the players, *Time* reported.[17] Regardless, the wins reflected the Soviets' abilities.

As they had been in the past, at the 1952 European championship Baltic players were again crucial to the Soviet Union's success. And months later in Helsinki, four of the team's twelve players were Lithuanians, while three others were Estonian. Combined, the two countries boasted populations fifteen times smaller than Russia's, yet they provided more than 50 percent of the Soviet team's players. This resulted from their strong basketball traditions.

Before World War II, Latvia, Lithuania, and Estonia had won three European championships among them. Lithuania, with less than four million people, was particularly strong, taking the European title in both 1937 and 1939—in no small part because of the efforts of Frank Lubin. By 1940, when Russia annexed Lithuania, basketball was already entrenched as Lithuania's national sport. The Baltics produced so much talent, in fact, that had it not been for Russian bias, there likely would have been more than seven Baltic players on the 1952 Soviet team. In an interview forty years after the Helsinki games, Heino Krussi, an Estonian on the first Soviet Olympic basketball squad, said that many good Baltic players could have helped the team, but they did not have visas. He recalled that the great Arvo Putmaker, an Estonian who ended up exiled to Siberia, was unable to get a visa to Moscow to try out for the team. Krussi's teammate Ilmar Kullamit, also Estonian, concurred. He remembered there being many good players at a Soviet training camp that took place in the Baltics, but when the group was told that in order to play on the Olympic team, they would have to go to Moscow to fill out paperwork, not everyone went.[18] Most native Estonians, as well as those from other Baltic countries, considered the Russians invaders and were not anxious to travel to Moscow for various reasons, fear of exile among them.

This distaste for Russian subjugation points to an important irony under the surface of the Soviet Union's basketball program. Most of the Baltic players that Stalin and his cohorts relied on to showcase the Soviet Union to the world opposed Soviet rule. This put the Baltic athletes in a difficult position when it came to playing on the Soviet national team. When Krussi and Kullamit, two of the Estonians on the 1952 Soviet Olympic squad (the other was star player Joann Lissov) were asked decades afterward if playing under the Soviet name meant that they had betrayed their country, they did not take umbrage at the difficult question. They understood the delicacy of the situation. Krussi answered that it was not completely fair to charge them as traitors just because they were athletes. He said all Estonians had Soviet passports, but it did not matter what was in one's pocket or on one's shirt. "What is important is we knew we were Estonians in our heart," he explained.[19] These comments demonstrate how, when it came to basketball, the Soviet Union relied heavily on the hearts of people they had not won, to win the hearts of people throughout the world.

Soviet basketball did not rely only on Baltic talent; it also borrowed from Baltic style. The Baltic countries had won their collective three European championships by utilizing a "disciplined pattern offense with chess-like precision. Nothing was left to chance: this was solid, academic basketball," according to the Soviet historian Yuri Brokhin.[20] In *Serious Fun*, the Soviet historian Robert Edelman expressed similar sentiments by quoting Russian Anatolii Pinchuk, the leading pre-glasnost basketball writer, who described the Baltic school as "using the maximum of rehearsed combinations and the minimum of improvisation. In short, Baltic basketball is a solid academic game."[21] This disciplined, scrupulous style worked well, particularly after the performance of Bill Russell at the 1956 Olympics, when the Soviets increasingly coupled it with the utilization of players that were, in comparison to the Soviets' 1952 team, more versatile, more athletic, and taller.

In the 1950s, the efficiency of the Baltic game helped polish the Russian style, which was more rugged and rigid, though its players were physically fit and played a bit faster. Comparing the differences, Brokhin writes that in Russia, "the strict, scientific style lost to a raging ad-lib." Together, these styles, combined with a little ball control and attacking from Georgia, melded into a "powerhouse hybrid of short but hard-driving" basketball stars, as Brokhin describes it.[22] In Helsinki, the Soviets had a team that seems to have fit that description rather well. However, the "short" stature of the Soviet squad would become a liability against the U.S. team's centers Kurland and Lovellette, who were both nearly seven feet tall. Thus, after the tournament, Soviet officials implemented a frenzied search for exceptionally tall players.[23]

The Soviets' 1952 European title in Paris came just months before the Olympics, and it challenged the assumption that America would cruise to the gold medal. Fortunately for the United States, the Olympic basketball committee had worked for several years on developing a strong team. In 1949, banking on repeat success, the committee adopted an approach similar to the one that had been used for the selection and training of the 1948 Olympic team. An eight-team qualifying tournament made up of the nation's best amateur squads was scheduled for the last week in March 1952. In a slight change, this time, the field consisted of all four semifinalists from the AAU's national tournament, the two NCAA tournament finalists, the

NIT champion, and the champion of the National Association of Intercollegiate Basketball (NAIB). For the first time, the YMCA champion did not receive a spot in the Olympic qualifying tournament.

Originally, the committee pegged Madison Square Garden as the host of the qualifying tournament, but the Kansas City Public Activities Association, looking to capitalize on the event's popularity, made an offer to stage the tournament in the Kansas City Auditorium. Eager to maximize profitability, the basketball committee allotted two first-round games to Kansas City.[24] It proved a wise decision. Dr. "Phog" Allen's University of Kansas team led the bill at the Kansas City Auditorium and helped attract sellout crowds.

Coach Allen's Kansas squad came to the 1952 Olympic trials after having just won the NCAA tournament, led by their center Lovellette, who scored a record 141 points in four tournament games. It was a bit ironic that the tall Lovellette powered the Kansas team, given that throughout the 1930s and 1940s, Dr. Allen had supported raising the basket to twelve feet to combat the advantage of height in basketball.[25] But by the late 1940s, Coach Allen had given up on deriding "glandular goons" in favor of utilizing their talents.

With Lovellette, Kansas was considered a challenger at the Olympic qualifying tournament to the AAU's leading National Industrial Basketball League teams: the NIBL champion Caterpillar Cats, sponsored by the Caterpillar Tractor Company out of Peoria, Illinois, and the runner-up Phillips Oilers, still led by Bob Kurland.

Sure enough, all three qualified for the semifinals in Madison Square Garden, along with the NIT champion LaSalle. Kansas did put up a fuss, however, before attending the semifinals. The issue arose when, after Kansas won its opening-round contests in the Kansas City Auditorium, Phog Allen declared that his team would not set foot in Madison Square Garden unless one of the three referees calling his team's semifinal contest came from the West. With their plane warming up and their bags packed, the Jayhawks waited for hours in protest in the lobby of Kansas City's Muehlebach Hotel until Phog's demands were met.[26] The spat raised tensions yet again between the AAU-laden basketball committee and Allen, who in 1936 had referred to the AAU brass as "oceanic hitchhikers." Finally, the U.S. Olympic Basketball Committee chairman Howard Hobson, having worked the phones, assured Coach Allen that a Midwestern official would make up part of the officiating crew.[27]

Satisfied, Phog Allen and his Kansas squad headed for New York City to battle LaSalle in what the *New York Times* characterized as a "dream" game because it pitted the champions of the nation's two elite collegiate basketball tournaments against each other.[28] In this instance, the NCAA proved superior, but just barely. Powered by forty points from the Hoosier native Clyde Lovellette, Kansas came back from a thirteen-point halftime deficit to beat the Tom Gola–led Explorers 70–65 in front of more than 11,000 fans. Back in Lawrence, on the University of Kansas campus and along Massachusetts Avenue, Jayhawk supporters lit bonfires in celebration, and "a crush of cars brought the town to a halt."[29] In the other semifinal, the Caterpillar Cats knocked out the qualifying tournament's defending champion, the Philips Oilers, 64–50, thereby pitting Caterpillar versus Kansas for the championship.

In a thrilling final played in front of over 18,000 fans, Caterpillar edged out Kansas 62–60. The win gave the AAU its third straight Olympic qualifying tournament victory. Caterpillar went into the game with more height and experience, as its roster was packed with former collegiate stars, but Phog Allen's Jayhawks nearly pulled off the upset by again relying on the exploits of Lovellette. In the closing seconds, with the score tied, however, the usually sure Lovellette dribbled down the court and missed a shot from point-blank range. "All I had to do was give it to Bob Kenney, and he lays it off the backboard and we win. I felt terrible," Lovellette recalled. By 2008 the legendary hooper, who helped Kansas get a title, his nation and Doc Allen a gold medal, and himself three NBA titles as a pro, still seemed irked by the miss, telling the author: "We had the game won and I had the ball. And I blew the shot. And I had two Kansas players on each side of me . . . Peoria rebounded, kicked it out to Howie Williams, he took about three or four dribbles, fired the ball up—we lose." He added, "It would've been really icing on the cake if we'd have got him [Coach Allen] as head coach."[30]

Howard "Howie" Williams, who capitalized on Lovellette's miss by racing to the other end and tossing in the winning basket for Caterpillar, was a fellow Indiana native and had starred in college at Purdue.[31] His game-winning shot reverberated widely. The day after, more than 2,000 fans greeted the Cats as they arrived back in Peoria, and thousands more lined the streets as a parade of about 150 automobiles carried the team through town.[32]

In a way, the final was a formality for the players, because the night before it took place, the basketball committee had released the Olympic roster. But the winning team's coach earned the right to coach the Olympic team, and this was a motivation. And as it happened, that coach became Peoria's Warren Womble, who was just thirty-two years old. Ironically, as a youngster growing up in Oklahoma, Womble had actually been a fan of Phillips. But Phillips spurned his attempts to join the squad after his college days at Southeastern State College, where he had played under Bloomer Sullivan, an Iba protégé who also stressed fundamentals. (Womble's time at Southeastern was interrupted by World War II.) After getting rebuffed by Phillips in 1948, Womble played for the Cats and then two years later became the squad's head man. For such a young man, this unlikely path would deliver an Olympic opportunity that "had eluded coaches who had devoted their lives to the game," as the basketball historian Adolph H. Grundman has put it.[33]

Most assumed that Dr. Allen would serve as Womble's assistant, and he ultimately did—but not without some controversy first. In an unprecedented development, the executive board of the United States Olympic Association (USOA) decided to challenge Allen's placement as assistant coach. The *Washington Post* reported that because of the "public utterances and actions, past and present, of the stormy petrel of the basketball courts, some members of the executive board will ask for a careful review of Allen's status as coach." The AAU-leaning executive members argued that it was merely precedent, not rule, that the runner-up coach in the Olympic qualifying tournament take on the Olympic assistant coaching duties, and that technically, according to the Olympic Constitution, no person could coach until approved by the executive board. It is a "privilege, not a right," the board argued.[34] The posturing was a way for AAU officials to punish Allen for his years of challenging the organization's position as America's leader of amateur basketball on the international stage. In the end though, Phog Allen did serve as the assistant coach.

From Caterpillar, the basketball committee chose five players: Dan Pippin, Frank McCabe, Marcus Freiberger, Ronald Bontemps, and Howie Williams. Two made it from Phillips—Bob Kurland and Wayne Glasgow.

Seven players from the 1952 NCAA-champion Kansas Jayhawks squad, a team whose players have continued to get together through five decades, earned roster spots. Those seven were the dominant Clyde Lovellette, William Lienhard, Robert Kenney, William Hougland, who played in both the 1952 and 1956 Games, Dean Kelley, Charles Hoag, and John Keller. Hougland and Lienhard had received military orders by the time they went to the Helsinki Games. "They were drafting everybody for the Korean War ... I just happened to be in ROTC, so when we [Hougland and Lienhard] went to the Olympics, we were really officially in the military," Hougland explained. "We should have gone to the service right out of college." In order to play in the Olympics, both players "had to get [the military's] approval," and then, upon returning from Helsinki, Hougland says, "Bill [Lienhard] and I both went right into the service."[35]

There were no African American players on the 1952 U.S. Olympic basketball team. Black players had enjoyed a measure of success in the AAU for several years, highlighted by the selection of the AAU's Don Barksdale for the 1948 Olympic team. And a few black players, like Rutgers's Paul Robeson, who graduated in 1919; George Gregory, who earned the first NCAA All-American honors by an African American in 1931 at Columbia University; and Barksdale at UCLA in the 1940s, enjoyed success in the collegiate ranks. In addition, Earl Lloyd, Chuck Cooper, and Nat "Sweetwater" Clifton integrated the NBA in 1950–51. But clearly, in the 1950s, prejudice in the sporting arena, as elsewhere, remained a major problem. In 1952 the Caterpillar Cats had no black players, and Kansas's Coach Allen was not as progressive as some other collegiate coaches. In 1996, the longtime University of Kansas radio voice Max Falkenstein, who called Jayhawk games for more than fifty years from the 1940s to the 1990s, summed up Phog Allen's attitude toward minorities:

> Doc Allen used to joke, "You've got to fight fire with fire. If the other team has a Jewish player, you've got to get a Jewish player ... if they've got a Polish player, we've got to get a Polish player ... if Kansas State has a black player, we've got to get a black player." So they went to Wichita and got La Vannes Squires to play at Kansas. He was the first black to play at Kansas.[36]

Such a policy was obviously prejudiced, but it also indicated how the open nature of sports competition could help minorities overcome artificial barriers. Teams looking to compete with the established stalwart college teams did indeed call on players from historically marginalized ethnicities and races, especially African Americans, forcing coaches such as the reluctant Dr. Allen to adapt or lose out. Dr. Allen adapted, and he would reap the benefits of his pragmatism in 1955 when he recruited Wilt Chamberlain to Kansas.

Among those on the United States' Helsinki roster, Lovellette and Kurland, a holdover from the 1948 team, led the way. Kurland was a known commodity who could be counted on for his leadership and consistent play. The six-feet-nine-inch, 250-pound Lovellette was less polished but carried huge potential. He came to deliver on it.

As with the 1936 star Joe Fortenberry, Lovellette's height caused him to turn inward as a youngster growing up in Terre Haute, Indiana. Shy in the classroom, he found solace on the court. Then, at the University of Kansas, he grew into his body and matured socially, turning from a shy farm boy into an extrovert. He even hosted a Wild West themed radio show on campus. On the court at Kansas, he improved his touch, and as a pro with the NBA's Minnesota Lakers, he became one of the league's early big men to effectively step away from the basket to utilize the outside shot. Given his exploits in the 1952 NCAA tournament and his strong showing at the Olympic qualifying tournament, expectations were high for him in Helsinki. He struggled in early round Olympic contests, however, and at one point he was benched for unenthusiastic play and for having had a run-in with Kurland in practice. But he rebounded from his early struggles to lead the U.S. team in scoring, delivering crucial baskets at opportune times in the later rounds.[37]

For a few weeks after the Olympic qualifying tournament, concern surfaced that Lovellette might not even play at the Games because of a three-year, $50,000 offer from the Milwaukee Hawks of the NBA.[38] This offer reflected the rising salaries of professional athletes, an escalation that had generated enough alarm a year earlier that the U.S. government's Salary Stabilization Board appointed a special panel to investigate the fairness of such large percentage increases.[39] The contract proposal also indicated the NBA's increasing ability to outbid NIBL teams for top collegiate talent. However, Lovellette decided to stay with the AAU's Oilers, which kept him eligible for the Olympics. He joined Phillips Company as an "employee" for $12,000 a year, partly because Boots Adams, the Phillips president and Phog Allen's good friend, had mentored Lovellette at Kansas. As the Phog Allen biographer Blair Kerkhoff puts it, "Big Clyde felt an obligation." Asked in 2008 if he ever really thought he would not join Phillips or attend the Games, Lovellette said no. "I had my mind set up that . . . I was going to Phillips Petroleum Company." And he certainly seems glad he did make it to Helsinki. "You take the championships from high school to college, pros and the Olympics, and I always tell the people that the greatest experience that I had was playing in the Olympics."[40]

After Lovellette announced his intention to stay and play on the U.S. Olympic team, the Milwaukee Hawks manager, Ben Kerner, further complicated the matter, however. Kerner claimed that Lovellette had told him that the Oilers had promised to put Lovellette on the payroll while he played in the Olympics. "I wonder how Brundage, with his strict amateur ideas, can hold still for this kind of stuff," Kerner asked sardonically.[41] True or not, the episode suggested the incongruities of Olympic amateurism in the United States. These incongruities were often overlooked by the AOA, even as Americans commonly derided Soviet Olympic participants for being professionals. The AOA, for instance, referred to Soviet Olympians as "'drafted' athletes" but allowed NIBL-affiliated players to participate in the Games.[42]

With Lovellette on board, the newly named U.S. team was split into two squads, one consisting mainly of AAU members and the other made up mainly of collegians. The teams were then sent on an exhibition tour consisting of four games, with the first stop in the basketball-loving town of Hutchinson, Kansas. There, townspeople had responded with rabid enthusiasm after learning their town would host an exhibition game, gobbling up 9,000 tickets for a 7,000-seat venue within forty-eight hours. As a result, the pleasantly surprised basketball committee decided to give Hutchinson two more contests, so three of the four exhibitions took place there. The Hutchinson Chamber of Commerce helped assure that all three games were played in front of near-capacity crowds, despite sweltering one-hundred-degree heat. All told, the contests generated $30,000 for the U.S. Olympic Committee. The fourth exhibition game, played in Peoria, added an additional $2,400 to the coffers.[43] The exhibition series solidified basketball's role as an important contributor to U.S. Olympic funds.

The basketball committee devised other ways to generate funds as well. During the 1951–52 basketball season, colleges and AAU teams routinely asked spectators to make small donations for the American Olympic effort. Given that the U.S. Olympic movement still relied on donations from American citizens (the first Olympic television contract with CBS did not materialize until 1960), high schools throughout the country did the same. Upwards of $10,000 poured in.

The basketball committee did garner funding from a few corporate sponsors, especially Converse and Spalding. As in 1948, the U.S. Olympic team was outfitted in Converse's robustly selling Chuck Taylor basketball shoes, and again the company made sure to advertise its relationship with the team that "flashed" across courts.[44] Meanwhile, the U.S. squad's "official" ball was provided by Spalding. These companies were long-standing stalwarts in the sporting goods industry, but they faced increasing competition in the 1950s as the popularity of sports and their associated products grew. For instance, Chicago's Wilson Company, which started as a meatpacking entity, was enjoying strong growth in its sporting-goods division, a component of the business established in 1917. By 1956 Wilson had fifteen factories devoted to the production of sporting goods in ten different U.S. cities, and its sporting-goods division surpassed Spalding in total employees.[45] Wilson's growth in this area indicated the potential of sports-related business.

Not satisfied with reaping financial support only from intrasquad exhibitions, donations, and corporate partnerships, the committee also enlisted the help of Abe Saperstein and his Harlem Globetrotters, who agreed to donate the proceeds of a couple of exhibition games to U.S. Olympic basketball. In the early 1950s, the Globetrotters counted as the world's most popular basketball team. In 1951 a record number of people, roughly 75,000, came out to watch the 'Trotters perform in Berlin's Olympic stadium—as well as to get a glimpse of Jesse Owens. During the summer of 1952, the Globetrotters lived up to their name by setting out on a State Department–backed road trip that covered some 51,000 miles as the team visited thirty-three countries in four continents. In the end, the team played in front of an estimated 1.5 million fans that summer, showcasing the groundbreaking creativity that made it famous.[46]

The Globetrotters' popularity even reached behind the iron curtain. The 1952 U.S. Olympic basketball player William Hougland recalled that, as far as high-level American-style basketball, "the only people they [Soviet players] had ever seen—and this is what we heard from them—they had seen the Globetrotters. That's about the extent of basketball that they had really seen."[47]

Ultimately, after all expenses, the U.S. Olympic Basketball Committee handed the USOC a check for over $100,000 to support the Olympic cause.[48] Basketball officials were satisfied with the economic success of their pre-Olympic plan and held high hopes that the selection process and exhibition schedule would lead to another gold medal.

In July 1952, on a Pan American World Airways flight that symbolized the budding global age, the U.S. hoops squad traveled by air to the Olympics for the first time. Regarding that flight, Hougland said, "We didn't think a thing about it . . . The thing that was important was that we got to go. How we got there was not very important." He did add, however, that, "The planes then were prop planes." Therefore, the multiple-stop flight "took you a long time to get there."[49]

On July 8 the U.S. basketball players, having been trained for basketball and been "briefed" on behavior—"what to do and what not to do" in dealing with the Soviets so as not to put the United States in a "bad light"—landed in Helsinki.[50] This gave them ample time to get acclimated to Finland before the first game, which was slated for July 25. During the two and a half weeks before that first game, Coach Womble and Coach Allen ran practices in front of large, enthusiastic crowds.[51] "We practiced outside. The skins against the shirts," Hougland explained.[52] During these sessions, the squad often shared practice time with other national teams. Hobson noted that the United States, hoping to improve international relations and to promote basketball in all countries, looked to help the other teams in "every way possible."[53] And strategically, it was during this time that Coach Womble decided to adopt the platoon system originated by Brown and Rupp in 1948. It called for playing the Kansas players together as one unit and the AAU players on the other unit, as often as possible.[54]

Twenty-three countries entered a team in the Olympic basketball tournament. The field represented nearly every part of the world. Ten arrived with an automatic bid for the final field of sixteen, including the top six finishers from the 1948 Olympic tournament: the United States, France, Brazil, Mexico, Uruguay, and Chile, a group that reflected the Americas' past dominance in international basketball. Argentina received a spot in the final sixteen as well, for winning the 1950 world championship, which included a victory over the AAU's strong Denver Chevrolets team. The Soviet Union and Czechoslovakia, the two finalists from the European tournament, and the host-country team Finland also received automatic entries. The remaining thirteen teams competed in a pre-Olympic tournament for the final six spots.

Adding uncertainty to the final determination of the sixteen teams for the Olympic tournament was the complex issue of mainland Communist China and Taiwan. In the weeks leading up to the Games, FIBA struggled to determine the best course of action. Initially, FIBA had decided to reserve a spot for both in the Olympic basketball tournament, partly because the IOC took so long to decide the issue. But the IOC did not officially announce its decision to allow athletes from either country to participate, albeit not as representatives of separate nations, until July 17, 1952, which was too late for them to enter the qualifying tournament for basketball anyway. Plus, the IOC rescinded its offer, only to offer it again a short time later.[55] In the end, neither Taiwan, which ultimately boycotted the Games, nor China, whose forty-one Olympic athletes showed up ten days after the Games started, participated in the 1952 Olympic basketball tournament.[56]

The Chinese question was a difficult one. The original IOC vote allowing mainland China to participate in the Helsinki Olympics had taken place the day after Avery Brundage was named president of the IOC. Brundage, a former two-sport All-American in track and field and basketball at the University of Illinois and a 1912 Olympian in the decathlon, had worked his way to the post after serving first as the AAU president and then as the head of the U.S. Olympic Association. He was an exceedingly skilled administrator whose career in high-level amateur sports ultimately spanned six decades. In 1952, his controversial decision to facilitate Communist China's entrance into the Olympic movement was perceived by many leaders as a victory for Mao Zedong. The outraged Nationalist Chinese, who in 1949 behind leader Chiang Kai-Shek had fled to Taiwan, perceived the decision as a betrayal by the West. "As a protest against such an unlawful decision, the Chinese National Olympic Committee has decided to withdraw from the 1952 Games," Taiwanese representatives declared.[57] Communist Chinese attaché Sheng Shih-tai responded by declaring his government the only effective government in China.

Leaders in the West were not pleased with Brundage's quick work in bringing China into the Olympic fold either, especially since it came at a time when China had not yet garnered admittance to the United Nations and the Korean War still raged.[58] Three years earlier, the U.S. State Department had criticized Mao Zedong's government as a Soviet puppet regime that "could not even pass the test of legitimacy . . . it is not Chinese." And in 1951 the *New York Times* condemned the Chinese Communist government as a "compact little oligarchy dominated by Moscow's nominees [the Beijing-Moscow accord was still in effect]." That same year, General Douglas MacArthur had summarized China's turn to Communism as "the greatest political mistake we have made in a hundred years in the Pacific . . . I believe we will pay for it for a century."[59] In other words, many folks did not meet Brundage's Olympic acceptance of China warmly.

The question of how to deal with Communist China at the Olympics reflected the quandary the West faced in deciding how to deal with it more broadly. As the relationship has developed, the story of China, the West, and the Olympics has become an important part of basketball's rise— however, this would not happen until the early 1970s, when the United States and China, rather ironically, found common ground in their shared desire to contain the Soviet Union.[60] From the table-tennis diplomacy of 1972 to Yao Ming, sports have played an integral role in that interaction.

On July 19, 1952, the Helsinki Games opened with a record seventy nations and more than 5,800 athletes participating.[61] As had been the case with London, political factors had influenced the IOC's decision to choose the host city. During World War II, Finland fought fiercely to remain outside the sphere of Soviet rule. The daring forays of its famed skier-soldiers who glided through the snow carrying out guerilla-style raids on Soviet camps symbolized its homeland defense.[62] Technically, Finland emerged from World War II neutral, but it stood as a beacon of democratic freedom abutting the iron curtain. Looking to reward the Finnish for their refusal to submit to Soviet rule, the western-dominated IOC had awarded the Games to Helsinki. The *New York Times*'s Allison Danzig reflected America's respect for the Finnish by writing that the Opening Ceremonies marked the realization of a dream for Finland, a people "brave of heart."[63] The *Saturday Evening Post*'s Collie Small maintained that most Finns were eager to host the Olympics because they offered Finland a chance to attract investment and tourists and to show the western world they were an independent, freedom-loving people.[64]

Critics griped, however, that Helsinki was not yet capable of hosting and pointed out that Helsinki maintained only 4,000 hotel beds when projections estimated that more than 100,000 visitors would attend the Games. However, as had been the case in London four years earlier, such cries proved unwarranted. The willingness of Finns to house athletes and guests in private homes averted the potential logjam. Sacrifices like this were not uncommon: even American corporations like Coca-Cola were able to overcome the remoteness and diminutiveness of Finland. Though the country lacked a local Coca-Cola bottler, Coca-Cola brought in 30,000 cases of Coke from the Netherlands on the MS *Marvic*, which served as a kind of "floating stockroom" for the athletes and spectators.[65] Ultimately, the Finnish people, like the English before them, silenced the critics.

Almost a week after the Helsinki Games Opening Ceremonies, the Olympic basketball tournament commenced. The U.S. team opened its quest for gold with a 66–48 win over Hungary in a rather poorly played affair. Kurland finished with only four points and "stumbled and fumbled constantly before fouling out." The promising young Lovellette did not fare much better, managing to score only seven. Fortunately for the United States, Dan Pippin, a six-feet-four-inch wingman, played well, deftly tipping in missed shots en route to leading the team with fifteen points.[66]

The *Washington Post*, for one, was more impressed with the Soviet Union's 74–46 drubbing of Bulgaria on opening day than with the U.S. victory. Coach Womble concurred. "We looked mighty ragged out there today," he told the *Post*, adding, "That Russian team looked good to me."[67]

Willard Greim, the acting FIBA president, and Vincent Farrell, an American referee at the Games, posited after the Hungary game that the U.S. team may have struggled with its shooting because of the international ball, "which looks like, and is made the same as our soccer ball."[68] Bob Kenney, the U.S. team's second-highest scorer in Helsinki, did not blame the performance on the ball, but he did explain that it "didn't bounce true most the time. So it was hard to dribble."[69] Though surely not the U.S. squad's only concern, the basketball in Helsinki did cause problems for American shooters—much as the Berg ball had caused problems at the Berlin Games. The Helsinki ball was decidedly different from the ones elite players in the United States commonly used. By 1952, the American firm Spalding touted its "famed research and manufacturing facilities" for producing basketballs with "top grain leather," "pronounced pebbling," and "deeper, wider channel seams . . . for finger-tip control."[70] At the tournament's end, Greim reported that cost had determined the differences in European and American basketballs. Stitched together with twelve pieces of leather, the European ball could be bought in Britain for the equivalent of nine dollars in local currency, while the stitchless, American-made basketball was "expensive and takes dollar currency," he explained.[71] Still, issues with the ball should not overshadow the abilities of the teams in Helsinki, in particular the South American squads of Uruguay, Brazil, and Argentina. An impressed Hougland told the author that the South American squads were the most capable of playing with the U.S. team.[72]

After beating Hungary, the United States played Czechoslovakia. Months earlier in the European Championship, the Czechs had lost to the Soviets by only one point, but in this game the United States won handily. Kurland powered the American effort by scoring fourteen points, but Lovellette continued to struggle, scoring only nine. During the game Coach Womble abandoned the platoon system of substitution in favor of simply playing the players that he thought could best do the job.

A few weeks into their stay and with a 2-0 record, by all accounts the players were enjoying themselves in Helsinki mightily. The Finns treated them very well, and surely the benefits of competing in the same building as the weight lifters and boxers, among them 1952 Olympic middleweight champion Floyd Patterson, helped matters. "In our building was a sauna. That's where the lady poured the water on the hot stones," Hougland reminisced. "Well, we had one where we went, and all the wrestlers and the boxers and ourselves, that's where we all would go down there and get in that, because that was something—we'd never been in one of those before."[73]

To round out opening-round pool play, the United States met the speedy Uruguayan squad. Uruguay used a zippy passing game and measured shot selection to stay relatively close before falling 57–44. Kurland led the way yet again, contributing twenty-one points. He had to carry double duty in the contest because Coach Womble benched Lovellette, citing a lack of enthusiasm. "I don't know Lovellette too well, but Phog isn't satisfied

6. Bob Kurland and Marcus Freiberger in Finland's Tennis Palatsi, where much of the basketball action took place. Photo by Nat Farbman. Time & Life Pictures Collection/Getty Images.

with the boy's work. So we had no other choice than to use men who are working harder and playing better," explained Womble.[74]

Though the press seems to have overlooked it, an earlier skirmish between Lovellette and Kurland had affected the scenario. "I had a run-in with Bob Kurland in practice . . . We got in each other's face, probably over a stupid thing in practice. And I got called down. And it was like one of these: 'Well, if you're gonna call me down and you don't call him down then you're picking on me,'" Lovellette explained to the author. "Then I get my dauber down and I thought, 'Well, shoot, it was both of our faults, we should've talked together and, you know, hashed it out.'" In turn, Coach Allen "decided that I needed some hardwood time. Really didn't enjoy it very much," Lovellette remembered. "I think I pouted." But the benching lit a fire under him. "I always wanted to give him [Coach Allen] 110 percent when I played . . . he was like a father figure away from home, and I really enjoyed him. And I didn't want to do anything to hurt him. And I think I hurt him. And I wanted to make up for it. And I apologized to him and did everything I could. But then the only thing I could think of is, 'Go out there and show him that I still wanted to give him the best I had.'"[75] And that Lovellette did. From then on, he simply dominated the tournament.

The win over Uruguay moved the United States into the second phase of the complicated tournament structure, where it was slated to play the Soviet Union. This matchup marked the first in a series of games between these two world powers that would span four decades. The stakes were high, and interest piqued. "You knew this. You read the papers," Lovellette said regarding the cold war and the game.[76] This initial contest generated so much attention that officials decided to move it from Helsinki's quaint Tennis Palatsi into the more spacious Messuhalli II, where more than 4,000 spectators crammed in to watch the action. Many more thousands would gladly have paid the five-dollar top-ticket price to see the game.[77]

Much attention had already been paid in the American popular press to the cold war rivalry, especially regarding Soviet behavior at the Games. The *New York Times's* Danzig had stated after the Opening Ceremonies that, whatever the Russian "designs," Russia's "attitude thus far has been correct." He added that Russian athletes had "fraternized to a surprising degree with those of the Western nations."[78] Not all reporters were so kind, though. Arthur Daley wrote an op-ed piece early in the Games arguing that the ability of the Olympics to transcend chauvinism and nationalistic interests was in jeopardy because of the unforeseen levels of Soviet politicking. Daley noted that the Russians and their satellite nations set up quarters far away from the Olympic Village, putting distance between them and the western nations in Helsinki. In addition, Daley wrote that the Russians met noncommunist arrivals at the Helsinki airport with cold, unfriendly stares.[79]

The *U.S. News & World Report* also criticized the Soviet decision to live outside of the Olympic Village. It was an unusual setup. At the Soviet Union's request, Finland had agreed to let the Russians and hundreds of members of its satellite delegations stay in college dormitories in Otanieme, a forested town eight miles from the Olympic Village. Once in Otanieme, Soviet officials went so far as to separate Russian athletes from satellite athletes. All told, the Soviet Union sent some 700 representatives to Helsinki, only 370 of them athletes. They sent their own cooks, waiters, trainers, managers, doctors, chauffeurs, and other personnel. *U.S. News & World Report* asserted that many in the Russian delegation performed the dual role of keeping an eye on the Soviet athletes, since "all are not the devoted Communists Moscow would prefer."[80] Such claims from American media were common throughout the cold war, but for various reasons, fear of reprisal among them, few athletes actually defected during the forty-year struggle.

As for Russian media coverage of the Olympics, Harrison E. Salisbury, reporting from Moscow for the *New York Times*, gave Americans a summary of its tone. He wrote that Soviet papers like the *Pravda*, *Izvestia*, and other state-run dailies trumpeted the Opening Ceremonies as an opportunity to "call to Soviet athletes to win world championships and demonstrate the superiority of Soviet sport over that of bourgeois countries." *Izvestia* reminded readers that sports in bourgeois countries, especially the United States, were being utilized to prepare "cannon fodder for a new, aggressive war." At the same time, *Izvestia* apparently maintained that the Soviets utilized sports positively on behalf of the "struggle for friendship and security of the people for peace in the world."[81]

Izvestia did not limit its criticisms of the United States to merely calling them bourgeois. They attacked American film as well, saying U.S. interests had unfairly monopolized filming of the Olympics with the creation of the Olympic Film Company. In addition, *Izvestia* reported that the United

States denied the *New York Daily Worker*, a socialist/communist paper, media credentials to cover the Games. In a common tactic, Soviet papers attempted to capitalize on the United States' unfortunate history of race relations by highlighting racial issues. Not finished, the paper attempted to stoke colonial rivalries as well by criticizing the Games for having only three Indonesian participants. Needless to say, the tone of Russia's coverage, as did America's, captured the tense competition occurring on multiple fronts between the East and West during the cold war.[82]

The packed Messuhalli II arena created an electric atmosphere as the players readied for action. Keeping with tradition, before the tip-off, the Soviet and U.S. teams formed into straight lines facing each other near midcourt. Then a Soviet player handed American captain Dan Pippin a Russian banner. Embarrassingly, the U.S. squad, unprepared for this facet of international protocol before arriving, had no gifts on hand. After the one-sided exchange, the teams shook hands and returned to their respective benches. With the starters back on the court, a French referee tossed the ball up at midcourt for the center jump and the game got underway.[83]

Spurred by Otar Korkija, a powerful, bald, mustache-wearing Caesar Romero–type character who was known for exciting crowds by "jumping for non-existent balls, plunging feet-first into the crowd, and faking stomach cramps,"[84] the Soviet Union had won all of its previous games in Helsinki. And against the United States, it used aggressive forays to the basket to keep pace early on.[85] Then, at the five-minute mark, Korkija collided with Lovellette. Korkija received the brunt of the collision and was carted from the floor. He returned in the second half, but by then, the outside marksmanship of Robert Kenney and his backcourt mates had opened the middle for Kurland and Lovellette. The United States pulled away soon after Korkija's exit and led 39–22 at the intermission.

In the second half, the Americans used their height advantage to increase the lead, while foul trouble mounted for the Soviets, forcing them to go to their bench. In its first four games the Soviet Union used only five or six players, but against the United States, four Soviet players had fouled out by the middle of the second half (four fouls constituted disqualification). The United States had its share of foul trouble too, losing five players to fouls before the final buzzer. However, their depth enabled the Americans to manage foul problems more effectively.[86] By the closing moments of the game, the supercharged atmosphere in the arena had dissipated as the United States led by a wide margin: it would go on to win 86–58 in a lopsided victory.[87] It was a physical affair. "We had some skirmishes right there on the court with Russians. Sometimes it wasn't very pleasant," Lovellette recalled. "The referees stepped in real quick if there was any kind of a face-off." Still, the game ended amicably, with the athletes shaking hands afterward.[88] The following day, the *Literary Gazette* in Moscow carried a piece by the prominent Soviet writer Anatoly Sofronoy that emphasized the fraternization that had taken place between American and Soviet athletes at the Games—however, the article apparently ran among others that leveled sharp criticism at the referees.[89]

To many Americans, the win over Russia could not have come at a better time, as the U.S. Olympic contingency lagged behind the Soviets in the "unofficial" overall medal count. The Soviet Union's medal success had caught Americans, and much of the rest of the world, off guard. According to the historian William J. Baker, "Western sportsmen were astonished." The *New York Times*'s Daley echoed the attitude of many Americans before the Games when he had wondered why the Soviets had opened their usually discreet government to the attention of the Olympics "in the face of remote chances for victory."[90] According to Baker, had more information about Soviet tactics been available in America, the Soviets' performance would have been less shocking.[91]

The Soviets certainly did not seem all that surprised. Confident after the first few days of the Games, they had tried to capitalize on their successes by getting the IOC to make the medal count official. On July 28, 1952, the Soviet contingency submitted the proposal to the International Amateur Athletic Federation (IAAF), but with dissent led by Brundage, the proposal met defeat. However, a Soviet official, unfazed by losing the vote, announced to the press, "We are certain to win," adding that international sports were of "great importance" to Russia.[92] His statements proved premature. The United States came back in the Games' final days to narrowly win the unofficial team title.[93] This conflict over whether to have an official overall medal count provides yet another example of how the Olympics served as contested turf in the ideological battles of the cold war. But often lost in these chauvinistic squabbles in ensuing years were the favorable conditions that the Olympics and basketball offered to liberal capitalist nations and the innovative companies that increasingly partnered with the Olympics, regardless of who won events.

Coming off of its win over the Soviet Union, the U.S. basketball team set a new Olympic scoring record with a 103–55 victory over Chile. Lovellette, finally playing up to expectations, paced the squad with twenty-five points. Apparently, Coach Womble's benching had caught Lovellette's attention. But then, the United States nearly lost to Brazil. Technically, before the Brazil game, the United States had already qualified for the final-four medal round, so Coach Womble decided to sit Kurland out. The U.S. still wanted to win, yet Brazil posted a two-point lead at the half, 26–24, marking the first time the U.S. Olympic basketball team had found itself on the wrong end of the score at intermission. Brazil gained its lead by using "ball-control" tactics. The strategy, which employed a deliberate, hard-cutting offense, utilized Brazil's quickness and worked against the United States' size advantage.[94] Flustered, Lovellette did not score in the first half; however, he played much stronger in the second. Brazil kept the score dangerously close, but the United States squeaked by 57–53, thanks in no small part to Lovellette's eleven second-half points.[95]

In other action, Argentina suffered an upset at the hands of Uruguay, which meant the Argentines would face the United States in the first game of the final-four medal round. The Argentine loss, combined with the Soviet Union's 78–60 win over Chile, which was powered by Korkija's thirty-eight points, put the Soviets in the other semifinal game against Uruguay.[96] All four teams had played seven games in seven days to reach the final four. It had been a taxing schedule, and the toughest tests were still ahead. If America could handle Argentina and the Soviet Union could beat Uruguay, the much-anticipated cold war gold medal game would materialize.

Analysts assumed that against the United States, Argentina would mimic Brazil's ball-control tactics, especially since Argentina had nearly upset the United States using a similar strategy in the 1948 Olympics. Instead, Argentina played an up-tempo game. Accustomed to fast-paced action, the United States obliged and raced ahead to a 14–0 lead. Argentina regained its composure and stayed relatively close the rest of the way, even coming within a few points on numerous occasions though the United States never relinquished its lead. Fortunately for Womble and company, Lovellette played well yet again. His work in the paint helped the United States hold on for a 43–39 halftime advantage, and he continued his excellent play in the second frame, ultimately tallying a game-high twenty-five points in the 85–76 win.[97]

The victory, coupled with the Soviet Union's close win over Uruguay, set up the wished-for gold medal contest between the Americans and Soviets. But first, there was a rematch between Argentina and Uruguay for the bronze medal, and it turned ugly. Some thought too much foul-calling had already contributed to tension among teams at the Olympic tournament: it was speculated that the language barriers between referees and players, as well as the different styles of referees and players from different parts of the world, contributed to this. Even before the Argentina Uruguay brawl, the American referee Vincent Farrell had been punched during a game, which led to the suspension of two Uruguayans. But in this second game between Argentina and Uruguay, the number of fouls called reached new levels. By the game's end, only seven players between the two teams had not fouled out. (Argentina was down to three players, Uruguay to four.) Much more troubling, before all the foul-outs, a brawl broke out between the two squads. "Spectators and team officials poured onto the court" as a result, and it took "ten Finnish policemen to restore order and clear the court." In the end, Uruguay won the bronze.[98]

The second contest between the two cold war giants took place on August 2, 1952, in front of another capacity crowd at the Messuhalli II. Hobson asserted that there was a tension in the air "seldom equaled in any athletic competition." Farrell and Greim described the scene in *The Amateur Athlete*, writing, "The house was jam-packed with spectators, and the electric tenseness prevailed."[99]

In their first matchup, the Soviets had tried to run with the U.S. team and ended up losing big. This time, they borrowed a page from Brazil's handbook and implemented a strategy of ball control, only to the extreme. Starting their five fastest players, the Soviet Union held the ball constantly. Their coach allowed only occasional forays to the basket by Korkija and Butautas, and the result was a mind-numbing exhibition of keep-away. Hobson summed it up afterward, saying that the "fastest action for the . . . forty minutes" occurred when the teams exchanged gifts before the tip-off.[100] The *New York Times* remarked that the action was so boring it "took on the character of a truce meeting in Korea."[101]

The United States struggled with the painfully slow tempo. Ten minutes into the affair, the score was only 4–3, and the Americans had made just one of their first fourteen shots. In the first half, the United States hit only seven of thirty-two shot attempts.[102] The *Washington Post* figured that the Americans "tightened a bit" after finding themselves down 7–4 with eleven minutes gone in the first half, though they did manage to lead 17–15 at halftime. As indicated by the halftime score, the Soviet Union struggled too. Its tactics hurt its own chances to score, helping the United States stifle the scoring ace Korkija.[103]

The second half saw even fewer points, and the United States continued to shoot horribly. For the game, it made just thirteen of sixty-five shots, a woeful 20 percent average. "We had to take outside shots against the Russians in the finals," Hougland, who scored five baskets in the final, recalled. "All my shots were outside." Meanwhile, the Soviet Union, connecting on only eight of forty-four attempts, registered an even worse shooting average—18 percent.

In that final game, Hougland said that the Kansas players played together a lot "primarily because our defense was something different than most people were playing." The half-court pressure defense Kansas played called for the guards to keep the opposition from "making the pass to the forwards . . . That was what really made us win the NCAA tournament," he maintained. In Helsinki, Hougland remembered, "The first game we played them [the Soviets] was easy. The second game they just held the ball—wouldn't shoot." It was understandable to him, though. "They just wanted to win. And they were tough. We fought like hell."[104]

Not until the last six minutes, though, with the help of some timely baskets by Kenney and Glasgow, did the United States extend its lead to six. With a "sizable" advantage finally in hand, the Americans implemented their own stall tactics. Incredibly, the Soviets became upset at the Americans for stalling. One Soviet player protested by taking a seat on the court during play. The protest did not last long, though, as the Soviet coach reprimanded the player, who then quickly stood up.[105]

The United States won the unsightly affair 36–25, and cooler heads prevailed in the game's aftermath as both sides shook hands and posed for pictures.[106] Lovellette, more than making up for his early struggles in the tournament, led the U.S. team in scoring again with nine points, while the wily veteran Kurland added eight.[107] In his postgame comments, Dr. Allen said that the "Russians played the best type of game for her purposes because she had tried a fast game in the previous game with the United States and lost by a big score." He characterized the Soviets' tactics as "an exact copy of the stall and freeze game used by Oklahoma A&M."[108]

The Soviet stall tactic would prove to have an important legacy, as it surely contributed to FIBA's 1956 decision to institute a thirty-second shot clock—a method of speeding up the game first implemented by the professional NBA, which in 1954 had adopted the innovative twenty-four-second shot clock. For decades, U.S. basketball organizations and FIBA had consistently responded to demands for action by combating the stall and encouraging more scoring. The shot clock, first used in the 1960 Games, was yet another step in this process.

Other rule changes were underway. Just as the Helsinki Games were ending, FIBA's President Greim, who held that post until 1960, told the media about changes that had already been agreed on, saying, "We are continuing to make progress toward getting the game in line with advances in technique such as in the United States." One new rule said that when teams were assessed fouls near the end of games—which had previously given them the option of either going to the free-throw line or taking the ball in from out-of-bounds (which a team often chose to do as a stall tactic)—they now had to shoot free throws. FIBA also decided that a player could commit five fouls before disqualification, instead of just four. As reported by the UP, an aim of FIBA was to keep referees from overpenalizing "fast-shooting, hard-passing teams such as the United States."[109]

Given that the Soviets were still relatively new to the international basketball landscape and that their most dominant inside player, Korkija, was only six feet and four inches (depending on the source), it would seem reasonable to assume that the Soviet Sports Ministry came away rather satisfied with the Soviet Union's performance in Helsinki. But that was not the case. Consensus held that the U.S. game was light years ahead of the Soviets'. Officials marveled at America's low-post play and powerful dunks and decided something needed to be done. Thus, the "poor showing" against the United States in Helsinki inspired the Sports Committee to usher in a new era of Soviet basketball.[110]

In preparation for the next Olympiad, the Soviet Union conducted a

TABLE 3. 1952 U.S. Men's Olympic Basketball cumulative stats

NAME	G	FGM*	FTM-FTA	(%)	PF	PTS/AVG
Clyde Lovellette	7	39	21-26	.808	21	99/14.1
Robert Kenney	7	27	22-28	.786	14	76/10.9
Robert Kurland	7	24	19-26	.731	19	67/9.6
Ronald Bontemps	8	16	25-28	.893	11	57/7.1
Dan Pippin	8	23	10-14	.714	18	56/7.0
Marcus Freiberger	7	15	14-18	.778	25	44/6.3
William Hougland	8	20	8-15	.533	19	48/6.0
Wayne Glasgow	6	10	7-7	1.000	17	27/4.5
William Lienhard	4	5	6-8	.750	12	16/4.0
Howard Williams	8	11	5-9	.556	15	27/3.4
Frank McCabe	6	6	6-9	.667	13	18/3.0
Charles Hoag	7	8	4-6	.667	13	20/2.9
John Keller	2	1	1-1	1.000	1	3/1.5
Melvin Kelley	6	1	2-5	.400	10	4/0.7
USA TOTALS	8	206	150-200	.750	208	562/70.3
OPP. TOTALS	8	118	170-250	.680	180	406/50.8

* Figures for field goals attempted are not available.

virtual nationwide roundup of tall teenagers. Working from the physical model displayed by Kurland and Lovellette, the Soviets searched the countryside for tall potential stars to combat the United States at its own game. Coaches were commissioned to "pick them up on the streets and at the movies, in stores and in subway stations, and promise their height in gold for appearing on the courts."[111] The race for basketball supremacy had kicked into high gear. What soon became apparent, however, was that the basketball model was fluid, because as the Soviets scoured the countryside for tall people, younger "American Gullivers"—in particular Bill Russell—were hard at work on their way to transforming the sport yet again.

4

THE RUSSELL MODEL REVOLUTIONIZES THE
INTERNATIONAL GAME IN MELBOURNE

Within a year of the 1952 Helsinki Games the political climate changed in
both the United States and the Soviet Union. In America the hysteria of
McCarthyism had slowed, while in the Soviet Union the death of Stalin
ushered in less-belligerent leaders. That same year, 1953, a convention took
place in Geneva between the United States, Great Britain, France, and the
Soviet Union, all possessors of a hydrogen bomb. The weapons produced
a mood that helped shift the young cold war into a phase of "peaceful
coexistence." The shift worked to resituate the battles of the cold war in less
dangerous cultural spheres. As the historian William J. Baker has put it, of
all the acceptable alternatives to war, "competitive sports loomed large."[1]

With the playing fields open terrain for cold war competition, countries
set their sights on the next Olympiad, slated for November 1956 in Melbourne, Australia. In 1954, for instance, President Eisenhower proposed
a script for a televised proclamation declaring the first annual National
Olympics Day, which was supposed to prepare the United States for Mel-

bourne. His proclamation read, "The world will again see that in sports, as in education, in economics, in politics, in every realm of life, regimentation runs a poor second to free enterprise."[2] And for both the United States and the Soviet Union, basketball was a central piece of their Melbourne plans.

In 1955 President Eisenhower invited basketball wonder Bill Russell to the Oval Office for a meeting on physical fitness. Ironically, Russell had to wait three days to pick up the invitation because he first needed to scrounge up the $1.50 in gas money and the $0.50 he needed to cross the Bay Bridge to get it. But he ended up receiving it and ultimately decided to accept. Other leading athletes attended the meeting as well, such as Willie Mays and Bob Cousy, but Russell was the only collegiate amateur present. A *Time* article about Ike's sports meeting highlighted that fact. It also claimed that during the meeting, Russell promised Ike he would remain an amateur until after the Games.[3] Later on, though, Russell denied that Ike had asked him any direct questions about the Olympics. Regardless, most saw Russell's inclusion in the proceedings as an indication of Eisenhower's hope that Russell would indeed participate in the Games. Undoubtedly, Ike recognized Russell's potential impact as an amateur in Melbourne.[4]

Sure enough, once Russell made it to Melbourne, he dazzled crowds with his revolutionary play. Describing him as a "phenomenon entirely new to the Southern Hemisphere," *Sports Illustrated* counted Russell among a select few 1956 Olympians who "made an indelible mark on [the Australian] public awareness."[5] In the process, he also provided the world with a new physical model for how the big man played basketball. Russell's Olympic teammate Bill Hougland summed up his influence on basketball by stating, "Mikan and Kurland, they changed the game. And then when Russell came, he changed the game."[6] The more versatile and athletic Russell model of play contributed to basketball's rise in the second half of the twentieth century.

As with the United States, in the Soviet Union, preparations for Melbourne had been put in motion soon after the conclusion of the Helsinki Games. The ushering in of new Soviet leadership enhanced its already energetic sports movement, eventually leading to the creation of the Spartakiad of the Peoples of the USSR, a massive sporting spectacular held in Moscow. The Spartakiad served as a kind of internal Olympics. Basketball and soccer did not receive as much attention as other sports at the festival because their regular seasons were given more importance.[7] But even so, daily crowds at the 1956 Spartakiad in Lenin Stadium, a mammoth edifice on the banks of the Moscow River, totaled more than one hundred thousand.[8] The huge crowds indicated that the Soviet Union's post–World War II strategy to engage the West in international sporting events had heightened national interest in competitive sports. As the historian Robert Edelman has noted, in the postwar Soviet Union, "The audience for all sports expanded."[9]

The Soviet Union continued its success on the basketball court, too, especially at the European championships. In front of partisan throngs at the 1953 European championship, held in Moscow's Dinamo stadium, the Soviet squad, again composed mainly of Baltic players, beat the competition in convincing fashion. Every session of the eleven-day tournament drew crowds of 30,000, and the Soviet Union's championship solidified its status as Europe's preeminent basketball power.[10]

Not yet satisfied, though, Soviet sports officials continued their work hunting down unusually tall humans. It was not an easy task. The All-Union Ministry of Physical Culture and Sports (hereafter the Sports Ministry) became discouraged when the efforts did not produce immediate results. In fact, the dearth of tall basketball talent prompted the Sports Ministry to take the rather unusual step of launching an official investigation to discover why Russia was "ravaged with retarded growth." Theories abounded. One claimed that size was proportional to the pace of daily life, and since Westerners ran around all day in a capitalist rat race, they were taller.[11] Alas, more respected scientists argued that Westerners' well-balanced diets, pure drinking water, and immunity to infectious diseases contributed to their size.

Undaunted by the lack of progress, the Soviets kept looking, and eventually, their efforts paid off. Before the Melbourne Games, the Sports Ministry ultimately procured two veritable giants. First, there was Vrais Akhtaev, an astonishing seven-feet-seven-inch, 350-pound powerhouse who arrived on the Soviet basketball scene a couple of years after Helsinki. Soviet basketball had never seen a player anywhere near his size. Before Akhtaev signed with Alma-Ata of the Russian professional league, the tallest players in the league stood at about six feet five inches. Opposing teams went to ridicu-

7. Vrais Akhtaev at a basketball competition in Moscow. Photo by Lisa Larsen. Time & Life Pictures Collection/Getty Images.

lous lengths to combat Akhtaev's height, including stacking a player on another's shoulders in a "pyramid" scheme. Others simply sent in lackeys to steal Akhtaev's shoes and uniform before the game. Unfazed, Akhtaev would come out in street clothes and play anyway.[12]

Akhtaev began his athletic career as a shot-putter, throwing a respectable forty-one feet, but he tired of the monotony of slinging the shot around. He next tried his hand at volleyball, only to purportedly become discouraged by fears that he would hurt his opponents with his ferocious kills. Soviet officials then persuaded him to turn to basketball, where he still towered over everybody, only just a little less so. Soon, stories regarding Akhtaev started to reach the United States, especially after he scored forty-seven points at Moscow's Spartakiad against a Turkemian team. In that game, the *Washington Post* reported, a couple of Turkemian players ran into Akhtaev, but he remained unmoved, while they "bounced off, gave him a terrified look, and retreated."[13]

The Turkemians may have been surprised by Akhtaev's immovability, but many Soviets were already well aware of his ferocious on-court reputation. Frustrated by players elbowing him, hitting him in the legs, and jostling him, he had been known to pick a player up and hold him against the backboard until he apologized. When word of the discovery of the Soviet Union's other basketball giant, Ivan Krumminch, reached Akhtaev, he is said to have exclaimed, "I'll teach that bastard to go and play basketball." But in truth, Akhtaev was a sensitive fellow, self-conscious about his freakish size. He carried a picture of a nearly nine-foot-tall Englishman in his wallet as a kind of reminder that he was not alone and penned long letters to his diminutive mother, who lived in a remote mountain village.[14]

The other giant, the seven-feet-four-inch, 360-pound Krumminch, was discovered in Latvia where his family dwelled in the forests. A lumberjack by trade, Krumminch did not play his first game of basketball until he reached twenty-four years of age. Despite the late start, he caught on quickly and skyrocketed through the Soviet basketball ranks. He went on to earn the nickname "Breadwinner" for his stellar play over more than a decade on the Soviet National Team.[15]

Really, these two were not the Soviet Union's only giants. Both Stassis Stonkous and Arkadi Votchkarez measured nearly seven feet tall as well. As the Melbourne Games approached, U.S. head coach Gerald Tucker told the press that he had friends behind the iron curtain sending him clippings on Soviet big men. Incredulous, he said, "I noticed that in some stories he was 7 feet 2 inches tall. Then he was 7' 3" and finally 7' 6½". I said to myself: 'Good Lord, this must be a growing boy.' It turned out that they were different men although the names sound all alike over there."[16] Reports such as this only added to the aura surrounding the budding cold war basketball rivalry. As it happened, Krumminch, Stonkous, and Votchkarez played in Melbourne; Akhtaev did not.

As the Soviets collared big men in the lead-up to Melbourne, in the United States, debates over amateurism continued to take place and the college game continued to improve, though the AAU remained strong. As for the amateurism debate, in the months following the 1952 Olympics, questions resurfaced regarding the legitimacy of U.S. amateurs from the AAU. R. G. Lynch was among those who considered the AAU's industrial leagues, such as the NIBL, to be populated by virtual professionals. In 1952 Lynch, the sports editor of the *Milwaukee Journal*, had astutely pointed out the irony of Avery Brundage's admonishment in Helsinki of "foreign violators of the amateur's code" (Lynch was referring to a lengthy letter Brundage had penned that charged Argentina's Olympic basketball team with accepting "prizes of considerable value" after a win). In response to this, Lynch argued that before Brundage tried to "clean up the world," he should "look at what is going on in his own backyard."[17]

Lynch wondered what type of compensation Brundage thought the NIBL offered players, considering they were turning down professional enticements that included $15,000 signing bonuses in order to play in the NIBL. And he declared that "the exploitation of industrial basketball for advertising and sales promotion is a black eye for amateur sports, and the manner in which a hasty coat of whitewash was applied to industrial players just before the Olympic tournament is a scandal." Lynch also maintained that the "special investigators" investigating the industrial players "almost gagged" on items in their own report, namely, that the Phillips Petroleum Company refused to reveal the salaries it paid its players, and that the Phillips players spent sixty-three days away from their job during the year, despite an AAU limit of twenty-one days. Lynch lampooned the Phillips Company's "impossible" explanation that it thought the rule meant no more than twenty days per trip, not only because Lynch thought the excuse made little sense, but also because the chairman of the AAU basketball committee, Louis G. Wilke, worked as a Phillips executive and therefore should obviously have known and understood the rules. Continuing, Lynch pointed out that the Phillips team's 1952–53 schedule suggested the company still apparently "misunderstood" the rule because its players were slated to miss a minimum of fifty-four days. He rhetorically and effectively asked his readers, "Does Mr. Brundage think this is amateur industrial basketball? Or exploitation of a supposedly amateur game to advertise and promote the sale of gasoline?"[18]

Avery Brundage responded to Lynch with a letter thanking him for his efforts to improve the NIBL. Brundage also touted his own labors to combat amateur violations, writing, "I have been fighting the same battle for thirty years. I think it can safely be said that if it was not for the efforts of those of us who believe that amateur sport must be kept clean, pure and honest that conditions would be far worse than they are today." However, Brundage then curiously asserted that he could not agree with Lynch's claim that "a basketball player who accepts a permanent job is being paid more than he would receive as a professional player."[19] He concluded by stating that the AAU was "trying to solve this problem and I hope it will do so soon."[20]

Brundage's claim that the AAU was working to solve amateur abuses seems particularly implausible, however, in light of an article written four years after this flare-up, in January 1957 in the *Wall Street Journal*. This rather candid article about the Denver Chicago Truckers of the NIBL showed that little had been done to change the AAU's practices, let alone hide them. The title alone, "A Truck Line Tries Basketball to Draw Executive Trainees," suggested as much. The article reported that the Denver Chicago trucking company had lured ten former collegiate basketball players to their company by "giving them a chance to supplement their earnings through basketball." Company president George J. Kolowich told the *Wall Street Journal* that the chartering of a DC-3 plane and a budget of nearly $100,000 for the team were worth it, given the team's ability to advertise the company and to recruit employees. Players could make up to $1,200 dollars per year in extra hours spent on basketball as part of their incentive package, which was no small matter considering the average professional "hardly could hope to pull down much more than $6,000 a year."[21]

That same month *Time* highlighted Kolowich's hiring of Johnny Dee from Alabama to coach his team, and the company's offer to lure the Minneapolis Lakers' second-round pick, Terry Rand, which included an all-expenses-paid sojourn to law school in addition to a salary, fringe benefits, and sizable bonus. As *Time* noted, part of Kolowich's dream was seeing his team, or at least a good portion of it, "going to the 1960 Olympics." Not surprisingly, NBA brass did not appreciate the competition. President Maurice Podoloff of the NBA told *Time*, "At least we admit we're pros."[22]

Murray Olderman, a sportswriter for the *Detroit News*, picked up on the amateurism issue in March 1953. He reported that in 1948, Don Barksdale was paid $600 a month by the AAU's Oakland Bittners and "set up an ice cream business, beer distributorship, and disc jockey show." Olderman said that Barksdale had turned down a $20,000 offer from a New York pro team to capitalize on these opportunities afforded him as an amateur. As a further example of the AAU's borderline behavior, Olderman claimed that the owner of Philadelphia's professional basketball club, Eddie Gottlieb, had Walt Davis, the 1952 Olympic high-jump champion and basketball star out of Texas A&M, "in the bag" until AAU officials topped his offer. Gottlieb maintained that after hearing overtures from the AAU, Davis came back and said he wanted "$19,000 for two years and $500 for a fur coat for his wife." Davis ended up in the AAU's NIBL. Olderman pointed out that a short time later, the "new oil man" Davis and the Phillips Oilers' Bob Kurland were nominated for the prestigious Sullivan Award, given annually to the person, or people, most responsible for the advancement of amateur sport.[23] Obviously, there were some inconsistencies in the U.S. amateur system, yet it was the commercial thrust of American amateur basketball, along with innovative players like Russell, that helped forge the modern characteristics of the sport.

Amateur issues aside, other noteworthy developments took place on the U.S. basketball front in the years between Helsinki and Melbourne. Most important, the barriers holding back African Americans in sports relaxed. The Supreme Court's landmark 1954 *Brown versus Board of Education* decision, aimed at ending segregation in the classroom, reflected that changing racial climate. The following year, Rosa Parks refused to move to the back of a bus in Montgomery, Alabama. In basketball, African Americans built on the sport's two landmarks of 1950. That year, the City

College of New York became the first team to win the national collegiate basketball championship with a black player on its roster, and Earl Lloyd became the first black player in the NBA. As the fifties progressed, more and more black players earned college scholarships and an increasing number earned their living on the hardwood after school.

Things did not change overnight, however. In fact, the *Wall Street Journal* reported that the South initially felt "nettled" by the landmark 1954 Supreme Court decision, to which it reacted by increasing segregation through curbing what had been a relatively lax attitude regarding white southern teams traveling north to play teams with blacks.[24] But within a few years of this initial over-reaction, important firsts took place throughout the South in sport, many of them spearheaded by basketball. For instance, in 1958 at a collegiate basketball tournament in Charlotte, North Carolina, Guy Rodgers, an All-American from Temple, and two of his teammates became the first African Americans to stay at the ritzy hotel the Temple team lodged in for the event. The players also dined in a restaurant usually off limits to blacks, and during the games, black fans could be seen cheering alongside whites. The *Wall Street Journal* described the tournament as the "splashiest non-segregated contest Charlotte has seen" and maintained that it "points up a subsidence of racial tensions in at least one area of life in the South— sports."[25] There was still plenty of progress to be made, but times were changing.

As opportunities through sport increased for African Americans, a young and unheralded Russell worked to take advantage of them. During the 1952–53 college basketball season, he honed his skills day after day in a small gym near the campus of the University of San Francisco, the only school to have offered him a scholarship.[26] Burning with an intense drive that has stayed with him his entire life, Russell soon changed the game. His style called for versatility and speed, and it kept the United States well ahead of the international basketball curve at the Melbourne Olympics.

Russell stands among the greatest to ever play the game, but in his younger days, few recognized his potential. As a high school player with pogo-stick legs, an awkward body, and small frame, he did not make the varsity squad until his senior year. His brother, a star football player, received more press in high school. Even after a productive senior season, Russell attracted little attention from major college coaches. He could use both hands—partly because when he was a youngster, an uncle had taught him to throw left-handed in hope that one day his nephew would blossom into a major league pitcher—and he stood within two or three inches of seven feet, but coaches dismissed Russell for lacking an offensive game and for not possessing the necessary build.[27] Finally, Phil Woolpert, head coach of the University of San Francisco Dons, having watched Russell in an all-star game after his senior season, decided to take a chance on the homegrown string bean. It paid off. In one of the most remarkable turnarounds in NCAA history, Russell led the small Dominican school from relative obscurity to back-to-back national championships in 1955 and 1956.

In hindsight, Woolpert's decision to sign Russell seems quite sensible. But when he did so, Woolpert was not only taking a chance on an underappreciated player, he was ignoring the racial status quo. Unfortunately, his contribution to integration has largely been overlooked. A prison counselor before coaching the Dons, Woolpert had an uncanny eye for talent and a willingness to sign black players that many of his colleagues did not share. He not only discovered the great Bill Russell but also signed an overlooked K. C. Jones that year. Both played on the 1956 U.S. Olympic basketball team and are now members of the Naismith Basketball Hall of Fame. And Russell and Jones were not the only African American Dons. While much attention is given to the 1966 Texas Western team for winning the first national championship with an all-black starting five, many times in 1956 Woolpert put five African Americans on the floor at the same time.[28]

Even for the progressive Bay Area, the Dons were ahead of their time. During their first championship season with Russell and Jones, in 1954–55, California, Stanford, and Santa Clara sported all-white rosters.[29] Hal Perry, a guard on that team, summed up Woolpert's courage, saying, "He deserved as much interest and respect as any coach . . . He went through hell. Very few people knew it. As far as they knew, he was a coach and that was it." According to Perry, Coach Woolpert confided in him that there were people within the university who wanted him fired, but given Woolpert's success, they could not justify it. Woolpert received hate mail, and opposing coaches called him what were supposed to be derisive names, like "Saperstein," a reference to Abe Saperstein, the native Chicagoan who had started the Harlem Globetrotters, and who was Jewish.[30]

Still, Woolpert and Russell did not always agree about the best way to play. Stylistically, Woolpert preferred more traditional methods of play than Russell and Jones commonly employed. In fact, it is the players and their assistant coach Ross Giudice who deserve a portion of the credit for developing the Dons' vaunted full-court press, which was anchored by Russell. "Coach taught us how to play defense, but we took it a step further with our creativity," Jones explained. As for the Dons' trademark fast break, Russell told *Sports Illustrated* in 2006, "He [Woolpert] believed about the fast break like Woody Hayes thought about the forward pass—that three things could happen, but two of them were bad." Surprisingly, Russell claims the Dons never even practiced the fast break, "But, of course, we used it from the start of every game." In large part, the differences between Russell and Woolpert stemmed from their difference in age. When Russell leaped into the air to block shots, the more traditional Woolpert would say, according to Russell, "But that's not the way it's supposed to be done. A defensive man is not supposed to leave the ground." In analyzing Russell's methods, perhaps Woolpert did not fully understand that Russell was changing the rules, not merely violating them. Despite these differences, though, Woolpert and Russell respected each other. In 2006 Russell said of Woolpert, "I always knew he was a good and decent man."[31]

It was because all NCAA freshmen were ineligible for varsity action that Russell spent his first year at the University of San Francisco in relative obscurity fine-tuning his skills in St. Ignatius High School's little gym, where the Dons practiced. There, he increased his astonishing leaping ability, mastered his timing on blocked shots, and became more comfortable with his gangly body. By the time he was a junior, Russell's defensive wizardry, his ability to outlet passes to teammates seemingly anywhere on the court, and his consummate team play brought national acclaim. People marveled at his ability to run the court like a guard, and he so dominated the glass that the collegiate lane was widened to twelve feet before he left school.[32] In addition, his ability to grab a shot at nearly any point in its arc baffled referees, who struggled to apply the new goaltending guidelines.

As early as 1955, fans looked eagerly toward the prospect of Russell leading the U.S. team at the next Olympiad. There was a problem, however. The Games were not scheduled to take place until November 1956, during Australia's summer, rather than in the customary summer months of the northern hemisphere. Therefore, people worried that Russell, not wanting to cut into his first professional season, would not suit up for the Olympics. The possibility of losing Russell to the professional ranks before having the opportunity to showcase him to the world at the Olympics seems to have motivated President Eisenhower to invite the young wizard to the White House in the summer of 1955. Following the meeting, speculation grew that in addition to playing basketball, Russell might even try as well to combine his ability to high-jump over six feet seven inches and run the 440 in 49.6 seconds to train for the 440 hurdles in Melbourne. Russell told *Time*, "I'd have an advantage over the other boys. They have to jump over the hurdles. All I have to do is walk over them."[33] It seemed he would play, but then, following the Dons' second NCAA title in 1956, offers for Russell poured in from the professional ranks, and speculation that he would become a pro mounted again. Saperstein of the Globetrotters, which attracted over 42,000 to a game at Yankee Stadium that year and boasted branch offices in London, Paris, and Tokyo, told the papers he planned to offer Russell $50,000. In his autobiography *Go Up For Glory*, Russell claims that in reality, Saperstein offered $17,000 and did not treat him with much respect.[34] Regardless, in the end, Russell waited to turn pro until after the Olympics even though it meant notably less in earnings for him during his first professional season.

Ironically, even though Russell and his fellow African American team-mates K. C. Jones and Carl Cain were willing to serve in Melbourne as virtual ambassadors for the American way of life and sacrifice some of their professional salaries in so doing, racial injustice continued to intrude on their lives before, during, and after the Games. As noted, some racial inroads had been made, but these three African Americans still played for the United States at a time when Jim Crow laws maintained systematic segregation in the South and de facto segregation plagued the North.

In his autobiography *Second Wind*, Russell recalled that when he was a youth, "the cops in Oakland stopped me on the streets all the time, grilled me and routinely called me 'nigger.'"[35] At McClymonds High School he struggled with the low expectations, despair, and lack of funding found in many inner-city schools, until one day he had an epiphany that assured him that he was all right. Yet even with the epiphany, racial slights continued to plague Russell. On the way back home after his 1955 meeting with Ike in the White House, Russell and his family drove through the South and had to deal with segregation. As late as 1962, after leading the Celtics to five of the NBA's previous six titles, he visited some old friends and family in Monroe, Louisiana, driving a brand new Lincoln convertible. En route he and his two sons were turned away at restaurant after restaurant, and they couldn't find a decent hotel to accommodate them. Finally, he and his boys resorted to putting the top up on the Lincoln and sleeping by the side of the road.[36]

In 1966, his first year as player and coach of the Boston Celtics, a Madison Avenue firm offered Russell a spot in an ad for Johnson & Johnson. The offer was a reflection of the changing times, but even it was tinged with racism. An ad executive told Russell, "You know, the advertising industry has been backward in bringing blacks into the field . . . It's been a long time coming, I know, but we want to get some blacks into advertising." The problem occurred when he told Russell they could pay him only "scale." When Russell questioned the rationale of paying him the same as any model right out of school, the executive told him, "Look, we're going out on a limb, and we need some black stars to help us. Don't you want to be the first black American featured in a national ad?" To this, Russell responded, "I refuse to pay again for what you said was your backwardness," and he declined the offer.[37]

Of course, despite the prejudice, the United States also offered Russell remarkable opportunities—not just for an African American but for anybody. In 1966 he was not merely the lone African American head coach in the NBA; he stood as the first black head coach in the history of major professional sports in America. And he counted as the NBA's highest-paid player at $100,000 per year before getting an additional $25,000 for coaching.[38] As for endorsements, many more and better offers have come his way since the Johnson & Johnson overture. Though Russell has not hesitated to point out racial slights, he has noted how rapidly some things changed. When he first joined the Celtics in 1957, he was the only black player, but by the late 1970s, when he served as the general manager and coach of the Seattle Supersonics, Russell's team had only two white players. If not for the ability of sports to function as a meritocracy, such a dramatic shift would have been unlikely.[39]

As an Olympian, Russell had issues with how he was treated, but he attributed the issues more to the way the AAU-laden U.S. Olympic Basketball Committee ran things than to racial prejudice. Russell asserts that the basketball committee told the players not to make any statements that might "be embarrassing to the United States . . . Then they proceed to place us in situation after situation where we were segregated or embarrassed." On their exhibition tour, he thought Olympic officials and assorted folk enjoyed finer suites, extra travel expenses, and more cultural exchanges than the players, and he did not appreciate it when Brundage, just before the team left for its flight from Los Angeles to Melbourne, declared that Russell "should guarantee he will continue as an amateur or he shouldn't compete in the Olympics." The comment led Russell to reply, "I'm more of an amateur than anybody on the Committee . . . You'll have to kick me out. I won't quit." So Russell had both to stand his ground as an amateur and to deal with racial injustice in America in order to represent the United States at the Olympic Games—in addition to already having agreed to a $6,000 pay cut from Red Auerbach's Celtics, on a prorated $22,500 contract.[40]

With the Olympics slated for November, other concerns than those about Russell's status emerged. As noted, one of the more pressing was that, if the basketball committee went with the old system of selecting players, then some members of the 1956 NCAA national championship team's roster, in this case the San Francisco Dons, would have been forced to travel to Melbourne right in the middle of their academic year and at the beginning of their basketball season. Thankfully, the committee chose to send a team of collegiate all-stars that had just finished their collegiate eligibility to the Olympic trials, rather than sending representatives from a single team, avoiding this potential problem.[41] An additional advantage to the collegiate all-star system was that a larger number of the nation's elite players could represent the United States in the Olympics. The policy worked so well that collegiate stars from various schools became a staple component of U.S. Olympic basketball for the next thirty-two years.

The U.S. basketball committee had chosen the first week of April and Kansas City's Municipal Auditorium for the trials, which would essentially be a four-team round-robin tournament. The collegiate all-star squad was composed of fourteen players who had been selected based on the votes tallied by members of the National Association of Basketball Coaches (NABC) for the *Collier's* year-end all-American basketball team.[42] The AAU champion Buchan Bakers and runner-up Phillips 66ers, which had won the 1956 NIBL title averaging 90.2 points per game, joined the collegians in Kansas City, along with a team made up of all-stars from the U.S. Armed Forces.[43] The committee planned to pick players from all four squads, with extra weight given to the trials' champion and runner-up. Ultimately, the tournament built on the success of the previous two trials, as it attracted huge crowds and generated substantial cash for the USOA. It also featured a high level of competition. The *Washington Post* characterized the event as "what may well be the greatest basketball tournament in history."[44]

However, not everyone thought the trials were run fairly, Russell among them. Russell had little respect for the way the AAU operated. He described the U.S. Olympic Basketball Committee, which was made up of members of the feuding AAU and NCAA, as partaking in "the greatest bit of sugar-'n-spice-in-the-mouth-and-bourbon-in-the-belly-carney-type-conning since Barnum and Bailey." He wrote that the AAU's Vickers Petroleum team offered him $500 to play in the trials, but instead he chose to play for the NCAA team for $2 a day. He feels strongly that during the action, the referees favored the AAU squads in an effort to strengthen its representation on the Olympic team. And, he maintained, "They succeeded."[45]

Regardless, the tournament was an economic success and helped set the stage for further growth. In addition to attracting huge numbers of fans, it attracted corporate sponsors in more visible ways. Ads in the 1956 Olympic qualifying tournament's official program show this. For example, Converse ran an ad for its legendary Chuck Taylor All-Star basketball shoes, which featured a "traction molded outsole and pivot button" for "non-skid traction and longer service." The shoes, manufactured in the United States by the Converse Rubber Company, were the latest model in Converse's forty years in the shoe business.[46]

The year 1956 marked a period of robustness for basketball shoe sales. While Converse touted its wares at the trials, Spalding was offering an imitation Converse basketball shoe that featured a "special Spalding cushioned sport arch and heel" and "large size non-rusting telescope eyelets."[47] And fellow competitor Pro-Keds ran ads featuring its "United States Royal" basketball shoe with patented "Powerlift" technology. These "United States Royal" shoe ads included endorsements from the likes of basketball stalwart George Mikan, who was dubbed "The Mr. Basketball," along with a number of prominent coaches.[48] Taken together, the ads serve as indicators of the basketball shoe's mushrooming status.

Though the basketball shoe was not yet packed with the cultural currency it was soon to gain, there were other indications pointing to its potential. In the 1950s, with time for sports and leisure increasing in American culture, the movie star James Dean sported Converse's Jack Purcell shoes in *Rebel without a Cause*. And in schools across America, fashion mores were loosening. This helped the sneaker's popularity to surge. Jonathon Wolford, the curator of the Bata Shoe Museum in Toronto, argues that at this time, "the sneaker was an integral part of the first distinctly marketed youth fashion and cultural movement in American history."[49] He may have overreached, but not by much. And the U.S. Olympic team, clad in Chuck Taylors, played a role in this process, though not as profoundly as subsequent American teams.

Converse resonated internationally, too. In 1956 Clifford Wells, coach of Tulane University, recalled that on a layover on Wake Island during a U.S. Special Services–sponsored trip to Asia to conduct basketball clinics for the Eighth Army and Far East Air Force, "we found several hundred Guamanians [people from Guam who worked there] playing basketball on outdoor courts, all of the players equipped with white All-Star Converse basketball shoes."[50] At the 1956 Melbourne Olympics, the *New York Times*'s Allison Danzig noted how highly the Soviet players, undoubtedly attracted by the American style of play and the quality of their shoes, valued the Chuck Taylors offered to them by the U.S. team as a gift.[51]

On the court at the trials, Bill Russell powered the collegiate all-stars to a win in their first game over the AAU champion Buchan Bakers from Seattle. In the other opening-day game, the armed forces pulled off a 78–77 upset over the AAU runner-up Phillips. With both of their teams losing on day one, it looked as if the AAU's reign as Olympic qualifying tournament champion was nearing its end. But the AAU quickly showed it was not ready to surrender its supremacy, as Phillips rebounded with two straight victories, including a four-point win over the college all-stars. In the win over the collegians, Phillips big man Chuck Darling, formerly of the University of Iowa, played well in tallying twenty-one points to Russell's nineteen.[52] On account of a complicated tiebreaker, the win made Phillips the champion of the trials. This gave the AAU its fourth straight Olympic qualifying tournament championship—in other words, every Olympic qualifying tournament up to that point. For Russell, the loss to Phillips marked his first defeat in sixty games.[53] In fact, the loss and subsequent tiebreaker that gave Phillips the trials championship count as the only tournament Russell failed to win over a nineteen-month period in which he won the NCAA championship, an Olympic gold medal, and an NBA title, a feat that remains unmatched.

In the end, the basketball committee chose five players from the champions, Phillips, as mandated, and then seven "at-large" players from the rest of the field.[54] Darling, Burdette Haldorson, high-scoring forward Robert Jeangerard, shooting guard James Walsh, and Bill Hougland came from Phillips. As a collegian Hougland had starred at Kansas, and he played in the 1952 Olympics; his selection in 1956 made him the second American, after Kurland, to play on two U.S. Olympic basketball teams.[55] In 1955 Haldorson and Burdette had starred together on Colorado's only NCAA Final Four team in school history, which lost to the Russell-led Dons in that year's semis. The U.S. Olympic Basketball Committee selected three players from the college all-stars—San Francisco's Russell and Jones, and the University of Iowa's Carl Cain, all African Americans—as well as three from the U.S. Armed Forces team: Gilbert Ford, William Evans, and the prolific Ron Tomsic, formerly of Stanford University. In Tomsic's case, his selection offered quite a reprieve from the mundane duties he carried out in the air force as a Public Information Officer stationed in Madison, Wisconsin. But he had endured an arduous route to become an Olympian, playing over fifty games as he moved through the air force's selection process. Throughout his life, he would consider the moment when he was finally told that he had made the squad, in a Kansas City hotel lobby at about three or four o'clock in the morning, "one of the biggest thrills of my life, that and receiving the gold medal."[56] Rounding out the team was Dick Boushka, a stalwart AAU player in the 1950s who had been added to the Buchan Bakers from the Wichita Vickers when the Bakers qualified for the Olympic trials (at that time, an AAU team that qualified for the Olympic trials could add four AAU players to its roster).[57] Along with Russell in Melbourne, Jeangerard, Tomsic, and K. C. Jones averaged double figures.

The squad could have been even stronger, particularly down-low, had NCAA institutions let the AAU use its players more readily. Some collegians could compete in the AAU championship, but certain conferences disallowed their players from doing so. For instance, as the basketball historian Adolph Grundman has noted, in 1956 the AAU tried to get the Kansas freshman Wilt Chamberlain on an AAU team for the championship tournament, thereby potentially making him eligible for the Olympics, but the Big Seven conference refused to waive its rule forbidding freshman from doing just that. Seattle University also refused to budge in the case of Elgin Baylor, so the possibility of fielding a legendary frontcourt trio of Chamberlain, Baylor, and Russell was missed.[58]

On account of his team's championship, the head coach of Phillips, Gerald Tucker, assumed Olympic head coaching duties, while Bruce Drake of the armed forces became his assistant.[59] To coach the armed services team, Drake had taken a one-year leave from his coaching duties at the University of Oklahoma, where he had manned the sideline for the previous seventeen. At Oklahoma, Gerald Tucker had actually played for Drake, in 1943 and then again in 1947, after returning from service in World War II. As a player, Tucker earned All-America honors.[60] The long-standing relationship between Tucker and Drake worked well in Melbourne. Tucker had absorbed much of Drake's coaching strategy when he played for him. It emphasized clever passing within the framework of Drake's popular ball-control "weaving" offense, known as the "Drake Shuffle."[61] The U.S. Olympic team implemented elements of the weave, but rather than deliberateness, the team integrated extreme speed into the equation, helping it set scoring records in Melbourne.

With the U.S. team set and reports of Soviet excellence circulating, anticipation for the Games mounted. Just weeks before Melbourne's Opening Ceremonies, most pundits tempered their predictions of how the U.S. basketball team would fare, despite the fact that the team had displayed its talent with an undefeated ten-game exhibition schedule that had culminated in Indianapolis with a convincing 73–60 win over the Phillips Oilers.[62] In the pre-Games buildup, *Sports Illustrated* touted the brand of ball played in Russia, France, Brazil, and Uruguay, while Hans-Dieter Krebs of Germany wrote in the *Converse Yearbook* that high-scoring Czechoslovakia was arguably Europe's top team. Krebs also acknowledged the Italian squad, which was coached by the American Jim McGregor, formerly of Whitworth College. By then Italy boasted a robust basketball scene, with 15,000 registered players, four stadiums featuring capacities of 5,000 or more, and a men's league sponsored by "large factories" in which games sold out commonly. *Sports Illustrated* argued that the Soviet Union's size and shooting ability made them the top contender to unseat the United States, while France rated high because of its stellar defense and rebounding, and Brazil and Uruguay caused fits for other teams with their "race-horse style of play," though against the United States, *Sports Illustrated* admitted, both teams would likely need to slow it down. Overall, Coach Tucker concurred with *Sports Illustrated*'s analysis of the quality of international play. "In the past 20 years the rest of the world has become basketball-conscious to such an extent that the sport now ranks among the favorites of a score of nations," he told reporters.[63]

In addition to recognizing an improved international standard of play, prognosticators assumed that the most common strategy employed against the United States would be the stall, given that Brazil had nearly upset the United States at the 1952 Olympics by slowing the game down, and the Soviet Union had used similar tactics with a modicum of success in that year's Olympic final. Coach Tucker told *Sports Illustrated* he intended to combat this with "hard, aggressive defense. We will press the opposition and keep pressing." This, along with Russell, whose agility and reflexes "make him perhaps the first true defensive genius the game has known"; the "mercurial" guard K. C. Jones; the "high-scoring" Darling; and the "speedy" Tomsic, encouraged *Sports Illustrated* to ultimately predict that the United States would prevail.[64]

It was a smart prediction, especially considering that the value of speed had increased soon after the Helsinki Games, when FIBA made further rule changes that encouraged fast play. As it had previously, in 1953 FIBA took its cues on the rule changes largely from the United States, as is evidenced by the fact that the wording of the new rules conformed closely to that of the 1953 U.S. amateur rulebook. However, the most notable rule change FIBA adopted was the implementation in 1956 of a thirty-second shot clock. The NBA had adopted a twenty-four-second shot clock in 1954, and though a shot clock was not used in Melbourne, from a broader per-spective, it reflected how commercial considerations had helped spur the adoption of rules that encouraged faster play for basketball internationally. In Melbourne, FIBA left unchanged the dimensions of its twelve-foot-wide lane.[65] FIBA's wide lane was an early example of how it could lead the way in encouraging speedier, more open play.[66]

8. Australia's Exhibition Building basketball venue. Note the hand-operated scoreboard on the platform behind the basket. Courtesy of the *Herald Weekly Times* Photographic Collection and the National Library of Australia.

So, with a faster international tournament expected and predictions made, the U.S. team set out for Melbourne. There they were to play in the Exhibition Building, where hammers clattered in the stands hours before the opening tip-off because it was being outfitted with a state-of-the-art roof that featured an open-air component. Just a few months before the Games, the Australians had decided to outfit the building with the roof to better accommodate the demand for tickets. They barely finished the job. In fact, the tight schedule kept officials from printing basketball press passes for the new venue until moments before the first game. *Sports Illustrated*'s Andre Laguerre reported that these were minor annoyances, but they "evaporated in the warmth of Australian kindliness and enthusiasm." And ultimately, during the Games, the Exhibition Building attracted over seventy-three thousand spectators.[67]

Politically, though tensions between the United States and Soviet Union had thawed a bit since the 1952 Olympics, two important events took place just before the 1956 Olympics that heightened cold war friction. First, in late October the Suez Canal crisis erupted. Armed with weapons from Russia, Egypt had moved to seize control of the Suez Canal, which had been used freely until then as a passageway for oil destined for industrial nations in Europe. Israel responded on October 29, 1956, by attacking Egypt, and then two days later, Great Britain and France intervened to make sure the passageway remained open. Looking to maintain stability, the Soviet Union and United States formed an unlikely union as they stepped in to negotiate a cease-fire. The effort proved successful, but Egypt, angry over the outcome, called for a boycott of the Olympics if the aggressors were not banned from participating. When these demands went unanswered, Egypt, Lebanon, and Iraq decided not to go to Melbourne, thereby firmly establishing the boycott as a political weapon in the modern era of the Olympics.[68]

Another political flare up caused even more disruption. On October 23, 1956, Hungarians took to the streets to protest their communist government, which emanated from Moscow. As Russian tanks moved in to squelch the rebellion, some Hungarian athletes, after hearing word of the rebellion en route to Melbourne, had their ship turned around. By the time they made it back to Eastern Europe, however, Russia controlled the port. Denied entrance, they decided to head back to Melbourne and take part in the Games. Other athletes that managed to participate in the rebellion fled to Czechoslovakia, where they were torn between trying to get back home, despite the prospect of strong reprisals, and heading on to Melbourne to compete. Most chose to compete in the Games because in Melbourne, an anonymous Hungarian athlete explained to *Sports Illustrated*, they could "tell the world about our wonderful adventure."[69] At the Opening Ceremonies word surfaced that Hungarian athletes planned to sabotage the Soviets' entry by hiding and then emerging with placards reading "murderers."[70] This did not happen, but in the Olympic Village, angry Hungarians did rip Communist insignias off of their uniforms, and a water polo match between the two nations turned violent.[71] As a way of protesting Soviet actions in Hungary, Switzerland, Spain, and the Netherlands chose to withdraw from the Olympics, too. International tensions reached such a pitch that many athletes, officials, and spectators in Melbourne wondered whether the Games would take place at all. Brundage, who had declared

9. Bill Russell and Chuck Darling in Melbourne with the Yugoslav wrestler Boris Vukov. Courtesy of the *Herald Weekly Times* Photographic Collection and the National Library of Australia.

the IOC's distaste for using the Games for political purposes, "whether right or wrong," refused to give in to such suggestions. "If we held up the Games every time the politicians made a mess of things we would never have them," he declared.[72]

Concerns about who would take up quarters in the Olympic Village arose too. To the surprise of many, the Soviets ended up staying there.[73] Still, the Russians were closely guarded. U.S. Olympian Tomsic remembered that "whenever the Russians went off the Village there was always two or three people with them. There was always someone with them and so they were always intrigued that we could come and go as we pleased."[74]

Despite the cold war issues, the Games opened with more than 4,000 athletes from a record sixty-eight nations in attendance. Opening day started with persistent rain, wind, and chill, but just in time, the skies parted, and the opening ceremonies took place under sunshine and seventy-five-degree weather.[75] By all accounts, Australia, a country of sports lovers, put on a fabulous show as a record crowd of over 100,000 packed into the Melbourne Cricket Grounds to watch. The U.S. Olympic basketball player Burdette Haldorson recalled a warm reception: "Australians loved Americans because we saved them from being invaded by the Japanese," he said in 2008, noting that it has not always been that way in recent years for U.S. teams abroad. But in 1956 in Australia, "When we marched into the stadium for the Opening Ceremony . . . Oh the crowd, it was just a huge ovation."[76]

The Americans met with kindness throughout their stay. Thanks to the Phillips Company's willingness to fly all its players (not just those who made the actual Olympic squad), along with a guest, to Australia, Margie Jeangerard got to watch her husband Bob play in Melbourne in person. "It was shortly enough after the Second World War that the Australians absolutely loved Americans . . . 'We love the Yanks, they saved us,' that type of thing," she remembered. "I got that when I was in a hotel sitting down to breakfast." She would be sat at a table with local folks, "And every time I opened my mouth . . . whoever I was sitting with, would say 'Oh, you're American. We love the Yanks.'"[77]

Some 200,000 more people enjoyed the opening festivities on television thanks to the city's three "new television receivers," made operational just over a week before the Olympics.[78] Enthusiasm for television coverage was strong. As the Games wore on, antennas sprouted up all over the city to capture the television signals. Even visiting military ships and periscopes on submarines sprung television aerials, which allowed navy crews to follow "every development of competition while afloat as well as ashore."[79]

In the United States there was widespread interest in securing footage of the Melbourne Olympics as well. Bob Mathias, one of President Eisenhower's personal representatives at the Games, interviewed American athletes for a series of exclusive films that were distributed within weeks after the Games closed. In addition to Mathias's work, a feature-length color film covering the Olympics was released soon after. If Americans did not want to wait until after the Games for footage, they could watch highlights on television in a series of six half-hour installments that aired in the States over the course of the Olympics, the first of which was released only two days after the Olympics opened. To pull it off, tapes were flown halfway around the world to Hollywood, where workers raced around the clock to edit them.[80]

Highlighting the Olympic movement's growing international significance, more than 800 credited reporters covered the Games, making it the biggest press story ever to emanate from the Australian mainland. Ninety desks, duplication machines, and typewriters with typefaces for five different languages filled the main press room. "Teleprinters" fed results from sporting venues into the pressroom, where the twelve "duplicating" machines printed off about 1,200 copies of each result.[81] As for radio coverage, the British Broadcasting Corporation led the way. They recruited Australian linguists to deliver eyewitness accounts around the clock to London via shortwave radio. These accounts were also rebroadcast in an astounding forty-four different languages on the BBC's worldwide external services.[82]

On the basketball court, of all the opening-game performances at the Exhibition Building, the United States team, spearheaded by Russell, demonstrated an unsurpassed combination of speed and size. This enabled them to emerge in the early going as the consensus favorite. Utilizing the pressure defense planned by Coach Tucker, the Americans beat Japan in that opener 98–40, even though, as Koh Koide of the Japanese Amateur Basketball Association noted, basketball in Japan after the war had enjoyed opportunities to improve. (Koide maintained that contests "with U.S. occupation forces and the Hawaiian AJA team," which visited in 1950, brought the "one-handed shot, various styles of weaves and superior dribbling" to Japan.[83])

Following its win over Japan, the United States handled Thailand 101–29 and then won in record-setting fashion, 121–53, over the Philippines, marking the highest scoring effort by a single team in the Olympics to that point.[84] Overall, the scores of the 1956 Olympic tournament were notably higher than those in previous Olympiads, especially the United States' near one-hundred-point average. The higher scores reflected the effect of rule changes over the years, as well as the increased skill, speed, and overall athleticism of basketball players throughout the world.[85]

In the next phase of the ridiculously complicated pool-play system that FIBA utilized for the tournament, the United States faced two seemingly tough tests, first against Bulgaria, which had only one blemish on its record, and then against the undefeated Brazil. Yet the United States disposed of both with relative ease. Its 85–44 victory over Bulgaria stirred up some controversy when referee Charley Sien of Singapore ruled Russell's "tap-in shot" illegal. The term "tap-in shot" was used to describe Russell's tactic of tapping the ball into the goal while it hung just above the rim. Technically, FIBA rules allowed this maneuver, though none of the international referees in Melbourne had likely seen a player work above the rim the way Russell did.[86] After the game, Coach Tucker attempted to persuade officials that Russell was making contact with the ball when it "still is above the rim and [that he] releases contact before it touches the hoop." Apparently he was persuasive, because officials judged the maneuver legal for future contests.[87] The United States followed its win over Bulgaria with a convincing victory over Brazil, 113–51.

Boasting a 5-0 record, the United States next faced the Soviet Union. The game marked the third encounter on the Olympic stage for these cold war foes and, as had their other matchups, it attracted huge interest. Despite having endured a close loss to France without Krumminch, the Soviets were still considered the United States' stiffest competition. Thousands of fans crammed into Melbourne's Exhibition Building to watch the action. When the game began, the atmosphere was at a fever pitch even though, technically, both teams had already qualified for the final-four medal round. The *New York Times* reported that great anticipation filled the air as the crowd waited to see if the Soviets could beat "the United States at a game the Americans invented."[88]

Some of the excitement was muted, however, when fans realized that Krumminch, still mending, had not suited up. Nonetheless, the Soviets' other big men helped them stay close in the first half, especially Arkadi Votchkarez. He scored twenty points in the game despite never even having entered an Olympic contest up to that point. Votchkarez outshined Stassis Stonkous, another of the Soviets' centers, who, before the contest, had been the team's leading scorer.[89]

At halftime, holding onto a 39–32 lead, the United States decided to implement a pressing defense in order to open the action and increase the tempo of play. The strategy paid off: the United States scored forty-six points in the second half, while smothering the Soviets on defense. The contest showed how, though the Soviets had greatly increased the size of their squad since Helsinki, the United States had upgraded its speed. As a result, the Soviets seemed to plod around the court as Russell and company maneuvered with relative ease. Russell led his team with twenty points on the way to an 85–55 victory.[90] Even more noteworthy, Russell's ability to block shots, jump-start the fast break with outlet passes, and run the court allowed the Americans to maximize the effectiveness of their extended defense. Russell's performance showed how a big man could dominate a game on both ends of the floor, with a degree of speed and agility heretofore unforeseen. Emphasizing Russell's defense in particular, Tomsic summed up Russell's effect on the team by saying, "He changed the whole nature of the game, really."[91]

Despite the U.S. team's dominating performance, as the semifinal medal round was set to begin, questions persisted about who would win the gold, especially since the Americans had not yet encountered the Soviets with a healthy Krumminch. Some argued that the Soviet Union should not have even remained in contention for the gold, because it had suffered an earlier loss to France in addition to its loss to the United States. However, a series of convoluted rules involving pool-play records and margin-of-victory tiebreakers made them eligible. This did not sit well with Coach Tucker. He said the Olympic tournament should be "a double elimination affair instead of this silly round-robin kind of thing." He also noted that, though the United States had just beaten the Soviets handily and the Soviet Union had lost to France, if the Soviets won the following night and then were to upset the United States, they would win the gold medal with two losses to the United States' one.[92]

Regardless, the semifinals featured the United States, Uruguay, France, and the Soviet Union. All of these teams had built strong basketball traditions, and the geographic distance separating them demonstrated basketball's widespread popularity. Still, the United States soon showed that the rest of the world still had a long way to go. In its opening game of the medal round, the Americans dismissed any notion of international parity as naïve with a 101–38 win over Uruguay. Tomsic led the well-rounded attack with eighteen points, while Russell only played for fifteen minutes of the affair. The game marked the fourth time in the Olympic tournament that the U.S. team score surpassed the century mark.[93] The new selection process, which had combined college all-stars with stars from the AAU and armed forces, demonstrated the extent of America's basketball superiority.

In the other semifinal game the Soviets, playing with a healthy Ivan Krumminch, rebounded from their earlier loss to France with a 56–49 victory. Leading the way with twenty-seven points, which accounted for nearly half of his team's total, Krumminch proved pivotal, signaling his presence to the U.S. squad in the process.[94] The Soviet Union's victory set up the second straight gold medal contest between the cold war's primary foes. With Krumminch healthy and the gold medal on the line, enthusiasm skyrocketed.

A capacity crowd and energized atmosphere greeted the players for the contest—already the fourth matchup between the United States and Soviet Union in their relatively young series. Before the opening tip-off, the teams lined up across from each other and exchanged gifts. The Soviets gave the American team stamps, while the U.S. squad offered white high-top Chuck Taylors. The pregame gift exchange generated little postgame comment in the papers, but, as mentioned, the *New York Times*'s Danzig did note, almost in passing, that the Soviets "prized the footgear above all else."[95] Nearly fifty years after the Games, Tomsic remembered as much, saying, "We'd see them [the Russians] around the village . . . what they really wanted from us was our shoes . . . you know, our basketball shoes because they didn't have the same technology at that time."[96] Both comments were simple observations, but they serve as early indicators of the ability of U.S. corporations to capitalize on basketball to attract people to basketball-related products. In this case, the American style and the business acumen and technical capabilities of its corporations had combined to attract the Soviet players to American basketball shoes. By 1964, in fact, Soviet officials placed an order with Converse for forty-six pairs of its famous Chuck Taylor high-tops to outfit its national team.[97]

After exchanging the gifts, the starters met at half-court for the tip-off and the game commenced. All told, the argument that the Soviet Union's communist government was a slow-moving bureaucracy that stifled innovation, while the United States' capitalist system rewarded speed and creativity, worked as an apt analogy for what played out on the court. Ivan Krumminch was simply too slow for Russell and his mates—they ran so well that the Soviet giant often found himself on the wrong half of the court while the United States finished plays on the break. The lumbering Krumminch was not the Soviet Union's only problem. Its entire team lacked the speed needed to stay with the United States, which enabled the Americans to race to a 56–27 advantage at the half and an eventual 89–55 victory. The final score could have been even more lopsided had the Soviets not implemented slow-down tactics to keep the United States under one hundred points.

Coach Tucker declared afterward that the U.S. squad was "the best basketball team I have ever seen," and he voiced dismay over criticism back home that the team had encountered inferior competition, asking, "What more do they have to prove? They would be equal to any team in any league anywhere . . . I don't want to get involved in anything controversial, but they are the best amateur team—the best ever."[98] He was right. Sure, Haldorson described the competition in Melbourne as a "cakewalk."[99] But the 1956 team faced a stiffer challenge than earlier U.S. teams, and yet it dominated more convincingly. Hougland, who played in both the 1952 and 1956 Games, said, "I think the competition got better" between the two Olympiads, but he also noted that in Melbourne, "we had two big centers, Russell and Chuck Darling. And nobody had seen anything like Russell. . . . All we did was just go press [half-court] the hell out of people. If they got around us, you didn't worry about it because they weren't gonna get a shot inside." He described Russell as a "phenomenal athlete, plus a phenomenal competitor."[100] But the team is often overlooked in debates

TABLE 4. 1956 U.S. Men's Olympic Basketball cumulative stats

NAME	G	FGM-FGA	(%)	FTM-FTA	(%)	PF	PTS/AVG
Bill Russell	8	46-96	.479	21-27	.778	5	113/14.1
Robert Jeangerard	8	45-74	.608	10-11	.909	9	100/12.5
Ron Tomsic	8	34-92	.370	21-25	.840	12	89/11.1
K. C. Jones	8	32-75	.427	23-27	.852	11	87/10.9
James Walsh	9	27-61	.443	19-21	.905	17	73/9.1
Burdette Haldorson	8	28-58	.483	13-15	.867	14	69/8.6
Dick Boushka	8	27-68	.397	10-10	1.000	12	64/8.0
Chuck Darling	8	22-44	.500	12-15	.800	7	56/9.3
William Evans	8	21-55	.382	12-18	.667	11	54/6.8
Bill Hougland	8	20-51	.392	6-6	1.000	5	46/5.8
Gilbert Ford	8	17-44	.386	5-7	.714	14	39/4.9
Carl Cain	2	1-5	.200	1-2	.500	2	3/1.5
USA TOTALS	8	320-723	.443	153-184	.832	119	793/99.1
OPP. TOTALS	8	137-415	.330	91-130	.700	163	365/45.6

regarding the best amateur squads of all time, a debate that usually focuses instead on the 1960 and 1984 U.S. Olympic teams.[101] Yet with a still-standing Olympic record 52.1-point average margin of victory, the 1956 team should undoubtedly be considered among the best.

Following the gold medal game, a reporter asked Russell, "How was it, Bill?" Russell replied, "Who was it said: 'I came, I saw, I conquered'?"[102] Indeed he had. Russell's personality, talent, and skill influenced his team's play, contributing greatly to the squad's creativity, athleticism, and teamwork, all of which endeared it to the adoring crowds. In retrospect, the 1956 squad's chemistry seems palpable, much like the attitude and style emanated by the Russell-infused Boston Celtics, who won eleven of thirteen NBA championships in the late 1950s into the 1960s. Evidence of this Olympic chemistry continued after the Games, too, when all of Russell's teammates, save Carl Cain, who was still convalescing from a sore back, attended his wedding.[103]

Driven by Russell's athleticism and charisma, the 1956 Olympic team contributed to the popularity and expansion of basketball worldwide. Fans flocked to the basketball venue to catch a glimpse of the action, especially Russell. His ability to block shots without fouling, to run the fast break, to dominate the boards, and to slam-dunk garnered repeat ovations from the crowds. Even his offensive game, though not considered his strongest asset, sparkled in Melbourne as he led the team in scoring and shot 78 percent from the free-throw line.

Russell won over even the Soviets, who were not only awed by his play but also seemed to find him likable. Soviet players went out of their way to embrace him after the final game, a sign of great respect. And two years later, in a telling indication of the effect of Russell's exploits in Melbourne, the Soviets showed up for a basketball tour of the United States with a revamped roster stacked with more versatile and speedier six-feet-seven to six-feet-ten-inch players. The shift to the Russell model started a long-standing international trend, in Europe in particular, that emphasized more dynamic big men. Just as he had changed the college game, in leading the United States to the gold medal at the Melbourne Olympics, Russell provided a new international model for a basketball player.

5

BASKETBALL ACCELERATES AS ROBERTSON, LUCAS, AND WEST RUN THROUGH ROME

Between Melbourne and Rome, the site of the 1960 Olympiad, the world took a huge leap forward toward the modern technological era. In 1957 the Soviets launched the world's first satellite, making the 1960 Games the first to take place with a satellite orbiting Earth and raising alarm across the United States that it was falling behind its cold war foe technologically, militarily, and culturally. A longer-term legacy of the Sputnik satellite, however, was the ushering in of an international communications revolution. As it happened, the 1960 Games were also the first to receive widespread television coverage. Complementing this, groundbreaking data processors, precursors to the modern-day computer, quickly churned out results for media outlets. All of it hinted at the potential of technology to provide instant coverage of athletic events and streamlined highlight packages to every corner of the globe, reaching billions immediately.

At the same time, the 1960 Olympic basketball tournament highlighted the international trend in basketball that encouraged fast action, high scores, and increasingly spectacular highlights. Oscar Robertson, Jerry West, Jerry Lucas, and company, who got set loose in Rome by Coach Newell, shone particularly brightly. In the ensuing decades, basketball's action-packed characteristics continued to work well with the escalating speed and clarity of the era's technological advances.

The U.S. television network CBS paid $394,000 to broadcast the Games and commenced its coverage with a simple one-hour highlight package during the not-so-coveted 9:00 p.m. to 10:00 p.m. time slot on the East Coast. Even so, this set an important precedent. As Richard Pound, a member of the IOC and at one time the negotiator of Olympic broadcasting contracts, put it in 2006, "In the course of a single generation, the power of television has made the Olympic Games the most universally watched event in well over two hundred countries."[1] This does not mean that Olympic television resonated in 1960 at all like it does now, however. When asked if he encouraged his family back home to watch Olympic basketball on television, the 1960 U.S. Olympic basketball coach Pete Newell told the author, "I didn't even know they [CBS] were doing it . . . I had no idea it was going to be on until someone told me." He added, "I don't remember ever being interviewed by them."[2]

On CBS's first day of coverage, Americans saw footage of the Opening Ceremonies from the previous evening as well as same-day highlights from the boxing and swimming venue. To accomplish the same-day feat, the network flew tapes overseas in the early afternoon, quickly put together a highlight package, and then aired it to millions across the country.[3] Americans soon familiarized themselves with the Rome Olympics' biggest stars, some already well-known, such as the basketball standout Oscar "The Big O" Robertson, others less so, such as a nineteen-year-old boxer named Cassius Clay and a young woman named Wilma Rudolph who had spent much of her childhood fighting illness. Remarkably, Robertson, Clay, and Rudolph spent their early childhoods within 150 miles of one another's birthplace; Oscar in tiny Bellsburg, Tennessee; Rudolph in Nashville, Tennessee; and Ali in Louisville, Kentucky.[4] As African Americans from humble beginnings in the South, their success demonstrated the merit-based nature of sports. For basketball in particular, Robertson's ability to, at six feet five and 200 pounds, play virtually all five positions, especially point guard, provided the international game with a new physical model for guards.

In 1950 Americans owned a total of 5 million television sets; by 1960, that number totaled 50 million, and sports boomed as a result. The flickering black-and-white images CBS aired from the Rome Games, remarkable at the time, seem woefully inadequate by modern standards, but this should not diminish their importance. As the cold war rivalry unfolded and technology improved, cold war powers tried to use television to advocate their respective ideologies. Yet America largely led the way technologically, and few television events since World War II have offered a better opportunity for promoting liberal capitalism than the Olympic Games, with its cultural currency, merit-based nature, liberal leanings, commercialism, and the visibility of its stars.

Along with the burgeoning technological advances, other precedents awaited as the Rome Olympics approached: namely, the stage was set for record-breaking participation in a relatively peaceful world. Ironically, atomic power had contributed to calls for peaceful coexistence, and in the late 1950s, there were signs of thawing in the cold war. This had encouraged the United States and the Soviet Union, in a show of goodwill, to sign agreements to exchange cultural, educational, and technological expertise. Plans to host track-and-field meets and wrestling competitions soon followed.[5] The interaction helped pave the way for a visit by Soviet premier Nikita Khrushchev to America in the fall of 1959. Exchanges occurred in basketball, too, through international tournaments and exhibition tours.

Still, the United States and Soviet Union aggressively competed against each other militarily, culturally, and economically. Americans continued to measure themselves against the Soviets, while in Russia officials hung signs seemingly everywhere proclaiming things like, "We shall overtake and outstrip the USA, in per capita production of meat, milk, and butter!"[6] Furthermore, the aforementioned Soviet launch of Sputnik had ignited a high-stakes "space race." The race was still on by the summer of 1960, as evidenced by the U.S. government's announcement during the Rome Olympics that the air force intended to send a monkey into space.[7] Both nations had also been stockpiling arms.[8] Then, on the eve of the Rome Games, tensions were ignited with the announcement that the Soviets had shot down a U-2 reconnaissance plane. Two days before the Games ended, Soviet premier Nikita Khrushchev sailed to America for a speech at the United Nations, "where he pounded his fist and railed against America and the West."[9] Less problematic for the United States was the Sino-Soviet split.[10]

The two leading cold war foes competed on the basketball court as well. In 1958, a year after launching Sputnik, the Soviet Union scored two hardwood victories when it won the World Championship on American soil in San Diego, California, and then beat the U.S. Air Force basketball team at an international tournament in Santiago, Chile, by a lopsided score, 62–37. After the loss in Chile, *Time* reported that "Communists everywhere hailed it as another landmark in Khrushchev's campaign to overtake the United States in everything from meat production to widget manufacturing." The magazine also noted that a leftist Chilean newspaper declared, "When it comes to shooting at the moon or at the basket, the United States cannot keep up with Russia." And the legendary Soviet coach Stepan Spandarian said, "We won, because we did what we planned to do."[11]

A big part of the Soviets' basketball success—in addition to the fact that they did not face America's best players at these events—resulted from their decision, following their drubbing in Melbourne, to field a team with more versatile players who, while still tall, also possessed speed. Working off of the Bill Russell model, rather than the Kurland and Lovellette model, Soviet officials wanted a team that was quicker on rebounds, faster in the open floor, and better at driving to the basket. As a result, players such as the six-feet-ten-inch Viktor Zubkov, who was tall and agile, were developed to complement, if not surpass, Ivan "the Breadwinner" Krumminch.

Another factor affecting the Soviet scenario was FIBA's adoption of its famed trapezoid-shaped lane for the 1960 Olympic tournament. U.S. Olympic coach Pete Newell suggested to the author that the new lane was a result of FIBA's desire to have international teams compete better against the United States. While the trapezoid lane often gets credit for helping Europe develop versatile big men, Newell makes the point that by the 1980s and 1990s, the lane had exerted a cost on European basketball as well: namely, the dearth of talented post players throughout Europe's basketball history. When FIBA adopted the new lane, "they knew they could not play the same game [as the Americans]," Newell maintained, because with the trapezoid lane, "you can't play a center post because of the angles of these lines [on the trapezoid lane]."[12] (Incidentally, in 2008 FIBA decided to do away with the trapezoid lane in favor of the extended rectangle—it also added an NBA-style charge line and moved back its three-point line as a way of "encouraging teams to attack more and to have high scorings," according to FIBA president Bob Elphinsto.[13])

In the middle of the 1959–60 U.S. basketball season, just several months before the Rome Olympics, Zubkov and speedy playmaking guards Maidon Valdmanis and Guran Minashvili showcased the Soviet team's new look during a series of games versus NIBL teams in America. The Soviets finished the tour with a 2-4 record but played nearly every game closely and impressed U.S. onlookers. While in the States, Krumminch garnered much attention from the U.S. media as reporters regaled readers with stories of his massive size and unlikely rise to the top of the Soviet sports world. *Newsweek* noted that a mere five years before the tour, Krumminch "didn't know a jump shot from a double dribble." In Madison Square Garden, following one of the Soviet team's losses, Krumminch was asked whether he enjoyed being seven feet three. *Newsweek* reported that as he squirmed a bit preparing to respond, "his muscles that he has developed chopping pine trees in the Latvian forests rippled." Finally, Krumminch answered by simply saying, "Not especially." When asked if he was teased as a child, he reportedly answered, "Nyet, I was too strong to be kidded."[14] The media loved it. But the real story of the trip was not Krumminch: it was the Soviet Union's increased stock of multifaceted big men and its more agile play overall.

One win in particular, over the defending NIBL champion the Denver D-C Truckers in front of a sellout crowd of 10,500, served as a statement of arrival for the revamped Soviet team. Aficionados came away from the game impressed with the Soviet Union's arsenal of weapons.[15] In addition to the six-feet-ten-inch Zubkov, the Soviets boasted two other six-feet-ten players in their frontcourt, both of whom, like Zubkov, could run better than the former lumberjack Krumminch.[16] After seeing the new Soviet lineup, people again questioned the United States' ability to defend its Olympic title. G. Russell Lyons, chairman of the AAU Basketball Committee, declared, "The Russians will be the team we must beat to win the Olympic title in Rome."[17] Pete Newell, who would soon take on the head coaching duties for the United States' 1960 Olympic team, came away impressed as well.

The Soviet squad impressed more than just Americans: after the trip,

Russia's chief communist youth newspaper, the *Komsomolskaya Pravda*, claimed that the Soviet basketball program was closing the gap enough to possibly take the gold in Rome.[18] And the Soviet coach Stephen Spandarian said, "The contests between the Soviet and U.S. teams were like a struggle between equals. The decisive advantage the Americans once had no longer exists."[19]

Much to the AAU's surprise, the Soviet tour, even with the sellout game in Denver, disappointed financially. The average turnout per game of nearly 7,000 people fell short of expectations. However, the lower-than-expected gate sales reflected the changing basketball landscape within the United States more than disinterest in the Soviet team. A talent shift away from the AAU in favor of the purely professional NBA had been occurring for several years. The NBA's rising popularity enabled its owners to attract NCAA players with more lucrative contracts than the corporate-backed NIBL teams could offer, which in turn increased the NCAA's competitiveness at the Olympic trials. Similar shifts were developing between the NCAA and AAU in other sports, leading to a period of particularly tense and protracted power struggles for control of amateur athletics. Eventually, a number of prominent people, from FIBA secretary-general R. William Jones to IOC president Avery Brundage to General Douglas MacArthur to President John F. Kennedy, became involved in the conflicts.

The rivalry between the AAU and the NCAA intensified in 1960 when the Swedish national basketball team, planning to play a tour against collegiate teams in the United States, was denied official sanctioning by the AAU.[20] The episode highlighted basketball's expanding internationalism and the NCAA's and AAU's intentions to control that growth. For a number of years the NCAA-dominated National Association of Basketball Coaches (NABC) had established rules for amateur hoops in the United States and Canada. But by the late 1950s, with the bulk of elite amateur talent within NCAA stables, the NABC wanted to seize control of amateur basketball on a broader international level.[21] Therefore, the NABC had supported efforts to bring the Swedish National team to the United States as a way of challenging the AAU's hold on United States involvement with international competitions. In turn, the AAU, acutely aware of the eroding public interest in its product, decided to meet the challenge head-on by rejecting the Swedish trip. It was a stubborn, narrow-minded response by the AAU to the challenge of dealing with the burgeoning international market for basketball while also coping with a loss of talent at home. Over time, the AAU's efforts to retain control of U.S. basketball by turning inward proved no match for basketball's ever-growing international appeal in an increasingly connected world.

The conflict carried over to the Rome Games, where NCAA representatives put forth a proposal asking FIBA to recognize the NCAA as the official international sanctioning body for amateur basketball in the United States.[22] FIBA, which had already demonstrated its ambivalence during the Swedish national team conflict—when General-Secretary Jones criticized the AAU's handling of the Swedish incident, while FIBA President Greim voiced support for the AAU—continued to send conflicting messages. So did the IOC, which, rather than choose between the AAU and the NCAA, decided to shelve the issue in order to give the two organizations time to resolve their differences. Considering that the AAU had represented the United States in FIBA for the previous twenty-four years, the *New York Times* accurately viewed the IOC's decision to shelve the matter as a victory for the NCAA.[23] Yet shelving the issue mollified few. Eventually, in the early 1970s, the NCAA did gain nearly total control of international basketball through an association called the American Basketball Association of the United States of America (ABA/USA), mainly because its talent pool was superior.

While a resolution of the rift between the NCAA and the AAU took time, the new-look Soviet team's performance in the United States during the winter of 1959–60, coupled with the unavailability of Wilt Chamberlain for the Rome Games, raised more immediate concerns for amateur basketball in the United States. As early as 1957, Chamberlain had fueled hopes in the United States that he would participate in the Olympics when he told the *Washington Post* that he planned to join the AAU in 1959 "with an eye toward the Olympic Games." Chamberlain added, "I also figure I can make the Olympic team in track. If I set my mind to it, I think I can high jump 7 feet, I'm also toying with the idea of trying for the decathlon."[24] The thought of Chamberlain, with his strength, wingspan, and leaping ability, patrolling the lane for the United States excited people, but the vision did not materialize. After Chamberlain's junior year, he decided to accept a contract with the Harlem Globetrotters, thus ending his status as an amateur.

Pressing ahead, the U.S. Olympic Basketball Committee implemented a tryout process for Rome similar to the one that had been utilized in Melbourne. The 1960 trials took place in late March and early April in Denver, Colorado, the weekend after the NCAA tournament championship. In one of the few changes to the qualifying process, eight teams received invitations rather than four. The best squads of the eight-team field were the NCAA University all-stars, the NCAA national champion Ohio State University Buckeyes, the NAIA all-stars, the AAU champion the Peoria Caterpillar Cats (who were coached by former Olympic head man Warren Womble), and the AAU runner-up Akron Goodyear Wingfoots.[25] The NCAA University all-stars, coached by Pete Newell, boasted a particularly formidable lineup powered by Robertson, West, and Terry Dischinger, while Lucas and John "Hondo" Havlicek led the Ohio State Buckeyes.[26]

With hindsight, it seems obvious that the collegiate all-star squad constituted the trials' strongest team, but that was not the prevailing viewpoint at the time. "College players were considered prima donnas in those days," Newell recalled. "The general feeling was that they'd fall apart against the AAU teams with a bunch of veterans who had worked together." No collegiate squad had ever won the Olympic qualifying tournament. Furthermore, as Coach Newell explained, "The AAU controlled the dates, the sites, the officials . . . I mean, I was scrambling up to Denver along with Jerry Lucas and Oscar Robertson, because we'd just finished the NCAA tournament two days before. No wonder the college teams found it impossible to make all the adjustments." Continuing, Newell said, "The AAU had it all their way. They were the teams who had been playing together, under international rules, and their officials were under big pressure from the corporations [Phillips Oil, etc.] to put AAU players on the Olympic team."[27]

In the end, though, the collegiate all-stars did prove superior. They won the Olympic qualifying tournament in convincing fashion, serving as an indication of the talent shift occurring in the NCAA's favor and ending the AAU's twenty-year reign as qualifying tournament champions. The AAU's Peoria Cats did make it to the finals, but the nucleus of the Olympic team came from the NCAA's ranks. From a financial standpoint, the tournament again delivered notable profits, as net receipts for the three-day affair totaled over $46,000.[28]

The NCAA University all-stars' qualifying tournament victory made Pete

Newell head coach of the 1960 Olympic team, while Warren Womble, the 1952 U.S. Olympic head coach, took on assistant duties.[29] With Newell's appreciation for pressing defenses and his willingness to adapt to his players' strengths, he proved an ideal coach for the 1960 squad. Before Rome, Newell had already elicited credit for innovative coaching. In 1947–48, as coach of the University of San Francisco Dons, his San Francisco teams became known for their "press defense." In addition to using his guards in a forward, pressing fashion on defense, Newell earned national repute for his teams' help-side defense. This involved defensive players that were away from the ball positioning themselves so as to help the on-ball defender, if needed. As he had done with the reverse-action offense, Newell gave Needles much of the credit for developing the principles of "weakside help."[30] In Rome, Newell used pressure defense and adapted his offensive style to fit players such as Robertson by giving them more space to operate.

Of course, it made sense to accommodate Robertson. He was the standout player at the Olympic trials, and in Rome, he became the next great basketball Olympian to emerge from America's cultural cauldron of opportunity, competitiveness, diversity, and innovation, despite the stubborn existence of racism. As early as 1959, *Sports Illustrated*'s Jeremiah Tax summed up Robertson's abilities well, writing, "It is the bright miracle of sport that the hearts of a whole city—occasionally, a nation—can be lifted and quickened by the accomplishments of such a gifted youngster in a simple game."[31] At six feet five inches and 200 pounds, Robertson changed the point guard position. He dribbled, passed, and scored like few had ever done and with a size that few thought possible. As Coach Newell described it, Oscar "could play any kind of game."[32] Perhaps no better example of Robertson's abilities is to note that he averaged nearly a triple double over the course of his prolific NBA career. As had happened with Russell, the emergence of The Big O marked an important stage in the evolution of basketball. In fact, the Robertson model has proven harder to emulate than the Russell model. Not until Earvin "Magic" Johnson in 1992 did a point guard play at the Olympics with size, skill, and versatility comparable to Robertson's.

Yet, despite his successes, Robertson's life, much like Russell's, was tinged by racial prejudice. There are many parallels in fact, in the lives of Robertson and Russell. Both were born in the South, only to spend the bulk of their childhoods north of the Mason-Dixon Line. Both helped keep America atop the basketball world by revolutionizing the game at the Olympics. And both spoke openly and sometimes controversially during and after their professional careers about America's troubled history of race relations.

Despite the prejudice both endured, the deep-seated ideal of equal opportunity could not forever be denied to black Americans, and neither could the talents of people such as Barksdale, Russell, and Robertson. Fortunately for the United States, these two forces, the country's ideals and the talent of its citizens, were loosening impediments to a fuller flowering of its potential. In the opening paragraph of his autobiography Robertson recognized as much, writing, "I've always thought that a wonderful thing about sports is that they give everyone a chance . . . That's one of the wonderful things about America as well. This country promises everyone a chance. It is a promise that has not always been kept. But the promise has always been here, a shining beacon down the road."[33] Still, it is hard to overstate the irony of the fact that first Barksdale, next Russell, and then Robertson, in these early years of the cold war, played important roles in America's desire to showcase its cultural ideals abroad, while suffering from racism at home.

Not long after moving from Tennessee to Indianapolis, Indiana, at the age of four, Oscar developed a love for basketball. As a youngster he pretended that a hoop hung on the trunk of a tree in his front yard. Unable to afford a real ball, he aimed jump shots at the imaginary rim with rolled-up socks held together with string or with a ball of rags. Later on, Oscar and his older brother Bailey got memberships at the local YMCA, where they honed their skills. Near their house, they turned an empty lot into a basketball court. It became known as the "Dust Bowl" because of the dirt, dust, and clay players kicked up when competing on it. The Robertson boys played many sports growing up, but Oscar recalled that in Indianapolis, "basketball was the emperor of them all. Guys played sunup to sundown." Oscar even took it a step further by playing late into the night in his home. "You couldn't sleep at night," Robertson's mother said once, "with that basketball going all the time. Bump! Bump! Bump!"[34]

After middle school, Robertson followed his brother to Crispus Attucks High School, where his hard work turned into astonishing success. That success was recognized at the turn of the millennium when The Big O was named the Hoosier state's best scholastic basketball player of all time, no small feat considering Indiana's illustrious high-school basketball history, which includes John Wooden, Clyde Lovellette, Larry Bird, and Glenn Robinson, to name a few. The distinction is all the more remarkable given that Robertson commenced his remarkable career at a segregated high school with no gym.

In September 1927 Crispus Attucks, built to accommodate 1,000 students, opened its doors to educate over 1,350 mostly black students. In later years even more students attended its overcrowded halls, Attucks would soon transform itself into a bastion of black progress and neighborhood pride. The historian Randy Roberts, in *But They Can't Beat Us*, a book about Robertson and Crispus Attucks, notes that soon after its opening, the school that was created as "a monument to racism" had ironically transformed itself "into a symbol of black pride." Hundreds of doctors, lawyers, and educators earned their scholastic education there, as well as a slew of jazz musicians, including J. J. Johnson, Slide Hampton, Wes Montgomery, Jimmy Coe, and Jimmy Spaulding. The students learned under a dynamic group of educators, many of them with PhDs. By the 1930s Crispus Attucks was also excelling on the athletic field, and in subsequent decades sports "came to define the school."[35]

In 1954, Robertson's sophomore year of high school, Attucks lost in the final eight of Indiana's state tournament to an all-white team from Milan, the small town memorialized in the 1986 movie *Hoosiers*. The following year Robertson led Attucks to the state championship. That year's final was the first Indiana state championship game to feature two all-black teams, a sharp contrast to the racial makeup of Milan's storied squad. In 1956 Oscar led Attucks to another state championship. But along with all the great memories of their championship runs, Robertson also remembers that after their 1955 championship, Crispus Attucks had to take a different parade route through the heart of downtown Indianapolis than the one used the previous year by Milan, a team not even from Indianapolis. Instead of going through downtown, Crispus Attucks paraded through "Naptown," the predominantly black section of Indianapolis. Later, Robertson learned that Mayor Alex Clark had met with Attucks officials beforehand and, voicing concerns about rioting, suggested the different route. Robertson wrote years later that such slights did not go unnoticed: "They took our innocence away from us."[36]

When his remarkable high-school career came to an end, Robertson attended the University of Cincinnati, thanks in no small part to an ill-fated recruiting trip to Indiana University.[37] Cincinnati boasted a rather modest basketball tradition. Its first postseason appearance did not come until 1950, and it would not appear in its first NCAA tournament until after Robertson's arrival, which made Robertson's ability to lead Cincinnati to the upper echelons of the NCAA basketball landscape somewhat akin to Russell's effect on the University of San Francisco.

In the spring of 1959, shortly after Cincinnati's Final Four loss to California, Oscar's mother fell ill with a kidney ailment. Her condition quickly turned serious, and she had to undergo an emergency surgery. The operation was successful but came with a huge price tag. To pay for the bill, Oscar's mom returned to work the day after her surgery. Still, The Big O did not jump at the Globetrotters' overtures. (He thought Saperstein underpaid players anyway.) Instead, he bided his time, telling his mother, "Someday, if I am able, I will do all I can for you."[38] The following year, true to his word, he took Cincinnati to the final four a second time and led his country on the basketball court at the Olympic Games. Then he took care of his mother.

Jerry West, hailing from Cabin Creek, a small town in West Virginia, starred alongside Robertson in Rome. To appreciate just how country West's humble beginnings were, one needs only to look at the title of a 1969 biography of him penned by Billy Libby, *Mr. Clutch: How a Hillbilly Kid Became an Olympic Champion and Pro Basketball Superstar!* As with Robertson's, West's family did not live in luxury. As one of six kids in that family, West has recalled, "We never went on vacations and we didn't have a car, we didn't have a lot of things that those families you would think are part of the American lifestyle [had,] and my lifestyle didn't involve that."[39] But in Cabin Creek, West, who grew into a six-feet-three sharpshooter, honed his dribbling and shooting skills on dirt courts for hours, and it is from there that he earned the moniker "Zeke from Cabin Creek." After rewriting West Virginia's scholastic record book in high school, West pleased his fellow statesmen by heading to West Virginia University and leading the relatively unheralded Mountaineers to the national championship game in 1959. Although his team lost to Coach Newell's California Bears in the title game, West earned Final Four MVP honors that year.

As West worked and matured, West Virginians from Cabin Creek to the State House came to celebrate him. For instance, in the summer of 1960, before West left for the Olympics, the town of East Bank changed its name to "West Bank" for a day. And after West returned from Rome, the governor of West Virginia invited him to visit the capitol. When West showed up, he said, "I'm Jerry West. I have an appointment with the Governor," to which the receptionist replied, "You don't have to tell me who you are. You're better known than the Governor."[40]

After Rome, "Zeke" enjoyed a spectacular career with the Los Angeles Lakers, garnering all-NBA recognition ten times in his fourteen years as a professional. The Los Angeles *Daily News*'s Kevin Modesti, who grew up in Los Angeles, summed up West's impact on youths there by recalling that during his childhood, "You chose white sneakers with three black stripes for your first basketball shoes because that's what Jerry West wore. You shot jumpers from just above your right eyebrow because that's how Jerry West did it."[41]

Though he was obviously gifted, when West tried out for the 1960 Olympic team, he had not yet recognized his full potential. In fact, after a bad game early in the trials, he nearly gave up on his Olympic hopes. When the young West voiced his dejection, Coach Newell pulled him aside and told him that if he was not on the Olympic team, then Newell was not coaching the team.[42] "But that was Jerry," Coach Newell remembered, referring to West's humility. His humility was coupled with an introspective nature that had become a central part of West's personality after he lost his closest brother in the Korean War. After his brother David's death, which all too painfully brought the East-West tensions to the Wests' home, Jerry West recalled, "all of sudden I became very introspective . . . became almost not talking, I was so quiet." He found solitary contentment practicing basketball.[43]

The other player to star alongside The Big O and Zeke from Cabin Creek in Rome was Jerry Lucas, who, Coach Newell said, partnered with Jerry West to make "the best two-man game you ever saw."[44] Lucas is also quite possibly the most eccentric American Olympian of all time. A middle-America marketer's dream, Lucas was tall, dark-haired, and handsome. He grew up in Middletown, Ohio, and attended Middletown High School, where he broke Wilt Chamberlain's all-time scholastic scoring record with

2,460 points. At six feet eight, Lucas set himself apart with his ability to play inside or out. Adding to his allure, his father worked as a pressman for a Middletown printing firm. Better yet, as nearly every college in the nation vied for his services and rumors swirled that some schools had offered everything from jobs for family members to paying off the family mortgage, Jerry chose Ohio State because, "State was the only school that talked to me first about my education . . . I wanted an academic scholarship and that's what I have."[45] The media loved it, along with just about everything else about Lucas.

In December 1958, just two months into Lucas's sophomore year, *Sports Illustrated*'s Jeremiah Tax, who a couple of years earlier had written a less-glowing article about Robertson that The Big O thought was racially tinged, wrote a cover story touting the fact that Lucas ranked among the nation's top five in scoring, rebounding, and field-goal percentage. Tax also celebrated the boy wonder's golden image. After noting his "deep-set eyes furthering the impression of intense seriousness," Tax credited Lucas with shunning lucrative offers during his recruitment in high school by "cutting himself off from everything but basketball and schoolwork." The article also pointed out that Lucas's academic prowess had carried over to Ohio State University, where as a freshman, he carried a heavy forty-nine credit-hour load with forty-two of those hours resulting in As. To compliment the story, *Sports Illustrated* ran a picture of Lucas studying diligently in the Beta Theta Phi fraternity library with the caption: "No 'Quick Study,' Lucas Earns High Marks through Hard Work." In another picture, readers could glimpse a romantic shot of Lucas lying in the grass enjoying a "rare relaxed moment with classmates near State's Mirror Lake."[46] Two years later, in 1960, Lucas graced the cover of *Sports Illustrated* again, this time as the magazine's "Sportsman of the Year."

It was not only the media that loved Lucas. Corporate America wanted to get their hands on the golden boy, too, but it had to wait until he turned pro. When he did, Lucas endorsed everything from shoes to insurance in classic, wholesome ads. As an example, an Equitable Life Assurance Society print ad treated the reader to action photos of Lucas and a still shot featuring his golden smile, all complimented with lengthy prose about the "Phi Beta Kappa" star's numerous athletic feats. Lucas was everybody's all-American.

However, as would be the case with many of the idealistic images from the 1950s, epitomized by television shows such as "Leave It to Beaver," Lucas's reality was much more complex than the rosy depictions found in *Sports Illustrated*. In the 1990s the magazine admitted as much, writing that its earlier portraits of Lucas had "belied an imperfect home life." In actuality, during his childhood, Lucas's family struggled to cope with his father's drinking. After his playing days were well over, Lucas told *Sports Illustrated* of stormy, booze-induced extended-family gatherings: "When my father's brothers and sisters came through the front door . . . I basically went out back," he recalled.[47] It got so bad that in 1959, his parents divorced.

As for the hard work in the classroom, that too proved an exaggeration. John Havlicek, who roomed with Lucas at Ohio State, said later that during their first months together, he "never saw him [Lucas] open a book and feared he wouldn't last the quarter." It was not that Lucas refused to work hard— when compelled by a subject, Lucas worked diligently—it was just that he did not *need* to study hard. What Havlicek did not know (at the time) was that Lucas was relying on his prodigious memory to earn his high marks. While in the NBA, Lucas's elephantine memory became legendary as stories circulated of him memorizing the first 500 pages of the Manhattan phone book or the names of selected members of the studio audience on Johnny Carson's *Tonight Show*.[48] He claims to have entirely memorized the film *The Godfather*.[49] On the plane during road trips with the Knicks, Lucas used to keep a running tally in his head of each player's standing in team poker games because Coach Red Holzman disallowed gambling.

Lucas's talents were not limited to basketball and memorization, however. While playing in the NBA, he put his outsized memory and work ethic to use in a number of other endeavors. Early in his career, he opened a chain of fast-food restaurants and somehow found twelve hours per day to devote to the enterprise, including penning the 270-page training manual himself. He used to tell people at Ohio State that he was going to be a millionaire by the time he was thirty. Thanks to his restaurants and basketball, he was, but, thanks again to his restaurants, he had also lost a million by the time he was thirty. Later, Lucas said he learned to handle it all with a certain degree of aplomb: "I thought for a good number of years that I had to make a million. Well, I've made it and lost it. I don't think about it anymore," he told *Sports Illustrated*.[50]

In maybe the most unlikely turn of events in Lucas's peculiar life, near the end of his professional career, during his 1971–72 season with the New York Knicks, he attempted to become a world-class magician. Lucas had wowed his teammates with a wide array of magic tricks and illusions for years. But in 1971–72, a time during which he continued to demonstrate his versatility on the hardwood by alternating between forward and center as he helped the Knicks win the NBA championship (which made him the first player to win a championship in high school, college, the Olympics, and the NBA), Lucas declared his intention to actually *become* a magician. In fact, he told reporters that he intended to become "the greatest magician in the world . . . I've studied the subject inside and out."[51] Ultimately, he wanted to turn his magic into a teaching tool for children. His big break materialized when song man and a developer of television talent named Don Kirshner, known also for managing The Monkees and The Archies, saw Lucas performing his "alphabetizing" on the *Tonight Show* with Johnny Carson. (In a matter of seconds, Lucas can rearrange the letters of virtually any word in the English language into alphabetical order.[52]) Looking to capitalize on the children's program revolution jump-started by *Sesame Street*, Kirshner asked Lucas to collaborate on a three-hour network television special entitled *The Jerry Lucas Super Kids' Day Music and Magic Jamboree Show* featuring the NBA star's myriad talents.[53]

As if that was not enough, during the 1973–74 basketball season, which was Lucas's last as a professional, he became a best-selling author. With Harry Lorayne he wrote *The Memory Book*, which immediately spent a year on the *New York Times* best-seller list. Even for Lucas, that last season turned out to be busy. He also divorced his Ohio State sweetheart and then, despite the book's success, parted company with Lorayne, who Lucas said "was interested in making a buck . . . I was interested in making a difference."[54] That same year, as Lucas walked off the court after a game, a friend handed him a Bible, which would jump-start yet another interesting facet of his life. For the rest of the season, in between games and practices, and with his curious roommate Phil Jackson looking on, Lucas went about trying to commit the entire *New Testament* to memory. He claimed he did.

Soon after his religious awakening, Lucas married the Christian singer Sharalee Beard and published a primer on committing scripture to memory. He started speaking at churches and schools, both to evangelize and to promote his teaching techniques for children, called the Lucas Learning System. During a sermon in Cincinnati in 1988, Lucas saw his father in the crowd. They had kept in touch over the years, but only sporadically. When their eyes met, Lucas said, "It overwhelmed me. He hasn't touched a drop since." A year and a half later, his parents remarried.[55]

Lucas's own second marriage did not fare as well, but he did find love again and continued to promote his memorization learning technique into the new millennium. In 2003 he told *Sports Illustrated* that occasionally, an overture rolls in from a television network that realizes he would make a colorful analyst, but Lucas defers. "If I did TV, I'd be passing up what God has called me to do . . . Even if it happens after I'm gone, I know this will change education and millions of lives," he explained.[56]

This trio of Robertson, West, and Lucas made up the nucleus of what is considered one of the greatest amateur teams of all time. And what an unlikely trio it was: a young African American man from the South who grew up poor in Indianapolis and attended a segregated high school; a white farm boy who grew up poor in the Appalachia of West Virginia; and a middle-class, everybody's All-American from Middletown, Ohio, who dealt with his own issues underneath the golden-boy image. Too often, basketball analysts and historians have called basketball a city game. This trio shows that it is a city game, but it is also much more than that. Basketball can work most anywhere, and at the 1960 Olympic Games, this trio, especially Robertson, pushed international basketball forward.

Joining West, Robertson, and Lucas on the 1960 Olympic squad from the collegiate ranks were the six-feet-six-inch wingman Terry Dischinger of Purdue University, who was just nineteen years of age at the time and counted Robertson and West as idols; the six-feet-eleven-inch Darrall Imhoff of the University of California; the six-feet-two-inch forward Jay Arnette of the University of Texas; and Walter Bellamy, a six-feet-eleven-inch center from the University of Indiana who became the first pick in the NBA draft in 1961.[57] The lone spot awarded to a member of the armed forces squad went to the six-foot-tall guard Adrian Smith. From the NIBL came the Peoria Cats' Allen Kelley, a five-feet-eleven-inch guard, and the six-feet-eight-inch forward Bob Boozer; from Phillips came the six-feet-seven-inch Burdette Haldorson, which made him a two-time basketball Olympian; and from the Wichita Vickers came the five-feet-eleven-inch guard Lester Lane, a former defensive back at Oklahoma State.[58] In another example of Newell's adroit handling of his star-studded roster, he made the high-scoring Lane the starting point guard, moving Robertson to the wing. As Newell explained, if he did not start Lane, he would have started five All-Americans, causing him to worry about teamwork. Coach Newell said that when he asked Lane if he wanted to get good minutes, Lane just asked for a chance to play, so Newell told him, "I'm going to make you the point guard and you're going to run that team on the court." Lane said, "I'll go out and sit down if you want me to," Newell recalled, adding, "Hell, he was so great." In short, Lane functioned as a role player. "He [Newell] was looking for teamwork, a difficult thing when you've got so many stars out there. That move really helped us out," Robertson said afterward.[59]

With the roster set, the team trained at West Point for just under a month. They stayed right alongside the cadets in the Academy dorms and ate at the mess hall. Given that Newell grew up in Hollywood during the Roaring Twenties and his Olympic roster included stars like Robertson and West, it seems reasonable to figure that he approached his job as Olympic coach with a laid-back air. But Newell had only around twenty-eight days to train the team before setting out for Europe, and by nature, Newell was a worrier.[60] He worried so much during his career that some took to calling him "Panicky Pete." Beginning in the late 1950s, he routinely drank twenty cups of coffee a day and smoked three packs of Chesterfields. In fact, the stress of coaching contributed to his decision to retire from the collegiate ranks—he announced his plans to retire in January 1960 before becoming the U.S. Olympic head coach.[61]

Newell's habits are easier to understand when one considers that he served in the Pacific during some of World War II's most vicious fighting. He enlisted in 1942 and by 1944 was involved in the second Manila Operation. His crew was also in the harbor nightly during the landing on Okinawa, "and this was some of the damnedest fighting you ever saw," Newell remembered. One night a kamikaze headed for the ship behind him, came within a stone's throw of his ship, "And then, bang! All we saw was a puff. The anti-aircraft guns hit him [the kamikaze]," Newell recalled. He estimated his naval experience "aged me at least ten years. I was so lucky to have a wonderful woman like Florence [his wife] and a nice place to raise our family."[62]

Newell was also fortunate to end his coaching career with such a talented roster. Even so, the 1960 Olympic team could have been even stronger had the committee chosen Havlicek, among others.[63] In *The Big O*, Robertson wrote that at the time, he disagreed with the decision not to include Havlicek on the Olympic team, as well as Lenny Wilkens.[64] In his 2001 autobiography, Wilkens, who went on to become a great player in the NBA, its all-time winningest coach, and the 1996 U.S. Olympic coach, wrote that despite earning co-MVP honors in the important 1960 East/West All-Star game for college seniors, he did not get invited to the Olympic trials. Before the all-star game, he received a letter that said the game would be important in determining who made the Olympic team, and he went to the game with a strong desire to do just that. "During my senior year, my basketball goal wasn't the NBA, it was the Olympics," Wilkens, who did not watch his first NBA game until after he got drafted, explained. He said it was hard for him to ignore that concerns about a racial ratio had likely played a part in his not being invited to play on the team. He also noted the disproportionate influence wielded by the AAU's NIBL in getting its players selected.[65] Robertson too directed his angst at the AAU, which he thought carried unwarranted influence. He asserted that the AAU players, whom he did not consider as strong as Havlicek or Wilkens, tried out as "amateurs" by working for corporations like "Phillips or some other oil company, or Goodyear tire for example . . . But they were really pros; they got paid to play basketball, and the jobs were their front."[66] Though some may argue that the term "front" is a bit strong, Robertson's argument carries some weight. Havlicek's absence from the Olympic squad in particular was an oversight, and the granting of such power to the AAU in the selection process was becoming anachronistic. Still, seven players from the NCAA did make the 1960 Olympic team, an indication that the organization was clearly surpassing the AAU.

Newell too had issues with the way the committee chose the team. Initially, after the collegians won the trials, Newell was told that only five members of his team would go to Rome (the trials champion was guaranteed five to seven spots).[67] "I knew my history. I knew that at least six players were always taken from the team that won the trials, sometimes eight or nine," he said later (that was incorrect, though—no team by then had landed more than seven spots on an Olympic squad, nor had six always been chosen from the trials champion). According to Newell, when he asked the committee how they could change the rules so suddenly, a committee member started to say, "Well, we think . . . ," at which point Newell reportedly interjected with, "Well, whatever you think, then you should coach the team . . . But we beat the hell out of your goddamn AAU teams every night, so I must be doing something right." Newell was so upset that "At that point, I didn't give a damn if I coached the Olympic team or not." In fact, he told the author, "If I took the players they wanted me [to] . . . I wouldn't have even been there [at the Olympics]."[68]

"I had battles with 'em," Newell said about the AAU-laden section committee. After he stated his demands to the committeemen, "They didn't want me to be the coach, but they couldn't do anything about that." Two players in particular that Newell pushed for were the twenty-eight-year-old Adrian Smith, who came to the Olympic team from the military and had starred in college at Kentucky, and Darrall Imhoff, a junior center who had played for Newell at the University of California. Newell got both on the squad, but it was not easy. With regard to Smith, Newell said, "They didn't want to take him." Describing the pressure involved in the choosing of the roster, he explained, "All these different companies . . . had star teams and players and they get their company names all over the place [if their players got chosen]."[69]

Still, Newell's protestations worked as the committee shifted gears, permitting six men from Newell's squad at the trials onto the Olympic team, as well as Smith. But he had to wait to find out exactly who those players were, as well as who else would join the roster. As the committee deliberated and he awaited word outside the meeting room, Newell remembered being approached by *Sports Illustrated*'s Jeremiah Tax. "What's going on?" Tax queried. "I don't know. I'm probably not gonna be the Olympic coach, for one thing," Newell recalled telling him. By Newell's estimation, he and Tax "downed about a gallon of coffee and a highball or two" before finally, at about two o'clock in the morning, the committee called him in. Ultimately, he got mostly what he wanted in Robertson, West, Imhoff, Dischinger, Arnette, and Bellamy—Lucas made the seventh collegian. "Still, I felt wronged," Newell told Jenkins. "And if you look around the collegiate game at that time, you realize what might have been."[70]

As part of its preparation for the Games, the Olympic squad played exhibition tilts against the Cleveland Pipers of the NIBL, which was coached by the eventual Hall-of-Famer John B. McClendon, who, upon taking the reins of the Pipers in 1959, became the first black coach of a prominent, integrated team in America. As it happened, amid a packed house of some 4,700, McClendon's team utilized its "four-second rule" speed game, which required all players to get to the offensive half of the floor within four seconds of gaining possession, to win the first of two contests against Newell's squad by the score of 101–96. The victory marked the first loss by a full Olympic team to another amateur outfit ever. In the second tilt, in front of a frenzied 6,500 spectators in Morgantown, West Virginia, the U.S. Olympic team delivered a seemingly vengeful 91–69 rout of the Pipers. Still, the Pipers' win warrants attention. It shocked many. In fact, according to McClendon's biographer Milton S. Katz, "McClendon carried film of the game with him because fellow coaches could not believe that his team had won." However, as an exhibition affair and perhaps because McClendon was black, the game did not get much coverage. The *Atlanta Daily World*'s Marion E. Jackson, for one, thought it should have received more. He called the game "the untold 'Big Story of 1960 Sports'" and wondered if it got "buried for the most part . . . because J. B. McClendon is a Negro?"[71]

Upon wrapping up the pre-Games training in the United States, the team flew to Europe on a plane that, Newell remembered, "had, I think, fifty seats and sixty players." In one row sat a U.S. Olympic shot-putter and a discus thrower, with a third guy squeezed in. "I couldn't believe it," Newell said.[72]

Before settling in Rome, the U.S. team played a series of exhibition games in Switzerland. Large crowds enthusiastically turned out to catch a glimpse of the American team. Traveling with the squad, Arthur Daley of the *New York Times* reported that basketball was undergoing a rise in popularity abroad and claimed that some major European championships could draw crowds of 50,000 spectators.[73]

Switzerland offered a less intense phase of training. Newell recalled the time Lester Lane and Adrian Smith, two "handsome-looking" gents, went out to mingle with folks on one occasion. "It's a beautiful day, it was. And they came back and they're beaming," Newell recalled. Apparently, Lane and Smith had gone out to walk around with a camera that didn't work—they did not have film. This did not keep them from going up to young ladies, though, and asking them to take a picture. As one of the two fiddled with the camera—acting like they were trying to get it to work—the other got to put his arm around a young lady for a bit. "And they did that for about two hours," Newell remembered. That type of fun stopped once the Olympics got underway. "Once we got to Rome it was all work," Newell said.[74]

In addition to promoting basketball, the tour served as a useful tool to familiarize players with the nuances of the international game. Many FIBA rules still differed from those in the United States. Under FIBA guidelines, personal fouls committed behind half-court did not lead to a foul shot, even if the offending team had committed over ten fouls. During a game in Switzerland, Coach Newell said that Spain popped in six layups on his squad before his team smartened up to that rule. Pausing after the ball went out-of-bounds in international rules could also be costly because the person inbounding did not need to wait for the referee to hand him the ball, as long as possession was not in question. This rule, along with FIBA's thirty-second shot clock and widened lane, exemplified how some FIBA rules had moved ahead of NCAA rules in encouraging faster, less crowded play. However, NBA and NIBL rules still encouraged an even faster game than FIBA's.

The pre-Olympic exhibition tour also gave Coach Newell the opportunity to develop a more offensive-minded game plan. In contrast to the defensive-minded squads he'd led at California, Coach Newell knew that his Olympic team lacked size, but it could run, shoot, pass, and dribble better than any other amateur team in the world. Therefore, he planned to exploit these offensive strengths. Also, recognizing that FIBA rules had increasingly rewarded fast play, and that this complimented his team's strengths, Newell skillfully adapted his style to his talent as well as to FIBA's rules. West thinks the attention heaped on the 1960 Olympic team's star players has overshadowed the job done by Coach Newell. He recalled that Newell "was a defensive coach, and now he had to coach a lot of offensive ballplayers. He had to make adjustments to his basic philosophy."[75]

On August 25, 1960, the Games opened with yet another record of more than 7,000 athletes representing eighty-five participating nations. To prepare for the Opening Ceremonies, Rome had undergone major renovations, including the building of highways and landscaping on a "breath-taking scale." State-of-the-art facilities were erected for the events, and reports glowed with approbation for the results. Over 100,000 fans from around the globe attended the vibrant opening show, and before the Games even began, spectators had paid roughly $3,200,000 on tickets to the various upcoming events. This prompted *Time* magazine to assert, "By any standard, the games looked to be the greatest in history."[76] After the opening, Daley reported that Indians had worn yellow turbans, Bermudans Bermuda shorts, Bulgarians blue suits, and the Afghanistan team gray slacks and white jackets. More than 5,000 pigeons were set free, just as Giancario Peris lit the Olympic flame with a torch that had passed through more than 1,000 hands en route to Rome.[77] In addition to the spectators, millions across the world watched the ceremonies thanks to television. Daley summed up the evening by writing that Italy pulled off the opening celebration "as flawlessly as an IBM machine."[78] The grandiose show demonstrated that hosting the Olympics provided an opportunity for a nation to showcase its prosperity and to demonstrate its modernity within a universalistic framework.

Despite their grandeur, Rome's Opening Ceremonies were not free of political shenanigans. For instance, as the American contingency walked past the Italian president's box seat, it continued its tradition of not dipping the American flag. Not to be outdone, the Soviets decided not to dip either. Members of the Taiwanese delegation, still at odds with Communist China and upset with the IOC's decision that it had to attend the Games as Formosa rather than the Republic of China, whipped out a handmade banner during their march that read "under protest." Germany marched under one flag, even though its Olympic team consisted mainly of athletes from West Germany, and Muslim teams such as Egypt marched only with men, since its women were not allowed to participate.

The U.S. basketball team took the court for its first contest a day after the Games opened. It played that day with another unfamiliar Olympic ball, which still differed notably from the American standard. "You had to use whatever ball they played with in that country," Newell explained in an interview with the author. "And this one was really strange. It was basically an 18-piece ball that had no pebble on it, and it was smaller than the ones we were used to." As Newell recalled, "Our first practice, the damn ball, it was awful. You know, it was light and airy. And Oscar didn't say anything;

he just took a ball down to the basket and started banking shots. And he got to the point where he couldn't miss on a bank shot. And pretty soon he had the other players doing that, using the glass."

As a sign of the ball's effect, Robertson and West, both of whom usually shot well over 80 percent from the free-throw line, shot under 70 percent from the stripe in Rome.[79] Still, the squad proceeded to breeze through its first few games, scoring points at a record pace. Home-team Italy and Japan, a crowd favorite with no player taller than six feet two, along with Hungary and Yugoslavia, were the first victims of the U.S. onslaught. Of those, only Italy held the Americans to under one hundred points, though the Italians still lost 88–54. The Italy game was never really in question, but the Italians did score the game's opening baskets, which, given that it was the U.S. team's first game, caused West to think, "Oh my gosh, what have we got ourselves into here?" The next time he recalled looking up at the scoreboard, the United States led something like 22–4.[80]

Particularly impressive was the United States' 104–42 victory over Yugoslavia in which Purdue stand-out Terry Dischinger propelled the balanced U.S. attack with sixteen points. Uruguay fell next in another high-scoring affair, 108–50, as the United States continued to thrive under Newell. Given the team's talent, Newell had emphasized more isolations and back-cuts than he usually did at California. "Whether it's cutting to the basket, going one-on-one, whatever, you want to isolate a player with superior ability on the defensive man and basically clear the way," he explained.[81] His strategy delivered record-setting results.

It was after the Uruguay game and because of the United States' early domination that, in a remarkable turn of events, a number of basketball officials from various nations yet again attempted to ram legislation through FIBA limiting the height of players. Ambrosie Padilla of the Philippines led the 1960 effort to limit the height of contestants, this time to six feet two. He claimed Asians would cease entering basketball teams in the Olympic tournament if the rule was not passed. Nineteen countries actually signed the petition, including Puerto Rico, Japan, and Australia.[82] However, due to opposition led by the United States, it did not pass.

In other early action, the Soviets escaped with a 62–61 victory over Brazil and then responded by handling Yugoslavia with relative ease, 88–61. They too demonstrated scoring prowess, especially with an impressive victory over Puerto Rico, 100–63. During the game with Puerto Rico Albert Valjtin, yet another "huge" Soviet center, caused a delay when he shattered the glass backboard after going up for a blocked shot and grabbing onto the rim. He left the game dripping blood, but was fine.[83] With both cold war giants winning, anticipation for another matchup between them heightened. As they had in Melbourne, the Soviet Union and United States soon met in the second phase of pool play.

An overflowing crowd of more than 4,000 poured into Italy's Palezzetto dello Sport, or little sports palace, to view the much-anticipated affair—the fifth Olympic tilt between the two. Many more would have attended had it been scheduled in Rome's larger Palezzo del Sport, which had a seating capacity of 15,000 and was filled for the United States' championship rounds. Landing tickets to this preliminary-round game proved so difficult that the U.S. Ambassador to Rome, James D. Zellerback, had to call in a favor from Avery Brundage so he and his family could attend. Gold and bronze medalist shot-putters Dallas Long and Bill Niedler showed up ticketless, but Newell conjured a plan to get them in: he gave them USA basketball warm-up suits and plopped them at the end of the bench—they even warmed up.[84]

Robertson summed up the atmosphere by writing, "The Cold War was underway, and our two nations were mortal enemies, so the hype for the game was unbelievable."[85] West, who played very well, recalled, "We'd heard so much about some of their players. They were real big. Had a real big team, but it was a war . . . It got very, very physical."[86] Coach Newell did not ignore the cold war implications of the game: he told his team that the affair meant more than a mere basketball contest between two teams; it pitted ways of life against each other.[87]

The Soviets had heard plenty about the Americans, too. Throughout the Olympics, Dischinger remembered, "Eastern bloc countries . . . They'd have somebody with a camera at all of our practices."[88] And Eastern bloc nations studied more than American tactics. As in Melbourne, they were attracted to American basketball shoes as well. Dischinger recalled, "All the Eastern bloc nations and the Soviets wanted our shoes."[89]

On the court against the Soviets, the Americans were plagued by early foul trouble. Newell's crew took some time to adapt to the Soviet Union's hard-driving and fast-paced tactics. However, Robertson thought the international officials, Bozhidar Takez of Bulgaria and Roger Weber of Switzerland, were in over their heads, afraid that real war would break out on the court. "They called all kinds of fouls: even the slightest contact drew a whistle," he remembered. Coach Newell and Dischinger, who ultimately fouled out, also found the refereeing a bit peculiar. The game did end, however, with thirty fouls called on the Soviets to the United States' twenty-eight.[90]

Relying on the relatively agile Viktor Zubkov, who tallied nine straight points for the Soviets right before intermission, and Genidin Voljov, both of whom were around six feet ten, the Soviets basically did not even use Ivan Krumminch. The strategy caused some problems for the United States, which went into halftime holding onto a slim seven-point margin thanks to a Soviet surge late in the frame that came while Robertson, West, and Lucas rested.[91] It seemed that the Soviets' decision after Melbourne to emphasize speed as well as height was working.

Coach Newell went into the locker room pondering how to approach the second half. He decided to come out attacking rather than play conservatively, a crucial decision that again showed his ability to adapt to his team. With his late-1950s University of California squads he might have played it safe, but recognizing the Olympic team's strengths, he decided to unleash its athleticism and allow his guards and wings to apply pressure on both ends of the court. The decision paid off. Utilizing a full-court press, the United States opened the second half with a 28–4 run. Newell remembered that the Russians could "not get the ball past the midline."[92] Afterward, Newell said, "We couldn't rely on the officials . . . the Russians, the officials, everyone else."[93] Robertson characterized the ferocious stretch as "one of the greatest displays of pressure defense of all time."[94]

Following the devastating run, the United States cruised to an 81–57 win. As it turned out, the Soviet coach Spandarian had been wrong: the gap between the two main cold war foes had not disappeared. The Soviets struggled to play Krumminch because of the speed of the game. "Within three minutes, he was out of the game," Newell recalled of one stretch. "We had stolen the ball twice, maybe three times, and we made the basket and they hadn't even got to the midline yet."[95]

Though the Soviets had worked on increasing their skills and developing more versatile big men, the United States still maintained speed and skill advantages that proved pivotal. Sure, the Soviet Union had improved its frontcourt deficiencies in speed, but it still could not match the United States' level. In addition, the United States was able to exploit its size advantage in the backcourt, and was further aided by its superior ballhandling and passing—particularly that of Robertson, who keyed the United States' second-half domination.

Just as in 1956, when the Soviets had not anticipated the speed, agility, and skill of Bill Russell, in 1960 they had no answer for Oscar Robertson's revolutionary combination of size, speed, ballhandling, shooting, passing, and power at the guard position. In Robertson, they faced a multiskilled, six-feet-five-inch, 200-pound man who could play any position on the floor. When the Soviets tried throwing two or three players at him, he adapted by finding open teammates. If he was not given extra attention, he made the Soviets pay with bruising drives to the basket or pull-up jump shots. Describing Robertson, Jerry West recalled:

> I had never played against him in college, and I had never encountered anyone as advanced as he was at such a young age. He had a skill level and degree of confidence that was beyond my comprehension . . . The rest of us on the team had to grow, but he was already there. I had absolutely no confidence in myself. I was a typical immature young man. I did have a lot of energy and enthusiasm for the game, but I was not a consistent player on a day-to-day basis. Not like Oscar.[96]

West was underrating his own ability, but the point stands. Oscar Robertson distinguished himself in Rome as one of the greatest amateur basketball players ever.

After the U.S. victory over the Soviets, only one game stood between them and another shot at gold. It was a final four pool-play game against the host Italians, and the United States encountered an Italian team energized by a fervent, sellout crowd. Given the tremendous demand for tickets to the game, Italian officials had decided to move the contest to the 15,000-seat Palezzo Del Sport.[97] Backed by the raucous crowd, the Italians opened with spirited play in a high-scoring affair. At halftime the United States led by only eight points, 56–48, but in the second half the Italians had trouble maintaining their energy level, and the Americans took advantage en route to a 112–81 win. Lucas, West, and Robertson, who scored twenty-six, twenty, and eighteen points, respectively, proved too much for the Italians to handle over the course of forty minutes.[98]

Despite just having secured the right to play in the gold medal game, which was slated for the next night, the U.S. team, still clad in its warm-ups, realized it had no ride back to the Olympic Village. Players and coaches ended up walking to the bus station and boarding a bus, with Coach Newell telling the driver, "'Olympico Village'—that's the best Italian I could come up with." After a while, the driver dropped them off and pointed down a dark road that the players peregrinated on for about eight blocks before finally making it back to the Village at around 2:00 a.m. Their game against Brazil was less than twenty hours away. Newell recalled, "We tried to make jokes about this thing, but inside, I was really seething, because I knew what happened. It turns out the bus had been there, but a bunch of AAU people were around, wanting to go home, and they just said, 'Let's take this bus. They can get another one.' It was like that throughout the Olympics."

Newell did not tell the media about the incident, but late that morning just after he and his team finally made it back to the Village, he apparently woke up "everybody in administration . . . There were about five doors, and I was so damn mad I kicked every one of 'em. I could see them later, these meek AAU guys and their wives, peeking out their doors. Oh, I made a hell of a racket. And I spiced it up with language they could understand."[99]

In all practicality, because of the complicated pool system implemented for the 1960 tournament, the win over Italy virtually assured the United States the gold medal. Without dissecting the nuances of the short-lived system, suffice it to say that in the final game against Brazil, the United States was assured of the gold medal as long as it did not lose by scores of points. This proved no problem as the U.S. team raced ahead of Brazil 50–24 in the first half and then cruised to a 90–63 victory.

The United States won convincingly even though Walt Bellamy, who had emerged as the "backbone" of the team's frontcourt efforts, was ejected after sending a Brazilian to the floor with an accidental elbow that had not even elicited a foul. Lucas led the way with twenty-five points, including a flurry of baskets in the first half that helped the United States open a 16–2 lead in the game's first five minutes. Still, the game marked only the third time the United States had failed to score one hundred points. "Our last

10. Oscar Robertson in action versus Brazil in the gold medal game. Photo by Popperfoto. Popperfoto Collection/Getty Images.

one was not our best. I'm glad it's over," Newell told reporters afterward.[100] Brazil deserves credit for its play; West counted it as the "best-schooled team" the United States met.[101] Brazil finished the Games with a bronze medal.

The Soviet team elicited jeers upon receiving the silver medal, while West and Robertson's receptions of gold for the United States generated cheers. "It was a moment of jubilation for me," Robertson said later. With he and West both coming from humble beginnings, and yet with "one black and one white, with all the troubles that were going on in the country at that particular time, which people don't like you to talk that much about, the race relations then. For [the two of us] to stand there and take that medal for the country, it meant a lot."[102]

The gold medal solidified a spot in the history books for the 1960 U.S. Olympic team as one of the best amateur squads of all time. Even with all its stars, Dischinger said the definitive characteristic of the group was "we were really a team—played the game as a team." As a nineteen-year-old in Rome, he learned from his teammates that "If you got open, they gave you the ball."[103] The team won every game by twenty-four points or more and finished with an average victory margin of just over forty points. Five years after the Rome Olympics, seven players from the 1960 squad played in the NBA All-Star Game. In 1988 a special commemorative article on the 1960 team ran in *Sports Illustrated* that counted the 1960 team, along with the 1984 U.S. Olympic team, as the greatest amateur outfit.

More important than the 1960 U.S. team's exact ranking among the best amateur outfits in history, the Rome Olympics showed that the trend toward a more open, faster, and higher-scoring style of basketball had become international. Not only could the United States and South America play swiftly, but by 1960, nearly all of Europe and the Soviet Union could, too. The encouragement of fast play was evident in FIBA rules and in the scores of Olympic contests. For example, building on the scoring prowess of the 1956 team, the 1960 U.S. squad averaged an Olympic record 101.9 points per game, a shocking total when compared to the United States' 1936 per-game average of 38—just twenty-four years earlier. The United States was not alone in accelerating the pace either. In Rome, U.S. opponents averaged 59.5 points against them, compared to 1936 when opponents averaged just 17.3 points per game against the American squad.

TABLE 5. 1960 U.S. Men's Olympic Basketball cumulative stats

NAME	G	FGM*	FTM-FTA	(%)	PF	PTS/AVG
Oscar Robertson	8	51	34-50	.680	24	136/17.0
Jerry Lucas	8	66	4-6	.667	23	136/17.0
Jerry West	8	46	18-27	.667	19	110/13.8
Terry Dischinger	8	37	20-29	.690	23	94/11.8
Adrian Smith	8	30	27-32	.844	19	87/10.9
Walter Bellamy	8	25	13-19	.684	22	63/7.9
Robert Boozer	8	23	8-13	.615	18	54/6.8
Lester Lane	8	20	7-9	.778	18	47/5.9
Darrall Imhoff	8	18	2-7	.286	20	38/4.8
Jay Arnette	8	9	5-6	.833	16	23/2.9
Burdette Haldorson	8	11	1-4	.250	12	23/2.9
Allen Kelley	5	2	0-0	.000	7	4/0.8
USA TOTALS	8	338	139-202	.688	221	815/101.9
OPP. TOTALS	8	179	118-205	.576	221	476/59.5

* Figures for field goals attempted are not available.

Still, Robertson and his teammates demonstrated that the United States continued to produce the most revolutionary advances in the game. Subsequently, in conjunction with the ever increasing role of television and transnational business, basketball's speedy, innovative action enhanced its popular appeal at the Olympics and elsewhere. In turn, basketball stars and basketball-related products became more known.

6

IN LIBERAL, POSTWAR TOKYO, TEAMWORK, TELEVISION, AND A COLD WAR TILT FOR GOLD

If you had to name an American who would have fully appreciated the historic significance of Tokyo hosting the 1964 Olympic Games, you might choose General Douglas MacArthur. MacArthur was crucial to Japan's successful post–World War II rebuilding efforts, and he played a role in assuring that the United States fielded an Olympic team there in 1964.

In 1962 President Kennedy had requested that General MacArthur, an avid lover of sports, come out of seclusion from the New York hotel where he was passing his final years to negotiate the ongoing AAU and NCAA dispute. Differences between the two bodies had escalated, threatening America's ability to field an Olympic team. As a mediator, General MacArthur, in quintessential fashion, helped settle a point of contention during the negotiations by asserting that he had stated his opinion "as clearly as I can make use of the English language. This decision is final." And so it was.[1] With MacArthur's help, the NCAA and AAU managed to put aside their differences for Tokyo. Unfortunately, General MacArthur died a few months before having a chance to see his efforts celebrated at the 1964 Olympics.

Surely, when the Tokyo Games did commence, it would have pleased General MacArthur to see Americans competing. He may even have watched the U.S. basketball team, led by Princeton's Bill Bradley, play against Japan in Tokyo's new, shell-like, 4,000-seat National Gymnasium Annex. Designed by the famed architect Kenzo Tange and supported by only a single gigantic pillar, the Annex was a central feature of Tokyo's Olympic venue construction. The *Chicago Tribune* described it as "an excellent and modern building, the best in all Olympic competition so far."[2] The fineness of the building reflected basketball's popularity in Japan, which in turn had resulted in the emergence of a more skilled Japanese Olympic team, as evidenced by its respectable 4-5 record at the Tokyo Games. MacArthur deserves some of the credit for basketball's postwar resurgence in Japan, too: his policy to "actively" promote modern sports after the war led to the restructuring of the Japan Basketball Association.[3]

MacArthur's legacy was alive in Tokyo in other ways. By the time the Games opened, Japan was in the midst of a massive economic boom. Infusions of cash from the United States, particularly during the Korean War, and the General Agreement on Tariffs and Trade (GATT) spurred this surge in Japan's economy, which had lain in a battered state after World War II. In 1947 leading noncommunist countries in the United Nations had implemented the first version of GATT with the intention of reducing trade barriers. Led by western, democratic-styled countries with market-based economies, the goal of GATT was to foster the emergence of an international economy of nations trading with each other, without restriction, in an open market. Only then, many believed, "could democracies endure and world peace prevail." In 1955 Japan joined the countries cooperating in GATT, and its decision proved beneficial. In 1950 Japan produced 12.6 percent of the world's GNP; by 1970 that figure had nearly doubled to 21.0 percent.[4] The Games did not hurt this economic activity. In preparation for them, Japan built a $470 million superhighway, expanded Tokyo International Airport at a cost of $555.6 million, dug twenty-five new subway miles, completed a $55 million monorail refurbishment, and constructed state-of-the-art hotels. The pop singer Sayuri Yoshinaga captured the spirited time in Tokyo with a widely played song that included the following lyrics.

Fresh morning comes . . .
Why is Tokyo so appealing and attractive?
Why does it make one dream?
Because, with all its flowery streets,
Tokyo marks a fresh start as a new Tokyo this year.[5]

And Japan's economy continued to mushroom after the Games.

Japan's economic growth opened opportunities for U.S. businesses look-ing to either sell goods to Japan or, attracted by its cheap labor, to make goods there. Amid this environment, the multipurpose basketball sneaker became a front-line item sold to Asian consumers and produced there. One of the earliest Americans to capitalize on this was Phil Knight. By the spring of 1962, he was already aware of the economic opportunities offered by Japan's cheap labor pool. Though just an MBA student at Stanford, he knew of the recent sales growth in the U.S. market of Japanese-made Nikon cameras and did a class project that posited the advantages of producing running shoes in Japan. The company he conjured as a graduate student at Stanford became Nike. Though it would take more than a decade, ulti-mately, basketball and the Olympics became key entry points for Nike to the marketplace.

During travels to Asia after graduate school in the summer of 1962, Knight noticed that imitation Adidas shoes, like the ones he had writ-ten about as a student, were being sold in Japan by Onitsuka Company, under the rather fitting name Tiger. Onitsuka Company's principal owner, Kihachiro Onitsuka, had founded the business after fighting for the Japa-nese Imperial Army in World War II. Following Japan's defeat, he was low on money, uncertain of his future, and devastated that his country had lost. It was an old army friend who suggested he try making athletic shoes. Benefiting from Japan's booming economy, Onitsuka soon became a prosperous shoemaker. He dominated the Japanese basketball market with his patented "suction-cup sole," an innovation that came to him one night while eating octopus. As a soldier, Onitsuka had been taught to hate the United States. But once he visited America, on his way home from the 1960 Rome Olympics, he was surprised to find that he liked it. He marveled at the nation's skyscrapers, work ethic, and "most of all, Converse's Chuck Taylor hi-tops."[6]

In Japan in 1962, Knight inquired about Onitsuka Company, and near the end of his trip, he decided to visit its headquarters in Kobe.[7] The timing of Knight's visit was fortuitous, because the shoe industry was perched on the cusp of tremendous growth. Having already sold $49 million in footwear in the United States that year, Onitsuka Company sought growth and thought the Tokyo Olympics offered a great opportunity to showcase its products. Soon Onitsuka formed a partnership with Knight that symbolized a changing world, one more devoted to the quest for profits in an open-market economy than to wide-scale conflict, and one where global exchange, thanks to technological advances, was constantly increasing.

As Knight planted the seeds for Nike, the U.S. government fumed over America's overall poor showing at the 1960 Olympics, especially given the string of cold war setbacks that followed the Rome Games. These setbacks signaled a possible tilt toward the Soviet Union in the cold war's ideological struggle. Cuba's communist revolution, the construction of the Berlin wall, the disastrous Bay of Pigs invasion, and the Cuban Missile Crisis all heightened American unease. To offset these developments, sports ambassadors like John J. Kurch, spokesman for the American Legion, called for closer cooperation between the public and private sector in aiding American athletes. Proposals calling for government aid for athletes had previously reached the Congressional floor, but the recent cold war developments created a more receptive atmosphere for Kurch's message.[8]

Hubert Humphrey, the liberal Democratic senator from Minnesota, echoed calls for increased government assistance for Olympic athletes in a January 1963 article in *Parade* magazine. He charged the Soviets with turning the "once-idealistic Olympics into an ideological battlefield." To combat this, Humphrey asked Congress to supply economic aid to Olympic sports rather than rely on private and corporate funds. He prescribed increased physical fitness for youth, a National Junior Olympics meet catering to the sports not necessarily popular in America, and the integration of females into athletics. Senator Humphrey reminded readers that the cold war was a "relentless struggle between freedom and Communism [embracing] almost every level of life from spacemen to sputniks."[9] Thinking in similar terms, President Kennedy had, early in his presidency, appointed Charles "Bud" Wilkinson to run the newly formed President's Council on Physical Fitness, a move that reflected Kennedy's lifelong interest in promoting fitness.[10] But after Kennedy's assassination, the movement lost momentum, and the American tradition of relying on private funding for its Olympic team remained intact.

The lack of direct federal funding for the U.S. Olympic team did not, however, affect basketball as much as nonrevenue sports. In America's open-market Olympic environment, basketball thrived because of its popularity, which enabled it to make money. The sport's mass appeal gave the U.S. Olympic Basketball Committee a wealth of talented players to choose from and a useful supply of cash. Consequently, the committee, through its Olympic trials and exhibition games, continued to generate excess funds for use by the USOC to support other sports.

Still, basketball did need better cohesion among its governing bodies. Just weeks after the Rome Olympics, Coach Newell emphasized this, as well as the need to recognize politics as an element of sports. Referring to his experience in Rome, Newell told reporters, "Since basketball is a universal game, our group was able to become friendly with athletes from all over the world . . . We found, in talking to all of these athletes, that, to them, the United States is a wonderful image. We stand for strength, for strength in sports, strength in politics, strength in economics." Continuing, Newell argued that to maintain this position of strength, the United States needed to combat Soviet tactics; tactics that he said undoubtedly mixed politics with sports. One of the main remedies urged by Coach Newell was to improve relations between the NCAA and AAU. In addition, he advocated using government funds to support international basketball events between Olympiads.[11]

Though Newell wanted more, there was already funding available for international basketball events through the State Department. In fact, in the 1950s and 1960s the State Department used sports in a variety of cultural programs aimed at fostering exchanges with other countries, especially those countries under Communist rule or in Africa. In August 1964, Nicholas Rodis, a special assistant for the State Department, reported that "all over the world American athletes are working side by side with American Foreign Service officers in a remarkable United States foreign policy program." Rodis argued that sports were a "vigorous force" in international relations. As an example of the State Department's efforts to export American culture, he highlighted a trip by an NBA all-star team behind the iron curtain to

Poland and Rumania under the Cultural Presentations Program.[12] These programs buttressed the growth of international basketball, but the real source of basketball's growth stemmed from the attractiveness of its action and the efforts of private enterprise to capitalize on that.

In the spring of 1963, the U.S. Olympic Basketball Committee met, still in need of the cohesion Newell recommended. The 1963 committee was made up mainly of men from the AAU and from the newly formed Basketball Federation of the United States of America (BFUSA), an NCAA-friendly body meant to challenge the AAU as the official sponsor of the nation's amateur talent internationally. Just before the meeting, BFUSA had won an important decision when FIBA, led by secretary-general R. William Jones, ruled that the AAU and BFUSA could exercise "independent sanctioning power on the local, national, and international level concerning international basketball club competition." FIBA also gave each "a roughly 50 percent voice in the Olympic selection process."[13] Ultimately, BFUSA and the AAU decided, with a few exceptions, to keep intact the selection process that had created the stellar 1956 and 1960 Olympic squads.

One notable change the committee did enact dealt with determining the head coach. For the Tokyo Games, the committee unanimously decided to select the coach in advance of the trials in order to give him time to study international rules, view film of potential opponents, and to objectively rate players at the trials. Adolph Rupp was recommended initially, but he did not receive a majority of votes from the U.S. basketball committee; so instead, the group picked Henry "Hank" Iba, the head coach of Oklahoma A&M (now Oklahoma State).

Iba ranks as one of basketball's most influential basketball coaches. His coaching family tree extends to every corner of the nation and has included such stalwarts as Don Haskins, Eddie Sutton, Nolan Richardson, and Gene Keady. He lived to coach. Legend has it that at the age of eighty-five, Iba could be found in Stillwater, Oklahoma, diagramming offensive plays.

Judging by his lifelong body of work, it is hard to argue with Iba's effectiveness. He remains the only coach to lead more than two U.S. Olympic basketball teams; he did so three times in 1964, 1968, and 1972. He won 767 games over the course of his illustrious career with teams known for methodical deliberateness on offense and stifling man-to-man defense. He prided himself on emphasizing the fundamentals, man-to-man defense, minimal dribbling, and probing motion offense. As part of his defense, Iba's teams gained repute for the implementation of his "swinging gate" tactics, which emphasized individual, on-the-ball pressure buttressed by a flowing rotation scheme on the help side. In an interview with the author, Larry Brown said that as coach of the 1964 team, "Iba was unbelievable."[14] However, by the end of Iba's reign as Olympic coach in 1972, critics argued that he was too old, unable to relate to the new generation. They said the game had passed Iba by.

Even in his first stint as Olympic coach, Iba reflected an earlier era. This is understandable. In the early 1920s in Eaton, Missouri, there were only ten people in Iba's graduating high school class. Eaton High did not even field a basketball team until Iba arrived as a freshman and helped organize one. He took up coaching in 1927, worked his way through the high-school ranks, and became the head coach of Oklahoma A&M in 1934. There, he used old-fashioned discipline to build A&M's reputation as a defensive-minded outfit that played with patience on offense. Kurland, who played for Iba at Oklahoma A&M, said, "He has the reputation of being a hard, but yet an extremely fair, man." The towering former Olympian recalled times during his career at A&M when, after a difficult loss, Coach Iba called spontaneous practices that lasted until nearly midnight. He also attested to Iba's penchant for "'chewing the ears' of one his players if they did not act as gentlemen on and off the court." But Kurland added, "You should know that he believes that law, not confusion, is the dominating principle of the universe, and you can believe that he has put his family, his school, his team, and his players before his personal interests. If this is being a hard man, then he is a hard man."[15]

For many years while Iba was at Oklahoma A&M, one of his coaching rivals was Kansas's Dr. "Phog" Allen. Though rivals, Dr. Allen and Iba shared a love for basketball, and both tirelessly promoted the game. Allen had pushed to get basketball on the Olympic program, and in 1938, the forward-thinking Iba opened the more than 6,000-seat Gallagher Hall at Oklahoma A&M, which was derisively called "Iba's Folly" before becoming the envy of nearly every athletic program in the nation. Despite their shared love of basketball, however, Allen and Iba were critics of each other. Dr. Allen disliked Iba's emphasis on center post play and screening and the tendency of Iba's teams to play deliberately on offense. He nicknamed Iba's offense the "barnacle of basketball."[16]

By the 1960s, criticism of Iba's methods had increased. By then the game was much faster and the rules more conducive to higher scores. Some thought Iba's methods too slow, and a review of Olympic statistics reflects that Iba teams did indeed play more methodically than preceding teams. Still, though Iba's college teams were known for his methodical offensive game, his Olympic teams did play a relatively high-scoring brand of basketball. The first two Olympic teams he coached, in Rome and then in Mexico City, averaged 78.2 and 82.6 points per game, respectively. Those numbers were lower than the spectacular 99.1 and 101.9 points-per-game averages produced by the 1956 and 1960 U.S. Olympic basketball teams, but they were not low averages by international standards in the 1960s. The criticism of Iba's tactics does seem more warranted when applied to the 1972 Olympic team, however, a team notorious for its lack of offense. Yet that team did average 73.4 points per game.[17]

With Iba in place as coach, the 1964 Olympic trials were staged in April at St. John's University in conjunction with New York City's hosting of the World's Fair. For the first time, all of the trials teams were a collection of standouts from each of the four participating organizations, and no team was guaranteed a certain number of slots based on how it finished. All told, eight "all-star" teams competed (three from the NCAA, two from the U.S. Armed Forces, two AAU squads, and one NAIA team).[18] According to the NCAA executive director Walter Byers, the AAU and armed forces had tried to limit the field to four teams (one each from the NCAA, AAU, NAIA, and armed forces) but the NCAA managed to expand the field to eight teams "only through the perseverance of our delegates," which in turn enabled the NCAA to showcase its "wealth of basketball talent."[19] Byers's claim about the NCAA's abundant basketball talent in comparison to that of the AAU was correct, but his tone reflected the ongoing tensions between the two amateur basketball bodies. Nonetheless, the Olympic trials were a commercial and strategic success.[20]

The biggest adjustment players had to make at the trials was adapting to international rules. One difference involved the absence of the "bonus," which in the United States awarded players free throws after a certain number of fouls. Under 1964 FIBA rules, the ball was taken out of bounds no matter how many fouls the offending team had committed, except on shooting fouls or any foul in the last five minutes of the game (when all fouls resulted in free throws). Without needing to worry about putting the opposition in the "bonus," teams could afford to play ruggedly until the last five minutes. Also, there was still no strict midcourt demarcation yet in the international game and therefore no "over-and-back" rule as practiced in the United States. These FIBA rule differences effectively slowed down the game.

As noted though, by 1964 FIBA, which boasted 110 national members, had sped up notably.[21] Three FIBA rules in particular encouraged faster play than the college game. First, its lane was 19 feet ⅜ inches across at the baseline, tapering off to 12 feet across at the free-throw line. Second, in 1956 FIBA had, as noted, adopted a thirty-second shot clock.[22] And finally, FIBA continued to allow teams to inbound the ball at their own discretion in instances where possession was not in question. In contrast, the NCAA maintained a much smaller lane: twelve feet across at the free-throw stripe and only seven feet across in the ten-foot section closest to the rim; it did, in fact, resemble a key. At that time the NBA lane measured sixteen feet across, and it was a perfect rectangle from the free-throw line down to the rim. The NCAA also had no shot clock—it did not adopt one until 1985, and that was originally a forty-five-second clock—and teams received the ball from the referee for every inbound, except after made baskets.

Another important difference players and coaches faced under FIBA rules involved the calling of a timeout. Rather than simply alert the referee, coaches had to signal the scorer's table of their desire for a timeout, which would come at the next dead ball. This rule would play a pivotal role in the controversial 1972 final between the United States and the Soviet Union.

At the 1964 trials the AAU's two teams were named "the Stars" and "the Stripes." Aware of the AAU's overall decline in talent, most had dismissed the chances of either team winning the tournament. But in the first round of action, the Stars, led by Pete McCaffrey and the Chicago Jamaco Saints' George Wilson, upset the NCAA Blues, a team that featured six players from John Wooden's undefeated 1964 NCAA national championship UCLA squad, including the college player of the year, Walt Hazzard.[23] In its next game, the Wilson-led AAU Stars played Cinderella again, this time upending the NCAA Whites, which boasted NCAA standouts Joe Caldwell of Arizona State, Cotton Nash of Kentucky, and Paul Silas of Creighton. If the Stars could win against the star-studded NCAA Reds, featuring Princeton's Bill Bradley, Texas Western's Jim "Bad News" Barnes, Jeff Mullins of Duke, and

Wally Jones of Villanova, it would find itself in the position to finish as the top-ranked team at the trials. Improbably, and thanks in no small part to Wilson's nineteen rebounds, the AAU's Stars did win again, returning the Olympic Trials championship to the AAU for the fifth time in six tries.[24]

As a scholastic prep, Wilson had played at Chicago's predominantly black John Marshall Metropolitan High School. Inspired by Oscar Robertson, from there he headed to the University of Cincinnati, where as a sophomore he helped the Bearcats win a national championship. But after his senior year in 1964 he initially missed out on an invitation to the Olympics. The NCAA chose Ron Bonham, Cincinnati's leading scorer, rather than Wilson. Wilson's Cincinnati coach, Ed Jucker, did end up successfully lobbying to get Wilson an invite, but it took a while, and by then, Wilson had agreed to play AAU basketball, which is how the AAU became his route to the Olympics. Ultimately, Wilson's Olympic experience would become his crowning basketball achievement. He won a high school state championship, a collegiate national championship, and played seven years in the NBA, but in 2009, the man who had been nicknamed "Jif" in 1958, because his leaping ability reminded folks of the kangaroo that first appeared on Jif peanut butter labels that year, recalled, "The Olympic experience is the greatest thing ever."[25]

The AAU's strong showing, coupled with the fact that long-time AAU advocate Russell Lyons served as chair of the Olympic basketball committee, enabled the organization to place five players on the 1964 U.S. Olympic team without much rancor. They were: Pete McCaffrey, George Wilson, Jerry Shipp, Dick Davies, and Larry Brown, who went on to coach at Kansas, numerous places in the NBA and American Basketball Association, and for the U.S. Olympic teams in 2000 and 2004. At the 1964 trials Brown impressed onlookers with his fearless and seemingly ceaseless drives to the basket.[26] The five AAU players were joined by the NCAA's Bradley, Joe Caldwell, "Bad News" Barnes, Melvin Counts, Hazzard, and Mullins and by the NAIA's tournament MVP Lucious Jackson, who averaged twenty-four points per game at Pan American College. These collegians proved prolific as they ultimately accounted for four of the Olympic team's top five scorers in Bradley, Jackson, Caldwell, and Barnes.[27] However, the team's top scorer, Jerry Shipp, who had scored abundantly as a collegian at Southeastern State College, did come from the AAU.[28] Some rather strong players did not make it, among them Billy Cunningham, Rick Barry, Gail Goodrich, and Willis Reed.[29]

The 1964 U.S. Olympic team averaged six feet five inches, 204 pounds, and twenty-three years of age, rather young compared to the Soviet Union's average age of twenty-seven. And the squad boasted five African Americans, the most to date. Hank Vaughn, an offensive-minded coach who led the AAU Stars to its improbable trials championship and just weeks earlier had led the Akron Goodyear Wingfoots to its first AAU national championship, earned assistant coaching duties alongside Coach Iba. So too did legendary African American coach and proponent of the fast-break game John McClendon, who in 2007 Larry Brown described as "probably as fine a coach as we've had in our sport . . . one of the nicest, brightest guys ever."[30]

Iba came away pleased with his team, telling reporters, "I got what I wanted. I feel we can play very well under international rules." He had not enjoyed complete autonomy in choosing players, but he had looked for ones that he thought worked well within his system, and he held great sway with the selectors. Continuing, Iba said, "We've got good shooters from the fringe area, about twenty-five feet out. We have guards who can drive and open up the middle, particularly in the last few minutes of the game. And another important factor is that we have versatility. We can swing players like Wilson, Mullins, and Bradley around." Still, he warned, "The American people think this will be easy. It won't."[31]

The team boasted a bevy of solid players but no revolutionary superstar. Fittingly, in Tokyo, the outstanding characteristic of the squad was its balance, unlike the 1956 and 1960 Olympic teams, which had boasted particularly dominant individuals in Russell and then Robertson, West, and Lucas. In 1964 the top five scorers averaged between 8.5 and 12.4 points per game. This balance was also related to the team's magnificent passing, which was noted time and again by analysts and was a crucial element of its success, considering it lacked a dominant player. Among its best passers were Bradley, Hazzard, and Brown. Brown credited Iba for that: "We practiced before or after every game," he recalled. As for defending, rebounding, and sharing the ball, Brown felt Iba had "instilled that from day one."[32]

If you had to choose the key cog in the 1964 team, Bill Bradley rates highly. Bradley grew up in Crystal City, Missouri, where early on, he dreamed of playing college basketball and demonstrated, as *People* magazine put it, "his uncanny ability to focus." With his sneakers weighted down by ten pounds of lead, he shot baskets for three and a half hours nearly every day after school. To improve his ballhandling, he taped cardboard underneath his glasses so they could function as blinders, keeping him from looking down at the ball as he worked through his drills. Bradley's parents made sure their son's discipline carried into the classroom. Commenting on his upbringing, Bradley said, "My parents always made me go to my room, close the door and study. They also made me practice the piano."[33]

In college at Princeton, Bradley's discipline paid off in spectacular fashion. During his junior year, the 1963–64 season, he led the nation in scoring with a 32.3 points-per-game average and excelled in his studies. He even found time to teach Sunday school.[34]

In the summer of 1964, while training for the Olympics, Bradley also interned at the congressional office of Richard Schweiker, a Republican from Pennsylvania. He even helped the presidential election campaign of the former Pennsylvania governor William Scranton, another Republican. That summer Bradley saw Congress support the Gulf of Tonkin Resolution, setting the stage for increased U.S. involvement in Vietnam, and he watched the Senate pass the Civil Rights Act. The soon-to-be Republican presidential nominee Barry Goldwater did not support the civil rights legislation, whereas attorney general Robert Kennedy, who had delivered a speech that summer to the interns, did. On the night the Civil Rights Act passed, not long before he went to Tokyo, Bradley said he walked out of the Senate chamber realizing his sentiments were with the Democratic Party (though Southern Democrats had played a pivotal role in delaying civil rights legislation). Fifteen years later, in 1979, the thirty-five-year-old Bradley became the youngest sitting senator in the United States, as a Democrat.[35] In 2000 he lost a bid for the Democratic presidential nomination to Al Gore.

The year 1964 proved busy for Bradley. While working on the Hill and preparing for Tokyo, he garnered distinction as one of the nation's thirty-two Rhodes Scholars, who were given stipends to pursue graduate studies in England. Bradley's decision to accept the Rhodes scholarship was not great news for the perennially inept New York Knicks, who had territorial rights to Bradley and had planned to take him with its top pick. The franchise picked him first in the NBA draft anyway because, as a Knicks representative explained, "We couldn't keep our franchise if he decided to turn pro with some other club two years from now." Estimates figured that Bradley could demand a $200,000 salary in his first three years were he to turn pro, a figure notably higher than the $20,000 to $30,000 that had been offered to top prospects like Clyde Lovellette just twelve years earlier.[36] But Bradley went to London as a Rhodes Scholar and then played for the Knicks when he returned.

When the Olympic Trials ended in the spring of 1964, the U.S. team did not meet again until September 1 in San Francisco. However, five Olympians did go on a State Department–funded and AAU-led trip to the Soviet Union: the AAU's Shipp, McCaffrey, Davies, Brown, and the NCAA's Barnes. Goodyear's Vaughn coached the squad and was assisted by McClendon.[37] First, the touring team traveled to Poland, where it split a pair of games against the Soviet squad. Then, in late April, the team headed to Russia. In the first of two games there, the Soviets asserted their basketball strength again, beating the United States 82–65 in front of an estimated 16,000 fans in Moscow Hall and raising concerns in America about the United States' ability to win the gold in Tokyo. On defense, the Soviets proved more than capable in confronting the hard-driving Americans, and on offense, they demonstrated their improved skills and versatility with strong play from Korneyev, Volnov, and Baylei, all of whom the United States would face in Tokyo.[38] The two losses, first in Poland and then in Russia, marked the first defeats of a U.S.-sponsored team by the Soviet Union in seven years.

It seemed the Soviets were reaping benefits from the changes they had made after Rome. Losing as they had in Rome was unacceptable to Soviet officials, and shortly afterward, Soviet personnel paid for it with their jobs. Top Soviet basketball official Nikolai Semashko was the first to go, while Coach Spandarian followed soon after. Only five players from the 1960 team returned in 1964. After the Rome Games, *Komsomolskaya Pravda*, which months before them had argued that the Soviets had closed the basketball gap and could take the gold, charged Semashko with "trying to obscure the facts of the loss to the United States" and Spandarian with "misleading the people about the relative strengths of the two teams."[39] Spandarian was also criticized for spending too much time on paperwork, which resulted in his team's poor discipline and "un-Soviet individualism while the Americans ran a happy, smooth cooperative." The *Komsomolskaya Pravda* reporter and basketball expert Viktor Grigoriev accused Semashko of believing Spandarian's fanciful claims that the Soviets had reached U.S. levels, when in reality the team was "inadequately prepared physically, tactically, and especially, technically." Grigoriev added, "The fast break, once our most dreaded weapon, is now used only sporadically, and chiefly against our weakest opponents."[40]

Alexander Gomelsky replaced Spandarian as head coach of the Soviet team. A diminutive Jewish fellow who stood only five-feet-five-inches tall, Gomelsky manned the Soviet Union's sideline during its wins against the visiting Americans in 1964. He was just getting started on a lengthy, successful, and tumultuous career in Soviet national basketball. That illustrious career included stints as the coach of the Soviet Olympic team in 1964, 1968, 1980, and 1988, when he won gold. For more than thirty years he also guided a number of Russia's leading trade-union teams. By the end of his career, he was considered the father of modern Soviet basketball, gaining the nickname "Papa," and had earned the moniker "Silver Fox" in America for his grey hair and cunning tactics.[41] His teams utilized disciplined teamwork and emphasized speed.

While the Soviet basketball team endured criticism for losses in Rome, Vaughn's team faced a wave of it following its two losses on Communist soil. The State Department did too. In late April the *Washington Post* noted that "criticism has been directed at the State Department in recent months for allowing United States athletic teams of questionable quality to appear abroad and 'injure the American image.'" The State Department disagreed, however, telling the *Post*, "The American team now in Russia is a first-class outfit, not far from being up to Olympic standards. The truth of the matter is that it is going to be mighty tough beating the Russians from here on, and our best informed authorities are beginning to face up to the facts." Even so, more than winning was at stake. The State Department and its critics thought that success in basketball suggested a robust and successful society.[42]

On October 1, 1964, following Olympic training in Hawaii and exhibition tilts, Iba and company boarded a flight to Tokyo. They were headed to an Olympic festival fraught with a number of important political issues related to the cold war. In particular, the Tokyo Games indicated the growing importance of "emerging nations" in Asia, Africa, Latin America, and the Near East to cold war foes. All of these areas offered the United States and the Soviets, not to mention the Chinese, desirable markets and were considered important to national security. The U.S. involvement in Vietnam demonstrated this. As a result, given their westward leanings, the health of the Olympics was important to America's efforts to gain influence throughout the world, especially among emerging nations.

Both the Soviets and Americans made efforts to garner influence in these areas of the world. Two years earlier, for the fourth Asian Games slated for Indonesia in 1962, the United States, eager to gain favor with Indonesian President Sukarno, offered to help mollify Indonesia's economic woes and infrastructure issues by building a highway linking the harbor of Jakarta to the city's main sports complex. At the same time, the Soviet Union offered Indonesia a substantial line of credit.[43] As many "emerging" nations learned to do during the cold war, Indonesia played both sides by accepting both offers.

A year later, in November 1963, the first Games of the New Emerging Forces (GANEFO) took place with fifty nations participating. The United States and Europe were not present, save France. As a result of concerns that participation in GANEFO could jeopardize eligibility for the Olympics, most countries did not send their top athletes. Still, the games were an important political statement. Indonesian President Sukarno recognized this and affirmed in his opening statement, "Let us declare frankly that sport has something to do with politics. And Indonesia now proposes to mix sport with politics." The formation of the GANEFO was one of a number of delicate global political issues, including the growth of the North Atlantic Treaty Organization (NATO) and South Africa's apartheid policies, that posed a threat to the Olympic movement. The IOC responded by pushing for a common policy to maintain the Olympic movement's standing in the world of amateur sports.[44]

It is fitting that Indonesia played such a prominent role in GANEFO, for Indonesia's relationship with the West over the past fifty years reflects well the complexities inherent in the global age. On one hand, the Olympics have tended to support human rights and liberal markets. On the other, the Olympic movement has worked to attract nations even if they do not represent those ideals, under the notion that the Games operate outside of politics and by their nature will facilitate cooperation and peace. For much of the second half of the twentieth century, Indonesia represented the Olympic movement's willingness to accept nations that flouted its political ideals (Indonesia opted out of the 1964 Games but returned in 1968). By the early 1990s, however, Indonesia embodied a wholly different set of issues. Rather than functioning as a direct competitor of western, liberal nations, Indonesia started to become more open politically and economically but also came to symbolize what many considered to be the exploitation of labor markets by corporations based in liberal capitalist nations.

On the eve of the Tokyo Games other parts of Asia created problems for IOC President Avery Brundage, too. Ultimately, North Korea joined Indonesia in opting out of the Tokyo Olympics over issues involving GANEFO.[45] China squabbled with the IOC over Taiwan and did not attend yet again, while Taiwan was forced to compete under the name Formosa and to take the "Republic of China" script off of its uniform.[46] Taken together, these various issues indicated that sports were coveted terrain among world powers aiming to convince others that their way of life offered the best opportunity.

On October 10, 1964, Tokyo opened the Olympic Games majestically. During the Opening Ceremonies, 10,000 balloons and 8,000 doves rose into the sky as more than 5,500 athletes from ninety-four countries, both records, paraded in front of 75,000 cheering fans.[47] Hosting marked a huge moment for Japan, and the country strove to deliver in spectacular fashion. From Tokyo, *Sports Illustrated*'s Jack Olsen reported that more than a year of arduous preparation had gone into the proceedings, as the Japanese knew the Games could be the "maraschino cherry on Japan's post-war dignity." Word from higher-ups had gone out in Tokyo stipulating that "urinating in the streets was gauche, and airport workers were told to cease and desist the practice of lounging around the air-conditioned airport in their underwear." Turkish baths received orders to curb extracurricular activity. The Japanese even put up posters warning young Tokyo women who went out on dates with visitors from other countries to ask: "Is this man actually offering me an honorable proposition. Or is he only interested in deceiving me so he can enjoy me as his Tokyo wife while he is here?"[48]

Japanese Emperor Hirohito, who nineteen years earlier had urged his countrymen to lay down arms, to accept the handover of power to General MacArthur, and to work toward peace, watched the proceedings from a box seat as the exhaust of five jet planes from Japan's Air Self-Defense Force formed five interlocking circles in the sky to represent the Olympic rings. Avery Brundage addressed the crowd in idealistic prose stating that at the Olympics, there is "no injustice of caste, of wealth, of family, of race. On the sports field everyone stands and falls on his own merits. The great lessons of the Olympic movement are here for all to see."[49] The preparations paid off. The U.S. media praised Tokyo for staging a fantastic opening for the Games.

The Opening Ceremonies also gave Japan, and by extension other liberal capitalist nations, a chance to highlight technology that signified the new global age. In Tokyo, International Business Machines (IBM) installed "the most advanced information network ever assembled for computing and distributing athletic scores." It could deliver results "within minutes after an event ends."[50] It portended things to come.

Other telecommunications advances were exhibited. Satellite television, for instance, had made important inroads leading up to the Tokyo Games. In July 1962 a satellite launched by Telstar Communications, a U.S.-based company, jumpstarted the era of satellite television. The satellite signaled a day in the not-so-distant future when, as stated by a business executive writing in the *Washington Post*, "In the grass shacks of Tahiti or the igloos of the Aleutians and in the marble palaces built by Bourbon kings—all of them can see 'Wagon Train' at the same time."[51] Then, in July 1964, Japan announced an agreement with the United States to launch a satellite named Syncom III that would enable live telecasts of the Olympics to be broadcast to the United States and Europe.[52] The Japanese government wanted to use the project to demonstrate its technological advancement and its cooperation with the United States, and to showcase Japan to the rest of the world. The ability of satellites to beam images across the globe led the *Washington Post* writer Dave Brady to declare that "the fantastic may become feasible by the time the Olympic Games open in Tokyo October 10." He also asserted that "the U.S. State Department would look favorably on the project, envisioning the international propaganda value of such an accomplishment."[53] His comments hinted at the power of the satellite, especially when partnered with events such as the Olympics. Sure enough, in July 1964 COMSAT announced that it had completed arrangements with NASA, the U.S. Defense Department, the Japanese government, and the Japan Broadcasting Corporation to broadcast Olympic action. In discussing the agreement, COMSAT explained that it was "acting at the request of the State Department," which held that television coverage of the games was "in the national interest."[54]

One of the few criticisms of the Opening Ceremonies was leveled at NBC for carrying them on a three-hour delay. Japanese officials and the U.S. State Department preferred a live telecast to "illustrate scientific collaboration between the countries and to improve Far East relations." Japan voiced its displeasure to the State Department after NBC decided to air the Opening Ceremonies at 1:00 a.m. West Coast time.[55] NBC's decision to delay showing the Opening Ceremonies until such a late hour demonstrates that the Games had not yet then reached the level of coverage afforded them in the twenty-first century, but that does not mean network interest in the Olympics was muted. On the contrary, NBC paid $1.5 million for the right to broadcast the Tokyo Games, a 308 percent increase from the $395,000 paid by CBS for Rome.[56] Of course, the level of coverage would pale in comparison to future efforts. As Brown recalled, friends and family reported that rather than show entire basketball games, NBC mostly showed "just parts" of them.[57]

Besides the delayed NBC feed, it seems as if one of the only other things not to go as planned on Tokyo's opening day was Mel Counts having to resort to wearing his Chuck Taylor Converse shoes as he walked around the track because American officials could not provide dress white oxfords in the size 16EE.[58] Counts sported his Chuck Taylors again the following night, when the U.S. basketball team took the floor for its opening game against Australia, a game the Americans won 78–45. The final score against Australia, given the lack of a dominant star on the U.S. team, had led to tepid predictions from prognosticators in America before the Rome Games. Counts summed up this attitude years later by writing, "Somehow, we showed up at the Olympics as the underdog to a lot of people," suggesting that the team had played splendidly.[59] But many observers, especially Coach Iba, thought the team played sloppily against Australia. "We'll have to fight for our lives," he said, looking ahead. "The rest of the world is advancing in basketball with mighty strides, and the American majority of superiority keeps shrinking." The United States did flash some brilliance, especially with its pristine passing. The *New York Times*'s Daley commented on one "spectacular" dish from Hazzard to Bradley underneath that led to a basket, but he also noted that such plays were not the norm. Daley was most impressed with the AAU players, pointing out that they were "much more familiar with international rules than the collegians"; he called them the "solid men on the squad."[60]

In contrast to the United States, the Soviet Union impressed mightily on basketball's opening night. Sporting a younger and faster team than the 1960 version, the Soviets piqued interest with a "racehorse" style of play in an 87–52 victory over Canada.[61] In a new role coming off the bench, Ivan "the Breadwinner" Krumminch offered the Soviets an intimidating option if one of their starting big men got into foul trouble. His mere presence still resonated with U.S. players. Using a little exaggeration to explain Krumminch's effect years after the Games, center Mel Counts wrote that Krumminch's size and strength were so foreboding that during his younger days in the Latvian forest, "I don't think he had to saw the trees down; he could just tear them out by the roots and load them on the truck by his hand." Even by 2007, Larry Brown still considered Krumminch the "biggest man I ever saw."[62]

Looking to keep pace with the Soviets, the United States won its next three games with relative ease, although it beat Peru by just fifteen points. The Soviets also carried out a string of victories, however, capped by an impressive win over a respected Puerto Rican squad, 82–63. After four games, both cold war powers were undefeated.[63]

Coming off their dismantling of Uruguay, the U.S. men faced their stiffest test yet in Yugoslavia. As a nation, Yugoslavia was an enigma during much of the cold war. Under General Tito, it partnered with neither the United States nor the Soviets; instead, Tito preferred recognition as one of the "nonaligned" nations. In the meantime, Yugoslavia managed to build an impressive basketball tradition.

Before Tokyo, the Yugoslavian team had placed third in the European championships behind the Soviet Union and Poland. And though they had not fared well in Rome, in January of 1964, Yugoslavia's head coach Boris Kristancic, captain of the 1960 Yugoslavian Olympic team, had visited the United States to learn new methods. He spent two weeks with Adolph

Rupp at the University of Kentucky, watched the Boston Celtics in action, and stopped by the University of West Virginia for tips. Kristancic told the American media, "We draw about 12,000 for our league games in an open-air stadium in Ljubljana, and we charge top prices. You can see that basketball is most popular in our country."[64] Yugoslavia, like the Soviets, wanted to produce versatile big men and in time did so rather effectively. Coach Kristancic's efforts to learn from the United States demonstrated the influence of the American game on Yugoslavia's basketball development. That same year, 1964, Red Auerbach brought an NBA all-star team to Europe and even Cairo. In 1988, the "preeminent" Yugoslavian basketball writer recalled, "The change in my country and other European countries came after the NBA team came in '64. Heinsohn, Cousy, Russell, Havlicek, Sam Jones, Bob Pettit, Oscar Robertson, Tim Gola, Jerry Lucas. They taught us how to play."[65]

Ultimately, in Tokyo, the United States beat Yugoslavia 69–61, but Yugoslavia's improvement was evident.[66] With just under four minutes remaining, in fact, Yugoslavia cut the U.S. lead to four. Then, with the United States in possession, the shot clock was dwindling down as George Wilson held the ball. Surveying his tightly defended teammates, Wilson, who averaged a modest 5.4 points and shot just 32.6 percent for the tournament, decided it was time to rise up and launch a jump shot. It found the net. "To this day, I wonder what would have happened had I not made those jump shots," Wilson said decades later. Iba told reporters that the game showed the difficulty of extending the United States' forty-three-game Olympic winning streak. As it happened, that night the Soviets struggled too, beating the much-improved Japanese squad by a score of only 72–59.[67]

After escaping with a victory over the feisty Yugoslavians, the United States pounded Brazil 86–53, and then South Korea, 116–50. The U.S. team's 116 points against South Korea marked the most points scored by one team in the tournament, surpassing the 105 points Estonia had scored against South Korea earlier.[68] The American team's scoring prowess suggests the charge that Iba's penchant for a controlled tempo greatly limited the U.S. Olympic team's ability to score has been overstated, at least in 1964.

Awaiting the United States in the semifinals was Puerto Rico, one of the surprise teams of the tournament. As a U.S. territory with a population of just under four million, less than that of Kentucky, Puerto Rico's Olympic basketball prowess was nothing short of amazing. Led by Jaime Frontera and Ruben Adorno, Puerto Rico came into its semifinal game with five straight victories thanks largely to its fast-paced style.[69] But against the United States, the Puerto Ricans abandoned their fast play in favor of a controlled tempo. The tactic worked in the first half as Puerto Rico led at the intermission by one point, 24–23. In the second half, the United States opened up its offensive game and yielded only eighteen points, leading to a 62–42 win that set the stage for another gold medal showdown with the Soviet Union.[70]

Going into its game against the Soviets, questions swirled about the U.S. team's chances. Critics said that this team was not as strong as America's 1960 version, especially when it came to outside shooting. Even the U.S. Olympic Committee chairman, Leon Williams, a former Big Ten commissioner, voiced concern. "We must win basketball," he said. "I am concerned about this sport. This is a sport we never have lost. Yet the Russians look very good, and we haven't been overly impressive. Frankly, I'm worried." To make matters worse, Mullins, one of the team's top long-distance shooters, had to sit out with a sore knee. Before the contest, Lou Rossini of New York University, who also coached the Puerto Rican Olympic team, said, "The Russians have speed and size . . . and I don't think the United States can win if it gets behind."[71]

On the Soviet side, which was rocked by news of leader Khrushchev's resignation during the Games, prognosticators were fairly upbeat. Reporting from Rome for the Estonian periodical *Edasi*, R. Protokollid Taru stated that "before the game everybody thought never before had the teams been so equal." Even the Russian coach Alexander Gomelsky sounded overtly optimistic in the pregame remarks, brashly declaring that in the finals, "there will be a surprise for everyone . . . We are fed up with finishing second."[72] By that point the United States had won forty-six games in a row and five straight gold medals, with three of those gold medals coming in championship matchups against the Soviet Union.

As in the past, tickets for the game were hard to come by. A wealth of buyers pushed the street market price for Tokyo's most coveted ticket to $125. Intensity was in the air as thousands of fans, among them Japan's newly married Prince Hitachi and Princess Hanako, packed into Tokyo's National Gymnasium Annex for the tip-off. Few in the electric atmosphere knew that Larry Brown nearly did not make it to the tip. With tickets scarce, he had given his Olympic pass to Fred Hansen, a gold medalist in pole vault. The plan almost backfired when Brown got held up by Olympic personnel as he tried to enter the stadium, "I almost didn't get in . . . Coach Iba was so mad at me," he recalled.[73] Overall, the reaction to the game reflected basketball's allure for both the common folks and the elite, and hinted at its potential global reach. With satellites in the air, IBM's "information networks" setting the stage for future advances in computer technology, NBC cameras filming the action, both squads featuring players clad in Chuck Taylors, and both teams' penchant for fast play, the conditions that made basketball a global phenomenon were on display.

The United States started the game down 4–0, vitalizing Soviet hopes for a victory. Minutes later, however, the United States took the lead 16–15 on a play that signified the 1964 team's trademark passing. The play developed after a Soviet missed a shot. Bradley grabbed the rebound and zipped a nifty pass up along the sideline to Hazzard, who found Lucious Jackson alone under the basket for an easy score. *Sports Illustrated*'s Jack Underwood reported that the play seemed to ignite the American squad. Soon afterward, Larry Brown drove in for a reverse layup and then fed Joe Caldwell for a wide-open jump shot that connected. Brown delivered again moments later, this time by dropping in a twenty-foot jump shot. Suddenly, the United States led 27–18. At that point the game was as good as over, especially since the United States' defensive tactic of sending two players Krumminch's way was limiting the big fellow and because Soviet sharpshooter Travin, torrid in the first half, was benched by Gomelsky in the second for committing an intentional foul, which he had done in frustration after his nose was bloodied on a drive to the basket.[74]

In the locker room following the 73–59 victory, Brown felt relief. Before the tip, he remembered "being scared." Looking at the medal for some time after the game, he said, "It's worth $12, that's all . . . And you couldn't buy it from me if you had a million." Forty-three years later he still considered it "probably . . . the greatest accomplishment for me." Counts summed up the difference in the teams, saying, "The Soviets, like a lot of teams from other countries, were a lot more mechanical, less creative and freelancing, than we as Americans were."[75]

After the loss, Estonia's R. Protokollid Taru noted that the U.S. team

TABLE 6. 1964 U.S. Men's Olympic Basketball cumulative stats

NAME	G	FGM-FGA	(%)	FTM-FTA	(%)	PF	PTS/AVG
Jerry Shipp	9	52-102	.510	8-10	.800	16	112/12.4
Bill Bradley	9	34-66	.515	23-24	.958	29	91/10.1
Lucious Jackson	9	36-75	.480	18-25	.720	20	90/10.0
Joe Caldwell	9	40-80	.500	1-6	.167	17	81/9.0
Jim Barnes	8	31-58	.534	6-12	.500	19	68/8.5
Melvin Counts	8	22-44	.500	9-12	.750	17	53/6.6
George Wilson	8	15-46	.326	13-19	.684	24	43/5.4
Pete McCaffrey	9	21-42	.500	4-6	.667	28	46/5.1
Larry Brown	9	14-31	.452	9-10	.900	17	37/4.1
Walt Hazzard	9	14-44	.318	6-6	1.000	13	34/3.8
Richard Davies	9	11-21	.524	9-14	.643	15	31/3.4
Jeff Mullins	8	8-12	.667	2-4	.500	6	18/2.3
USA TOTALS	9	298-621	.480	108-148	.730	221	704/78.2
OPP. TOTALS	9	167-571	.292	100-165	.606	233	434/48.2

"averaged one inch taller, jumped higher, and dominated on the boards, were faster and passed better." The Estonian magazine *Kehakultuur* ran an article titled, "As Usual Silver Medal," arguing that the USSR should "think about bringing younger players to Mexico [the site of the 1968 Olympics]." Striking an optimistic tone, however, *Kehakultuur* did assert, "If four or five years ago the U.S. team was a lot stronger than what we saw in Tokyo, we can say everyone is catching up."[76]

Following the contest, the *Chicago Tribune* accurately declared that the Soviets "discovered again that all players must possess scoring skills as well as ability to handle the ball on attack and move with agility on defense."[77] America's ability to churn out players who could pass and dribble with a deftness and pace superior to others gave American basketball special allure. Even though the 1964 Olympic team was not as dominating as the 1960 team, it still remained the runaway standard-bearer internationally.

In rather short order, the attractiveness of basketball's action and the international reach of television came to saturate the sport and its associated products with meaning and facilitated exchanges on a global scale. As an example, throughout the 1960s and 1970s Brown remembers requests from overseas players for American stuff, from blue jeans to shoes. "Our equipment was huge" to players because we were "so far ahead in that regard." It was coveted stuff to Brown, too. He said that getting a pair of Chucks as a kid "was the biggest thrill for me," and getting a pair of free Chucks for the Olympics thrilled him as well.[78] Brown also recalled that in Tokyo, word had it that the Soviet player Aleksandr Petrov was wearing the same pair of Converse shoes an American player had given him in 1960. Through events like the Olympics, increasing numbers of consumers, not just players, across the globe became attracted to products made by sporting-goods firms such as Converse, Adidas, Puma, and later Nike.

Soon after Tokyo, Soviet players also came to covet the wealth professional players in Europe and America could earn, which was an indication of those places' prosperity. Indeed, the rising stakes were evident in Tokyo as NBA teams could hardly wait to hire some of the American Olympians. In fact, Brown said that while he and his mates were *still* in the locker room after winning the gold, NBA personnel maneuvered to sign guys.[79] Soon, Soviet players would look for similar freedom to capitalize on their talents.

7

HAYWOOD SHINES AS SATELLITES, CABLE, AND SHOES MATURE IN MEXICO CITY

In a year that Martin Luther King Jr. and Robert Kennedy were assassinated, unrest over the Vietnam War flared, and violent protests broke out in the United States, Mexico, and elsewhere, the 1968 Olympic Games in Mexico City boasted a record-setting 112 participating nations. Those Games also showcased new standards in television, became coveted terrain for shoe companies seeking endorsers, delivered numerous world records in track and field, thanks in part to the thin air, and saw an unheralded nineteen-year-old from the Deep South named Spencer Haywood wow observers with his fierce slams and dominance of the basketball lane.

In 1966 the American Broadcasting Company (ABC) landed U.S. and Canadian television rights to these Games for a record $4.5 million.[1] Around $5 million more in production costs were needed to bring the games to American and Canadian living rooms, and that figure does not even include the use of about $8 million in equipment, including forty color cameras, nine mobile truck units, and twelve videotape machines. ABC also utilized shots from an additional eighty cameras employed by other members of the television "pool," which included Telésistema Mexicano (a group of three Mexican networks), the Japanese network NHK, and the European Broadcasting Union (EBU). To handle lines of communication between these entities and to help the network's own workforce of more than three hundred people, ABC hired thirty interpreters as well.[2]

The effort, which was led by Roone Arledge, delivered forty-two hours of Olympic coverage over a seventeen-day period, and for the first time, almost all of it was live and in color. Beforehand, Arledge said ABC's efforts would be "the biggest live remote telecast in television history." Along with live broadcasts and color cameras, ABC utilized instant-replay, stop-action, slow-motion, and split-screen techniques, all of which helped foster an upsurge in the popularity of sports television.[3]

In addition to advances in television production, technological maturation continued in the field of satellites. The Mexico City Games brought about a new standard for international satellite television with its roughly 225 hours of total programming.[4]

The improvement in television production and the rise of satellite usage would help propel sports to remarkable heights. Commenting on the boom in June 1967, *Time* noted that the Sunday edition of the *Los Angeles Times* devoted forty-eight columns to sports, compared with fourteen to music and seven to art, while Americans spent $46.5 billion on leisure activity the previous year. All this and more led *Time* to the rather obvious declaration that "sport has become big business." As a further indication of sports' popularity, ways to supplement the athlete's diet abounded. *Time* noted that Florida University's football coach Ray Graves was giving his players a drink consisting of glucose, sodium phosphate, sodium chloride, potassium chloride, sodium bicarbonate, calcium cyclamate, and citric acid that researchers at his university had developed. In the 1990s that drink became known around the world as its maker encouraged the globe's citizens to "Be like Mike" (Michael Jordan) and drink Gatorade.[5]

Improvements in other areas that would contribute to the rise of sport worldwide occurred as well, namely, the growth of sporting-goods companies, especially those in the shoe business. To garner a larger market share, these companies were paying higher sums to ally themselves with superstar athletes. At the 1968 Summer Games the issue of amateurism resurfaced when reports emerged that Adidas and Puma were jockeying for influence among athletes by offering up large amounts of cash for sponsorship. Sometimes their jostling continued right up to an athlete's event. A rumor circulated in Mexico City that one athlete entered the tunnel leading to the Olympic Stadium wearing a pair of Adidas and came out the other end wearing Pumas.[6] The shoe wars emphasized that footwear had become a crucial point of entry for sporting-goods firms looking to increase visibility.[7] And Knight's unheralded Nike corporation would soon prove that basketball, with its artistic movement and hip allure, would be the key entry-point in sport.[8]

In Mexico City, though, the U.S. Olympic basketball team still wore Converse's Chuck Taylors. During the 1968 Games, Converse ran ads in periodicals like *Sports Illustrated* and *The Amateur Athlete* touting its shoes. "Just because the U.S. Olympic team will wear Converse basketball shoes, should you? Darned right!" Converse wrote. The company also evoked the U.S. team's ability to execute "lightning-fast breaks" during the "fierce and fast" Olympic basketball tournament, "because every team is out to beat the world."[9] These ads aimed to capitalize on the human attraction to competition, to innovation, and to speed, as demonstrated in the game of basketball.

In the 1950s and 1960s in particular, Converse's image was indeed resonant. The 1968 basketball Olympian Spencer Haywood serves as a great example of this. Shoes were a big part of Haywood's life. Throughout his entire childhood, he received only one Christmas gift—a pair of shoes. He recalled that in the poor, rural town of Silver City, Mississippi, where he had grown up, shoes were "symbolic" for folks.[10] In contrast to big-ticket items like cars, shoes offered poor people an opportunity to demonstrate a certain level of success and assert an identity. When Haywood entered high school, his mother knew that her son yearned for a real pair of basketball shoes, so she decided to treat Spencer by buying a pair of "ugly green canvas sneakers." They cost $5.00, but she was able to buy them for $3.00 and the promise of a pecan pie.[11] The following season, Haywood's coach gave him an upgrade, a pair of Chuck Taylors. As Spencer put it, the Chucks were his first "true" pair of basketball shoes. Lacing up the wondrous shoes as a young man, Haywood thought, "I had arrived."[12] After Mexico City, Haywood endorsed products himself—imbuing them with the type of cultural currency he had associated with Chuck Taylors as a youth.

Though Haywood felt like he had arrived when he laced up his first pair of Chuck Taylors, by the end of the Mexico City Olympics, he really had arrived. Before the Games, however, the 1968 team was known more for the names missing from its roster than those on it. The most notable absences were Lew Alcindor and Elvin Hayes.

In 1967 the Brooklyn native Lew Alcindor, a lengthy seven-feet-two-inch center, dominated the NCAA ranks while leading UCLA to the national title. Alcindor was so effective other schools persuaded the NCAA to forbid dunking for the 1967–68 season. The no-dunking rule failed to slow Alcindor, though, as he proceeded to lead UCLA to another national title. That year, Hayes, a six-feet-nine-inch power forward out of Houston University, challenged Alcindor for recognition as the most dominant college big man. They squared off in two epic battles. The first, in January at the Houston Astrodome, took place in front of a record-high indoor crowd of over 52,000 fans. Credited by many as the game that turned college basketball into a major sport, it was the first NCAA contest to be broadcast on national television. Alcindor and Hayes's second meeting came in the NCAA semifinals. Alcindor fared better that time as UCLA beat Hayes's Houston squad convincingly, 101–69. The prospect of the two starring alongside each other on the U.S. Olympic team's frontcourt excited basketball fans, but it soon became clear that neither would suit up in Mexico City. The 1968 U.S. Olympic basketball player Bill Hosket remembers getting *Sports Illustrated* shortly after making the team and reading that his squad would probably be the only Olympic team to lose. "I thought, 'What have I signed up for?'" Hosket told the author. "Basically, it [the *Sports Illustrated* prediction] was because we didn't have a center, or a known center."[13]

Other stars that could potentially have suited up for the 1968 Olympic team were three prolific guards: "Pistol" Pete Maravich, Calvin Murphy, and Rick Mount. Maravich and Murphy had led the nation in scoring during the 1967–68 college basketball season with astounding 43.8 and 38.2 averages, respectively, while Mount, a sophomore shooting guard from Purdue, had scored 28.4 points per game. With big men like Hayes and Alcindor and even Wes Unseld teaming up with such prolific guards, many thought that the 1968 U.S. Olympic squad could be as potent and thoroughly dominating as the teams of 1956 and 1960. But none of these collegians played on the 1968 team, which makes the actual squad's performance in Mexico City even more striking.

The absence of so many stars highlighted how the growth of professional and collegiate basketball posed a challenge for the Olympic movement. In addition to the fact that the Mexico City Games were to take place in the fall (thereby cutting into the time that some would-be Olympians would otherwise have spent with NBA teams), part of the problem in getting NCAA players on the team stemmed from the quixotic position IOC President Avery Brundage held regarding professionalism. Brundage maintained that even if a player had not yet turned pro, he was ineligible for the Olympics if he *intended* to turn pro right after the Games—despite Brundage's acknowledgment that "intent is a very difficult thing to prove." It was an unrealistic and baffling stance that caused players and professional leagues to approach the subject with the utmost delicacy. For instance, NBA president Walter Kennedy tried to convince collegiate players who intimated a desire to play in the Olympics that they would face no pressure to sign a contract from the NBA beforehand, but he could not specifically assure any one person directly, because that would suggest the player intended to turn pro. Thus, college players were put in the awkward position of having to make sure that they did not suggest too strong an intention to turn pro at the same time that they were also trying to gauge the NBA's level of interest in them. It made no sense. "Suppose they ask a boy who has gone out for the Olympic team if he has made a verbal commitment to turn pro. If his answer is 'no' and they later find out that he has, what would they do?" Kennedy posited to the *Chicago Tribune*.[14]

Rather understandably, Hayes cited this lack of cooperation between the NBA and the IOC as one of his reasons for turning pro. He made that decision in late March, after his Houston Cougars lost in the NCAA tournament to UCLA. Hayes, who was married and had a son, told reporters, "If I go to the Olympics and get hurt, I have nothing. Nothing would come to me or my family, it would be zero-zero . . . I don't want to be a failure to my mother or my family. I'm not thinking of myself." Discounting suggestions that he was motivated by the African American Olympic boycott movement that had arisen, Hayes said, "It's not color nor anything like that. It's my own decision. I only hope the public can understand my problem."[15] A short time later, he signed a three-year $440,000 deal with the San Diego Rockets; the contract indicated the rising commercial stakes of professional basketball.

Hayes's decision to sign with the NBA's San Diego Rockets elicited an outcry of criticism from people, including prominent sports figures, who thought he should represent his country in Mexico City. Hayes tried to quell the criticism five days later by announcing that all of the proceeds from a ten-game summer basketball tour he intended to lead were earmarked for the U.S. Olympic basketball team.[16] A few days later, Boston Celtics General Manager Red Auerbach provided a voice of support for Hayes, telling reporters:

> I don't blame him. For one thing, he has a lot of money and his future at stake . . . Besides, the handling of the Olympic basketball team stinks. Ask Bill Russell who was on the 1956 Olympic team. Bill says he would never do it again. They pick about twelve players and nine coaches who really live it up while the athletes have trouble making ends meet. I had another player who made an Olympic team and he was given $5 a day for nine days—$45 in all. He said that when he got back he was so broke he couldn't afford to walk down the ship's gangplank.[17]

Auerbach went on to accuse the American Basketball Association (ABA) of raiding college campuses for talent that otherwise might have competed for the U.S. Olympic team. "I get calls all the time from college coaches who tell me that the ABA has been approaching their stars. We [the NBA] don't draft boys until their eligibility is completed—just like football."[18]

As Auerbach suggested, the actions of the ABA, an upstart professional league rivaling the NBA, did affect the availability of players for the Olympics. But in a larger context, the league also helped basketball immensely. Considered one of the "wackiest most colorful and strangest professional sports leagues ever," the ABA gave basketball the three-point shot, the red, white, and blue ball, and the slam dunk contest. As Terry Pluto, author of a book on the ABA, has noted, the league infused basketball with energy, athleticism, and innovation. The attractiveness of the ABA's style, especially to the all-important youth market, was demonstrated by the sale of some thirty million red, white, and blue basketballs over the course of its eight-year existence and with the popularity of its groundbreaking slam dunk contest.[19] Larry Brown, who played and coached in the league, said the ABA provided more jobs for professional hopefuls, "opened" the game, and "gave little guys more opportunities."[20]

The league deserves credit for enhancing basketball's allure, and by 1976 the NBA showed it recognized as much by agreeing to combine the leagues. Eventually, the NBA would adopt many components of the ABA model, most notably the three-point shot. The changes promoted faster, more innovative, and higher-scoring play, which in turn affected college and FIBA rules. For instance, just as FIBA had done with the NBA shot clock in 1956, it took cues from the NBA on the three-point shot, implementing it for the 1988 Olympic tournament.

An even more problematic issue facing the U.S. Olympic Basketball Committee, other than a lack of cohesion with professional leagues and parsimonious treatment of its players, was the proposed African American boycott of the 1968 Games led by the San Jose State sociologist Harry Edwards. Edwards's boycott movement came during a tumultuous time in American history. Throughout the land, youth agitated, whether against the war in Vietnam or racial injustice at home. Between the 1964 Tokyo Games and Mexico City, race riots in the American cities of Los Angeles, Detroit, and Newark left dozens dead. In January 1968, the Tet Offensive, launched by the Vietcong and North Vietnamese, highlighted the seemingly endless violence in Vietnam. In April 1968, after the assassination of Martin Luther King Jr., Washington DC went up in flames.[21] In June of the same year, Robert Kennedy was assassinated, and then in August, white and black alike protested at the Democratic National Convention in Chicago, which resulted in violent confrontations between police and demonstrators, all of it caught on television.

During this period of racial and political tumult, African Americans had increased their numbers dramatically on the basketball court, making the sport a place of prominence for them. Whereas in other facets of life artificial barriers to success limited opportunity, on the playing fields, there were fewer racial barriers holding people back. As an example of this, in 1966, Don Haskin's Texas Western team was the first NCAA champion to start five black players as they beat Adolph Rupp's University of Kentucky team, led by a young Pat Riley. Within a few years of that victory, the Southeastern Conference (SEC) was fully integrated. Given the prominence they gave to many African Americans, sports like basketball became a vehicle for activism.

Lew Alcindor represented this well. In early March of 1968 UCLA announced Alcindor's decision to not attend the Olympics, citing scholastic reasons. Most figured, though, that his support of the African American boycott was the more likely reason for his absence.[22] The *Washington Post's* William Gildea stated as much when he responded to UCLA's announcement by writing, "More reasonable is the assumption that he favors the boycott, for his actions do it a service." Although academics were a concern, since Alcindor would have missed a quarter of classes at UCLA had he gone to the Games, Gildea was right to assert that Alcindor favored the boycott. Fifteen years later Kareem Abdul-Jabbar, as he was then known, admitted as much, writing, "I fully supported the idea; I felt no part of the country and no desire to help it look good." Jabbar did admit there were legitimate points to be made in the international arena, but added, "If white America was going to treat blacks poorly, then white America could win the Olympics on its own."[23]

Gildea was also correct in asserting that Alcindor's support for the boycott benefited the movement.[24] A *Newsweek* article demonstrated this. "Negro athletes" had "stunned" administrators at numerous colleges with their calls for black coaches, trainers, cheerleaders, and a "new black dignity," *Newsweek* reported. The magazine specifically noted that the United States "is likely to lose the Olympic basketball title for the first time because Lew Alcindor of the University of California at Los Angeles and other black stars boycotted the trials,"[25] The attention Alcindor brought to the cause showed how basketball could give young African Americans a national voice, otherwise a rare commodity.

People from all over tried to talk Alcindor out of his decision to stay home, such as the Hollywood star Kirk Douglas. But when American media men came down on those associated with the boycott effort, Abdul-Jabbar recalled, "I became even more resolved not to involve myself in their jingoism." He stands by his decision not to play and has expressed his admiration for John Carlos and Tommie Smith, who, following their respective first- and second-place finishes in the 200 meters in Mexico City, famously held up their black-gloved fists during the playing of the National Anthem. "My passive gesture had cost me a lot—I was deluged by hate mail calling me an uppity nigger and a traitor—and I knew their active statement, in the public eye of that hurricane, would cost them much more. I think of them as patriots," he wrote.[26]

The power of the boycott was also evident in that it not only garnered the attention of Americans, but of people overseas too. Dr. Charles V. Hamilton of Chicago's Roosevelt University, who coauthored with Stokely Carmichael the influential *Black Power: The Politics of Liberation*, recognized as much when he said, "The boycott expresses our concern for the plight of most of our people in this country. And it gives the problem international visibility."[27] When word of the possible African American boycott surfaced in Tokyo, Japan's Sports Federation Chief, Tetsuo Ohba, fretted, "The Negro super-stars made the Games worth seeing." Neil Allen of London's *Times* asserted that the boycott was "hitting at middle-class America, the social force most perpetuating racism—telling it that no longer can sport be excluded from goals of assimilation."[28] Of course, Edwards's message involved much more than just sports. In fact, though there were racial problems within the sports world, one of Edwards's main points was that assimilation needed to occur more speedily in areas outside of sports and, therefore, it was through boycotting sports that African Americans could push for change elsewhere.[29]

Ultimately, the results of the boycott were mixed. A number of prominent black athletes came out in support of the movement, including the former Olympian Bill Russell, who attended the 1968 U.S. Olympic basketball trials in Albuquerque with Edwards. Yet not all blacks backed the cause. Among the more prominent African Americans against the movement were Willie Mays, Jesse Owens, and several female track athletes. Emmet Taylor, a track athlete from Ohio University in Athens, Ohio, summed up a common argument of those who opposed the boycott when he told *Ebony*, "I think a boycott would be more detrimental to the Negro's cause, because there is less discrimination in athletics."[30] *Newsweek* noted that John Wooden, whom the magazine credited with maintaining peace on his UCLA teams by allowing his black athletes to express racial pride with their haircuts and clothing, disagreed with the boycott. "I feel it's outside influences trying to use the Negro athletes," Wooden explained. Wooden was not soft on racial issues either. In 1947 his Southern Indiana team boycotted the NAIB tournament because it did not allow black players. The next year his team integrated the tournament. IOC president Avery Brundage, as one might expect, did not support the boycott. He stated, rather condescendingly, "It seems a little ungrateful to attempt to boycott something which has given them such great opportunity."[31]

The 1968 U.S. Olympic basketball team assistant coach John B. McClendon, the first black man on the coaching staff of a U.S. Olympic basketball team and a hugely successful coach whose name, had he not spent the bulk of his career restrained by prejudice, would be evoked with the likes of Iba, Rupp, and Allen, also did not support the boycott. Considered a civil rights pioneer by his biographer Milton Katz, McClendon thought the Black Youth Organization, which supported the boycott, had a cause but was "without a cause in Mexico." As Katz explained it, McClendon thought America could correct itself systematically if pressed to.[32]

All told, forty-four African Americans participated in the Olympic basketball trials held in Albuquerque. Charlie Scott and Joseph "JoJo" White, both black and both eventual Olympians, commented on the situation while trying out. "As far as I'm concerned, there is no boycott yet," Scott said. But he added, "I'm not going to be the only Negro out there. I'll go along with them. But if it's scattered, my choice is to play." White did not give as much wiggle room. "I make up my own mind, and I've decided to play," he told *Sports Illustrated*. "I don't care if I'm the only one. They can go ahead and boycott; I'm playing." Many African Americans did not show up for the trials, but rather than emphasize the boycott as the main reason for their absence, most gave other reasons, such as signing a pro contract, injury, exhaustion, or an inability to take time away from their studies.[33] As for Edwards's prediction that just five African Americans would end up on the roster, it proved correct.

The trials took place at the University of New Mexico's new, $1.5 million stadium that could seat over 14,000 fans. Nearly entirely underground, the engineering marvel was dubbed "The Pit." A tunnel large enough to accommodate a pickup truck connected the playing floor to separate training rooms, locker rooms, and storage rooms. Over 55,000 cubic yards of earth were moved and 28,000 yards of concrete poured to build the structure.[34] It was a physical testament to basketball's growth over the previous thirty years.

It was in "The Pit" that Iba, who the U.S. Olympic basketball committee had again named head coach, first noticed the eighteen-year-old Haywood. Legend has it that Haywood made the team in the opening moments of the trials in the layup line. Recalling the scenario years later, Haywood said he was told that Coach Iba, already concerned about a dearth of big men, "made his decision after watching me almost tear down the backboard in warm-ups." Others noticed Haywood as well. Pointing out that twenty or so of the NCAA's top players did not attend the trials, *Sports Illustrated*'s Curry Kirkpatrick credited Haywood and his junior college mates with providing "the only excitement in an otherwise listless three days of basketball."[35] Iba labored to get Haywood on the team. He faced some resistance from members of the selection committee over Haywood's youth, but with the help of McClendon, Iba prevailed.

For a country that wants to stand for opportunity, Haywood rose to Olympic glory fittingly. He capitalized on the absence of players like Alcindor and Hayes in a fashion as spectacular as it was unexpected. Few would have predicted greatness for Haywood early on, as he was born two months early and sickly in abject poverty in Silver City, Mississippi. That is, unless you put stock in hands. Family and friends noticed right away that his huge hands appeared to have "an extra joint, a fourth bone" on each finger. Upon seeing the young baby's hands, Charlie Battle, a neighbor of the Haywoods, supposedly exclaimed, "Look at that boy! This boy is going to be a great cotton-picker, ain't he? Whooo-eee!" Haywood's Aunt Harriet said, "Oh precious God, look at them baby's hands. This baby is blessed, this boy is special. He's got them healing hands."[36]

Silver City was a small town in the Deep South. As late as the 1950s some southern farm owners still hired mostly black laborers to pick cotton manually, rather than using mechanization. Silver City was one of those places. The town also struggled with race relations. As a youngster Haywood remembered white folks at a Silver City country club grabbing their rifles, running outside, and firing off shots "yelling and ya-hooing," when they heard of Kennedy's assassination. "I had never seen white people act so happy," he recalled.[37]

In "Old" Silver City, the black section of town, people were particularly poor. And since the Haywoods were poor by "Old" Silver City's standards, they were poorer than poor. For Spencer and his siblings, Christmas presents came in February because that was when other kids in town threw away toys that they had grown tired of. Eventually, the throwaways made it to the landfill behind the Haywood's home. Then, Spencer and his older brother Andrew picked through the garbage for discarded gems.[38]

Early in his adolescence, Haywood took a liking to basketball. "We played constantly, always on dirt courts. We walked miles and miles to find a game, played all day, and walked back home," he said. Before high school, Haywood, who was six feet six by the age of thirteen, had caught the attention of McNair High School basketball coach Charles Wilson, who later pushed Haywood hard, making him work out in weighted shoes so he could reach his full potential.[39] Haywood left Mississippi a short time later, though, in May 1963, when he used $17.50 that he had saved to take a bus to Chicago alone. His journey eventually led to Detroit, where he moved in with James and Ida Bell and attended the 60-percent white Pershing High School. In 1967 the Pershing Doughboys, with Haywood leading the way, became the first public Michigan high school in thirty-seven years to win a state basketball championship.[40] By that year nearly every major NCAA university and coach in the nation wanted Haywood, including Kentucky's Rupp, who by then seemed willing to accept a black player.

Initially, Haywood committed to play at the University of Tennessee. Had he attended, he would have become the first black basketball player in the school's history. But he did not. "Difficulty" arose in processing his application. Ultimately, Haywood grew fed up and headed off to Trinidad Junior College in Colorado.[41] Following his first season at Trinidad, during which he scored and rebounded at a torrid pace, Haywood was chosen to try out for the junior college all-star team, which was slated to compete at the Olympic trials. So he had not even played an NCAA basketball game by the time he tried out in "The Pit."

Joining Haywood and the other junior college all-stars on his trials squad in Albuquerque were AAU all-stars, armed forces standouts, and forty-eight NCAA collegians. Initially, the pool of NCAA players was much larger, but after workouts and exhibition games in Indianapolis, Louisville, and Evansville, the selectors trimmed the number to forty-eight.

High-scorers Maravich, Mount, and Murphy counted among those chosen to continue trying out in "The Pit."[42] Expectations for the trio were high. Mount and Maravich, in particular, had turned in strong performances at their workouts in Indianapolis two weeks earlier.[43] And on the first day of action in Albuquerque, Mount delivered on those expectations, scoring twenty-one points to lead all scorers—he averaged just over eighteen points per game at the trials. Maravich did not fare as well, though. He managed only six points in his opener, and his NCAA Blues lost to the Haywood-led Junior College All-Stars. Ultimately, neither made the Olympic team. Mount and Maravich lost out seemingly because of their relative youth and issues with their style.

Maravich's style, especially, caused problems with the Iba-directed coaching staff. Criticism of Maravich from various camps had been brewing for some time. Though he filled up stadiums across the South with his phenomenal ballhandling and nifty passing, some coaches thought his style was overly individualistic. Even John Wooden, a longtime advocate of the fast break and proponent of the college shot clock, did not particularly care for Maravich's style. A few weeks before Albuquerque he admitted that Maravich was a "great basketball player" but also said, "I would much rather have balanced scoring. I want my players to score and I want Lew [Alcindor] to score—but not at the expense of the team."[44]

John Bach, who later assisted Iba at the Munich Games, was Maravich's coach in Albuquerque, and he hardly played him. When Maravich did play, he struggled.[45] But he still managed to amaze. Bill Hosket played alongside Maravich in Albuquerque and remembers one sequence in particular. It occurred near the end of a first half when Bach had finally decided to give Maravich a go. Hosket recalled:

He [Maravich] comes across half-court and he stops and he's like five feet inside of the line [half-court] . . . And he shoots a two-hand set. He let this ball go and I just couldn't believe it . . . It hit up in the corner of the backboard. And everybody kind of turned when he threw it and it shot out of there like a boomerang and Pete was great at following his own shot and he catches it at the foul line on the fly—just follows this rocket he threw up there. And he shoots a jumper, just caught it and shot, didn't even look anywhere else and just caught it and put it back up. And now we kind of reacted to this first thing flying back over our heads. Now we see he shoots it again and I'm going to the offensive glass and the ball . . . just starts spinning around the hoop and everybody . . . like mistimed whatever was going on. Well the ball drops straight down . . . it fell down toward the floor. And everybody's going for this ball and Maravich went in and dug it out and starts dribbling out toward the right corner with his back to the basket and threw it up over his shoulder and made it. I mean God, he's one for three, he's got two rebounds. This whole thing was like six, seven seconds long . . . I was actually laughing on the floor. I could not believe this. And Johnny Bach's wearing his white shoes and I looked over toward the bench and he's just sitting there shaking his head like, "What are we going to do with this kid."

Hosket maintained that Maravich "really loved the sport. And he loved to play." Though Maravich was known for his scoring, Hosket considered him a "phenomenal passer" and also thought Maravich was "real emotional." Hosket said, "I remember at night he went out and lost a dance contest—Calvin Murphy won a dance contest in a local place in Albuquerque and Pete was upset he lost that. He was having a tough week. But he was entertaining."[46]

In 1972, Maravich's biographer and apparent supporter Bill Gutman argued that not everyone appreciated Pistol's "magical game." Some, like Bach, preferred "the old virtues of grin-'n-bear-it basketball," he wrote.[47] Iba's attitude toward Maravich was similar, and it reflected a generation gap between older basketball aficionados and the younger players, who were taking the sport in a new direction. In time, the allure of youthful, innovative, and flashy play like Maravich's transformed the sport and became more commonplace.

While the cutting of Mount and Maravich surprised many, the committee's rejection of Calvin Murphy may be its most peculiar decision (though, of the three, Hosket thinks that the sharp-shooting Mount would have fit best with Iba).[48] After averaging 38.2 points at Niagara, Murphy played solidly in Albuquerque. *Sports Illustrated*'s Kirkpatrick claimed that Murphy appeared "woefully inexperienced in [his] floor games."[49] But Murphy did help his NCAA Whites to a 2-1 record. Some suggested that coming from Niagara had limited his visibility before the trials, but other players from small schools gained spots, and Murphy was a known commodity beforehand. In early April, just days before Murphy was cut, Red Auerbach described him as "the only college player—including Alcindor and the rest—I'd pay to see. The kid is simply a genius. He can do everything. I think he can make the pros right now."[50] Yet Murphy apparently could not overcome his sophomore status.

Only one sophomore, Charlie Scott, a less-heralded six-feet-five-inch forward from North Carolina, made the squad. The first African American to play for the Tar Heels, Scott was, according to Kirkpatrick, "the most versatile and spectacular player of the trials," a strong endorsement considering Haywood's performance.[51] Other collegians joining Haywood and Scott were Donald Dee, a six-feet-seven-inch forward from St. Mary of the Plains (Junior) College, the only other junior college player to make it, and four NCAA Division I players: "JoJo" White of Kansas, a six-feet-three-inch guard; Houston's center Ken Spain, who at six feet nine and 240 pounds was the team's largest player; Glynn Saulters, a six-feet-two guard from Northeast Louisiana; and Hosket, the six-feet-eight-inch forward from Ohio State.

From the AAU came forward James King, a "great defender" who had played for Iba at Oklahoma State, and veteran guard Calvin Fowler, the squad's elder statesmen, of the Goodyear Wingfoots.[52] By that time, the National Amateur Athletic Union Basketball League (NABL), unable to cope with the competition for players from the NBA and the two-year old American Basketball Association (ABA), had shrunk to only four teams. Still, the AAU held enough sway on the U.S. basketball committee to wrangle two spots on the squad.[53] Three players from the U.S. Armed Forces earned positions as well: the guard John Clawson; the wide-shouldered and hard-nosed forward Michael Silliman, who later served in Korea and who, in 2003, Bob Knight said "may still be the best player I've ever coached on a college team"; and the guard Michael Barrett, a navy seaman, the team's lightest player at a mere 155 pounds, and a veteran of international basketball. (The previous year at the World Games in South America, Barrett made a shot as time expired to give the United States a 59–58 victory over the Soviet Union.)[54]

After naming the squad, Iba announced a plan to convene the Olympians in Alamosa, Colorado, for high-altitude training, with late September and early October exhibition games against professional teams in Cincinnati, New York City, and elsewhere to follow. "We haven't the strength, we haven't the defense yet, but we have finesse and speed. We will have team unity, and that is very important," Iba told reporters. That Iba built the team on finesse and speed suggests he was not limited to playing a center-dominated "barnacle" style of basketball.[55] Certainly, Iba's assistants, Henry Vaughn of the AAU's Akron Wingfoots and McClendon, were not averse to the fast game. In fact, McClendon had helped develop it.[56] Still, the 1968 team did average fewer points than had the three previous American Olympic teams.

Before meeting in Colorado for their high-altitude training, a number of Olympians, including Barrett and collegians Scott and Haywood, set out for an AAU-sponsored, ten-game exhibition tour of Eastern Europe. The tour started in Yugoslavia then headed to Russia, before ending in Finland. In Ljubljana, Yugoslavia, the American team dropped two straight games to Yugoslavia's national team.[57] The losses contributed to concerns about the Olympic squad. From Yugoslavia, the team went to Minsk, Russia, where, according to Haywood, much of the enthusiasm for the trip wore thin. North Carolina's Scott in particular did not take kindly to Russia. He thought the steaks, which were served up for the team three times a day, tasted a bit peculiar, and after some inquiry, he learned that the meat came from horses. Already thin, Smith lost fifteen pounds the rest of the tour, eating nothing but ice cream and Coca-Cola.[58] Though their spirits were dampened, in Minsk the U.S. team did avenge its earlier losses to Yugoslavia. A tilt with the Soviets followed.[59] The United States won that one too, giving the team the round-robin championship.

From Minsk, it was on to Moscow for two more games against the Soviets. Moscow's bleakness caught Haywood off-guard: "I started to get the impression that Blacks in Mississippi weren't the only oppressed and disadvantaged people on earth," he recalled. Adding to the discomfort, Haywood noted that no one on the team had mollified their pangs for home or the sting of defeat by finding a little romance. But then in Russia's capital, Ken Spain, a bruising center from Houston, met a young lady. He invited her to his room and invited Haywood up as well. Haywood in turn invited Scott. Soon word spread, and other teammates started to congregate outside the room, banging on the door. When Haywood and company did not answer, a few even tried to climb around the edge of a window in an adjoining room. After a while the banging got louder and louder and Spain, Scott, and Haywood noticed Russian voices. One of the players called out, "Who's there?" An emphatic answer came back, "KGB!" Nervously, they opened the door. Two KGB agents hustled in, took the lady by the arm, and walked her out. The whole episode was too much for Scott, who was already terribly homesick. He broke down crying the next day, telling Haywood, "I ain't never cried in my life, Wood. I'm through. I don't care if they kick me off the team, I'm goin' home." And he did, but he was not kicked off of the Olympic team for it.[60]

In Moscow the United States lost both games to the Soviet national team, prompting a *Washington Post* headline that read, "Russians Beat United States, Stay Wary." Commenting on the wins, Soviet coach Alexander Y. Gomelsky told the *Post*, "Of course, the victory is a big and honorable one. But we should not cherish any illusions . . . The Americans, after checking their qualities in action, and we, as well, will draw conclusions. Although their Olympic lineup has already been announced, they probably will replace three or four players and reinforce their team."[61] The United States did not replace three or four members of their Olympic team, but the trip did elicit concern, both regarding American chances in Mexico City and whether the State Department should send losing teams abroad. Those suggesting that the State Department should only send winning teams abroad, however, tended to disregard the advantages of engaging other nations in the cultural milieu of a sport like basketball, win or lose.

Ever since the Soviets played in their first Olympic basketball tournament in 1952, basketball's popularity had grown throughout Russia and its satellites. And in areas where it was already hugely popular, like the Baltics and Georgia, it had continued to thrive. As examples of this, in 1956 Moscow's 14,000-seat Palace of Sport opened. A few years later an 11,000-seat Sports Palace boosted basketball further. Meanwhile, Lithuania's 4,500-seat Sporthalle and Estonia's 3,000-seat stadium in Tallinn could not accommodate demand. During this time, Alexander Gomelsky's local army team in Riga, Russia, which became one of the strongest in Europe, and rival Vladimir Kondrashin's Spartak Leningrad team routinely played to sold-out crowds. By 1968 the Soviet Union boasted 3,065 stadiums with at least 1,500 seats, compared to 1,020 such stadiums in 1952.[62]

The increase in basketball's popularity had continued to pay dividends in the quality of the Soviet Union's play, as evidenced by Haywood and company's tour. Coming into the 1968 Mexico Olympics, the Gomelsky-led Soviets had recently won the 1967 European championship and the 1967 FIBA World Championship in South America. These successes raised Soviet expectations for Mexico City. In Estonia's *Kehkultuur*, author A. Tobi reported that of eleven journalists asked to predict the outcome of the 1968

Olympic basketball tournament, six predicted the United States would win and five picked the Soviet Union. Tobi noted that a "U.S. basketball person" he had talked to said the Soviet Union's world championship team was the best he had seen. In addition, Tobi pointed out that the United States had only placed fourth at the 1967 world championships and had played three games in Russia before Mexico City, dropping two of them. "USA players were great individuals, not great team players," he declared.[63]

The 1968 Soviet Olympic squad was younger than its predecessor, averaging just under twenty-four years of age compared with twenty-seven in Rome. It was also taller, with a remarkable mean of six feet seven. In addition, the roster featured two players over seven feet, Vladimir Andreyev and Sergei Kovalenko, a twenty-one-year-old student from Tbilisi who stood seven feet two. In comparison, the six-feet-nine Spain was the United States' tallest player. Gomelsky declared his team the tallest and strongest yet to come out of the Soviet Union. "The Americans will have at least one equal opponent at Mexico City—our team," he maintained. "I do not contend that we will win for sure, but I do believe that we have equal chance with the Olympic champions."[64] As a complement to their height, the Soviets boasted quickness and accurate outside shooting.

In contrast to the impressive Soviet resume, the American team's resume was murky. The squad did win its tune-ups against NBA squads (save an overtime loss to the Cincinnati Royals in which Oscar Robertson, according to Hosket, simply seemed to be declaring, "'Not here. It's not gonna happen here tonight by a bunch of kids.' And he dominated us.") But the NBA teams had not yet had their training camps for the upcoming season, and the Olympic squad still seemed to have some holes. After the U.S. team's win in its final tune-up against the New York Knicks, however, Iba did somewhat optimistically tell the *Washington Post*, "We're not as strong physically as some of our Olympic teams of the past, but we've got the best shooting team ever and they're very quick. Our biggest problem will be rebounding."[65]

Others voiced less optimism. Given the Soviet team's height, agility, and accuracy, and the absence of many American stars on the U.S. team, many predicted that this Olympic basketball tournament would be marked by parity and, ultimately, the first U.S. loss. The *Washington Post* called the 1968 team the first to enter the Olympic tournament as an underdog. *Time* rationalized its skepticism by noting that a "24-year-old Army captain

[John Clawson] and a 28-year-old rubber company foreman [presumably the twenty-seven-year-old Fowler]" would be joining Haywood in the starting lineup. *Time* also claimed that the team seemed ill-prepared to handle the taller Russians and Yugoslavs. Striking a similar tone in its Olympic basketball preview, the *Amateur Athlete* warned, "The reader is respectfully reminded that the United States is not always represented by its best players. Such players as Lew Alcindor, Lucius Allen, and Mike Warren of the UCLA quintet could beat any Olympic team itself."[66] But in hindsight, it is clear the prognosticators misjudged the squad. Hosket thinks much of the team's success came from its weeks in Alamosa, Colorado, where they trained in virtual isolation and where two-a-days and strategy meetings were the norm.

Upon deboarding the small prop plane that he took to Alamosa—with a couple of cowboys—Hosket met Iba on a humble airport runway. Coach Iba greeted him and said, "I've got you rooming with Haywood. That doesn't bother you, does it son?" And I said, "No sir, not at all." Later, Hosket learned from trainer Whitey Gwynn that Iba had "agonized over two or three days" over how to make the rooming assignments. "That's how much he was on detail," Hosket explained. "He wanted to make sure he had everybody right for what position they played and what kind of guys they were and probably racial balance and they probably worried about everything." (As for Hosket and Haywood, they got along swell. When they would run into each other in pro ball years later, Haywood would still call Hosket "roomie.") On the Alamosa trip, Hosket maintained, "Obviously, part of the reason we won those Olympics is the fact that we did go to Alamosa, Colorado, that we were isolated and he [Iba] turned twelve decent basketball players into a great team. I mean, the man was remarkable." Explaining Iba's tactics, Hosket said, "Everything was regimented and very much geared from the defensive end of the floor . . . He was an absolute taskmaster."

Hosket was particularly impressed with Iba's handling of Haywood: "Watching what he did with Spencer Haywood was just an absolute clinic. He turned him into an absolute force over a four- or five-week period and was on him constantly. I mean it was amazing how much he barked at him." When Haywood had first been selected for the team, Hosket said people around Ohio State "didn't even know who he was." As folks in Columbus and throughout the rest of the world soon learned, Haywood helped the U.S. squad not only by dominating inside offensively, which was highlighted by his vicious slams, but on defense as well, as the team could funnel players to him as he prowled the lane.[67] Still, it was with outside expectations relatively low that the squad traveled to the Games.

In addition to concerns about the squad's ability, yet another uncertainty faced the U.S. team as the Mexico City Olympics neared—whether the Games would even take place. Days before the Opening Ceremonies, political protests in Mexico City put them in jeopardy. It was just the type of scenario the IOC had dreaded when it chose Mexico City, a major metropolis in an emerging nation, as host. From the outset, the IOC was excited at the prospect of Mexico being the first "emerging nation" to host the Games, but wary of unpredictability. The concern had seemed unwarranted, however, considering that for five years Mexicans had rejoiced, or so it appeared, at the idea of hosting. Posters hung throughout the city celebrating the Games, and billboards read "Anything is Possible with Peace." But then, domestic political issues, not directly related to the Olympics but related to the global era, erupted when thousands of students, along with many women and children, gathered at Mexico's Plaza de las Tres Culturas to protest the military occupation of the National Polytechnic Institute. Parallels were drawn between the Mexican protest and student protests earlier that year in the United States and in France.[68]

The incident was another indication of the tumultuous times, not only in North America but across the world. In yet another example of this, in Czechoslovakia, on the nights of August 20 and 21, over 200,000 Soviet troops and 5,000 tanks stopped liberal Czechoslovakians from carrying on their policies of "socialism with a human face." In response to the Soviet Union's incursion, the IOC's Jan Staubo of Norway asked Brundage to revoke the Soviet Union's and East Germany's Olympic membership. But Brundage responded to these events in usual fashion, stating, "If participation in sport is to be stopped every time the politicians violate the laws of humanity, there will never be any international contests." The historian Allen Guttmann, no apologist for Brundage, wrote that he did have a point: "How could a humane and peaceful world be a precondition for the Games that were meant to contribute to the creation of a humane and peaceful world?" Guttmann asked.[69]

Even with the political turmoil, the Games opened in relative peace and splendor in Mexico City's magnificent Olympic Stadium. Over 100,000 spectators from across the globe watched some 6,000 representatives from 112 nations march in the opening ceremony. Armed guards stood at the ready outside the stadium, and there were 5,000 plainclothes officers in and outside the venue.[70] Fortunately, the full complement of their services was not needed. ABC carried the events live as satellite technology beamed images of the Opening Ceremonies across the globe. Bob Ottum of *Sports Illustrated* reported that these Games were possibly the most beautiful ever put on. He noted that flowers and official señoritas in party dresses met visitors at venues and that gardens along highways leading up to the Olympic Village spelled out "XIX Olympiad".[71] Norma Enrique Basilio, a young Mexican female athlete with a penchant for jazz, lit the Olympic flame. When asked how women's roles would change in the modern world, she stressed the prospect of more "independence."[72] All told, the successful staging of the Games proved a triumph for Brundage, who navigated the Czech crisis, the threat of the African boycott (which ended in the IOC revoking its invitation to South Africa on account of that nation's apartheid policies), the African American boycott, and the Mexican student protests with the Olympics intact.[73]

On the basketball court, the U.S. Olympic squad opened with three straight resounding victories against lesser-regarded foes Spain, Senegal, and the Philippines. Of the United States' first three opponents, the Philippines stayed closest, at least for the first ten minutes. Still, the United States won that game with relative ease as well, 96–75, led by Hosket, Spain, and Dee's play on the interior.[74] But the rest of the U.S. pool included Italy and Yugoslavia, both considered possible medal contenders, as well as a strong Puerto Rican team.

In its fourth game the United States faced an undefeated Yugoslavian squad that featured two tall forwards, the most fearsome of which was the six-feet-eleven-inch Kresimir Cosic. Cosic was an early example of Yugoslavia's success, similar to the Soviet Union's, in cultivating multi-skilled big men. Known for his versatility, including "exquisite ballhandling," "thirty-foot lookaway passes," and "fifteen-foot jump hooks," as the *Boston Globe*'s Bob Ryan described it, Cosic played with creative flair. "He was 6-11 and he loved to get out and handle it," recalled Dave Gavitt [the U.S.

national team basketball coach for the boycotted 1980 Games]. In 1996 Cosic, a former Brigham Young University All-American who had died in 1995, was posthumously inducted into the Naismith Memorial Basketball Hall of Fame. By that time, Cosic, who was raised in Croatia and served as that country's ambassador to the United States in the mid-1990s, had won one gold medal and three silvers (one of them as the 1988 Yugoslavia coach), earned first team All-Europe distinction seven times, and garnered credit for legitimizing, as Ryan put it, "European basketball talent in the eyes of the nit-picking Americans." After his career, a slew of tall, versatile players from what was then known as Yugoslavia played in the NBA, including Dino Radja, Toni Kukoc, and Vlade Divac.[75]

In front of a raucous crowd at Mexico City's Sports Palace in 1968, the U.S. and Yugoslav teams went back and forth in the opening minutes. Then, with the score 12–11, the United States registered a 6–0 run, giving them a seven-point advantage. Behind the strong play of JoJo White, who knocked down jump shot after jump shot over the tall Yugoslavians, the Americans played steadily the rest of the half and went into the intermission ahead 36–28. Keeping Yugoslavia at a comfortable distance throughout the second frame, the United States won 73–58. Surprisingly, Haywood was one of the only players to struggle, as he finished with just seven points. But his teammates overcame his uncharacteristically modest numbers in another well-balanced effort.[76]

Upon following up the Yugoslavian victory with two high-scoring blowouts of Panama and Italy, the United States faced Puerto Rico to get to the semifinals—and nearly lost. Puerto Rico, known for its speed and shooting, went ahead in the early going, and though it surrendered the lead before the half, at intermission, only one point separated the two teams. In a close second frame, the United States maintained an edge for a tight 61–56 victory, keeping them undefeated. "The toughest game we had was Puerto Rico . . . most of those guys had played in the United States. They played a more similar style to what we did," Hosket said. If not for a dominating twenty-one-point performance by Haywood and strong play from Silliman, the United States, with more than fifty times the number of people and a thousand times the land mass of Puerto Rico, would likely have lost. But even with the Puerto Rico game, Hosket said, "I never felt like we were going to lose." He just felt so well-prepared. Iba would meet

11. Spencer Haywood goes up for the ball in the United States' tilt with Brazil in Mexico City. Photo by Hulton Archive. Hulton Archive Collection/Getty Images.

with players by position before games, and then he would meet with the whole team. "He would tell you about the guys you were going to play against, what they liked to do. He would break it down into minutiae," Hosket explained.[77]

In front of 23,000 fans the United States won its semifinal tilt 75–63 over Brazil, which came into the contest with a 6-1 record—its only previous loss having come against the Soviets. Powered again by "JoJo" White, touted by the *New York Times* as "the man behind the movement" and for his "cool, disciplined play which embodied the qualities Iba sought," the United States jumped out to a 24–8 lead. Building the early advantage was doubly important, because the crowd seemed eager to adopt Brazil as the sentimental favorite.

In the other semifinal game, Yugoslavia, cheered on by a partisan crowd, scored a shocking 63–62 upset of the Soviets. Yugoslavian head coach Ranko Zeravica characterized the win as "vital for the morale and pride of our players and people." His team used a furious late-game rally for its one-point victory, prompting the *New York Times* to assert that the game "had as much drama as any event of this two-week athletic extravaganza."[78] Yugoslavia's upset meant that for the first time in sixteen years (excluding the 1960 pool-play format), the gold medal game would not feature the United States versus the Soviet Union.

In that gold medal final, Yugoslavia gave the United States moments of uncertainty. Actually, concern arose the night before the game when word surfaced that Spencer Haywood had fallen ill. On game day Iba told reporters he expected Haywood to play, but added, "He is real sick and should be under a doctor's care." An Associated Press report surely echoed the thoughts of many when it asserted that if the sickness notably slowed Haywood, the results would be "disastrous." But Haywood did play, and a sold-out, rollicking crowd of some 25,000 fans were treated to a hard-fought affair.[79]

Against a Yugoslavian squad with big men that Hosket described as "mechanical in nature but they were really powerful," the score swayed back and forth the entire first half. The first frame ended with the United States clinging to a 32–29 lead. Then Coach Iba took his team "somewhere underneath the stands" to implore them to forget about the first twenty minutes and concentrate on the fundamentals. Like Coach Newell in 1960, Iba also decided to increase the pressure in the second half. His team responded with a ferocious 17–0 run to open the second frame. JoJo White and Haywood, who *Sports Illustrated* said was "destined to become a Bill Russell for the next few years," led the onslaught. The *Chicago Tribune* described the action as the "fastest and best by any U.S. team in seven Olympic finals," and the blitz gave the United States a 49–29 advantage, leading to a 92–61 win. After the game, Yugoslavia's Coach Zeravica, sounding rather baffled, said, "The Americans take in their hands, the uhhh, the activities. After that, with our morale coming down, it is difficult to do anything with these Americans." He added, "They have the best defensive team we have ever seen . . . We tried to slow down the game, but they came out in the second half and were too fast for us." The win brought the United States' overall Olympic record in basketball to 74-0 and resulted in its seventh straight gold medal.[80]

In the end, the wealth of America's basketball talent overcame the absence of Kareem Abdul-Jabbar and Elvin Hayes. From those who had predicted defeat, approbation poured in. *Time* gave the team credit for proving its mettle in beating Yugoslavia twice and praised Coach Iba, dubbing him the "grand old man of basketball." *Sports Illustrated*, highlighting Iba's experience, noted that about the time Iba started his career at Oklahoma State, Yugoslavia's Coach Zeravica was being born.[81]

Haywood's fame, in particular, skyrocketed. Haywood's meteoric rise from virtual unknown to international basketball superstar was complete. Pressmen credited him with making people forget about the absence of Alcindor and Hayes. Iba said, "Perhaps we were fortunate they didn't play. Probably it was easier to build team unity with the boys we had. And I think we had as good a team as the United States ever had." Still just nineteen years old, Haywood's potential seemed limitless. Olympic veterans declared that Haywood could turn himself into the "best basketball player in history." Iba declared that Haywood certainly deserved a place among America's all-time Olympic greats and that with experience, Haywood could become "the best basketball player there ever has been."[82]

However, after the Olympics, Haywood's life took some troubling turns. In the years immediately following the Games, things were not so bad. At the University of Detroit he averaged an astounding thirty points and twenty-two rebounds. Then in 1969 he went "hardship" to take care of his mother and nine siblings and was selected in the first round by the ABA's Denver Rockets, who by then were coached by McClendon. In Mexico City, McClendon and Haywood had become friends, and in 1969 Haywood had contacted the Denver Rockets' owners about playing for the Rockets "because Coach McClendon was there" (As noted, NBA rules at that time stipulated that players needed to wait until their class graduated to become NBA eligible, while the ABA allowed a player to sign earlier in "cases of extreme hardship"). During the 1969–70 ABA season, Haywood led the league in scoring and rebounding, and his team finished first in the division even though McClendon got fired during the season after a 9-19 start.[83]

On the outside, things seemed fine. During the summer of 1972, by then a millionaire and a member of the NBA's Seattle Supersonics, Haywood ran a "poverty camp" for roughly one hundred young players too poor to go to a regular basketball camp. While starring on the Supersonics, he also pursued his interest in jazz by hosting a radio program on a station he partly owned and worked towards completing his college degree.[84] But he also experienced the ups and downs of fast living. Haywood's world began to unravel in 1975 when he was shipped from the Supersonics to the New York Knicks for $2 million. In New York, Haywood married a glamorous African supermodel from Somalia named Iman (who later married David Bowie) and bought a fur coat, a home on Park Avenue, a Rolls-Royce, and a few lines of cocaine. Slowly, the vice-grip of the narcotic took hold of his life.

Tiring of Haywood's act, in January 1979 the Knicks traded him to the New Orleans Jazz for the relatively unknown Joe C. Merriweather. Eight months later he was traded again to the Los Angeles Lakers. Jim Murray recalled that at the time, many considered the trade a big break for Haywood. In Los Angeles, so the theory went, he could join a team with rookie sensation Magic Johnson, make a run at a championship, and regain control of his life. Instead, Haywood discovered "the joys of free-basing . . . The baskets stopped dropping. The rebounds went untaken." During the Lakers NBA finals series in 1980, Haywood woke up one morning late for practice, popped some pills, and then fainted during warm-up stretching. He was voted off the team and given no share of the Lakers' playoff money (he would receive half of this share years later).[85]

TABLE 7. 1968 U.S. Men's Olympic Basketball cumulative stats

NAME	G	FGM-FGA	(%)	FTM-FTA	(%)	PF	PTS/AVG
Spencer Haywood	9	64-89	.719	17-38	.447	15	145/16.1
Joseph White	9	46-98	.469	13-16	.813	16	105/11.7
Michael Silliman	9	35-78	.449	11-12	.917	18	81/9.0
Charlie Scott	9	25-49	.510	22-32	.688	20	72/8.0
Bill Hosket	8	31-49	.633	7-16	.438	23	69/8.6
Calvin Fowler	9	26-44	.591	6-10	.600	24	58/6.4
Michael Barrett	9	26-56	.464	4-8	.500	17	56/6.2
Glynn Saulters	8	16-30	.533	10-10	1.000	9	42/5.3
Donald Dee	7	13-33	.394	7-12	.583	13	33/4.7
Ken Spain	8	15-17	.882	5-14	.357	11	35/4.4
John Clawson	8	13-25	.520	3-4	.750	9	29/3.6
James King	8	5-10	.500	4-6	.667	20	14/1.8
USA TOTALS	9	315-578	.545	109-178	.612	195	739/82.1
OPP. TOTALS	9	200-513	.390	105-158	.665	240	505/56.1

From there, Haywood bounced to a team in Europe and underwent a difficult divorce before overcoming his toughest foe, drugs. His turnaround occurred one night when, as he sat parked in his Rolls Royce overlooking the Detroit River contemplating suicide, he determined instead to cast away the drugs. From that point he turned himself into a "man on a mission." With much of his own money, he started the Haywood Foundation to deter kids from meandering down the wrong path and to encourage prisoners to overcome drug addiction. Business endeavors helped him pay for his causes. In 1990 Haywood told Murray, "You have to help people; it's part of your own recovery. If you can live with others' suffering, you're not a whole man yourself."[86] In 1992 he penned an illuminating autobiography with Scott Ostler called *Spencer Haywood: The Rise, The Fall, The Recovery.*

Haywood's personal woes have not diminished the effects of his and his teammates' Mexico City performance on the international game. The impact was clear, judging by the Soviet Union's reaction. In the wake of the loss, Communist Party chief Leonid Brezhnev stated the orders for the newly named head of the Committee for Physical Culture and Sports,

Sergei Pavlov, matter-of-factly: "International standards for our sports must be improved." The Soviet trade-union paper *Trud* expressed exasperation, writing that the Soviet basketball players were "giants" and their "coaches had everything," but the team played too many "passionless games." The *Trud* attributed the lackadaisical performance to the "easy life."[87]

As had happened before, the versatility, and especially the speed and athleticism, demonstrated by the U.S. squad counted as the key difference between it and the other top contenders. As a result, the Soviets redoubled their efforts to develop versatile, agile big men and quick, deft guards who could shoot.

By continually pushing the game toward faster and more skilled play, the U.S. Olympic team remained a key contributor to an international basketball style that was attracting legions of fans within a universalistic sports community of increasingly global reach that featured competition, commercialism, and individuality. Even the absence of the college game's biggest stars at the Mexico City Olympics could not stop that.

8

MAYHEM IN MUNICH

The Munich Games opened on August 26, 1972, with 7,000 athletes representing a record 121 nations. Eighty thousand spectators packed into West Germany's Olympic stadium for the Opening Ceremonies, and an estimated 800 million more watched the proceedings on television. Thousands of additional spectators, rather fittingly, sat upon a mountain of rubble created by the bombs of World War II to peer over the stadium walls and view the action.[1] The festival highlighted the changed economic and political landscape that emerged after World War II, the technological advances that had occurred, and how sports had become so ubiquitous internationally—celebrated by the poor and rich, common and elite. In fact, the stadium itself, designed by Günter Behnisch and Frei Otto, stood as a symbol of democracy and opportunity to its creators, in contrast to the 1936 Olympic Stadium. Meanwhile, as *Time* reported, among the throngs drawn to "Munich's gala atmosphere" was "an older, more pecunious group: the international set, complete with titled leaders . . . Prince Philip, Princess Margaret and their highnesses, Rainier and Grace."[2]

According to the *New York Times*'s Red Smith, the Opening Ceremonies were free, at least outwardly, of political, racial, and social undertones. This, Smith believed, could serve to "heal some of the wounds of the past— slurring the memory of the 1936 Olympics in Berlin, which Adolf Hitler's propagandists turned into a Nazi carnival."[3] But his sentiments proved a little optimistic. While the Munich Games did indeed go a long way toward healing past wounds, they would be most remembered for opening new ones, on and off the playing field. For in Munich, the United States versus Soviet Union basketball final ended in the most controversial fashion of any major basketball championship in history. And much worse, midway through the Games, terror wracked the Olympic Village as Palestinian gunmen killed a total of eleven Israeli athletes and trainers, striking a blow to the Olympics' image of international brotherhood. Nonetheless, the Olympic movement, as it had after Berlin, remained intact.

Enabling the hundreds of millions to watch Munich's opening were important milestones reached by the satellite industry just a few years earlier. In 1970, Hughes Space and Communications Company (HSCC), started by the American Howard Hughes, moved forward with plans to operate a domestic satellite system with the intent of sending programs to local cable television operators. Earlier, the HSCC had helped create the Syncom satellite series, and for the next thirty years the company helped lead the way in satellite technology.[4] Rather quickly, innovation and capital investment by companies like HSCC, complemented by liberal FCC guidelines promoting competition, gave the United States an edge in the burgeoning international satellite technology.

The United States' lead in telecommunications was evident with ABC's coverage of the 1972 Olympics, which pushed technological standards and the total number of Olympic viewers to new heights. To capitalize on the burgeoning relationship between sports and television, ABC had paid $12.5 million for broadcast rights in Munich.[5] Armed with new, innovative equipment, ABC technicians condensed two weeks and over 1,200 hours of action into three hours of primetime that aired each weeknight, with even more coverage on the weekends. By renting time from a Communications Satellite Corporation (COMSAT) satellite, the network delivered much of that action live and in color to American living rooms. Roone Arledge, president of ABC Sports, continued his groundbreaking broadcasting techniques, including an emphasis on the individual athlete to give the audience a rooting interest.[6] It was not an easy task to deliver the kind of programming Arledge wanted. Leading up to Munich, ABC executives traveled to Germany over twenty times to negotiate with German officials about the style of broadcast they intended to deliver. ABC vice president Chuck Howard explained, "My biggest problem was insisting that ABC bring its own cameras. The Germans fought this concept in the beginning, but relented. Our argument is that we wanted to 'Americanize' our coverage—dwell more on individuals if the situation requires it."[7] This emphasis on the individual turned not only into an Olympic trend but a television trend—one that complements a core liberal value, individualism.

America's lead in telecommunications would prove especially important in subsequent years. China reflects this. In 1971 it reached out to the United States through "table tennis diplomacy," setting the stage for "the opening of long-severed diplomatic relations between the two countries."[8] President Richard Nixon reportedly celebrated the breakthrough with a bottle of Courvoisier, while Henry Kissinger told the president, "This is the most important communication that has come to an American president since the end of World War II." According to the historian James Mann, Kissinger later added to that already profound assessment by saying, "The American opening to China was the country's greatest watershed since the Civil War."[9] Within a couple of decades, China's economy had liberalized and grown, while its involvement in the Olympics had increased and basketball's popularity had skyrocketed. In turn, as Brook Larmer wrote in 2005 in the journal *Foreign Policy*:

> The foreigners who began trickling into China in the 1990s carried different symbols of their faith: the Nike swoosh, the NBA logo, highlight films of a miracle man named Michael Jordan—all played to the hip-hop soundtrack of global youth culture . . . Hoping to crack the last great untapped market on Earth, the new evangelists peddled a vision of sports entertainment, a pleasurable commodity that channeled the values of freedom, competition, and individual heroism.[10]

Of course, important differences between China and the United States exist politically. Few doubt, however, that U.S. culture, at least, has resonated powerfully in China, and telecommunications have played an important role in this.

Adding to the dynamic telecommunications industry, in the late 1960s cable television had emerged as well. Noteworthy growth occurred a short time later when, in 1970, the FCC passed liberal guidelines for the industry, enabling cable to become a "major competitor of the existing over-the-air broadcasting system." By 1971 2,800 cable systems served some 30 million American homes.[11] Further marketplace competitiveness led to capital investment: more cable lines were laid and innovations ensued, helping turn the United States into the world leader in cable television as well as satellite. This proved a boon to basketball.

As American capital and innovation positioned the country to lead the technological age, basketball also continued to grow. By the early 1970s basketball stars like Jerry West, Julius Erving, Clyde Frazier, and Spencer Haywood were household names, endorsing a wide range of products from cars to toothpaste. The influence of basketball stars on the market was particularly evident by a surge in the popularity of the basketball shoe. In the early 1970s Walt Frazier, nicknamed "Clyde" because his fine clothing reminded a New York Knicks trainer of Warren Beatty's portrayal of Clyde Barrow in *Bonnie and Clyde*, helped spawn a shoe craze by popularizing the Puma Suedes that he sported during Knicks games. Frazier also endorsed the suede Pumas in ads that read, "Straight-up cool." By associating with Clyde Frazier, Puma was also allying with popular culture, because at the time, Frazier was considered the American embodiment of hipness.[12] The Puma "Clydes" demonstrated that basketball shoes were taking on a greater prominence and that African Americans were overcoming barriers in commercial endorsements while lending an increasingly hip element to basketball and its attendant culture.

Frazier's popularity became comical. In September 1972 he was invited to appear at a *women's* shoe store called The Grand Stand that specialized in platform dress shoes as high as six inches. Describing the scene, the *New York Times* reporter Angela Taylor wrote, "The Grand Stand was mobbed, mostly with autograph hunters who nearly ripped Mr. Frazier's clothes off until somebody thought to barricade him behind the rail of bleachers." A year earlier, *Time* ran an article on the expressionism and the visibility of athletes in which it pointed out that Frazier's salary was over $100,000 salary when combining his Knicks pay, endorsements, business interests, and speaking engagements; the magazine noted his penchant for squiring his girlfriend "around the discotheque circuit in his 'Clydemobile' . . . a far cry from the Ford Pinto he pushes in TV commercials." The sporting world, *Time* concluded, now harkened back to "the Hollywood of yesterday."[13]

Endorsement deals such as Frazier's were not possible for collegiate and Olympic amateurs, but this does not mean that amateur basketball in the 1970s did not have cultural resonance. In fact, it seems that collegiate stars carried comparable, if not more, influence than the pros. It was during the second half of the 1970s that the NCAA basketball tournament became a "major television spectacle."[14] Consequently, companies became intensely interested in outfitting amateurs in their products, whether they were playing for their college or at the Olympics.

With the college game thriving and top-level AAU weaker, eleven of the twelve 1972 Olympic basketball players came from the NCAA. This domination of the amateur talent had helped the NCAA change the format of the Olympic Trials. Rather than taking place in late March or early April, the 1972 trials were slated for mid-June in Colorado Springs, mainly so attendees did not have to miss classes, but also to give the committee time to determine which collegiate stars planned to attend. All told, sixty-six players from the NCAA, NAIA, AAU, junior colleges, and U.S. Armed Forces received invitations to the trials. Each group had a quota, and the NCAA's twenty-eight player allotment was far and away the largest. Ultimately, fifty-nine of the invitees convened on the United States Air Force Academy campus, 7,200 feet above sea level. There the players were assessed by members of the Olympic basketball committee and most importantly by Hank Iba, who, despite a mandated retirement from Oklahoma State in March of 1970, had been named head coach of the Olympic team once again.[15]

The number of collegians that chose to turn down invitations to the trials was high again in 1972, partly because of time-commitment issues, but mainly as a result of professional teams angling to sign players, especially ABA teams, which commonly signed underclassmen. The NBA and ABA still did not have an agreement in place with the Basketball Federation of the United States of America (BFUSA) enabling them to sign a player without forcing him to sacrifice his amateur status. Consequently, this forced players to choose between professionalism and the Olympics, even though their first professional game would not take place until after the

Summer Games. This contributed to the Olympic committee's struggle to determine which twenty-eight players to invite. Iba came away from the whole process quite discouraged. In March of 1972, he told the *Washington Post*, "If the pros sign all the boys we'd like, and they seem determined to do so, we are going to have to scramble to keep competitive." Continuing, he said, "We can't survive in this situation. We're a little bit chesty as to our participation in the Olympics."[16]

Part of Iba's pessimism also stemmed from the depletion of the AAU's stables. By 1972 Goodyear and Phillips did not sponsor teams in what was then the NIBL, and the NABL had just six teams. This meant that the United States did not have many older players with international experience to choose from.

By the spring of 1972 it was clear that the United States would be without many of its top amateurs in Munich. Virtually all of the NCAA's brightest stars, including Bob McAdoo, David Thompson, George McGinnis, Len Elmore, Julius Erving, and Bill Walton, chose not to play in the Games. As Lew Alcindor had been four years earlier, the UCLA center Bill Walton was the biggest loss. His announcement not to play came after the 1972 season, when Walton's doctor, Robert Kerlan, diagnosed the six-feet-ten-inch star with severe tendonitis in both knees, recommending rest until the fall. Some pundits were not surprised to hear that Walton would not play and suggested that other factors had contributed to his decision, as he was known to oppose the Vietnam War. In reporting Walton's absence, a writer for the *Washington Post* noted that in the spring of 1972 Walton had elicited a fifty-dollar fine, plus one year's probation, for participating in an antiwar demonstration.[17]

Few if any reporters in 1972, however, drew a connection between Walton's previous experience with U.S. basketball, as a member of the national AAU U.S. Armed Forces team that played in the World Championships in Yugoslavia, and his decision not to play in Munich, but Walton did so himself in a 1994 autobiography. For those World Championships, a few years before the Munich Games, twenty-five players agreed to try out. As a seventeen-year-old, Walton, who stood six feet ten and a half and weighed 190 pounds, was the only attendee not in the army. A coach that Walton refused to name, but whom he characterized as "the most abusive man I had ever met in my life," ran the try-out camp. Apparently, among this coach's more egregious acts was a penchant for telling players that if they did not play well enough to make the team, "I'm going to personally sign your orders for combat duty in Vietnam." According to Walton, those who did not make it did indeed end up in Vietnam.[18]

That experience apparently affected Walton's response to overtures from the U.S. Olympic Basketball Committee to play on the 1972 team. Walton said he told "The Suits" that he did not intend to drop out of UCLA at any point or go through any "boot-camp tryout session . . . If they wanted me to live in Army barracks, sleep in tiny beds, eat at mess halls and play in a bunch of meaningless exhibition games, I wasn't interested." Ultimately, the committee and Walton could not agree on a plan.[19]

Given the 1972 U.S. Olympic team's struggles on the interior, many were drawn to speculate, following the Munich Games, that had Walton been on the team, things might have turned out differently. For his part, Walton said in his 1994 autobiography, "I wish I had been on that team." He disagreed, however, with those who blamed him for the U.S. team's eventual loss. It "wasn't my doing. I merely became a postdefeat whipping boy, one in a long line of excuses provided by people who ran what was then called the U.S. Olympic Basketball Committee," he asserted. Walton did say that FIBA erred in putting seconds back on the clock in the controversial gold medal game's closing seconds (which we will get to), but he also believes that "the suits" share part of the blame.[20]

Along with Walton, the loss of McGinnis and Erving certainly hurt, too. They were signed by the ABA before exhausting their NCAA eligibility. For well over a decade, the NBA had complied with a "verbal understanding" with the Olympic basketball committee in which the league agreed not to sign players before the Games ended. That changed when the ABA became stronger and began to compete with the NBA for players.[21] By 1972 the ABA was four years old and changing the sport in a number of ways. Julius Erving epitomized this. Known as "Dr. J," he became the signature player of the freewheeling league, winning the ABA's MVP award three times by 1975.[22] As noted, the ABA's contributions to basketball enhanced the sport's popularity, but for the 1972 Olympic team, the most notable sign of the ABA's presence was its poaching of potential Olympians. The ABA even managed to take one potential Olympian—Jim Chones, the starting center on an undefeated, top-ranked Marquette team coached by

Al McGuire—*during* the 1971–72 college season. Chones left school with six games remaining in the season to sign a professional contract with the New York Nets.[23] To make matters worse for Iba at the trials, USC's Paul Westphal was injured.

Not surprisingly, this left Iba concerned. "If the people of the United States knew the depth of impact of Olympic competition on other countries, they would see [to it] that we had the best performers possible," he warned the public a month after Chones had signed with the ABA. Later, in June of 1972, he reminded Americans, "We'll be playing against some players who were in the 1964 Olympics. We've sent coaches over there, we've sent players, we've done all we can to help them. Those other countries are hungry and we better realize our task won't be easy."[24]

As in 1968, Iba did not worry alone, especially because, in addition to the U.S. team's missing out on top talent, in the years leading up to Munich, reports of improved levels of international play surfaced with more regularity. First, in 1970 at the World Championships in Ljubljana, Yugoslavia, the United States placed a disappointing fifth. Sure, the U.S. world championship team was less talented than the expected U.S. Olympic roster, but even with a less talented roster, Americans did not expect their team to finish fifth in international play. It seemed that the years of sending coaches abroad, the diffusion of the game, and the influence of American players throughout the world had increased the quality of play.

It was not just the influence of American collegiate tours or national team exchanges that helped diffuse basketball. By the early 1970s, an increasing number of Americans were playing professionally in Europe. Beginning in the mid-1960s, industrial teams and sports clubs in countries like Italy, France, Belgium, and Spain had sponsors that were "anxious to upgrade the sloppy play and win new friends and publicity for their teams." As a result, they had increasingly recruited "U.S. college stars" with offers reaching up to $30,000 for six months of play. Perhaps the earliest example of this occurred in 1962 when Spain's Real Madrid club recruited the six-feet-eight-inch Wayne Hightower out of Kansas, who left the Jayhawks a year before becoming NBA eligible, played one productive season in Europe, and then returned for a long professional career in the United States in the NBA and ABA.[25] In 1969 *Time* estimated that one hundred American professionals played in Europe and reported that, though some may have found the style a bit slower than and not quite as slick as that in America, "the affection of the European fans makes up for the shortcomings on the court." Sometimes that affection could get out of hand, like the time in 1966 that souvenir-mad Italian fans apparently rushed onto the court after a championship game and "stripped an American player right out of his shoes, socks, shirt and shorts."[26]

In the spring of 1971 further indications of an improved international standard emerged when an Olympic developmental team, made up largely of collegians, went to Russia, Poland, and Finland. Penn State's Johnny Bach served as an assistant coach on the trip, as he would a year later for the U.S. Olympic team in Munich. He came back from Russia worried about the United States' chances in the upcoming Games. "Their [the Soviets'] jump shooting, passing, the crispness of what they do is amazing—and alarming. Their defense is especially admirable, aggressive with great individual responsibility," he told the *Washington Post*. Bach recalled that during one pregame warm-up, the Soviet team watched quietly as the U.S. all-stars put on a dunking display, led by Maryland freshman Tom McMillen, who ended up playing on the 1972 Olympic team. Unfazed, the Soviet team then proceeded to "do the same thing, and as well, with all the twisting back-to-the-basket frills." According to the *Washington Post*, the episode demonstrated how the Russians, like the Japanese, have "copied our styles of purity—from films, clinics and our best players from past Olympics—Jerry West, Jerry Lucas, and Bill Bradley."[27] The Soviet team admitted as much, as did others, such as Yugoslavia, which borrowed U.S. tactics throughout the 1960s and onward and employed them at the Munich Games, and which helped Yugoslavia perform splendidly in Montreal in 1976.

Bach also pointed out how physical the international game was, since, in his words, you could "foul for profit." Bach was referring to the international rule which stipulated that on all nonshooting fouls before the last five minutes, the ball had to be taken out of bounds, which thus led to rougher play. By contrast, in the United States, teams were allowed to work their way into the bonus, receiving free-throw opportunities after a certain number of fouls each half.[28]

Soon after Bach's Soviet tour, the United States encountered another setback on the international stage. This time they were upset by Brazil at the Pan-Am Games. Featuring USC's Paul Westphal and Bob McAdoo, the United States finished the tournament with a 2-1 record but failed to advance out of its pool as a result of a bizarre tiebreaker. This would mark the first time the United States did not win the Pan-Am Games.

Finally, there was another, more nuanced problem that some thought adversely affected the United States' chances in Munich: Coach Iba. Nearly sixty-eight years old by the time of the trials, he came to them out of touch with a new generation. As the historian Chris Elzey put it, "The Iba style and philosophy did not exactly jibe with the free spirit of the early 1970s college generation." While most respected Iba for his long career and record number of wins, by 1972, his autocratic tendencies, aversion to high-scorers, reluctance to switch on defense, and lack of appreciation for the fast break raised concerns. Many considered him an anachronism. For instance, the *Washington Post*'s Neil Attner astutely observed, "His court strategy contradicts the playground-style atmosphere of international basketball."[29] Ironically, FIBA had borrowed that international "playground style," presumably meaning higher scoring, from the United States, but now, with Iba at the helm, it looked like the United States was abandoning its trademark speed game. Yet Iba's successes in past Olympics enabled him to wield considerable influence in 1972, pushing to the fringes dissent from members of the basketball committee that could have worked to balance his tendencies. For example, as reported by the *Washington Post*, the U.S. Olympic Basketball Committee, undoubtedly influenced by Iba, chose not even to invite the NCAA's number one and number two scorers, Dwight Lamar and Richard Fuqua, to the trials, "because of their attitudes."[30]

In addition to noting Iba's distaste for scorers and other stylistic concerns, critics argued that Iba's autocratic ways reflected a coach out of touch socially with the current generation, with his curfew and aversion to players meandering off campus. As another example of this, Attner noted that part of Iba's selection methods included scrutinizing player behavior in the dorms and the locker room. Iba liked to have "good" trainers who reported back on player behavior, and he watched etiquette at the dinner table. "You can't believe the petty things these people are worried about. They almost kicked one guy off the Pan-American team for not standing right during the National Anthem. This is all work, no fun for them," an unnamed coach at the trials told Attner.

Attner maintained that Iba remained aloof during the trials. He apparently sat high in the stands "surrounded by assistants and reporters, lecturing, telling stories, forgetting names, [and] recalling past triumphs" as he evaluated the new players. "He rarely talks to the players," Attner criticized. These conditions did seem to take a toll on the players. One anonymously told Attner, "I guess it's a privilege to be here. But I don't know if I'd come back again."[31] Six players left the first week. Trying to defend Iba's methods, another coach said that Iba merely wanted to avoid another scenario like the one at the Pan-Am Games, when "Some players came in with 'I'm a star, don't touch me' attitude. There were discipline problems and a lot of friction." It was partly the loss at the Pan-Am Games and the perceived attitude of the Pan-Am players that motivated Iba to give players personality tests before their Olympic workouts began. "I'll take a player who has the right attitude and incentive over a more talented athlete," he explained. There were, of course, plenty of folks who admired Iba's tactics, just like former Olympians Larry Brown and Bill Hosket do.[32]

Although opinions about the effectiveness of Iba's tactics varied, one thing most could agree on was that the emergence of another superstar at the trials, akin to Haywood's emergence in Albuquerque four years earlier, could have allayed the various issues hurting U.S. chances in Munich. But early returns were not promising. "So far no Haywood has emerged, and the non-college players have been mostly unimpressive," Attner reported. Doug Collins, a lengthy, sharpshooting guard from Southern Illinois, did impress, especially when he scored thirty points in one game, but not as resoundingly as had Haywood. At the center position Swen Nater, UCLA's backup to Bill Walton, earned distinction en route to leading all scorers in Colorado Springs. But still, no superstar emerged.[33] This was particularly apparent in the frontcourt, as evidenced by the analysis of Phoenix Suns guard Clem Haskins, who said, after playing the Olympians in an exhibition game, "There just doesn't seem to be anyone there to take charge . . . They need a big guy to take charge."[34]

Many observers thought Maryland's Tom McMillen, who had been one of the most recruited high school basketball players and who would later become a member of the U.S. Congress, would make it at center. Before selection day, Attner claimed that McMillen was virtually assured of a spot on the team because he was one of Iba's favorites. "You couldn't ask for a better attitude than the one McMillen has. He's always hustling, and he's a perfect gentleman. And can he ever shoot," Iba had said during the trials. McMillen averaged 15.1 points and shot 53 percent from the floor, but he got cut in Colorado.

Another big fellow, Kermit Washington, came on strong late, which gave him an outside chance of making the squad. However, it was possible that statements he had made during the trials to a reporter from a home-town Washington DC paper about the difficult conditions Iba instituted in Colorado would hurt his chances. The article in question was headlined "Kermit Washington: I Pity the Guys Who Make the Team." This was not exactly the kind of sentiment Iba was looking for. It does seem that Kermit's comments cost him, because he did not even make the alternate list.[35]

As for the rest of the selections, many spots were undetermined until the final hours. Approximately twenty-one members of the U.S. basketball committee had met every night after the previous four sessions, using a com-plicated statistical system to rate the players. One might assume the final Saturday night meeting served mainly to summarize previous sentiments, but a basketball official told Attner, "The intrigue has yet to come to a head at the daily meetings. They're saving the best for last. That's why the final meeting usually lasts to the wee hours." Commenting on the difficulties of filling out the roster, another unnamed coach said, "Once you get beyond the first six, politics start to enter the picture. It's hard to say what they'll end up with after the bargaining is done." According to Attner, "Politics, racial considerations and international basketball experience will influence player selections from a talent pool already weaker than in past Olympic years."[36]

Ultimately, among the final selections were Big Ten Player of the Year Jim Brewer of Minnesota and Mike Bantom of St. Joseph's, both of whom could play at the center or power forward position; the guard Ed Ratleff of Long Beach State; Ken Davis of Marathon Oil, the only AAU player to make the roster; Kevin Joyce of South Carolina; and Doug Collins of Illi-nois State, the nation's third-leading scorer with an average of more than thirty-two points per game. All of those selections were expected.

Players who had not been not considered certainties going into the trials but made the team nonetheless included centers Swen Nater of UCLA and Dwight Jones of Houston, and forward Bobby Jones of North Carolina. Two lesser-known players selected were Missouri's six-feet-seven-inch John Brown, an All-Big Eight performer but not a household name, and the even less-heralded Tom Henderson of San Jacinto Texas Junior College. Henderson was one of Iba's special selections. "Not many have heard about Henderson. At six feet two inches, he can rebound with the big boys. He can shoot and he can handle a strong, small forward on another team real well," Iba explained.[37] During the Olympic tournament, the *New York Times*'s Neil Amdur described Henderson as "an obscure junior college guard, and one of those brilliant products of New York's countless playgrounds." Iba told Amdur that he chose Henderson because he "had the type of leadership and type of enthusiasm and pride we needed on our team."[38] In Munich, Henderson led the team in scoring, along with Dwight Jones, proving yet again Iba's penchant for using his special selections wisely. Another surprise selection was the seven-feet-four-inch sophomore center Tom Burleson from North Carolina State, whom Iba called "half mean."[39]

The 1972 team was the youngest in U.S. Olympic history, but also the tallest, with an average height of six feet seven inches. North Carolina State's Burleson stood tallest (though he was considered a bit frail), while Davis, at six feet one inch, was the shortest. With Collins and Ratleff as backcourt options, Iba could put two six-feet-six-inch guards on the court. Still, he wanted an even bigger team. Noting that international rules allowed for more body contact, he told the *Chicago Tribune*, "We just aren't big enough and strong enough to outmuscle any of our opponents in Munich." Nonetheless, the 1972 team, even without a superstar, was talented. Ten of the team's twelve players were selected in the first round of the NBA draft.[40]

A noteworthy snub on the final Olympic roster, considering his solid play at the trials, was McMillen. Though he had taken a liking to McMillen, Iba pressed for the more versatile Bobby Jones of North Carolina. It was a surprise, given Iba's preference for center-dominated play, and that McMillen was considered an "establishment player," a reputation he had solidified at the trials when, rather than join the chorus of players complaining about the conditions, he chose to read a book on positive thinking. But "the committee picked according to the type of player Iba wanted and McMillen somehow never fit in," an official at the meetings divulged afterward.[41] In the end, the strong play of Nater had hurt McMillen's chances the most. With Burleson and Brewer virtual locks, taking four centers was a difficult proposition, and the committee decided Nater had beaten out McMillen for the third center spot.

Born in Holland, Nater came to the United States at the age of nine under uncommon circumstances. His mother left for America after a divorce but left Swen and his sister behind at an orphanage because of money problems. He was not reunited with his family until six years later, in a surprise reunion on the television show *It Could Be You*.[42] Though he had spent the past two years at UCLA in relative obscurity backing up Bill Walton, scouts were aware of him by the time of the trials. Both the NBA's Portland Trail Blazers and the ABA's Floridians had thought highly enough of his potential to draft him after the 1971–72 collegiate season, even though he still had one year of eligibility remaining. Professional teams loved Nater's ability to shoot and knew that at any other school besides UCLA the six-feet-eleven-inch center would have played regularly.

Initially, Nater stated his satisfaction with making the team. "It's an honor to do something for my country after all it has done for me," he told reporters. But his attitude soon changed. When the team arrived in Hawaii for training camp, problems arose right away. "The first day I was there I started to wonder about the whole situation. I tried to stick it out. Maybe I'd get used to it. Instead, I got weaker and weaker. I couldn't rebound. I couldn't do anything," Nater explained later. He claimed his problem stemmed from Iba's stubborn refusal to let him eat at any time other than a half-hour after workouts. "We'd practice from about three to five o'clock, and we'd have to eat by five-thirty. We were eating in the mess hall with the sailors. The same thing at lunch. We'd practice from ten to twelve and have to eat by twelve-thirty." Apparently, Nater simply could not force himself to eat so quickly after practice; as a result, he lost fifteen to twenty pounds in five days, and so he quit the team. Although Nater's departure might sound rash, it should be noted that Iba did run a tightly regimented camp. "No one saw the beach or took a swim. It was almost warlike the way they worked," Bach said of the team's stay in Hawaii.[43]

Nater said he did not want to quit, but when he broached the subject with Iba, asking for permission to eat at a later time, Iba refused. Nater stressed to reporters that his weight loss provided the impetus for his departure, but he mentioned that the conditions in Hawaii were subpar, citing dirty bathrooms and roaches on the barracks floor. With no sense of irony, Nater said of the accommodations, which thousands of sailors had endured over many years, "I would have overlooked the conditions.

But they shouldn't be. After all, we were the U.S. Olympic team."[44] Nater remains the only person to quit the U.S. Olympic basketball team in this fashion. At the same time, he also remains highly respected by UCLA folks like John Wooden and Bill Walton.

Nater's departure opened a spot for McMillen, who took his place in Hawaii and finished camp without incident.[45] Missouri's Brown, however, did not. Near the end of workouts, he reaggravated on old foot injury; this eventually led to surgery, causing him to miss the Olympics. He was replaced by the six-feet-eight-inch forward James Forbes of the University of Texas El-Paso.[46] Although he was the last man to join the team, Forbes averaged 5.1 points per game in Munich and would end up playing a pivotal role during the controversial final seconds of the gold medal game.

With the team finally intact, the group prepared for a five-game, nationally televised series of exhibitions against professionals. In the first game in Dayton, Ohio, the U.S. Olympic team displayed stellar defense en route to beating a collection of NBA professionals led by Oscar Robertson and Spencer Haywood, 65–52. Houston's Dwight Jones led the U.S. squad with eighteen points. In its fourth exhibition tilt, the U.S. team met a group of ABA players led by Julius Erving at the home of the Carolina Cougars, who were coached by former Olympian Larry Brown. Iba's men stayed unbeaten with an 82–76 overtime win against Brown and Erving, thanks to thirty-two points by Doug Collins, eighteen by Long Beach State's Ratleff, and crucial overtime blocks and baskets by Jones. On the whole, the team was pleasantly surprised with its exhibition play, but concerns still emerged. "They didn't have too much trouble with us. But they're going to have trouble with Russia. This isn't the same team we had in '68, that's for sure," the Cleveland Cavaliers guard Butch Beard told the media.[47]

In Munich, the team opened its defense of the gold medal against Czechoslovakia, taking the floor to loud cheers. With fierce defense at the forefront, it won with relative ease, 66–35.[48] Iba's no-switching, man-to-man defense allowed a meager three baskets in the entire first half. On offense, Iba's special selection, Tom Henderson, led the way with sixteen points, complemented by Dwight Jones's fifteen. Afterward, Jones told reporters he was motivated by a newspaper article in West Germany that suggested the IOC kick the United States out of the Olympics, particularly out of basketball. When Jones mentioned the article, a West German media man attempted to explain it by saying, "We in this country get tired of the U.S. basketball team winning all the time. It gets boring to us."[49]

Though encouraged by the performance, in his postgame comments Iba cautiously stated, "We still don't know if we can be competitive for forty minutes . . . To beat teams like Cuba and Brazil, you've got to be competitive all the time."[50] Others also had reservations about the win, and questions arose about the United States' offensive firepower. In the previous few Olympiads the United States had usually posted large scores in its lopsided wins. But against the Czechs, the U.S. team did not score even seventy points. Basketball aficionados knew that Czechoslovakia had presented only a nominal challenge and that the United States was in a tough bracket, with stiffer opening week games against Cuba and Brazil awaiting them.

Backstories informed the contests between both Cuba and Brazil. The team for Cuba, a nation long considered a cold war adversary of the United States, was not only considered a gold-medal threat in Munich but had also made it to the medal round at the Pan-Am Games ahead of the United States based on a points-per-game tiebreaker. And the Brazil game gave the United States, especially Dwight Jones, who had played on that Pan-Am team, a chance to avenge its loss a year earlier. A packed crowd of 6,000 rowdy fans attended the matchup against Cuba, which had won its opener over Egypt 105–64. Inspired to right the Pan-Am debacle, D. Jones treated the crowd to a stellar offensive performance in leading the United States to a 67–48 victory. The United States' vaunted defense starred again as well, using a number of different schemes in the first half to hold the fast-break-ing Cubans to just twenty-one points.[51]

With Brazil up next, Iba and company had little time to enjoy their win. Before the game, Coach Iba had intimated that it could mark the first U.S. loss in Olympic basketball history. In the first half of the bruising affair, which the *Chicago Tribune* characterized as a "rough game that did little for the Good Neighbor Policy," both sides struggled to score, making it look like it might end in a U.S. defeat. The opening frame ended with a tie of twenty-six apiece; after intermission, the Brazilians opened up a 43–36 lead. Later, the Brazilian coach Togo Soares said, "When we were seven ahead, I thought we would win." But Henderson, who led the United States with twelve points, made two key jump shots to start a rally, and down the stretch Doug Collins, Ed Ratleff, and Jim Brewer provided the United States with crucial plays that helped propel the team to a 61–54 win. However, once again, the game highlighted the U.S. team's lack of frontcourt dominance and its struggles to score points. "There were times tonight when I was really thinking that this might be the one," Iba admitted.[52]

Following the hard-fought win, the United States faced yet another formidable foe in Spain. In a tightly contested game, the Americans won by a misleading margin, 72–56. Still, the win gave the United States a 6-0 record and kept its winning streak intact. The team followed the Spain game with a 99–33 win over Japan.[53]

Keeping pace, the Soviets also entered the semifinal round with a 7-0 record, but just barely. In their final preliminary round game they escaped a rollicking matchup with Puerto Rico, a team that had utilized a high-scoring, fast-breaking style to win its first four games in crowd-pleasing fashion and had quickly turned into the tournament's Cinderella story. That players culled from a population of only three million people could compete with such giants as the Soviet Union and the United States seemed improbable. The Puerto Rican team's ability to do just that made them the "darlings" of the Games. Their game against the Soviets was a wild, offensive battle that saw the teams score 187 points combined. In the end, Alexander Belov's thirty-seven points helped save the Soviets from defeat as they beat Puerto Rico 100–87.[54] Still, Puerto Rico's popularity with fans in Munich's modern *Basketballhalle* epitomized the allure of fast-paced basketball.

As for the Soviet team, by 1972 it had a bevy of more versatile big men. The twenty-one-year-old, six-feet-eight-inch Alexander Belov in particular epitomized the tall, multidimensional player that began to dot the Soviet roster after the team's introduction to Bill Russell in Melbourne. "Now there must be more speed and better endurance," Soviet assistant coach Sergey Bashkin explained. "We are trying to do more American style. We have translated the books of your Red Auerbach and your Adolf Rupp, and they tell us much. We are sorry we have no book of your coach Iba." Gennardi Volnov, Modestas Paulauskas, and the six-feet-three-inch Sergei Belov, were three of the Soviet Union's other leading players. Sergei Belov, no relation to Alexander, was considered the "Jerry West of Russia" and was arguably the team's best player, while Bashkin has noted that on a tour of the United States, Paulauskas was enticed by several professional coaches with big-money offers to defect.[55] Even so, Alexander Belov represented the crown jewel of the Soviet crop. Some already considered him the team's best player, and he had loads of potential as well. Before the Munich Games, the Yugoslavian team members said Alexander Belov was the best player to ever oppose them.[56]

However, the basketball drama created by the prospect of another meeting of these two cold war foes, each of whom shared records of 7-0 and needed only one more win to make it to the gold medal showdown, was eclipsed by the terrorist attack carried out by Palestinians at the Olympic Village, an event that rocked the world. Looking to strike a dramatic blow for their cause, the terrorists strategically chose the Olympics as a target, and the world stood stunned that such a bold, murderous attack could take place at the Games. The terrorists' plan entailed taking Israeli Olympic athletes and personnel hostage, then demanding the release of jailed comrades in exchange. Those plans ended in tragic fashion. All told, eleven Israeli athletes were killed, as well as five of the eight kidnappers and a German police officer. The attack is considered a watershed moment in the Israeli-Palestinian conflict as well as in the larger clash between liberalism and radical Islam.

After the initial shock, the question became whether or not the Olympics should go on. Directly following the assault Israeli prime minister Golda Meir denounced the "lunatic acts" and asserted that it was inconceivable that the Games could continue while "our citizens are under threat of being murdered in the Olympic Village."[57] However, Avery Brundage, apparently speaking for his fellow colleagues at the IOC, declared: "The Games must go on."[58] They were postponed for a day and then they did.

When they resumed, a tough Italian squad boasting a 5-2 record met the United States on the hardwood. Italy had emerged from a formidable bracket that included the Soviets and Yugoslavia, which gave the team confidence. Before the opening tip, Italian coach Primo Giancarlo asserted that his team enjoyed a "definite advantage" over the United States for having come out of the tougher pool. He also claimed that his team was prepared, especially for Mike Bantom, because he had coached an Italian team during the previous basketball season that toured the United States and had encountered Bantom and his Saint Joseph's team. "I know all about Mike Bantom," he declared.[59] But the Italians were beaten 68–38. Again, the

U.S. defense was the story. By yielding only thirty-eight points, the squad brought its points-against average to forty-three per game, a remarkably low number by 1970s standards. In the other semifinal, the Soviets escaped Cuba 67–61. Sergei Belov paced the Soviet squad, delivering crucial plays down the stretch. As a result, of six Olympics in which both attended, a fourth U.S. versus Soviet gold medal basketball final materialized.[60]

Of those four, the Munich final undoubtedly ranks as the most controversial. In fact, it remains the most controversial major basketball championship of all time. A slew of oddities attended the affair. To begin with, on account of the terrorist attack, the game took place a day later than expected, and it started at the ridiculously late hour of 11:45 p.m. Munich time. Two years earlier, ABC, counting on the dramatic cold war matchup that ultimately materialized, had requested the late tip-off in order to air the game during New York City's primetime. Therefore, the game started on September 9, 1972, just before midnight, and it did not end until after 1:00 a.m. the following day. In addition, players, fans, and officials lingered about the stadium well past 3:00 a.m., awaiting final word from a huddled group of FIBA officials who were attempting to determine whether the outcome should stand.[61] Few Americans thought it should. The *Chicago Tribune* characterized the late-game decisions made by the referees and FIBA secretary-general R. William Jones as "the greatest three-second violation in the history of the sport."[62]

Despite the late hour, a partisan crowd of over 6,500 crammed into the *Basketballhalle* to watch the physical and tenaciously defended game. Not surprisingly, in the first frame, the United States struggled to score, which enabled the Soviets to lead 26–21 at intermission. More trouble came for the United States in the second half, especially when, with 12:18 remaining, the Soviet Union's Mikhail Korkia and the U.S. team's Dwight Jones were ejected after the two tussled while wrestling for a loose ball on a rebound. Given that Jones was leading the United States in scoring, the ejections particularly angered American onlookers. Many thought the referees had been duped by the antics of Korkia—the less-talented player, but a starter for the Soviets—who had embroiled Jones in a fracas.[63] Even before Jones was tossed, however, the second half had not opened well for the United States. A stunning, pressure-induced run to open the stanza, reminiscent of the ones turned in by the 1960 and 1968 U.S. Olympic squads, would have been fitting. But this did not occur. Iba decided against unleashing his team's full-court potential, opting instead to continue a half-court game. In turn, both teams continued to struggle for points. After Jones's departure, the Soviets built a ten-point lead. The United States cut that lead to six, but then, with just over six minutes remaining in the game, the Soviets made a basket for an eight-point advantage. At that point, U.S. prospects looked dim. Given the game's slow scoring, overcoming this deficit was a major challenge.

With several minutes remaining and facing imminent defeat, Coach Iba finally decided to switch tactics and implement a full-court press. The Soviets did not score another field goal until the final seconds of the game, and that one was the most controversial field goal in Olympic history. Afterward, critics pointed to the success of the pressure defense to argue that the United States should have played a full-court game throughout. Others have defended Iba, like assistant coach Don Haskins, who well after the Munich Games said, "Mr. Iba told me all summer long that the Russians would choke at the end, and that's when we started to press." But mainly there were critics—and these were not only outsiders. Over thirty years after the final, Ratleff said, "We had the wrong coach. They brought in a bunch of thin, fast guys. You're talking about guys who loved to score, who never passed up shots in college. But he made us slow it down and make all these passes."[64] Such criticism has warrant, particularly as it relates to Iba's timing in choosing to apply full-court pressure against the Soviets. That he did not do it earlier, say at the start of the second half as he had in the Mexico City final, seems an obvious tactical mistake.

But to be fair, Iba's previous Olympic squads, in 1968 and 1964, had averaged 82.1 and 78.2 points per game, respectively, demonstrating that Iba-coached teams could score relatively often. Yet in Munich, the team managed just 73.4 points per game, which is lower than the averages of the previous four Olympic squads. This suggests that criticism focusing on Iba may be overdone. Looking more closely at the team's statistics reveals that, in addition to the relatively low team-scoring average in Munich, no individual on the 1972 U.S. Olympic team averaged even *ten* points per game there—a distinction no other U.S. Olympic team has had. Furthermore, of the team's top four scorers in Munich, none averaged sixteen points per game or higher in any of their professional seasons. (Doug Collins did average over twenty points in one NBA season, but he was the team's fifth-leading scorer in Munich.) In comparison, Spencer Haywood from the 1968 team averaged more than twenty points per game over the length of his thirteen-year professional career, and his teammate "JoJo" White averaged over seventeen points per game during his twelve-year NBA career. Statistically speaking, the 1972 Olympic team's offensive skills were lacking in comparison to those of previous Olympiads: this contributed as much as did Iba's tactics to its scoring struggles.

Another part of the puzzle that often gets overlooked is the Soviet Union's improvement in playing fast. In Munich, Coach Vladimir Kondrashin's Soviet squad averaged roughly ninety points per game. Kondrashin, who took Gomelsky's place supposedly on account of the Soviet Union's third-place finish at the 1970 World Championships, demanded tough defense and ball control in an offensive half-court set, but he also seemed to more readily embrace the fast break than Iba. (Gomelsky still had a strong influence on the 1972 Soviet team, which was composed mainly of members of his Central Army Sports Club (CSKA) team: he referred to the players as "my boys." It has been suggested that the main factor affecting Soviet officials' decision to replace Gomelsky was their concern that he planned to defect in Munich.[65]) The two decades of building the Soviet basketball program with heavy influence from the American style of play had produced a better Soviet squad.

Still, no one can deny that the full-court pressure paid immediate dividends. When the United States finally applied it, the Soviets started to rush shots and turn the ball over. Capitalizing on this, the Americans pulled within two points at 44–42 after Kevin Joyce made two quick shots. With less than ten seconds remaining and the Soviets leading 49–48, an Alexander Belov shot was blocked by McMillen, which resulted in A. Belov being trapped near the baseline, some ninety feet from his basket. He threw an errant pass that Doug Collins swooped in front of and grabbed near half-court. Collins charged to the basket, drawing a hard foul. Later, Collins said he was "KO'd for a few seconds."[66] Groggy, he stepped to the free-throw line—down one point with three seconds remaining in the gold medal game. He made the first. The partisan crowd erupted in cheers as television play-by-play man Chris Schenkel said, "This place goes insane. Doug Collins has tied it up." Then, just as he was about to release the ball for his second attempt, a loud horn at the scorer's table inexplicably sounded. It did not faze Collins, however, as he proceeded to make the second free throw, putting the United States ahead by one point with three seconds remaining.[67] It had been a remarkable comeback. The American team, which scored just over thirty points in the game's first thirty minutes, had scored seventeen in the game's final ten minutes. But there were still three seconds remaining.

Things got murky after Collins's second free throw. According to 1972 FIBA rules, a team could not call a time-out after the second free throw: if a coach wanted a time-out, he had to signal the scorer's table before the referee handed the ball to the free-throw shooter for his second free throw. If the coach did not signal the scorer's table, the rules stipulated that the team must inbound the ball from underneath its own basket. In Munich, a coach could alert the scorer's table for a time-out via two methods: pushing a button on the bench that set off a red light or walking over to the scorer's table and signaling for a time-out in traditional fashion. Since no such light had appeared between Collins's first and second free throws, and Coach Kondrashin did not appear to signal for one manually, the Soviets took the ball out from underneath their basket after Collins made his second attempt.

However, Coach Kondrashin claimed that he had pressed the button to signal for a time-out before Collins's first free throw. Then, according to him, when officials at the scorer's table asked Kondrashin if he wanted a time-out called right away, he shook his head somewhat disgustedly. As a long-time coach, he thought it should have been obvious that he wanted the time-out following Collins's first free throw. That way, he could address his team and develop strategy based on whether or not the first free throw had gone in. "The idiots, they wanted to give me the timeout before the first free throw; of course I refused," he said later.[68] The Soviet historian Yuri Brokhin notes that this statement is the key to understanding the bizarre chain of events that followed, because it seems that while the scorer's table took Kondrashin's refusal of a time-out before Collins's first free throw to mean that he no longer wanted a time-out at all, Kondrashin himself apparently figured they should have known he wanted his time-out after Collins's first free throw. This unclear exchange has also been offered as a possible reason for why the buzzer went off just as Collins shot his second free throw. It was when the referee handed Collins the ball for his second free throw that Soviet assistant coach Bashkin claims he realized that this meant no time-out had been granted. Thus, he ran to the scorer's bench screaming, "We called a time-out, dammit!" According to Bashkin, the official scorers then "immediately turned on the siren, but it was too late . . . Luckily, FIBA Secretary William Jones saw the whole thing and stood up for us."[69]

Whether it happened that way or not, the Soviet players on the court did not appear to realize their coach wanted a time-out, because after Collins made the second free throw, Alshan Sharmukhamedov took the ball out-of-bounds. As Sharmukhamedov did so, Coach Kondrashin pleaded with the scorer's table. Then, as the seconds ticked away and with the Soviet team in a seemingly impossible position to win the game (as noted, the ball was inbounded some ninety feet from the Soviet basket), other Soviet personnel started to spill onto the floor demanding a time-out. Many observers would later wonder why this did not elicit a technical foul, but rather than call a technical foul for coming on the court during play, Brazilian referee Renato Righetto stopped the action with a second remaining. In turn, the Soviets continued to claim that the officials had denied them their time-out, while the Americans asserted that since FIBA rules did not allow coaches to call time-outs during play, the game therefore should not have been stopped.[70] Righetto did not acknowledge the Soviets' claims that they had called a time-out, but he also did not explain why he was awarding the Soviet Union another opportunity to inbound the basketball with a second remaining even though it was Soviet personnel that had initially come onto the court during play.

In the midst of the chaos, the most bizarre turn of events occurred when suddenly, FIBA secretary general R. William Jones, who had been watching the game in the stands, came onto the court and gestured to the officials at the scorer's table to put three seconds back on the clock, giving the Soviet Union another chance to replay the final seconds. Mystery surrounds Jones's actions. Later, he admitted that he had no jurisdiction, but he also insisted that his instructions to put three seconds back on the clock were correct. However, as the historian Chris Elzey notes, in 2000 Borislav Stankovic, the head of FIBA, argued that Jones had intruded in an "absolutely legal" fashion.[71] Regardless of whether Jones technically had the

12. The U.S. team celebrating what it thought was a victory in Munich. Photo by
AFP. AFP Collection/Getty Images.

light to come on the court, it certainly was an uncommon move. Years later,
Tom McMillen drew an appropriate analogy, saying that Jones's actions
would be the equivalent of NBA commissioner David Stern emerging from
the stands and walking onto the court in the final seconds of an NBA Finals
game to overrule a decision by the officials. Noting the absurdity of this,
he said, "David Stern just doesn't come out of the stands."[72]

Even more peculiarities occurred. For unclear reasons, play resumed
before three seconds were put back on the clock. In the meantime, the U.S.
squad had set up its defense again, while the Soviets prepared to inbound
the ball for a second time. This time, Ivan Edeshenko, despite seeming to
illegally step over the out-of-bounds line, sent a long pass down the court
to a hopeful teammate, only to have it deflected. The ball fell harmlessly to
the ground and the U.S. team rejoiced in euphoric joy, "jumping up and
down excitedly." Watching the cheers and thinking the game had ended,
Schenkel told viewers, "It's all over. Wow, what a finish! The United States

has won its eighth consecutive gold medal. This place has gone crazy!"[73]

But as they celebrated, the Bulgarian referee Artenik Arabadjian, looking perplexed, asserted that he had blown his whistle before the horn sounded because he had handed the ball back to the inbounder Edeshenko before the timekeeper had reset the clock properly.[74]

Coaches Iba and Haskins, realizing what was transpiring, vociferously protested, decrying the unprecedented maneuvering of Jones and the subsequent reset by Arabadjian. Coach Haskins wanted to end matters right then by taking the team off the court. But Iba, concerned that such action could lose the gold medal on an appeal, chose to stay. "I don't want to lose this game later tonight, sitting on my butt,"[75] he told Haskins.

So the Soviets took the ball from out-of-bounds a third time. This time it appeared that referee Arabadjian pointed to McMillen and then back at the baseline, intimating that McMillen should back away from the inbounder. In an HBO documentary, McMillen said that Arabadjian had said as much, while Arabadjian claimed he said no such thing. Remembering Iba's warnings to the team about the referees, to be safe, McMillen did move all the way back to free-throw line, giving Edeshenko a clear view ahead. "We were conscious the game could be won by hook or crook. I was afraid of a technical being called on me," McMillen told David Wharton of the *Los Angeles Times* years later.[76] With McMillen stepping away, Dwight Jones on the bench because of an ejection, Jim Brewer on the sideline nursing a concussion that he received with twelve minutes to play, defensive-stopper Bantom fouled out, and a clear view, Edeshenko then threw a strike all the way down the center of the court, toward Alexander Belov, who was flanked by Forbes and Joyce.[77] All three lunged for the basketball, but Belov had favorable position. As the players vied for the ball, Belov snagged it out of midair, and Forbes went to the ground. Belov landed several feet from the basket in the middle of the lane, then quickly turned and shot a layup over Joyce, who had backed away slightly, not wanting to foul. Thousands of fans in the arena and millions more watching television sets around the world watched the ball sink through the basket. The United States had lost. Its basketball dynasty was over. Reporting from Munich, Neil Amdur said that after the ball went in, the crowd looked "stunned and confused" and "chaos ensued." Belov simply dropped to his knees and cried.[78]

13. After the Soviets' third opportunity to inbound, Alexander Belov lays it in. Photo by Rich Clarkson. Time & Life Pictures Collection/Getty Images.

Furious, Iba rushed to the scorer's table. As he did so, several American players walked around in a daze, while Forbes wept openly.[79] Twenty years later, Forbes, who had ended up on the team as a result of Brown's injury, wrote, "When I got back to school at UTEP, I'd go in my room and close the door and not come out. I'd lie there and just think about it. My mind would play tricks and I'd start thinking, 'If someone else had been back there, would it have happened?' Just think about it. We were jumping and we were hugging, feeling such exhilaration one moment, and the next we were in a state of shock. And then came the anger, and the anger just goes and goes and goes." Iba refused to sign the official scorecard, explaining, "I've never seen anything like this in all my years of basketball."[80]

Around 2:00 a.m., the United States filed an official protest maintaining that the referees had acted properly when they stopped action with one second remaining on the clock but had violated the rules in putting three seconds on the clock (after the second buzzer had sounded). This should not have been done, according to the protest, particularly because the people that ran onto the court were Soviet coaches and players. The U.S. Olympic Basketball Committee chairman W. K. Summers delivered the appeal to a five-member jury made up of representatives from Italy,

Puerto Rico, Cuba, Poland, and Hungary: three from Communist nations and two from western ones. As expected, the final vote went along party lines, with communist Cuba, Poland, and Hungary voting to uphold the final score, and Italy and Puerto Rico voting in favor of the United States. This led many in the American media to claim that partisan leanings had affected the outcome. At a press conference called to announce the decision, American media members fumed at the protest committee chairman, the Hungarian Ferenc Hepp, assuming that he'd favored the Soviets. (Hepp had taken the post only after Egypt's Abdel Moneim Wahby had stepped down following Egypt's departure from the Games.) However, if the press had looked closer, they could have learned that Hepp had earned a doctorate from the University of Iowa, had many friends in the West, and had reportedly lost members of his family to Russian aggression during Hungary's short-lived 1956 revolt. According to Elzey, "He despised the Soviet Union."[81]

Yet during the boisterous news conference, Hepp could not deny that FIBA rules disallowed putting time back on the clock. Rather than focusing on that, though, he emphasized the discretion of Brazilian referee Renato Righetto in making the decision to put time back on the clock. However, *Righetto* did not think the game had ended properly, and he too refused to sign the official scorebook. American journalists had a hard time enduring Hepp's hollow responses. When he hesitated to reveal the vote tally, one journalist called him "a goddamned liar," another shouted, "Are you kidding?" and a third hollered, "We're not mentally retarded. Can we get an honest answer?" A U.S. Olympic Committee official asked, "How can you penalize the U.S. team for the Russian team coming on the floor?" Then, unexpectedly, a German official took the floor to argue that because the scorer's table had not insisted that only one second remained on the clock, Righetto had to listen to FIBA Secretary Jones when he ordered officials to put three seconds on the clock. Later that day, when Jones was confronted with the charge, he denied having anything to do with the final decision.[82] Months afterward, though, he admitted the role he had played in influencing the game, and he can be seen in footage of the game holding up three fingers.

Before the protest committee even voted, the U.S. players had stated their decision not to accept a single silver medal. Those medals remain sealed in a vault in Lausanne, Switzerland. Ten years after the Munich Games, letters from the IOC arrived at the homes of the U.S. players, asking them to reconsider and accept the medals, with one condition: all of the players had to agree to accept the medals or else none would receive them. The players did not accept the offer. Letters arrived at the players' homes once again in 1986, and again they delivered the same verdict. In a curious footnote, Sports Illustrated's Gary Smith reported in 1992 that while ten of the twelve players told him they voted no, USA Basketball claims that the first time around, only three players voted no and the next time, only two did.[83]

Since 1972, general consensus in the United States has been that the American team was robbed. But according to the Russian historian Robert Edelman of the University of California at San Diego, the events surrounding the final moments of the game are not as controversial as people think. He maintains that, as the Soviet Union prepared to take the ball out for the second time, the clock briefly showed fifty seconds remaining, which suggested confusion. Additionally, he points out that since the footage shows Secretary General Jones holding up three fingers during the chaos that ensued, three seconds should have been put on the clock the first time play was resumed. Furthermore, Edelman asserts that the final horn seemed to come too quickly on the second inbounds pass, when the Soviet Union had thrown the ball in with only one second remaining. He told David Wharton of the Los Angeles Times, "It was obviously a poorly supervised game. But I don't think it happened the way many people remember it." Edelman added, "The thing that bothers me as a historian is [that] this idea of the United States being cheated has lived on and has never been challenged with any kind of research."[84] However, Edelman's claim that the game was "poorly supervised" grossly understates the scenario. No other major basketball championship in history has ended in such bizarre fashion, and R. William Jones's actions remain unmatched. The ending was not merely poorly supervised; it was chaotic, confusing, and without precedent.

Ultimately, though, the legacy of the 1972 final does not rest in the nuances of what transpired in its final moments. Yuri Brokhin sums it up well when he asserts that, no matter what one thinks of the waning moments, the game demonstrated that the technical and tactical aspects of basketball had matured outside of the United States and that the Soviets had played basketball on par with U.S. amateurs. On the surface, this appeared to give the Soviets a cultural victory in the cold war. However, although the game reflected cold war tensions, it also reflected a world increasingly interested in competing within an international sporting community led by liberal capitalist, universalistic views—a world in which basketball was a shared attraction to hundreds of millions.

The rise of international sports, basketball in particular, was facilitating cultural exchanges and promoting a common desire for western products. This was suggested by the Soviet and Yugoslav coaches' ready admission that they had borrowed heavily from American basketball style and also by the fact that one of the Soviet Union's star players had earned renown as the "Jerry West" of Russia. Soon after the Munich Games, reports of a controversy involving the 1972 Soviet basketball team also hinted at this process. In October 1973 the *New York Times's* Hendrick Smith reported that the gold medal Soviet team had become "the scandal of the Soviet sports world," as it had received a slew of negative press in the Soviet Union for acting like spoiled "prima donnas" and for losing the European Championship for the first time in nineteen years to Spain. More glaring, a number of Soviet players from the Munich team faced court appearances for smuggling western goods from their international tours into the Soviet Union, a practice that was taken for granted by Soviet athletes as a privilege. *Time* picked up on the story as well, noting that *Komsomolskaya Pravda*, the state-run newspaper, had charged Soviet Basketball Federation officials with creating "a climate of total permissiveness." In addition, *Pravda* applauded the Soviet government's consideration of court action against certain players, asserting that after a recent trip, "the national team returned home burdened not with a heap of victories but with a heap of unprecedented customs violations."[85]

The Soviet basketball players were not the first to face scrutiny for customs violations. A few years earlier, a Soviet soccer team had returned from a trip to the West with illegal appliances, radios, textiles, and other off-limits items.[86] Such exchanges gave Soviet sports stars a firsthand look at western prosperity: this could be a powerful experience for a Soviet. The story of Boris Yeltsin's shock upon seeing the abundance of food at a Houston supermarket in 1989 is probably the most famous example of this.

According to the *New York Times*'s Smith, *Komsomolskaya Pravda*, presumably speaking for party officials, seemed particularly upset about the Soviet team's loss at the 1973 European championships. After that loss, it even stated for the first time that the Soviet team had not played particularly well in 1972 against a U.S. team that was "not the best team the U.S.A. could have put forward." In addition, *Komsomolskaya Pravda* suggested that the Soviet players had come to expect exemption from political indoctrination and other liberties. Essentially, the team had become "absolutely unaccountable to any social authority."[87]

Compounding matters, Soviet players were already being enticed with offers from NBA teams, and those offers would only come more frequently in ensuing years. This reflected the forces of globalization and the influence of the prosperity of liberal, open-market economies in the sports world. Both proved a tough opponent for socialist indoctrination. Isolating athletes from the West would become increasingly difficult in subsequent years as satellite technology improved, the reach of transnational corporations like Nike expanded, and moguls such as Ted Turner escalated efforts to lure Soviet athletes and attract Soviet consumers. It was this legacy, which the Munich tournament contributed to, that proved more important than the 1972 tournament's controversial ending.

Even Mike Bantom, who had delivered a powerful indictment against the United States before the Games, could not deny certain realities after Munich. Bantom's pre-Games comments were reminiscent of the strong rhetoric offered by Harry Edwards during the 1968 boycott movement. Bantom said:

> I'm playing for myself only. I don't really consider myself a member of the U.S. team. I'm no patriot. I'm going to Munich because my family can use whatever I get out of it. I can't buy this "Win medals for your country" jazz. There's no glory in Munich for the people of North Philadelphia. They're too busy trying to stay alive to worry about the Games. They don't really share much in the country's glory, do they?

The statements reflected the continuation of racial discrimination in the United States, even if conditions in some areas, such as endorsement opportunities for African American athletes, had improved and basketball had given some young African Americans a voice.

TABLE 8. 1972 U.S. Men's Olympic Basketball cumulative stats

NAME	G	FGM-FGA	(%)	FTM-FTA	(%)	REB/AVG	PF	PTS/AVG
Tom Henderson	9	39-74	.524	5-6	.833	18/2.0	20	83/9.2
Dwight Jones	9	34-68	.500	15-22	.682	51/5.7	26	83/9.2
Mike Bantom	9	29-72	.403	11-22	.500	44/4.9	33	69/7.7
Jim Brewer	9	26-62	.419	16-24	.667	64/7.1	20	68/7.6
Doug Collins	9	25-59	.524	16-22	.727	21/2.3	19	66/7.3
Tom McMillen	9	24-72	.333	13-16	.813	39/4.3	16	61/6.8
Ed Ratleff	9	27-68	.397	4-6	.667	29/3.2	26	58/6.4
Kevin Joyce	9	21-56	.375	6-6	1.000	11/1.2	28	48/5.3
James Forbes	9	23-45	.511	0-4	.000	28/3.1	18	46/5.1
Bobby Jones	9	14-23	.609	9-10	.900	25/2.8	14	37/4.1
Tom Burleson	8	10-27	.370	7-12	.583	15/1.9	13	27/3.4

Still, Bantom came away from Munich less belligerent toward America. In 1992 he told *Sports Illustrated*'s Gary Smith:

> Being an American is something that makes me feel proud. My whole philosophy started changing in those Games—I'm a true believer in our country now. I don't say that blindly . . . I'd never been out of the country before we went to Munich. Once you got to that Olympic Village, you couldn't help but think about the United States in relation to hundreds of other countries. The Cubans couldn't speak to us. The Soviets and the East Europeans dressed and acted like robots. Then I'd look at us, and we were all such diverse personalities. I realized you can choose your aspirations in America without becoming a clone. We open things up to allow individuals to strive; we make it possible for our people to be great. I was never in another protest after coming home from the Games.[88]

Obviously, this does not mean Bantom suddenly disregarded all problems in the United States or that there were not issues, racial or otherwise, to overcome; it indicates mainly that participating in Olympic basketball provided Bantom with a new frame of reference from which to measure ways of life. In time, sports such as basketball, along with the increasing connectedness of the globe, would give more and more people that same opportunity.

9

TRADEMARK SPEED RETURNS IN MONTREAL, THEN POLITICS INTRUDE IN MOSCOW

In 1976, during a game against Italy at the Montreal Olympics, Coach Dean Smith did not notice that one of his players was wearing Adidas shoes rather than Converse's Chuck Taylor's. But afterward, a USA basketball official pulled him aside and asked, "Don't you know Converse paid for our team to wear their shoes?" Indeed, Converse had "donated" $170,000 for the right to advertise its shoe as the one the U.S. Olympic squad had "selected for use."[1] Coach Smith felt like he needed to resolve the situation, so he spoke with the offending player, telling him that if he wore the wrong shoes again, he would not play. Yet Smith's private warning did not settle the matter entirely, because later on, just before the U.S. Olympic basketball team took the floor for the 1976 gold medal game, the situation arose again. This time two different players, Scott May and Adrian Dantley, decided to wear basketball shoes other than Converse. Rather than distract the team, Smith decided to let it go.[2] These episodes highlighted the new preferences players were developing for athletic shoes, whether owing to technical reasons, the opportunity to make a cultural statement, or both. (In Dantley's case, he said that the Adidas model "was just a better shoe . . . a better fit on my arches".[3])

In the 1970s, the rise of the athletic "sneaker"—a rise that basketball helped propel—was striking. Less than a decade before the Montreal Games, high society had deemed the sneaker unworthy of a gentleman, but by the mid-1970s, everyone from older ladies to school kids to business folks trekking to work on Wall Street was wearing them. Basketball played a role in that process partly because of the attractiveness of the sport's action and partly because sneakers and high-tops were so comfortable and useful. In 1973 the *New York Times* noted that "the lowly sneaker has become a lofty status symbol among Brooklyn schoolboys." At that time, you could still by Pro-Keds or Converse for around ten dollars, which the majority of kids did. But if you really wanted to make an impression, you sported a pair of twenty-dollar, all-leather Pumas endorsed by the great New York Knickerbocker, Walt "Clyde" Frazier. Explaining "Clyde" Frazier's influence, ESPN.com's Ralph Wiley wrote in 2005, "My story's simple: I blame Walt Frazier for everything. I blame Walt Frazier for it all, from the way I walk, to the way I watch hoop."[4]

In Montreal it was clear that as the sophistication and prominence of athletic shoes advanced, so too did the relationships between shoe companies and athletes. Adidas and Puma representatives displayed this as they basically swarmed athletes. The inside of Montreal's Diplomat Hotel, a hub of Olympic activity, served as a virtual epicenter of action for the jockeying shoe firms. Puma set up a huge store there, luring Olympic athletes who happened to be passing by with free merchandise.[5] Not to be outdone, Adidas rented an entire wing of the Ramada Inn that abutted Montreal's Olympic stadium and armed its reps armed with a budget estimated at $7 million, a staggering amount compared to the $5,626.90 Nike spent on giveaways in Montreal. A *Chicago Tribune* headline during the Games read: "The Great Sneaker War, '76: Bigger Stakes—and Giveaways."[6]

With détente out of favor, satellite and cable technology advancing, and the role of sports in forging an international global culture expanding, the shoe firms' efforts to recruit athletes in Montreal reflected the high stakes. And the basketball competition, given the controversial 1972 gold medal game, featured particular cold war–infused intensity.

Even before Montreal, the Soviet–United States basketball rivalry was re-ignited when a string of much-publicized games in April 1973 took place between the two in America. Though this was not the Olympics, many Americans saw the games as an opportunity for revenge. The six-game cross-country series featured a noteworthy cast of American amateurs and a Soviet team consisting primarily of the players that had beaten the United States in Munich. And it attracted many fans.[7]

The series almost did not take place, though. It had nearly come unhinged just a couple of months earlier when the tired NCAA/AAU rivalry erupted again. The problem arose when the NCAA barred its coaches and players from participating in the exhibition because it was sponsored by the AAU.[8] In an attempt to explain the decision, the NCAA's Tom Hanson rather callously told the *Washington Post*, "The AAU can't commit those kids. They have no control over them. It wouldn't be very attractive unless they have the outstanding college kids like Walton, Jones, and McMillen." However, as it soon found out, the NCAA did not have complete control over players either. Under pressure, the NCAA ultimately reversed its decision to bar its own players from the exhibitions, but many of those players decided not to play anyway.

Even before the NCAA relented, Munich Olympians Dwight Jones and Tom McMillen had stated they would most likely not participate; Jim Brewer had announced as well that he did not intend to participate, offering as reasons his reluctance to miss school and the recent completion of a hard season. Meanwhile, a representative for Doug Collins told the *Washington Post* that he wanted to participate but had already signed a pro contract. Collins did not seem overly excited about the series, however. He told the *Post*, "There's nothing to prove, but other people might think there would be."[9] In the end, Bobby Jones and Thomas Henderson were the only two Munich Olympians to suit up on the American all-star squad that played the visiting Soviets.

Still, in the series' late April opener, over 17,500 ribald spectators packed into the Los Angeles Forum to watch. Bob Cousy coached the U.S. team and came away surprised by the physicality of the international game. "I've never seen anything like that out there, especially under the basket," he told reporters. Led in scoring by Providence's Ernie DiGregorio, who had not even been asked to try out for the Munich squad, the United States won in convincing fashion 83–65. DiGregorio scored fourteen points, as did center Swen Nater, who had presumably regained the weight he lost in Hawaii. Most did not expect Nater to play as much as he did for Cousy, but after Bill Walton suffered a knee ligament injury in the first half, Nater filled in admirably. Nater's 1973 performance only increases speculation about what the outcome might have been in Munich had he played, let alone had Walton.[10]

The 1973 series showed that the U.S.-Soviet rivalry had stoked interest in international basketball, but an actual Olympic rematch was needed to settle the score properly. Therefore, Americans continued to look ahead toward Montreal. Adding to the intrigue, the cold war took some rather interesting turns between Munich and Montreal, especially regarding the role of emerging nations. By the mid-1970s the oil embargo by the Organization of Petroleum Exporting Countries (OPEC), ongoing issues in Cuba, and the United States' inability to keep a Soviet-leaning regime from taking over in Angola caused the U.S. strategy of détente to fall out of favor. Even Henry Kissinger, one of the strategy's architects, said in 1976 that détente "is a word I would like to forget." Consequently, the United States and Soviet Union moved toward an increasingly confrontational posture as the Montreal Games approached.[11]

To meet the 1976 Olympic basketball challenge, in 1975 the ABA/USA basketball committee, made up of Henry Iba, Red Auerbach, and Pete Newell, among others, had selected North Carolina's Dean Smith to coach the Olympic team. With Smith at the helm, for the first time in sixteen years someone other than Iba would patrol the U.S. sideline.

Ironically, Smith had played at Kansas in the early 1950s for Iba's rival, the flamboyant and creative Dr. "Phog" Allen. Recalling his days at Kansas, Smith wrote, "In Forrest C. 'Phog' Allen and his invaluable assistant, Dick Harp, I had met two of the most interesting basketball authorities the game has ever known. It was impossible to play for those men and not learn something."[12] As a coach, Smith advocated the fast-paced style Allen preferred, in contrast to Iba's more methodical approach. As Dantley explained to the author, "Dean Smith was a great coach, very organized. He emphasized defense first; then fast break off of that." If the break faltered, the team played a motion "passing game."[13]

Smith was given the freedom to pick his own assistants; he chose his longtime sidekick at North Carolina, Bill Guthridge, and a young African American from Georgetown named John Thompson. Upon accepting assistant duties, Thompson, who in 1964 lost a chance to play for the Olympic team to Oregon State's Mel Counts, had his chance to win Olympic gold. But with the increasing globalization of the game, the relative youth of the U.S. squad, and the fact that a number of star collegians were not participating, winning back the gold would be no small task.

That task was made even more difficult in the spring of 1976 when Kent Benson, the starting center on Indiana's undefeated 1976 national championship team, announced that he would not be available for the Games owing to wrist surgery. A number of other star players simply declined invitations to try out, among them All-American guard John Lucas and center Robert Parish, who chose not to participate out of fear that a potential injury might hurt his draft status.[14] The absences of Parish and Benson were particularly troublesome because they played center, the 1976 team's weakest position. And Parish and Benson were just two of ten top-level NCAA big men that were six feet ten inches or taller and did not attend the trials. Other notable absentees included Marques Johnson, Wally Walker, and Sip Brown. Compounding matters, the United States needed to contend with improving, older, and more experienced European club players, in addition to the Soviets. Players in Western Europe could still play in professional leagues as "employees" of the corporation that sponsored their team, thereby maintaining their amateur status. These corporate "employees" were basically professionals. Nonetheless, the system enabled older European players to remain eligible for the Olympics, helping make the U.S. team the youngest squad among the contenders by a wide margin.

Ultimately, sixty American players, headlined by Indiana's Scott May, North Carolina State's Kenny Carr, and Notre Dame's Adrian Dantley, attended the trials. During the first week of competition, in June at North Carolina State University, Dean Smith put the attendees through grueling two-a-day workouts. He came away impressed with the work ethic of Indiana's May and Quinn Buckner, both important members of Bob Knight's undefeated national championship team the previous season. They made the final Olympic squad, along with Dantley; Carr; North Carolina's Walt Davis, Phil Ford, Mitch Kupchak and Tom LaGarde; Duke's Tate Armstrong; Ernie Grunfeld of Tennessee; Phil Hubbard of Michigan; and Steve Sheppard of Maryland.

By the summer of 1976, Brundage's rule stipulating that players with stated intentions to play professional basketball would be rendered ineligible for Olympic competition, even if they had not signed a contract, was no longer in effect, but Olympic players still had to wait until after the Games to sign their professional contracts. Dantley, May, Kupchak, and Buckner did just that, thereby risking injury for the chance to play in Montreal. "I thought hard on it for a long time . . . I decided it could only help me," Dantley told reporters a month before the Games, and a few weeks after he was selected sixth in the NBA draft.[15]

Depth in the frontcourt emerged as Smith's biggest concern, even though *five* seven-footers were cut from the Olympic team.[16] Smith and fellow committee members did not think some of those cut had the speed and mobility necessary to thrive given FIBA's wider lanes and Smith's schemes, so they selected a smaller, faster team. Kupchak and LaGarde were the team's only true centers. Coach Smith did claim he wanted to put one of the seven-footers that did not make the final cut on the squad, but he was overruled in committee. "This is not the team I handed in. I differed in three places with the final selection by the ten-man committee, but I won't say where. I will say I had a seven-footer on my list," he told the *New York Times* after the team was announced.[17] "You and I know that, by international standards, this squad does not have the size you would like," Smith admitted. "It will be [a problem] at defensive center and with shot-blocking. Rebounding will be the key."[18] But he added, "Size is only a problem on defense—not offense."[19]

Of Coach Smith's two centers, Kupchak was the strongest. He won 1976 ACC player of the year honors before the Montreal Games and was a proven player. In Montreal he averaged more than twelve points and five rebounds and shot better than 60 percent from the field. As it turned out, the six-feet-ten-inch LaGarde, who was a year behind Kupchak at North Carolina, also turned in a strong performance in Montreal. He shot thirteen of eighteen from the field and 88 percent from the free-throw-line en route to averaging just under seven points per game. The play of both assuaged frontcourt concerns as the Olympics progressed. To further bolster the frontcourt, Smith also asked Adrian Dantley and Phil Hubbard, both undersized, to play inside. They too performed well.[20]

On paper, the team seemed formidable offensively, considering that every player save Buckner, who had played a distributing role as the point guard at Indiana, had averaged more than fourteen points per game the previous season. Furthermore, May, Carr, Dantley, and Grunfeld all had averaged more than twenty-three points per game. Still, Coach Smith received a rash of criticism when it was announced that seven players from the ACC, four from North Carolina alone, had made the team. "A team of monkeys throwing darts at the entry list could have come up with a better group of players than the Olympic selection committee chose," charged Robert Markus in the *Chicago Tribune*. "It's simply not a representative team. We're sending the Atlantic Coast all-stars to play the Russians." Markus went on to note that the ACC champion had lost to DePaul in the NCAA's first round, while the conference's runner-up was pummeled by Alabama.[21] To be fair, though, Smith would have taken Indiana's Benson had he been available, and though he was allowed to advise the basketball committee on the kind of players he preferred, Coach Smith did not select the entire roster. "In fact, I lost several arguments," he asserted.[22] In addition to missing out on the seven-footer he wanted, Smith finally admitted that among the other two he had unsuccessfully pushed for was another Hoosier, the shooting guard Bob Wilkerson. "Bob Wilkerson was definitely one I wanted and didn't get," he said in late June.[23] So it could be argued that Smith's first choice would have been to have four Indiana Hoosiers.

Even with the presence of such high scorers as May, Carr, Dantley, and Grunfeld, at first glance, it did not appear that a star would anchor the team. That is because most did not fully appreciate Dantley's ability. Throughout his scholastic, collegiate, and to an extent even his pro career, people underrated Dantley. At every step in his career in both high school and college, Dantley recalled, the critics had claimed: "he's too small."[24] In Montreal he changed many minds, though, by turning in one of the best performances in U.S. Olympic basketball history.

Unlike Olympic basketball stars of past Games, such as Robertson, Russell, and Haywood, Dantley did not shock people with astounding physical feats. He did not have Robertson's versatility and he couldn't block shots like Russell or dunk like Haywood. He was not an excellent shooter either. But he was a good shooter, a solid ballhandler, a strong rebounder, and, when necessary, he could dunk. He excelled at craftiness, and did most everything else well, in a workmanlike fashion. And he produced. In the previous college basketball season Dantley had led Notre Dame to the NCAA Final Four. He finished his remarkable collegiate *career* with averages of 25.8 points and 9.8 rebounds, despite standing at only six feet three inches. Later, in the NBA, he won rookie of the year honors by averaging 20.3 points and nearly eight rebounds; averaged over twenty-four points in his thirteen-year Hall-of-Fame career; and finished ninth in career NBA points and in the top twenty in career field-goal percentage.

Dantley's work ethic was influenced by his grandfather. Dantley grew up in Washington DC in a household that consisted of his single mother, three aunts, and his grandparents. His family did not enjoy material wealth, but they made up for it with love and an appreciation for a day's labor. Dantley's grandfather spent time with him. "He'd come home from work, we'd watch TV," Dantley recalled. They could just hang out. And every two weeks on payday, his grandfather bought his grandson a case of Payday candy bars. It was a symbolic gesture not lost on the budding star.[25]

While Dantley grew, he also came to admire basketball prep stars from the Washington DC area, including Dave Bing, Elgin Baylor, and Austin Carr, who also played at Notre Dame under Digger Phelps. In 1975, after he had made it to Notre Dame, Dantley got his first major international basketball experience when the Fighting Irish played against the Soviets. The game gave him confidence heading into the Olympics. "I was more physical than they were. I don't see how they are going to stay with our quickness and mobility," he told the *Washington Post* shortly after getting selected for the Olympic team.[26]

Many pundits were not as optimistic about the U.S. Olympic squad. Citing subpar frontcourt play and underrating Dantley, pessimistic predictions poured in, and one *Washington Post* headline read, "Weak Middle May Spell the End of U.S. Olympic Basketball Reign." The *Post's* Paul Attner, calling the team "the weakest the United States has ever fielded for the world's premiere amateur athletic competition," suggested that it might not win a medal at all. According to him, this U.S. Olympic team would struggle to win even against a squad made up of the collegians that had declined invitations to the Olympic tryouts, let alone those that had accepted and not made it.[27] But he was not all negative. Attner did express excitement at the prospect of Coach Smith taking the reins of the United States' fast and quick roster because he thought Coach Smith could capitalize on "this era of run-and-shoot basketball players" better than Coach Iba. It was an astute observation. Beyond that, Attner liked the team's two excellent point men, Buckner and Ford, to go along with the slew of forwards led by Dantley and May. Attner also noted that the 1976 team could look at the U.S. championship at the 1975 Pan-Am Games in Mexico City a year earlier for confidence. Still, he pointed out that the previous summer, a U.S. all-star team had lost four international games, two to the Russians and one each to Italy and Yugoslavia.[28]

A string of exhibition games before the Olympics provided more opportunities to gauge the team's potential. On June 18 the squad lost to coach Larry Brown's Denver Nuggets of the ABA, 108–100, but the following night it scored a solid victory over the Nuggets, 98–85. Brown came away impressed. "They played unselfishly, with style and enthusiasm. If you utilize twelve people and are flexible, you can accomplish a lot," he said.[29] The following week the United States won an exhibition tilt against the Israeli national team in an encouraging performance. The scores of its early games suggested that in Montreal the team would indeed capitalize on the "run-and-shoot" style saturating the American game.

But then in Mount Prospect, Illinois, the U.S. squad struggled to beat a team characterized by the *Chicago Tribune* as a "pick-up squad of pros built around Bob Love."[30] The 94-90 squeaker raised further questions. "This is the first time I haven't felt encouraged after a game," Smith admitted in his postgame remarks. Cliff Ray, a former Chicago Bull who played for Golden State, gave a cautious appraisal of the United States, saying they were "weak at center."[31] And Ray Meyer, the legendary DePaul coach who manned the sideline for this "pick-up" professional outfit led by Bob Love, said, "They don't have a real strong center, and that may hurt them against the Russians, who are extremely physical." Yet Meyer also noted that the wider trapezoidal international lane, which fanned out three and a half feet on each side from the free-throw line to the baseline would open the action. This opened action, theoretically, would help mitigate the United States' weakness at the center position. "Their style of play is suited to the wider lane. They pick well away from the ball and try to keep the middle open," Meyer explained.[32]

In July, with its exhibition schedule complete, the results mixed, the U.S. players traveled to Montreal. They arrived in a host city that had recently endured much negative press. Montreal mayor Jean Drapeau had dreamt huge for the 1976 Olympics, which, he legendarily claimed, "can no more have a deficit, than a man can have a baby."[33] But the financing was government-driven, and the Montreal Olympic Organizing Committee did not efficiently utilize open-market tactics, like limiting advertising relationships and competitively bidding out those limited relationships.[34] Therefore, as the Games approached, major cost overruns and missed deadlines accrued.[35] In April, *Forbes* estimated the city's bill, for facilities alone, at $1.3 billion—nearly double initial estimations.[36] As it happened, Montreal's Olympic Stadium came to be called the Big Owe; the debt incurred in building it was not paid off in full until thirty years after the Games—a special cigarette tax serviced a bulk of that debt.[37]

Montreal's woes were especially troublesome considering the difficulty it had faced in earning the right to host. In a process that highlighted cold war tensions, Montreal had won the right over Moscow and Los Angeles by prevailing in a dramatic run-off—mainly because it was an acceptable alternative to the other two cities.[38] The IOC said Montreal offered a neutral option to the United States, which was suffering international backlash over Vietnam. In regard to the Soviet Union, the IOC maintained that it was too new to the Olympic movement compared to a country like Canada.[39] Despite IOC proclamations, however, the fact remained that up to that point, the modern Olympics had taken place only in Europe or North America, except for the 1960 Games, which took place in Japan, a strong western ally. Furthermore, they had not been originally awarded to any nation other than a theoretically liberal one (the IOC initially awarded the 1936 Berlin Games to the Weimar Republic). The history of the IOC's choice of hosts echoes the Olympic movement's westward leanings. Practically, this could not continue. And sure enough, in 1974 the IOC chose Moscow as host of the 1980 Games.

Making matters worse for Montreal, just days before the Games opened, political issues flared. African nations were upset with the IOC's refusal to ban New Zealand, even though its rugby team was touring apartheid South Africa. This led to a mass boycott by African nations.[40] Many African American athletes in Montreal expressed sympathy for the movement.[41] All told, thirty-two nations boycotted the Montreal Games, most of them African. Taiwan counted among the boycotters, too. They withdrew when

China, a coveted Canadian trading partner, pressured the Canadian government to disallow Taiwan from competing under the name the Republic of China.[42]

Given the acrimony that arose over choosing a host city, additional cold war tensions, and other attendant political issues in the summer of 1976, some critics questioned the entire Olympic movement—particularly its commercialism and nationalism, and even suggested that the Olympic Games simply cease. The *New York Times* asked whether the Olympics, "as presently organized, are worth holding." Pointing to patent exploitation of the athlete by state governments, hypernationalism, and issues over professionalism and amateurism, its editorial board answered, "We think they are not."[43]

But just a couple of days earlier the *New York Times* had carried an article penned by David B. Kanin that offered a different view. Kanin said the Olympics went a long way in promoting the established international political system, and he called the opening march "the most lavish celebration of the international political system in use today." At the same time, he noted that strong undercurrents against the status quo did emerge at the Olympics, as evidenced by the uprising in Hungary that occurred just as the 1956 Olympics got underway and the Suez crisis, which became "a showcase for amity between the Americans and the suddenly friendly Russians." He also pointed out the Soviet Union's and the United States' efforts to arrange contacts through sports exchanges to argue that the Olympics have been a "remarkably active part of the political world."[44]

Two months earlier, in the academic journal *Intellect*, Kanin had expressed similar sentiments, asserting that sports are a "form of intercultural relations which attracts the interest of a mass public" and noting that most people involved in the "transaction" took part indirectly through the media. Furthermore, he argued, participation in international sporting events offered nations a chance to thaw relations and interact in a "safe" way, as in the case of the United States' and China's "ping-pong diplomacy." Sports allow these cooperating nations to compete within agreed-upon standards, he concluded. Kanin admitted that international sports did not always work seamlessly, as evidenced by the rough play that marred the Soviet basketball trip to the United States in 1973, but claimed that such issues came from a different idea of what constituted "fair play," rather than an ineffectiveness of sports. According to Kanin, even boycotts could be viewed positively, because they gave nations an opportunity with an avenue of dissent that would not likely be "avenged by the use of force." Though, in essence, this enabled sports to work on the periphery of politics, Kanin predicted that as the magnitude of intercultural transactions increased, sports, as a representation of the international political system, would increasingly be "an instrument in the creation of mass perceptions in international relations."[45] He was right.

In the mid-1970s advances in telecommunications continued to help turn sports into a potent instrument in creating mass perceptions in international relations. And America's willingness to provide a market economy that encouraged innovation and competition helped it lead the telecommunications industry globally.[46] That the Soviets felt threatened by the United States' dynamic telecommunications industry was evident in the spring of 1974 when the Soviet Union, trying to guard against western "imperialism," encouraged developing nations to put pressure on the United Nations (UN) to curb satellite usage. Indeed, some third world countries did pressure the UN to restrict the acquisition and dissemination of photographs taken from satellites that revealed the "natural wealth, especially rich mineral reserves, in independent countries." The Soviet Union also expressed concern with a U.S. partnership with India that allowed Indians to beam shows off of U.S. satellites, as well as an American agreement with Japan, which was in the process of negotiating with American companies to establish Japanese satellite television. In fact, the major obstacle of the Japanese plan was not capital investment, of which the United States had plenty, but concerns of "spillover" content from Japan to other countries like China, the Soviet Union, and North and South Korea. At the UN, Moscow backed a blanket rule that, had it passed, would have disallowed any nation from transmitting into another country without that state's "prior approval." The UN formed an Outer Space Committee to write up guidelines regarding such issues. Clearly, the Soviet Union's aversion to American leadership in telecommunications reflected the cultural potency of the industry.[47]

As satellite technology advanced, so did cable television, which was capable of receiving satellite signals from around the globe and sending them across its vast underground cable networks. Though during the mid-1970s the cable industry tussled with the networks, struggled with high interest rates, and faced a landscape overcrowded with numerous small companies, the cable subscriber base grew impressively from approximately 5.3 million in 1970 to 12 million in 1976, the latter of which roughly translated to 15 percent of U.S. homes. Charles Dolan's 1973 launching of Cablevision helped spur this growth as did the 1976 launch of Home Box Office (HBO). That same year, Ted Turner, a media, billboard, and sports magnate, helped invigorate the cable industry as well by launching WTBS. Aired nationwide via satellite, it was the first of the so-called superstations.

Recognizing early on the role sports played in attracting viewers, Turner emphasized sports programming. Consequently, by 1988 he had fostered relationships with basketball players and government officials associated with the Soviet Union's Olympic basketball team and his NBA franchise, the Atlanta Hawks. He realized that signing Soviet players and sending his Hawks to play exhibition games in Russia encouraged the expansion of his media empire. And in many respects, as the satellite and cable industries matured and their relationship with sports grew, Soviet concerns that the dissemination of satellite images from the United States would not work to its advantage materialized.

The United States' dynamic telecommunications industry enabled it to lead the way in 1976 Olympic television coverage, evidenced by the $25 million ABC paid for broadcast rights in Montreal and the more than eighty hours of coverage it provided. All told, roughly 50 percent of American television viewers watched the prime-time broadcasts, while companies paid on average $72,000 per minute for advertising time during them. These companies did so with the hopes of linking "their products to the noblest ideals of athletic competition—and at a staggering cost." *Time* called ABC's broadcasting efforts the "most ambitious TV project in history." Those efforts included the use of twenty-five color cameras, including five mobile unites and four Electronic Sports Gatherers, described as "minicameras with backpack power sources," which had never before been used for live Olympic broadcasting. ABC also constructed "a prefabricated, soundproofed TV headquarters" replete with "two full-sized studios, control rooms and a telecine center with twelve videotape machines and a slow-motion converter." And the network employed an estimated fifty-four tape editors to organize the coverage. In addition to these expenditures, which totaled roughly $10 million, ABC was aided by the Canadian Broadcast Company's (CBC) 104 cameras and the Canadian Olympic Radio-TV Organization (ORTO), which sent up to twelve live signals simultaneously "to broadcasters from 70 countries—that will be beamed abroad via three satellites," as *Time* explained. Characterizing the effort, the ABC planning director Geoff Mason said, "We've created a monster—but a friendly one."[48]

Ultimately, ABC's Roone Arledge was credited with pulling off the coverage "with technical professionalism of the highest order." And in doing so, Arledge continued to emphasize the individual story. ABC's Mason explained the strategy to *Time*: "The Olympics are much more than two weeks of moving bodies. This is a convocation of mankind unique in the world, and we have to get that across. The participants are talented people, and to bring them out as people is as important as broadcasting the events." To accomplish its goal of delivering the Games in an "up close and personal" way, the network spent eighteen months interviewing close to seventy athletes in twelve nations.[49]

On the hardwood, in Montreal's new, 4,500-seat Desmarteau Center, where the Olympic basketball tournament opened play amid the remarkable global attention that the Olympics had generated by 1976, early returns suggested that those who had predicted subpar play from the relatively unheralded American collegians were mistaken. In an opening round 106–86 victory against a highly regarded Italian team, Phil Ford showed "spunk and dexterity" handling the bulk of point-guard duties, while Mitch Kupchak, Scott May, and Adrian Dantley, who led the team with twenty-two points, provided the bulk of the scoring. Coach Smith voiced his "surprise" and pleasure with the performance, saying that the U.S. team "displayed all the enthusiasm, poise, and confidence of an experienced team. After all, we're going up against teams that have been practicing six hours a day all year long."[50] Though that was an exaggeration, the American performance was impressive. The game marked the first time the United States had eclipsed the century mark at the Olympics since Rome, harkening back to memories of earlier American Olympic performances, especially those from 1956 to 1964. The team's trademark speed and high scoring had returned to the Games.

Altogether, the opening day of action, particularly for the United States, the Soviets, and Puerto Rico, demonstrated the international trend toward higher scoring. On the same day the United States beat Italy, the Soviet Union made an offensive statement of its own with a 120–77 victory over Mexico and Puerto Rico scored an upset by beating a favored Yugoslavian team.

Butch Lee of Marquette scored fifteen points for Puerto Rico in its upset win. Raised in New York City, Lee grew up practicing on that city's renowned playgrounds. When asked after the Yugoslavia upset why he was not playing for the U.S. team, Lee responded, "Nobody asked me." Fortunately for Lee, he had been born in Puerto Rico and could pursue his Olympic aspirations from his native land.[51]

A few days after Lee's performance against Yugoslavia, the United States almost paid for having overlooked him, when, in a thrilling, fast-paced shootout, Lee nearly led Puerto Rico to an upset of the United States. He dazzled onlookers with thirty five points, making an amazing fifteen of eighteen shots from the field. His performance led to more inquiries into why Lee did not even receive an invitation to try out for the U.S. team, especially considering that five of his Marquette teammates attended the trials. Years later, the former Olympian and U.S. Olympic Basketball Committee member Bill Hosket explained, "At that time the budget didn't allow you to bring every college player that you thought could make the team. They [the committee] were very selective because of budget concerns on how many people they could even invite to the trials." Hosket remembered that the committee wanted to hold the trials near a big airport to save money on flights so that they could invite more players. But still, they could not invite everyone. Members of the committee would talk to college coaches and, "I think Al McGuire told one of the guys that Butch was like my third or fourth best player on my team," Hosket said.[52] Regardless of why it had happened, not getting invited to the U.S. Olympic basketball trials motivated Lee.

Yet, despite Lee's heroics, in the closing seconds the United States held on against Puerto Rico for a 95–94 victory, with the pivotal basket coming when Adrian Dantley swooped in for a tip-in with the United States down by one point. Recalling the game, Dantley said, "Puerto Rico was a tough one . . . They weren't intimidated by us." He pointed out that Puerto Rican players, like Lee, played in the United States and played an American-style game.[53]

A day after its close call with Puerto Rico, the United States rebounded with a win over the strong Yugoslavian squad. The 112–93 final score suggests that the United States had an easy time, but it was a bruising contest. First-half action saw extreme physicality as together the teams were whistled for forty fouls—or one every thirty seconds. Down 55–51 at the end of the opening frame, the United States again faced a possible upset, thanks in no small part to another stellar individual performance, this time by the Yugoslavian Drazen Dalipagic.

Dalipagic so impressed onlookers that he garnered an invite from Red Auerbach to the Boston Celtics' training camp a couple of months later. At the Celtics camp, Dalipagic nearly earned distinction as one of the first to commence what later became a wave of European players to the NBA, but both the Celtics and Dalipagic struggled to overcome the language gap. "He was NBA star material," Auerbach lamented afterward. "His only drawback was his inability to communicate with the coach and his fellow players."[54] Still, his tryout portended things to come.

No such language issues confronted Dalipagic and the Yugoslavian team in Montreal, and his efforts in helping forge Yugoslavia's halftime lead caused the U.S. team to search for answers. As in past Olympiads, Coach Smith decided to increase the pressure in the second half. And, as before, the tactic delivered positive results as the United States opened the second half with eight straight points. By the end of the frame, it had scored sixty-one points while holding Yugoslavia to thirty-eight.[55] Though not quite as magnificent as the second halves turned in by Robertson and company in 1960 and Haywood and company in 1968, it was a thoroughly dominating run that exemplified the American basketball traditions of extreme speed and skill.

The win over Yugoslavia appeared to put the United States on another gold medal game collision course with the Soviets, who continued to beat opponents convincingly. Both teams finished preliminary round action undefeated at 5-0 and were on opposite sides of the semifinal brackets. (In its other preliminary round action, the United States registered a forfeit win over absentee Egypt and an 81–76 victory over Czechoslovakia, a score that in this instance misled in the other direction since the outcome was not really in doubt in the closing minutes. Nonetheless, after the Czechoslovakia game, Smith did say, "We could have used some more poise out there."[56])

In the semifinals the United States faced a Canadian squad coached by the United States' Jack Donohue of Holy Cross University, while the Soviets were pitted against Yugoslavia. Donohue kept his team close in the first half. In fact, the Canadians led 32–26 with only four minutes remaining in the opening stanza, but the United States then reeled off eight straight points en route to a 95–77 victory that, again, highlighted its speed. In one decisive stretch to start the second half, the *Washington Post* wrote, the United States "literally ran" to a twenty-point advantage.[57]

In postgame comments Coach Donohue joked to the media, "I'm a United States citizen . . . and I'm awfully upset that we won't be getting a chance to play the Russians." He was referring to the unexpected victory—unexpected to many Americans, that is—Yugoslavia had managed over the Soviet Union, 89–84, in the other semifinal, which denied the United States a chance to redeem its loss in Munich. Dantley remembered that he and his mates were also "kind of disappointed Yugoslavia beat Russia" because of what had occurred in 1972.[58]

Yugoslavia beat the Soviets by mimicking the United States' speedy methods, including those of, ironically enough, the 1972 team. Indeed, Yugoslavia's adoption of the American fast break had proved successful before the Montreal Games, as they had beaten the Soviets five straight times leading up to them. In addition to utilizing their speed in Montreal, the Yugoslavs were able to hold the seven-feet-two-inch Soviet big man Vladimir Tkachenko, known as a gentle but effective giant, to two points. It also did not hurt that the clutch-shooting Sergei Belov, who starred against the United States in Munich, fouled out with four minutes remaining. "The Russians have trouble with quick guards," the Yugoslav coach Mike Novosel explained in his postgame remarks. "When we tour the United States every year, we watch players from high school to the pros. Yes, we copy their fast style. It is one of the reasons we win."[59]

For the gold medal game, in front of a sold-out crowd, it looked like the U.S. players would face another stiff test from a Yugoslavian squad imbued with American style. But the United States' speed, teamwork, and game plan ultimately proved too much. Having watched Yugoslavia beat the Soviets with the help of superb outside shooting, one particular move that Coach Smith implemented paid immediate dividends—his decision to play more man-to-man defense than usual. The strategy helped the

14. A battle for the ball between Yugoslavia and the United States during the gold medal game. Photo by AFP. AFP Collection/Getty Images.

United States score the game's first eight points, and the team did not stop there. Sticking with its pressure defense, America built a comfortable 44–22 advantage with six minutes left in the first half. Quite simply, the team had "everything running real well," Dantley explained.[60] The fast start helped it win the gold rather comfortably, 95–74.

Dantley led the United States in the final with thirty points, even though he missed a portion of the second half when he sustained an injury to the face. All told, he made thirteen of nineteen shots and even guarded Yugoslavia's highly regarded Cosic, who tallied only fifteen points.[61] Following the win, the *Washington Post*'s Kenneth Denlinger praised the U.S. team for accepting roles, enduring tough practices when the soon-to-be-pros could have made money working clinics, and for unselfish play.[62] Although it lacked a flamboyant superstar, the 1976 squad had left an indelible mark on the Olympics with its splendid display of grit, teamwork, and fast action. At the same time, individual excellence could be seen in Montreal, whether through Arledge's masterminding of ABC's coverage, through Dantley's splendid play, or through the shoe industry's focus on endorsing superstar players. As the stature of basketball stars increased and their personas and styles became associated with certain products, opportunities for self-expression would gain further importance, even if that expression was often allied with a transnational firm.

The gold medal victory over Yugoslavia in Montreal helped soothe the disappointment of Munich, but for those still wanting a direct Olympic rematch with the Soviets, the wait would prove long. By the time the United States won the 1976 gold, the IOC had already notified Moscow of its selection as host of the 1980 Olympics. Immediately after the announcement, speculation of a U.S. boycott mounted. The *New York Times*'s Red Smith called such speculation useless, writing, "Trying to predict how politicians and playground directors would behave four to eight years hence would be sheer madness."[63] But as it turned out, those predicting a U.S. boycott were correct.

Though the official decision did not come until the spring of 1980, by 1979 the prospects of U.S. participation looked dim. America had sent teams to the Soviets' Spartakiad, including a hastily organized group of basketball amateurs that consisted largely of second-tier players whose "brilliant improvisations" still managed to draw "large crowds, even to their practice sessions."[64] However, that year Jimmy Carter admitted on the television program *Meet the Press* that he had asked the USOC to boycott the Olympics if they were not moved to another location, unless the Soviet Union withdrew from Afghanistan by February 1980 (it had invaded in the summer of 1978). By January 1980 the Soviet Union had not withdrawn. As a result, *Time* wrote rather pessimistically, "The fact is there is probably no single action short of war that would punish Moscow more than to have the Olympics taken away or spoiled."[65] (The Winter Olympics did, of course, take place that year in Lake Placid, New York, the site of the improbable United States' run to gold in hockey.)

Some who supported a boycott of the Soviet Summer Games claimed that the Soviets were carrying out rampant human rights abuses. In the months leading up to the 1980 Olympics, reports surfaced of crackdowns by the Komitet Gosudarstvennoy Bezopasnosti (KGB) on dissidents. The *National Review* charged the Soviet Union with carrying out an "especially severe purge of dissident groups" in order to "ensure that when the thousands of foreign visitors and athletes arrive, everything will look peachy." Pressure placed on the IOC from political agitators advocating human rights exemplifies how the terms of such debates with regard to the Olympics have historically assumed respect for liberal principles.[66]

Still, outside of Great Britain's Margaret Thatcher, the suggestion to move the site gained few supporters. It was not the USOC's prerogative to move the Olympics—that power rests with the IOC—and the IOC held firm to the Brundage tradition of arguing that the Olympics function outside the realm of politics. Lord Killanin, the head of the IOC, had claimed early in 1980 that moving the Games was "virtually physically impossible" anyway, and when the U.S. boycott was officially announced, he voiced his displeasure. Others did too. During the boycott debate, the IOC official Jean-Pierre Soisson said, rather dubiously, "The Olympics are a sporting event, not a political affair."[67]

In the end, sixty-four other nations, including West Germany and Japan, boycotted the Moscow Games along with the United States. France and Great Britain did attend, though during the opening ceremonies, Englishman Dick Palmer carried the Olympic flag rather than England's in a show of protest. As expected, Soviet officials did not appreciate the USOC's decision to boycott or Carter's support of that decision. One Soviet newspaper editor said of Carter, "He is going too far. This has nothing to do with Afghanistan. It is America's pure anti-Sovietism coming out again."[68]

The boycott meant the 1980 Olympic basketball tournament did not attract the attention it otherwise would have. The prospect of the United States finally having the opportunity to avenge the Munich loss on Moscow's soil would have undoubtedly engendered great interest: it had certainly gotten the attention of Bob Knight, who wanted to coach the U.S. squad on Soviet hardwood and had Newell in his corner. But ultimately, after the issue was "hotly debated" by the Dean Smith–led U.S. Olympic Basketball Committee, the job went to Providence head coach Dave Gavitt.[69] (An international incident at a basketball tournament in Puerto Rico—more on that later—likely hurt Knight's cause.)

Another reason that sending a U.S. squad to the Olympic Games in Moscow would have elicited considerable attention was that by then, college basketball, and the NBA for that matter, was enjoying a surge in popularity, thanks in no small part to the impact of Larry Bird and Earvin "Magic" Johnson, both of whom starred in the 1979 NCAA final that drew a 24.1 rating for NBC. Those ratings dipped slightly the following year for the NCAA final, but were still quite strong at 19.8. Among the stars of that 1980 NCAA final between UCLA and Louisville was the Final Four's Most Outstanding Player, Louisville's Darrell Griffith—just the type of player NBC would have liked to see perform in Moscow. Darrell "Dr. Dunkenstein" Griffith had been the only high school player to try out for the 1976 Olympic team. He did not make that team but did register an astounding forty-eight-inch vertical leap at the tryouts. The LA Times's Jim Murray once wrote of the high-flying Griffith, "He's not a guard. He's a satellite."[70] NBC had paid $87 million for the right to broadcast the 1980 Games, and the network planned to provide a record-setting 150 hours of Olympic action.[71] But those plans got scrapped with the boycott. (NBC did recover its rights fees "since the U.S. government had not allowed the network to actually cover the Games." However, NBC had neglected to purchase insurance for its pre-Games costs.[72])

So rather than providing an unprecedented level of Olympics coverage and thereby enabling other stations, like the upstart ESPN, to deliver highlights of a 1980 Olympic basketball tournament that seemed certain to garner groundbreaking attention, both the media and the athletic sector needed to formulate a plan on how to proceed postboycott.[73] Dave Gavitt, who had named UCLA's Larry Brown and Dee Row of the University of Connecticut as assistant coaches, decided to proceed nonetheless with the basics of his original trials plan, which had included inviting sixty-four players to North Carolina State for a mid-May tryout.[74] And the U.S. Olympic Basketball Committee set to work organizing an alternative series of games for the U.S. team. The eventual plan called for the 1980 squad to play five exhibition tilts versus NBA all-star teams in major cities and one contest versus the 1976 Olympic team.

When the trials came to an end on May 23, the U.S. basketball committee announced a team that was headlined by All-American Mark Aguirre of DePaul University and that featured a trio of standout freshman: Sam Bowie of Kentucky, Rodney McCray of Louisville, and Isiah Thomas of Indiana. Alton Lister of Arizona State joined Bowie at the center position, while Maryland's forward Buck Williams, LaSalle's Michael Brooks, Utah's Danny Vranes, and North Carolina's Al Wood complemented Aguirre as forwards. Kansas's Darnell Valentine, Notre Dame's Bill Hanzlik, and the versatile six-feet-six-inch Rolando Blackman of Kansas State rounded out the U.S. backcourt.[75] (Darrell Griffith, among others, chose not to try out.) And the squad's 97–84 victory at Los Angeles's Forum in the opening game of its series suggested that another high-scoring American Olympic team would have represented the United States in Moscow.[76]

As for the 1980 Olympic basketball tournament, after upsetting the Soviet Union on its own turf, Italy faced Yugoslavia for the gold medal. This marked the first time that neither team in the Olympic basketball final hailed from the United States or the Soviet Union, and in that precedent-setting final, Yugoslavia, competing in the gold medal game for the second straight Olympiad, proved superior in winning 86–77. On the team was Kresimir Cosic, the former BYU standout who had played for Yugoslavia against the United States for gold in Mexico City and who ended his career having played in four straight Olympiads for his country, from 1968 to 1980. He finished that impressive Olympic career with two silver medals (1968 and 1976) and one gold (1980). "The Russians had dominated international basketball in the '60s, and right through Munich in '72," Gavitt maintained. "But the '70s belonged to the Yugoslavs, and Cosic was the key player. He was the leader of that team."[77]

TABLE 9. 1976 U.S. Men's Olympic Basketball cumulative stats

NAME	G	FGM-FGA	(%)	FTM-FTA	(%)	REB/AVG	PF	PTS/AVG	AST
Adrian Dantley	6	43-80	.538	30-36	.833	34/5.7	12	116/19.3	10
Scott May	6	42-80	.525	16-18	.889	37/6.2	17	100/16.7	12
Mitch Kupchak	6	30-49	.612	15-20	.750	34/5.7	16	75/12.5	6
Phil Ford	6	29-54	.537	10-12	.833	13/2.2	17	68/11.3	5
Quinn Buckner	6	22-44	.500	0-0	.000	18/3.0	19	44/7.3	18
Kenny Carr	6	20-36	.556	1-2	.500	19/3.2	13	41/6.8	6
Tom LaGarde	6	13-18	.722	14-16	.875	11/1.8	18	40/6.7	1
Phil Hubbard	6	12-23	.522	1-1	1.000	23/3.8	18	28/4.7	3
Walt Davis	6	10-21	.476	6-6	1.000	10/1.7	14	26/4.3	12
Ernie Grunfeld	6	9-18	.500	3-4	.750	4/0.7	9	21/3.5	15
Tate Armstrong	6	5-7	.714	6-8	.750	2/0.3	0	16/2.7	2
Steve Sheppard	6	3-7	.429	3-4	.750	6/1.0	2	9/1.5	1

Yugoslav head coach Ranko Zeravica told the press in postgame remarks, "A question who is best, the Yugoslavs or the U.S.A., is being disputed. So, we must meet and find out."[78] The comments demonstrated that there was a U.S. presence in Moscow despite its absence.

Overall, the scores of the 1980 Olympic basketball games showed how internationally the sport had sped up. In fact, the scoring was so abundant that it suggested a pace more akin to the pro game in America than the college game, especially given that the NCAA still had not adopted the shot clock. In 1984 another change FIBA adopted in the wake of the NBA was the three-point shot, which the NBA legalized for its 1979–80 season. In addition to the adoption of the three-point shot, which would not take effect until the 1988 tournament, in an effort to lessen the physicality of the game a bit, FIBA decided to decrease the number of team fouls it takes to put a team into the one-and-one "bonus" from eight to seven. FIBA also chose to have a five-second dribbling rule put into effect for the 1988 Games.[79] So, to be sure, the college game resonated internationally as well, but, as with the AAU's industrial leagues decades earlier, the NBA was influencing FIBA significantly. Ironically, within a couple of decades it would be FIBA that influenced the NBA.

TABLE 10. 1980 U.S. Men's Olympic Basketball cumulative stats

NAME	G	FGM-FGA	(%)	FTM-FTA	(%)	REB/AVG	PF	PTS/AVG	AST	BLK	ST
Michael Brooks	6	29-57	.509	21-32	.656	36/6.0	14	79/13.2	11	0	9
Sam Bowie	6	29-49	.592	11-19	.579	41/6.9	12	69/11.5	12	14	0
Mark Aguirre	6	26-54	.481	16-24	.667	30/5.0	14	68/11.3	16	1	9
Al Wood	6	27-43	.628	6-12	.500	17/2.8	11	60/10.0	2	4	5
Isiah Thomas	6	22-55	.400	14-17	.824	12/2.0	19	58/9.7	37	0	10
Rolando Blackman	6	22-54	.407	4-6	.667	28/4.7	5	48/8.0	14	1	5
Danny Vranes	6	17-33	.515	7-11	.636	17/2.8	16	41/6.8	4	1	4
Darnell Valentine	6	14-30	.467	6-8	.750	12/2.0	4	34/5.7	17	1	14
Buck Williams	6	9-23	.391	11-16	.688	24/4.0	8	29/4.9	5	4	3
Alton Lister	6	5-14	.357	0-0	.000	6/1.0	8	10/1.7	1	0	0
Bill Hanzlik	6	5-14	.357	1-3	.333	6/1.0	4	11/1.8	7	1	5
Rodney McCray	5	1-3	.333	1-2	.500	4/0.8	2	3/0.6	4	2	0
USA TOTALS	6	206-429	.480	98-150	.653	233/38.8	117	510/85.0	130	29	64
OPP. TOTALS	6	192-421	.456	72-126	.571	201/33.5	132	456/76.0	136	30	71

10

AIR JORDAN ARRIVES AND THE GENERAL DELIVERS IN LOS ANGELES

With the benefit of hindsight, the rule changes that basketball underwent in the several decades before the 1984 Los Angeles Olympic Games seem almost to have been custom-made for Michael Jordan. The widening of the lane, addition of the shot clock, more liberal interpretation of traveling, imposition of a ten-second limit in which to pass half court, and the limiting of players to three seconds in the lane all opened the game for speedier action, more forays to the basket, and more innovation. Even so, no one could have conjured Jordan. The superlatives used to describe him over the years could fill a book. Maybe the sociologist Harry Edwards's characterization of Jordan sums it up best: Edwards said that if he were in charge of introducing an alien being "to the epitome of human potential, creativity, perseverance and spirit, I would introduce that alien life to Michael Jordan."[1] As noted in the introduction, the historian Walter LaFeber put Jordan's popularity into perspective in 1999 by referencing a poll of Chinese schoolchildren that placed Jordan second among the twentieth century's greatest figures.[2]

Such descriptions, however, did not appear until well after the LA Games. In 1984 people understood that Michael Jordan was good; they just did not know he was destined to become the greatest basketball player ever. Sure, Jordan had won back-to-back player of the year honors at North Carolina, but at the Olympic trials in the spring of 1984, most observers thought Patrick Ewing had the most potential. Besides Ewing, much of the press's attention went to Charles Barkley, already dubbed the "Round Mound of Rebound." And in late April of 1984 the *Chicago Tribune*'s Bob Logan, echoing the sentiments of most Chicagoans and most members of the Bulls management, had written that the seven-foot center Hakeem Olajuwon was the player every NBA team wanted in the upcoming draft. Logan also listed five players the Bulls might choose in the third slot— Jordan was not even mentioned.[3] However, by June 17, Logan did predict Jordan would be the Bulls' selection, asking, "Is he [Superman] here at last?"[4]

Over the course of that Olympic summer Jordan suggested he might just be. And in time, he would play a key role in opening basketball to its full potential, thereby allowing it to affect popular global culture dramatically. Though telecommunications and marketing helped build Jordan's legend, this should not overshadow the allure of his ability to play basketball artfully. Like most great art, he expressed powerful, seemingly dichotomous ideas simultaneously when he played: explosive athleticism with fine skill, grace with ferocious competitiveness, and teamwork with individuality. And much as they do with great art, people have struggled to pinpoint the exact nature of Jordan's brilliance. For example, at the Los Angeles Games, Spain's head coach resorted to saying Jordan looked more like rubber than a man.[5]

It would take a player of Jordan's magnitude to raise himself and his Olympic teammates above the domineering presence of the U.S. team's head coach Robert Montgomery Knight. The highly successful, highly controversial Knight, from Indiana University, earned the right to lead the 1984 U.S. Olympic basketball team in May of 1982. As a collegian, Knight was a teammate of Jerry Lucas and John Havlicek at Ohio State. He went on to coach at West Point before commencing a thirty-year stint as head coach of Indiana University, where he won three national championships and posted a .735 winning percentage before being fired in 2000 largely for his outbursts of anger. Later he coached at Texas Tech University. During his career, he enjoyed a close relationship with Pete Newell, the 1960 U.S. Olympic basketball coach. It was a relationship that dated back to 1969, and one that Knight has described as that of "father-son." Jerry West characterized Newell's and Knight's closeness after being asked to compare his 1960 Olympic team with the 1984 squad by answering, "You might as well start out by understanding that it was the same guy coaching both teams." Knight credits Newell, as well as Coach Iba, with lobbying other ABA/USA committee members to give him the reins of the 1984 team. For Newell, it made complete sense—he considered Knight the best coach in college basketball.[6]

Knight was a controversial choice. Nicknamed "The General," he had a penchant for making historical references to actual generals, often hard-driving ones, such as George S. Patton. Like Patton, Knight's deference and sense of responsibility were accompanied by an outsized ego, a deep trough of unpredictable anger, and autocratic methods. He represented the relentless taskmaster college coach who emphasized team play over the individual. It was a creature formed in part as a result of an NCAA system ostensibly based on a bizarre mutation of the old British amateur ideal. The system limited the agency of NCAA players, while granting far-reaching powers for its coaches.

Knight's outbursts and tactics became legendary. He has been known to curse with abandon, throw a chair on the court during a game, lash angry tirades at members of the media, and even grab a player's neck. In 1979, as coach of the U.S. Pan-Am team, he became involved in an international basketball imbroglio that led to his arrest on charges of assaulting a police officer. After the incident, Arturo Gallardo, head of the Basketball Federation of Puerto Rico, wrote a letter that ran in the *New York Times* accusing Knight of entering *Puerto Rico's* locker room after the United States had beaten Puerto Rico to give the Puerto Rican team "a verbal lashing, stating they only had one worthwhile player."[7]

Knight could also show considerable sentiment, though, such as his willingness to praise predecessors and mentors. Plus, Knight's Indiana teams succeeded, and he had earned the respect of his peers and many of his players; as a result, he became the Olympic coach. He took the job seriously, approaching it as a general might approach battle. He told

Newsweek, "I think about the millions of men who were drafted in world wars and told, 'Here's your responsibility.' I've accepted this job in the same sense. It's a tremendous honor, and I'll accept whatever comes with it. As I think about it, I like to keep it simple: I want to coach the best team in the world for two weeks."[8]

According to Knight, from the moment of his appointment to the end of the Los Angeles Games, not a day went by that he did not think of some aspect or detail of his Olympic plan. "The Olympics is a no-choice situation for an American basketball coach. You've got to win . . . I thought we'd win. I thought we *should* win. I believe we *had* to win. And I'll never have a greater honor," he said afterward.[9] Knight thought the United States *had* to win because the tournament was larger than basketball. He was defending America's way of life. "I want us to be able to represent American competitiveness and American basketball, in that order, to the nth degree," he told reporters during the opening week of the Games.[10]

Knight's antics, coupled with his undeniable on-court success, made him a divisive figure as pundits tried to predict the effect he would have on the U.S. team. Critics claimed that Knight's shenanigans served no purpose but to feed his ego and wondered whether his deep reservoir of anger would ultimately hurt the Olympic team. Supporters argued that he was a masterful tactician whose actions were intended to mold his players into the best team possible.

To run his system, Knight wanted specific kinds of ball players. "I want players who are good athletes or possessors of excellent basketball skills. Ideally, I look for a combination of the two. But I need a guy who accepts his role in a disciplined offense and plays hard man-to-man defense," he explained.[11] His style was rooted in the fundamentals, motion offense, and man-to-man defense of the kind taught by Iba. But a common misconception about Knight is that he advocated a slow, deliberate offensive approach. This was not true of Knight's teams at Indiana, especially when they were stocked with athletes, and it certainly was not true at the Los Angeles Games, where the U.S. team averaged 95.4 points. Knight's vaunted motion offense may have emphasized team play but, as was so with Dean Smith's and John Wooden's schemes, team play did not mean slow action or low point totals.

Knight had a number of things working in his favor to help him accomplish his mission as the LA Games approached. Basketball was booming nationwide, especially NCAA basketball, as evidenced by the 61,000-plus spectators that attended the 1982 NCAA Men's Final Four, a U.S. record for the sport.[12] And a number of superstars filled the collegiate ranks, most notably Ewing, Barkley, and Jordan. They helped continue the rise in the popularity of NCAA basketball generated by Larry Bird and "Magic" Johnson in the late 1970s.

All of these stars' legends, especially Jordan's, were helped during the 1980s by maturation in the satellite and cable industry, at home and abroad. In April of 1981 the FCC had given the Communications Satellite Corporation (COMSAT) permission to move forward with plans to "beam programs directly from satellites to individual rooftops equipped with special dish-shaped antennas." The *Washington Post* predicted the demand for direct-to-television satellite signals would come mainly from "places that are not now served by cable systems and that get poor reception from regular stations."[13] This referred mainly to rural areas of America, but soon, those sentiments applied to places across the globe. In 1981 Gustave Hauser, chairman of Warner Amex Cable Communications, had summed up the state of the industry, saying, "We are building cable now about as fast as human and technological resources are available . . . It's going to cost billions of dollars. You can't wire America for nothing." Fortunately for the United States, the FCC was continuing to promote an environment that encouraged growth. In the early 1980s some predicted fifty million American cable subscribers by 1990.[14] As it turned out, there were roughly fifty-two million cable subscribers by then.

The implications of satellite technology were particularly strong because they posed problems for countries looking to control content.[15] Given its capital reserves, business acumen, technological know-how, and the attractiveness of its film and sports stars, this worked in the United States' favor. Over time, the success of satellite television brought American basketball and attendant corporate ads into the homes of billions of people across the globe, including those behind the iron curtain. For instance, in the spring of 1985 the *Washington Post* noted that since the inception of Rupert Murdoch's British "superstation," dubbed the Sky Channel and on which sports played an important role, advertisers like International Business Machines (IBM), Proctor & Gamble, and Mars Inc. had shown keen interest in the prospect of global advertising. According to the *Post*, global advertising offered companies a chance to move away from regional attempts to reach consumers and toward a universal theme aimed at turning their brands into worldwide forces.[16] To reach as many potential consumers as possible, these transnational corporations emphasized advertising during sports programming.[17]

For most of these multinational corporations, China, with its more than 1 billion people, was a particularly coveted sphere. The 1984 Olympics would provide a unique opportunity for businesses to reach China's populace because, for the first time since 1948, the country had decided to participate fully in the Games. China's presence in the LA Olympics was part of leader Deng Xiaoping's plan to return his nation to the status of a global superpower. To survive in a global economy led by liberal capitalist nations, all of which celebrated sports, Deng began opening China's market, which in turn at least modestly increased personal liberties. Deng also put an emphasis on sports.[18]

China's other two Olympic basketball appearances had come in 1936 and 1948, before Chiang Kai-shek's exodus to Taiwan (China had nearly participated in 1952, but uncertainty on the part of both the IOC and China caused them to miss out on the basketball tournament). So, in all practicality, the 1984 Games marked "Communist China's first major presence in the Olympics," as *Time* put it.[19] Political, economic, and cultural differences had caused China's decades-long absence, but by 1984, the increasingly commercial IOC enthusiastically welcomed a changing China back to the fold. Its attendance marked a monumental shift for the Communist nation. From the late 1950s to 1978 (before Deng took over), China had withdrawn or was banned from nearly all international sports federations, much like the pre–World War II Soviet Union. China did enjoy international success in ping-pong during that time, but little else. But with Deng ushering in a new era, as Brook Larmer has asserted, Chinese leaders "knew real respect would come only when China could compete with Western powers in the 'big balls'—soccer, volleyball, and basketball—and in the most illustrious of all sporting events, the Olympic Games." Therefore, Deng endorsed China's "Gold-Medal Strategy" for the LA Olympics.[20]

Under Deng, China's economy grew at a phenomenal rate, and though winning a gold medal in basketball in LA proved unrealistic, China's basketball prospects brightened quickly nonetheless. In fact, they had brightened several years before the LA Games, though few outside the Shanghai Sports Commission noticed, when the six-feet-ten-inch Yao Zhiyuan and six-feet-two-inch Fang Fengdi, both former Chinese basketball stars, welcomed a baby boy they named Yao Ming to their family. As Larmer has noted, news of Yao's birth quickly made its way to the zenith of the Shanghai Sports Commission. For two generations, Chinese officials had singled out Yao's forebears for training in China's Communist sporting system, modeled on the Soviet system. A Shanghai coach told Larmer, "We had been looking forward to the arrival of Yao Ming for three generations."[21] Without the changes that Deng had made, Yao would not have ended up playing for China at the Olympics. When he finally did suit up for China, Yao personified the success that Communist partymen, especially Deng, had wrought by bringing about change. However, at the same time, Yao reflected the difficulties the Communist party faced in retaining authoritarian control while opening China's economy.

In the mid-1980s, even before the emergence of Yao, multinational corporations maneuvered to capitalize on the newly accessible Chinese consumer. One way to ramp up their commercial presence in China was through purchasing advertising time on China's lone television station, especially during the LA Games. Peking's Central China Television station planned to show six hours of daily Olympic coverage, and multinationals gobbled up the advertising slots.[22]

With the advances in television in the 1980s enabling advertisers to reach more consumers, and the Olympic movement expanding, the price tag for Olympic broadcast rights increased. The U.S. television station ABC paid the LA Olympic Organizing Committee (LAOOC) $225 million to broadcast the 1984 Games, a figure that nearly tripled NBC's $87 million bid for Moscow.[23] To deliver more than 180 hours of coverage, ABC utilized over 3,500 employees at twenty-three separate venues, 208 cameras, and 660 miles of cable.[24] Estimates that ABC would reap, including international rights, roughly $300 million in broadcast revenues, one-third of which would go the IOC, proved about right. The Olympics had clearly become a sound investment, considering the boost the Games have historically given to a network's fall schedule.[25]

The exorbitant fees ABC paid the IOC for broadcast rights meant that the network played a pivotal role in financing the Olympics. This put it in a good position to direct the nature of the coverage and select preferred prime-time events. The planning was precise. For instance, before the LA Games, IOC officials were already pressuring national governing bodies of various sports to schedule morning finals for the *1988 Seoul Games*, so that those finals could air in prime time in the United States. The *Chicago Tribune* noted that one network official bluntly said, "They [the IOC] know where the money is."[26]

Of course, not everyone appreciated the television coverage of the LA Games. The Soviet Union's state-run *Pravda* called the Games nothing more than an extended Fourth of July celebration. "The spirit of peace, of international friendship—essential elements in the Olympic tradition— was replaced in Los Angeles by an atmosphere of crusading nationalism," *Pravda* wrote. Since the Soviets boycotted these Games, Soviet brass limited media coverage largely to shots of medal winners and to criticism. But the Soviet Union's virtual blackout of the Games was not completely effective. Reports of increased trips by Estonians to Finland were attributed to the airing of the Olympics in Finland.[27] The 1984 Olympics did, in fact, attract the largest global television audience for a single event up to that time—an estimated 180 million Americans alone watched part of ABC's coverage, breaking the old record of 160 million for the 1976 Montreal Games and the 1983 miniseries "The Winds of War."[28]

Still, a number of U.S. commentators did not like the coverage of the Olympics either. For instance, Rajiv Desai, writing in the *Chicago Tribune*, credited ABC with its use of "Super Slo Mo" technology, which he thought worthy of a gold medal, but bemoaned ABC's broadcast decisions and wondered whether the Soviet news agency Tass was correct in its assessment that the Games were merely "crass commercialism."[29] ABC responded to such criticisms by emphasizing that the international feed it provided differed from the one it offered domestically.[30]

In addition to television, a relatively new component of the telecommunications industry, the personal computer figured prominently among the throng of advertising that helped ABC turn a record $75 million profit from its Olympic coverage. By the mid 1980s the popularity of the personal computer had surged in Western nations. In the United States alone there were roughly 30 million PCs compared to 50,000 in the Soviet Union.

Apple, Texas Instruments, Compaq, and IBM counted among the leading computer companies that touted their products during the LA Games, and virtually all of them expanded their advertising initiatives for the Olympics.[31] The Games provided an opportunity for companies like these to showcase their innovative products and, by extension, the abundant liberal capitalist marketplace.[32]

Affordable, accessible personal computers represented the latest global technological advancement to emerge from democratic-based, market-oriented nations. As the 1980s and 1990s progressed, the computer, in coordination with the Internet, cable television, and satellite technology, created new platforms for instantaneous coverage of the exploits of superstar athletes, such as Michael Jordan clad in Nike shoes. Taken together, the power of these technological advances, as the cold war historian LaFeber has asserted, "changed the lives of people around the world and, in so doing, brought down the Communist system, which could not adjust to this revolution."[33]

At the same time, Peter Ueberroth's Olympic financing model gave the Games an even stronger commercial thrust, helping both the Olympics and basketball attract more people. Ueberroth implemented some basic open-market principles in his private-sector-driven plan to host the Games profitably. For instance, Ueberroth made the three major networks, plus the upstart ESPN, pay a nonrefundable $750,000 just to participate in a blind bidding process for broadcast rights. The record $225 million bid from ABC resulted. "When [LA Olympic committee member] David Wolpor and I opened the envelopes from the television officials, and ABC bid a substantial amount of money, that's when I knew we were in very, very good shape," Ueberroth said. An additional $61.8 million poured in from international television rights. Ueberroth also decided to limit the number of firms that could gain distinction as an official Olympic Games sponsor, and large bids for these exclusive relationships materialized as well.[34] Since the LA Games, the IOC has basically co-opted the Ueberroth model (taking responsibility, and thereby influence, from municipal Olympic organizing committees in the process) to leverage the Games financially and control more closely how the Games get broadcast and marketed to the world.[35]

Before Coach Knight could take the 1984 U.S. Olympic team to Los

Angeles to play in front of ABC's record-setting television audiences, however, he needed to pick the squad. From April 17 through April 22, seventy-four Olympic hopefuls traveled to Indiana University's Assembly Hall for tryouts. There, Knight and his assistants, C. M. Newton, Don Donoher, and George Raveling, along with a number of coaches invited to oversee the workouts, including Purdue's Gene Keady, Michigan State's Jud Heathcote, and Creighton's Willis Reed, assessed the players. Noteworthy NBA personnel watched too, among them Wayne Embry, Pete Newell, Jerry Colangelo, and Stu Inman.[36] Though he played an active role in their planning, Knight oversaw much of the trials in Iba-esque fashion, from a scaffold above the courts, which also evoked images of "the remote and godlike Bear Bryant in his tower of the Alabama football fields," as *Newsweek*'s Pete Axthelm described it.[37] Knight did meet with the other coaches each morning and night to critique players, but by keeping a physical distance, he could create a powerful type of luminary influence on the proceedings.

Knight and his cohorts cut the number of players to about thirty for the last two days of the trials. Then they separated the surviving players into four teams to compete in a round-robin tournament dubbed the "final four." Understandably, decisions on players did not always come easily; they were critiquing a talented bunch. At the forward position alone, nine talented players at the trials later enjoyed splendid professional careers. Included among them were North Carolina's Sam Perkins, Oklahoma's Wayman Tisdale, the high school player Danny Manning, Oregon State's A. C. Green, Villanova's Ed Pinckney, San Diego State's Michael Cage, DePaul's Tyrone Corbin, and Auburn's Chuck Person and Charles Barkley. That list does not even include Maryland's Len Bias, who, along with North Carolina's Kenny Smith (left wrist surgery) and Kentucky's Sam Bowie and Melvin Turpin, turned down an invitation to try out.[38] Commenting on the intensity of the competition, Tyrone Corbin said, "It's fun and scary at the same time." Forward Antoine Carr of Wichita State, who had just spent a season in Italy's top professional league, also attended. (Because Carr played in a European professional league and FIBA counted its players as employees of the respective corporate sponsors of its teams, he was eligible for the U.S. team.) Speculation held that Knight and company thought Carr's strong personality and year in the European pro leagues could disrupt team morale. Carr was cut after the weekend scrimmages.[39]

Though not as numerous as the forwards, the centers faced stiff competition too. Granted, Georgetown's Patrick Ewing came to the trials as one of a few, if not the only, player who was certain to make the team. But outside of the Georgetown seven-footer, the competition was fierce, especially between Southern Methodist's seven-foot Jon Koncak and Arkansas's six-feet-ten-inch Joe Kleine. The two had lockers alongside one another at Assembly Hall but did not speak to each other before workouts. "My fiancé told me if they took him not to come home," Koncak jokingly told reporters.[40]

The guard positions proved hardest to decide. Originally, Knight intended to cut the group to sixteen or eighteen players after the first week, but to further evaluate the guards, he kept twenty, including Duke's Johnny Dawkins, Gonzaga's John Stockton, Louisville's Lancaster Gordon, Georgia's Vern Fleming, Cal-State Fullerton's Leon Wood, and the Indiana freshman Steve Alford. After the first few days, Wood, a member of the 1983 U.S. Pan Am team, and Alford, known for his shooting, had demonstrated capabilities at point guard. Early reports also had the six-feet-six-inch, 280-pound Barkley emerging as a dominant force inside, and Michael Jordan apparently seemed incapable of missing a shot.[41]

The selection process seemed participatory, given the daily coaches' meeting, but Knight reigned supreme. Indicative of this, on the second day of the trials, the *Washington Post*'s John Feinstein could not find any of the nine men technically charged with selecting the Olympic team on hand. He reported that when one professional scout asked, "Where's the selection committee?" the scout was told, "The selection committee is standing on that tower over there," and then motioned him toward Knight atop the scaffold.[42] Though the story slightly overstated the situation, since Knight did listen to his coaches in their daily strategy meetings, he did exercise final say over who would make the team. Dave Gavitt, chairman of the selection committee, admitted as much when he told Feinstein, "In the past, we've always tried to give the coach what he wants, but we've gone through the laborious exercise of going over every single player . . . This time, Bob will come to us with the team intact and say, 'This is the team I want.'"[43]

Knight opened the "final four" weekend scrimmages to the public, and in a demonstration of the state of Indiana's storied enthusiasm for basketball, the scrimmages attracted frenetic, sold-out crowds. Knight thought the spirited crowd in Assembly Hall gave the players "an idea of how enthusiastic the support was going to be for them from fans just like these across the United States."[44] Sure enough, the team received another indication of just how strongly Americans, especially native Hoosiers, supported them in early July when more than 67,000 people came to the Indianapolis Hoosier Dome to watch the Olympic team play an *exhibition* game against a collection of NBA stars that included the Indiana legends Larry Bird, Isiah Thomas, and Mark Aguirre. In a poignant display of basketball's popularity, the contest marked the largest crowd to watch a basketball game in U.S. history. And Jordan, who finished with twelve points, did not let them down.[45]

Bill Hosket, the 1968 Olympian and member of the U.S. Olympic Basketball Committee for the 1976 Games and the boycotted 1980 Games, credits Knight with filling USA Basketball coffers with the exhibitions he scheduled. Knight helped with the economic woes, so USA basketball didn't have to "worry about 'where we can we hold the trials and how many uniforms do we have,'" Hosket explained.[46]

Plenty of examples of the college game's popularity existed outside of the Olympic exhibitions. In the mid-1980s ESPN reached 25 million homes, and its staple fare, college basketball, was so coveted in one Kansas town that when a cable operator dropped ESPN because of fees, picketers showed up at the operator's offices to protest—they got ESPN back in three days.[47]

The record-breaking crowd present for the exhibition game did not leave the Hoosier Dome disappointed. Michael Jordan wowed fans with two moves that, the *Chicago Tribune*'s Phil Hersh gushed, "only air traffic controllers could track." Jordan also executed an "explosive" dunk over the Houston Rockets' Robert Reid. His graceful yet explosive highlights epitomized the essence of basketball's aesthetic allure. Knight lived up to billing too, drawing a technical after telling the referee Hank Nichols, "I've seen you bad before, but never this bad." And, as they would in all nine of their exhibition games, the U.S. Olympic squad won the affair in high-scoring fashion, 97–82.[48]

In addition to Jordan, Patrick Ewing, who had struggled up to that point, garnered praise for his strong play in the Hoosier Dome. Against the Boston Celtics' Robert Parish and Kevin McHale, he scored eleven points and snared five rebounds in sixteen minutes. "People might think

I was upset," he said afterward, referring to not playing in the team's previous game. "But Coach Knight is the coach, and I don't have any problem abiding by what he says."[49]

Part of Ewing's struggles stemmed from Knight's motion offense, in which centers played more like forwards and were depended on for screens. When setting screens for wing players, the forwards often got pulled away from the rim, so mobility and accurate shooting from ten to fifteen feet from the basket became important assets. Explaining Ewing's struggles, John Thompson, his coach at Georgetown, also noted that the perimeter emphasis of the international game put uncommon demands on true American centers like Ewing and Tisdale. "There is more emphasis on perimeter defense instead of so much shot-blocking. Foot movement becomes more important in guarding people," Thompson noted.[50]

Thompson's comments indicated the maturation of the international game. By 1984, many European teams had taken the agility associated with the 1956 Russell model and successfully added outside marksmanship to it. Europe's wider lanes, shot clock, and its recently adopted three-point shot, coupled with its club system for elite youths, which allowed youngsters to play virtually year-round under these liberal rules with well-organized club teams that were often affiliated with professional ones, helped in the development of more versatile and more mobile centers moving forward. By the 1990s this versatility helped many international players find work plying their craft in the NBA. In turn, the imports affected the American game. The decades-long process represents basketball's fluid, dynamic diffusion as opposed to the one-sided descriptions offered by some.[51]

In addition to demonstrating the popularity of the college game, the Hoosier Dome exhibition contest, with Bird, Thomas, and others playing, also showcased an NBA on the cusp of dramatic changes. In the late 1970s and early 1980s, the league had struggled with charges of drug infestation and violence. LaFeber noted that Newsweek called the league "the sorriest mess" in sports and that CBS ran the 1980 NBA Finals on tape delay after prime time.[52] Despite television issues, NBA salaries and endorsement deals did continue to increase during its supposed dark days—which suggests more vitality in the league than is traditionally granted to it during this time. Still, in 1983 Dave Checketts, a former vice president of the NBA who then worked for Bain & Co., a Boston management and consulting firm, advised clients not to pay $18 million for the Boston Celtics franchise. Checketts said later, "The league looked like it was heading for disaster." At the time, a young lawyer named David Stern disagreed with Checketts's analysis, arguing that the NBA offered great opportunity. Time would show the accuracy of Stern's position. By 1991, analysts estimated the value of the Celtics organization at $100 million to $125 million.[53]

The NBA named Stern its new commissioner in February 1984, and he quickly, along with Jordan, Bird, and Magic, turned the league into a thriving entity. By the new millennium, the league enjoyed spectacular international reach, and most considered Stern the ultimate commissioner. As early as 1991 *Sports Illustrated*'s E. M. Swift wrote, "No one disputes that Stern is now the best commissioner in sports, the best in the history of basketball and every bit the equal of the best sports commissioners of all time."[54] And Stern had not even carried out his most successful act. That occurred in 1992, when he utilized the Olympic platform to propel his stars to spectacular international fame, which was ironic since the NBA had not played the lead role in getting its players eligible for the Games. FIBA did.

In mid-July, Knight finally cut the team down to its final twelve players. Ewing, Jordan, Mullin, and Perkins headlined the roster. Koncak and Kleine made it too, as did the six-feet-nine-inch Jeff Turner of Vanderbilt University. None of these three were considered super-talents; in fact, the *Boston Herald*'s Charlie Pierce labeled them "the great white fleet."[55] The six-feet-nine-inch Wayman Tisdale helped bolster the frontcourt. Complementing Jordan and Mullin in the backcourt were the six-feet-four-inch Alvin Robertson; the defensive specialist and point guard Leon Wood; the six-feet-five-inch Vern Fleming of Georgia; and the young, six-feet-one-inch Steve Alford. Knight chose the relatively unheralded Wood because of his ballhandling skills and opted for Alford's shooting over Stockton's passing, explaining that since he knew teams would play a zone defense against the United States, he emphasized shooting over ballhandling.[56] It was a simple theory that makes sense. International rules allowed zone defense, and international teams commonly played zone to contend with the United States' speed and athleticism. Stocking the roster with shooters was a practical way to combat this. Surprisingly, selectors overlooked this basic strategy at the 1988 Seoul Games, again at the Athens

Games in 2004, and then again, shockingly enough, at the 2006 World Championships in Japan. (In 1988 the United States attempted only 45 three-pointers compared to their opponents' 126. In 2004 and 2006 not a single player on either roster could be found among the NBA's top *thirty* three-point shooters in the preceding season. Only one player, reserve Shane Battier in 2006, could be found among the NBA's top *fifty*.)

To many, the two biggest surprises Knight delivered were his decisions to retain Alford and cut Barkley. The retention of Alford caused considerable debate, since he was a relatively unproven freshman, and many thought Louisville's Lancaster Gordon had outplayed him at the trials. The *Washington Post*'s Robert Fachet characterized the response to Knight keeping Alford as "outrage."[57] Meanwhile, the decision to cut Barkley remains one of the most controversial in Olympic history.

Few disagreed that Barkley played well enough at the trials to make the team. The players knew it and the coaches knew it. "He's the toughest I've ever played against," Tulane's John Williams told reporters. "He was possessed. You just didn't see people other than Dr. J get a rebound at one end, go downcourt by himself, dunk the ball to finish the play," Rod Thorn, who was the Chicago Bulls' general manager at the time, recalled.[58] Michigan's Tim McCormick gushed, "Barkley's been dominant. Three or four times a day, you see the backboard shaking. You look back and you see Barkley walking away."[59] Part of the awe Barkley's thunderous dunks inspired stemmed from the effect of Assembly Hall's new breakaway rims. To keep players from bending the rim on dunks, the breakaway technology enabled the rim to recoil. As a result of the snap-back action, dunks of sufficient force by players like Barkley caused a loud noise, making the impact of the dunk even more striking. The *Washington Post*'s Michael Wilbon concurred with the praise heaped on Barkley. During the trials he wrote, "When Charles Barkley, six feet six inches, 284 pounds, becomes an Olympic basketball hero sometime in late July . . ." Wilbon simply assumed it would happen.

But Barkley's weight was an issue. In the same article, Wilbon reported that early in the trials, when asked about his poundage, Barkley humorously responded, "I really don't eat that *much*. I just, more or less, tend to eat all the time. If I could go into a room and peel some of this stuff off of me, I'd come out looking like Hercules." This attitude did not necessarily gel with the response Knight had given when asked if a fat player had ever played for him, which was "Not for long."[60] Some wondered if Barkley could even make the first cut after Knight also said half-facetiously, half-seriously that he wanted Barkley to trim down to 215 pounds.

Concerns about Barkley's weight had not suddenly arisen at the trials. During the previous collegiate season, his weight had led many to question whether he was sufficiently motivated to achieve the physical conditioning required for the game. Although Barkley shot 64 percent from the field en route to winning Southeastern Conference (SEC) player-of-the-year honors, he had somehow also managed to *gain* fourteen pounds during the year, going from 258 to 272. This seemed impossible to critics, but those critics did not realize that with Barkley, the seemingly impossible was actually quite probable. For instance, just four years earlier, as a senior in high school, Barkley had stood just five feet ten. Not until after a Christmas holiday tournament that year did more than one junior college recruit him.[61] The odds, then, of Barkley turning into the SEC player of the year and a certain first-round pick were ridiculously low, but he had done both at Auburn, becoming a "cult figure" and national curiosity and garnering the classic nickname "Round Mound of Rebound" in the process.[62] During the trials, the *Chicago Tribune* noted Barkley's attractive persona, describing him as the "center of attention wherever he goes." Attempting to explain his appeal, the paper quoted Barkley's coach at Auburn, Sonny Smith, who said, "Charles gives every fat person in the world hope. He scores loud, spectacular baskets." In reference to Barkley's engaging, humorous personality, Smith said that he thought Barkley "boosts his weight if it improves the interview."[63]

In the final analysis, it appears that Bob Knight was one of the toughest critics of Barkley. Knight says he cut him because Barkley did not have the desire to play well and had not lost enough weight. The Olympian Leon Wood has suggested as much, saying, "I don't think he [Barkley] wanted to spend another two or three months playing under the tutelage of Bobby Knight." Murmurings of a power struggle emerged, as did hints that this had perhaps played a role in Knight's decision. For example, Barkley had apparently challenged Knight once about a double standard when the coach showed up late for a practice.[64] In his autobiography Knight claims that rather than lose nine pounds as requested, Barkley returned from the seventeen-day interval between the first and the second part of the trials eleven pounds heavier. In addition, Knight asserted that after Barkley's professional stock climbed during the first session of the trials, "I don't think he was excited about playing on the Olympic team. I think pro basketball was on his mind."[65] But in 1984, Knight admitted that before the trials commenced, Barkley went out of his way to call him to ask what weight Knight preferred for him—not exactly the action of someone not interested in making the team. Knight told the *Post*'s Wilbon that he did not tell Barkley the weight he preferred him at "because I wanted him at about 215 pounds." Surely, Knight did not really expect Barkley to weigh 215 pounds, but it is also not certain that he would have taken Barkley at 265. No matter what, Knight's emphasis on Barkley's weight suggested a disinclination to keep him and a lack of appreciation for Barkley's style. Barkley's ability to play fast, agilely, *and* with power that few could match separated him from others. Charles Barkley at 215 pounds is not Charles Barkley. Later, Coach Smith said, "I've always thought if the Soviets were playing, then Charles would have been on that team."[66]

The Soviet Union's decision not to participate in the Games had come during the course of Knight's extended tryouts. Up to the announcement, the Soviets had given little indication that they intended to boycott, no matter how dubious the West remained. But in May they proved the doubters correct. As part of their reasoning for not attending, Soviet officials rather unconvincingly charged the Reagan administration with doing little to protect their athletes in Los Angeles, even though the U.S. government had spent $100 million on security for the Games. Earlier that month, the Soviets had also accused the Reagan administration of "direct connivance with anti-Communist groups."[67]

One of the specific security concerns the Soviets noted was the appearance of badges on the streets of Los Angeles that read "Kill a Russian." Even IOC President Samaranch, who felt compelled to respect the Soviet Union's security claims though he realized the politics behind them, thought the badges provided the Soviets with a scapegoat. "Forget the Communists. Even for me, from Europe, it is very difficult to understand how, in a city where the Games will be, you can sell badges that read, 'Kill a Russian,'" Samaranch said. He added that it was hard to believe Californians were "naïve enough to provide them [Soviet officials] with the excuse they needed." At the same time, Samaranch coyly admitted that the true reason for the boycott lay elsewhere. "I had always known that sports and politics did not live on separate planets," he told reporters.[68]

Really, the boycott was expected. After it was announced, *U.S. News & World Report* predicted that American and Soviet relations would remain in a deep freeze until the November presidential election, which the Soviets hoped would end in Reagan's defeat. Malcolm Toen, a former ambassador to Moscow, claimed that "they [Soviet officials] feel, in their twisted view, that somehow this [the boycott] will hurt Ronald Reagan's chances of being re-elected."[69]

Though the boycott announcement was scarcely surprising, many simply did not want to ponder the LA Games without the Soviets, especially if a number of Eastern bloc countries joined them in not attending. Dreading a ratings debacle, many ABC officials met the boycott announcement with denial. Citing the fact that the Soviets had already spent $2 million in nonrefundable fees for Olympic broadcasting and satellite time, an ABC spokesman told the *Washington Post* that the network believed the Soviets would still attend.

But not everyone at ABC feared the Soviet Union's absence. Roone Arledge pointed out that, whether or not people wanted to admit it, "the vast majority of our television audience looked on the Olympics as a competition between nations . . . the more Americans we could count to win gold, the greater our success."[70] Therefore, he did not fret over the Soviet absence as much as many of his ABC cohorts and other U.S. corporations associated with the Olympics did.

Ultimately, the Soviet absence was not nearly an irreparable setback to the new, market-based financing model developed for the LA Games. The 1984 Olympics turned a profit of over $200 million for the LAOOC, the first for a host city since the 1932 LA Games, and ABC set ratings records. Furthermore, thanks to Ueberroth's leadership, the corporations that financed the LA Games ended up revolutionizing the way the Olympics got funded. It was a remarkable turn of events. In 1983 *Time*'s Tom Callahan asserted, "Growing so hugely expensive that they have been threatening to collapse under their own deficits, the Games have not been at such risk since AD 394." That made Ueberroth's success in putting on "a private Olympics without government subsidies" so important.[71]

Like some of the ABC brass, Coach Knight had met the boycott announcement with some denial. But by late July he was resigned to the fact that the Soviets did not intend to come. "Who cares that they're not here," he told reporters then. "They stole a game from us in 1972, didn't make the finals in 1976 and didn't win in 1980 in their own backyard. If we'd have had the good sense to go to Moscow, they wouldn't have even won a medal."[72] The tone of Knight's remarks betrayed a desire, held by most everybody else, to see a U.S. versus Soviet rematch in basketball. But it was not to be.

Still, the Games went on, and Los Angeles opened them with grandeur on July 28, 1984. When LA had hosted the Olympics fifty-two years earlier, President Herbert Hoover chose not to attend, and tickets for the Opening Ceremonies cost three dollars. In 1984 President Reagan watched the opening from a box seat, and tickets averaged roughly two hundred dollars. An 11,000 person choir sang the Olympic hymn, and thousands of peace doves were set free.[73] Hundreds of millions watched on television—by the end of the 1984 Games, an estimated two billion from across the globe had tuned in. At one point during the opening festivities, the more than 8,000 athletes from a record 140 nations joined hands while an orchestra played Beethoven's "Ode to Joy."[74] Arledge recalled the plans for the mind-boggling display: "84 pianists in white tie and tails would bang out *Rhapsody in Blue* on 84 concert grands; a 750-member all-star college band would march across the coliseum green while an 11,000-voice chorus sang Woody Guthrie and Michael Jackson tunes; and a spaceman wearing a jet pack would land on the 50-yard line, after which 92,500 spectators would perform card tricks. And that was just the first twenty minutes."[75] A better platform to showcase U.S. prosperity seems hard to imagine. Of course, a one-time display of grandeur could not endure, but the economic activity, opportunity, and dizzying array of products emanating from the dynamic, competitive marketplaces of liberal capitalist nations did.

Many viewed the Opening Ceremonies positively. *Sports Illustrated*'s Kenny Moore portrayed a celebratory mood, reporting that Sam Perkins high-fived a gowned-and-turbaned Sudanese man and noting that the U.S. athlete Willie Banks summed it up when he said, "Everyone radiated fantastic love and friendship."[76] Yet not everyone shared in Moore's jubilant analysis. Frank Deford, writing an op-ed piece in *Sports Illustrated*, characterized the Opening Ceremonies as an "overlong halftime show." Clearly not a fan of the Arledge-inspired television coverage, he proceeded to level criticism at ABC, the LAOOC, and American fans for supernationalism. To augment his point, Deford quoted Monique Berlioux, a Frenchwoman and director of the IOC, who said, "They are like children . . . We have in French a word for this—chauvinist."[77]

Given her remarks, it is not too hard to imagine what Berlioux might have thought of Coach Knight after the U.S. team's opening round victory over China, when in the press room he commenced a rather lively flirtation with the team's translator, Marie Hidalgo. The flirtation would last the duration of the Games. Hidalgo, a Paris-born émigré who had attended the Sorbonne, came to LA four years before the Olympics in hopes of making it big in Hollywood. She was randomly assigned to translate for the American squad's first postgame press conference. Fortunately for her, Knight was in a good mood after that game because the United States had won in resounding fashion over China, 97–49, a score that suggested America's speed would stand out at the tournament.[78]

As it happened, China's relative inexperience was exacerbated during the contest by its shorthandedness: the team was now without its longtime center, the seven-feet-eight-inch "tower of power" Mu The-chu, known in America as Mr. Mu, who had retired a year earlier. Also missing was the seven-feet-two-inch Hang Peng-san, Mr. Mu's replacement, who had died of a heart attack months before the LA Games.[79] Still, the game was hugely important to China and basketball as a global sport because it came at a time when dynamic changes were occurring in China: as noted a bit earlier, the opening of China economically and its decision to embrace Western-based sports movements like the Olympics.

At the postgame press conference, Knight was forced to cede the floor to Hidalgo as he waited for her to translate his statements. But his buoyed spirits helped him wait patiently rather than give her a dose of his legendary temper. He even shot her a wink and then later requested that she translate for all of the U.S. team's postgame conferences. No one objected, and she took the job even though people warned her about Knight. "I didn't know anything about him. I'm ignorant about basketball. Then all these people came up to me and said, 'Don't you know about Bobby Knight?' So then I got kind of scared," she told reporters.[80]

At the press conference following the team's second victory, Knight brought Hidalgo flowers. Then the next day, after another decisive win, he brought her a U.S. team t-shirt and even helped her put it on. Later, though, Hidalgo got a taste of his colorful, controversial lexicon, and she responded by refusing to translate the word "ass" into French. Another time, Knight, in the middle of a rant, warned her not to fall too far behind. She said, "I don't know if I can remember everything you said." When he replied, "There wasn't a lot of it that was real important," she said okay, and they just moved on.[81] The media loved it, and so did Knight.

In that second game, the United States had beaten Canada, and then in its third, Uruguay, scoring 89 and 104 points, respectively. The team's scoring removed any concern that Knight's emphasis on fundamentals would stifle the opportunities for athletic players like Jordan. After the U.S. team's win over Uruguay 104–68, the Uruguayan coach Ramon Etchamendi said, "Perhaps if we played five against seven." While against Canada, in front of another disappointing crowd of just over 12,000, Jordan led the way in a rout, prompting the Canadian coach Jack Donohue to say, "I think this is the best basketball team I've ever seen."[82]

The U.S. basketball players were not the only Americans faring well at the LA Games, and ABC was reveling in the successes. Some did not appreciate that. As the basketball team prepared for its fourth game, this one against France, the IOC's President Samaranch delivered a "stern message" of rebuke to ABC for what the committee believed to be its biased coverage of the Games. From a domestic perspective, an ABC official, on the condition of anonymity, told the New York Times that the United States was "cleaning up (in medals), and that's what we're covering." Indeed, the United States had won twenty-eight of the sixty-one medals awarded. But ABC stressed that, from a global perspective, it aired separate international feeds. Still, the New York Times noted that England's Daily Mail, London's Guardian, and France's Le Monde all characterized ABC's coverage as "self-centered."[83] The comments reflected how the United States' lead in the television industry gave them the ability to focus on certain events and to highlight American stars. Yet it also showed a potential downside to the United States' global lead in telecommunications and economics as countries increasingly came to view America as overindulgent and self-absorbed. As it turned out, on the basketball court, Knight and company probably did little to mollify

Le Monde as they beat France 120–62 on the day the paper published its criticisms. Steve Alford led the barrage with eighteen points. It was only the third time in Olympic history, and the first since 1960, that the United States had scored 120 or more points.

In other action, Yugoslavia beat Brazil 98–85 in a fast-paced affair indicative of the South American style, and Italy prevailed against Australia 93–92. At that point, the United States, Spain, Italy, and Yugoslavia were all 4-0 with only one game remaining in pool play. In its final pool game, the United States faced Spain. To promote the matchup, which was to be aired in prime time, ABC ran an ad in the *New York Times* featuring Michael Jordan.[84]

In an effort to combat the United States' athleticism, Spain opened the contest in a zone and stayed in it most of the game. The tactic did not keep the Americans from continuing to score at a torrid clip, however: they finished the first half with forty-six points, thanks mainly to a dominating performance by Jordan, who made nine of eleven field goal attempts, several of them dunks. But Spain scored abundantly too and trailed by only five points at halftime, 46–41.

In the opening minutes of the second half, Spain continued to stay close, and then, with 15:55 left in the game and the United States up by only three, Jordan left with an ankle injury. Up to that point, Jordan's exploits had given the United States a slim lead. Without him, the squad's chances looked bleak. But Jordan's teammates responded to his injury by reeling off a 36–14 run, opening a twenty-five-point lead.

Chris Mullin, one of the shooters Knight had made sure to stock his team with, led the charge as, against Spain's zone defense, a wealth of shooters proved advantageous. In addition, Mullin, though not known for his defensive prowess, contributed six steals, while Ewing and Perkins asserted themselves on the boards, helping the United States enjoy a 47–22 rebounding advantage for the game. After enduring the wrath of Knight in the first half, Leon Wood also played a strong second stanza, finishing with twelve points and twelve assists. And to everyone's relief, Jordan's injury was not serious. He returned for the closing minutes of his team's 101–68 victory. "I would say our defensive play in the second half was better than in the first," Knight said afterward, in an obvious understatement.[85]

Though others turned in strong performances as well, the game functioned as a kind of international coming-out party for Jordan, who finished with twenty-four points and shot a remarkable twelve-of-fourteen from the field. Summing up Jordan's impact, the *New York Times*'s Michael Moran wrote that, thus far, the Olympics had served "only to demonstrate that Jordan defies description in more than one language."[86] In *Time*, a week before the Spain game, Roger Rosenblatt opined, in analyzing the Los Angeles Olympics and why Americans love sports so much, "Everything Americans wish to believe about their national character is housed in sports: vitality, spontaneity, the bursting of bonds." Rosenblatt also asserted that much of the appeal centered on individual heroes, like Jordan, and he emphasized that this allure came about because "these displays of individual worth are simply beautiful."[87] In LA Jordan was showing that he, more than any other player in history, embodied the artistry of basketball.

The win over Spain pushed the U.S. record to 5-0 and put the team into the final eight, single-elimination medal-round. To the surprise of many, West Germany awaited the United States in the medal round opener. West Germany had lost its first three games but rallied to win its last two to earn a berth in the quarterfinals. At the start of the game, the West German coach Ralph Klein advised his squad, led by University of Washington players Detlef Schrempf and Christian Welp and the Indiana center Uwe Blab, to use as much of the thirty-second shot clock on offense as possible. On defense, West Germany followed Spain's lead by playing a zone to combat the United States' athleticism.

In the opening minutes, West Germany kept the game close at 14-14, but a 15–2 run keyed by Steve Alford gave the Americans a cushion. West Germany was unable to mount a serious challenge from that point on. Still, it was a hard-fought game. Fouls plagued the opening frame, and Knight let the officials know of his displeasure. He bickered with them and even jawed with West Germany's Coach Klein throughout the half. "This is a travesty for a game on this level, for both American and German players . . . I thought the officials were incredibly bad for both teams," Knight said afterward.[88]

In the second half, West Germany's zone kept the United States from pulling away for its customary blowout. This tactic stymied Jordan, in particular, for the first time in the tournament. He finished only four of fourteen from the floor and turned the ball over six times. Coach Knight reamed Jordan after the game. Perkins recalled, "It was the first time Coach did that to him." All the players seem to have respected Jordan mightily, and several told him not to worry about it. According to Perkins, "it propelled Michael."[89] Even at that age, Jordan seemed to know better than to let a reaming keep him down.

Picking up the slack against the West Germans, with a performance that went a long way in vindicating his selection as an Olympian, Alford led the team with seventeen points on seven-of-twelve shooting.[90] His marksmanship was beneficial in combating West Germany's zone.

In its quarterfinal tilt, Canada scored a stunning upset over Italy, 78–72, in another game plagued by fouls—especially in Italy's case as three of its key players, including Dino Meneghin, fouled out. The upset win meant Canada would face the United States next. In addition, Spain and Yugoslavia both advanced in high-scoring games, setting up a semifinal matchup between the two.

Like Spain and West Germany, Canada implemented a zone to slow the United States, but, also like Spain and West Germany, Canada found that this did not produce the desired result. In his first start, Chris Mullin thwarted the zone by making outside shots on his way to twenty points.[91] Having met the challenge of a zone for three straight games, Knight was clearly reaping the benefits of his emphasis on shooting. "The United States always had the best players. They didn't always have the best team in the Olympics. Now they do," Canadian coach Donohue said after his second lopsided loss to the United States.[92]

In the other semifinal, Spain capitalized on the struggles of the young Yugoslavian star Drazen Petrovic to win in an upset, setting up another matchup with the United States, this time for the gold medal. Much like in its first meeting with Spain, the United States displayed great teamwork and speed on offense and defense en route to a convincing 96–65 win. In the opening minutes, the Americans left little doubt of the game's outcome by making twelve of their first fourteen shots. The win gave the 1984 team an average margin of victory of 32.1 points, putting it alongside the 1956 and 1960 squads as the best amateur teams of all time. The point differential was all the more impressive considering that internationally, the level of basketball had advanced dramatically since the Rome Games.

Immediately following the game, with the national anthem playing over the stadium speakers, U.S. players hurried over to Coach Henry Iba. Standing at a distance, Knight lifted his thumb in the air, signaling the players to pick up the legendary coach. As the players carried Iba on their shoulders, the crowd roared and tears welled up in Knight's eyes.[93] He considers it one of his proudest moments in coaching. The gesture showed the complexity of Knight's character.

Knight had endured ample criticism on a number of fronts: for selecting Alford, for the rampant use of four-letter words, and for over-disciplining his players.[94] Yet he had achieved his goal, and America's. Knight had helped show the world a new incarnation of American basketball and American competitiveness, and it was hard to argue with the results.

But winning the gold medal did not mean Knight suddenly turned into a kinder, gentler man. In the postgame press conference, he showed that his confrontational tendencies were unaffected when he lobbed a few verbal shots at the Soviets. "The Russians can't play defense," he said. Then he offered up a review of the Soviet Union's performances at an earlier European tournament, during which it had struggled with Italy, Spain, and Yugoslavia. "You tell me the Russians can play with these guys?" Knight asked, referring to his own players. To a degree, Coach Antonio Diaz-Miguel of Spain concurred. Had the United States and Soviet Union played for the gold medal, he would predict a U.S. victory, he said, but he did add that it would be a "good game to watch." That such a debate surfaced right after the U.S. team won the gold medal demonstrated that its inability to prove its mettle against the Soviets had slightly lessened the 1984 U.S. Olympic squad's legacy.

As for Jordan, he continued to steal the show, and gracefully. Even before the final game, Ken Denlinger wrote, "Why be wishy-washy about this: The United States men clinched the 1984 Olympics on Feb. 17, 1963, the day Michael Jordan was born."[95] Indeed, Jordan was the key to the team's success. And in the final, as he had all summer long, Jordan turned in a spectacular individual performance while still managing to partake in a fine team effort.

Earlier in the LA Games, Coach Diaz-Miguel said of Jordan, "He's like a robot. He's not a man." Later, an interpreter clarified that Diaz-Miguel had meant that Jordan was like "rubber."[96] It was an important distinction, for Jordan was no robot: his seeming elasticity and springiness compared

15. Michael Jordan airborne at the 1992 Olympics. Photo by Dimitri Messinis. AFP Collection/Getty Images.

more aptly with something more fluid, like the plastic man in flight. "He's like an airplane," Diaz-Miguel said in awe after the final. "Everybody else is on the ground, he hangs up there when he should come down. In the air, he runs. Most valuable player for them. Michael Jordan." The *Chicago Tribune's* Bob Verdi, trying to explain an eventual trademark move, wrote that as Jordan drove towards the basket, "he took a flying 8-count, above glazed Spanish eyes, then bore in on the basket and stuffed it. Chicago will love him." Teammate Leon Wood explained, "That was Michael's 'rock-abye moonwalk' maneuver."[97] The descriptions indicated the effect Jordan's actions could have on the human mind.

Bird and Magic deserve credit for bringing the NBA back from the brink, but Jordan deserves credit for taking the league to incredible new heights. As noted, a few years before he arrived, bankrupt teams and drug scandals had diminished the number of viewers to such an extent that CBS aired the finals late in the night on tape delay. By the time Jordan left, the NBA was nearly a $3 billion business.[98]

Jordan's impact on the city of Chicago, not to mention the business model of the NBA, set new standards. In 1998 *Fortune* attempted to quantify the economic effect of "all the Jordan-influenced business—the sneaker and apparel sales, the higher television ratings, the increased game attendance, the endorsement value, the videos, the cologne, and the rest of it." After exhaustive number crunching, the magazine estimated a $9.53 billion impact, $5.2 billion on Nike alone.[99] In short, Jordan changed the commercialism of basketball and the sport's cultural significance.

As noted in the introduction, Scott Bedbury, head of Nike advertising from 1987–94, counted people's desire to belong, as well as a "near-universal desire for greater personal freedom," as among the key emotional connections a brand can make with its customers.[100] Nike, along with its advertising partner Wieden & Kennedy, deserves credit for not only recognizing Jordan's ability to connect in both ways, but finding effective methods to express it.

In the mid-1970s, escalating sales of athletic shoes had intensified competition between shoemakers. Converse and Uniroyal, who led among U.S.-based manufacturers, battled for market share with their staple basketball shoes, Uniroyal's Pro-Keds and Converse's Chuck Taylors. But both of these models were still made with canvas, and the biggest complaint among consumers stemmed from deficiencies in their durability.[101] As a result, higher-end leather-bound sneakers, like those made by Adidas and Puma, rose in popularity, and small companies, such as Nike, focused on delivering even higher-quality shoes with more innovative designs, gnawing away at the market-share.[102] As a company, Nike had initially catered to the subtle demands of runners, and this carried over into its heavily promoted basketball line in the 1970s. Nike invested in delivering shoes of the highest quality, with "the best nylon, the best cement, the best rubber . . . a heel wedge, a soft midsole, and leather instead of vinyl."[103] With attention to design and product visibility enhanced through its relationships with basketball players, Nike would continue to grow for the rest of the decade.

An important part of Nike's growth plan entailed landing big-name endorsers, especially basketball players. By the mid-1970s the endorsement climate had changed dramatically from just a few years earlier, when free shoes and merchandise had satisfied most athletes. Nike CEO Phil Knight knew that to capture market-share going forward, he would have to pay highly visible superstars to wear his shoes. And, given basketball's urban appeal, its ability to attract youths, and the versatility of high-top shoes, he targeted hoops. In late 1974 Nike considered making a power move in the basketball market by offering $100,000 to Kareem Abdul-Jabbar, but it opted instead to sign a group of players for less money. The players made up the Nike Pro Club and shared in sales royalties at the end of the year. Among the first members of the club were former gold medalist Spencer Haywood, Rudy Tomjanovich, Elvin Hayes, Paul Silas, former Olympian Lucius Allen, and Austin Carr. At the end of the Nike Pro Club's first year, each member received a royalty check in excess of $8,000, well above the contract-stipulated minimum of $2,000. The club worked quite well for Nike too. By 1976, Nike basketball shoe sales had nearly quadrupled.[104]

It was during the summer of the 1984 Olympics that Nike raised the stakes and broke industry norms with its bet on Jordan. In LA, the U.S. Olympic team had worn Adidas shoes—the first time in Olympic basketball history an American team had not chosen Converse. But this had no impact on Nike's decision to go after Jordan aggressively. By 1983, the company had already spent an astounding $26 million a year for basketball players to endorse Nike products, "more than any ten sneaker companies put together."[105] Despite this, however, Nike was struggling to compete with the big players in the shoe market. Thus, Nike decided to gamble on the affable, "telegenic" Jordan with the largest basketball endorsement deal of all time: five years for $2.5 million, along with royalties over certain thresholds. It was a lot to rest on one man, and Nike knew it.[106] Nike had wanted Jordan before the Olympics began, but his performance there surely buoyed the firm's confidence in him. As it turned out, Nike got him cheaply.

From the beginning, the coupling of Jordan with Nike's marketing and design abilities succeeded. Keeping with the Nike tradition, the first Jordan shoe departed from the norm. It featured a radical red-and-black color scheme incorporating the Nike swoosh.[107] When that first Air Jordan shoe came on the market, the *Washington Post* explained, "The medium-high leather sneaker will have an air pad," and then added, "It should help the wearer jump, but there's no guarantee it will help you match Jordan's hang time."[108] The sneaker has never been the same since.

The technology incorporated into the first Jordan model signified a staple component of Nike: innovation. Nike's emphasis on design has largely been overlooked, given the attention heaped on its renowned marketing campaigns. The air pocket indicated the design emphasis. Nike had brought the waffle sole to the market in 1977, and then, two years later, it introduced a polyurethane bag filled with a gas of large molecules that cushioned the sole. It was in 1987 that Nike found a way to remove sections of the midsole so that people could see the air pocket. Advances to other parts of the shoe had occurred too, jumpstarting competition between "Reebok, Nike, Adidas, and other new entrants to see who had the best shoe laboratory."[109] Nike's attention to technological innovation has played an important role in its rise to ascendancy in the shoe industry. And as its sales grew in the 1980s and 1990s, Nike continued to stress this component of its business—in the mid-1990s Nike tripled its research and development budget and employed more than three hundred designers, compared to Reebok's sixty and Fila's forty. Nike's Advanced Engineering Group, with ten in-house engineers and ten top-shelf researchers and designers, was a kind of special operations wing on the front line of innovation. Some of the designers, such as Tinker Hatfield, ultimately gained their own renown in popular culture.[110]

By the end of its first year the Air Jordan line tallied $130 million in sales,

TABLE 11. 1984 U.S. Men's Olympic Basketball cumulative stats

NAME	G	FGM-FGA	(%)	FTM-FTA	(%)	REB/AVG	PTS/AVG	AT	BK	ST
Michael Jordan	8	60-110	.545	17-25	.680	24/3.0	137/17.1	16	7	12
Chris Mullin	8	38-67	.567	17-22	.773	20/2.5	93/11.6	24	3	14
Patrick Ewing	8	31-56	.554	26-35	.743	45/5.6	88/11.0	4	18	6
Steve Alford	8	38-59	.644	6-7	.857	26/3.3	82/10.3	26	0	12
Wayman Tisdale	8	27-50	.540	15-23	.652	51/6.4	69/8.6	3	7	6
Sam Perkins	8	29-50	.580	7-8	.875	43/5.4	65/8.1	10	5	7
Alvin Robertson	8	26-40	.650	10-14	.714	22/2.8	62/7.8	20	0	17
Vern Fleming	7	23-45	.511	8-17	.471	19/2.7	54/7.7	19	1	9
Leon Wood	8	14-24	.583	19-24	.792	16/2.0	47/5.9	63	0	3
Joe Kleine	8	10-16	.625	7-8	.875	16/2.0	27/3.4	3	2	1
Jon Koncak	8	11-25	.440	4-8	.500	19/2.4	26/3.3	1	2	3
Jeff Turner	8	3-15	.200	7-9	.778	17/2.1	13/1.6	6	1	3
USA TOTALS	8	310-557	.557	143-200	.715	318/39.8	763/95.4	195	46	93
OPP. TOTALS	8	185-475	.389	136-194	.701	290/36.3	506/63.3	119	9	51

a staggering amount for one athletic shoe. As *Sports Illustrated* noted, theoretically, this sum made the Air Jordan line the fifth-largest shoe company in the United States. Later models sold considerably more.

The quality of Nike shoes and the company's hipness translated into sales not only in urban areas but across white suburbia, and eventually to the distant reaches of China. From 1982 to 1995, Nike sales roughly doubled, while the money spent by consumers on its product nearly tripled. By 1992 the company, powered by the exploits of the six Olympic Dream Team members it had under contract, especially Jordan, generated $3.4 billion in revenue. By that time already, one in four Nike sneaker sales occurred overseas, yet domestic sales were still "booming."[111] By 1996 the company's sales topped $5 billion, while its focus turned increasingly global.[112] Other corporations, such as Coca-Cola and McDonald's, saw their own international reach enhance dramatically during this time, too. An important thing all three of these corporations had in common during the 1990s was an employee named Michael Jordan. The universal appeal of his exploits on the basketball court made him the quintessential spokesman, not just for these corporations, but for an expanding global culture rooted in liberal values and featuring a dynamic, participatory marketplace. You could sense this at the LA Games.

11

ODDITIES IN SEOUL OPEN THE
LANE FOR THE DREAM TEAM

In 1984 the IOC passed legislation that allowed individual sporting federations to determine eligibility guidelines. Since then, sporting bodies have tended to let professionals participate in the Olympics. In 1986, FIBA's World Congress voted to decide the matter for basketball. For European leagues, the vote was not all that momentous, as their professionals had competed in the Olympics for years. This resulted from the classification of players in European leagues as "employees" of the corporate sponsor of each team rather than as professional basketball players. But for the United States the ramifications were potentially momentous, because it could have allowed NBA players to participate in the Olympic Games. The 1986 FIBA vote, though, upheld the status quo by a slim five-vote margin, keeping NBA players out of the Olympic fold. However, FIBA General Secretary Boris Stankovic, who wanted to see NBA players at the Games, predicted that it would be only a matter of time before FIBA made NBA players eligible.[1]

He was right. The measure passed three years later. (Interestingly, FIBA's U.S. representative, ABA/USA, voted against it.) And by the time it did get passed, the struggles of the 1988 U.S. Olympic basketball team, capped by a loss in the semifinals to the Soviets, had convinced many Americans that sending NBA players to the Olympics was a good idea. As *Time* magazine noted shortly after the 1988 Games, "Failure in Seoul has fueled the argument that NBA pros, currently banned under amateur rules, should be allowed to play in the Olympics."[2] This would be the lasting legacy of the 1988 Olympic team, a fittingly peculiar legacy for a team surrounded by a number of oddities.

In hindsight, it is striking that FIBA head Stankovic was the principal figure pushing for the acceptance of U.S. professionals into the Olympics. Given the momentous effect of the 1992 Dream Team as well as NBA commissioner David Stern's global master plan, it seems sensible to assume that in the mid-1980s, the NBA would have pushed FIBA hard to let NBA stars get showcased at the Games. However, the NBA seems to have not realized the potential effect that Michael Jordan, Larry Bird, Earvin "Magic" Johnson, and the rest could have at the Olympics. As Russ Granik, deputy commissioner of the NBA from 1985–2006 and a principal figure in USA basketball throughout the 1990s, told the author, though in 1987 the NBA did have talks with FIBA, those talks were "not about the Olympics." (They focused instead on developing tournaments, such as the 1987 McDonald's Open in Milwaukee between the Milwaukee Bucks, the Soviet National team, and the Italian professional club Tracer Milan.) Granik stated flatly, "We were never engaged in any conversations of any kind about the NBA playing in the Olympics until FIBA had actually adopted it." To this, he added, "Playing in the Olympics was not something we aspired to or thought about much."[3]

In the summer of 1987, Gary Bettman, vice president and general counsel of the NBA, did admit that the NBA would "be delighted" if the Olympic opportunity arose, but he also made clear that the NBA was "not pushing for it."[4] Stankovic, however, was. To him, including NBA stars in the Games would raise the quality of the Olympic basketball tournament and enable FIBA to showcase the increasing number of international players in the NBA. Granik explained Stankovic's vision by saying that Stankovic thought, "If you're going to hold yourself out as running the championship of the world, then you had to have the world's best players." Granik added, "It always impressed me as his [Stankovic's] vision . . . that this was something he wanted to happen while he was in charge of FIBA."[5]

Some were unhappy and charged that commercial considerations were influential in bringing NBA players into the Games. Not surprisingly, among these critics were members of ABA/USA, which surely realized that the moment the NBA received admittance, the ABA/USA's influence over U.S. Olympic basketball would cease. "FIBA got $600,000 from the IOC from the Olympic TV money," Bill Wall, executive director of the ABA/USA and an advocate of keeping NBA players out of the Olympics, made sure to point out in 1987. "They see an NBA [expansion] franchise going for $32 million . . . They know there is a lot of money out there, and they think a lot of it will stick with FIBA."[6]

But Wall had plenty of critics himself, and those critics thought that his fears about the NBA caused him to make odd decisions in 1988, particularly during the initial phase of the Olympic trials held in May in Colorado Springs. Indeed, Wall's actions contributed significantly to the peculiarities surrounding the 1988 U.S. Olympic basketball team.

Most glaring was the media blackout he implemented in Colorado Springs. To be fair, 1988 Olympic coach John Thompson, who was known for secluding his Georgetown teams before big games, had encouraged the blackout—(Thompson maintained that the media distracted his players), but Wall enforced it. And though he claimed to support it for the same reason as Thompson, pundits questioned his real motivation. A source suggested to *Sports Illustrated*'s Scott Wolff that Wall's blackout actually stemmed from a fear of losing out to Stern's NBA. In turn, Wolff wrote that Wall's actions had "to do with a desire to maintain control of a fiefdom that rewards him handsomely, sends him to exotic ports of call and permits him to exercise his power more or less arbitrarily every quadrennium or so." Wolff also sarcastically noted that apparently, the fifty NBA scouts permitted to watch the action, along with shoe company representatives and at least one agent, did not cause distractions. Wall responded to such statements by saying, "I'm 57 years old. I'm not going to have this job much longer anyway."[7]

In the end, the main effect of the blackout was to generate negative coverage of the Olympic team. Media members that managed to circumvent it were still so annoyed by it that they did not focus on the players vying for Olympic spots. For instance, once he managed to get into the trials, Wolff told readers that he was quickly stopped by one of Wall's "henchmen," who allegedly told him, "You can't talk to anybody. The policy is that you are here for observation only."[8] Such stories took attention away from the team.

Wolff also wrote of the time that one of Wall's staffers stopped the *Rocky Mountain News*'s Teri Thompson on her way to the ladies' room. The staffer reportedly told Thompson it was necessary to check the restroom for players before she entered. Baffled, she said, "Look, it's the *ladies'* room." The staffer checked anyway. Jere Longman of the *Philadelphia Inquirer* compared the ABA/USA to mayflies. "They live for two weeks and die," he wrote. The *New York Times, Boston Globe,* and *Philadelphia Daily News* didn't even send people to the trials.[9]

Seeing shoe company representatives at the trials irked the media members even more. Wolff's mention of their presence reflected not only the slight media members felt, but also indicated the influence multinational corporations such as Nike and Reebok now wielded. Throughout the 1980s, the sneaker industry had continued to skyrocket, and basketball maintained a leading role in driving that growth. From 1982 to 1989 the number of pairs of sneakers sold in the United States rose from 183.6 million to 379.5 million. During that time, Reebok emerged as a major challenger to Nike, with its sales soaring from $35 million in 1982 to nearly $200 million in 1985. Both companies surged ahead of Converse, and both emphasized basketball.[10]

Nike in particular continued to form close allegiances with basketball to propel its growth. Jordan counted as the most visible figure representing the relationship between the sneaker market and basketball in the 1980s and 1990s, but many other prominent figures also endorsed basketball-related products, among them John Thompson. As it happened, Thompson maintained a particularly revealing relationship with one of the shoe company representatives allowed into the trials, Nike's Sonny Vaccaro. The relationship exemplified the role shoe reps and college coaches played in promoting sneakers, and a perturbed media pointed it out.

Thompson and Vaccaro did make an odd pair. In the 1960s Thompson had been a star player at Providence, and as a member of the Boston Celtics, he had won two NBA championships backing up Bill Russell. In

1972, Thompson became head coach at Georgetown, where he would enjoy marked success that led to his induction in the Naismith Memorial Basketball Hall of Fame. Vaccaro, on the other hand, was jobless in 1977, divorced, nearly broke, and barely scraping together a living in Las Vegas by gambling on sports.[11] He had worked in basketball in the 1960s, for an agent who recruited players to the ABA, but he struggled to find consistent work in the 1970s.

Then, in 1978, he asked Phil Knight for a job, telling him that he thought he could "probably get all the major college teams in the country to [wear Nike shoes]."[12] "The guys at Converse ruled college basketball then, but they were vulnerable," Vaccaro recalled. Knight agreed to meet with him. Remembering the encounter years later, Knight said, "I was charmed by Sonny . . . We had been beating our brains in trying to get a foot in the door in this game. Then this little, portly, Italian fellow comes around and says he's going to burn down the walls for us. When we saw his relationships with coaches in action, that he could produce . . . And then these massive orders for shoes began pouring in. We gave him all the room he wanted."[13]

Within four months of his hiring, Vaccaro had signed twenty coaches, a period he later referred to as his "kamikaze sweep." By the late 1980s he enjoyed relationships with sixty college coaches and twenty high school coaches. Offering endorsement contracts to the college coaches and loads of free merchandise to the high school ones, he expected them to outfit their teams in Nikes.

Given Thompson's success and the slew of stars he coached at Georgetown, Vaccaro worked at cultivating a particularly close relationship with him. It worked. "I don't deal with a lot of people closely, but Sonny and I are very close," Thompson said in 1988. Georgetown, incidentally, wore Nikes. Vaccaro was also quite close with George Raveling, one of the assistants Thompson had handpicked for the 1988 Olympic team. In fact, Vaccaro stood up for Raveling at his wedding.[14] Because he had access to the trials, Vaccaro was likely able to begin forming relationships with the Olympians he'd targeted as potential endorsers, and sure enough, many of them later became Nike employees, most notably David Robinson. Critics suggested that the coziness of Vaccaro with Thompson, Raveling, and others indicated an NCAA Division I system that had become overly commercialized and exploitative of its players.

Whether or not this was true, the 1988 Olympic trials still saw Wall police a media blackout with vigor, while a former washed-up-Vegas-gambler-turned-shoe-company-representative enjoyed access to Thompson and his assistants, Raveling and Mary Fenlon, as they evaluated players.

Thompson had made it to the trials as Olympic coach after leading Georgetown to the apex of college basketball with his patented full-court aggressiveness on defense, complimented by dominant frontcourt play. In 1984 Georgetown won the national title; the following year, they lost in the championship game. Then, in May of 1986, ABA/USA committee members voted for Thompson as Olympic coach. "I don't win many popularity contests with some positions and stands that I take. And that's one of the many reasons I'm very flattered that so many people said I should be the next Olympic coach," Thompson told the press at the time.[15] Given basketball's improved quality internationally, its popular appeal, lingering cold war emotions, and that Thompson was the nation's first African American Olympic head basketball coach, the stakes were magnified for him at the Seoul Games.

A year before the trials, Thompson explained that he wanted players who fit with his style. "I don't know any other way to coach. It's important to me to get a group of people who want to get out there and be quick."[16] In addition to looking for quickness, he emphasized the need to select the players that would make the most cohesive unit, rather than a collection of all-stars.[17] With stiffer competition facing them from abroad, the selection process became even more important.[18]

The main threat remained the Soviet Union. Its 1988 team, led by the versatile seven-feet-three-inch center Ariydas Sabonis, was one of its strongest ever. Other teams posed challenges as well. At the 1987 Pan-Am Games in Indianapolis, Denny Crum's talent-laden squad, led by Navy's David Robinson, Danny Manning of Kansas, the seven-foot-tall Pervis Ellison of Louisville, and the sharpshooting Rex Chapman of Kentucky, lost to Brazil in the finals, 120–115. And at the 1987 World University Games, the U.S. team, coached by Mike Krzyzewski and featuring the All-American Sean Elliott of Arizona, Kansas State's Mitch Richmond, and Duke's Danny Ferry, lost 100–85 in the finals to Yugoslavia. "We were just not as good as Yugoslavia . . . They're an excellent team. Three seven-footers. A starting lineup with everybody six foot five and above. They're really good, and they've played together for a long time," Krzyzewski said in the spring of 1988. "I think that John's [Thompson] got a tough job. A real tough job."[19]

The improved international standard of play provided a conundrum that mirrored a problem of the expanding open market. As basketball's popularity mushroomed globally (a development that so many in America wanted, from the State Department to the Nike boardroom), the competition for supremacy increased as well, as did the stakes. The *New York Times*'s Peter Alfano summed up the growing importance of Thompson's job as Olympic coach by writing that because basketball had become "as American as apple pie," and because U.S. popular culture stretched across the globe, as evidenced by the pervasiveness of "Dallas" reruns and the golden arches, the U.S. Olympic basketball team had "no room for failure."[20] On the court, maybe it seemed so. But from a broader perspective, heightened basketball competitiveness at an event like the Olympics, within a world featuring a participatory marketplace and with mushrooming openness, was a good sign. Some realized this. For instance, in an interview with *Time* in 1987, the former Olympic coach Pete Newell offered a rather sensible reaction, asserting that after decades of diffusion, "Now there are good basketball players in Japan, the Philippines, Turkey, Israel, Lebanon, all over Western and Eastern Europe, Africa, almost everywhere. We're not going backward; they're just coming forward. I don't think that's so bad."[21]

Still, the cold war had not yet ended. Few people realized that the Soviet Union was teetering on the brink of collapse. And though the firm stance President Reagan had taken against the "evil empire" in the early 1980s had been mollified a bit by the time the Seoul Olympics took place, the rivalry between the two cold war foes' opposing ideologies, both in the press and in the minds of Americans, continued. For example, just months before the Seoul Games, Thompson railed against the Portland Trailblazers for helping the Soviet team by rehabbing Sabonis's ailing Achilles heel. Portland had chosen Sabonis with its first-round draft pick in 1986 and, hopeful that one day he would play in the NBA, wanted him healthy. Thompson told the *Oregonian*, "Realistically, I see Sabonis as being a fulfillment of Lenin's prophecy: The capitalists are selling [the communists] the rope that they can hang us with. I feel we're being used. We are in direct competition with them. To prepare Sabonis to play against us just isn't right."[22]

Thompson's comment was provocative, but instead of strengthening the

Soviet sports machine, the actual effect Sabonis would have in the NBA would be the reverse. First of all, Sabonis is Lithuanian, and Lithuanians did not appreciate Russian subjugation. Secondly, Sabonis wanted badly to play in the NBA, and since he was a hero in his homeland, that meant thousands of young Lithuanians dreamed of playing in the NBA, too. In 1998 his Soviet doctor, Kestutis Vitkus, a Lithuanian as well, explained, "It is every basketball player's dream, everywhere in the world, to play in the NBA." Sabonis's hero was, in fact, Larry Bird.[23]

Furthermore, even if a healthy Sabonis carried the Soviet Union to the gold medal in Seoul, the international sporting community and the Olympic movement helped showcase the prosperity and innovation largely of liberal nations. As examples, Nike, Reebok, and Adidas marketed their dizzying array of products throughout the Seoul Games and outfitted numerous teams— including the Soviet basketball team, which wore Adidas even though the Soviet Union produced more shoes than anyone in the world. The Soviet squad sported Adidas because, as LaFeber put it, Soviet-made shoes "fell apart in weeks or rotted in warehouses because nobody wanted them."[24]

Many did disagree with Thompson's confrontational rhetoric. His statements were too divisive, particularly for those aiming to build business relationships with the Soviets, such as NBA commissioner Stern. "I'm glad he is not our secretary of state conducting our foreign policy," Stern immediately responded to reporters. "The concept that basketball could be used . . . as a way for the two countries to achieve a better understanding of each other is very exciting for us. I'm sorry that Coach Thompson does not share that view of the world." Larry Weinberg, the owner of the Trail Blazers, weighed in as well, calling Thompson's rhetoric "off base, way off base," and declaring that it "flies in the face of what our president has been trying to urge. Our president is traveling to Moscow for a summit meeting. Our president is not doing this to fulfill one of Lenin's prophecies. He's doing this in the best interests of world peace."[25] Though one could argue that Stern and Weinberg were willing to overlook legitimate issues with the Soviet Union because of their desire to do business with it, the emergence of Mikhail Gorbachev in 1985 had changed America's relationship with the Soviets. By February 1988, Reagan recognized as much, saying that the Soviet Union was no longer "an evil empire."[26]

As for Stern's global designs, by the mid-1980s the international basketball stakes were rising. In 1987, the NBA already held TV contracts with forty countries and licensing agreements with Europe, South America, and Asia.[27] By 1988, the league maintained television agreements in seventy-five countries, "on every continent except Antarctica, ranging from the obvious, like Italy, Spain and France, to the esoteric, like Qatar, a small, oil-rich country in the Persian Gulf," as explained by *Sports Illustrated*'s Rick Reilly. That year the NBA estimated that 200 million households outside the United States could receive significant coverage of its regular season. In the ensuing years, Stern scheduled more exhibition games in other nations as he positioned the league to possibly locate a franchise abroad.[28] So Stern's reaction to Thompson's comments regarding the Soviets made some sense.

Thompson, however, preoccupied with his role as the Olympic basketball coach, wanted every advantage he thought he could get on the court. He understood that, as he put it, "Portland was just trying to protect its investment. I understand it's a business. I love our system—I'm a capitalist." But he also said, "We've got to draw the line. I've always been accused of having an us-versus-them mentality, and I'm proud in this case—because it *is* us versus them."[29] Yet his worry about the advantages the Soviets might enjoy over his team kept him from appreciating how, in the larger scheme of things, Portland's association with Sabonis actually contributed to a newer, more open global basketball environment.

In addition to criticizing the NBA for aiding Sabonis, Thompson accused the league of helping to train the Soviet team by allowing it to come to the United States for a ten-day tour that included scrimmages against NBA teams. "The NBA has been very helpful to our opponents," he said in August 1987 on NBC's *Today* show. "Presently they are training the Soviet team." He also griped that the Soviet team enjoyed the advantage of already practicing together while the U.S. squad would not convene until August 1988.[30]

Thompson's concerns did not end there. On the eve of the Seoul Games, he voiced displeasure with the growing professionalism of Europe's Olympic participants, adding that the United States could not disregard this or the improvement of other countries. "The Romans always won, too, didn't they?" he asked sardonically. With the media boycott and other disliked operating procedures implemented by Coach Thompson and his staff in mind, *Sports Illustrated*'s Wolff responded by writing that it looked "well, as if an empire were in its late stages."[31]

Thompson also questioned the start date of the Seoul Games (in late September), which, in his opinion was unfair to college players. "Here's the exploitation of the athlete that we preach so much about. Now we're missing school for our country. Is it all right?" he asked.[32] Known as a disciplinarian and players' advocate at the same time, Thompson added, "The NCAA rules say that in the school year, they cannot work to make money. These kids are making a tremendous sacrifice."[33] In fact, it remained unclear how the NCAA intended to handle the issue until just before the Olympic trials, when in May of 1988 the NCAA announced the passage of special legislation that waived the full-time enrollment requirement for the fall semester for Olympians.[34] Taken together, Thompson's numerous concerns suggest that he felt immense pressure to succeed, and understandably so.

On the court at the May trials, the biggest question mark was a seven-foot graduate of the U.S. Naval Academy named David Robinson. Dubbed the "Aircraft Carrier" by Al McGuire, Robinson, keenly bright and multitalented both on and off the court, had spent the previous year working for the Navy as a civil engineer. As a senior at Annapolis during the 1986–87 basketball season, he had set the national NCAA record for blocked shots, and in June 1987 the San Antonio Spurs had selected him as the first pick in the draft. Yet before he could join his new team, Robinson needed to complete two years of service in the Navy. This made him eligible for the 1988 Olympic squad, but it also meant he had no team to play for during the 1987–88 season. Thompson worried that the layoff would cause rust. In the summer of 1987 he warned Robinson, through reporters, not to sit around eating Navy chow during his time off. "Was it Terry Mills who said he went from 205 to 235 lifting weights?" Thompson asked reporters dubiously. "I need to find that set of weights."[35]

As expected, by the time the trials began, Robinson did look a little rusty. In fact, even before the trials commenced, the manager of the Olympic team, Bill Stein, watched Robinson's Navy squad endure a pounding at the Armed Services tournament. Stein told Thompson, "David couldn't get down the court three times in a row." Alarmed, U.S. basketball officials quickly created a training regimen for Robinson to follow in Annapolis and hastily organized a European tour to precede the Seoul Games. However, though Robinson struggled with conditioning and his timing at the trials, there was no doubt he would make the team.

Following the Colorado Springs portion of the trials, fifteen others joined Robinson in moving on to the next round of the selection process, slated for June on the Georgetown campus. The NCAA player of the year Hersey Hawkins from Bradley, the sharpshooter Danny Ferry of Duke, and Danny Manning of the national champion Kansas Jayhawks team headlined the others. In addition, ten players were chosen to participate in the hastily organized June European trip, thereby giving these players another opportunity to earn a spot in the second phase of the trials at Georgetown. Among the notables not selected for the Georgetown camp or for the European trip were Notre Dame point guard David Rivers, Michigan's six-feet-eight-inch shooter Glen Rice, and Purdue's Troy Lewis, a three-point specialist.[36] In hindsight, considering that a dearth of shooters would be a problem for the United States in Seoul, the absence of Rice and Lewis looms larger.

Initially, Thompson had planned for some of his Georgetown players and some of George Raveling's USC men to accompany Robinson on the European tour. But when Thompson decided he needed more time to assess how to fill a few of his Olympic roster openings, the tour became an extended tryout for a number of players, among them guards Steve Kerr of Arizona, who ended his NBA career with the highest three-point percentage in league history, and Rex Chapman of the University of Kentucky, a schoolboy legend and noteworthy marksman. Performing well in Europe would not necessarily guarantee a player a spot on the Olympic team, but it could improve his chances, and these hopefuls were expected to attend.[37]

Chapman, maybe more than any other player, including Robinson, arrived in Europe with enormous hype. Sporting remarkable leaping ability, he had captured the attention of basketball fans and even graced the cover of *Sports Illustrated* in January 1987. And just before the initial phase of the trials in Colorado Springs, Chapman had announced his decision to turn pro after just two years at Kentucky. When he arrived in London, the *Guardian* referred to him as "sexy Rexy."[38] The international reach of his stardom, aided by satellite technology, reflected the heights to which college basketball had ascended.

In Colorado Springs, before the European trip, however, Chapman had struggled, so the trip was viewed as an opportunity for him to bounce back.

"He came into the trials probably under more pressure than any other young man there . . . I hope he can relax [in Europe] so we'll have a chance to see the way he can play," Thompson told the press.[39] Instead, in Europe Chapman's struggles continued. By the time the team made it to Spain, a Basque daily referred to him as a player on the roster only "por condicion de blanco," or, in other words, because he was white.[40]

In the end, five players who went to Europe, in addition to Robinson, garnered invitations to the final tryout camp at Georgetown. UNLV's Stacey Augmon, center Alonzo Mourning, a recent high school graduate headed to Georgetown, and Virginia Tech's Bimbo Coles were among them.[41] Chapman and Kerr did not make it. Considering Chapman's difficulties in Europe, it is understandable that he was cut, even though the U.S. probably could have used his shooting. However, the absence of Kerr, who would become one of basketball's all-time great shooters, proved in hindsight to be particularly costly in Seoul—especially given the injury that sidelined shooter Hersey Hawkins and when considering Mullin's and Alford's importance four years earlier in Los Angeles.

To Thompson's credit, he did select Hawkins and the unheralded Dan Majerle of Central Michigan, both marksmen. Of the two, Majerle had come into the Olympic trials the least heralded. But by the end of the Colorado Springs session, Thompson told reporters, "His name kept coming up. He plays good, hard defense, he fights over screens, which will be very important in Seoul, and he can shoot the outside shot."[42] Furthermore, it seemed that Coach Thompson wanted Duke's sharpshooting Danny Ferry. Had all three gone to Seoul, perhaps the United States' shooting woes would not have been so glaring. Unfortunately, Ferry had to leave the Georgetown tryout camp in July because of a knee injury. Amid the criticism of Thompson for not bringing enough shooters to Seoul, the loss of Ferry to injury is commonly overlooked. Of course, he could have reacted to Ferry's injury by inviting another shooter, such as Kerr, back to camp.

Ultimately, the final U.S. Olympic roster looked a lot like Thompson's Hoya teams. It was stocked with quick athletes and featured a dominant center in David Robinson. Eight of its players were chosen in the first round of the NBA draft. On the downside, in addition to lacking shooters, Robinson's form remained in doubt.

At the guard position, Thompson's point man at Georgetown, the quick, defensive-minded Charles E. Smith IV, made the team, along with Virginia Tech's Vernell "Bimbo" Coles, Iowa State's Jeff Grayer, Georgia's Willie Anderson, Hawkins, and Kansas State's Mitch Richmond. It was an athletic group with solid penetration capabilities and considerable length, particularly with Anderson, Richmond, and Grayer, all of whom were six feet four inches or taller. But together, these six guards would shoot only twenty-nine three-pointers over the course of eight games in the 1988 Olympics, or less than one three-point shot per man per game. Granted, Hawkins would have shot more than eight three-pointers had he not suffered the injury that sidelined him after the first four games in Seoul, but still, shooting was not an overall strength of the guards. Statistics bore this out. At the 1988 Games, the first in which the three-point shot was allowed, the United States' opponents shot 126 three-pointers while the American team shot just 45. In comparison, the 1992 Dream Team shot 187 three-pointers.

The forwards Thompson settled on were led by Dan Majerle, the only U.S. player to shoot more than nine three-pointers in the Olympics and the team's leading scorer with a 14.1 points per game average. The defensive-minded Stacey Augmon of the University of Nevada Las Vegas, J. R. Reid of North Carolina, Charles D. Smith of Pittsburgh, and Danny Manning of Kansas made up the rest of the forwards. Robinson counted as the team's only true center.

As noted, the squad's potential weaknesses may have mattered little in Olympiads before the 1970s; however, by Seoul, the improved level of play globally left little room for error on the hardwood. The reemergence of Alexander Gomelsky as the Soviet coach, along with the Soviet team's talented players, suggested that the Soviets would provide a particularly stiff test. As it happened, in Seoul, Gomelsky would deliver his "most important—and final—triumph" as he unified an ethnically divided and freedom-hungry team by "persuading Mikhail Gorbachev to allow the players to sign with clubs outside the country provided they won the gold medal."[43]

Gomelsky's return served as yet another example of the unpredictable world of Soviet sports. Officials had asked Gomelsky to sever ties with Soviet basketball in 1985, even though with him, the team had won six European championships. He was preparing for his seventh when informed of his removal, ostensibly for having lost the World Championship with the then twenty-one-year-old Sabonis, but more likely because Soviet officials feared Gomelsky planned to defect and disapproved of his business dealings. No official explanation was given, just rumors that he had "trouble going abroad." In 1993 Gomelsky told the *Moscow News* he was removed in 1985 for political reasons: "How could it be otherwise?" he asked, meaning that his record on the court clearly had not warranted his removal. Oddly, it was not the first time Gomelsky had faced removal as coach; he had been fired and rehired a number of times.[44]

It does seem that Soviet officials worried about Gomelsky's attraction to the West, and it seems that most within the Soviet basketball circle reckoned that Gomelsky's firing stemmed from political considerations rather than performance. But Gomelsky's starting point guard on the 1988 Soviet Olympic team, Tiit Sokk, thought there was more to the story. "He [Gomelsky] was not always fired for basketball reasons," Sokk said. He was involved "in something that at the time was illegal, but now is considered business. He was involved in different deals involving money, he was clever . . . fired for reasons outside basketball," Sokk maintained.[45] However, it seems more likely that concern about Gomelsky heading West, his Jewish heritage, and his contentious relationships with some high-level Russians led to his removal. The expatriate Dan Peterson, who coached in Italy in the 1970s and 1980s, explained to *Sports Illustrated* both Gomelsky's persona and his complicated relationship with higher-ups, saying, "He [Gomelsky] was a wily little guy, politically shrewd, considered one of the 100 most powerful men in Russia, disliked by many, connected with higher-ups in the Politburo. A ruthless winner, a brilliant guy."[46] Ultimately, Soviet officials knew he could coach, so he was rehired for Seoul.

In Gomelsky, the Soviet team had a seasoned, proven coach to complement Sabonis and the sharpshooting Sarunas Marciulionis, a fellow Lithuanian. Furthermore, the Soviets had Sokk, considered the top point guard in Europe and maybe the best point guard in European history. Hailing from Estonia, Sokk, along with Sabonis and Marciulionis, continued the rich basketball tradition of the Baltics, which provided the Soviet national team with the bulk of its players over the course of its thirty-six years of Olympic basketball. Sokk said that when he made the national team in 1986, basketball was the national sport in both Estonia and Lithuania and that making the Olympic team was difficult. "It was harder to make the final twelve in the Soviet Union than it was to win the European championship," he explained.[47]

When asked by the author in 2003 if he harbored any mixed feelings about playing for the government that had subjugated his native country, Sokk said: "Not really any mixed feelings . . . Sport was the only way to get abroad." He pointed out that the national team was a "way to get better in basketball—only choice. It was the highest level at that time; now you can get to Europe and go to the NBA." Still, he claimed he felt no resentment for not having had such opportunities. "No, it was all I knew. That was it. Making the top twelve in the Soviet was the top," he said. He also claimed little political pressure was put on the players. We "felt no cold war pressure. It was sports, not politics." He admitted that he had heard of times when, "if two players were equal, they would pick the Russian over the Baltic player, or really over any player outside Russia," but by 1986, "this was not a problem . . . It was near the end of the cold war, so it was a good time for them [people outside of Russia]."[48] Though a force in Europe, Sokk was not sought by NBA teams in the same fashion as some of his teammates, like Marciulionis, who described quite a different scenario. In 1992 Marciulionis recalled, "On the Soviet team we had to hide ourselves. They controlled us. We had good relations in 1988, but on that team we knew if we didn't win we might have personal intrigues."[49]

In an interview during the 2008 Beijing Olympics, Sergei Tarakanov, the general manager of Russian basketball and a 1980 and 1984 Soviet basketball Olympian, maintained that it was harder to manage players in the postcommunist Russia than in earlier times, because the players had "choice." By the 1990s they could make money overseas, so getting them to play on the national team did not always prove easy. When he played, Tarakanov explained, "it was almost like being in the Army . . . You just followed the orders. You were always under such pressure." As a player, Tarakanov did not like the lack of freedom. "I'm more of a Western guy, always liked freedom," he explained. He told Adrian Wojnarowski of two occasions in which he had threatened to quit. Apparently, officials bluntly told Tarakanov, "You'll go so far away in the Army."[50]

In the second half of the 1980s, though, for Soviet players coveted by the NBA and with aspirations to play in Stern's league, such as Marciulionis and Sabonis, times were becoming more hopeful. The ushering in of

Gorbachev as leader of the Soviet Union in 1985 led to the implementation of his *glasnost* plan, which called for a liberalization of the economy, and *perestroika*, which called for Soviet publicity and political openness to "encourage individual initiative." As the cold war historian LaFeber has noted, Gorbachev was not an anomaly. He represented a generation that realized the need to reform its economy and politics to keep up with the "technological changes (computers, satellites, instant international television coverage) that were revolutionizing Western societies."[51] As a result, by the late 1980s, Marciulionis and Sabonis could reasonably harbor hope for their NBA aspirations. Indeed, *Sports Illustrated*'s Jack McCallum noted in 1988 that *glasnost* and *perestroika* "have brightened the prospect that athletes from the USSR will be allowed to ply their trade in the United States." He reported that plans were underway to send the Soviet Union's top players to the NBA, although McCallum voiced doubt about the willingness of communist officials to allow such a major move.[52]

Not all were as doubtful as McCallum, however, such as the Portland Trail Blazers, which, counting on Gorbachev's liberalization plans to give them access to Soviet players, had chosen Sabonis with the first pick in the 1986 NBA draft. Meanwhile, the Atlanta Hawks targeted Marciulionis. Atlanta Hawk general manager Stan Kasten, under the direction of media mogul Ted Turner, worked tirelessly in the mid-1980s on securing Marciulionis's rights. Turner's interest in Marciulionis stemmed from the "extensive business dealings" he had with the Soviets."[53] Most notably, in 1986 Turner had worked with a Soviet partner to broadcast the Goodwill Games from Moscow. Modeled after the Olympics, the Goodwill Games, as suggested by their name, were intended to foster peace while simultaneously giving firms the opportunity to attract consumers. Turner's TBS superstation, which reached nearly 35 million homes by 1985, held exclusive U.S. broadcasting rights to the Goodwill Games as part of the deal.[54]

For Turner, getting Marciulionis on the Atlanta Hawks offered a pathway to further penetration of the Soviet market. Yet signing him proved difficult. Referring to the mixed signals Soviet officials sent him during the negotiating process, Kasten said, "You are optimistic and pessimistic, clearheaded and confused, all at the same time."[55] McCallum described the process as riddled with challenges for everybody involved: government officials, league representatives, the growing agent industry, and the players themselves. There were language barriers, currency differences, cultural adjustments, obligations to national teams, and haggling with lawyers.[56] The process served as a reflection of the issues involved in engaging previously closed communist nations that were undergoing liberal changes and an opening of their markets.

A key component of the negotiations was the Soviet Union's cabinet-level All-Union Ministry Physical Culture and Sports, a branch of the Soviet government with thousands of employees. Bob Wussler of Turner Broadcasting explained the ministry's pervasiveness, saying, "If it sweats or wears Adidas, the ministry has a hand in it." In addition to the Ministry of Sport and Physical Culture, Turner Broadcasting and Hawks officials had to deal with both Goskomsport and Sovintersport, which were additional governing bodies beneath the ministry in the Soviet Union's bureaucratic sporting maze. Then there was the local sports ministry in Lithuania, all of them wrangling over who would get what percentage of a player's contract.

Technically, McCallum reported, if the Hawks succeeded in securing Marciulionis's rights, the contract would be with Sovintersport, not him. The system was not the American way, but Wussler accepted it. "That's their business, but obviously we want guarantees: that the player receives enough money to get a home, a car, enough to eat, English lessons, those kinds of things," he said. Wussler admitted that navigating the bureaucratic maze was cumbersome. As TBS and Hawks officials scuttled to and from the Soviet Union in the hopes of striking a deal, he explained, "There's never a shortage of people to say 'no.' What we need is someone to step in and say 'yes.'" Marciulionis concurred, telling *Sports Illustrated*, "I want to go to Atlanta. And I want to go soon."[57]

In addition to working on securing Soviet talent, Turner's Atlanta Hawks became the first NBA team to play in the Soviet Union. Following the 1988 NBA season, the Hawks played the Soviet national team in three Soviet cities. The reaction was phenomenal. Fans packed stadiums to watch the action, gobbled up NBA merchandise, and hunted down autographs. In Lithuania, 5,000 fans showed up for a *practice* session.[58] The response showed that the NBA had reached behind the iron curtain. It also indicated basketball's ability to provide a gateway to potential consumers.

During the tour, Soviet fans were pleasantly surprised to see their team compete well against the vaunted NBA. Yet, though all of the main Hawks' players participated, McCallum questioned just how hard they played. Indeed, some of the players openly wondered why they had traveled 110,000 miles for three games.[59] Executives at TBS and NBA commissioner Stern had no such gripes, however. They commiserated with Soviet officials, acutely aware of the potential growth a lifted iron curtain could offer. As McCallum reported, topics broached between the American business leaders and Soviet brass included television, franchising rights, and the prospect of Soviet players coming to the United States.[60] Of course, from Thompson's narrow vantage point, such trips simply aided the opposition.

As part of Coach Thompson's final preparations for Seoul, the U.S. Olympic basketball team played a series of nine exhibition games against various concoctions of NBA stars. The Olympians won the bulk of them, but even in victory, some troubling trends emerged. After the team won its third straight, the *Chicago Tribune*'s Skip Myslenski raised some legitimate questions and pointed out some flaws. First, he wondered who would emerge as the main point guard, since neither Smith IV nor Coles had distanced himself from the other. Second, Myslenski noted that Robinson continued to show signs of rust. Robinson admitted as much to reporters following the third exhibition game, saying, "I'm confused. I expected to come along faster . . . I'm trying not to let it get to me, but basically it's hard to see what the coaches are driving us to do." Other players voiced uncertainty and confusion about Thompson's desires as well. Barkley, who played for the NBA stars, noticed it on the court, too, saying afterward, "They're so tentative, it's ridiculous. They're not ready to go to war yet." Myslenski asserted that Thompson's grueling schedule, which had included a month of two-a-days, had caused fatigue. Finally, and most important, he speculated that this may have compounded what had become the United States' most disturbing problem: shooting, which he characterized as "just this side of miserable."[61] Myslenski's emphasis on the shooting woes proved incisive.

In its fifth exhibition game, on August 22, the United States suffered a 90–83 loss to a group of NBA stars stacked with members of the 1988 Detroit Pistons, a team known as the "Bad Boys." More than 16,000 attended the game, the first played in the Pistons' new Palace of Auburn Hills. Thompson appreciated how hard the NBA stars played. Two days earlier, the U.S. team had won a laugher in Ohio by thirty-three. "They [the NBA players] were very physical, and I was glad to see it," he told reporters after the Pistons game.[62] Thompson knew that the international game allowed more physical play off the ball than most college players were accustomed to. The 1987 Pan-Am team had learned as much. "It's a lot more physical, so you need some strong, big people, and with the three-point shot, you have to get some good outside shooters . . . They [officials] all allow a lot more physical contact away from the ball," Pan-Am assistant Jerry Jones had explained.[63] Yet, while the game in Detroit provided the squad with needed experience against physical play, it also exhibited some of the U.S. team's weaknesses mentioned by Myslenski and raised concerns about how the team would respond to the more physically mature players they would soon face in Seoul. Complicating matters further, as the team headed to Seoul, rumors of disarray, stemming from Thompson's taxing schedule and the shielding of his players, plagued the U.S. squad. As a result, questions swirled on the eve of the Seoul Games.

There was uncertainty even about where the U.S. team would lodge in Seoul. Some wondered whether Thompson, given his penchant for secluding his Georgetown teams, particularly during the NCAA tournament, intended to do the same with the Olympic team—especially since Thompson had cried foul when the U.S. Army had asked that its soldiers be given permission to watch practice in Seoul in exchange for the U.S. team's use of a post gym.[64] As early as 1986 Thompson had addressed the issue of seclusion, saying, "I don't think that I'm so crazy that over in Seoul, South Korea, I'll be outside the [Olympic] Village."[65] But people still wondered. As it turned out, the U.S. team did stay in Seoul's Olympic Village.

Along with the other Olympians, the team lodged in a city that had spent $3 billion in preparations since winning the right to host the Olympics in 1981. Seoul finished those preparations, intended to demonstrate its "arrival" on the international scene, ahead of schedule. Parts of the effort to showcase its growing economy included an update to its subway system, the building of a 750-acre Olympic park, and the construction of an Olympic stadium that seated 100,000. Many of its venues were available for the 1986 Asian Games and had already elicited "lavish praise."[66] Seoul also became wired in the process. Overall, the Olympics enabled South Korea to stand as an example of the prosperity that could come with liberalizing a nation's economy and represented a trend of the 1980s in which countries increasingly turned to a more open market.

From India to China to South America, many nations emphasized competition and more freedom within their economies, even if limited political rights continued. In the case of South Korea, the coupling of the Olympics with its liberalizing and booming economy had major ramifications. As the historians James F. Larson and Heung-soo Park have argued, the massive public works, telecommunications advancements, and transportation networks that resulted from the Olympic effort positioned the country to compete well in the global economy and ultimately aided liberal reform.[67]

More than a decade after the Seoul Games, Peter Petri and Carl Shapiro, of Brandeis University, used the example of the 1988 Games to argue that the IOC should allow Beijing to host the 2008 Games. Petri and Shapiro reasoned that in the early 1980s, when Seoul earned the right to host, its human rights record may have been worse than that of China in 2001. But a year before the 1988 Games took place, more robust unions, student demonstrations, and ultimately democratic changes swept across South Korea, ending a military dictatorship. Petri and Shapiro admitted that South Korea's democratization had unique factors, but they also argued that the democratization reflected "the awakening of political consciousness in an emerging economic power, and the leverage of international opinion in an interdependent world."[68] They recognized that the Olympics were not the key factor in South Korea's political upheaval but argued that the Games had an important effect. Furthermore, they saw similar potential for the same changes in China. "If China wins the Olympics, the international media will scrutinize every aspect of its life and work and will surely offer a prominent stage to those oppressed by their government," they argued.[69] The longer-term ramifications for China of hosting the 2008 Games remain to be seen, but there is little question that on balance, the Olympics and its associated values function as an argument in favor of liberal economic and political policies and did so in Seoul.

At the same time, however, the selection of Seoul as Olympic host in 1981 had generated mixed feelings among South Koreans. They wanted to showcase their country on the international stage, but throughout the 1980s many South Koreans also grew weary of the strong-arm tactics of militant leader Chun Doo Hwan. South Korea was considered a western ally in the cold war, but many South Koreans questioned the IOC's decision to legitimize Hwan by giving him the Olympics.[70] By extension, feelings of anti-Americanism increased as U.S. leaders were also accused of legitimizing Hwan, especially when President Reagan welcomed Hwan to the United States just over a year after the 1979 Kwangju prodemocracy movement had ended tragically, with an estimated several hundred to several thousand activists losing their lives as a result of the actions of South Korea's repressive leaders.[71]

Still, the liberal values pushed by South Korea's growing middle class, the growth of which occurred, ironically, as a result of the liberalization of South Korea's economy by Hwan's regime, were aided by the Olympic movement. As Larson and Park have argued: "From a political communication standpoint, the national commitment to host the Seoul Olympics played a key role in this process of democratization and the ongoing resolution of tensions between the competing opposition groups and the ruling party, dominated by the military."[72] Larson and Park point to the acceptance of direct presidential elections and virtually all other opposition demands in June of 1987 as an example of this. "It is widely accepted that it was the prospect of massive international media attention surrounding the Seoul Olympics that led them to the June 29 declaration," they asserted.[73]

The situation in South Korea showed how people could, at the same time, harbor resentment for U.S. foreign policy, which they thought undermined the freedom they yearned, while valuing the liberal ideals that were supposed to stand as the hallmark of liberal nations like the United States. This helps explain the opinion poll results found in the work of historians such as Joseph Nye, which indicate an attraction to U.S. culture and its political liberties but an aversion to U.S. foreign policy.[74] The situation also demonstrated how American culture can serve U.S. interests even at times when its leaders make foreign policy decisions that seem to contradict liberal values and raise anti-American sentiment.

Ultimately, conservative estimates are that worldwide, 460 million people watched Seoul's Opening Ceremonies on television. For the first time in the United States, they watched them on NBC. The network had won the bidding for broadcast rights with an offer just over $300 million.[75] In the end, NBC's bid proved about right, as the network made $30 million for its efforts.

An Arledge protégé, Dick Ebersol, who had defected to NBC, and Michael Weisman, the thirty-eight-year-old executive producer of NBC sports, helped lead the network's winning Olympic bid. Ebersol's and Weisman's success in wrestling the Games from ABC enabled them to start their own Olympic legacy, which came to rival Arledge's. Ebersol, in particular, garnered national repute in the ensuing years for NBC's Olympic coverage. Not only did he turn the Olympics into a substantial moneymaker for his network, but he increased the number of Olympic viewers dramatically. Ebersol did this partly by continuing the Arledge tradition of focusing on individuals and, as Arledge had as well, implementing a number of technological advances, such as split-screen coverage. By the middle of the first decade of the twenty-first century, former USOC spokesman Mike Moran said Ebersol's footprint on the Olympic movement was "as large as anyone's on any level."[76] Overall, even given the time difference affecting U.S. viewership and with NBC's "subtler form of boosterism," the Seoul Olympics set broadcast records by nearly all measures. One hundred sixty nations tuned in, with major countries devoting ten to twelve hours of coverage per day. The Games showcased the latest technology and attracted an estimated 10 billion viewers (counting repeat viewers) over sixteen days.[77]

The United States opened the Olympic basketball tournament with a forty-four-point win over Spain, spurred by David Robinson's sixteen points, eleven rebounds, and four blocks. Afterward, the Spanish coach Antonio Diaz-Miguel said the United States was "magnifico" and "much better" than the United States' 1984 team. Yet even though the win made the United States a favorite again, it did little to dampen speculation of internal discord. Rather than focus on the remarkable win, at the postgame press conference, American reporters fired pointed questions about rumors of team dissension, particularly the rumor that Manning had wanted to leave the squad.

"I didn't really feel like I wanted to quit. You just get tired of things," Manning remarked, and Georgetown guard Charles E. Smith, considered a reliable cog of the team, said, "They sometimes come to me for advice. I told them this. I told them that. I sometimes told them Coach Thompson doesn't know what he wants himself." Coach Thompson weighed in on the situation, telling reporters it was not all that unnatural to have some strife. Of the rumored defections, he said, "I heard all that crap. I don't worry about it . . . I'm a pain all the time. Fussin'. Moldin'. Tryin' to get a team together. So it's normal . . . I did hear about [Manning wanting to leave].

I think it's a bunch of crap. I discussed it with the team. J. R. [Reid] got up and said he wanted to leave, too. There's just a whole lot of fussin' and strainin' in a situation like this."[78]

It was an odd press conference for a team coming off of an impressive win. It seemed that the negative tone of the media's coverage, which emerged during the initial phase of the trials in Colorado, had carried over to Seoul; and that there was something to the rumors of player discontent. Even the good-natured Robinson confirmed this more bluntly later, telling *Gentleman's Quarterly* three years after the Games, "Thompson was a dictator. You had to go his way. It was always *his* gym, *his* team, *his* this . . . He wants you scared of him."[79]

In its second game the U.S. squad faced a lightly regarded Canadian team that had lost its opener to Brazil by sixteen points. Canada played the United States surprisingly tough, however. It trailed at halftime by only two points, 42–40, and at that point had grabbed more rebounds than the Americans, a supposed U.S. strength. Ironically, to pull out the win the United States relied on its biggest weakness, three-point shooting. Majerle, Hawkins, and Charles E. Smith made crucial three-point baskets in the closing minutes for a 76–70 victory.[80] Still, the affair hinted at potential problems. If the squad needed to rely on its three-point shooting to beat Canada, against stronger teams, it would probably have to as well. Smith made outside shots this time, but it was not his forte, nor was it an area of depth for the team. After Hawkins went down with a knee injury following game four, the outside shooting prospects looked even grimmer.

Nonetheless, the U.S. team won all of its preliminary round games to move to 5-0 as it readied for the single-elimination quarterfinals. Despite the team's success, though, the press continued to provide negative coverage. *Sports Illustrated* ran a story entitled "They've Won with No Fun . . ." in which Scott Wolff wrote that the U.S. team had been kept on lockdown since assembling in mid-July. He also reported that the situation had caused Manning to meet with his agent, Ron Grinker, several weeks before the Olympic tournament to ask about the ramifications of going AWOL—which caused that issue to resurface. Furthermore, Wolff noted that, while Russian coach Alexander Gomelsky captivated people during the Games by doing things like "giving a *USA Today* reporter a ride on the team bus after a practice" and conducting open practices, Thompson did little to ingratiate himself with the press. In fact, all of the various Olympic teams' practices were open to the public, "except guess whose," Wolff asked rhetorically.[81]

Though Wolff painted a rosy picture of Gomelsky, by the end of the preliminary round, the Soviets also faced some problems. As winners of the European championship earlier that summer, they had come to Seoul fairly confident. After their European championship, the outspoken Gomelsky had told reporters he thought the Soviets could beat the United States in Seoul even with an injured Sabonis: "I think so. I hope so. I don't know what the U.S. team is. Many people talk about it being a great team. I remember the United States losing the Pan-Am game against Brazil. Brazil was a good team, but not great." As evidenced by Wolff's reportage, Gomelsky's confidence had buoyed his spirits in the days leading up to the tournament. In turn, he ingratiated himself with the media and turned himself into their darling, opening his practices and entertaining the American press with colorful remarks. However, Gomelsky's air soured after Yugoslavia, coached by the 1968 Yugoslav Olympian Kresimir Cosic, soundly beat the Soviets in preliminary round action, 92–79. Following the loss, Gomelsky refused interviews, telling reporters only that he planned to "have an announcement tomorrow." His players shunned the media as well.

Led by the seven-foot-tall center Vlade Divac, the six-feet-ten-inch guard Toni Kukoc, and the six-feet-five-inch guard Drazen Petrovic, the 1988 Yugoslav team, not unlike the Soviet squad, represented the results of basketball's global diffusion. The versatility of Divac, Kukoc, and Petrovic in particular indicated the maturation of the international game. As his coach Cosic did, Divac embodied the versatile, crafty big man that Europe began cultivating in earnest after Russell's Olympic performance in 1956. Meanwhile, Kukoc, nicknamed "the waiter" for his deft passing and who shared some Cosic-type qualities, also had elements of his game in the mold of Oscar Robertson and Magic Johnson. Petrovic's shooting conjured thoughts of Jerry West. *Sports Illustrated*'s Wolff described the young and brash Petrovic as a European guard with U.S. skills, comparing his "panache" with Ernie DiGregorio's and his frontcourt skills with those of the former Olympian Phil Ford, "only Petrovic is bigger than either of them." Nicknamed "the dalmation sensation," the athletic Petrovic led the "funkier-than-thou," as Wolff described them, Yugoslavs in scoring at the Olympic tournament.[82] These types of European players were making indelible contributions to the physical models of how to play basketball, which would come to affect U.S. style.

Earlier that summer, Thompson had come back from the European qualifying tournament and asserted that Yugoslavia looked better than the Soviets. His sentiments appeared true after the Yugoslavs beat the Soviets in Seoul. Outside of stopping Yugoslavia's big three, the most glaring problem the Soviets encountered in the game was Sabonis, who struggled with his mobility and could "jump but a few inches off the floor." Yugoslav coach Dusan Ivkovic reluctantly admitted, "I can say only he was once a great player, but after his injury, he doesn't play so well at this moment."[83]

In medal-round action, the United States opened with a sound defeat of Puerto Rico, 95–59, behind eighteen points by Danny Manning. As a result, finally, after sixteen years, the long-anticipated Olympic rematch between the Soviet Union and the United States materialized, this time in the semifinals. Not surprisingly, pregame buildup focused on the rekindling of the long-time cold war rivalry. The actions in 1972 of FIBA Secretary General R. William Jones were scrutinized yet again, and the numerous other peculiarities that attended the Munich affair were rehashed. Asked by reporters, Gomelsky gave thoughts on the continuation of the 1972 saga: "The boys come back from Olympic Games in '72, and this is big story. All the people make them heroes . . . This is 15 [actually 16] years ago, but every day, every day, Russian people, journalists talk of this historic moment in Munich. Everybody knows Alexander Belov. This is good story." He also told reporters that his 1988 team was not as good as his 1984 team, but nonetheless he claimed to "have a chance now," intimating he knew something no one else did. But the Brazilian players Marcel Souza and Oscar Schmidt, who had played the Soviets, did not give Gomelsky's team much of a chance. Schmidt thought Sabonis's two Achilles injuries had slowed him down. "He cannot jump. He suffers when he does. The United States will take it right at him," Schmidt predicted. Souza warned the Soviets not to run with the United States; if they do "it will be a covenant of death."[84]

For over a year, Thompson had prepared for this game. In November 1987 he even missed an exhibition game between his own Georgetown Hoyas and the Canadian national team in order to scout the Soviets, who were playing the same night in Las Vegas.[85] But he had not planned on the injury to Hersey Hawkins that would bring a glare to the United States' dearth of shooters; and he had not prepared for the early foul trouble that Manning, who finished scoreless for the game, would encounter against the crafty, disciplined Soviets. Both of these problems contributed to the United States' ten-point halftime deficit.

Meanwhile, the seasoned Soviet squad, quarterbacked by the savvy Sokk, had little trouble handling the Americans' pressure defense, and the Soviets' wealth of shooters created problems for the United States. In the first half Rimas Kurtinaitis and Marciulionis drained three three-pointers apiece, propelling them to their 47–37 lead.[86] At the midway point, the United States' ineffective pressure defense had resulted in only one fast-break basket. The first half's relatively high score was especially disturbing. In their 1972 victory the Soviets were happy to play a slow game. In 1988 the Soviets showed that they had learned how to beat U.S. amateurs at their own game in the Olympics.

Though the contest remained relatively close most of the second half, the Soviets continued to control the bulk of the action, winning in rather workmanlike fashion, 82–76. Sabonis finished the game with thirteen points and thirteen rebounds. Afterward, the Portland Trail Blazers, which held Sabonis's NBA rights and for which he would one day play, received calls blaming the franchise for the U.S. loss. The *New York Times* ran a quote from the Trail Blazers' physician Dr. Robert Cook, who thoughtfully maintained, "If we're not prepared to beat the Soviets in their best health, we don't deserve to win. Withholding athletic care is no avenue to a gold medal." Regardless of the phone calls to the Blazers, it seems the vast majority of Americans concurred.[87]

For the Soviets, years of traveling to America to learn the collegiate and professional game had paid off. Gomelsky admitted as much in post-game remarks. Referring to the Soviet Union's trips to the United States and games against the Hawks in the Soviet Union, he said, "We have nice competition. It was very good preparation."[88] Thompson had figured as much. And it was not just the several years leading up to Seoul that had prepared the Soviet team: sixteen years earlier, Gomelsky had talked about translating the works of Auerbach and Rupp. The win was really a culmination of decades of preparation.

16. The Soviet Union posing for a gold medal photo, before the "clandestine" photo Sarunus Marciulionis and his fellow Lithuanian teammates would take. Photo by Joe Patronite. Getty Images Sport Collection/Getty Images.

To get the gold, the Soviets still had a big hurdle—the Cosic-coached Yugoslavs that had beaten the Soviets in preliminary round play and won four of the teams' previous five meetings. But this time the Soviets rolled to victory, led by Marciulionis's twenty-one points and Sabonis's twenty points and fifteen rebounds, 76–63. The United States faced Australia for bronze. Rather than come out deflated, the team rebounded with a convincing 78–49 win. Thompson graciously said, "The players have done everything I've asked of them. I wanted us to be emotional against Australia because I didn't want to go out on a losing note."[89]

Revealingly, right after winning the gold medal, Marciulionis, Sabonis, Rimas Kurtinaitis, and Valdemaras Chomicius, the four Lithuanians on the 1988 Soviet team, risked punishment by sneaking off to a side room for a clandestine photograph. The photograph occurred immediately after Russian officials had gathered the Soviet players for an "official" team picture. In 1992 Chomicius told the *Boston Globe*'s Bob Ryan that the secret picture "was our team picture . . . We are Lithuanian now. We were Lithuanian then. We were never Russians." By 1992, Marciulionis could also speak openly about life under Soviet rule, especially about the time he was forced to give a speech that defended Russian occupation and discouraged freedom. "They forced people to come and listen," Marciulionis explained in 1992, by then a millionaire playing in the NBA. "I was told if I did not read it I would be failed in all my classes at university and I would not be allowed to have an apartment. I read it. It was the most embarrassing moment of my life."[90] His story—and Lithuania's, of course—would not end there.

In the United States, the loss to the Soviets magnified criticism of Thompson's handling of the players, tactics, and lack of shooters. Certainly, there were legitimate criticisms to be leveled, but the *New York Times*'s Peter Alfano made an important point immediately after the defeat. Unlike Knight, who had relied on Ewing and Jordan, Alfano asserted, "Thompson did not have a superstar on his roster."[91] Outside of Robinson, the professional careers of Thompson's Olympic players bore the claim out. In addition, Thompson faced stiffer competition. NBA coach Lenny Wilkens emphasized this when he wrote that "the 1988 Olympic team didn't lose because John Thompson was the coach. It was simply a matter of the world's pros catching up to our college kids; there was nothing John Thompson could have done about that."[92] To be sure, the Soviets did not attend the LA Games, and the overall level of international play had improved by Seoul. Still, a number of unnecessary and seemingly disruptive decisions by Thompson and Wall plagued the team, while a number of personnel moves warrant questioning.

For Robinson, the loss to the Soviets marked the second time in as many years that he was the featured player on a U.S. national team that had failed to win in international competition. Nonetheless, he still came to have a profound impact on basketball, and in 1992 he won an Olympic gold medal. In 1990 he became the chief spokesman for Nike's now iconic Force line of basketball shoes. Wieden & Kennedy spent $15 million on a "Mr. Robinson's Neighborhood" marketing campaign that celebrated Robinson's intellect, Renaissance-man personality, along with his exploits on the basketball court. The campaign was wildly successful. Robinson's biographer Jim Savage wrote that Nike watched in amazement as Robinson grew "larger than life." Nike started to think he could potentially rival Jordan as a shoe salesman. And by all accounts, the image propagated by Nike fit the real persona.[93] Throughout his life, Robinson has donated millions to charity and striven to embody moral values. As we will see, he

TABLE 12. 1988 U.S. Men's Olympic Basketball cumulative stats

NAME	G	FGM-FGA	(%)	3PM-3PA	(%)	FTM-FTA	(%)	REB/AVG	PTS/AVG	AST	BLK	ST
David Robinson	8	40-69	.580	0-0	.000	22-30	.733	54/6.8	102/12.8	7	19	9
Danny Manning	8	40-70	.571	0-0	.000	11-13	.846	48/6.0	91/11.4	6	3	5
Mitch Richmond	8	29-60	.483	1-4	.250	12-18	.667	27/3.4	71/8.9	17	0	10
Hersey Hawkins	4	11-20	.550	5-8	.625	8-8	1.000	4/1.0	35/8.8	0	0	2
C. E. Smith IV	8	28-59	.475	4-9	.444	9-11	.818	10/1.3	69/8.6	16	0	7
C. D. Smith	8	23-40	.575	0-0	.000	16-20	.800	33/4.1	62/7.8	2	6	1
Bimbo Coles	8	23-44	.523	0-0	.000	11-13	.846	14/1.8	57/7.1	7	0	11
Jeff Grayer	8	24-45	.533	3-6	.500	4-9	.444	27/3.4	55/6.9	2	3	7
J. R. Reid	6	14-30	.467	0-0	.000	8-13	.615	20/3.3	36/6.0	2	3	3
Willie Anderson	7	16-25	.640	0-2	.000	3-31	.000	13/1.9	35/5.0	6	4	6
Stacey Augmon	6	3-6	.500	0-0	.000	1-2	.500	11/1.8	7/1.2	0	1	5
USA TOTALS	8	299-551	.543	19-45	.422	116-158	.734	299/37.4	733/91.6	74	40	73
OPP. TOTALS	8	167-453	.369	41-126	.325	115-166	.693	201/25.1	490/61.3	74	11	36

still faced criticism, though, through his relationships with multinational corporations, namely, Nike.

Regardless of strategic shortcomings in 1988, even the critics seemed to recognize that times had changed; that regardless of the issues with U.S. decision-making, the mature, super-skilled European players would continue to fare well against collegians. This gave the 1988 team its most prominent legacy. The Soviet loss gave credence to the argument that the time had come to allow NBA players into the Olympics. The loss in Seoul made Stankovic's and Stern's job of selling people on the idea of NBA players in the Olympics easier.

There had been support for professionals before the loss. Along with NBA brass, the players' association had already changed course by deciding to support the idea.[94] Even John Thompson in 1987 had voiced support for the idea, a somewhat controversial stance since the system helped NCAA basketball. "If you were coaching, would you want Larry Bird?" Thompson asked rhetorically.[95] Before Seoul, Thompson and Stern were in the minority, however. But afterward, sentiment in support of, or at least in acceptance of, NBA players competing at the Olympics increased. Sure enough, in 1989 FIBA opened the door, and the NBA stepped through.[96] Upon Gomelsky's death in 2007, Stankovic said, "It is fair to say that Gomelsky and his success in 1988 might have been a final catalyst for this decision."[97]

With the stage set for a U.S. Olympic team stacked with the world's greatest professionals, NBA players quickly improved the standard and accelerated the diffusion of basketball. Gomelsky recognized this could happen right after his 1988 gold medal victory, when he was asked about the specter of NBA players participating. He answered, "I am a basketball man. I think is good. I know Larry Bird, Magic Johnson, and Michael Jordan is not possible to beat this year. Maybe after ten years is possible."[98] Indeed, in 1992 Bird, Johnson, and Jordan played together at the Olympics. By that time, the iron curtain had raised, giving Marciulionis an opportunity to enjoy one of the proudest moments of his life and helping the Dream Team demonstrate in particularly dramatic fashion basketball's dynamic role within a reshaped world driven by the tenants of universalism and market-based economics.

12

BASKETBALL BEDLAM IN BARCELONA

When the 1992 U.S. Olympic basketball team arrived at the luxurious Hotel Ambassador in Monte Carlo a week before the Barcelona Games, the hotel's managers scoffed at suggestions that they might need to enhance security, assuring all that their experience hosting rock stars and kings and princesses had ably prepared them. Then, as the *Hartford Courant*'s Alan Greenberg put it, "the team showed up." Soon after it did, hotel officials were apologizing for the disorderly mess as the fans and media who had flocked to the hotel converged on Michael Jordan, Larry Bird, Magic Johnson, and the rest. "The magnitude of this basketball royalty, they had not understood," Greenberg wrote.[1]

The experience in Monte Carlo gave Olympic officials an indication of the enormous response the team would receive in Spain. So when the American players journeyed from Monte Carlo to Barcelona, Olympic officials flew them first to Reus and then had them driven to Barcelona. This allowed the team to avoid the 3,000 to 4,000 fans that had gathered at the host city's airport in anticipation of its arrival. Still, once the players made it to the Olympic Village to get their accreditations, a mob enveloped them. Rather than shield the players from the onslaught of people, *security guards* angled for autographs; so did many of the other Olympic athletes. Space became tight as people jostled for position. "Of all the things we've experienced . . . the stampede at the village was the most frightening," the U.S. Olympic team coach Chuck Daly said later.[2]

With the Berlin wall down and the iron curtain lifted, a record 172 countries attended the "New Order Olympics."[3] And at them, the Dream Team epitomized basketball's global reach and raised the basketball standard for everyone—a standard that, by the turn of the millennium, international teams would strive for as successfully as American ones, if not more so.

Three forces—liberal capitalism, technological innovation, and basketball—blossomed with exquisite timing in Barcelona, enabling the phenomenal response to the U.S. team, from fans across the globe to burgeoning transnational corporations. David Burns, president of the Chicago-based Burns Celebrity Services, said, "No doubt about it, this is the biggest, most expensive marketing deal in the history of sports." Deputy secretary general of the USOC and marketing legend John Krimsky maintained, "There are young people out there who think the Olympics are one big basketball tournament."[4]

The response caught the NBA off guard. "We completely didn't understand what the demand [for merchandise] would be," NBA chief marketing officer Rick Welts explained. Within four years of Barcelona, the NBA, whose marketing division USA Basketball had hired to market its gear, would make U.S. Olympic basketball team apparel available in seventeen countries, compared to seven in 1992. By 1996, the league's total global merchandise sales amounted to roughly $3 billion, up from $1 billion in 1990.[5]

In short, the Dream Team changed basketball forever. Almost immediately, it accelerated the improvement of basketball players across the globe as well as the growth of the sport's international market. In turn, it benefited the NBA and FIBA, as well as firms like Nike and Adidas. In hindsight, this seems obvious, but again, it was not Stern's international designs that proved pivotal in bringing about the Dream Team. It was Boris Stankovic, the head of FIBA. And given the Olympic basketball tournament's continued popularity since 1992 and international teams' strong showings against USA basketball in the first decade of the twenty-first century, Stankovic's vision looks exceedingly brilliant, having produced as it did a win-win situation for FIBA and the NBA.

Firms had long associated themselves with Olympic sports; it is just that the Dream Team brought these relationships to a new level. Forty different companies, spending an estimated $40 million, emerged as promotional partners of the squad. Fourteen of those went through USA Basketball, paying $750,000 apiece (ever since NBA players have become eligible for the Olympics, the NBA has functioned as USA Basketball's marketer). Twenty-six others aligned themselves with the team using separate licensing agreements. These figures do not even count the money spent by corporations like Nike, which circumvented official association with USA Basketball by making its own ads featuring the stable of six Dream Team players it had under contract: Jordan, John Stockton, David Robinson, Charles Barkley, Scottie Pippen, and Chris Mullin. These Nike men were featured in commercials depicting them as larger-than-life cartoon characters smashing everything in their path. Also excluded from the figures is the spending of numerous publications like *Sports Illustrated* and *USA Today*, which, in an effort to increase readership, set up games and gift promotions centered on the Dream Team. Sponsors, official and otherwise, hocked everything from posters to peanuts, hats to pins, shoes to trading cards; if you could imagine it, you could probably find it.[6]

The three biggest stars driving the Dream Team phenomenon were, of course, Bird, Magic, and Jordan, all three remarkable American tales. Bird, a six-feet-nine-inch white marksman capable of deftly utilizing both hands, passing with great subtlety, and making off-balance shots seemingly all over the court, grew up poor in a rural part of Indiana. Magic, an African American, was a charismatic six-feet-nine-inch point guard who grew up in a lower-middle-class, two-parent home in Lansing, Michigan. Not endowed with great explosiveness, Johnson made up for it with amazing deceptiveness, adroit ballhandling, fine court vision, and underappreciated quickness. Finally, there was Jordan—the most artful and effective player of all time. In Wilmington, North Carolina, Jordan grew up in a quintessential American home. His father, like so many African Americans in the 1960s and 1970s, worked his family into the middle class through the military.[7]

Together these three great players proved, as had Fortenberry, Russell, Robertson, West, and Haywood, that a superstar basketball player could conceivably come from any place, under any condition. A big difference between the Dream Team standouts and these earlier stars, however, was that by 1992, a basketball standout could become one of the most recognizable faces on the planet.

Bird grew up in West Baden and French Lick, two small towns abutting each other in southern Indiana. His parents bounced from job to job, struggling to get by from month to month, commonly earning just over $200 a week between them. Eventually, his father's drinking led to a divorce. Soon afterward, his father spiraled into a deep depression. When Bird was nineteen, his father, in debt and facing legal difficulties, took his own life—according to Bird, his father deemed the social security money his family would get in return more valuable than his life.[8]

Nonetheless, Bird does not recall an unhappy childhood. He knew his family was poor, but he felt as if most everybody else in French Lick was too. His four brothers and his sister kept themselves busy playing sports. "There never was a day we didn't do *something*, whether it was baseball, basketball or football," Bird remembered as an adult. Surprisingly, he did not pay much attention to basketball until the rather late age of thirteen, when he visited extended family in Hobart, a small town in northern Indiana. As he walked around town, some boys asked young Larry to join them in a pickup game. He obliged and started sinking shot after shot. The kids asked him what team he played for and could not believe it when he told them he played for no team. From that day on, Bird was hooked on hoops. He made the "B team" the following year as a freshman, and by the time he was a sophomore, he said, "Basketball was all I thought about, all I wanted to do . . . I would play at 6 a.m. before school. I would duck into the gym between classes to get a few shots up and play again after school into the early hours of the next morning, feeling that sleep was a rude intrusion on my practice time."[9]

After a brief stint at Indiana under Bobby Knight, he left school and headed back to French Lick. There, Bird worked at a gas station and then for the street department, picking up trash once a week as he pondered his future.[10] A slew of coaches, including Bill Hodges, the head coach of Indiana State, a school just over fifty miles from French Lick, continued to recruit Bird during this time. It seemed that Hodges showed up in West Baden nearly every day. He would appear unannounced at the Laundromat or at the Birds' home. It got so bad that one time Bird's mom slammed the door on him. Bird appreciated Hodges's persistence, however, and he had visited Indiana State and liked it. Later, Larry Bird, his older brother Mark, and their friend Kevin Carnes traveled to Indiana State to scrimmage with the team. When Bird and his crew showed up ready to play wearing jeans, Hodges offered them some shorts, but they deferred. As Bird put it, "We never played in shorts back home." Apparently, Hodges was "horrified."[11] But everyone in the gym soon learned that you *can* wear jeans and still play basketball, and a few years later, with Bird enrolled, they found out that the Indiana State Sycamores could make it to the national championship game.

In that national championship game, Indiana State faced the Michigan State Spartans and their star, Earvin "Magic" Johnson. Raised in Lansing, Michigan, not far from the campus of Michigan State, Johnson wrote in 1992, "I grew up in the kind of black family that people today worry is disappearing."[12] Magic had six siblings, and his parents worked hard to provide for their large family. Magic's father toiled at two full-time jobs, and his mother worked as a custodian and waitress, among other things. Johnson said that his parents "believed in hard work" and that his father did not believe in "handouts." As an adult, Johnson attributed his work ethic to the example set by his father, and his colorful, magnetic personality to his mother: "People talk about my smile, but my smile is her smile."[13] That smile remained intact even after Magic announced in November 1991 that he had contracted the HIV/AIDS virus, most likely from promiscuous sexual activity. The announcement brought the stark realities of the virus's infectiousness to Americans of all sorts. Some voiced concern about Johnson playing basketball with HIV, in the NBA and the Olympics, but ultimately, he did both. And since his announcement, Johnson has crusaded for HIV/AIDS prevention, preaching safe sex and education as the globe's most recognizable carrier of the virus.

As with Bird and his reflections on West Baden and French Lick, Johnson considered Lansing a great place to grow up. "It wasn't the suburbs, but it wasn't the ghetto, either," Johnson explained. Not surprisingly, basketball played a big part in his life early on. Johnson learned much about the game from his father, whom he idolized as a youngster. Like Bird's mentor in high school, his coach Jim Jones, Magic's father emphasized the total game: inside and outside shooting, blocking out, playing defense, passing.[14] Both Bird and Magic benefited from their mentors in developing their dazzlingly versatile games. Also like Bird, Johnson became obsessed with working on his skills, though he did so at a much earlier age. "No matter what else I was doing, I always had a basketball in my hand," Johnson recalled. "I remember waking up when it was dark outside and wanting to play ball so badly that I'd just lie there, looking out the window, waiting for daybreak."[15] Together, Bird and Magic deserve credit for enhancing basketball's popularity to a point that enabled Jordan to take the game even further.

While Bird and Magic came to Barcelona in the twilight of their spectacular careers—Bird, hampered by back problems, told reporters just before the Games got underway, "I've been retired for four years, only nobody knows it yet"—Jordan did not.[16] He came to Barcelona in his prime, capable of personifying at this most opportune time the uncommon confluence of forces that flowered in Barcelona. Cut from the varsity team as a sophomore in high school only to hit the game-winning shot three years later as a freshman for North Carolina in the NCAA national championship game, Jordan possessed world-class athleticism, uncanny skill, court awareness, and a seemingly unmatchable competitive drive that enabled him to stand out even on the greatest team ever assembled. Chuck Daly admitted as much: "Not even close. Whenever he wanted to, he could just take over."[17]

Gauging his prominence, the journalist and historian David Halberstam has noted that during his career, Jordan sold shoes to help people fly, Big Macs to help them eat, and Gatorade to quench their thirst; he "was nothing less than a New World seigneur." Just about everybody wanted Jordan to sell everything, from hot dogs to perfume, and he would ultimately end up having to turn away endorsement deals that would have been inaccessible to most African Americans in the 1950s and 1960s.[18] This unique status motivated the sociologist David Andrews to compile and edit *Michael Jordan, Inc.*, a book of essays from distinguished minds that was intended to "make sense of a celebrated figure, whose public existence graphically exteriorizes a late capitalist order defined by the convergence of corporate and media interests."[19]

As had been the case for his fellow Olympians Russell, Robertson, West, Bird, and Magic, Jordan was not born into such lofty status. With the help of hardworking parents, opportunity, an indefatigable work ethic, creative genius, athletic grace, technological innovation, marketing savvy, and a sport that enabled all of these traits to be displayed to the rest of the world, Jordan turned himself into a global icon. And his presence on the U.S. Olympic team in Barcelona played a pivotal role in this. Though much of his fame came through his exploits in the NBA, his rise to a global icon of mammoth proportions is, in no small part, due to his participation on the Dream Team. Halberstam recognized as much, writing, "In a way, it was the 1992 Olympics that lifted Michael Jordan's fame to another level, because of the worldwide focus on the American team, known as the Dream Team."[20]

This worldwide visibility meant that all of the Dream Team players had endorsement relationships with some shoe and apparel company. In fact, throughout the late 1980s and into the 1990s, shoe companies had continued to more effectively leverage the cultural appeal of their products. Jordan's Nike line reflected this best of such efforts. With the success of the 1985 Air Jordan campaign, Nike's advertising budget ballooned over the next eight years from $20 million to $150 million, and, as Donald Katz has noted in *Just Do It*, Nike ads became global sensations during this time. Indeed, the original 1985 "Jordan Flight" commercial set off a national shopping spree "replete with long lines, hoarding, sales far above retail price, secondary street markets, [and] traumatic disappointments over the limited supply." Future Nike commercials landed the producer Jim Riswold a spot on *Newsweek*'s list of the one hundred most significant people in American culture.[21]

In his work, Riswold focused on developing an "urban," or "black," image.[22] One of his most famous spots featured Spike Lee, as Mars Blackmon, and Jordan, with "style reeled in from the farthest edge of urban hip, and with the best of all good hearts," as Katz has described it. So popular were the commercials that few did not know of Mars's love for Jordan and his shoes. In 1993 Jordan summed up the comprehensive impact of the Nike marketing campaigns, saying, "What Phil and Nike have done is turn me into a dream."[23] But it was not easy to stay on top. The money that the shoe market generated made for an increasingly competitive industry.

As Nike's Geoff Hollister noted in 1998, "You've got to come up with great stuff all the time. You miss just one season, and you can flatten out just that quickly." The shoe industry analyst Faye Landes echoed those sentiments, emphasizing the need to stay fresh: "Coolness. That is the issue; that's something that I worry about constantly."[24]

In addition, the sheer volume of sales and the visibility of the industry's superstar endorsers put the basketball shoe at the center of debates involving a wide range of topics, from cultural values to labor in the global age. Interpretations varied. As the sociologists Stephen Papson and Robert Goldman have explained, "As one of the most visible and most desirable brand images, Nike—and in particular, Michael Jordan and Spike Lee—has received an exaggerated share of sensationalist finger-pointing for the acquisitiveness inspired by consumerism among the poor."[25] In 1993 the intellectual Michael Eric Dyson argued that the sneaker "symbolized the ingenious manner in which black nuances of cool, hip, and chic have influenced the broader American cultural landscape."[26] He also asserted, however, that the sneaker epitomized the "worst fears of social production of desire, and represents the ways in which moral energies of social conscience about material values are drained by the messages of undisciplined acquisitiveness promoted by corporate dimensions of the culture of consumption." Furthermore, "while sneaker companies have exploited black cultural expressions of cool, hip, chic, and style, they rarely benefit the people who both consume the largest quantity of products and whose culture redefined the companies' raison d'etre." Ultimately, Dyson claimed that the situation was compounded by the ineffectiveness, defensiveness, or indifference of spokespeople like Jordan and Bo Jackson regarding issues of black-on-black violence related to the products they endorsed.[27]

Others offered analyses similar to Dyson's, but these critiques seemed to overlook that the vast majority of people buying Nike's high-priced products in America were white. In 1991 Nike estimated that whites purchased 87 percent of its products sold in the United States.[28] In discussing similar charges of indifference leveled at David Robinson, Jim Savage, his biographer, noted that, "It was pointed out that the vast majority of hundred-dollar basketball shoes were not sold in inner cities, but to affluent white suburbanites." However, Savage said, "The criticism [of Robinson] continued unabated."[29] Some critics seemed even to suggest that sneakers perpetrated violence. In addressing this charge, Papson and Goldman reasonably suggest that it "displaces attention from the mundane sociological forces at work in our inner cities."[30] Regardless of where one stood on the issue, that shoes played a prominent role in the debate over such weighty issues highlighted their prominence.[31]

Few disputed that Jordan, the most visible athlete of the time, was portrayed as a heroic figure imbued with ethical values and that Nikes sold all over the world because of him.[32] As an indication of this, the academic James Twitchell included the Nike ad campaign for the Jordan Flight line in his list of "Twenty Ads That Shook the World," drawing parallels between the Jordan Flight marketing campaign and the American frontier, the transcendent meaning of the Sistine Chapel, and the human yearning to soar. He also credited Nike with developing the "hero as product."[33] Nike's ad man Dan Wieden lent some legitimacy to Twitchell's frontier comparison when he said that the remote, "cut-off" nature of Portland, the main home for the Wieden and Kennedy firm, was crucial to the advertising agency's work, as well as the agency's willingness to challenge authority.[34] The success of Wieden and Kennedy's campaigns, the sociologist Marshall Blonsky has maintained in *American Mythologies*, enabled the agency to go around the world to market "Nike's image of America."[35] Jordan, of course, was out front.

Even Dyson acknowledges that Jordan has "attained unparalleled cultural status because of his extraordinary physical gifts, his marketing as an icon of race-transcending American athletic and moral excellence, and his mastery of a sport that has become the metaphoric center of black cultural imagination." Though Dyson has claimed that the scope of Jordan's social influence was limited to the black body, he has also noted that Jordan's career "symbolizes possibility itself."[36] Others put similar limitations on the influence of Jordan and other Dream Team members: in the late 1990s, the scholars Kay Schaffer and Sidonie Smith asserted that while there was no doubt that Jordan had helped improve race relations in the United States, they still questioned whether he had helped the image of the average black man.[37]

Sports Illustrated's E. M. Swift argued in a similar vein in 1991 when he penned an article entitled "Reach Out and Touch Someone: Some Black Superstars Cash in Big on an Ability to Shed Their Racial Identity." In the article, Swift compared the struggles of African Americans to receive fair treatment in the endorsement market up through the 1970s with the remarkable endorsement earnings that year of Jordan (an estimated $15 to $20 million) and Magic Johnson, who, he said, had "traded his good name and winning smile to Pepsi, Kentucky Fried Chicken, Converse, Campofrio (a Spanish meat company), Nintendo and Spalding, among others, for some $12 million." Swift also pointed to Charles Barkley's deals with Nike and Gillette and David Robinson's relationships with Nike, Casio watches, Franklin sporting goods, and Brock Candy to assert that one of his Mr. Robinson's Neighborhood ads should read: "Today's word is color-blind." David Green of the Chicago-based McDonald's corporation asserted as much, telling Swift, "The public, especially young people, is color-blind in terms of its athletic heroes." Green added, "They look at these guys as great athletes who do superhuman things. They don't look at color at all."[38] Yet, while Swift acknowledged that the endorsement market had become more accepting of African Americans, he also suggested that to endorse products, these stars had to shed their blackness, thus intimating that blackness constituted a monolithic state of being.

In his article, Swift talked with Marvin Bressler, a sociologist from Princeton, to gauge how this acceptance of African Americans in the endorsement market had come about. Bressler said, "I do think there's been a kind of general, abstract improvement in race relations in this country, more of a willingness to recognize merit." But he added, "It has no implications for race relations as such . . . It's long been the case that whites have acknowledged the athletic excellence of blacks without giving up a whole series of prejudices in other areas." Swift finished his article with the assertion that the effects of color-blind marketing were "largely nil," and suggested that in effect, whites were telling all of the athletes who worked for them, "Come play for us. Just use the backdoor."[39]

However, the suggestion that African Americans have, over the course of the past several decades, excelled at basketball and then merely exited through the backdoor overlooks some basic facts. Many great African American players, from Robertson to Russell to Julius Erving to Magic Johnson, have done quite a bit more than that. In fact, Johnson maybe better than any other Dream Team member works to counter the argument that basketball perpetuates, or even exacerbates, racism and the suggestion that in endorsing a product, an athlete must shed his or her blackness. Magic has used the cultural and economic capital gained through his exploits on the basketball court to do much more than simply play and leave through "the backdoor."

Johnson's business success has been no mistake. In 2001, the Lakers owner Jerry Buss said, "Anyone who thinks Magic is a success in business because of his personality doesn't know business." That same year, *Sports Illustrated*'s Jack McCallum noted that ever since Johnson started his yard-cleaning franchise as a ten-year-old in Lansing, Michigan, he had dreamed of building a business empire. By 2001 he had. Not only that, but he had also helped show major U.S. corporations, such as Starbucks, TGI Friday's, and Loews movie theaters, that their businesses could thrive in African American communities. For instance, the Starbucks and the Loews movie theater he opened in Harlem in 1999 and 2000 were quickly followed by stores from Old Navy, H&M, and MAC cosmetics.[40]

Even before this, Magic had worked to leverage his wealth and visibility and to utilize his business relationships. In 1994 he started the Johnson Development Corporation (JDC), which soon became an inner-city phenomenon. By 2004, the business reporter Marc Hequet noted, Johnson's company maintained partnerships with seventy Starbucks locations, six theaters, and one TGI Fridays, and "only three underperforming Starbucks and one TGI Fridays have closed over the years." As a private entity, Johnson's corporation does not publish revenues. Regardless, Hequet argued, "Johnson's success has shown other retailers that setting up shop in minority neighborhoods isn't social work—it's just good business."[41] Magic Johnson not only left the court through the front door, he has opened the door for many others.

Joining Bird, Magic, and Jordan in Barcelona were other greats in their own right. At the forward positions were Charles Barkley, a six-feet-five, 250-pound force; Karl Malone, a six-feet-nine, powerful forward in his own right; Chris Mullin, the six-feet-seven silky shooter who had played in the 1984 Games; and finally, the youngest Dream Team member of all, six-feet-eleven Christian Laettner out of Duke, who was selected over Shaquille O'Neal as the lone collegian. At guard, Clyde Drexler and Pippen, both six-feet-seven versatile wingmen, and the six-feet-one point-man Stockton complimented Jordan and Magic. The seven-feet-one Robinson,

17. Magic Johnson, Scottie Pippen, Patrick Ewing, Michael Jordan, and Charles Barkley—not a bad bench. Photo by Mike Powell. Getty Images Sport Collection/Getty Images.

a 1988 Olympian, and the seven-foot-tall Patrick Ewing, a 1984 Olympian, manned the center position.

About a year before USA Basketball named the bulk of the Dream Team, Chuck Daly, winner of the 1989 and 1990 NBA titles as the head coach of the Detroit Pistons, was chosen to lead the squad. Daly, who was from a humble background, started his coaching career in 1955 at the high school level in Punxsutawney, Pennsylvania (yes, home of Groundhog's Day). Before that, he had been a standout on his high school team in Kane, Pennsylvania, played college basketball at Bloomsburg State, and been drafted into the U.S. Army. In the army Daly served in Tokyo as a medical corpsman, and while there, he went to his first basketball clinic. Ironically, Bruce Drake helped run it. That Daly would one day come to share with Drake the distinction of being an Olympic basketball coach was not something he likely figured on while attending the clinic.[42] From the high school ranks, Daly moved to the college level as an assistant coach at Duke.

It intrigued the Olympic selection committee that Daly had coached at all three of those levels. In addition, Daly was considered a "player's coach." The influential U.S. Olympic Basketball committeeman C. M. Newton explained that he wanted someone players liked to play for. "I thought Chuck commanded that respect," Newton wrote. Daly made a point to note, though, that he did not give up all discipline when coaching pros. His style did, however, mean that there would be no arduous two-a-days for the Dream Team and that Daly would attempt to make the experience of being on the greatest Olympic basketball team ever assembled an "enjoyable" one on and off the court. This, he thought, would help maximize performance.[43]

Because they were known commodities as players and owing to their sensitivity about their time commitments, rather than being expected to try out, the Dream Team players were invited to join the squad. "What sense would it make to invite Michael Jordan or Magic Johnson to a one-week tryout? Everyone knows what they can do!" Daly wrote.[44]

A Games committee that the now NBA-led U.S. Basketball Olympic Basketball Committee had formed was charged with doling out the invites. As it happened, Daly did not have a major influence on this committee. In some ways, Daly explained, this helped relieve pressure on him and perhaps limited the prospect of an NBA player who was not asked to join the team trying to exert revenge on Daly's Pistons squad. Of course, Daly also admitted that "coaches like to pick their players." Ironically, a bulk of the "heat" he did get regarding selection came from the absence of three of his own players, all of whom were "disappointed" about being left off the original ten-player list of Dream Team selections. The three Pistons left off were Joe Dumars, a classy jump-shot artist with strong defense; Dennis Rodman, an agile rebounder and defender; and, particularly noteworthy, the Pistons' point guard Isiah Thomas (more on that later). In April 1991 Daly did provide USA Basketball with a comprehensive list of players that he thought should warrant consideration for the team, but C. M. Newton and Rod Thorn took the lead on player selection (even though the committee also boasted some NBA general managers). The trick was paring down the list that C. M. Newton eventually put together. Just trimming it to five players per position "was rough, but shortening the list even further was rougher," Newton explained. Ultimately, Daly got a team that, among other things, had flexibility and versatility. This was something Daly had told the committee he wanted.[45]

Once USA Basketball had determined the top ten players it wanted for the team, in September 1991 (Clyde Drexler and the collegiate choice Laettner were chosen in the spring of 1992), the committee next needed to ask those players if they would indeed suit up. That job went to USA Basketball vice president Russ Granik and Rod Thorn.[46] Granik recalled that the NBA players embraced the Olympic opportunity, and so did NBA owners, provided they got acceptable insurance for their players against the risk of injury. "What we heard from the star players was, you know, If you can get A, B, and C to do it, I'll do it," Granik said. "Not surprisingly to me, but to I think a lot of people, the top players really got into the idea because they'd never really had a chance to play together."[47] The stars did indeed come out. Virtually all of the Dream Team members will eventually be enshrined in the Naismith Memorial Basketball Hall of Fame.

Ironically, Stockton, a conspicuous cut in 1984 under Knight, emerged as perhaps the most eye-catching pick for Barcelona. Stockton, who stood only six feet one inches tall and was also relatively skinny, looked and seemed rather unassuming. However, underneath that veneer was an intensely competitive man. In fact, his backyard basketball battles with his brother Steve often turned so bloody that they earned the nicknames Cain and Abel. That roughness was balanced by the Stockton family's Catholic faith, which they practiced in an Irish, working-class neighborhood in Spokane called the "Little Vatican." In his unlikely climb to the top of the NBA, Stockton tallied spectacular statistics while starring alongside Karl Malone on the Utah Jazz. Yet many figured Isiah Thomas, winner of two NBA championships to Stockton's none, was more deserving than Stockton of a spot on the Dream Team roster. Widespread reports maintained that Jordan, though, did not want Thomas on the team. Jordan's distaste for Thomas apparently stemmed from the "freeze out" Thomas has been credited with leading against the upstart Jordan at the 1985 NBA All-star game. However, Russ Granik, the former NBA deputy commissioner and president of USA Basketball told the author that reports of Jordan's influence on the Thomas decision have been "vastly exaggerated." He admitted that "picking the team was difficult," but maintained that the "issues were much more complex than whether Michael wanted Isiah, which is how some portrayed it."[48]

Owing to the losses of earlier U.S. basketball teams, in the summer of 1992 the Dream Team needed to qualify for the Olympic Games before heading to Barcelona. To do so it had to finish first or second in the "Tournament of Americas." For marketers and television executives, not to mention USA Basketball, the additional games meant more opportunities to capitalize on peoples' fascination with the squad. To do that, USA Basketball bought the rights to host the "Tournament of Americas" for $5 million from a Brazilian event organizer, who had purchased them from a Pan-American amateur body. USA Basketball also controlled the North American television rights to the contest. By owning the tournament's rights and with the help of the savvy NBA marketing group, with which it had partnered, USA Basketball made the "Tournament of Americas," in marketing parlance, "ambush proof," meaning that it maneuvered to keep companies unaffiliated with the Olympics from capitalizing on the Dream Team's popularity by taking ad time. Since USA Basketball was in control, it could reserve all commercial segments for Dream Team sponsors.[49]

USA Basketball also moved the "Tournament of Americas" to Portland, Oregon, where a friendly crowd met the Dream Team in its first official games in the quest for gold. A huge amount of money was on the line in Portland, since the Dream Team's quest could have ended there: a costly proposition for a company like Skybox, whose total investment in the Dream Team was about $7 million.[50] Fortunately, the United States breezed through the games with ease, and its opponents did not appear too upset. In Portland, Bird signed copies of his book for Brazilian players, and Magic was shocked when players posed for pictures with him as he guarded them *during* the game. Such unlikely scenarios hinted at what lay ahead in Barcelona.

The Dream Team's training sessions intensified a week before the Games, in Monaco, where it stayed at the renowned Hotel Ambassador in rooms that ran about $900 a night, a fact that elicited criticism from people who thought such high-class living was out of step with the Olympic ideal. Johnson characterized the play in Monte Carlo as "easily the best basketball I've ever seen or been a part of." However, Bird thought the squad's greatest single workout had actually come earlier in the summer—the day after the Dream Team lost its first scrimmage to a group of college all-stars. Returning that next day a bit more serious, the Dream Team opened with a 30–2 run against the college all-stars. "Those kids opened our eyes pretty good," Bird recalled. "From that day on, we picked it up."[51]

Once in Barcelona, after confronting the Olympic Village stampede, most of the Dream Team members went to the Opening Ceremonies, where they stole the show despite a spectacular ceremony. Athletes from all over the globe (Puerto Rico, the Netherlands, China, and more) broke ranks during the opening march to meet the players, especially Magic Johnson. They wanted to take pictures with him and his contagious smile; they wanted autographs; they simply wanted to see the larger-than-life stars that so many had watched on satellite television over the years. As the crowd gathering around him and his mates grew, security guards and other officials, George Steinbrenner among them, pleaded with some of the best athletes in the world to wait for another time to request autographs from Magic.[52] But the *New York Times* reported that Magic did not disappoint, flashing his smile seemingly the entire time as he obliged their requests.

Few expected that any team would mount even a nominal challenge to the American squad, but outside of the Dream Team, the tournament was rather competitive. As the Croatian coach Peter Skansi noted, in games not involving the United States, "Anybody can win." Among the leaders of the rest of the field were the Unified Team and Lithuania, which together comprised most of the remnants of the former Soviet squad; and Croatia. None of these three teams had existed in the previous Olympiad.[53] As a result of the speed and timing of political developments, the IOC had ruled that Russia, along with the former satellites that chose to, could compete together under the banner of "Unified Team." Those satellites that chose not to be a part of the "Unified Team" had the right to compete independently.

Ultimately, twelve former Soviet republics participated on the Unified Team. Although early reports indicated that the "wild capitalism" that had engulfed much of the region when the iron curtain lifted had delivered mixed economic results, the Unified Team, with the help of a sponsorship by Adidas and creative fundraising methods, fielded an Olympic squad that fared remarkably well, considering the circumstances. From a basketball perspective, the team's biggest pre-Olympic triumph was convincing Igors Miglinieks and Gundars Vetra of Latvia to play under the "Unified" banner.[54]

The Unified Team was not successful, however, in luring talent from Lithuania. Eager to come out of the shadows and oppression of Soviet rule, Lithuanian stars enthusiastically represented their nation's basketball prowess in Barcelona. Aryvidas Sabonis jumped at the chance to play for his homeland; so did the Golden State Warriors' star Sarunas Marciulionis, who had parlayed his million-dollar NBA contract into business opportunities in his homeland—sports clinics, a hotel, and a sports bar—and whom the Lithuanian assistant coach Donn Nelson described as "the Elvis of Lithuania."[55]

It had been a long time in coming. In Barcelona, the Lithuanian coach Vladas Garastas remembered how, as a seven-year-old in 1939, he had watched the Lithuanian national team win its second straight European championship. He could still recall one of the team's players saying, "We all know that this was not the first Lithuanian great victory on the basketball court, but we also believe that it will not be the last." As the Lithuanian coach fifty-two years later, Garastas could help make this sentiment come true. In fact, before the Games, Lithuania had already scored a shocking victory by beating the Unified Team by *forty-six* points in the European Olympic qualifying tournament in Badajoz, Spain. "Yes, we wanted to win by 52 points," the Lithuanian player Valdemaras Chomicius admitted later. "Fifty-two years, 52 points. But it is difficult to win by 52 points over Unified Team." Marciulionis acknowledged that if all the former Soviet satellites and Russia played together, their odds against the Dream Team would increase. "But we have freedom now. On the Soviet team, we had to hide ourselves. They controlled us . . . January 13 [the main date marking Lithuania's 1991 independence movement] was a terrible night, but the people who died were heroes," he said. "Sometimes you have to lose something to pick the right way. It is very hard in my country today. There are shortages of groceries, shortages of everything. It will get worse before it gets better."[56]

Croatia was led by the New Jersey Nets shooting guard Drazen Petrovic, the forward Dino Radja, who had recently been drafted by the Celtics, and Toni Kukoc, to whom the Chicago Bulls' Jerry Krause had offered a sizable contract in an effort to lure him to Chicago. Later, Mike Krzyzewski would point to the Croatian team as a further example of the Dream Team's particularly good timing. Not only had the splintering of the Soviet Union scattered players to various teams, but the 1990 world champion Yugoslavian team was broken up with the disintegration of Yugoslavia in 1991. Surely, the Dream Team would still have won had a "unified" Yugoslavian team competed in Barcelona, but the absence of one enabled a more pronounced American dominance. Rather than playing a team with Kukoc, Petrovic, and Radja, along with the Serbians Vlade Divac and Predrag Danilovic, both of whom played on the new-fangled silver-medal-winning Yugoslavian team in 1996 and both of whom averaged double-digit figures in the NBA, the Dream Team faced only a Croatian team. As for Divac and Danilovic, and any other Serbian and Montenegrin players, for that matter, the crisis in the Balkans had prevented them from fielding a team at the 1992 Games. Not until 1994 did FIBA, taking its cue from the United Nations, allow Serbians and Montenegrins back into the Olympic fold.[57] Though the Unified, Lithuania, and Croatia teams came into the tournament with the best odds of pulling off an upset of the Dream Team, everyone figured that their real battle would be against each other for the silver medal.

In their opening Olympic contest, the Dream Teamers faced a completely overmatched Angolan squad, but the 116–48 defeat was overshadowed by an elbow Charles Barkley threw at an unsuspecting Angolan by the name of Herlander Coimbra, whom Harvey Araton described in the *New York Times* as a "174-pound economics student from a third-world, war-torn nation." Coimbra told reporters afterward that back home, he had spent many nights watching "Sir Charles" via satellite and was surprised that Barkley would "make violence" with him. Of course, had he been watching Barkley closely, he might have been less surprised. For Barkley's part, he claimed Coimbra had hit him on the head as he went in for a dunk and tried to downplay the incident by telling the press they would not understand; that it was a "ghetto thing." And as if that were not enough, he drew even more ire for joking, "Well, he might have pulled a spear on me." That the Barkley elbow came during an Olympic record 46–1 run by the Dream Team did not help, either—the one point came from the free throw awarded to Coimbra for the elbow. Following the game, "Sir Charles" did promise to make up for his poor sportsmanship and went out of his way to pose for a picture with Coimbra, who, none the worse for wear, eagerly posed with the "Round Mound of Rebound."[58]

Despite the elbow incident, during the first week of the Games, Barkley turned himself into a standout personality on the Dream Team. *Sports Illustrated* ran an article on Barkley's brash, freewheeling, mammoth persona. "He has become, at once, America's greatest Olympic ambassador and its greatest potential nightmare, a man who can turn a grimace into a smile—or vice versa—in an instant," Jack McCallum wrote. Barkley went to many Olympic events, as did other Dream Teamers (especially Magic), all of them drawing crowds wherever they went. At night, Barkley walked Barcelona's hot and happening promenade, mingling with folks until the street cleaners got to work, as McCallum described it. "I can't just sit in my room and do nothing. Sure, it's a pain in the butt to sign autographs and be bothered all the time, but I'd rather walk around and be bothered than sit around. As far as I'm concerned, it's fun going around and meeting people." Actions like this and Magic's enthusiastic support of other U.S. teams went a long way in dispelling the team's image as "isolationists," McCallum noted. And people loved it. A Spanish teenager told McCallum, "I hear this Barkley supposed to be a bad guy. I think he is a nice guy."[59]

Following Angola, the Americans faced the solid Croatian squad led by Toni Kukoc (known as "the European Magic Johnson"), Petrovic, and Radja. Beforehand, Petrovic said the game had been on his mind since it was announced three weeks earlier. He told reporters going into the affair that he would consider "anything within 25 points" a success. Of all the Dream Teamers, Scottie Pippen was likely the most motivated for this game. His Chicago Bulls owned Kukoc's draft rights, and owner Jerry Reinsdorf and general manager Jerry Krause had refused to renegotiate Pippen's contract as they awaited word on Kukoc's response to their contract offer to him. At the time, Kukoc was intimating that he intended to come to Chicago in about a year. Krause had offered Kukoc a five-year, $13 million deal, while Pippen made only $700,000 per season. Pippen wanted to prove that he was not only better than Kukoc, but dominatingly so. And he did.

Throughout the game Pippen, and to an extent Jordan, hounded Kukoc. In the end, Kukoc finished with a measly four points in thirty-five minutes, on two of eleven shooting from the floor. He delivered five assists, but he also turned the ball over seven times. Petrovic and Radja tried to pick up the slack, scoring twenty-two and twenty points, respectively, but it was nowhere near enough as the Americans won 103–70. "I never saw that kind of defense before," Kukoc lamented afterward. Radja told reporters, "We knew before we didn't have any chance. It's an honor to play against Jordan and Magic. We run a little, sweat a little. I don't think they played fifty percent." For stretches of the game, however, the team played above

50 percent, especially Pippen. He told reporters, "I couldn't put Krause on the court, so this was the next best thing. I would have bought a big-screen TV for him."[60]

More controversy began to engulf the Dream Team the following day, though, as debate erupted over what sweat suit, Reebok or Nike, the Dream Team members intended to wear on the medal podium. The USOC's code of conduct stipulated that all of the Dream Team members should wear a Reebok sweat suit (though Jordan had crossed that portion out when he signed his intent to play). USOC spokesman Mike Moran said, "The money we're getting from Reebok is going to assist thousands of athletes in training." But Barkley and Jordan, preoccupied with their own feelings of loyalty to Nike, which had paid both handsomely, responded by reiterating their decision not to wear the Reebok suits. This prompted Moran to assert, "This is the ultimate in separating themselves from the rest of the U.S. team."[61] Many observers pointed out that the spat served as another example of commercialism gone awry.

Russ Granik, who had met with Jordan and Jordan's agent David Falk before the Games to discuss such matters, admitted to the author, "We did have, you know, a bit of an unfortunate misunderstanding that involved the shoe companies and the players." Explaining the scenario, Granik said, "People thought that Nike was unhappy because Reebok was the sponsor of USA basketball at the time . . . I really think the players were kind of acting on their own." Commenting on shoe firms, Granik said, "The companies understood that Reebok had paid for certain rights . . . I really think on a corporate level they all understood." Continuing, he stated, "But some people just got, I think . . . maybe got a little carried away in trying to be loyal to their relationships."[62] If so, it certainly seems that, considering the boon that the Dream Team provided to Nike in subsequent years, it would have behooved Nike to actively encourage Jordan and the others, very early on, not to make a big deal out of the sponsorship issue. Instead, the issue led to critical coverage of both Nike athletes and the firm itself.

Certainly, the episode also placed further emphasis on the relationship between athletes and footwear firms. Another prime example of the spotlight that the Dream Team brought to this relationship occurred when the issue of athletic firms' international labor practices flared, and Jordan and Nike figured prominently in the debate. One article in particular that fueled the firestorm was written by Jeff Ballinger in *Harper's* and concerned Nike's practices in Indonesia. It ran, not so coincidentally, in August 1992, the same month the Dream Team regaled fans across the globe with its play.

As we have seen, from its inception in the early 1960s, Nike aimed to profit from the utilization of cheap labor. Within a decade after Nike had tapped Japan's labor pool, wage levels had increased in its open marketplace, leading many Japanese corporations to look to South Korea for cheaper labor. Knight followed suit. In 1976, Nike penned a contract with one of the largest manufacturers in South Korea, Sung Hwa Company. According to Strasser and Buckland, this deal offered the opportunity to "catapult a discount factory [Sung Hwa] into a whole new technology, and contribute nothing less than a new base upon which Korea could industrialize."[63] In many respects, that is exactly what happened. By the late 1980s, many of South Korea's previously low-wage workers had earned enough within South Korea's growing economy to create a burgeoning middle class. This middle class helped propel a prodemocracy movement that won the right to "form independent unions and strike." In turn, "Nike's work force won higher pay." But, in one of the more problematic trends of open-market economics, these higher wages encouraged Nike to look elsewhere for cheap labor, and Nike generally found that labor in countries that did not have liberal governments, such as Indonesia.[64] Yet even many of these nations, such as Taiwan and Indonesia, did ultimately move toward a more liberal society as their markets opened.

It was in the late 1980s, a time during which constitutional rights, unions, and economic prosperity had increased workers' wages and freedoms in South Korea, that Sung Hwa moved many of its production lines to Indonesia. Nike apparently had no objections to this.[65] Nike's decision to move to Indonesia, particularly in light of that nation's history with the GANEFO games and its tenuous relationship with the United States throughout the cold war, was in some ways disappointing. In the Indonesian President Suharto, Nike was turning to a regime that clearly did not subscribe to American values, the very ones Nike had championed in its marketing campaigns.[66] The move suggested that there was an ugly side to global capitalism as Nike came under pressure for the exploitation of poor Indonesian laborers who worked under an autocratic regime with few rights.

In August 1992, when Ballinger's *Harper's* article ran, Nike did not seem too concerned with addressing global labor issues. But Nike's image consciousness and the popularity of its star endorsers eventually forced the company to push for change from its subsidiaries—albeit, seemingly only after political agitators brought these practices to the public's attention and Nike saw that inaction could hurt its bottom line. In 2002 Wieden and Kennedy's Hal Curtis said, "The labor thing was a punch to the gut for the brand, and it took a couple of years to recover."[67]

Some attention had been placed on Nike's international labor practices before Ballinger's *Harper's* article. But the timing of Ballinger's piece, coupled with its potent simplicity, heightened national awareness of the issue. The article shocked readers by reporting that Indonesian women and children employed by Sung Hwa made fourteen cents an hour with virtually no labor rights. Based primarily on a pay stub Ballinger obtained, the article showed that a woman had worked sixty-three hours of overtime for Sung Hwa during one pay period and received an extra two cents per hour for her efforts. Ballinger also reported abusive and coercive measures at the facilities. As Randy Shaw noted in *Reclaiming America*, the article helped inspire activism promoting fairer labor.[68]

It took time to deliver results, though, and without continued political agitation, important changes may not have occurred. In the decade following Ballinger's report, Nike endured nearly constant scrutiny. At first, it turned inward, but in 1998 Nike took some concrete steps toward addressing its labor issues. The bad press and its effect on sales seem to have spurred these actions.[69] As is it turned out, however, the measures taken in 1998 did not satisfy all the discontented parties, so just after the turn of the millennium, further initiatives were implemented. The effects of these initiatives, while not entirely ideal, have shown some positive developments.

In 2001 a group of scholars put together a comprehensive work on the issue of "sweatshop" labor, entitled *Rising above Sweatshops*. In it, Laura P. Hartman and Richard E. Wokutch noted that by 2001, Nike generated revenue totaling nearly $10 billion, manufactured roughly 175 million pairs of shoes per year, and employed more than 550,000 workers in roughly fifty-two nations. The book also pointed out that of Nike's more than 800 contracted suppliers, more than 400 were located in Asia. Thanks to the attention brought to Nike's substandard labor practices beginning in 1988,

Hartman and Wokutch claimed that the firm played a role in Indonesia's incredible increase in minimum wage from 1988 to 1996—from $0.86 to $2.46 per day, a 300 percent increase during a period that saw a 205 percent rate of inflation. Furthermore, the authors noted that by 2001 Nike had implemented a management audit intended to measure contractors' abilities to comply with Nike's labor standards. They called the new auditing instrument "in-depth" and credited Nike with "focusing on global consistency" that included "a significant global labor practice team that visits factories on an everyday basis."[70]

Further indicating the effects of pressure placed upon Nike to live up to the values that it was supposed to embody, in 2005 Nike became one of the most transparent transnational corporations on the planet with its decision to publish all reports on all of its subcontractors.[71]

Following Pippen's stellar play in the victory over Croatia, the Dream Team faced another squad with an NBA star, Germany's Detlef Schrempf, who also played for the Indiana Pacers. For the affair, the United States was without the services of Magic Johnson, who strained his right knee, and John Stockton, who broke a small bone in his foot. Before the game Barkley proclaimed that he might play some point guard, since he counted as the third-best at the position, behind Pippen and Jordan. Daly, continuing to thoroughly enjoy himself, said Barkley's claim was "frightening but true," adding that although he had thought about playing Barkley at the point, "I didn't think he knew enough about the offense." It hardly mattered, though, as the Dream Team beat the Germans 111–68. Jordan displayed his remarkable versatility by starting at point guard, tallying eight assists and nine points in the game's first twelve minutes. Yet Larry Bird was the story of this game as he soothed his back pain enough to pour in nineteen points in twenty minutes of action.[72]

The Dream Team then set an American Olympic scoring record with a 127–83 drubbing of Brazil. Pippen again demonstrated his defensive prowess, limiting Brazil's high-scoring Oscar Schmidt, who had scored frequently against American collegians in previous tournaments, to eight of twenty-five shooting. In the postgame press conference, Schmidt said, "It is not funny to go inside against them." Earlier in the summer at the "Tournament of Americas" in Portland, word surfaced that Schmidt and fellow Brazilian standout Marcel Souza had questioned the Americans' focus. In Barcelona, the Dream Team members seemed to be using Schmidt and Souza's comments for motivation, not to mention to have some fun. "I've been thinking about Oscar all week. In the middle of my backswing, I think, 'Oscar, Oscar,'" Barkley told reporters. "If we said something about the other teams, they'd use it against us. We're just like other teams. We're human. We need motivation," Johnson explained. Really, Souza and Schmidt had great respect for the Dream Team, and the American players knew it. In Portland they had asked Bird to sign his autobiography for them. Bird obliged, writing jokingly in Schmidt's, "I want you one-on-one in French Lick." To Souza he wrote, "You're lucky I wasn't in Indianapolis," a reference to the U.S. team's 1987 loss to Brazil at the Pan-American Games in Indiana.[73]

In other action, Lithuania lost to the Unified Team to the surprise of many. The game was, of course, packed with political tension as Lithuania, the main contributor of talent to Soviet teams during the cold war, aimed to avenge its treatment at the hands of the Soviets with a symbolic victory over the Unified Team at the Olympics. The game had started out much like Lithuania's forty-six point win against the Unified squad earlier in the summer. With just over fifteen minutes remaining, Lithuania led 54–35, but suddenly, the Unified Team, led by Tikhonenko and Migilinieks, who made a flurry of threes, carried out a spectacular comeback. Both players had received negative press in their native Latvia for opting to play for the Unified team. After the win, Migilinieks defended his decision. "These are not Communists. This is not the Red Army. These are my friends," he asserted. The Unified Team's pragmatic coach, long-time Soviet coach Gomelsky, also defended the Latvians' decisions to play for him. In internationalist fashion, he explained to reporters, "They play with the Unified Team and try to make good contract for themselves." Though both teams expressed respect for each other following the game, the loss devastated the Lithuanians. Donn Nelson said later that for ten minutes in the postgame locker room huddle, no one spoke a word.[74]

China also made news. In addition to its regimented elite-level athletic programs at home, known for being brutally demanding, China had implemented a far-reaching plan to send coaches and athletes to the United States to learn from top-flight American coaches. China's integration into the international sporting community was not seamless, however. In Barcelona, during a 100–84 loss to the Unified Team, China's star player Ma Jian was benched for the game's final five minutes. An unnamed basketball official told the *New York Times* that his benching was retaliation for Ma's decision to leave the national team and enroll at UCLA.[75] The situation hinted at tensions that could arise as China continued its transition to a more market-based economy and its star players began to assert the independence that comes with a more open economy.

This difficult balance China was attempting between openness and control was tested again years later when Wang Zhizhi became the first Chinese player to play in the NBA. Zhizhi came to America in 2001 and within about a year had caused Chinese officials to go "ballistic" for not reporting to the Chinese national team—Zhizhi, apparently enjoying this freedom in the United States, had chosen not to play for the national team at that year's World Championships but did play in an NBA summer league, looking for a new contract. That contract soon arrived to the tune of $6 million over three years with the LA Clippers. That summer Zhizhi did try to mend relations with the Chinese government, but as Hannah Beech reported in *Time-Asia*, the government ultimately expelled him from the national team for "indifference to the interests of the nation," and undertook a "smear campaign" against him. Quixotically, in 2006, once it became clear that Zhizhi's NBA career had not taken off and his contract with the Clippers had run out, he was accepted back on the Chinese team under the condition that he apologize publicly for not having joined it earlier. Zhizhi then played for China at the 2008 Beijing Games. The tensions in China were also on display in dramatic fashion in 2004 when Yao Ming drew rebuke from Chinese officials for supposedly speaking too individualistically after a loss.[76]

In Barcelona, the United States continued to win with relative ease throughout the rest of the preliminary round action and went into the quarterfinal medal round without being tested. With Magic and Stockton back from their injuries, the Americans beat Puerto Rico 115–77. Despite its dominance, some claimed the Dream Team appeared lethargic, speculating that weariness may have resulted from criticism over not staying in the Olympic Village, or from the sweatsuit issue, or simply from having to practice. "It's getting rough out there right now," Charles Barkley admitted. "We just want to get it over with. I wish we could play a doubleheader tomorrow, just to get home sooner."[77] Still, lethargic or not, the team won by thirty-eight points.

Next, the United States faced the highly regarded Lithuanians. Being that it was the semifinals, the Dream Team tried to get more serious. Magic Johnson admitted that the intensity ratcheted up for the game. He told Jordan beforehand, "I don't you need you to be Michael Jordan tonight. I need you to be Air Jordan." He was. The Dream Team shellacked Lithuania, 127–76, proving yet again that all the hype surrounding the Dream Team was warranted.

Lithuania rebounded from the blowout loss rather quickly though, with a win against the Unified Team. The Lithuanian squad had gotten its opportunity to avenge its earlier loss because in the other semifinal, Croatia beat the Unified Team, 75–74, on two free throws made in the closing seconds by Drazen Petrovic. In marked contrast to Lithuania's loss to the Unified team several days earlier, joy abounded after it beat Gomelsky's Unified outfit. In the locker room Marciulionis cried tears of joy. The victory enabled Lithuania's 3.6 million citizens to see its team, clad in its Grateful Dead warm-ups (which the legendary band had donated to the cash-stripped squad), stand alongside the Dream Team for the medal ceremony.[78]

In the final, the Dream Team faced Croatia for a second time. By then, a compromise had been reached on the sweatsuit saga (Nike players would unzip the sweatsuit top to cover the Reebok logo), and other issues moved to the periphery. The focus was on basketball. Before the tip-off, $65 tickets were scalped for $2,500. According to the *Moscow News*, it was "worth the money" to see the NBA's finest stars.[79]

Croatia stayed around longer than most expected, and Kukoc turned in a much stronger performance, but the Dream Team ultimately dominated again. In winning 117–85, the squad surpassed the century mark for the eighth time in eight games. For the tournament, the Dream Team averaged 117.3 points per game, while yielding only 73.5, for a 43.8-point average margin of victory. No team in Olympic history has scored more and only the 1956 and 1964 teams, with 53.5 and 41.4 average margins of victory, respectively, can compare in point differential.

Overall, the Dream Team's scoring prowess and personality had complemented basketball wonderfully. Right along with the rise of globalization, in the twentieth century basketball had evolved into a fast-moving, high-scoring, innovative game that celebrated both teamwork and individual creativity. It had been a spectacular rise, and no team better reflected that than the Dream Team. Coach Daly summed it up following the gold medal win, saying, "This team was majestic."[80]

Yet debate over whether U.S. professionals should have partaken in the Games continued. Before the Olympics, many had thought not. As the *New York Times* reported, to some, the Dream Team epitomized the "overwhelming commercialization of the Olympics by the NBA's obvious use of this forum to push global expansion while its players broaden the market for $120 sneakers." Detractors noted that it was during a press conference at the Dream Team's expensive hotel in Monte Carlo, Monaco, that Magic Johnson announced his intention to end his twelve-year relationship with Converse because they had not invested heavily enough in him.[81]

During the Games, in *MacLean's*, Fred Bruning argued that more than the millions at stake in marketing dollars fueled the creation of the Dream Team. He credited George Bush with forging the team because, according to Bruning, with President Bush in the White House, the United States did not know who to view as enemies and no longer had a pretty war to watch on television (apparently referring to Desert Storm). Demonstrating a lack of basketball knowledge, he called the collegians' loss to the Soviets in 1988 shocking. And he criticized the United States' reaction to that loss by sardonically quoting Jordan, who had told *Newsweek*, "We've got to regain our sense of pride, our dignity." Bruning did admit a connection between big-time sports and national psyche, but he derisively argued that the United States saw basketball as its dominion, and that it must move to "liquidate all who question our supremacy on the slatted floor." Finally, he ominously warned, "Domination is fun—but dangerous."[82]

Months before Bruning's article, Carl Mollins, writing in *MacLean's* as well, said the original dream of recreating the ancient Olympics was "fading under modern strains," those being commercialism via television. Mollins did admit, however, that television had brought the Olympics, which by the author's own admission functioned as a peaceful global festival, to billions of people worldwide.[83]

In America, after the Games, Rob Morse wrote in the *Seattle Post-Intelligencer*, "The Dream Team, what a nightmare. Imagine how the poor

Croatian team feels." (Apparently he had not talked to them.) Even the best-selling author Stephen King questioned the merits of the Dream Team, writing in the *New York Times* that the promotion of the pros, with their "baggage of bad court habits, loud mouths and absolutely staggering basketball skills," fits well with the "last twelve years of American life, when the almighty buck swamped just about everybody's principles." And Fidel Castro said that the Dream Team had "nothing to do with the Olympic spirit."[84]

But many others took another view. Bill Walton weighed in during the trials with a piece in the *New York Times* arguing that basketball was a world game and that "the Olympics are a showcase; the planet's best should be there." Having NBA players at the Games, according to Walton, would also lessen the gap between U.S. basketball talent and the rest of the world. By sending over its stars, the United States would force international teams to raise their standards, rather than allowing those teams to become complacent while competing against lesser talent. "It will take time, but over the next ten to twenty years, the rest of the world will progress, and everyone will be better off."[85]

Harvey Araton of the *New York Times* pointed out that professional athletes from various countries had been plying their craft at the Olympics for years. He noted that Italian superstar skier Alberto Tomba, at the Winter Games, had paid for a helicopter to whisk him away from a private practice slope tucked away in the mountains to his races.[86] Of course, Araton could have easily noted that basketball players like Brazil's Oscar Schmidt and Croatia's Toni Kukoc and Vlade Divac had competed in the Olympics despite playing as professionals for years. Araton encouraged people to enjoy the confluence of events that brought the Dream Team together.

Many of the Dream Team's actual opponents expressed similar views. "For those fans who thought that sending NBA players to Barcelona was a mistake, I wish they could have seen how our opponents welcomed us, and how happy they were to play against us," Johnson wrote in his autobiography. In fact, it is hard to find a single *competitor* who did not appreciate the Dream Team's presence or its effect on raising the basketball standard internationally. Brazilian great Schmidt said afterward, "I loved it. They are my idols. I will remember this game for the rest of my life." Schmidt added, "For the basketball to grow, and to learn to play at the American level, they must send more teams like this to the World Cup and the Pan Am Games." His teammate, Souza, concurred. Former Soviet coach Alexander Gomelsky also agreed. He told reporters, "This is the best thing for world basketball. To play against the NBA, everyone can understand what the best basketball is like."[87]

By the end, most had come to appreciate the Dream Team for what it was: an extremely rare combination of human ingenuity, beamed globally to billions thanks to technological advancements, at an international festival of staggering popularity that signaled the flowering of a new global age. All of this happened within a relatively peaceful world that had moved toward free markets and democratic principles. In retrospect, the *New York Times* asserted that the 1992 Olympics, hailed beforehand as Games of peace and reunion, had delivered. South Africa participated for the first time since 1960 and Germany had marched under one flag, as did many former Soviet satellites. Furthermore, the paper noted, the Dream Team was the most identifiable part of the entire celebration.[88]

The Olympics, the era, and the Dream Team's outsized talent certainly aided the team's massive popularity. It also helped that the players genuinely liked each other. "Me, Scottie, Michael, and Magic played cards every night, all night. We'd start playing cards around eight o'clock, go until five in the morning, get three hours' sleep, and then go to practice," Barkley recalled. Unlikely friendships were struck, like the one between Larry Bird and Patrick Ewing. "We called 'em Larry and Harry," Barkley wrote. The players' fondness for each other helped them mix individual talent with collective action, enabling them to play as alluringly as any team in history. And they really seemed to care. "I almost broke down during the playing of 'The Star-Spangled Banner,'" Johnson wrote.[89]

Though it sometimes got lost in the hype, the artful basketball action displayed by these men played a pivotal role in the response to the Dream Team. "The Dreamers did more than just play well and win; they raised an entire sport to a new level before a global audience in the one competition whose importance transcends national boundaries," wrote the *Wall Street Journal*'s Frederick Klein. He added that they did it "over the objections of small-minded people of various countries, including their own." Klein effectively focused on the on-court action of the Dream Team in gauging its impact: "It's long been my view that basketball has benefited most from the sociological and technological changes that have swept American sports since the end of World War II, and has become our best-played game. But the virtuosity displayed by Michael, Magic, Larry, Charles, et al., in Barcelona, and at the Tournament of the Americas in Portland, Ore., before, surpassed anything seen previously."[90]

Bob Ryan of the *Boston Globe* marveled at the team's spectacular passing skills, calling it the squad's "most visible legacy." Indeed, the team finished the Olympic tournament with an astounding total of 239 assists. That amounted to almost *thirty* assists per game—considerably more than any other U.S. Olympic team. Assistant coach Mike Krzyzewski, after watching the Dream Team's marvelous ball movement against Spain, shook his head and said, "People may say it's overkill and all that, but there is no way anyone who professes to like basketball couldn't appreciate that."[91]

Based on the television ratings, it appears that many people from across the globe did appreciate it. The Dream Team attracted substantial viewing interest from the widest array of nations of any team or any other event at the Barcelona Games. And the basketball final, the authors of *Television and the Olympics* pointed out, "obtained the highest audience figures in such culturally and politically different countries as China and Mexico as well as high ratings in Spain, Italy, Romania, and more."[92]

Even the longtime sportswriter George Vescey finally came to see the positive elements of the Dream Team's efforts by the close of the Barcelona Games. Rather than focusing on the influence of multinational corporations, Vescey tried to remember stories of children from over one hundred countries wanting Dream Team T-shirts and noted that there are worse things than a photo-op with Magic Johnson. Upon final analysis, Vescey wrote, it was a "noble experiment, and it worked."[93]

It is hard to overstate the effect of the Dream Team on the international game. The predictions of Walton, Gomelsky, Schmidt, and others that the team would raise international standards proved correct. Most of the world's best players by the first decade of the twenty-first century—many of them from outside the United States—were inspired as youngsters by the Dream Team: players such as Dirk Nowitzki, Manu Ginobli, and Pau Gasol have all noted this. In turn, by the time they became adults, they too contributed to the direction of basketball throughout the world, including in America. In fact, rather startlingly, in the twenty-first century these

TABLE 13. 1992 U.S. Men's Olympic Basketball cumulative stats

NAME	G/S	FGM-FGA	(%)	3PM-3PA	(%)	FTM-FTA	(%)	REB/AVG	PTS/AVG	AST	BLK	ST
Charles Barkley	8/4	59-83	.711	7-8	.875	19-26	.731	33/4.1	144/18.0	19	1	21
Michael Jordan	8/8	51-113	.451	4-19	.211	13-19	.684	19/2.4	119/14.9	38	4	37
Karl Malone	8/4	40-62	.645	0-0	.000	24-32	.750	42/5.3	104/13.0	9	5	12
Chris Mullin	8/2	39-63	.619	14-26	.538	11-14	.786	13/1.6	103/12.9	29	2	14
Clyde Drexler	8/3	37-64	.578	6-21	.286	4-10	.400	24/3.0	84/10.5	29	2	19
Patrick Ewing	8/4	33-53	.623	0-0	.000	10-16	.625	42/5.3	76/9.5	3	15	7
Scottie Pippen	8/3	28-47	.596	5-13	.385	11-15	.733	17/2.1	72/9.0	47	1	23
David Robinson	8/4	27-47	.574	0-0	.000	18-26	.692	33/4.1	72/9.0	7	12	14
Larry Bird	8/3	25-48	.521	9-27	.333	8-10	.800	30/3.8	67/8.4	14	2	14
Magic Johnson	6/5	17-30	.567	6-13	.462	8-10	.800	14/2.3	48/8.0	33	0	8
Christian Laettner	8/0	9-20	.450	2-6	.333	18-20	.900	20/2.5	38/4.8	3	3	8
John Stockton	4/0	4-8	.500	1-2	.500	2-3	.667	1/0.3	11/2.8	8	0	0
USA TOTALS	8	369-638	.578	54-135	.400	146-201	.726	288/36.0	938/117.3	239	47	177
OPP. TOTALS	8	214-586	.365	57-187	.305	103-151	.682	180/22.5	588/73.5	109	13	104

players, as well as other international standouts, contributed to a sweeping reimagining of American basketball and ultimately, the implementation of new methods for American hoops. Americans started to reemphasize versatility, coordinated offensive action, help-side defense, and speed.

From a larger perspective, basketball serves as a frontline commodity and nexus of exchange in the modern global era—an era driven by market-oriented economies and one that has seen democratic-based governments increase in number. And as Larry Brown asserted, it was the Dream Team that really made basketball a "global sport."[94]

According to the historian Walter LaFeber, "The most globalized business in the world, and the most lucrative, is the drug trade. . . . But for legitimate businesses, sports is probably number one."[95] Unlike the drug trade, basketball in Barcelona was worth cheering for.

13

FROM UNDERRATED GREATNESS IN
ATLANTA TO THE GAP CLOSED IN ATHENS

During the 1996 Olympic Games, at which an underrated Dream Team II turned in an overwhelming performance, Michael Jordan visited to watch basketball and endorse a designer line of underwear. While in Atlanta, he predicted it would take ten years for the rest of the world to compete with the United States in hoops. Many thought his timeline too generous to international teams, but Charles Barkley, who played on Dream Team II, made similar statements in Atlanta. Barkley said that in 2000 the United States would likely fare well, but that by 2004, "we could be in trouble."[1] As had the longtime Soviet coach Alexander Gomelsky and Bill Walton, both Jordan and Barkley recognized that the quality of the international game was improving, and both men's prognostications about Olympic basketball would prove prescient. This was partly because as the Dream Team helped lengthen basketball's international reach, the quality of the international game improved.

Though in Atlanta the second Olympic version of the Dream Team won big, in relatively short order, international teams, such as Lithuania and Argentina—with their well-run offenses featuring fine passing, strong shooting, and versatility—did indeed close the gap with the United States. This, in turn, placed pressure on America to reemphasize the team game. And so, into the new millennium, teamwork and individuality continued their delicate coexistence, while the Dream Team's legacy became that of integration rather than domination.

A simple analysis of the statistics turned in by the disappointing bronze-medal U.S. team at the 2004 Athens Games indicates why America came to reevaluate its basketball ways. Consider two particularly troubling categories: shooting percentage and assists (which often directly correlate to the ability of a team to play together). In 2004 the U.S. team made 40 of 144 shots from the three-point line for a 31.4 percent average (no player among the NBA's top *seventy-five* three-point shooters was on the 2004 U.S. team's roster). By comparison, in 2000 the U.S. team made 54 of 128 three-pointers for a 42 percent average. In 1996 the United States shot 40 percent from the three.

As for assists, the 2004 team totaled 121, to the 2000 version's 153. Comparing the 2004 team's 121 assists with those of the 1996 and 1992 squads is even more striking. In 1996 the United States compiled *210* assists, while the original Dream Team dished out *239*, almost exactly doubling the 2004 total.

Dream Team II's assists total hints at its spectacular abilities. However, those abilities often went underappreciated because, while the popularity of Dream Team I accelerated the diffusion of hoops across the planet, in America, it would prove a hard act to follow. Almost immediately after Barcelona, this seemed apparent as people argued that, since the original Dream Team had successfully staked the United States' claim as the undisputed basketball superpower, the USOC should revert back to letting collegians compete. Leroy Walker, a leading candidate to become the next president of the USOC, did not call for a complete reversion to college players, but he did say he wanted a more open selection process with a balance of collegians and professionals. Walker emphasized that his comments were not directed at professionalism, which he considered an Olympic reality he had already accepted, but rather at the way players earned selection.[2] Regardless, his position surely met resistance from David Stern and other

NBA brass, who did not want to surrender their newfound opportunity to showcase their stars on the Olympics' international stage. In the end, the NBA kept its strong Olympic presence.

Five original Dream Team members—Barkley, Malone, Pippen, Robinson, and Stockton—played in the Atlanta Games. They were joined by the Orlando Magic's versatile, six-feet-seven-inch Anfernee Hardaway and seven-feet-one-inch, 301-pound center Shaquille "Shaq" O'Neal; the Detroit Pistons' six-feet-eight-inch Grant Hill; the Indiana Pacers' sharpshooting, six-feet-seven-inch Reggie Miller; the Houston Rockets' seven-feet Hakeem Olajuwon; the Seattle Supersonics' six-feet-four-inch Gary Payton (Payton replaced the Milwaukee Bucks' Glenn Robinson, who left the team because of achilles tendinitis in late June); and the Sacramento Kings' six-feet-five-inch jump-shot artist Mitch Richmond.[3] With eight players over the age of thirty, Dream Team II was slightly older than the Barcelona version. And the squad, coached by the African American Lenny Wilkens, counted eleven black players among its twelve-man roster, demonstrating that the days of unspoken racial balance were long gone.

Upon announcing the selection of the widely respected Atlanta Hawks' coach as head man for the U.S. men's Olympic team, C. M. Newton, the president of USA Basketball, described Wilkens as a "genuinely great human being."[4] Out of Brooklyn, New York, and a former star at Providence, Wilkens became the NBA's all-time winningest coach in 1995 and in 1997 would get named among the NBA's top fifty players of all time. He and John Wooden were the first two men to get elected into the Naismith Memorial Basketball Hall of Fame both as a player and a coach. Not bad for a guy who only played one half-season of high school basketball, helped support his family as a teenager with jobs like pouring concrete (his father passed away when Wilkens was five years old), and did not see an NBA game until after he was drafted into the league.

Although he was known as a players' coach with a mild air, Wilkens thought this label led folks to overlook elements of his coaching, and that at times, race might have played a factor in the characterization. "People assumed John Wooden was laid-back, too. How can you be laid-back and win as many games as we did? My players know differently," he said in 1998 just before his induction ceremony into the hall of fame.

Wilkens's rise as an NBA coach started in the late 1960s, and he remained in the business even though there were few jobs for African Americans during much of his career. Wilkens said his early success helped him stay on amid a less-accepting attitude towards black coaches, as did his resolution that he "wasn't going to be denied." This attitude reflected the grit behind his gentle manner. Still, the economic and political enthusiast did have a thoughtful, gentle way about him. And this made him likable to plenty of players.[5]

Getting the opportunity to coach the U.S. Olympic team moved him deeply. He also did not want to lose. He wanted gold for his country, he thought his team had the best talent, and he also wanted to show that an African American coach could win gold. Without Bird, Magic Johnson, and Jordan, who apparently told Wilkens he would have played had he "thought you really needed me," Wilkens thought his job was going to be tougher. Yet he knew he had depth. In fact, in an effort to show that he thought his roster was strong from top to bottom, Wilkens never started the same five players twice in the Olympics. Wilkens was concerned, though, as was USA Basketball, about the negative press that the 1994 U.S. team at the World Championships in Toronto had received. A glaring example of the criticized behavior was the time the Seattle Supersonics' Shawn Kemp swung from the rim while grabbing his crotch after a slam dunk. So Wilkens emphasized to the players that they should conduct themselves with humility.[6]

The 1996 U.S. men's team had two dominating centers, along with strong forwards, defensive stoppers in Payton and Pippen, and innovative, versatile wing players in Hill and Hardaway. And it boasted a bevy of shooters, always important in international competition. Given the team's ultimate performance in Atlanta —it won by an average margin of more than thirty points—the squad counts as one of the greatest teams ever assembled. But by Atlanta, the novelty of NBA players participating in the Olympics had worn off. Only a United States loss promised to galvanize people, and that did not happen.

Inevitably, as the 1996 Games approached, articles such as "The Thrill Is Gone," by Sports Illustrated's Jack McCallum and Richard O'Brien, began to appear. McCallum and O'Brien called Dream Team II a "tired" imitation of the original and argued that by keeping the same model, absurd expectations had "doomed" the second Dream Team "to a kind of failure."[7]

Their article and others like it symbolized the squad's dilemma: if it played lackadaisically, observers would complain about overly pampered stars, but if Dream Team II crammed home dunks and ran up the scores, critics would accuse them of ugly Americanism.

This dilemma made the media's response to Dream Team II somewhat understandable, but the lack of enthusiasm for the team was compounded by the actions of some of its players. For instance, unlike with the original Dream Team, reports surfaced in Atlanta of team members griping about the accommodations, playing time, and their treatment by the media. It seems that these reports had some merit: Barkley wrote afterward, "By 1996 . . . we had guys bitching about playing time, guys who made life miserable. It was so frustrating."[8] Shaquille O'Neal, for one, did write in 2002 that Wilkens had played him less than a minute in the gold medal game. "He's a great coach and all," Shaq said, "but I'm still upset."[9] To be fair, O'Neal was a great player, and he did play less than a minute.

In addition to rumors of player discontent and charges of pampering, for many critics, Dream Team II served as an embodiment of the rampant corporatism at the Atlanta Games.[10] When O'Neal signed a staggering 121 million dollar contract with the Los Angeles Lakers and then refused to talk about it at an Olympic press conference, preferring instead to wait until television screens flashing the Reebok logo flanked him, it was seen as indicative of the overt corporate presence.[11] As another example, the *Chicago Tribune*'s Terry Armour pointed a commercial barb at the Bulls' Pippen, arguing that although he should have rested over the summer, Olympic-related endorsements had motivated him to play.[12] During the Games, Rold Gold did unveil a television ad that Pippen starred in with *Seinfeld*'s Jason Alexander.[13] But that was nothing new. And players who chose not to play also faced criticism.

Before the Games started, the *Washington Post* detailed the business element of the U.S. men's basketball team and highlighted that the players were likely to earn about $100,000 each through a licensing deal. USA Basketball, strongly influenced by the NBA by then, had spearheaded the deal, which called for merchandise sales royalties of an estimated $5 to $7 million per year to be split between USA Basketball, NBA Properties (the league's marketing division), and the players. On certain USA Basketball products, the USOC earned a cut too. There were also, of course, separate marketing deals players struck with various firms, which had to navigate delicately, particularly if that firm was not an Olympic partner, in associating a player with the tightly guarded Olympic trademark. As Bob Williams, president of the Burns Sports marketing firm of Chicago, put it, "The advent of NBA basketball players and the Dream Team concept has created an enormous, newfound source of revenue for all parties involved."[14] With that in mind, and considering that other Olympic athletes had the opportunity for those types of royalty arrangements, it does not seem like the players' licensing arrangement was an extravagant deal.

Still, for other reasons, concern over too much commercialism flourished in Atlanta. Even IOC head Juan Antonio Samaranch, generally a proponent of commercialism at the Games, thought the corporate presence was overdone there. He noted that the financing provided by corporations made the scope of the two-week Olympic festival possible, but called for more balance. "This commercialization must be controlled and directed by organizing committees of the IOC," Samaranch declared.[15]

Sports Illustrated's Phil Taylor asserted rather appropriately that the negative coverage of Dream Team II overshadowed positive parts of the team's story, such as the fact that eleven out of the twelve Dream Team members agreed to donate their $15,000 gold medal bonuses to help rebuild black southern churches destroyed by arson (Olajuwon gave his share to the greater Islamic society of Houston). The Dream Team also brought Fallon Stubbs, who lost her mother and endured injuries herself in the Centennial Park bombing, to the Omni Hotel to visit with players; then, they brought her to the Georgia Dome stadium for one of their games.[16]

Compounding matters, the physical on-court presence of a guy like O'Neal, who averaged 9.3 points and 5.3 rebounds and shot 62 percent in Atlanta, personified the view critics had of America as a gargantuan, money-driven bully. Such critics likely saw O'Neal as a supersized mammoth muscling his way through the lane to dunk on people incapable of matching his power, in much the same way some critics thought America behaved on the international stage. But as with America, there is much more to O'Neal's story.

As it happens, in fact, looking at O'Neal's humble beginnings might give pause to those who would characterize him as a bully. At the age of eighteen, in Newark, New Jersey, O'Neal's mother, Lucille, gave birth to her "little warrior," which is the English translation of his Islamic name. She dreamed of going to college and nursing school, but instead set about raising her son. To do so, she went on welfare for a few months and then started working. Secretarial jobs with the city of Newark led to a romance with her eventual husband, Phil "Sarge" Harrison, an army sergeant. In the meantime, the little warrior was growing rather large, and he would continue to do so as the army family moved often—from New Jersey to Georgia to Germany and to San Antonio, Texas.[17]

By the time he finished high school, O'Neal was downright huge. Colleges came calling, and O'Neal ended up dominating for a few years at LSU. (LSU coach Dale Brown had actually started recruiting O'Neal at the age of thirteen after giving a basketball clinic at a U.S. military base in Wildflecken, West Germany. At that clinic Brown asked a young man, "Where are you from, soldier?" The six-feet-six-inch O'Neal replied, "I'm not a soldier. I'm thirteen years old".[18]) After college, O'Neal was the first pick in the 1992 NBA draft. Upon signing his first contract, he purchased homes for his mom and dad and another for his grandparents.[19]

By 1995 Newsweek had credited O'Neal with "redefining the merger with business and athletes" and observed that he had a global visibility approaching that of Mickey Mouse. In addition, the magazine commented on his outsized personality. "Basketball coaches say you can't teach a 48-inch vertical leap. Well, you can't teach an eight-inch smile, either, especially one like Shaq's that actually twinkles."[20]

By attending summer school in 2000, O'Neal fulfilled a promise to his mom and graduated from LSU. Then, in 2001, as a member of the Los Angeles Lakers, where he won three NBA championships, he received patrol training from the Los Angeles County police force.[21] He earned an MBA in 2005 and announced his desire to eventually earn a doctorate in criminal justice as part of his plan to pursue a postbasketball career in law enforcement.[22] That year newspapers across the globe, including New Zealand's Herald, carried reports of O'Neal getting sworn in as a reserve police officer with the Miami Beach Police Department.[23] Given his magnanimous personality, education, charity, and outside business interests, O'Neal shows yet again the great achievements that star black athletes have accomplished. Unfortunately, O'Neal's occasional verbal spats with his former coaches such as Phil Jackson, and former teammate Kobe Bryant surely have turned some folks off.

As with Dream Team II, if you could look past the overdone corporate veneer and logistical shortcomings of the Atlanta Games, positive elements emerged. With seemingly no major threats to global stability, the world enjoyed relative peace during the 1996 Olympics, and with a booming global economy, the world celebrated them in rather spectacular fashion. Nearly 11,000 athletes from 197 countries, both records, competed in front of 8.6 million spectators. An astounding 3.5 billion more people watched some part of the Games on television. Those spectators saw athletes from seventy-eight different nations win medals, compared to only sixty-six different countries in Barcelona.

Even after the 2000 Sydney Games, NBC's attraction of 208.6 million unique domestic viewers over the course of 171 hours of Atlanta coverage kept the 1996 Games as the "all-time champ" of any television event in American history.[24] Part of NBC's success, as with ABC's under Arledge, lay in its emphasis on "good, old-fashioned storytelling." Dick Ebersol, head of NBC sports, who had labored as a researcher decades earlier under Arledge, explained, "People can get the results from CNN or the internet. But they'll get the stories from NBC."[25]

In addition to NBC's coverage, the Atlanta Games displayed other examples of remarkable technological ingenuity, most notably in computer-related technology. By 1996 the growth of the Internet had provided another way for firms to capitalize on the Olympics' allure. And, though the World Wide Web was still relatively new, corporations implemented strategies to integrate it into their relationship with the Games. For instance, for Atlanta, the *New York Times* held forums on a Web site where people could opine on a wide range of Olympic topics.[26] Since Atlanta, the merging of traditional print and television coverage with the Internet has changed the accessibility of sports across the globe and provided new ways for the Olympics to reach viewers.[27]

Virtually all of the firms that showcased their lead in the ever-evolving world of technology at the Atlanta Games emanated from liberal capitalist nations, especially the United States. Not that the United States was alone—Japan, South Korea, and others were innovating aplenty—but U.S.

companies like Microsoft and Intel were leading the way. This may surprise some, since in the mid-1990s American businesses received ample criticism for failing to capitalize in the same fashion as Japanese firms on products such as the VCR. Yet in early 1994, research showed that American business competitiveness had produced something akin to what the *Wall Street Journal* characterized as "the trade version of Olympic basketball's 'Dream Team.'" The *Journal's* Daniel Stickberger argued that the free-market environment in the United States had enabled it to gain 37 percent of global sales and 48 percent of global profits by that time in globally competitive industries. In addition, he emphasized advances made by American firms in technologically intensive industries, particularly those made by Microsoft and Intel—two firms that he characterized as the most powerful technology companies on the planet.[28] To be sure, the technological innovations of firms like Microsoft and Intel, as we saw with satellite technology beginning in the 1960s, have added a new dynamic to the diffusion of the Olympics and basketball. And it certainly has not hurt USA Basketball that so many of the new technology and new media firms sprang from America.

Amid Atlanta's corporate façade, Argentina, Lithuania, and Croatia were among the Dream Team II's five preliminary round opponents. The U.S. squad commenced the tournament with a win, although it looked sluggish early on, over Argentina, 96–68, and then won easily over Angola.[29] Its third preliminary round matchup against a solid Lithuanian team ended in victory, too, 104–82. However, the *New York Times* headline about the game emphasized that Dream Team I had beaten Lithuania by a wider margin. In the accompanying article, the *Times's* Michael Moran criticized the United States for letting Lithuania hang around longer than expected, then griped that in the closing minutes of the affair, he thought it became "the obligatory dunkfest that inspired hundreds of flashbulbs and aroused corporate clients." Moran's treatment of the game highlighted the difficult situation Dream Team II faced: it would be criticized whether the game was close or a blowout. Sure, with Sabonis nursing an injury and playing only five minutes and with Marciulionis not playing at all because of swelling in his knee, Lithuania was shorthanded. But the United States did win by twenty-two points.[30]

A couple of days after beating Lithuania, Dream Team II scored a lopsided victory over China, 133–70, in front of a crowd of 34,417. It did so without Barkley, who took the night off, mainly to give court time to players that had complained about a lack of it. Though a blowout, the game marked another step in China's basketball development and, from a broader perspective, another milestone in its plan to liberalize economically and cooperate with the West.[31] And even though it lost to the United States, China did emerge from the preliminary round as a medal-round qualifier, the first time in history a Chinese team had done so. It was a particularly noteworthy accomplishment, considering China had not even qualified for the Olympic basketball tournament four years earlier.

By this time, the unsettling July 27 Centennial Park bombing had occurred. In response to it, Barkley said, "No SOB terrorist is gonna intimidate me." Tensions did rise, though, amid already high security. Wilkens and his staff worked to ease players' concerns; he did not want the experience spoiled for them and their families and was confident in the team hotel's security. But a few days later when a false bomb threat at the players' Omni Hotel came—by then Karl Malone had already sent his family home—people were anxious once more.[32] Security at the Games would only increase in subsequent Olympiads.

In quarterfinal medal-round action, the United States played Brazil, led by the thirty-eight-year-old (rumor suggested over forty) and legendary scorer Oscar Schmidt, playing in his fifth and final Olympics. In front of some thirty thousand fans, the national hero in Brazil and FIBA star in the European professional ranks finished with twenty-six points, keeping Brazil respectfully close in a 98–75 defeat. "Oscar was something. He has great rhythm, and he knows how to get a shot off with bigger guys in his face," Reggie Miller, the class-act Dream Teamer who starred for the Indiana Pacers and ranks among the all-time best shooters, said of Schmidt. The defensive attention Pippen and Hill gave Schmidt pleased the Brazilian star. "That's the best respect for anybody," he said afterward.[33]

A decisive win over Australia came next for Dream Team II, setting up a gold medal tilt with Yugoslavia, which had made it to the final game for the third time in six Olympics. Though relatively unknown to most Americans at the time, Yugoslavia boasted a talented roster—it included three players who played in the NBA at some point—Vlade Divac, Toni Kukoc, and Sasha Djordjevic—as well as Dejan Bodiroga, who received NBA offers.[34] Still, Yugoslavia's appearance in the final was remarkable

18. Charles Barkley and Vlade Divac vie for a jump ball in the gold medal game. Photo by Scott Cunningham. National Basketball Association Collection/Getty Images.

considering that the crisis in the Balkans had nearly caused the team to miss the Olympics.[35]

Before the gold medal game, Vlade Divac said his team had little chance on paper, but would play hard. Yet with fourteen minutes and five seconds remaining, the Yugoslavian team pulled to within one point. However, then, the United States responded with an impressive surge. The most decisive part of the run saw Dream Team II reel off nineteen points to Yugoslavia's three. Similar to the great run of 1960 spearheaded by Robertson, West, and Lucas, this one started with stifling defense followed up by aggressive forays to the basket. Ultimately, the United States won the gold medal game 95–69, but Yugoslavia's ability to keep it close for so long showed the improving international standard and led to further criticism of Dream Team II.

Criticism notwithstanding, Dream Team II finished the tournament with a gaudy 102 points-per-game average and won each game by an average of 31.75 points. That did not match the over 43-point average victory margin turned in by the original Dream Team, but it did reflect the team's excellence. Nonetheless, players felt the need to give an explanation for the team's performance. Karl Malone said, "You can't worry about the things that don't go well for you. We won the gold and that is what matters."[36] All things considered, it certainly seemed like Malone had a much more enjoyable experience in Barcelona.

Although critics argued over whether the team had won by too much or by too little, the reality that the 1996 Dream Team had simply faced stiffer competition seemed to get obscured. Barkley recognized this, though, explaining, "By 1996 you could really see the other countries coming up. The only real advantage we had now, and it was only four years later, was depth."[37]

The *Wall Street Journal*'s Frederick Klein echoed Barkley's sentiments, noting that the first Dream Team's opponents had recognized that playing against and watching America's best at the Olympics would help them. Furthermore, Klein wrote, "From the way the NBA has been drafting foreign players of late, it's clear the basketball gap between the U.S. and the rest of the world is shrinking, and the international exposure the league engendered by the Barcelona Games has to be a cause."[38]

The NBA presence on the U.S. Olympic team had raised the level of play in the rest of the world. With satellites beaming Olympic and NBA images to Moscow, Shanghai, Buenos Aires, and elsewhere, young players dreamt of playing at the level of their heroes.[39]

Coach Wilkens predicted in 1996 that the level of international basketball would change more quickly than most expected. Aware of the quality players international teams were turning out, he asserted that, with younger players coming into the NBA with less fundamental skills, "you're going to have future Dream Teams that probably won't be as accomplished as the ones that have played in 1992 and 1996."[40] As it happened, the next two versions of the "Dream Team" did pale in comparison to the first two.

Nonetheless, in many ways the improved international standard actually worked in the NBA's favor, as well as the Olympics' and even America's. Though some Americans vacillated between ripping the United States for dominating and then for barely winning, Michael Clough, a senior fellow at the Council on Foreign Relations and cochair of the Stanley Foundation's New American Global Dialogue, recognized the larger ramifications of basketball's globalization. Writing in the *Los Angeles Times*, he asserted that the 1996 bronze medal game between Australia and Lithuania served as "an example of how the richness of American society can be used to help the world."

Clough argued that in Atlanta, the Dream Team stood as the most visible sign of American athletic and cultural dominance, and that while some saw the team as symbolizing the worst part of the U.S. foreign policy—"a swaggering giant toying with its competitors"—he saw the potential for something else. He noted how Lithuanian Americans had contributed to Lithuania's success on the basketball court as far back as the 1930s when Frank Lubin, a star on the United States' 1936 Olympic basketball team, had coached and played there. Sixty years later in Atlanta, Clough noted that people such as the lawyer Alexander Domanskis, who played a lead role in organizing fellow Lithuanian Americans to support their homeland, could "take pride in the Olympic successes of both the United States and Lithuania."[41] This participatory relationship between the United States, Lithuania, and basketball could be translated to other nations, Clough suggested.

At the same time, Clough did not ignore the NBA's profit motive in joining the Olympic movement. Indeed, he admitted that over time, it was not in the NBA's best interest for the American Dream Team to completely dominate the competition, because interest in the tournament would wane. Instead, the NBA needed China, Brazil, and Lithuania to field competitive teams. In this way, he saw basketball as reflecting a world at a crossroads, in which the United States could strike an in-your-face attitude or "help transform the world in ways that may ultimately reduce its medal count at future Olympics, but will renew its sense of national purpose."[42] In his view, the Lithuanian Olympic basketball team represented the latter possibility at work. And sure enough, Lithuania soon lessened the United States' potential gold medal count by beating the Americans in basketball in 2004. At the same time, the growth of basketball in Lithuania, a U.S. ally, and elsewhere had not translated into a loss for the Olympics, the NBA, or America, for that matter.

Indeed, in 2006 NBA commissioner David Stern was actively encouraging international leagues to grow. It was not that he no longer wanted the NBA to play a role in international professional basketball, but he saw robust international leagues as complimentary to basketball and by extension the NBA.[43] Dramatic overseas NBA expansion could presumably come later.

To be sure, though, the NBA, affiliated corporate sponsors, and most Americans did expect the United States to remain basketball's gold standard, even within a more competitive environment. By the 2000 Olympic tournament, that desire would face a mighty challenge from NBA-laced opponent rosters. As a result, more profoundly than Atlanta, the 2000 Sydney Games came to represent basketball's improved global standard.

In Sydney, the Houston Rockets' Rudy Tomjanovich coached the United States. He had led the Rockets to the NBA championship in 1994 and 1995 and carried a reputation as a player's coach. As the Purdue head coach Gene Keady, an assistant to Tomjanovich at the Sydney Games, explained, "Rudy's a finesse coach, doesn't holler—perfect pro coach." Furthermore, he added, "Rudy is all about offense, fast-break; then run plays."[44] In this way, given that the previous two Olympic coaches, Daly and Wilkens, were also known as "players' coaches" who encouraged fast action, Tomjanovich fit the recent mold (in 2004, Larry Brown broke that mold).

Tomjanovich's team featured the high-flying six-feet-six-inch guard Vince Carter and the forward Kevin Garnett, who weighed just 220 pounds despite measuring six feet eleven inches. The guards were Ray Allen, a sharpshooter at six feet five inches, and Jason Kidd, the six-feet-four-inch, 212-pound NBA triple-double-maker. Helping Garnett anchor the front-court was the six-feet-ten-inch veteran center Alonzo Mourning. Shortly after the Games, Mourning would need a kidney transplant, and yet he returned to the NBA to win a championship in 2005 with the Miami Heat, a season in which he also donated his *entire* salary to a program designed to aid young kids in South Florida. The frontcourt also boasted the six-feet-nine-inch forward Antonio McDyess, a promising talent whose career would be limited as a result of knee injuries; the multiskilled six-feet-nine-inch Shareef Abdur-Rahim; and the six-feet-eleven-inch Vin Baker. These players gave the United States depth and versatility.

The six-foot-tall Tim Hardaway, a grizzled veteran with an effective step-back jump shot, and the six-feet-four-inch defensive stalwart Gary Payton supported Kidd at the point guard position. On the wing, the six-feet-five-inch Allan Houston, a proficient marksman, and the versatile six-feet-eight-inch Steve Smith gave the United States a group of guards with considerable length and diverse skill sets. Yet reviews of the U.S. team, before, during, and after Sydney, were decidedly mixed.

Despite the media's cool response to the 2000 U.S. men's hoops team, the media did largely celebrate the Sydney Olympics.[45] The Australians themselves had started celebrating well before their Games even took place, in the early 1990s when the IOC had selected Sydney as the host city. The announcement of that selection came at a press conference in Monaco, which prompted the Australian delegates there to shout, dance, cry, and hug. Back in Australia, millions took to the streets in raucous celebration. Prime minister Paul Keating said the decision put Australia "in the swim with the big boys." And Michael Knight, chairman of the Sydney Organizing Committee for the Olympic Games (SOCOG), declared, "We'll show the world what freedom really means at the dawn of the twenty-first century."[46] Given that Australia had been locked in a close competition with China for the right to host, these sentiments carried particular significance.

Australia's rabid enthusiasm showed how the 1984 Los Angeles model had changed perceptions about hosting the Olympic Games. At one time, hosting had been seen as relatively undesirable, but after LA, it became an opportunity for nations both to generate revenue and to convince the world of their importance in the global age—an age increasingly defined by technological advancement, open markets, and the spread of democracy. And indeed, the 2000 Olympics, held at a time when there was relative peace across the world, showcased Australia. Over 10,000 athletes from a record-setting 199 nations attended—roughly 3.7 billion additional folks viewed some part of the Games on television; this amounted to nearly every person with access to a television. No other event could elicit such attention and participation.[47]

Fittingly, NBC's Olympic coverage of the Sydney Games took broadcast standards to yet another level. Although it purchased the broadcasting rights during a slight economic downturn, NBC still paid $715 million for the Games, and the network quickly planned 441.5 hours of domestic coverage, which dwarfed the 171 hours delivered from Atlanta. Cable affiliates enabled NBC to carry the record load, as 279 of the over 441 hours ran on cable stations.

Orbiting the skies, the COMSAT World System provided NBC's domestic feed, while an NBC partnership with Telstra, which utilized the INTELSAT international satellite system, delivered an international broadcast.[48] The use of these satellites helped NBC deliver real-time results, despite Sydney's location on the other side of the world. In the end, over 180 million Americans watched at least some part of the Olympic action on television, along with the billions worldwide.[49]

The figures do not even include the millions more who accessed images and reports of the Games online. Even though many Internet technologies such as broadband video streamlining were just emerging or had yet to be created, Internet traffic added significantly to the media's coverage of the 2000 Olympics.[50] This would be only the beginning of the relationship between the Internet and the Games.

The first time NBC brought the 2000 U.S. Men's basketball team to living rooms across the globe, the squad played China. Viewers at home and in the sold-out stadium got to watch a Chinese squad boasting a humongous frontline—led by the lanky, seven-feet-four-inch, nineteen-year-old Yao Ming. The matchup, given the size of China's population, caused particular excitement for basketball brass, as evidenced by the attendance of numerous NBA and shoe company executives. And though the United States handled the Chinese squad in dominating fashion, 119–72, just about everybody came away impressed with China's bevy of fairly skilled seven-footers, especially Yao. Foul trouble limited him to fifteen minutes of play, but in his limited time on the court, he made a turnaround jump shot over Garnett, delivered a couple of assists out of the post, and blocked a layup attempt by Gary Payton. Tim Hardaway recognized the Chinese team's potential. "You look at the field today and China, to me, could pass Australia by, and give Canada a real tough time if they're not careful. China can play, man," Hardaway said.[51]

At the turn of the new millennium, the influence of Western culture on China was profound, and basketball was a key sport in that exchange. In 2001 entrepreneurial tracts by the likes of Bill Gates and Jack Welch sold briskly in China, and American movies enjoyed huge popularity there, as did the NBA. The *Financial Times* suggested that this cultural diffusion led to an emphasis on individualism in China, as opposed to the egalitarianism of twenty years earlier. On balance, this motivated the *Financial Times* to foresee a China that would continue to mature in a more liberal fashion, given that, "the changes sweeping Chinese society are more often echoes from the west than revivals from the country's '5,000 years of civilization' vaunted in official pronouncements."[52]

In 2005 Reebok launched an ad campaign that reflected this. It was the "largest integrated marketing and advertising campaign in nearly a decade," and it featured Yao Ming, along with the 2004 Olympian Allen Iverson and others. The campaign's tagline was "I Am What I Am." As Reebok explained, the campaign celebrated "individuality and authenticity."[53]

Following the U.S. team's victory over China, it won in lopsided fashion over Italy. Then came a match against a strong Lithuanian team led by Sarunas Jasikevicius that stayed close throughout. Though in the final minutes the outcome was not really in doubt, the United States' eight-point margin of victory was its lowest since NBA players had arrived at the Games.

Next was a lopsided win over New Zealand, and then a 106–94 high-scoring victory over France that gave the United States an undefeated record at the end of preliminary round action. Even so, the scores suggested that this batch of NBA stars would face a more challenging Olympic route going forward than had their predecessors.

In the quarterfinals, the United States did dispatch Russia in relatively easy fashion. The final score was 85–70, but the Americans controlled the action throughout. About 18,000 fans in Sydney's Superdome watched the affair, and their emotions vacillated between awe and displeasure. Vince Carter's aerial forays thrilled, particularly his dunk, often referenced as one of the most spectacular in history, over—literally over—Russia's seven-feet-two-inch Frederic Weis. "For me, that was probably the greatest play in basketball I've ever seen," Carter's amazed teammate Jason Kidd declared afterward.[54] But when Carter got angry that Evgueni Pachoutine had undercut him on a dunk attempt and then became embroiled in a shoving match with the Russian guard, fans booed—"as they do whenever the overpowering American machine flexes unnecessary muscle," the *Washington Post* maintained.[55] Such episodes indicated how fans and media both enjoyed Dream Team III and derided them, for showing off, for overindulgent individualism, and for representing a perceived elitist American attitude.

In their next game, the Americans nearly lost to Lithuania, with its tiny populace but outsized basketball tradition. With only a couple of seconds remaining in the game, just two points separated the teams, and Lithuania had possession. The partial crowd inside Sydney's Superdome, and surely Lithuanians across the globe, watched expectantly as Sarunas Jasikevicius came off a screen and launched a twenty-two-foot jump shot for the win. The crowd seemed to try to hope it in, just as many watching on television undoubtedly did as well, but Jasikevicius's high-arching, on-line shot bounced off the rim just short. Ray Allen said later that if the ball had gone in, "It would have haunted us for the rest of our lives." Jason Kidd speculated, "About 12 guys would have to change their identities. We'd all have to move as far away as possible. New Zealand would be my pick." Lithuanian assistant coach Donn Nelson also came away stunned, partly because no one on the Lithuanian team had even set foot at an NBA training camp, let alone made an NBA roster (that changed soon, though).[56] As an American with a strong connection to the game's history, Nelson had not known whether to hope for a miss or a make when Jasikevicius shot the potential game-winner.

As had happened with the U.S. team's other games in Sydney, criticism of the American players' behavior followed the near loss. Critics noted that during the game, Carter had needed to be restrained as he verbally sparred with a Lithuanian player; he drew further ire for raising his index finger to give the "number one" sign in the game's immediate aftermath—

even though the United States had won by just two points against a nation nearly *one hundred* times smaller (regardless of population differences, if you went player-by-player down each team's roster, it seemed the United States had the top twelve individual players). Along with others, the Lithuanian forward Darius Songalia, who during the regular season starred for Wake Forest, questioned the American team's postgame, center-court celebration, and he noted that only a few of the U.S. players went through the obligatory postgame handshaking. When asked about the "number one" gesture from Carter, Songalia said, "Maybe that's not telling me about American basketball players. Maybe that's more like, European basketball is getting closer to Americans."[57]

While in 1992 the media had seemed to revel in reports of Chuck Daly, Michael Jordan, and Charles Barkley playing golf together, fewer stories of that ilk appeared from Sydney. Negativity had become the focus instead, and even with the gold, this trend largely continued. Coach Keady became annoyed by what he perceived as the media's desire to "make stuff up." All told, he characterized the team's deportment as fantastic, telling the author, "No incidents, coaches had great rapport, played golf with Kidd, Allen, and Houston . . . All eleven guys hung out, Garnett had a bowling party, paid for everything. They didn't go out and party all night, they wanted to win the gold medal . . . You see, I was in charge of substituting players, I never heard any gripes . . . had to rotate all those players in and they still weren't disgruntled." As for the partisan crowd cheering against them, Keady said, "I didn't blame them . . . We didn't expect everybody to be for us."[58] But to many, the deportment of Dream Team III highlighted a U.S. weakness: overt individualism and arrogance.

In a way, the criticisms leveled at the 2000 American squad had played out on the court. Lithuania stayed close by utilizing the style that had made it an international power for years, whether as an independent nation or as a primary supplier of players to Soviet squads during the cold war. That style emphasized efficient, coordinated movement in its half-court offensive sets, persnickety shot selection, and selectively capitalizing on the fast break. "We were essentially five guys, moving the basketball," explained Nelson, who also argued that the United States in general placed too much emphasis on the one-on-one isolation game. "That's not what basketball was made to be. It's made to be a five-man game."[59] This did not mean

Lithuania played at a slow pace. Rather, much as had the motion offense of Dean Smith and Bob Knight, the Lithuanians' execution, crisp passing, and fabulous shot selection actually enabled them to score with regularity. The team's eighty-three points in forty minutes against the United States demonstrated this.

A key element of the Lithuania motion offense rested with the expectation that every player possess the capability to perform nearly every facet of it. Big players came out on the wing, guards posted up or set screens on the block, and virtually all players were expected to shoot outside and see the floor. The multifaceted nature of the Lithuanian style represented a trend that can be traced back to Bill Russell at the 1956 Melbourne Games. Sure, Russell did not have the most polished offensive game, but he showed the center position's potential for dynamism with his speed and defense. At the same time, as Pete Newell has suggested, Russell had been something of a catalyst for FIBA's decision to use a trapezoid lane, which in turn has promoted the development of wing-oriented tall players—at the expense of strong post-play. Particularly since the 1980s, Europe has proven successful in developing multidimensional big men. Players like Lithuania's Aryvidas Sabonis, Serbia's Vlade Divac, Germany's Dirk Nowitzki, and Spain's Pau Gasol have exemplified this.

Following Lithuania, France stood between the United States and the gold medal, and once again, the Americans flirted with defeat. With four minutes and twenty-six seconds remaining, France's Antoine Rigaudeau made a three-pointer to pull France to within four points, once again riveting the partisan crowd.[60] But the United States responded. In the closing minutes, Garnett scored a timely put-back and made a signature turnaround jump shot that was sandwiched between two Mourning free throws. Then, with 1:40 to play, Carter capped the win by elevating for an acrobatic reverse slam. It was fitting that Garnett, Mourning, and Carter figured in these pivotal plays down the stretch, since the threesome had led the U.S. in scoring in Sydney. This should not, though, obscure the shooting ability of Allen and Houston and the unselfishness of Kidd and Payton—which were also key in helping the United States win gold.

As NBA commissioner David Stern watched the 2000 gold medal game, he fielded questions about the state of international hoops. When asked if the U.S. would lose soon, he said he hoped it would happen "after I'm retired.

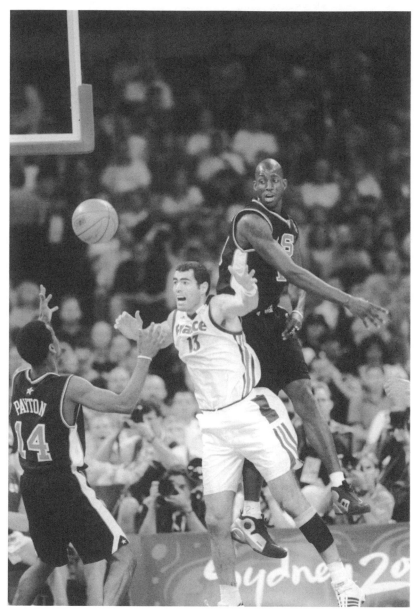

19. Kevin Garnett and Gary Payton in action versus France. Olympic Museum Collections. Copyright © IOC/Steve Munday.

The NBA is still the gold standard. But the reality is, the world is catching up. I'm sure there are some NBA scouts jotting things down and you may see some of these players in training camp." When told that Mourning did not think NBA players would lose at the Olympics in his lifetime, Stern said with a smile, "I don't know how long he's planning to live."[61]

Stern's attitude reflected his ambivalence about the rising international standard. On one hand, he surely preferred that American basketball remain the "gold standard," considering that the NBA was and is based in the United States. On the other, he wanted to expand the NBA to various parts of the globe and wanted the NBA to rank as a top international brand with followers spread all over the world. The flourishing of international superstars from a wide of array of places would be beneficial in achieving those goals.

In light of the close calls in Sydney, concern about the 2004 Olympic team abounded right after the 2000 Games. This concern moved into overdrive in the summer of 2002 when the United States finished seventh at the World Championships in Indianapolis, Indiana. At those World Championships, the U.S. squad not only lost for the first time since NBA stars were permitted to play, they lost three times. Granted, the sport's biggest American stars—Shaq, Kobe Bryant, Garnett, Allen, and Iverson—did not play, but a number of stars did, including Jermaine O'Neal, Paul Pierce, Ben Wallace, and Baron Davis. Yet they struggled mightily against teams such as Yugoslavia and Argentina, which featured rosters packed with current and future NBA players.

Players on the 2002 World Championships team expressed "shock" and said they were "embarrassed" by the losses. Some analysts emphasized that the team lacked cohesion and did not play hard, but others thought differently. Barkley said, "Everybody's going to come up with excuses saying we didn't send the best players, we didn't practice long enough. The simple fact is international teams are getting better. That's it. The bottom line is they're not in awe of us anymore." Continuing, Barkley observed, "I noticed a big difference from '92 to '96. In '92 they wanted to take pictures with us and things like that. It wasn't like that in '96. The only advantage we used to have was depth. The best teams could only put maybe three NBA players out there against us. In '96 they were able to put more NBA-caliber players out there."[62]

Though expecting more from U.S. teams made sense, from a sheer numbers standpoint, the influx of international players that had come into the NBA since Barcelona was staggering. And it highlighted an improved global standard. In November of 2002 the NBA boasted sixty-six international players from thirty-four countries, a 100 percent increase from just five years earlier.[63] By the 2006–7 NBA season, that number jumped to eighty-three. In 2002, at that time a Dallas Mavericks assistant coach, Donn Nelson attributed the surge to differences in the basketball systems of the United States and elsewhere. "If you're a good player [in Europe] you go to a club. Our best 16 or 17-year-olds might play four or five hours a day on a playground. In Europe, they're learning from coaches."[64]

In addition to European and South American nations, China played a visible role during this time in the trend toward internationalizing the NBA. In 2001 China's Yao Ming became the first pick of the NBA draft—the first number one pick in NBA history not to play for a team based in the United States before getting selected. And even before that, in 1999, Yao's fellow "Great Wall" member, Wang Zhizhi, was chosen by the Dallas Mavericks.[65]

It took two years to navigate various Communist Party issues, but finally, in the spring of 2001, Zhizhi made it to the NBA. When he did finally take the floor, the *Financial Times* noted its symbolic importance. In fact, that April of 2001, the paper saw Zhizhi's NBA arrival as one of two events, both ironically enough involving a man named Wang, that indicated the possible implications of China's rise in disparate ways. This prompted the *Financial Times* to dub that April "the month of two Wangs." As noted, Wang Zhizhi represented a more economically open and engaging China; he also soon showed the difficulty China faced in trying to be more global and more economically open, while still maintaining authoritarian political control. The other Wang was Wang Wei, reported in the West as a brash Chinese pilot who died in a collision with a U.S. spy plane. "While Wang the pilot has become a symbol in death of Chinese resentment of perceived American arrogance, the celebration of Wang the basketball star reflects the awe that many Chinese feel toward the icons of American society," the *Financial Times* astutely observed. Jing Jun, a professor of sociology at China's Tshinghua University, explained, "On one hand there is what I call an American fetish among people in China. On the other you have calls of 'down with America.'"[66]

On balance, though, because of the success of China's economic reforms, increased economic freedoms, and its appreciation of American culture, it seemed then as it does now that taking an optimistic view of the relationship between the United States and China would be worthwhile. At the very least, China's attraction to America's economic model and culture has helped foster exchanges complimentary to both.

In fact, as had Yao's efforts to make it to the NBA, Wang Zhizhi's struggle to make it there showed how China's desire to participate in events like the Olympics and participate globally in sports like basketball could nudge, or even push, the Communist Party toward more open positions. For instance, as Wang's three-year haggle to make the NBA unfolded, the IOC's decision to determine the host for the 2008 Olympic Games loomed. The Chinese government, a frontrunner for the task, wanted to host badly, and the Communist Party realized that the western-dominated Olympic movement preferred liberalization and openness. In 2001 Michael Coyne, a leading international sports lawyer and consultant to the China Basketball Association's Shanghai Sharks, maintained that the Olympic factor would help Wang. "Permitting him to leave and play in the US is not taken lightly, but denying him the opportunity to play in the NBA will send the wrong message to the IOC," Coyne explained.[67]

But the *Financial Times* speculated that other factors could affect the decision about Wang and the NBA, too. For instance, the paper thought George W. Bush's tougher stance on China could hurt Wang's chances to get to the NBA. Continuing, the *Financial Times* argued, "The Bush administration's decisions regarding the 'son of Star Wars' anti-missile programme as well as the sale of four US destroyers to Taiwan will be crucial to Sino-US relations. Any deterioration could prompt China to block Wang's move to Dallas."[68] That the analysis of how China approached the prospect of Chinese players joining the NBA involved such nuance revealed basketball's influence. In addition, the treatment of basketball and its relation to such weighty issues in publications like the *Financial Times* echoed the weight sports carried in the new millennium.

With this dynamic role of sports in mind, and given that the U.S. basketball team had just squeaked by in Sydney and then lost big at the 2002 Worlds, it is startling that the 2004 U.S. Olympic roster did not have a passing point guard or feature any of the NBA's leading shooters. Given that the international three-point shot, at twenty feet, six inches—until 2010, when FIBA's three-point line will be extended to twenty-two feet, two inches—is shorter than the NBA's, strong shooting makes for a lethal weapon in international play, especially for a commonly zoned team like the U.S. The decision not to bring a single player among the NBA's top *seventy-five* three-point shooters to Athens thus made little sense. To be fair, some shooters, like Richard Hamilton, were asked to play and declined, but the fact that a few declined does not mean that everyone would have.

These shortcomings contributed to the lack of awe opponents showed against the U.S. hoops squad at the 2004 Athens Olympics. The tournament opened, in fact, with a nineteen-point U.S. loss to Puerto Rico. By the end of the Games, the United States had lost three times—more than all of the previous Olympic teams combined. As noted, a simple statistical comparison between the 2000 Olympic team and the 2004 team in shooting and assists shows the problems. The squad did, though, manage to win the bronze medal.

Well before the losses in Athens, the Larry Brown–coached squad—he was assisted by the Spurs' Gregg Popovich, Clemson's Oliver Purnell, and the University of North Carolina's Roy Williams—elicited attention for its youthfulness. The outfit averaged 23.6 years of age, making it younger than any U.S. Olympic team since FIBA had deemed NBA professionals eligible for the Games. Sure it had some veterans, in the seven-foot-tall center Tim Duncan, the six-feet-seven-inch forward Shawn Marion, the six-feet-two-inch guard Stephon Marbury, and the six-feet-tall guard Allen Iverson. However, the six-feet-eight-inch forwards Carmelo Anthony and Carlos Boozer; the budding superstar wingmen Dwyane Wade and LeBron James, at six feet four and six feet eight inches, respectively; and the forwards Emeka Okafor and Amar'e Stoudemire, both six feet ten, were all twenty-two or younger. And, though relative veterans by comparison, the forwards Richard Jefferson and Lamar Odom, six feet seven and six feet ten, respectively, were just twenty-four. This youth, coupled with the personalities of Marbury and Iverson, made folks worry about the steadiness of the squad. Indeed, working with such youthful stars as Carmelo Anthony and LeBron James proved difficult for the taskmaster Brown, as did handling Marbury, whom Brown reportedly tried to remove from the team a week before the Games.[69] "We've got a heck of a challenge," Brown explained on the eve of the Games. "This is a young team, and we don't have much time together. . . . But if we do things the right way—if we share the ball and we play defense—then we have a chance to be pretty good."[70]

In the end, the challenge proved too tough for the group. Signs of a lack of cohesion had emerged at the end of the training period in late July. For most of that week, things seemed to go well, but the benching of Stoudemire, Iverson, and James for an exhibition tilt versus Puerto Rico on account of tardiness raised some concern.[71] After the Games, more stories about such issues would emerge.

Athens, the host city of the Games, was a symbolic destination for the U.S. team in two ways: it was not only the birthplace of democracy but also the ancient birthplace of the Olympics. The ancient Games of more than two thousand years ago had, in fact, directly inspired the modern-Olympic founder Pierre de Coubertin. "Believing that the ancient Greek heritage remained at the core of Western civilization and that modern sport in its moral characteristics . . . was largely continuous with ancient Greek athletics, Coubertin began to dream of a 'revival' of the Olympic Games on an international basis," the Olympic historian John MacAloon has explained.[72]

Ironically, the Greece of 2004 had been functioning under a democratic-style constitution for only twenty-nine years (a military coup, with support from the CIA, had disrupted the Greek government in 1967). But since having adopted that constitution in 1975, Greece had joined NATO and the EU, and enjoyed noteworthy prosperity.

Still, the Athens organizing committee got off to a slow start: during the build-up to Greece's symbolically pregnant Games, the IOC's chief investigator had to warn the committee repeatedly that unless it got to work, it would not be ready to host. Fortunately, by May 2004, those concerns had subsided.[73] And sure enough, in August, Athens delivered a successful Olympics that included a record-setting 201 nations and attracted over 20,000 members of the media.

The costs were extravagant. Security alone cost $1.5 billion, which included a "$312 million command-and-control center built by a U.S. consortium" that collected a "constant stream of video, audio and other data beamed from around Greece." In addition, there were Greek fighter planes and NATO surveillance aircraft, one thousand security cameras, blimps with probing eyes, and some seventy thousand security forces on hand. Total Olympic-related costs amounted to an estimated $7.2 billion to $12 billion, at least six times that of Sydney. But hosting the Olympics also led to major infrastructure improvement in Greece, from new highways and a massive increase in the area's rail service to a new airport.[74]

As alluded to, the most shocking of the U.S. team's three losses in Athens came in the opener against Puerto Rico. In that game, Brown's team was outscored, outrun, and outshot 92–73 by an American territory with a population of less than four million and a land mass 1,000 times smaller than that of the United States. The *Financial Times* stated that the U.S. team, during the woeful second period, looked "as though they didn't really care," and then summed up the shock many felt by asserting, "Losing was a possibility but only against a traditionally strong rival . . . not against an island that many Americans believe they own." Looking ahead, Brown said, "We have to become a team in a short period of time. Throw your egos out the window."[75]

The squad did respond with two wins over Greece and Australia, but neither by more than ten points. Then, in their fourth game, Brown and company succumbed to Lithuania—setting off celebrations in the basketball-rich Baltic nation. Donn Nelson, serving again as an assistant coach for Lithuania, had predicted that no team would beat the U.S. in his lifetime, but just in case, after the two-point squeaker against Lithuania in 2000, he had vowed not to coach against his homeland again. So it was from the Olympic Village that he watched, with conflicting emotions, as Lithuania dismantled the United States.

This time, Jasekivicius did not allow the game to come down to a last-second heave. During one stretch, he scored ten points in one minute and nine seconds of action. The points came on an assortment of jump shots and off-balance moves, including a spectacular four-point play. He finished the game with twenty-eight points, while Marbury struggled throughout, shooting just two of fourteen and finishing with eight points. By the contest's end, the United States had hit just eighteen of eighty-two three-point attempts for the tournament.[76]

As in 2000, in a lot of ways, the U.S. team's struggles in Athens reflected a natural consequence of the NBA's international aspirations. Following the game, the *Washington Post* noted that the "magnanimous" NBA had spent the last decade teaching the world how to beat us—for instance, since Dream Team I, Coach Daly had traveled to Spain and Italy twelve times to give clinics.[77] But again, the way the United States lost repeatedly in Athens, as at the 2002 Worlds, stood out.

A win over Angola, following the Lithuania loss, left the squad with a 3-2 record and the last-place seed in its grouping heading into the quarterfinal medal round. In other preliminary round action, China overcame struggles early in the tournament to register a big win over Serbia-Montenegro and thereby qualify for the medal round too.

The Chinese team was buttressed by a more experienced Yao Ming and coached by former Los Angeles Lakers head man Del Harris—his presence indicated how China looked toward the United States for inspiration in building its basketball program, while Yao showed that China could develop its own talent. The squad came to Athens with high hopes, and not just for Yao. Other players had high expectations as well, especially the seven-foot-tall Yi Jianlian, a future 2007 first-round draft-pick of the Milwaukee Bucks. Listed as being sixteen years old in Sydney, Jianlian had spent the previous season playing in China's top professional league and impressed in summer workouts leading up to Athens. His five blocked shots and seven rebounds in twenty-four minutes of action in an Athens warm-up tussle with Serbia-Montenegro drew praise. "He's better than me at 16. He can jump. If he keeps working hard, he can make it big," a gracious Yao said.[78]

In Athens, though, China came away with mixed feeling about its performance. Qualifying for the medal round for just the second time in its history registered as an important achievement, but the team's blowout losses in other games diminished that accomplishment. Moreover, the controversy that arose over comments Yao made after a loss to Spain, which hinted at the difficulty China faced in balancing its Communist ways while engaging the predominantly liberal capitalist global arena, did not help matters.[79]

Yao's comments were as follows: "I am really upset. I got hurt almost every time playing for the national team." He also said, "I cannot figure out the reason why [we played badly]. Were they [teammates] nervous? Or they would not take responsibilities? I just did what I could do."[80] The *Toronto Globe and Mail* reported that an unnamed Chinese official responded by declaring, "Now, he [Yao] has changed, he's more like an American, he dares to say anything." Officials were purportedly "very angry." In addition, the *Toronto Globe and Mail* asserted that one report out of China hinted that the controversy may have caused Chinese officials to "consider more deeply and carefully about sending players to the NBA again."[81] The swift rebuke of Yao's self-expression showed how China was grappling as it tried to simultaneously embrace the open market while limiting individual liberty. Ultimately, China did not disallow its citizens from playing in the NBA or implement any noteworthy punishment upon Yao. Neither action would have made sense in light of the more open course it had chosen.

In its first game of the medal round, the United States pulled out a 102–94 win over previously undefeated Spain, which was led by NBA star Pau Gasol. Before the affair, the *Financial Times* asserted that a U.S. loss would "be seen as one of the greatest failures in the history of U.S. sport."[82] But Spain did not play a zone defense as expected, and Marbury spearheaded the win with thirty-one points, the most by a U.S. Olympian in Olympic history and eighteen of which came from three-pointers. It was a bit ironic that Marbury delivered such a splendid performance, given that he epitomized for many the perceived me-first attitude of the NBA. His three-point shooting in this game hinted at how the tournament might have unfolded for the United States had the team shot well from the outside consistently. Instead, the Spain game stands as an aberration. By tournament's end, only one team in the entire Olympic field shot worse than the United States from three-point range.

In the semifinals the United States lost rather convincingly to the well-drilled Argentines, who boasted future NBA standouts Manu Ginobli and Andres Nocioni, along with a sharp-cutting offense and terrific passing. The Argentines followed the victory over the United States with an 84–69 victory for gold over Italy, which just about two weeks earlier had soundly beaten the United States in an Olympic exhibition.

Against Argentina, it did not help the United States that Tim Duncan, baffled by foul trouble throughout the tournament, fouled out. At the tournament's end, a frustrated Duncan said, "I'm about 95 percent sure my FIBA career is over," but not wanting to discourage others from playing for the United States in the Olympics, he added, "I'll try not to share my experiences with anyone."[83] Regardless of the role foul trouble may have played in the game, the United States simply got beat by a super-talented, well-oiled team. Afterward, China's state-run news agency, *Xinhuanet*, declared, "Twelve years after Michael Jordan, Magic Johnson and Larry Bird led the American senior basketball team to conquer the world, the era of the U.S. Dream Team was terminated." Continuing, *Xinhuanet* voiced the thoughts of most around the globe when it wrote that even though a number of top NBA players had not played for an array of reasons, "it was still shocking to find the American Dreamers so vulnerable."[84]

Even before the defeat, the *New York Times*'s Mike Wise noted, players and coaches were decrying things ranging from the way the team was "haphazardly constructed," to the breakdown of team play in America, to a lack of sufficient time for the team to prepare—the team did not start practicing for the Games, which opened on August 13, until July 26.[85] Coach Brown, for one, highlighted the lack of preparation; he also criticized his roster, as well the team's short preparation time. NBA commissioner David Stern was so irked by this that he traveled to Greece to deliver a barb Brown's way and defend the players.[86]

In Athens, Stern said, "This was a team that was put together by everyone, including the coaching staff." He also stated, "And this is a great team, so I don't buy the, 'Well, I'd like to have this, I'd like to have that.' . . . It's not about who didn't come. I'll tell you what, we're all in sports. You take your team to the gym and you play what you've got and then you either win or you lose. And this whining and carping is not fair to the young men . . . who are representing their country admirably and well."[87]

In fairness to Brown on the preparation issue, USA Basketball did soon change its methods in that regard. As for the roster selection, after the loss, the *New York Times*'s Wise did highlight some of the NBA players that had not ended up in Athens, noting that in all, "14 players effectively said no." Tracy McGrady and Ray Allen, he reported, stayed away for "security concerns." All-stars Jason Kidd and Jermaine O'Neal missed on account of late-season injuries, as did Vince Carter and Elton Brand, "though privately USA Basketball officials felt some of the reported ailments were dubious," Wise maintained. He said that Mike Bibby did not offer a clear, main reason for his absence, and that, with a free-agent contract looming, Kenyon Martin had not come because he did not want to risk injury. Richard Hamilton and Ben Wallace, who played for Brown in Detroit, had pulled themselves out of the running in June 2004. As for Kobe Bryant,

20. For just the second time, the United States finished in third place in the Olympic basketball tournament. Photo by Maxim Marmur. AFP Collection/Getty Images.

Wise wrote, "Bryant was committed, but pulled out when he realized his sexual assault case in Colorado would go to trial at the end of August." But really, the main problem was not an inability to get reluctant folks to sign on. Sure, getting a bulk of the best helps immensely, but America sent considerable talent to Athens. Two key parts of U.S. Basketball's problem rested with its failure to pick players that would mix their talents better and in not committing more time and energy to building a team.[88]

The anguish over the U.S. losses was assuaged when the squad, led by Shawn Marion's twenty-two points, delivered a bronze-medal victory against Lithuania. This mollified matters only so much, though. The losses in Athens had been too convincing. Still, the team drew praise for ending with a win. "If you don't get it done the way you expected to, I think it's important that you get it done the best way you can," Iverson said. The losses smarted, but Jefferson commented, "It's amazing how, as soon as you start to lose, everybody turns against you . . . we gave our all every single game." The team had come away with a medal. "That's what being an American and being a patriot is all about. You get knocked down, you keep going," Odom, who finished with fourteen points and seven rebounds, told reporters. And even though they had not won gold, Iverson, who drew praise for his attitude, continued to cherish the opportunity to suit up for his country at the Olympic Games. Iverson also gave credit to the opposition, saying, "A lot of people don't understand . . . how Smarty Jones loses a race . . . how Muhammad Ali lost a fight . . . But things happen, and people should understand—it's not easy over here."[89]

The Athens Games highlighted the quality of international hoops and a need for more U.S. teamwork. This does not mean that individuality ceased to be part of basketball's marketing, but even before the 2004 U.S. performance, there was evidence that the NBA recognized the need for a shift in American style. For example, before its 2001–2 season, the NBA adopted rules aimed to increase off-the-ball player movement. Most telling, the league allowed teams to play zone defenses, which could be played in FIBA action, in an effort to limit isolation plays on offense.

More indications of the shift came after Athens. In November 2006, for instance, Nike announced a grassroots initiative to completely restructure its summer basketball program for American youths. The plan, as the *Oregonian* described it, "will start promoting skill development and team play ahead of the individual, street-ball style that has permeated youth basketball in recent years." Part of the impetus for Nike's actions came from the competitive challenges international teams posed to the United States.[90] The rededication to teamwork in America was accompanied, ironically, by a return to speedier play, which also came as a result of international influence.

It still took, however, that major wake-up call in Athens for USA Basketball to change dramatically. The process has been painful for many American basketball fans, in some ways echoing the dynamic competitiveness within the increasingly integrated global economy. But, given that the United States had promoted basketball's diffusion since its creation and championed the open market for centuries, it did not make much sense to complain about increased competitiveness. It made more sense to respond to the competitive challenge with a better product. In 2008, the United States did just that.

TABLE 14. 1996 U.S. Men's Olympic Basketball cumulative stats

NAME	G/S	FGM-FGA	(%)	3PM-3PA	(%)	FTM-FTA	(%)	REB/AVG	PTS/AVG	AST	BLK	ST
David Robinson	8/3	34-50	.680	0-0	.000	28-40	.700	37/4.6	96/12.0	0	3	5
Reggie Miller	8/5	33-64	.516	17-41	.415	8-9	.889	8/1.0	91/11.4	17	0	8
Scottie Pippen	8/7	37-71	.521	8-23	.348	6-11	.545	31/3.9	88/11.0	26	4	13
Charles Barkley	7/4	31-38	.816	2-4	.500	23-32	.719	46/6.6	87/12.4	17	1	6
Mitch Richmond	8/3	25-54	.463	11-26	.423	16-19	.842	13/1.6	77/9.6	10	0	10
Shaquille O'Neal	8/3	31-50	.620	0-0	.000	12-23	.522	42/5.3	74/9.3	7	8	5
Anfernee Hardaway	8/1	25-44	.568	4-13	.308	18-25	.720	22/2.8	72/9.0	35	1	11
Karl Malone	8/4	29-51	.569	0-0	.000	9-17	.529	36/4.5	67/8.4	11	1	8
Grant Hill	6/1	22-36	.611	2-6	.333	12-16	.750	17/2.8	58/9.7	21	1	18
Gary Payton	8/6	14-37	.378	3-7	.429	10-19	.526	25/3.1	41/5.1	36	0	6
Hakeem Olajuwon	7/2	13-29	.448	0-0	.000	9-13	.692	22/3.1	35/5.0	8	3	6
John Stockton	8/1	10-19	.526	1-2	.500	9-11	.818	6/0.8	30/3.8	22	0	13
USA TOTALS	8	304-543	.560	48-122	.393	160-235	.681	305/38.1	816/102.0	210	22	109
OPP. TOTALS	8	190-452	.420	61-161	.379	121-174	.695	201/25.1	562/70.3	119	9	51

TABLE 15. 2000 U.S. Men's Olympic Basketball cumulative stats

NAME	G/S	FGM-FGA	(%)	3PM-3PA	(%)	FTM-FTA	(%)	REB/AVG	PTS/AVG	AST	BLK	ST
Vince Carter	8/5	41-81	.506	11-27	.407	25-36	.694	29/3.6	118/14.8	11	1	8
Kevin Garnett	8/5	37-68	.544	0-0	.000	12-19	.632	73/9.1	86/10.8	17	3	9
Alonzo Mourning	6/6	22-37	.595	0-2	.000	17-20	.850	25/4.2	61/10.2	8	14	1
Ray Allen	8/2	28-52	.538	10-19	.526	12-12	1.000	15/1.9	78/9.8	10	2	7
Vin Baker	8/2	23-36	.639	0-0	.000	18-31	.581	24/3.0	64/8.0	6	4	3
Allan Houston	7/4	18-38	.474	12-20	.600	8-10	.800	13/1.9	56/8.0	7	0	0
Antonio McDyess	8/2	27-40	.675	0-0	.000	7-15	.467	47/5.9	61/7.6	8	1	4
Shar. Abdur-Rahim	8/1	17-31	.548	0-1	.000	17-21	.810	26/3.3	51/6.4	1	0	3
Steve Smith	8/2	11-24	.458	4-9	.444	23-29	.793	19/2.4	49/6.1	11	3	2
Jason Kidd	8/4	16-31	.516	4-8	.500	12-15	.800	42/5.3	48/6.0	35	1	9
Gary Payton	8/6	15-43	.349	2-10	.200	12-17	.706	17/2.1	44/5.5	27	1	9
Anfernee Hardaway	8/1	15-39	.385	11-32	.344	3-5	.600	11/1.4	44/5.5	12	0	2
USA TOTALS	8	270-520	.519	54-128	.422	166-230	.722	341/42.6	760/95.0	153	30	57
OPP. TOTALS	8	187-479	.390	50-178	.281	163-239	.682	200/25.0	587/73.4	106	17	35

TABLE 16. 2004 U.S. Men's Olympic Basketball cumulative stats

NAME	G/S	FGM-FGA	(%)	3PM-3PA	(%)	FTM-FTA	(%)	REB/AVG	PTS/AVG	AST	BLK	ST
Tim Duncan	8/8	38-67	.567	0-2	.000	27-36	.750	73/9.1	103/12.9	13	10	6
Stephon Marbury	8/8	30-71	.423	10-31	.323	14-19	.737	10/1.3	84/10.5	27	0	7
Shawn Marion	8/0	34-64	.531	4-10	.400	7-9	.778	47/5.9	79/9.9	6	3	9
Lamar Odom	8/8	29-51	.569	4-8	.500	12-23	.522	46/5.8	74/9.3	11	5	16
Carlos Boozer	8/0	20-32	.625	0-0	.000	21-32	.656	49/6.1	61/7.6	3	1	6
Dwyane Wade	8/0	21-55	.382	0-3	.000	16-23	.696	15/1.9	58/7.3	19	3	17
Richard Jefferson	8/8	18-56	.321	6-23	.261	12-22	.545	22/2.8	54/6.8	8	3	2
LeBron James	8/0	19-32	.594	3-10	.300	2-2	1.000	8/1.0	43/5.4	13	0	6
Amar'e Stoudemire	8/0	9-16	.563	0-1	.000	4-8	.500	14/1.8	22/2.8	1	4	3
Carmelo Anthony	7/0	7-28	.250	2-11	.182	1-2	.500	11/1.6	17/2.4	0	0	2
Emeka Okafor	2/0	0-2	.000	0-0	.000	0-0	.000	3/1.5	0/0.0	0	0	0
USA TOTALS	8	259-564	.459	44-140	.314	143-214	.668	311/38.9	705/88.1	121	30	85
OPP. TOTALS	8	233-483	.482	86-195	.441	116-171	.678	225/28.1	668/83.5	88	19	45

14

RECLAMATION IN BEIJING

Millions came to them and billions watched them. Multitudes celebrated them, while many protested them. In preparation for them, billions of dollars were spent just to clean the air. Hundreds of millions more dollars went to just getting them launched. Virtually all of the world leaders attended, while thousands of "armed" citizen-soldiers stood ready to shoot silver iodide into clouds in order to manipulate the weather for them. Beforehand, the earth shook terribly. During them, a war erupted, and throughout, participants battled in the Water Cube and the Bird's Nest. All of this sounds a lot like something that would happen in a science-fiction story, but it is in fact a description of the 2008 Beijing Olympics, which witnessed epic performances from the Opening Ceremonies, to the swimming events in the Water Cube, to the track-and-field races in the Bird's Nest, to the basketball played by the Redeem Team.

Amid the dramatic scene, the Redeem Team, the nickname by which the U.S. men's Olympic basketball team became known, and its global stars, Dwyane Wade, LeBron James, Kobe Bryant, and the rest, managed to resonate with terrific force. Sure, in the United States, the affable, eight-time gold-medal-winning swimmer Michael Phelps dominated, but the Chinese loved the Redeemers. They cheered the team wildly, oohed and ahhed at its creativity and explosiveness, and mobbed its stars. Sales figures for the NBA jerseys of the Redeem Team players are a good indication of how popular the team was: even in China, Bryant's jersey ranked first, while four Redeemers made the top nine—all in front of Yao Ming, who ranked tenth. (Of course, it helped that, as Sarunas Kazlauskas, the [Lithuanian] 2008 Chinese national team coach hyperbolically put it, "You can find an NBA game any day of the season anywhere in China.")[1]

The U.S. Olympic basketball player Chris Paul described the team's reception in China, saying, "We're like the Beatles over here." His teammate Carmelo Anthony recalled, "In Athens, there was no excitement at all, except maybe when we got booed in the street . . . This is all different."[2] And the Redeemers returned the affection by producing hit after hit en route to a dramatic gold medal tilt with Spain.

USA Basketball was not the only entity that faced high stakes in Beijing. Host nation China had a lot riding on the Games, too—particularly in the political arena. In 2006, Human Rights Watch gave notice that it would "pay special attention to the 2008 Games."[3] The stakes were also high economically. As an indication of the 2008 Games' market potential, the Johnson & Johnson employee Brian Perkins explained his company's multiyear, multimillion dollar global sponsorship deal with the IOC by saying, "There are going to be over 4.5 billion [viewers] looking at Beijing and China with amazement." He added, "It's going to go beyond a sporting event. I think it will be a cultural, social, and economic event, the likes of which we won't see in another generation."[4] Ultimately, China's performance, given the various issues that arose during the Games, did not equal that of the Redeemers.

It had been a long journey to that gold medal game, though. After Athens in particular, USA Basketball had a lot to overcome. Its losses had come to represent more than just poor play: as noted before, Thomas Friedman, the author of *The World Is Flat*, used the 2004 U.S. Olympic team as a symbol of how excessive individualism could hurt America on a global stage that featured increasingly open economic models and intense competition.[5] Changing the perception that U.S. basketball reeked of arrogance and overt individuality, while returning America to the top of the international basketball landscape, became the lofty, albeit difficult, mission for the team.

To tackle the problem, the U.S. Olympic Basketball Committee created a new job, "Managing Director," and hired Jerry Colangelo for it. Reared in Chicago Heights, Illinois, Colangelo starred in hoops in the mid-1960s at the University of Illinois and then worked in marketing for the Chicago Bulls. At the age of twenty-eight, he became the general manager for the NBA's new Phoenix Suns franchise.[6] The numerous positions he held with the Suns in subsequent decades ultimately resulted in his being inducted in 2004 into the Naismith Basketball Hall of Fame. With his new post as managing director of USA Basketball, Colangelo was offered virtual control over USA Senior Men's Basketball outside of, as the reporter Jim Litke put it, "a badge reading 'New sheriff in town.'"[7]

In the summer of 2005, Colangelo convened a meeting with a kind of Dream Team of advisors that included Jerry West, Dean Smith, Larry Bird, and Michael Jordan. At this meeting, great emphasis was placed on the idea that the United States needed to create a team with all the necessary parts, rather than a collection of stars, so a three-year commitment to the team was required from future U.S. coaches and players. In time, Colangelo would meet "eyeball-to-eyeball" with each player he'd initially targeted to be part of USA basketball's pool of players. Though the three-year commitment was a hurdle in attracting folks, "what happened in Athens made my job a lot easier," Colangelo explained.[8]

Discussion in Chicago also took place about who should coach. Two names rose to the top: Gregg Popovich, an Air Force Academy graduate and the four-time NBA champion as coach of the San Antonio Spurs, and Mike "Coach K" Krzyzewski, a West Point graduate and the legendary coach of the NCAA powerhouse Duke Blue Devils. Considering both great candidates, Colangelo talked to each. Popovich had been an assistant at the Athens Games and still had some bitterness about the way things had gone there. He was also apparently a bit hesitant about the time commitment. On the other hand, Krzyzewski, who was shocked to hear that Colangelo had him in mind as head coach, voiced his enthusiasm and ultimately got the job.[9]

By the 2006 World Championships, a newfangled U.S. squad had formed. It included some young holdovers from 2004, such as Dwyane

Wade, LeBron James, and Carmelo Anthony—each of whom, to the chagrin of many, had been played sparingly in Athens. But the U.S. squad also had plenty of new faces to go along with its fresh attitude. It talked about cohesion as well as a need to return America to basketball glory. To put the challenge facing the team into perspective, Coach K had learned more about the history of the international game and strove to instill in his team a sense of that historical context, which he thought would lend credibility to the way he had them prepare. In addition, in revamping the national team, Coach K and Colangelo had, as Coach K frankly recalled, "borrowed from international teams like Argentina and Spain the need for familiarity with one another and for continuity."[10] Coach Krzyzewski even invited injured U.S. veterans from the Iraq War to visit the players at training. Some of the players were moved to tears.

However, there were still criticisms of the U.S. team. For instance, in a peculiar op-ed in *The Nation*, David Zirin pointed out that Colangelo supported an evangelical group and that Krzyzewski donated to the Republican Party. Zirin also suggested that Colangelo and Krzyzewski were using an unpopular war to build team cohesion, and he called having injured veterans visit the team "disturbing." The soldiers seemed to enjoy the visit immensely.[11]

On the eve of the 2006 World Championship, Krzyzewski summed up the new attitude: "Our go-to guy is our team." The U.S. team did seem to have a new energy and better cohesion at the championships, but even with its revamped roster, seemingly cooperative attitudes, and improved image, the previously undefeated United States lost to Greece in the semifinals. The victory caused "huge celebrations to break out all over Greece," and the prime minister, Kostas Karamanlis reportedly "cut short scheduled meetings to watch the end of the game." By winning, Greece proved yet again just how competitive international basketball had become. Still, the loss shocked many, particularly because the Greek team boasted no current NBA players, and it had repeatedly hurt the United States on a classic NBA play, the pick-and-roll. (Greece's six-feet-ten-inch forward Antonis Fotsis spent a short time in the NBA during 2001–2, and its six-feet-four-inch point guard, the FIBA star Vasileios Spanoulis, who scored twenty-two points in the Greek win, had a brief, albeit unfruitful, stay with the Houston Rockets in 2006–7.)[12] So even though USA Basketball, the NBA and its star players, and all of their commercial partners had committed to sending a winning team to Beijing, they still had to resolve some personnel issues and address the need for tactical improvements.

Corporate sponsors had bet big on U.S. players that summer of 2006. In the run-up to the World Championships, Gatorade launched one of the most ambitions marketing campaigns ever by plastering Wade's likeness on twenty million of its bottles—all destined for the Chinese marketplace. And that summer, Coca-Cola utilized LeBron James to compete with Gatorade's marketing push in Asia.[13]

With the stakes so high for so many, it seems odd that the U.S. Olympic team seemed to contain a fairly simple, easily fixable flaw (in addition to needing to defend the pick-and-roll more effectively): namely, the team did not include league-leading shooters. All told, the 2006 U.S. squad had only one player who had finished the previous NBA season among the top fifty NBA three-point shooters (Shane Battier at thirty-first). Among the shooters that did not make the final 2006 roster were the six-feet-six-inch Michael Redd (who did make the 2008 Beijing roster), the rookie J. J. Reddick, Mike Miller, and Bruce Bowen.[14]

In addition to exposing the need for personnel changes and increased focus on the behalf of the U.S. squad, the 2006 loss to Greece meant that the United States would have to qualify to participate in the Olympics by finishing among the top two teams at the 2007 FIBA Americas tournament. In a nod to the history of U.S. Olympic basketball—which Coach K had emphasized in preparation for Beijing—at the FIBA Americas tournament in Las Vegas, the U.S. team wore Nike uniforms that had the 1960 U.S. Olympic roster stitched on the inside.[15] With reminders of such legends as Robertson, Lucas, and West etched on their uniforms, the United States took the FIBA Americas title, thanks in no small part to strong play from the Cleveland Cavaliers' six-feet-eight-inch James, the Denver Nuggets' six-feet-eight-inch Anthony, the recently added six-feet-six-inch Kobe Bryant, and the marksman Michael Redd, whose off-the-bench shooting performance surely helped him land a spot on the 2008 U.S. team.

So too did Redd's attitude. Managing director Jerry Colangelo thought Redd epitomized what he was looking for. He loved to tell people of the first time, in 2005, that he met with Redd to gauge the shooter's interest in suiting up for USA Basketball. Redd had driven from practice with the

Milwaukee Bucks straight to Chicago for the meeting, so when he finally knocked on the door to Colangelo's hotel room, he was still wearing sweatpants. After the two exchanged greetings, Redd asked if he could use the restroom before getting started. When Redd came back out, he was nattily clad in a suit and tie. He had wanted to show how important it was to him to represent his country at the Games. "That was pretty darn impressive," Colangelo said.[16]

USA Basketball, and by extension, the NBA, came to the Games facing an eight-year championship drought in international competition—the United States had competed in the previous two World Championships and the 2004 Games without winning a title. A championship would lend a new measure of legitimacy to the NBA and the opportunity to further cultivate relationships with businesses.

For players, there was also the prospect of showcasing themselves for massive contracts overseas. In fact, during the 2008 Beijing Games stories broke about the prospect of international teams, unrestricted by a salary cap, trying to lure Bryant or James from the NBA for $30–50 million per season. "As players, the business of the game [is] evolving," Bryant maintained before a training session at Beijing Normal University, where the U.S. squad practiced at the Olympics. "I think free agency is now becoming a global thing." Though Bryant has not seemed able to captivate Americans in the same way Michael Jordan did, in China, Kobe's popularity was clear. His NBA jersey was the best-seller at Adidas stores, and in Beijing he "got serenaded with chants of 'Kobe! Kobe!' at airports" and was cheered loudly at the Opening Ceremony. This led the *Washington Post* to suggest that he was "arguably the most popular athlete in Beijing."[17]

The threat of NBA superstars jetting off to Europe led ESPN.com's J. A. Adande to predict a hastening of some type of merger between the NBA and FIBA's top professional league.[18] Yet even given this unforeseen potential side effect—that of star players getting recruited by FIBA—of David Stern's international vision, the Beijing Games still offered the NBA the opportunity to show people across the globe that its American-born and highly marketed stars warranted recognition as the finest. And in the end, the Redeemers, albeit infused with an international influence, delivered. The squad wove a team attitude together with jaw-dropping individual talent into a golden tapestry.

Nonetheless, in 2008 it seemed as if many Americans still simply expected a Dream Team–type performance from their basketball Olympians. The competitive environment had changed so much, however, that actually delivering that type of performance was not easy: it was just that, for most of the tournament, the Redeemers made it appear so. As the U.S. Olympic coach Mike Krzyzewski said in Beijing, "The thing that our American fans don't understand is that we've learned from other international coaches, from the way they conceive their systems, from individual players. We've always looked at it from an American basketball culture that we're always giving knowledge to the world. And that has changed. They're giving knowledge, and we're sharing knowledge of the game. To me, that's one of the best things about this whole experience [the 2008 Olympics], and I think the world sees that in us."[19]

The ESPN reporter Chris Sheridan saw firsthand the effort that the Americans put into the Beijing Games, but he also witnessed the abilities of the competition. During the tournament, he warned readers not to take wins for granted, stressing how the scenario had changed since 1992. Clearly, the Redeem team impressed him. Asserting that it was a disservice to the team to assume that a U.S. victory would be easy, Sheridan wrote, "They're [the Redeemers] the ones in the gym and the weight room for more hours than you could imagine; they're the ones staying up an extra hour or two to study DVDs of their opponents' tendencies. It's a disservice, too, to those coaches and scouts who stayed up until 4 a.m. local time Thursday [into the early morning of August 22nd] breaking down tape of the Argentina-Greece game, formulating a game plan, adjusting their scouting reports and depriving themselves of sleep." Whether or not everyone appreciated it, the fact is that it took a tremendous, years-long effort for the United States to win back the gold medal.

Even though the practices of international teams had motivated the United States to accentuate team play, from the Dream Team to the Redeem Team, individual expression continued to be vital to basketball's growth. Though it is hard to quantify, this in turn has affected how people view core values like individuality. China demonstrates this well. In interacting at events such as the Olympics and through sports like basketball, the United States and

China have generated a shared framework from which to pursue athletic and commercial interests within an international sporting environment that compliments universalism. This framework has enabled the United States to showcase its popular culture quite successfully, and basketball has helped lead the way.

From the 1990s onward, firms in industries ranging from sporting goods to cell phones to food have utilized basketball's appeal to reach consumers in China. In so doing, they have not just hired the likes of 2004 and 2008 Olympian Dwyane Wade to endorse products in China but have also personalized their basketball-related goods. For instance, in the late 1990s, as shoes continued to evolve as a form of individual expression, Internet start-ups put pressure on companies like Adidas and Nike to diminish the "time-lag" between the unveiling of a shoe and its appearance in local stores. "Personalization is a key area right now—and the web is ideal to make that happen, but developing that trend is still some way off," Charlie Brooks, press director for Nike United Kingdom, explained at the time. Marketing campaigns reflected an emphasis on individuality too. For example, though in 2005 Adidas shifted the marketing emphasis of its namesake basketball line toward team play, that same year, Reebok launched its "I Am What I Am" marketing campaign featuring Yao Ming.[20]

Yao Ming, in fact, represents the effects that liberal capitalist culture can have on China. As noted, at the 2004 Athens Olympics, it became clear that China's "prodigal" son had been reared to embody, as his biographer Brook Larmer has put it, "basketball with Chinese characteristics . . . no questioning of authority, no glorification of individual achievement, and little freedom to think for oneself." Thus, it was shocking to some in China when Yao made comments that Communist officials criticized as too individualistic. By that time, however, Yao had signed a lucrative endorsement deal with Reebok and spent most of the year in Houston, Texas, playing in the NBA—hardly the type of lifestyle Marx had envisioned for Communist citizens.[21]

In a 2006 cover article, *U.S. News & World Report*'s Bay Fang wrote about the rise of the Chinese consumer, asserting that the mindset of the relatively youthful and growing middle class in China was much different from that of their forebears. One young Chinese middle-class citizen, Sharmin Du, told Fang, "In the U.S., kids know what they like. But in China, no one in the past thought that way—what do I prefer? What do I like? I am just starting to figure that out now."[22] And much as had happened in the United States, in China, basketball was recognized as playing an integral role in the popular tastes of urban Chinese youths. Fang highlighted Adidas, whose sales in China doubled in 2004 and then doubled again in 2005, to show how important the China market had become for shoe firms. And Fang noted that in 2006, Adidas released a limited-edition Tracy McGrady basketball shoe in China rather than the United States. The shoe sold out in hours.

It was the Dream Team effect that compelled athletic firms, particularly Nike, Adidas, and Reebok, to enhance their use of basketball to attract consumers in China. In 1994 Nike started sponsoring entire school leagues there. Ultimately, its sales in China went from $8 million in 1994 to $450 million by 2006. Part of Nike's success stemmed from its hip image. Chinese consumers routinely ranked the company as the "coolest brand." In 2006, Terry Rhoads, who had been Nike's marketing analyst for twelve years, predicted that the company would grow even more, telling Fang that he saw a "perfect storm coming . . . The middle class is beginning to grow. Kids all use the Internet and see what their counterparts in the U.S. and Europe are listening to, what sports they play. They want to be part of a global tribe."[23]

Like Nike, Adidas responded to the Dream Team's Barcelona performance by developing innovative ways to attract Asian consumers. Part of its strategy included sponsoring street basketball tournaments throughout the Asian-Pacific area. The nature of street basketball promotes rugged, creative play and fits well with the improvisational nature of the sport. By the turn of the millennium, hundreds of teams participated in Adidas-sponsored street basketball tournaments all over Asia.[24] Street basketball represented basketball's ability to, on a global level, maintain a hip image while enjoying mainstream acceptance.

Others also capitalized on the game's appeal: for example, the upstart basketball apparel and footwear company, And 1. Started by young Philadelphian hoop enthusiasts (one a former Congressional staffer and some others MBA students), it grew rapidly in the 1990s and beyond. From its inception in 1993, a crucial component of And 1's growth came from its promotion of street basketball in the United States. By 2005 its products sold in more than 130 nations, and the firm sponsored four separate national basketball teams: New Zealand, Puerto Rico, Slovenia, and Turkey.[25] As much as any firm, And 1's growth has been directly related to basketball's improvisational possibilities and easy accessibility. As happened with American jazz in the first half of the twentieth century, these characteristics have also helped basketball attract people across the cultural and ethnic spectrum globally. The Dream Team and its subsequent versions have had a big effect on these developments.

At the 2008 Games, this only continued. In Beijing, Li Ning, a Chinese shoe firm privately started by the former Chinese Olympic gold medalist of the same name (the same Li Ning who lit the Olympic flame in Beijing's Bird's Nest Stadium to open the Games), showed how Asian firms were aiming to challenge the likes of Nike and Adidas. On its Web page, Li Ning the company, which listed on the Hong Kong stock exchange in June 2004 and boasted over $600 million in revenue in 2007, champions teamwork and innovation. Through its marketing, it has also promoted individuality. For instance, in 2006 when the Cleveland Cavaliers' Damon Jones became Li Ning's first NBA endorsee (Shaquille O'Neal signed with the firm in 2007), the ad campaign that Leo Burnett initiated on behalf of Li Ning and Jones encouraged local players to "create their own unique style of play." A similar chord was struck by Anta, a fellow Chinese company and rival firm of Li Ning, in its 2007 slogan: "Forge yourself."[26]

Shoe firms' efforts in China reflected basketball's appeal there, and perhaps no better example of this appeal occurred at the 2008 Olympics when China and the United States opened their Olympic tournaments with a game against each other. Outside of Wukesong Indoor Stadium, the Olympic basketball venue, hundreds of fans queued in the rain for hours eagerly awaiting the game's start. U.S. president George Bush, in Beijing, spoke to the Redeemers right before the opening tip-off and even joined their pregame huddle. His daughter Barbara and his father, the former president, also met the players beforehand. (There were reports that when LeBron James saw Bush Sr., he affectionately said, "What's up, pops?") Along with the president and his family, Chinese foreign minister Yang Jiechi and former U.S. secretary of state Henry Kissinger watched the contest. So too did over 18,000 others, some of whom reportedly paid five hundred dollars per seat. The clamorous crowd cheered loudly for both teams.

Won by the United States 101–70, the game may constitute the most-watched basketball tilt in history. "I've never felt anything quite like this. I've played in many big games, but the energy tonight was different," the 2008 NBA MVP Kobe Bryant marveled.[27]

According to CSM Media Research, some 184 million people in China alone tuned in to the game's television broadcast—even though the contest aired from 10:20 p.m. to midnight. Because of the multiple media platforms on which broadcasts of the 2008 Beijing Games were offered, assessing total viewership ratings for them is difficult, particularly in a vast area like China. But for perspective, the 184 million who watched this basketball game in China alone compares favorably to the estimated 148.3 million total American viewers that the record-setting 2008 Super Bowl attracted.[28]

The Wukesong Indoor Stadium itself represented the awesome potential of basketball in China. In January 2008 the NBA announced that NBA China had developed a design, marketing, and programming partnership with AEG, a Los Angeles–based sports marketing firm, and the Beijing Wukesong Culture and Sports Center. By then, the NBA had already consulted with the Wukesong Sports Center on the design of the Olympic basketball stadium, and plans were in place to eventually turn the stadium into an NBA-caliber arena, replete with suites, dining facilities, and other amenities. In addition to soliciting bids for naming rights, which some estimated could reach $100 million, AEG was charged with booking top-tier events as well as managing the arena's operations. Both the NBA and AEG saw the partnership as a first step in what would hopefully be a fruitful business endeavor. The president of AEG, Tim Leiweke, said that he wanted to "develop and run stadiums" throughout China. Meanwhile, the NBA's head of international business, Heidi Ueberroth, said, in regard to speculation that the NBA wanted to develop perhaps a dozen more similar stadiums in China, "We're getting approached." In addition, Stern suggested that the NBA could become affiliated with, or a sponsor of, a Chinese professional league.

"Ongoing dialogue" was also occurring between the NBA and China about a possible role for the NBA in the Chinese government's plan to install 800,000 basketball hoops in villages across its vast country, which boasted a basketball-playing population estimated by the NBA of about 300 million. And as if this were not incentive enough, according to *China*

Daily, China boasted an NBA fan base of an astounding 450 million people. Given that spending for athletic events and sporting goods accounted for roughly .2 percent to .3 percent of China's economy, compared to about 3 percent for Western nations, it's easy to understand why the NBA has wanted to tap into the Chinese enthusiasm for hoops.[29]

But in China, challenges for professional sports, even basketball, have remained. For instance, in 2008 Zhang Qing, the chief of Key-Solution Sport Consulting Co. in Beijing, told the *LA Times* that market rules did not yet fully apply to professional sports in China. Instead, the government-run "Sports Bureau" had considerable sway over sports-related commerce. And there was, of course, the issue of China's geopolitical relations. Nonetheless, the NBA and others were choosing to proceed with big plans.[30]

In picking Beijing as the host city for the Games, the IOC had taken a big chance. The committee hoped the Games would serve as a catalytic effect and improve China's human rights record, but it risked looking soft on authoritarianism, which was not in keeping with the Olympic charter. And sure enough, political issues flourished leading up to, during, and after the 2008 Games—particularly with regard to China's abysmal human rights record. This, in turn, affected coverage of the Olympics and the Redeem Team.

Though many were dubious of China's willingness to change, in the buildup to the 2008 games, many held out hope—a hope that even China seemed willing to encourage in 2002, when it claimed that the Games would "be open in every aspect," and in 2004, when it passed a constitutional amendment that supposedly would protect human rights and political critics.

As early as 2002, the IOC president Jacques Rogge said, "We are convinced that the Olympic Games will improve the human rights record" in China.[31] In 2007 Rogge addressed the human rights issue again by calling for a continuation of an "open door" policy with China. He did hedge his bets, though, writing, "The Games can only be a catalyst for change and not a panacea." In response to this, the Chinese political prisoner He Depu, sentenced to eight years for political activities and held by authorities in China's now-infamous Beijing No. 2 prison, managed to get a letter to Rogge—it had to pass through many hands first. In the 2008 letter, Depu reminded Rogge of his suggestion that the Olympics could be a catalyst for a nation to improve its human rights record but wondered if the situation, in prisons at least, hadn't actually gotten worse. His letter, he hoped, would help spur such a catalytic effect. Striking a similar tone in the buildup to the Beijing Games, Western publications ran headlines akin to the *Washington Post*'s "China Falls Short on Vows for Olympics" and the *Christian Science Monitor*'s "Games Spur Little Progress on Human Rights Front."[32]

Really, the issue had come to the fore the moment in July 2001 that China had earned the right to host. Critic asserted that the IOC's choice legitimized China's government despite that government's horrible human rights record.[33] And many considered China's gestures on the eve of that decision, such as the release of some political prisoners and the announcement of a redevelopment plan—both intended to persuade IOC voters that China was committed to improving its human rights record—as nominal.[34]

As it happened, in September 2006, China's *Xinhua* News Agency announced that it would ban any international news that undermined national unity, unsettled "economic and social order," or did other such things under similarly broad categories. Critics asserted immediately that the directive contradicted earlier "assurances from Beijing of looser controls ahead of the 2008 Olympic Games."[35] In December 2006 China did, at least publicly, switch its position, albeit under pressure from the IOC and human rights groups. In its retraction, China maintained that it would relax controls on international media through the 2008 Olympic Games, giving "foreign journalists . . . unprecedented freedom to travel and report within the country beginning next year." However, many predicted that this more open attitude would end shortly after the Games.[36]

In fact, it ended even before they had begun. Journalists who traveled to Beijing for the 2008 Games learned this rather quickly as they were denied access to Web sites about Taiwan, Tibet, Darfur, and Tiananmen Square, along with the homepages for Amnesty International, the *LA Times Olympic Blog*, and Wikipedia. Words like "democracy," "demonstration," and "Falun Gong" were red-flagged too. The IOC responded by putting pressure on China to ease up, and it did—but only to a degree. On August 1, 2008, China did receive some approbation from western media sources such as Reuters, which ran a story with the headline "Hu Stands by Games Pledges, Web Curbs Lifted." However, on August 5, the *LA Times Olympic*

Blog noted that its site was still one of many blocked in China.[37] During the Games, eight American demonstrators, along with a Briton and a German, got a firsthand taste of China's heavy-handedness when they were detained. Their arrests, along with other examples of China's Olympic clampdown, led the U.S. embassy in Beijing to make "an unusually strong statement attacking Chinese authorities for their handling of protests and dissent" on the day the Games closed.[38]

Although many griped beforehand that the Olympics should not have been awarded to China, others predicted that, though issues remained, the Olympics would still lead to more political freedoms there. Many called for a broader perspective when looking at China—in particular by comparing 2008 China to the China of just a few decades earlier. Certainly, when one considers China through a scope that stretches back to the cultural revolution of the 1960s and 1970s, it seems that China has made progress. Most obviously, from an economic standpoint, the China of 2008 bore little resemblance either to Marxist-style communism or Maoism. On the political front, however, there had not been nearly the same level of change. Some rather small victories, such as regarding Chinese land-owning rights, had been won.[39] Still, in 2007, the *Financial Times* had opined that China's "political system steadfastly resists reform."[40]

There was optimism, though. In an article published in the *Wall Street Journal Asia* just before the 2008 Olympics commenced, the political scientist Bruce Gilley shared his belief that the 2008 Games would create "new levers for positive change" on the human rights front.[41] And the United Kingdom's prime minister Gordon Brown, facing criticism for attending the Closing Ceremonies from the Liberal Democratic Party leader Nick Clegg, argued, "Support for the Games and engagement with China is not at the expense of human rights. It is integral to their promotion. China has made enormous social and economic progress over the last three decades, but much more remains to be done."[42]

Debate raged among intellectuals about whether it was better to continue to engage China and push for change at the current pace, with the expectation that more political openness would come through economic openness, or to push China much harder while continuing engagement, because change would not otherwise likely come—or to do something else altogether.[43]

Interestingly, the shoe business and the Redeemers figured into this issue in their own ways. Take for instance Nike's 1990s exodus from the by-then democratically reforming Indonesia, which reflected the "flying geese" theory of economic development. This theory maintained "that less-developed countries go up the production hierarchy as they pursue industrialization."[44] And it credits companies like Nike, not necessarily through an intention of their own, with helping bring a higher level of prosperity, labor rights, and ultimately more democratic-based politics to the very countries they have come to for cheap labor—like Indonesia and, earlier, South Korea. The situation, if one subscribes to the flying geese theory, creates a conundrum. On one hand, from a human rights standpoint Nike's motives to move to a place like Vietnam from Indonesia are bothersome. On the other, the possible unintended consequences of helping bring about more prosperity and political openness by moving to Vietnam are quite welcome.

Regarding human rights, the Redeem Team dealt less with labor-related concerns and more with China's close dealings with the Arab Sudanese government, which was charged by most western observers with carrying out genocide against mainly non-Arab "rebels" who had taken up arms in 2003 in Darfur on account of "neglect" by the central government). The human rights issue increased focus on America's dealings with "authoritarian capitalist" regimes like China. In 2007 Kobe Bryant did a public service announcement calling on people to "rise up and help" resolve the crisis in Sudan, and LeBron James supported that position in an interview on ESPN. He also promised, according to Yahoo! Sports' Dan Wetzel, a bigger statement in Beijing. For reasons that are unknown, this did not happen. However, the former U.S. Olympic medalist Joey Cheek, who organized Team Darfur—a collection of Olympic athletes united in their opposition to China's close dealings with the Sudanese government—did get his visa to China revoked just before the Games started.

The relative efficacy of an individual sportsman who does not hold any political office speaking out on political issues is up for debate, but James and Bryant both enjoy a level of worldwide popularity heretofore possessed by few other sportsmen, and it is interesting to speculate about what might have happened had they spoken out. A day before the Games opened, however, both suggested that no "bold pronouncements" would come from them regarding China's relationship with Sudan, although James did say, "Basic human rights should always be protected."[45] The situation reflected the difficulty all westerners, not just sportsmen, faced in deciding how to deal with China, which represented a new model of governance that few in the early 1990s had foreseen emerging in the way it did.[46]

The final roster of the U.S. Olympic basketball team was announced in June 2008. As noted, Bryant, James, Anthony, and the six-foot-tall Chris Paul made it; as did the guards Jason Kidd, who at six feet four came into the exhibition tilts and Olympic tournament with a 44-0 record in international play, Deron Williams, who was six feet three, and the shooter Michael Redd. Oddly enough, Dwyane Wade did not secure a roster spot until a strong June 2008 workout in front of Colangelo; injuries had caused the wingman to miss portions of the previous two NBA seasons, as well as the 2007 FIBA Americas. The doubts about Wade, who in 2006 was the NBA Finals MVP for the champion Miami Heat, motivated him to plan on "playing angry" in China.[47] Apparently, that included suffocating defense, nearly a point-a-minute offense, and splendid displays of skill and athleticism. In fact, perhaps the highlight of the whole tournament occurred when Wade chased down a ball that was headed out-of-bounds on the sideline and not only saved it but somehow managed to whip a thirty-feet-or-so, spur-of-the-moment pass to Bryant, who received it with two hands and tilted the ball behind his head before slamming it through the basket.

Down low, the roster boasted the six-feet-eleven-inch Dwight Howard, the six-feet-nine-inch Carlos Boozer, and the six-feet-ten-inch Chris Bosh. Though not meaty, Bosh appealed to Coach K—as the former Olympian Doug Collins noted during his work as a broadcaster for NBC Universal during the Games—because of his quickness and his wingspan in defending the pick-and-roll.[48] This would prove a huge benefit in games like the rematch with Greece that came about in Beijing. Rounding out the team at six feet nine inches and a gangly 215 pounds was the super utility man Tayshaun Prince.

Those were the final twelve that emerged out of a USA basketball pool numbering thirty-three players. Since Amar'e Stoudemire and Chauncey Billups had taken themselves out of consideration shortly before the team was announced, the decision to choose Prince rather than the six-feet-eleven-inch shot-blocking master Tyson Chandler generated the most debate. In bypassing Chandler, the team would be heading into competition with just three players who were considered either a center or power forward: this raised some concern. ESPN.com's Chris Sheridan for one thought it a mistake that could go down as a "singular example of hubris" on the part of Coach K and Colangelo.[49] In the gold medal game against Spain, the team's relative lack of size did cause some problems, but overall, the choice of Prince—who was ultra-versatile, contributed positively to team chemistry, and provided crucial baskets in the gold medal game against Spain—proved stellar. And as far as size was concerned, Coach K actually went even smaller than expected by playing Chris Paul and Deron Williams together in the backcourt. That too was effective.

Another potential problem with the team, one that received less attention, was its lack of good shooters. Sure, Williams and even Bryant would likely help improve overall shooting percentages in comparison with those of the 2006 U.S. team, but Redd was the lone player on the U.S. Olympic roster who finished the 2007–8 NBA season among the top thirty-five three-point shooters in the league. Players who might possibly have helped in this regard include Jason Kapono, who in the two NBA seasons before the Beijing Games had led the league in three-point percentage; Monta Ellis, a midrange jump-shot artist; and Raja Bell and Rashard Lewis, both of whom had finished among the NBA's top thirty in three-point percentage in the two NBA seasons before the 2008 Olympics.

Just a few days after the roster was announced, ESPN2 aired a five-part, three-hour-long documentary called Road to Redemption presented by Nike. Although the sum in question is not known, Nike provided financial backing to help NBA entertainment produce the series, which reflected the participating entities' market relationships: ESPN aired NBA games, NBA Marketing promoted USA Basketball, and all but one of the Redeem Teamers were under contract with Nike. Not surprisingly, then, the series did have something of the tone of a long commercial, but the unprecedented effort that had gone into creating and financing it also showed how important the Beijing Olympics were to all of these entities. As Nike brand president Charlie Denson said in the summer of 2008, "One of the things we've [Nike] talked about . . . was an ignition point for our basketball business . . . I think about what's going to happen in Beijing . . . we just think this year is special."

In addition, shortly after the team was announced, Nike helped stage an unveiling at Rockefeller Center of the specially designed Team USA basketball mesh uniforms, which Nike claimed were state-of-the-art, "more breathable," and a lighter weight than traditional ones. (Interestingly, a photo Nike made available of the U.S. team in its new uniforms elicited some online blog chatter. In the photo, Coach K's foot blocks almost entirely from view the shoes of Dwight Howard, the only non-Nike player on the roster.)

In keeping with its innovative past, Nike also publicized its creation of a shoe that several Redeem Team players would wear at the Games, called the USA Nike Hyperdunk. It too boasted a svelte design, weighing 18 percent less than the average Nike basketball shoe, and it was touted as the "lightest and strongest basketball shoe" in Nike's history. The shoe also had something Nike dubbed Flywire technology, which, apparently inspired by suspension bridge cables, "basically makes use of a strong Vectran thread [a fiber spun from a liquid crystal polymer] arranged in a fan-shaped pattern at anchor points around the shoe."

Nike even released an ad days before the Beijing Games began that interspersed Redeem Team practice highlights with Marvin Gaye's stirring rendition of the "Star Spangled Banner" at the 1983 All-Star Game. Coach K also blared the Gaye rendition over speakers at the start of a pre-Games practice in order to pump up his team. A Nike marketer emphasized the Redeemers' willingness to put aside "individual recognition" to represent their country as a team in Beijing; however, Nike did have LeBron James and Carmelo Anthony unveil yet more shoes—signature shoes for each individual—the Zoom LeBron VI and M5, respectively, just before the start of the Redeemers' gold medal game. The marketing hype and multi-layered business relationships led Tommy Craggs in *Slate* to maintain that USA Basketball was simply "the NBA wrapped in an American flag." Yet, while critical of the "boy scout troop" marketing of the Redeemers, even Craggs did ultimately admit that Colangelo's reforms of USA Basketball were "substantive."[50]

As it happened, since the Dream Team era, when it had faced labor issues in 1992, Nike had also made some substantive reforms. For years after the 1992 Barcelona Games, Nike battled legal challenges regarding international labor issues that had been brought to the forefront by Jeff Ballinger's article in *Harper's*.[51] Though Nike's initial response was to turn inward—for a while, the company even decided to curtail its social reporting—in time, it realized that such a strategy did not serve its best interests. So rather than receding further in a defensive, taciturn posture, Nike has chosen to be more open, and it seems to be confronting its labor-related issues with at least some significant positive changes. In 2005 Nike became arguably the most transparent major transnational corporation on the planet. That year it resumed the publication of its internal reports, which not only covered areas such as workforce diversity, the environment, community programs, and socially responsible investment, all independently reviewed by a committee of people from trade unions, nongovernmental agencies, academia, and the business community, but also broke new ground "in transparency by publishing a complete list of suppliers on its website." Nike, whose advertisements and whose endorsers often champion values associated with sports and the Olympics—open competition, individuality, innovation, collaborative action, and fair play—has decided that it is in its best interests to push for more corporate responsibility.

Nike also continued its wider-reaching worker education programs and micro-loan programs. The loan program had similarities to programs enacted by the 2006 Nobel Peace Prize winner, the economist Muhammad Yunus. Praising Nike following the announcement of its enhanced transparency, the *Financial Times* asserted that the company's "return to social reporting—particularly with the added level of disclosure in listing its suppliers—provides a forceful counter-argument to those who suggested the Kasky ruling [a court case involving Nike] would discourage corporate transparency." Hannah Jones, Nike's vice president of corporate responsibility, said, "We felt the risks of any future lawsuit were far outweighed by the benefits of transparency. Because if we've learned anything as a company, it's that closing down and not talking about the challenges and opportunities doesn't get you far."[52]

Nike's emphasis on assuming corporate responsibility in this fashion led the *Financial Times* to credit the company with pioneering a new model for corporate responsibility, from one focused on charitable donations or awareness of reputation management and risk avoidance, to one that "sees corporate responsibility as a way of improving its performance rather than just protecting its reputation. Factories that ensure workers are registered for social security benefits often become more productive as a result." Though many critics of Nike remain unmoved, such accomplished economists as Jagdish Bhagwati consider Nike a "fine" multinational corporation.[53] It seems that the liberal capitalist tradition, an event such as the Olympics, the general visibility of sport, and the outspokenness of political agitators can hold corporations like Nike to higher standards.[54]

Following an exhibition game blowout of Canada in Las Vegas, Nevada on July 25, 2008, the U.S. team flew to China. This U.S. team enjoyed rather different accommodations than had Coach Pete Newell on his flight to Rome in 1960: the 2008 team flew on a Cathay Pacific Airlines plane that had seats for the players that turned into beds.[55] Once in China, the team played a series of four exhibition games. The first two games of the four were routs over Turkey and Lithuania. The third game was against the Russian team, which was coached by a Jewish American, David Blatt, who had played under Pete Carril at Princeton and then played and coached in Israel and also coached throughout Europe.[56] Yet again the United States won big, even though Coach K did not think the team looked as sharp as it had in the previous two contests.

In those first three exhibition contests in China, the United States shot a solid 46.2 percent from the three-point line and 70.9 percent from the free-throw line, but in its last exhibition game, in Shanghai against Australia, things did not go as well. "Porous defense, inside and outside. Abysmal 3-point shooting. Bad free-throw shooting," bemoaned ESPN.com's Sheridan, and all of this had happened even though a sore ankle had kept Australia's seven-foot center Andrew Bogut, who played for the Milwaukee Bucks during the NBA season, from suiting up. One of Australia's other roughly seven-foot-tall players, Chris Antsey, helped his squad deal with Bogut's absence by scoring thirteen. Joining Antsey with Australia's scoring honors was the six-foot point guard Patrick Mills, fresh from a standout freshman season at the University of St. Mary's in California, who jetted all over the court. Meanwhile, the Redeemers shot just three of eighteen from beyond the three-point arc and twenty of thirty-three from the free-throw line. The United States did win, 87–76, but worry arose. Trying to downplay the matter, Coach K said, "I was concerned after the last game [against Russia] that they [the U.S. team] were already in Beijing."[57]

Soon after, the team did actually get to Beijing for the host city's eye-popping Opening Ceremony, at which five basketball players carried their country's flag—and none of these flagbearers hailed from the United States. China's Yao Ming, German's Dirk Nowitzki, Argentina's

Manu Ginobli, Russia's Andrei Kirilenko, and Lithuania's Sarunas Jasikevicius were the five: as leaders of their respective nations, Coach K thought, they illustrated basketball's global growth rather poignantly.[58] The opening featured a more than one-hundred-yard-long LED (light-emitting diode) screen that actually comprised 15,000 miniscreens; thousands of dancers in striking synchrony; and a torch lighting that was preceded by what looked on television like a walk through the air. The ceremony cost some $300 million and involved seven years of planning, as well as untold hours of rigorous rehearsal. According to the *Washington Post*, "draconian security deployments" had kept protestors at bay, and the 91,000 in attendance had been "carefully screened," but overall, the paper declared, "on Friday at least, barely anything" went wrong.[59]

Yet within just a few days of the start of the Games, the controlling side of China that makes so many Westerners leery came to the fore. It was revealed that some of the fireworks at the ceremonies had been false, that one of the singers had actually been lip-synching (the real singer had not been deemed attractive enough), and that the demonstration of diversity had been phony (rather than having fifty-six children from each of China's ethnic groups carrying flags, the majority were actually from the Han ethnicity). These revelations tempered the initial rave reviews of Beijing's Opening Ceremony. "Fake fireworks, a fake singer and now fake children at the Olympics opening ceremony," declared a Reuters report. For his part, ESPN's Rick Reilly maintained, "This is what comes from the IOC cashing in its moral ideals for its financial ones. You get an Olympics that pretends to be a nation's coming-out party in newfound freedom and enlightened openness, and you wind up with something as phony as Michael Jackson's nose." Other criticism of Chinese government tactics, such as arresting people for simply *applying* for permits to protest in designated areas, also appeared in the press. Eventually, the media pressure caused the Beijing Organizing Committee and Games spokesman to fire back, "So many criticisms in this room just reflect how biased some of the media are about China, how little some of the media understand China."[60] But that statement certainly did not stop efforts to report on human rights issues.

On the basketball court, the United States followed its opening round win over China by walloping Angola, a country that, in qualifying for the

Games, had continued its strong basketball tradition in Africa. The Angolans might have ended the Olympic tournament with a record of 0-5, but they seemed happy nonetheless to play the Americans. Harkening back images of the heady Dream Team days, members of the Angolan squad came up to LeBron James for pictures and autographs.[61]

Next up for the United States was a preliminary round showdown with Greece. Beforehand, the energy was palpable, and the United States was highly motivated to make a statement against the team that had defeated them two years earlier. And in a sold-out Wukesong Indoor Stadium—all of the U.S. games sold out—just under ten thousand spectators saw the United States do just that. Team USA pushed Greece's high pick-and-roll action away from the top of the key, and on the weak side, the United States met the pick-and-roll with pronounced help defense. Greece felt the pressure. Instead of the 101 points Greece had scored in the 2006 World Championships, this time, it tallied just 69 to the United States' 92. Chris Bosh in particular put his stamp on the game, finishing with eighteen points to complement his stellar defense. Bryant said, "Chris Bosh was terrific . . . he did a great job on the pick and roll and stopping their guards from penetrating."

The team's overall shooting against Greece was not stellar, however. The squad shot just thirteen of twenty-three from the free-throw line for a paltry average of 57 percent. And by the end of the Greece game, the United States had registered a meager 30.7 percentage on three-pointers for the tournament (it would shoot 41.9 percent from the arc for the rest of the way, which resulted in a respectable 37.7 three-point percentage by the tournament's end). Nonetheless, the win had avenged the United States' only loss from the 2006 World Championships, secured the team a berth in the quarterfinal phase of the Olympic tournament—from which point three straight wins were needed for gold—and gave the United States a 3-0 record going into a showdown with perhaps its greatest threat, the 2006 FIBA World Champion Spain.[62]

Those who feared that after the intense win over Greece, Team USA would experience a letdown against the undefeated Spain saw those concerns fade pretty early on. The Spanish team boasted the LA Lakers' seven-foot star center Pau Gasol; his seven-feet-one-inch brother Marc, who would soon arrive in the NBA himself; the Toronto Raptors' impressive six-feet-three-inch point guard Jose Calderon; the recently drafted, six-feet-four-inch and super-athletic Rudy Fernandez, who as a youngster had put a poster of Dream Teamer Clyde Drexler on his bedroom wall; and the former Memphis Grizzly player Juan Navarro, who stood six feet three. In addition, there was the seventeen-year-old, six-feet-four-inch Ricky Rubio, a top-five pick in the 2009 NBA draft, who would end up playing a big role by tournament's end. Spain had experienced role players, too—in particular, the six-feet-nine-inch forwards Felipe Reyes and Carlos Jiminez. But in this game, Spain's fine roster did not matter. The United States forced seventeen first-half turnovers, and Spain exacerbated its woes by trying to use the full-court press against the United States. This prompted ESPN. com's Sheridan to write, "If another team tries to use the full-court press against Team USA, it might as well walk off the court and forfeit."[63]

Early in the second frame, the United States pulled away further and ultimately registered a 119–82 victory. The game featured the United States' speedy team defense, spectacular fast-break capabilities, and individual skill, and it gave the United States a great chance at securing the top seed among its bracket of four teams for the quarterfinal phase.

Although its opener against China was broadcast on NBC, the Redeem Team's next three games aired in America on the USA Network, an affiliate of NBC. The contests were also streamed, as were all Olympic tourney basketball games, on an NBC Web channel devoted completely to basketball.

NBC's comprehensive plan to deliver a staggering 3,600 hours of Olympic coverage at huge costs had carried with it some uncertainty, but by the time the Redeemers met Spain in the preliminary round, indications were emerging that NBC would succeed in reaching record numbers through its multiple platform strategy. And by the Olympics' end, NBC would attract more than 211 million American viewers, an all-time U.S. record for a television event.

The network also turned a profit by selling over $1 billion in advertising after paying $894 million for its Beijing rights compared to CBS's $394,000 in 1960. In addition, NBC's cable ratings rose by 30 percent compared to the figures for Athens. Finally, the network broke "all kinds of records" for online broadcasting by landing 50 million unique Web visits and delivering a combined 10 million hours of video coverage online. Not unlike fears several decades earlier about whether television would detract from the gate, there had been some concern about online content taking a chunk out of television's performance. But NBC's results prompted NBC Universal CEO Jeff Zucker to assert, "Digital content does not cannibalize television."[64] China's state-run China Central Television (CCTV) also did quite well. Near the end of the Olympics, over 80 percent of Chinese households had accessed some of CCTV's coverage. The Morgan Stanley analyst Richard Ji called CCTV a "powerhouse in China" and said, "Global brands want to tap into China's consumer market." Given that firms such as Adidas and Coca-Cola advertised with CCTV and the NBA had a marketing relationship with the network, Ji foresaw global brands as "one of the biggest beneficiaries of the Olympics."[65]

The U.S. hoops team finished preliminary round play with a lopsided victory over Germany, a team woefully unable to match up with the United States even though it was anchored by the Dallas Mavericks' Dirk Nowitzki and the LA Clippers' Chris Kaman (Kaman grew up in Michigan but was able to suit up for Germany because his great-grandparents had lived there). Dwight Howard was unfazed by the duo of seven-footers; he sank nine of ten field goals for twenty-two points and grabbed ten rebounds.[66]

This win finished pool play, and fittingly, the U.S. swimming star Michael Phelps visited the U.S. basketball squad afterward to show support and congratulate the players.[67] The visit was another indication of how the Redeem Team had ingratiated itself with fellow Olympians, and the media made sure to cover it. The squad might have stayed in a luxury hotel, but the media made less of the team staying outside of the Olympic Village than it had with the beloved original Dream Team. And yet, like the Dream Team, this team had a high level of appeal. Stories abounded—such as those about Dwyane Wade and Michael Redd having bought churches for a parent, about the religious-minded Dwight Howard, or about the overall enthusiasm that the team had demonstrated in Beijing. In addition, players got good press from a media that largely embraced the team for deciding to visit the Olympic Village shortly after arriving in Beijing. And the fact that they were virtually mobbed at the village made it easy to explain why they were not staying there. Critics might call these efforts of the U.S. basketball players to "reach out" contrived, but the behavior seemed genuine and generated a good vibe between the U.S. basketball players and other Olympians.[68]

The United States opened the quarterfinal medal round with a walloping of Australia. The close exhibition tilt between the two that had taken place about two weeks earlier had raised questions about Team USA. However, in this game, an Australian squad that was, according to the on-site reporter Adrian Wojnarowski, "full of big talk" and had tried during the game to "lure the U.S. into a scrap with hard fouls and smart mouths," came up way short on the scoreboard, 116–85.

Even though the team had won with such a wide margin of victory and even though only two games now separated the United States from gold, reports indicated the players' focus remained steady. Tellingly, Wojnarowski reported that almost an hour after the Australia game, Paul, James, Anthony, and Wade were talking about sets and plays in the Wukesong Indoor Stadium, rather than having returned to their five-star hotel. Wojnarowski thought this reflected what he had come to observe—a team that had "invested itself completely into this tournament," one that was "taking teams and preparations with a stone-cold seriousness."[69] This report offered yet another example of the stark difference in the way the media covered the 2008 team as compared to 2004's.

On account of the Argentines' two-point win over Greece in another quarterfinal game, the United States faced them next. This gave Team USA a chance to avenge its 2004 loss to Argentina in the semifinals in Athens. For Bryant, this was fitting. Even before Argentina had squeaked by Greece, Bryant told Wojnarowski, "Argentina is the defending champs. You want to be able to play the guys that won it the last time."[70]

The game ended up being rather odd. The United States dominated early, racing ahead 34–13 by the end of the first quarter, but then it struggled in the second quarter. The Argentines cut the lead to 46–40 deep in the opening half, even though the San Antonio Spurs' acrobatic shot-conjurer Manu Ginobli had left the game in the first quarter with a gimpy ankle and the Chicago Bulls' Andres Nocioni wore a brace on a knee that obviously hampered him. As ESPN.com's Chris Sheridan noted, strong play down low by Argentina, by the likes of the Houston Rockets' Luis Scola, and a physical zone defense, which baited the United States into twenty first-half three-point attempts compared to just thirteen two-pointers, helped Argentina climb back into the game.[71]

In the second half, Argentina stayed relatively close for stretches, but from about midway through the third quarter, it never came within twelve points of the United States. Led by Carmelo Anthony's twenty-one points, the United States finished the game with a 101–81 victory. This victory seemed harder than the score indicated, and in a way, that made sense. As early as 1948, when Argentina lost to the U.S. Olympians by just two points, it had presented a challenge to the United States. In 1952 the otherwise dominant U.S. squad had beaten Argentina by only nine points, and though in 1996 Dream Team II had delivered a 96–68 win, in 2004, of course, Argentina had won 89–81. For Sheridan, the 2008 Argentina versus U.S. game provided a blueprint for Spain on how to approach the Redeemers: play lots of zone, be physical, and try to capitalize in the frontcourt.[72]

Indeed, Spain, which four years earlier in the Olympics had played man-to-man against the United States in a losing quarterfinal effort and had already tried a full-court press in Beijing, played a lot of zone against America this time. And down low, its big men Pau Gasol (twenty-one points and six rebounds), Felipe Reyes (ten points, seven rebounds), and Marc Gasol (eleven points, five rebounds) played well. But so too did Dwyane Wade, especially in the first half when Bryant and James both spent stretches on the bench with two fouls. In that opening frame, Wade, who ended the tournament as the United States' top scorer with a sixteen-point average in just eighteen minutes per game, scored twenty-one points.

At the midway point, the United States held a 69–61 advantage, which put the two teams on pace to combine for 260 points. Afterward, the AP's Brian Mahoney characterized the game as "devoid of defense"; however, although there were surely some defensive shortcomings, the scoring seemed more the result of great offense.[73]

Scoring tailed off a bit in the second half, but the drama did not. Spain kept within striking distance even though it was playing without injured star point guard Jose Calderon. And with just over eight minutes remaining, the twenty-three-year-old Rudy Fernandez, who was Spain's high scorer in the game with twenty-two points and who had rammed home an eye-popping slam on Dwight Howard in the second half, drained a three-point shot that tightened the score to 91–89, prompting a U.S. time-out. Coach K recalled that as the players came to the bench, he was thinking that "this team *was* worthy of winning and that I trusted who we had become." He believed that there is a time to call a play, and then there is a time to let them play, and breaking the huddle on this occasion, he simply told his team, "Just go out there and play."[74] From then on, the game was packed with uncertainty and any number of game-changing plays. In the end, the playmaking of James, Bryant, and Wade proved critical. Bryant in particular delivered several clutch plays down the stretch, whether a shot from the outside, the inside, or an assist. Perhaps biggest of all, with a little more than three minutes to go, Bryant connected on a three-point shot over Rudy Fernandez and got fouled. He sunk the free throw for a four-point play that gave the United States a nine-point cushion. Yet Spain netted the next five points, three of them on a big-time three-pointer by captain Jiminez that cut the U.S. lead to four. But then, on a kick-out from Bryant, Wade answered with a gargantuan three of his own. James then rebounded a Spain miss, and Bryant delivered a pull-up jumper in the lane. It was only a matter of time before the United States could celebrate a hard-fought gold medal win. As Pau Gasol said afterward, "They had to work for it." James concurred. "Every possession counted," he stated.[75]

For so many, the win meant so much. For Dwayne Wade, it meant redemption for the Athens loss, the chance to win gold for his country, and an opportunity to show that he had been counted out too soon. To be sure, it also likely meant the opportunity to make more money, and Wade had not denied that during the Games. But this team in general seemed to appreciate the Olympic experience for reasons that went beyond monetary gain. "To be a part of the 2008 Olympic team, to play with the best players in the world . . . it's just amazing," Wade said upon arriving back in the States.[76] He knew that the U.S. men's hoopers had been derided as "high-paid showboat athletes," and he was eager to show that they were much more than that.[77] He and his mates did.

Many Americans reveled in the Redeem Team's performance, but some had expected more from the team. ESPN.com's Scoop Jackson legitimately noted that the gold medal game had been close even though Calderon had sat out and Spain had relied heavily on a seventeen-year-old point guard in Rubio; he also mentioned Ginobli's injury in the Argentina game.[78] In offering such criticism, Jackson was not alone: indeed, it seemed as if a decent number of Americans still expected blowouts from their Olympic basketball teams. However, such sentiments overlook that in the 2002 World Championships and 2004 Olympics, with teams that had many very

21. Team USA reclaims gold. Photo by Garrett Ellwood. National Basketball Association Collection/Getty Images.

strong NBA players, the United States had gone a combined 10-6. With NBA-quality players dotting so many international rosters, it seems that Olympic tournaments dominated by the United States will more likely become the exception than the rule.

As billions turned their eyes toward Beijing for the 2008 Olympics and as all of those Games' attendant issues arose, people saw a U.S. men's basketball team that represented the popularity of sports in the modern era. With Wade, Kobe, and James out front, the team mirrored the delicate balance between the community and the individual, the dynamism that competition can generate, and the opportunity that sports provide. The squad's revamped roster and attitude also, ironically, reflected the influence of the international game on the nation where basketball was invented. In this sense, the game truly had switched from American hoops into hoops international.

However, there are still ways in which FIBA was adopting elements of the American game. Before the Beijing Games, FIBA announced rules changes that would be in effect in the year 2010. Among them, the trapezoid lane will become rectangular, much like the recently widened lane in the NBA. FIBA also decided to put a "no charge" arc around the basket to open up room for drives and elevation around the basket, another change that the NBA had already implemented. Finally, FIBA's three-point arc will be pushed back to within a half of a meter of the line already in use in the NBA. The NCAA, coincidentally, has also pushed back its three-point line, perhaps suggesting that FIBA has influenced it.[79]

It seemed evident, certainly by the summer of 2009, that playing on the U.S. basketball team in the Olympics had once again become a coveted opportunity, and one that could propel careers. In 2008–9, the NBA was dominated by those who had played in Beijing. The top five vote getters for that year's MVP award were LeBron James, who won it, followed by Kobe Bryant, Dwyane Wade, Dwight Howard, and Chris Paul—all members of the 2008 Olympic team. In addition, when Interbasket.net put out its list of the NBA's top-performing international players, every member of the top five had played in Beijing, or, as in the case of Tony Parker, had wanted to play there.[80] Furthermore, the Olympians of 2008 anchored nearly every contending team in the NBA, whether it was James's Cavaliers, Howard's Magic, Anthony's Nuggets, or Bryant's NBA champion Lakers.

Yet it seems that some still remain critical of having NBA players participate in the Olympics. Concerns about wear and tear have kept Lakers coach Phil Jackson from supporting having players there; his concerns are shared by Mark Cuban, the owner of the Dallas Mavericks. Surely, there is some risk, but the wear-and-tear theory appears to ignore the potential benefits that the Games offer players—such as the sharing of workout strategies that could enhance a player's longevity, and an increase in confidence and leadership abilities. In addition, the Olympics can help players stay fit while training with the world's best. Another concern of Cuban's is that the Olympics get to use the NBA brand and its assets too freely. According to him, the NBA should simply start its own international tournament.[81] In the late 1980s and into the 1990s, though, the NBA did try to get an international tournament to thrive—the McDonald's Open. It ceased operations in 1999.

The aforementioned performance of the Redeemers in the 2008–9 NBA season and the television ratings of that year's playoffs suggest that the Olympics can enable the NBA to raise its level of play at home while offering a unique opportunity to build goodwill and visibility on the international stage. In the wake of the tremendous number of viewers that the Olympic tournament attracted, the NBA delivered record-setting ratings for ESPN's and TNT's coverage of the 2009 playoffs. And that year, the global reach of the NBA continued to be the key factor that separated it from other domestic professional sports leagues.[82]

The key is to do the Olympics intelligently. The late Chuck Daly certainly got credit for doing just that with the 1992 Dream Team's stable of stars. And after Beijing, Coach K deserved credit for building upon the Daly model so that it still worked for the NBA's stars even though those stars faced an environment of increased international competitiveness.

By the summer of 2009, those who welcomed the resurgent performance of the NBA players at the Olympics in Beijing could look forward to a similar model for the 2012 London Games. Jerry Colangelo had announced his intention to remain as chairman of USA Basketball by then, while numerous Redeem Team members had expressed a desire to play in London and Coach K had agreed to man the U.S. sideline in England.[83] Perhaps in 2012 LeBron James will, like Jackie Robinson had in 1948 when Elizabeth was still the queen-in-waiting, find himself having high tea with Queen Elizabeth II. Given basketball's dramatic developments in the interim, what a connection those two points in time would make.

Surely, at the least, the Olympic basketball tournament serves as a far-reaching nexus of exchange—a peaceful movement that people all over the world share interest in. It includes contributions by coaches and players that span the globe. The performances of nations like Argentina, Lithuania, and China, and the success of international stars, such as Argentina's Manu Ginobli, China's Yao Ming, and Germany's Dirk Nowitzki, along with Wade, Bryant, and James, symbolize active international participation in basketball. And this integrated realm takes place within the context of a global culture and a sporting environment of phenomenal appeal that compliments universalism and openness.

So, to the individual sportsman, corporate employee, fan, political agitator, and consumer, whether watching Olympic basketball through traditional television broadcasts, streamlining broadband video over the Internet, receiving satellite signals beamed to a cell phone, or downloading images to an iPod: may we all continue to enjoy the action. It will be hard not to.

Ediz. Plurigraf - Via Flaminia km 90 - Tel. 0744 - 715946 - (Tr)

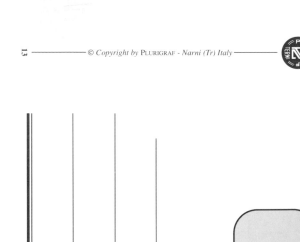

TABLE 17. 2008 U.S. Men's Olympic Basketball cumulative stats

NAME	G/S	FGM-FCA	(%)	3PM-3PA	(%)	FTM-FTA	(%)	REB/AVG	PTS/AVG	AST	BLK	ST
Dwyane Wade	8/0	47-70	.671	8-17	.471	26-41	.634	32/4.0	128/16.0	15	1	18
LeBron James	8/8	50-83	.602	13-28	.464	11-24	.458	42/5.3	124/15.5	30	8	19
Kobe Bryant	8/8	48-104	.462	17-53	.321	7-12	.583	22/2.8	120/15.0	17	4	9
Carmelo Anthony	8/8	27-64	.422	14-37	.378	24-29	.828	34/4.3	92/11.5	3	2	8
Dwight Howard	8/8	35-47	.745	0-0	.000	17-37	.459	46/5.8	87/10.9	4	7	5
Chris Bosh	8/0	24-31	.774	0-0	.000	25-29	.862	49/6.1	73/9.1	2	6	2
Deron Williams	8/0	23-52	.442	9-24	.375	9-10	.900	18/2.3	64/8.0	22	0	6
Chris Paul	8/0	19-38	.500	4-14	.286	22-24	.917	29/3.6	64/8.0	33	0	18
Tayshaun Prince	8/0	13-22	.591	6-11	.545	2-5	.500	15/1.9	34/4.3	2	1	3
Carlos Boozer	8/0	10-18	.556	0-0	.000	6-8	.750	15/1.9	26/3.3	2	0	2
Michael Redd	8/0	10-31	.323	5-18	.278	0-1	.000	9/1.1	25/3.1	4	0	2
Jason Kidd	8/8	6-7	.857	1-2	.500	0-0	.000	21/2.6	13/1.6	16	2	5
USA TOTALS	8	312-567	.550	77-204	.377	149-219	.680	332/41.5	850/106.2	150	31	97
OPP. TOTALS	8	222-551	.403	60-201	.299	123-156	.788	287/35.9	627/78.4	85	29	53

NOTES

INTRODUCTION

1. "The Final Tally—4.7 Billion Tunes in to Beijing 2008—More Than Two in Three People Worldwide," Nielsen Company press release, 5 September 2008, Hong Kong, http://blog.nielsen.com/nielsenwire/wp-content/uploads/2008/09/press_release3 .pdf (accessed 1 February 2009).

2. Originally, in 1936, FIBA was the International Basketball Federation (FIBB). Later, the letter A in FIBA stood for "amateur," though throughout the second half of the twentieth century just about everywhere, its top-level members did not compete as true amateurs. In 1989 FIBA dropped the word "amateur" from its official title but kept the abbreviated name FIBA.

3. *Daily News*, 11 August 1998.

4. *New York Times*, 26 July 1992.

5. Qtd. in Jack McCallum, "USA, Inc.," *Sports Illustrated*, 22 July 1992, 124.

6. David Halberstam writes that before Jordan's performance in Barcelona and the subsequent five years of mounting fame, he used to enjoy anonymity in Paris. After Barcelona, Jordan's popularity brought him tremendous riches and nearly universal recognition, but he lost Paris. He was mobbed wherever he went. David Halberstam, *Playing for Keeps: Michael Jordan and the World He Made* (Random House: New York, 1999), 4.

7. Walter LaFeber, *Michael Jordan and the New Global Capitalism* (W. W. Norton: New York, 1999), 27.

8. John Wooden, interview by author, 12 August 2006, Westwood CA, handwritten notes.

9. *Olympic Charter*, paragraph 2, http://www.olympic.org/uk/organisation/missions/ charter_uk.asp (accessed 20 March 2006); Phillip Hersh, "Rogge Stands Tall," *Chicago Tribune*, 11 April 2008, http://www.chicagotribune.com/sports/cs-11-hersh-on-olym pics-beijingapr11,0,4824776.story (accessed 15 April 2008). Barbara Keys has highlighted the "western" nature of the rise of international sport in the 1930s, the role of European and American members of the IOC in shaping international sport, and how international sport has promoted "universalism" and "commercialism," particularly since the 1930s. Barbara J. Keys, *Globalizing Sport: National Rivalry and International Community in the 1930s* (Cambridge: Harvard University Press, 2006), 4–5. In 2004, Richard Pound, an IOC member for decades and two-time vice president of the IOC, explained the modern Olympic movement by writing, "One of the principal objectives . . . is a commitment

to universality and the concept of human dignity, including freedom from all forms of discrimination, whether based on race, religion, color or gender." He recognized that challenges have arisen realizing the goals of carrying out the movement but added that the IOC had "one of the best records of any organization in the world" in practicing what it preaches. Richard Pound, *Inside the Olympics: A Behind-the-Scenes Look at the Politics, the Scandals, and the Glory of the Games* (Canada: Wiley, 2004), 115–16.

10. Pound, *Inside the Olympics*, 144–46, 168–71, 195.

11. Though the AAU was officially classified as amateur, in 1936 *Time* magazine quite plainly noted its commercialism. Explaining why Globe Oil sponsored its AAU team (the McPherson Oilers), *Time* asserted, "Like Universal Pictures' five, and thousands of similar groups in the U.S., they are a company promotion scheme." That year, members of the AAU's McPherson Oilers squad and the "Universal" team (sponsored by Universal Pictures) made up the first U.S. Olympic basketball roster. "Olympic Basketballers," *Time*, 13 April 1936, http://www.time.com/time/magazine/printout/0,8816,755998,00.html (accessed 7 October 2006).

12. Yuri Brokhin, *The Big Red Machine: The Rise and Fall of Soviet Olympic Champions* (New York: Random House, 1978), 135.

13. Pete Newell, interview by author, 23 June 2008, Ogden Dunes IN, tape recording.

14. These technological innovations came about partly because, as Martin Wolf, borrowing from William Baumol, has noted, "innovation rather than price competition is the central feature of the market process." Martin Wolf, *Why Globalization Works* (New Haven: Yale University Press, 2004), 51.

15. Thomas L. Friedman, *The World Is Flat: A Brief History of the Twenty-First Century* (New York: Farrar, Straus and Giroux, 2005), 250–51.

16. Robert Ray, *A Certain Tendency of the Hollywood Cinema, 1930–1980* (Princeton: Princeton University Press, 1985), 58.

17. Scott Bedbury, *A New Brand World: 8 Principles for Achieving Brand Leadership in the 21st Century* (New York: Penguin Books, 2002), 91–93.

18. Ray, *Certain Tendency of Hollywood Cinema*, 21.

19. Associated Press, "2008 Olympics Changes Events for U.S. TV," 26 October 2006, available from http://www.highbeam.com/doc/1Y1-99574216.html (accessed 11 August 2007).

20. "NBA Players from around the World: 2007–08 Season," 7 August 2008, NBA.com, http://www.nba.com/players/int_players_0708.html (accessed 1 February 2009); *Washington Post*, 28 August 2004; *Washington Times*, 11 August 2004.

1. AMERICAN HOOPS IN BERLIN

1. *New York Times*, 15 August 1936.

2. *Washington Post*, 15 August 1936.

3. Jim Needles, "Olympic Basketball," *Converse 1935–1936 Basketball Yearbook*, 15th ed. (Malden MA: Converse Rubber Company, 1935/36), 22–23 (Duplicate from the Edward J. and Gena G. Hickox Library, Basketball Hall of Fame, Springfield MA [hereafter referred

to as the Hickox Library], housed at the Notre Dame Archives, South Bend IN); Clair Bee, "Basketball Speeds Up," *Converse 1935–1936 Basketball Yearbook*, 15th ed. (Malden MA: Converse Rubber Company, 1935/36), 41 (Duplicate from the Hickox Library, housed at the Notre Dame Archives, South Bend IN). Holman noted eight Madison Square Garden doubleheaders that attracted some 100,000 spectators as examples of the rules' popularity. Nat Holman, "1934–35 Basketball Season Makes History in the East," *Converse 1934–1935 Basketball Yearbook*, 14th ed. (Malden MA: Converse Rubber Company, 1934/35), 20 (Duplicate from the Amateur Athletic Foundation Library, Los Angeles CA).

4. *New York Times*, 8 August 1936.

5. Brad Herzog, "The Original Dream Team," *Basketball Digest*, 22 June 2000, available from http://www.highbeam.com/library/doc3.asp?DOCID=1G1:65642441&num=1& ctrlInfo=Round15%3AProd%3ASR%3AResult&ao=&FreePremium=BOTH (accessed 20 August 2005).

6. Qtd. in Alexander Wolff, *Basketball: A History of the Game* (New York: Bishop Books, 1991), 196.

7. "Basketball: Favorite of 20,000,000 Popular All Over the World with Variations in Play and Rules," *Literary Digest*, 2 January 1937, 33.

8. Allen Guttmann, *The Olympics: A History of the Modern Games* (Urbana: University of Illinois Press, 2002), 53–54.

9. Barbara J. Keys, *Globalizing Sport: National Rivalry and International Community in the 1930s* (Cambridge: Harvard University Press, 2006), 4–5, 157.

10. David Clay Large, *Nazi Games: The Olympics of 1936* (W. W. Norton: New York, 2007), 8; Guttmann, *The Olympics*, 56–57.

11. Large, *Nazi Games*, 316–17.

12. Keys, *Globalizing Sport*, 157.

13. The sports historian Allen Guttmann argues that Brundage viewed the boycott as a movement driven by Jews. Allen Guttmann, *The Games Must Go On: Avery Brundage and the Olympic Movement* (New York: Columbia University Press, 1984).

14. Edward Lapchick, *The Politics of Race and International Sport* (Westport: Greenwood Press, 1975), xvi. Not everyone felt such warmth in Berlin. Brundage's comments contrast with those of the U.S. basketball player Art Mollner. Upon making it to Berlin, Mollner rode into the Olympic Village on a bus. According to Mollner, almost immediately, he and his mates "noticed hooks on the ceiling [presumably, he meant roofs] of our Olympic Village rooms. Those hooks were camouflage hooks, so we knew they were going to use this Olympic Village as a barracks for soldiers. But they were also looking forward to when they would go to war." Arthur O. Mollner, interview by George A. Hodak, May 1988, Westlake Village CA, http://www.aafla.org/6oic/OralHistory/OHMollner.pdf (accessed 17 September 2006).

15. The International Basketball Federation, or FIBB, the forefather of today's FIBA, gained recognition when men's basketball was included on the 1936 Berlin Olympic program. By 2006 FIBA had over two hundred members and was divided into five regional zones covering every continent except Antarctica.

16. As early as 1933 the American Olympic Association (AOA) came out against Berlin

as the host site, and in 1934 the New York Republican representative Emmanuel Celler asserted that Brundage "prejudged the situation before he sailed from America." Guttmann, *The Olympics*, 59. See also Duff Hart-Davis, *Hitler's Games: The 1936 Olympics* (London: Century Hutchinson, 1986), 15; "Shorts: 'Parliamentary Trick' Keeps United States in Germany Olympics," *Newsweek*, 14 December 1935, 27.

17. "Shorts: 'Parliamentary Trick,'" 27.

18. Clair Bee is credited with helping implement the three-seconds-in-the-lane rule, creating the one-three-one zone defense, and, as coach of the NBA's Baltimore Bullets, pushing for the twenty-four-second shot clock. From 1931 to 1951 his Long Island teams won 95 percent of their games.

19. Mollner interview.

20. Kay Schaffer and Sidonie Smith, *The Olympics at the Millennium: Power, Politics, and the Games* (New Brunswick: Rutgers University Press, 2000), 59.

21. Jews in Sports, http://www.jewsinsports.org/olympics.asp?sport=olympics&ID=99 (accessed 13 October 2004).

22. Mollner interview; Herzog, "Original Dream Team"; Large, *Nazi Games*, 278–79.

23. After the Olympics, Laemmle stopped backing the Universal AAU team, so the players, according to Mollner, "went over to Fox studio." Mollner interview.

24. Gene Johnson reportedly came up with the idea of Globe Oil sponsoring an AAU team in 1934, when he worked for the company as a sales manager. "Olympic Basketballers," *Time*, 13 April 1936, http://www.time.com/time/magazine/printout/0,8816,755998,00.html (accessed 7 October 2006).

25. The regional tournament system was so complicated that the committee hired Creighton University's athletic director, Mr. A. A. Schabinger, to run it. The NCAA teams were expected to participate in these regional tournaments at their own expense, and proceeds from the contests went to U.S. Olympic Basketball, not the NCAA. Finally, the committee deemed fourth-year seniors ineligible, though in February 1936 the committee made an exception to this rule. The exception allowed NCAA teams that had recently adopted the three-year rule, which barred freshman from playing varsity, to allow their fourth-year men to participate in qualifying action. *Los Angeles Times*, 3 February 1936.

26. *Los Angeles Times*, 2 April 1936.

27. Frederick W. Rubien, ed., *Games of the XI Olympiad: U.S. Olympic Committee Official Report* (New York: USOC Report of the American Olympic Committee, 1936), 166.

28. *Washington Post*, 4 March 1936; "West under East," *Time*, 6 January 1936, http://www.time.com/time/magazine/printout/0,8816,755998,00.html (accessed 7 October 2006). In March 1936, *Time* reported that Clair Bee's LIU squad had "suddenly replaced huge NYU . . . as New York City's basketball favorite." *Time* also noted that 13,000 fans had recently turned out to watch LIU play Rice Institute and listed Bee's squad among the Olympic trials contenders. "Long Island's Streak," *Time*, 2 March 1936, http://www.time.com/time/magazine/printout/0,8816,755998,00.html (accessed 7 October 2006).

29. Rubien, *Games of the XI Olympiad*, 166. Some stages of the process did do well—

for example, there was a strong demand for tickets at the University of Washington to determine the Pacific Coast collegiate representative—but on balance, the process fell well short of its financial goals. *Los Angeles Times*, 24 March 1936.

30. As a further indication of the sport's growth, that season NYU and Long Island University played games in Madison Square Garden against the likes of Purdue and Kentucky, and those contests generated phenomenal interest. "Basketball: NYU Quins Make It More Popular than Football," *Newsweek*, 18 January 1936, 30.

31. "Olympic Basketballers," *Time*, 13 April 1936, http://www.time.com/time/magazine/printout/0,8816,755998,00.html (accessed 7 October 2006).

32. In an interview in 1996, Francis Johnson said, "The oil refinery I worked for in McPherson told us if we went to the Olympics we wouldn't have jobs when we got back." Qtd. in Herzog, "Original Dream Team," n5.

33. *Los Angeles Times*, 6 July 1936.

34. "Olympic Basketballers."

35. *Los Angeles Times*, 6 July 1936; Jack Lippert, "Basketball's Greatest Show," *Converse 1935–36 Basketball Yearbook* (Malden MA: Converse Rubber Company, 1935/36), 43 (Amateur Athletic Library, Los Angeles CA).

36. Frank Lubin, interview by George A. Hodak, May 1988, Glendale CA, http://www.aafla.org/6oic/OralHistory/OHLubin.pdf (accessed 11 September 2006).

37. Lubin interview.

38. Lubin claimed he was six feet six and a half. See Lubin interview.

39. Lubin interview.

40. Lubin interview; Bob Phillips, *The 1948 Olympics: How London Rescued the Games* (Cheltenham: SportsBooks Limited, 2007), 144.

41. Lubin interview.

42. Lubin interview.

43. *Los Angeles Times*, 6 July 1936.

44. Blair Kerkhoff, *Phog Allen: The Father of Basketball Coaching* (Indianapolis: Masters Press, 1996), 111.

45. Mollner interview.

46. Kerkhoff, *Phog Allen*, 106.

47. Lubin interview.

48. In his interview with George A. Hodak, Lubin said the committee suspected him of having played semipro baseball, too, but that Goldstein helped deflect that suspicion by telling committee members, "'It wasn't Lubin.'" Therefore, as Lubin explained, "We were down to seven players and played seven players all the time." Mollner, in an interview with Hodak in the late 1980s, maintained that Goldstein reaped the benefits of not going to the Berlin Olympics by becoming the head electrician (of Universal) "and he's a millionaire today, living in Palm Springs," *Los Angeles Times*, 7 April 1936 and 5 April 1936.

49. Jon Mark Beilue, "Fortenberry Stood Tall in Basketball's Early Days," *Amarillo Globe-News*, 3 January 1999, http://www.amarillonet.com/stories/010399/spo_170-5537.001.shtml (accessed 29 May 2004).

50. Beilue, "Fortenberry Stood Tall"; Adolph H. Grundman, *The Golden Age of Ama-*

teur Basketball: The AAU *Tournament, 1921–1968* (Lincoln: University of Nebraska Press, 2004), 76.

51. Qtd. in Chris Broussard, "A Game Played Above the Rim, Above All Else," *New York Times* 15 February 2004, http://nytimes.com/2004/02/15/sports/basketball/15DUNK .html (accessed 15 October 2004).

52. Broussard, "Game Played Above the Rim."

53. *The Amateur Athlete*, no. 5 (May 1936): 14 (Amateur Athletic Union [AAU] Archives, Orlando FL).

54. Dr. Joseph A. Reilly, director of the Kansas City Athletic Club and a member of the Olympic Basketball Committee, accompanied the squad as team manager.

55. Lubin interview.

56. Mollner interview.

57. Bruce Jenkins, *A Good Man: The Pete Newell Story* (Berkeley: Frog, 1999), 11.

58. Jenkins, *A Good Man*, 14.

59. Jenkins, *A Good Man*, 15.

60. Kerkhoff, *Phog Allen*, 107–9; Oswald Tower, "Basketball Hits a New High," *Converse 1935–1936 Basketball Yearbook*, 15th ed. (Malden: Converse Rubber Company, 1935/36), 41 (Duplicate from the Hickox Library, housed at the Notre Dame Archives, South Bend IN).

61. Adolph H. Grundman, "AAU-NCAA Politics: Forrest C. 'Phog' Allen and America's First Olympic Basketball Team," *Olympika: The International Journal of Olympic Studies* 5 (1996): 118.

62. Grundman, "AAU-NCAA Politics," 118.

63. *Washington Post*, 6 May 1936.

64. However, oddly enough, into the late 1940s and early 1950s Dr. Allen funneled his players to the AAU/NIBL, particularly to his good friend and Phillips Petroleum president K. S. "Boots" Adams. Some in fact found the Adams-Allen friendship suspicious. Kerkhoff, *Phog Allen*, 110–13.

65. Grundman, "AAU-NCAA Politics," 118–19.

66. *Washington Post*, 6 May 1936.

67. Mollner interview.

68. *Los Angeles Times*, 7 April 1936.

69. Sam Balter, "Olympic Basketball," *The Amateur Athlete*, no. 10 (October 1936): 12 (AAU Archives, Orlando FL).

70. *Los Angeles Times*, 7 April 1936.

71. "Basketball: Favorite of 20,000,000," 32.

72. Keys, *Globalizing Sport*, 149; Large, *Nazi Games*, 278.

73. *Washington Post*, 2 August 1936.

74. "Olympic Games," *Time*, 17 August 1936, http://www.time.com/time/magazine/ printout/0,8816,755998,00.html (accessed 7 October 2006).

75. Keys, *Globalizing Sport*, 149.

76. "Do You Know That," *The Amateur Athlete*, no. 5 (May 1936): 14 (AAU Archives, Orlando FL); Keys, *Globalizing Sport*, 148; Ronald A. Smith, *Play-by-Play: Radio, Tele-*

vision, and Big-Time College Sport (Baltimore: Johns Hopkins University Press, 2001), 48.

77. Mollner interview.

78. Just before it did open, representatives from fourteen basketball nations settled a dispute between Mexico and the United States over how to organize the tournament schedule. The United States wanted a draw after each round, while Mexico wanted the loser of each game to have the right to pick its next opponent. The United States thought this would lead to too much squabbling among teams. In a 9–5 vote, the representatives ultimately decided on the "draw" method, which, as the *Los Angeles Times* noted, inserted "an element of luck into the championship." *Los Angeles Times*, 6 August 1936.

79. Needles, "Olympic Basketball," 22.

80. Needles, "Olympic Basketball," 23.

81. Balter, "Olympic Basketball," 10, 12.

82. Needles, "Olympic Basketball," 22.

83. Balter, "Olympic Basketball," 5.

84. Balter, "Olympic Basketball," 10.

85. *Chicago Tribune*, 14 August 1936.

86. Rubien, *Games of the XI Olympiad*, 167.

87. "Basketball: Favorite of 20,000,000," 32.

88. Balter, "Olympic Basketball," 10.

89. Balter, "Olympic Basketball," 10; Large, *Nazi Games*, 279.

90. "The History of Converse," Converse press release, http://www.converse.com/LiveFiles/7/11/Timeline.pdf (accessed 17 May 2005).

91. Balter, "Olympic Basketball," 10; Large, *Nazi Games*, 278.

92. "History of Converse."

93. *Wall Street Journal*, 11 February 1927.

94. Sol Metzger, "Basketball—The National Game," *Converse 1931 Basketball Yearbook—Section One* (Malden MA: Converse Rubber Company, 1931), 7. Reprinted from the *Country Gentleman*. (Duplicate from the Hickox Library, housed at the Amateur Athletic Library in Los Angeles CA).

95. Balter, "Olympic Basketball," 10.

96. Balter, "Olympic Basketball," 10.

97. Balter, "Olympic Basketball," 10.

98. *New York Times*, 15 August 1936.

99. Arthur Daley, *New York Times*, 17 August 1936.

100. Lubin interview.

101. Mollner interview.

102. Official Website of the Olympic Movement, http://www.olympic.org/uk/organisation/missions/charter_uk.asp (accessed 15 November 2004).

103. Keys, *Globalizing Sport*, 157.

104. Needles, "Olympic Basketball," 23.

105. *Washington Post*, 24 January 1937.

106. Newell credits the legendary USC basketball, baseball, and football coach Justin

"Sam" Baker with getting the center-jump rule abolished. Pete Newell, interview by author, 23 June 2008, Ogden Dunes IN, tape recording.

107. *New York Times*, 13 August 1936.

108. "Olympic Games," *Time*, 24 August 1936, http://www.time.com/time/magazine/printout/0,8816,755998,00.html (accessed 7 October 2006).

2. ADVANCING THE GAME IN POSTWAR LONDON

1. Robinson also met the Queen Mother, the monarchs' two daughters, Margaret and Elizabeth (the latter of whom would become the present queen of England), and Prince Philip, whom Robinson characterized as a "marvelous conversationalist." Jackie Robinson, interview by author, 27 July 2008, Ogden Dunes IN, tape recording.

2. Bob Phillips, *The 1948 Olympics: How London Rescued the Games* (Cheltenham: SportsBooks Limited, 2007), 143.

3. Vincent Boryla, interview by author, 16 July 2008, Portage IN, tape recording.

4. Pete Newell, interview by author, 23 June 2008, Ogden Dunes IN, tape recording; Joshua Fried, "Hank Luisetti Scored Big, and Changed the Game," *Stanford Magazine*, March/April 2003, http://www.stanfordalumni.org/news/magazine/2003/marapr/departments/examinedlife.html (accessed 29 June 2008).

5. Phillips, *The 1948 Olympics*, 145.

6. Phillips, *The 1948 Olympics*, 145.

7. James E. Coogan, "1936 Rules for Olympic Basketball," *The Amateur Athlete*, no. 3 (March 1948): 43 (Amateur Athletic Union [AAU] Archives, Orlando FL).

8. William J. Baker, *Sports in the Western World* (Urbana: University of Illinois Press, 1988), 261.

9. Thomas Doherty, *Cold War, Cool Medium: Television, McCarthyism, and American Culture* (New York: Columbia University Press, 2003), 3–4.

10. James Kane, *Converse 1947 Basketball Yearbook*, 26th ed. (Malden MA: Converse Rubber Company, 1947), 8 (Duplicate from the Edward J. and Gena G. Hickox Library, Basketball Hall of Fame, Springfield MA, housed at the Amateur Athletic Library, Los Angeles CA).

11. *Wall Street Journal*, 21 February 1945.

12. Allen Guttmann, *Games and Empires: Modern Sports and Cultural Imperialism* (New York: Columbia University Press, 1994), 107, 2.

13. Walter LaFeber, *Michael Jordan and the New Global Capitalism* (New York: W. W. Norton, 1999), 162.

14. *New York Times*, 14 August 1948.

15. Baker, *Sports in the Western World*, 269.

16. Michael Wallis, *Oil Man: The Story of Frank Phillips and the Birth of Phillips Petroleum* (New York: Doubleday, 1988), 183, 254, 403.

17. Edward Macauley, telephone interview by author, 7 April 2008, handwritten notes. Ed said that the decision not to go did not result from Saint Louis University brass worrying about players missing too much school. *New York Times*, 22 March 1948.

18. Robinson interview.

19. "Alex Groza," Big Blue History, http://bigbluehistory.net/bb/statistics/Players/Groza_Alex.html (accessed 2 August 2008); *Washington Post*, 27 October 1949; Adolph H. Grundman, *The Golden Age of Amateur Basketball: The AAU Tournament, 1921–1968* (Lincoln: University of Nebraska Press, 2004), 122.

20. *Washington Post*, 1 December 2007; Robinson interview.

21. *Washington Post*, 20 March 1948.

22. Asa S. Bushnell, *Report of the U.S. Olympic Committee XIV Olympiad, 1948 Games* (New Haven: Walker-Radcliffe, 1949), 144; Wallis, *Oil Man*, 449.

23. *Washington Post*, 2 April 1948.

24. Grundman, *Golden Age of Amateur Basketball*, 149.

25. Buck Jerzy, National Polish-American Hall of Fame and Museums, http://www.polishsportshof.com/hof55_complete.htm (accessed 28 May 2004).

26. Dave Kindred, "Big Man on Campus: 40's Basketball Great Bob Kurland," *Sporting News*, 30 March 1998, available from http://www.highbeam.com/library/docfree.asp?DOCID=1G1:20500719&num=1&ctrlInfo=Round15%3AProd%3ASR%3AResult&ao=&FreePremium=BOTH (accessed 20 August 2005).

27. Kindred, "Big Man on Campus."

28. John Paul Bischoff, *Mr. Iba: Basketball's Aggie Iron Duke* (Oklahoma: Western Heritage Books, 1980), 118.

29. Bischoff, *Mr. Iba*, 118.

30. Naismith Memorial Basketball Hall of Fame, http://www.hoophall.com/hallof famers/Kurland.htm (accessed 28 May 2005).

31. Kindred, "Big Man on Campus."

32. Wallis, *Oil Man*, 449.

33. *Los Angeles Times*, 31 March 1948.

34. Kerry Eggers, "Basketball Finds a Lion in Winter," *Portland Tribune*, 15 April 2005, http://www.portlandtribune.com/sports/story.php?story_id=28998 (accessed 27 July 2008); Alex Petersen, "Up Close and Personal: Remembering the 'Thrill Kids,'" *Beaver Eclips, OSU Alumni Association*, http://209.85.173.104/earch?q=cache:6fKcrk L9oUQJ:www.osualum.com/s/359/index.aspx%3Fsid%3D359%26gid%3D1%26pgid%3D504+Lew+Beck+basketball&hl=en&ct=clnk&cd=9&gl=us (accessed 27 July 2008); Jeff Welsch and George P. Edmonston Jr., *Tales from Oregon State Sports* (Champaign: Sports Publishing, 2003), 68, http://books.google.com/books?id=-VvQ8F8s_20C&printsec=copyright&dq=Lew+Beck+oregon+basketball+player+life+story&source=gbs_toc_s&cad=1#PPA68,M1 (accessed 27 July 2008).

35. Robinson interview.

36. Boryla interview.

37. *New York Times*, 28, 30 March 1948.

38. Boryla interview.

39. Boryla interview; "Vince Boryla: Consensus All-American," Indiana Basketball Hall of Fame, http://www.hoopshall.com/inductees/1986/boryla.html (accessed 26 July 2008).

40. Boryla interview.

41. *Los Angeles Times*, 3 February 1948; Boryla interview.

42. Don Barksdale, interview by Dr. Margaret Costa, 15 December 1991 (Unedited oral history, Amateur Athletic Foundation Sports Library, Los Angeles CA).

43. Grundman, *Golden Age of Amateur Basketball*, 115–16.

44. Barksdale interview.

45. *Chicago Defender*, National edition, 13 March 1948.

46. "The new NAIA, A Proud Past, A Dynamic Future," http://www.naia.org/campaign/history/history.html (accessed 19 January 2005). Clarence Walker, a reserve guard on John Wooden's Indiana Sate squad, became the first African American to play in the NAIB (later known as the NAIA) tournament in 1948. Wooden had boycotted the tournament the previous year because it did not allow African Americans to participate.

47. Grundman, *Golden Age of Amateur Basketball*, 35.

48. Barksdale interview.

49. Qtd. in *Oakland Tribune*, 3 October 2002.

50. He had actually played eight games for the Bruins a few years earlier, in 1943, after two years of junior college, but the army beckoned, and Barksdale did not return until 1946. Barksdale interview.

51. Barksdale interview.

52. *Chicago Defender*, National edition, 31 July 1948. Barksdale interview; Phillips, *The 1948 Olympics*, 146.

53. Barksdale interview.

54. Robinson interview.

55. Barksdale interview.

56. Grundman, *Golden Age of Amateur Basketball*, 111–12.

57. Bushnell, *Report of the U.S. Olympic Committee XIV Olympiad*, 144.

58. Robinson interview.

59. Barksdale interview.

60. Bushnell, *Report of the U.S. Olympic Committee XIV Olympiad*, 144.

61. Grundman, *Golden Age of Amateur Basketball*, 100.

62. Stanley Frank, "Let's Ditch the Olympics," *Readers Digest* 52 (June 1948): 115.

63. John Lardner, "Avery's Oilers," *Newsweek*, 12 April 1948, 80.

64. Grundman, *Golden Age of Amateur Basketball*, 122.

65. On the "fluttering" flag, see Joseph M. Sheehan's *New York Times* article of 15 July 1948; the Kurland quote is from Phillips, *The 1948 Olympics*, 144.

66. Guttmann, *Games and Empires*, 107.

67. Allen Guttmann and Lee Thompson, *Japanese Sports: A History* (Honolulu: University of Hawaii Press, 2001), 79.

68. *New York Times*, 14 August 1948.

69. LaFeber, *Michael Jordan and the New Global Capitalism*, 162.

70. In the Middle East, issues between the newly formed Israel and its Middle Eastern neighbors worsened during the Games. On 15 August 1948, with the Olympics in full swing, reports surfaced of an Arab attack on Israel. *New York Times*, 16 August 1948.

71. Bushnell, *Report of the U.S. Olympic Committee XIV Olympiad*, 147.

72. *Washington Post*, 25 July 1948.

73. Harris, *Converse 1948 Basketball Yearbook*, 8.

74. Robinson interview; Boryla interview.

75. Bushnell, *Report of the U.S. Olympic Committee XIV Olympiad*, 147.

76. Frank, "Let's Ditch the Olympics," 115.

77. Frank, "Let's Ditch the Olympics," 115.

78. Baker, *Sports in the Western World*, 264.

79. Bushnell, *Report of the U.S. Olympic Committee XIV Olympiad*, 10.

80. Baker, *Sports in the Western World*, 264–69.

81. Robinson interview.

82. Robinson interview.

83. Bushnell, *Report of the U.S. Olympic Committee XIV Olympiad*, 144; Phillips, *The 1948 Olympics*, 144.

84. Bushnell, *Report of the U.S. Olympic Committee XIV Olympiad*, 144; Phillips, *The 1948 Olympics*, 144.

85. Robinson interview.

86. Harris, *Converse 1948 Basketball Yearbook*, 8.

87. *Los Angeles Times*, 5 August 1948; *Washington Post*, 5 August 1948; Harris, *Converse 1948 Basketball Yearbook*, 9.

88. *Chicago Daily Tribune*, 8 August 1948.

89. Bushnell, *Report of the U.S. Olympic Committee XIV Olympiad*, 145.

90. Bushnell, *Report of the U.S. Olympic Committee XIV Olympiad*, 145.

91. *Chicago Daily Tribune*, 14 August 1948; Phillips, *The 1948 Olympics*, 147.

92. *Los Angeles Times*, 14 August 1948.

93. *Los Angeles Times*, 14 August 1948.

94. *New York Times*, 14 August 1948.

95. Robinson interview.

96. Boryla interview.

97. Bushnell, *Report of the U.S. Olympic Committee XIV Olympiad*, 144; *Chicago Defender*, National edition, 16 October 1948; Boryla interview.

98. However, the technology was primitive, and few people in Great Britain owned television sets.

99. *The Amateur Athlete*, no. 3 (March 1948): 29 (AAU Archives, Orlando FL).

100. Harris, *Converse 1948 Basketball Yearbook*, 8.

101. *The Amateur Athlete*, no. 9 (September 1948): 13 (AAU Archives, Orlando FL).

3. OPENING SALVO IN HELSINKI

1. Arthur Daley, *New York Times*, 10 June 1952.

2. William J. Baker, *Sports in the Western World* (Urbana: University of Illinois Press, 1988), 261.

3. *New York Times*, 3 August 1952.

4. Susan Brownell, *Training the Body for China: Sports in the Moral Order of the People's Republic* (Chicago: University of Chicago Press, 1995), 18.

5. The Russian attitude toward sport led some provincial governments to ban soccer, believing it a special relic of "bourgeois practices." The Supreme Council of Physical Culture, which valued competitive sport, did work to curtail these provincial "aberrations." Pierre Arnaud and James Riordan, *Sport and International Politics* (New York: E&FN Spon, 1998), 188.

6. Arnaud and Riordan, *Sport and International Politics*, 187–88.

7. Qtd. in Joseph A. Machiony, "The Rise of Soviet Athletics," *Comparative Education Review* 7, no. 1 (June 1963): 19.

8. Barbara J. Keys, *Globalizing Sport: National Rivalry and International Community in the 1930s* (Cambridge: Harvard University Press, 2006), 5.

9. The Soviet Union joined the IOC in 1951. James Riordan, *Sports in Soviet Society* (New York: Cambridge University Press, 1977), 15.

10. "Stalin's 'Iron Curtain' for Athletes," *U.S. News and World Report*, 25 July 1952, 44.

11. Yuri Brokhin, *The Big Red Machine: The Rise and Fall of Soviet Olympic Champions* (New York: Random House, 1978), 7.

12. D. Thoreau, "How Good Are Russian Athletes?" *Saturday Evening Post*, 19 July 1952, 26–27.

13. In May 1951 *Time* said that two years earlier, the Central Committee of the Communist Party had issued orders to Soviet athletes to "start winning world championships in all major sports." "The Coach Is Watching," *Time*, 7 May 1951 (accessed 6 February 2009, University of Chicago Regenstein Library).

14. Allison Danzig, *New York Times*, 20 July 1952.

15. *New York Times*, 6 May 1951.

16. *New York Times*, 6 May 1951.

17. "European Champions," *Time*, 21 May 1952, 76.

18. "Laupaev," *Eesti Paevaleht*, 3 August 2002, 16. Translated from the Estonian by Christian Makke.

19. "Laupaev," *Eesti Paevaleht*, 3 August 2002, 16. Translated from the Estonian by Christian Makke.

20. Brokhin, *Big Red Machine*, 139.

21. Robert Edelman, *Serious Fun: A History of Spectator Sports in the USSR* (New York: Oxford University Press, 1993), 145.

22. Brokhin, *Big Red Machine*, 139.

23. En route to their 1952 European championship in Paris, the Soviets won eight straight games. Bruising play down low by the Georgian star Otar Korkija and nifty passing on the perimeter propelled the Soviet squad. (According to *Time*, Korkija was six feet two inches. Other sources, such as the *Chicago Tribune* and the *Washington Post*, put Korkija's height at anywhere from six feet three to nearly six feet eight.) Korkija's energy matched the Soviet style of play well. The Soviets used outlet passes to jump-start the fast break, quick interior passing, and deft ballhandling, allowing them to emerge from Paris as the team most likely to challenge the United States at the Olympics. "European Champions," 76.

24. In the Kansas City Auditorium, the University of Kansas, the 1952 NCAA champion, beat the Southwest Missouri Teachers NAIB champs, 92–65. Phillips Co. (AAU 2nd place) beat the Fibber McGee and Molly squad (AAU 4th place) 50–48 in double overtime. At Madison Square Garden, LaSalle (NIT champion) beat St. John's (NCAA runner-up) 71–62, and the Caterpillar Tractor Co. (AAU champ) beat the U.S. Air Force (AAU 3rd place) 71–67.

25. Adolph H. Grundman, *The Golden Age of Amateur Basketball: The AAU Tournament, 1921–1968* (Lincoln: University of Nebraska Press, 2004), 144–45.

26. Blair Kerkhoff, *Phog Allen: The Father of Basketball Coaching* (Indianapolis: Masters Press, 1996), 172–73.

27. The referee brought in was Ronnie Gibbs, a Big Seven official from Springfield, Illinois. *New York Times*, 30 March 1952.

28. *New York Times*, 31 March 1952.

29. Kerkhoff, *Phog Allen*, 173.

30. Kerkhoff, *Phog Allen*, 174; Clyde Lovellette, interview by author, 2 July 2008, Ogden Dunes IN, tape recording.

31. *New York Times*, 1 April 1952. For the game, Ron Bontemps, a six-feet-three-inch "string bean," led Caterpillar with sixteen points, while Williams scored fifteen. *Washington Post*, 1 April 1952.

32. *Chicago Daily Tribune*, 2 April 1952.

33. Grundman, *Golden Age of Amateur Basketball*, 145–46.

34. *Washington Post*, 3 April 1952.

35. William Hougland, interview by author, 30 June 2008, Ogden Dunes IN, tape recording.

36. Squires played his first season of varsity basketball in 1952, but he played sparingly in Kansas's drive to the national championship and was not selected for the Olympic team. Harold Bechard, "An Interview with Max Falkenstein: The Voice of the Jayhawks for 50 Years Sunday," *Salina Journal*, 17 March 1996.

37. After the Olympics and his NBA career, Lovellette experienced some rough times off the court. He suffered from bouts of depression and bounced from job to job for years until he was in his late fifties, when he found some solace teaching and coaching at White's Institute, a school for troubled youth in Terre Haute, Indiana. "Lovellette Finds Niche in Life as Prep Cage Coach in Indiana," *Lawrence Journal*, 18 February 1982 (Edward J. and Gena G. Hickox Library, Basketball Hall of Fame, Springfield MA, hereafter referred to as the Hickox Library).

38. Some sources put the value of Milwaukee's offer at $60,000. In 1953 Lovellette did sign with the Minneapolis Lakers for a reported $20,000 and $5,000 signing bonus. He played in the NBA for eleven years, winning championships with both the Lakers and the Celtics. Kerkhoff, *Phog Allen*, 175.

39. *Wall Street Journal*, 22 August 1951.

40. Kerkhoff, *Phog Allen*, 175; Clyde Lovellette, interview by author, 2 July 2008, Ogden Dunes IN, tape recording.

41. *Washington Post*, 23 April 1952.

42. *Washington Post*, 5 August 1952.

43. Asa S. Bushnell, ed., *United States 1952 Olympic Book: Quadrennial Report U.S. Olympic Committee* (New Haven: Walker-Rackliff, 1953), 149.

44. Converse advertisement, "America's Best for America's Finest," *Converse 1952 Basketball Yearbook*, 31st ed. (Malden MA: Converse Rubber Company, 1952), back cover (Duplicate from the Hickox Library, housed at the Amateur Athletic Library, Los Angeles CA).

45. *Wall Street Journal*, 21 March 1952.

46. Ben Green, *Spinning the Globe: The Rise, Fall, and Return to Greatness of the Harlem Globetrotters* (New York: Amistad, 2005), 244, 248–52.

47. Hougland interview.

48. Bushnell, ed., *United States 1952 Olympic Book*, 149.

49. Hougland interview.

50. Lovellette interview.

51. Bushnell, ed., *United States 1952 Olympic Book*, 28, 150.

52. Hougland interview.

53. Qtd. in Bushnell, ed., *United States 1952 Olympic Book*, 150.

54. *Chicago Daily Tribune*, 12 July 1952.

55. *New York Times*, 18 July 1952.

56. Guttmann, *The Olympics*, 91–92.

57. *New York Times*, 18 July 1952.

58. *New York Times*, 18 July 1952.

59. The state department, *New York Times*, and MacArthur are all quoted in "China: The Mistake of a Century," *Time*, 21 May 1951, 32.

60. Michael Schaller, *The United States and China: Into the Twenty-First Century*, 3rd ed. (New York: Oxford University Press, 2002), 2.

61. According to the *Washington Post*, the 70,000 in attendance "cheered wildly for the big Scandinavian and American teams, but greeted Soviet Russia's first appearance with only polite applause." *Washington Post*, 20 July 1952.

62. The Finnish and Soviets signed a treaty in 1948 that allowed Finland to remain neutral in the East-versus-West power struggle. For all practical purposes, the agreement allowed Finland to maintain its democratic way of life.

63. Allison Danzig, *New York Times*, 20 July 1952.

64. In elections that took place a month before the Games, the Finnish citizenry voiced their support for democracy and the Olympics at the ballot box. The election resulted in no significant changes in Finland's democratic government, which the West considered a good thing. Collie Small, "Even the Russians Are Going to Play," *Saturday Evening Post*, 25 August 1951, 27.

65. "Coca-Cola and the Olympic Movement: A Long-standing Partnership," http://torchrelay.coca-cola.com/pdf/background_movement.pdf (accessed 25 May 2005).

66. *Washington Post*, 26 July 1952.

67. *Washington Post*, 26 July 1952.

68. Willard N. Greim and Vincent DeP. Farrell, "U.S. Olympic Basketeers Triumph,"

The Amateur Athlete, no. 9 (September 1952): 16 (Amateur Athletic Union [AAU] Archives, Orlando FL).

69. Robert Kenney, interview by author, 30 June 2008, Ogden Dunes IN, tape recording.

70. *The Amateur Athlete*, no. 11 (November 1952): 2 (AAU Archives, Orlando FL).

71. *New York Times*, 3 August 1952.

72. Hougland interview.

73. Hougland interview.

74. *New York Times*, 28 July 1952.

75. Lovellette interview.

76. Lovellette interview.

77. Bushnell, ed., *United States 1952 Olympic Book*, 150.

78. Allison Danzig, *New York Times*, 20 July 1952.

79. Arthur Daley, *New York Times*, 16 July 1952.

80. "Stalin's 'Iron Curtain' for Athletes," *U.S. News & World Report*, 25 July 1952, 42.

81. Harrison E. Salisbury, *New York Times*, 21 July 1952.

82. *New York Times*, 21 July 1952.

83. *New York Times*, 21 July 1952.

84. "European Champions," *Time*, 76.

85. *New York Times* 28 July 1952.

86. *New York Times*, 29 July 1952.

87. Kurland led the United States with fifteen points, while Lovellette, breaking out of his minislump, scored fourteen, as did Kenney. Stepas Butautas, one of Russia's three captains and the eventual father of Ramūnas Butautas, who became the head coach of Lithuania in 2006, led his team with fifteen points. Bushnell, ed., *United States 1952 Olympic Book*, 152.

88. *New York Times*, 28 July 1952; Lovellette interview.

89. *New York Times*, 29 July 1952. In another rare example of the Soviet press putting a positive spin on the Games, the youth newspaper *Komsomol Pravda* wrote, "In these days when the atom bomb and other weapons of mass destruction of population threaten the lives of mankind . . . the meeting of the youth of the whole world in brotherly sports competition has great significance." Qtd. in "Stalin's 'Iron Curtain' for Athletes," 42.

90. *New York Times*, 16 July 1952.

91. Baker, *Sports in the Western World*, 264.

92. *New York Times*, 31 July 1952.

93. *New York Times*, 29 July 1952.

94. Bushnell, ed., *United States 1952 Olympic Book*, 152.

95. *New York Times*, 31 July 1952.

96. *New York Times*, 31 July 1952.

97. Bushnell, ed., *United States 1952 Olympic Book*, 152.

98. *New York Times*, 2 August 1952.

99. Greim and Farrell, "U.S. Olympic Basketeers Triumph," 18 (AAU Archives, Orlando FL). "It looked like to me that their side was a little bit more than our side," Lovellette recalled of the number of fans. Lovellette interview.

100. Bushnell, ed., *United States 1952 Olympic Book*, 153.

101. *New York Times*, 3 August 1952.

102. Greim and Farrell, "U.S. Olympic Basketeers Triumph," 19 (AAU Archives, Orlando FL).

103. *Washington Post*, 3 August 1952.

104. Hougland interview.

105. Bushnell, ed., *United States 1952 Olympic Book*, 152.

106. *Washington Post*, 3 August 1952.

107. Bushnell, ed., *United States 1952 Olympic Book*, 152.

108. *Washington Post*, 3 August 1952; Kerkhoff, *Phog Allen*, 175.

109. *New York Times*, 3 August 1952; Manfred Stroker, *The Rules, 1931–2000* (Munich: FIBA, 2001), 94.

110. Brokhin, *Big Red Machine*, 135.

111. Brokhin, *Big Red Machine*, 186.

4. RUSSELL MODEL REVOLUTIONIZES IN MELBOURNE

1. William J. Baker, *Sports in the Western World* (Urbana: University of Illinois Press, 1988), 269.

2. Thomas Michael Domer, "Sport in Cold War America, 1953–63: The Diplomatic and Political Use of Sport in the Kennedy and Eisenhower Administrations," (PhD diss., Marquette University, 1976), 54.

3. "Along Came Bill," *Time*, 2 January 1957, 36–37.

4. Aram G. Goudsouzian, "Bill Russell and the Basketball Revolution," unpublished manuscript; Bill Russell, as told to William McSweeney, *Go Up for Glory* (New York: Coward-McCann, 1966), 36–37; "Along Came Bill," 36–37.

5. Andre LaGuerre, "World's Eye on Sport," *Sports Illustrated*, 3 December 1956, 15.

6. William Hougland, interview by author, 30 June 2008, Ogden Dunes IN, tape recording.

7. Robert Edelman, *Serious Fun: A History of Spectator Sports in the U.S.S.R.* (New York: Oxford University Press, 1993), 150.

8. Baker, *Sports in the Western World*, 169.

9. Edelman, *Serious Fun*, 117.

10. Edelman, *Serious Fun*, 145.

11. Yuri Brokhin, *The Big Red Machine: The Rise and Fall of Soviet Olympic Champions* (New York: Random House, 1978), 136.

12. Brokhin, *Big Red Machine*, 137. The *Washington Post* put Akhtaev's dimensions at seven feet six and a half inches and 404 pounds.

13. *Washington Post*, 7 August 1956.

14. Brokhin, *Big Red Machine*, 137.

15. Brokhin, *Big Red Machine*, 138.

16. *Washington Post*, 25 October 1956.

17. R. G. Lynch, *Milwaukee Journal*, 15 December 1952.

18. R. G. Lynch, *Milwaukee Journal*, 15 December 1952.

19. Letter from Avery Brundage to R. G. Lynch, 20 December 1952, Avery Brundage Collection, University of Illinois, Urbana IL.

20. Brundage to Lynch, 20 December 1952.

21. *Wall Street Journal*, 24 January 1957.

22. "Executives on the Court," *Time*, 11 February 1957, http://www.time.com/time/magazine/article/0,9171,809062,00.html (accessed 7 October 2006).

23. Murray Olderman, *Detroit News*, 1 March 1953.

24. *Wall Street Journal*, 18 March 1958.

25. *Wall Street Journal*, 18 March 1958.

26. Bill Russell, *Second Wind: The Memoirs of an Opinionated Man* (New York: Random House, 1979), 81.

27. "Along Came Bill," 36–37.

28. Paul Woolpert, interview by author, 22 January 2005, Yakima WA, handwritten notes.

29. Kelli Anderson, "San Francisco Dons: In Their Own Style," *Sports Illustrated*, 3 July 2006, 100; *St. Louis Post-Dispatch*, 6 February 2005.

30. *St. Louis Post-Dispatch*, 6 February 2005.

31. Anderson, "San Francisco Dons," 100.

32. "Along Came Bill," 36–37.

33. "Along Came Bill," 36–37. With his Dons team slated for a State Department–sponsored tour of Latin America during the track-and-field trials and his spot on the U.S. Olympic basketball team secure, Russell decided not to compete in the U.S. Olympic trials for high jump. He did not want to abandon his collegiate teammates in Latin America or take away an Olympic spot from someone else since he already had one.

34. Russell, as told to McSweeney, *Go Up for Glory*, 41; Bill Margolis, "Trotters Triple-Team the World," *Converse 1956 Basketball Yearbook*, 35th ed. (Malden MA: Converse Rubber Company, 1956), 18 (Amateur Athletic Library, Los Angeles CA).

35. Russell and Branch, *Second Wind*, 52.

36. Russell and Branch, *Second Wind*, 44.

37. Russell and Branch, *Second Wind*, 192.

38. "All the Credentials," *Time*, 29 April 1966, http://www.time.com/time/magazine (accessed 7 October 2006).

39. Unfortunately, Russell also said that as the lone black Celtic, "I was excluded from almost everything except practice and the games," while later on, his two white players with the Supersonics "were excluded from almost everything but practice and games." Russell and Branch, *Second Wind*, 188.

40. Russell, as told to McSweeney, *Go Up for Glory*, 46–47.

41. Adolph H. Grundman, *The Golden Age of Amateur Basketball: The AAU Tournament, 1921–1968* (Lincoln: University of Nebraska Press, 2004), 171.

42. In *Collier's*, Russell was the runaway pick for player of the year. *Washington Post*, 29 February 1956.

43. "Oilers Win Olympic Tourney, NIBL Title," *Converse 1956 Basketball Yearbook*, 35th

ed. (Malden MA: Converse Rubber Company, 1935/36), 22 (Amateur Athletic Library, Los Angeles CA).

44. *Washington Post,* 11 March 1956.

45. Russell, as told to McSweeney, *Go Up for Glory,* 45.

46. "Olympic Team Trials: 1956 Basketball, Kansas City, Mo. April 2–3–4," *Official Program of the U.S. Olympic Committee* (Edward J. and Gena G. Hickox Library, Basketball Hall of Fame, SpringfieldMA).

47. *Wall Street Journal,* 26 October 1956.

48. *The Amateur Athlete,* no. 12 (December 1952) (AAU Archives, Orlando FL).

49. Qtd. in Tom Vanderbilt, *The Sneaker Book: Anatomy of an Industry and an Icon* (New York: New Press, 1998), 13.

50. Wells showed a Converse-created basketball highlight film on his Asian journey that depicted action from the previous year. It was met with enthusiasm. Clifford Wells, "Basketball in the Far East," *Converse 1956 Basketball Yearbook,* 35th ed. (Malden MA: Converse Rubber Company, 1956), 23 (Amateur Athletic Library, Los Angeles CA).

51. Allison Danzig, *New York Times,* 3 December 1956.

52. *New York Times,* 5 April 1956.

53. *Chicago Tribune,* 5 April 1956.

54. Grundman, *Golden Age of Amateur Basketball,* 171.

55. *Washington Post,* 11 August 1956.

56. Ron Tomsic, Interview by Dr. Margaret Costa, unedited oral history, 11 July 1984, transcript (Amateur Athletic Foundation Sports Library, Los Angeles CA).

57. Bakers coach Fred Fidler thought at least one player on his AAU-champion roster, such as Charlie Koon, should have made it. As it happened, the Bakers thought UCLA's Willie Naulls, and the 1956 NCAA tournament MVP Hal Lear got overlooked too. Grundman, *Golden Age of Amateur Basketball,* 172–74.

58. Grundman, *Golden Age of Amateur Basketball,* 171–72.

59. Frank "Bucky" O'Connor was the NCAA's qualifying team coach. Drake earned coaching duties only after O'Connor, head coach of the University of Iowa Hawkeyes, whose team lost to Woolpert's Dons in the NCAA final in 1956, declined the assistant post. Both Woolpert and O'Connor would have had to miss a large part of their 1956–57 collegiate schedule had they agreed to attend the Olympics.

60. "Drake Joins Olympic Hoop Squad," *The Amateur Athlete,* no. 8 (September 1956): 18 (AAU Archives, Orlando FL).

61. Naismith Memorial Basketball Hall of Fame, http://www.hoophall.com/hallof-famers/Drake.htm (accessed 8 February 2005).

62. *Chicago Tribune,* 21 October 1956.

63. "Olympic Preview," *Sports Illustrated,* 19 November 1956, 87; Hanz-Dieter Krebs, "European Basketball," *Converse 1956 Basketball Yearbook,* 35th ed. (Malden MA: Converse Rubber Company, 1956), 19 (Amateur Athletic Library, Los Angeles CA); Jim McGregor, "Italian Basketball," *Converse 1956 Basketball Yearbook,* 35th ed. (Malden MA: Converse Rubber Company, 1956), 19 (Amateur Athletic Library, Los Angeles CA).

64. "Olympic Preview," 87.

65. Willard N. Greim, "International Basketball Meeting," *The Amateur Athlete*, no. 10 (October 1952): 19 (AAU Archives, Orlando FL).

66. In addition to these rule changes, FIBA offered membership to East and West Germany and to the All China Athletic Federation of the People's Republic of China and the Federation of the Republic of China (Taiwan) for the 1956 Melbourne Games in an effort to increase international participation. Greim, "International Basketball Meeting," 19 (AAU Archives, Orlando FL). In 1957 the NCAA extended its free-throw lane to twelve feet wide.

67. Laguerre, "World's Eye on Sport," 14; Jim McGregor, "USA Retains Olympic Crown," *Converse 1957 Basketball Yearbook*, 36th ed. (Malden MA: Converse Rubber Company, 1957), 20 (Amateur Athletic Library, Los Angeles CA).

68. Baker, *Sports in the Western World*, 269.

69. "Hungary's Heroes in Their Hour of Staggering Strain," *Sports Illustrated*, 3 December 1956, 23. The Soviets controlled the athletes' entrance via the Mediterranean, presumably at Rijeka, in modern-day Croatia.

70. LaGuerre, "World's Eye on Sport," 14

71. Baker, *Sports in the Western World*, 270.

72. Qtd. in Baker, *Sports in the Western World*, 270; LaGuerre, "World's Eye on Sport," 12.

73. "Russian Athletes Will Live in Olympic Village," *The Amateur Athlete*, no. 10 (October 1956): 6 (AAU Archives, Orlando FL).

74. Tomsic interview.

75. *Washington Post*, 23 November 1956.

76. Burdette Haldorson, interview by author, 25 June 2008, Chicago IL, tape recording

77. Margie Jeangerard, interview by author, 25 June 2008, Chicago IL, tape recording.

78. *New York Times*, 23 November 1956.

79. "Golden Melbourne," *Sports Illustrated*, 10 December 1956, 46.

80. "Bob Mathias Narrates Official Olympic Films," *The Amateur Athlete*, no. 12 (December 1956): 18 (AAU Archives, Orlando FL).

81. "800 Reporters to Cover Melbourne Olympics," *The Amateur Athlete*, no. 11 (November 1956): 28 (AAU Archives, Orlando FL).

82. "BBC to Broadcast in 44 Languages," *The Amateur Athlete*, no. 12 (December 1956): 18 (AAU Archives, Orlando FL). The massive attention afforded the Games demonstrated the world's passion for sports.

83. Koh Koide, "Basketball in Japan," *Converse 1956 Basketball Yearbook*, 35th ed. (Malden MA: Converse Rubber Company, 1956), 23 (Amateur Athletic Library, Los Angeles CA).

84. *New York Times*, 23 November 1956.

85. *New York Times*, 27 November 1956.

86. FIBA allows players to touch the ball if it is within the theoretical cylinder so long as the ball is not touching the rim.

87. *New York Times*, 28 November 1956.

88. *New York Times*, 28 November 1956.

89. *Washington Post*, 30 November 1956.

90. *Washington Post*, 30 November 1956.

91. Tomsic interview.

92. *Washington Post*, 30 November 1956.

93. *Chicago Tribune*, 1 December 1956.

94. *New York Times*, 1 December 1956.

95. Danzig, *New York Times*, 3 December 1956.

96. Tomsic interview.

97. Tomsic interview.

98. *Chicago Tribune*, 2 December 1956.

99. Haldorson interview.

100. William Hougland, interview by author, 30 June 2008, Ogden Dunes IN, tape recording.

101. "The Bucket Brigade of '60," a special article that appeared in the 29 August 1988 issue of *Sports Illustrated*, analyzed whether the 1960 or 1984 U.S. Olympic squad was the greatest amateur team of all time. The 1956 team received scant mention. Walter Bingham, "The Bucket Brigade of '60 (Special Advertising Section)," *Sports Illustrated*, 29 August 1988, 71, 73–74.

102. *New York Times*, 3 December 1956.

103. *Chicago Tribune*, 10 December 1956.

5. BASKETBALL ACCELERATES IN ROME

1. Richard Pound, *Inside the Olympics: A Behind-the-Scenes Look at the Politics, the Scandals, and the Glory of the Games* (Canada: Wiley, 2006), 167.

2. Pete Newell, interview by author, 23 June 2008, Ogden Dunes IN, tape recording.

3. John P. Shanley credited CBS for its "impressive technical achievement" of same-day coverage. *New York Times*, 27 August 1960.

4. Oscar Robertson, *The Big O*, (United States: Rodale, 2003), 128.

5. William J. Baker, *Sports in the Western World* (Urbana: University of Illinois Press, 1988), 271.

6. Jonathan A. Becker, *Soviet and Russian Press Coverage of the United States: Press, Politics, and Identity in Transition* (London: MacMillan Press and St. Martin's Press, 1999), 69.

7. In an interview about the expedition, Lieutenant General Bernard A. Schriever affirmed the United States' commitment to sending animals into space and expressed skepticism of Soviet claims that they could already send dogs into orbit and recover them. *New York Times*, 27 August 1960.

8. Walter LaFeber, *America, Russia, and the Cold War, 1945–2000* (Boston: McGraw Hill, 2002), 205.

9. David Maraniss, *Rome 1960: The Olympics That Changed the World* (New York: Simon and Schuster, 2008), xii.

10. LaFeber, *America, Russia, and the Cold War*, 213.

11. "Wither, Oh Wither?" *Time*, 27 January 1961, 52.

12. Newell interview.

13. Shan Lei and Zou Dapeng, "(China Sports) FIBA makes major changes on court and rules," *Xinhua News Agency*, 26 April 2008, available from http://www.highbeam. com/doc/1P2-16511840.html (accessed 23 June 2008).

14. "The 7-Foot-3 Russian," *Newsweek*, 7 December 1959, 100.

15. James Banks, "Russian Basketball Teams Strong," *The Amateur Athlete*, no. 1 (January 1960): 28 (AAU Archives, Orlando FL).

16. *New York Times*, 28 August 1960.

17. *New York Times*, 28 August 1960.

18. Walter Bingham, "The Bucket Brigade of '60 (Special Advertising Section)," *Sports Illustrated*, 29 August 1988, 71, 73–74.

19. Qtd. in "Wither, Oh Wither?" 52.

20. The NCAA, among others, protested the AAU's decision. *New York Times*, 25 August 1960; "Greim Defends AAU in Swedish Tour Hassle: Basketball Chairman G. Russell Lyons Explains Stand; AAU Record in International Exchanges Cited by Congress," *The Amateur Athlete*, no. 1 (January 1960): 17 (AAU Archives, Orlando FL). The AAU later asserted that it had fostered international exchanges with international teams, which had been so "inspiring" that they had been "included in the Congressional record." Banks, "Russian Basketball Teams Strong," 28.

21. *New York Times*, 1 September 1960.

22. *New York Times*, 25 August 1960.

23. *New York Times*, 1 September 1960.

24. *Washington Post*, 14 December 1957.

25. Adolph H. Grundman, *The Golden Age of Amateur Basketball: The AAU Tournament, 1921–1968* (Lincoln: University of Nebraska Press, 2004), 201–5.

26. Dischinger played his collegiate ball at Purdue University, where he set scoring records and added to the illustrious history of Purdue basketball players who have worn the number forty-three. In Rome, on top of averaging 11.8 points, Dischinger roomed with The Big O, who credited the Boilermaker with spending an inordinate amount of time sleeping.

27. Qtd. in Bruce Jenkins, *A Good Man: The Pete Newell Story* (Berkeley: Frog, 1999), 195–96.

28. Memorandum, "U.S. Olympic Basketball Trials, Denver Colorado" (Edward J. and Gena G. Hickox Library, Basketball Hall of Fame, Springfield MA, hereafter referred to as the Hickox Library).

29. Grundman, *Golden Age of Amateur Basketball*, 207.

30. Jenkins, *A Good Man*, 43–44.

31. Jeremiah Tax, "What Price Glory for Oscar? At the Summit of a fame he has achieved so early, Cincinnati's brilliant Oscar Robertson finds himself unable to relax and enjoy it," *Sports Illustrated*, 26 January 1959, 19.

32. Newell interview.

33. Robertson, *The Big O*, ix.

34. Robertson, *The Big O*, 10; Ira Berkow, *Oscar Robertson: The Golden Year 1964* (Englewood Cliffs: Prentice-Hall, 1971), 123.

35. Randy Roberts, *But They Can't Beat Us* (Champaign IL: Sagamore, 1999), 40.

36. Robertson, *The Big O*, 53–54. Triumphantly, upon the death of Ray Crowe, Robertson's coach at Attucks, his funeral procession went through the center of Indianapolis as the Attucks parade should have done nearly fifty years earlier. *Indianapolis Star*, 3 January 2004.

37. Robertson, *The Big O*, 64.

38. Robertson, *The Big O*, 114.

39. Interview of Jerry West, transcript, Amateur Athletic Foundation Library, Los Angeles CA.

40. Jerry West and Bill Libby, *Mr. Clutch: The Jerry West Story* (Englewood Cliffs: Prentice-Hall, 1969), 72.

41. *Chicago Daily News*, 15 July 2000.

42. Richard Hoffer, "Mister Clutch, Master Builder," *Sports Illustrated*, 23 April 1990, available from http://www.highbeam.com/library/doco.asp?DOCID=1G1:8904357&num=1&ctrlInfo=Round16%3AMode16a0%3ASR%3AResult&ao=&FreePremium=PREMIUM (accessed 24 August 2005).

43. West interview; Maraniss, *Rome 1960*, 236.

44. Newell interview.

45. Jeremiah Tax, "A Is the Grade for Lucas: On the Basketball Court and in the Classroom This Grave Yet Competitive Youngster Is an All-America Performer at Ohio State," *Sports Illustrated*, 11 January 1960, 34.

46. Tax, "A Is the Grade for Lucas," 34.

47. Alexander Wolf, "Jerry Lucas: Thanks for the Memory," *Sports Illustrated*, 30 June 2003, 60.

48. Wolf, "Jerry Lucas," 59.

49. *Hartford Courant*, 27 August 1972 (Hickox Library).

50. Wolf, "Jerry Lucas," 59.

51. *New York Times*, 30 July 1972.

52. *New York Times*, 30 July 1972.

53. Wolf, "Jerry Lucas," 59.

54. Wolf, "Jerry Lucas," 59.

55. Wolf, "Jerry Lucas," 60.

56. Wolf, "Jerry Lucas," 60.

57. Terry Dischinger, telephone interview by author, 31 July 2006, Chicago IL, handwritten notes.

58. Grundman, *Golden Age of Amateur Basketball*, 206.

59. Newell interview. The Robertson quote is from *The Big O*, 124–25.

60. Jenkins *A Good Man*, 201, 202.

61. Jenkins, *A Good Man*, 6, 182, 186.

62. Jenkins, *A Good Man*, 23–24, 37.

63. As noted earlier, Havlicek, from Lansing, Ohio, played alongside Lucas on Ohio State's 1960 national championship team. Bob Knight was on that team as well; he was a bench player.

64. Robertson, *The Big O*, 124, 125.

65. Lenny Wilkens and Terry Pluto, *Unguarded: My Forty Years Surviving in the* NBA (New York: Simon and Schuster, 2001), 60–62.

66. Robertson recalled that Pete Newell stayed up all night picking the team and that a lot of AAU guys were selected because of the AAU's influence in those days. Robertson, *The Big O*, 124, 125.

67. Grundman, *Golden Age of Amateur Basketball*, 206.

68. Jenkins, *A Good Man*, 197–99; Newell interview.

69. Newell interview.

70. Newell interview; Grundman, *Golden Age of Amateur Basketball*, 206–7.

71. The Pipers' John Adams, chosen as an Olympic alternate but who thought he warranted a roster spot, played for McClendon in the win. Milton S. Katz, *Breaking Through: John B. McClendon, Basketball Legend and Civil Rights Pioneer* (Fayetteville: University of Arkansas Press, 2007), 114–26.

72. Newell interview.

73. Arthur Daley, *New York Times*, 26 August 1960.

74. Newell interview.

75. Bob Ryan, "They're Baaack (History of U.S. Olympic Basketball Teams) (Special Advertising Section)", *Sports Illustrated*, 6 July 1992, available from http://www.highbeam.com/library/doco.asp?DOCID=1G1:12401055&num=6&ctrlInfo=Round16%3AMode1 6a0%3ASR%3AResult&ao=&FreePremium=PREMIUM (accessed 24 August 2005).

76. "To Do a Little Better," *Time*, 29 August 1960, http://www.time.com/time/magazine (accessed 7 October 2006).

77. *New York Times*, 26 August 1960.

78. *New York Times*, 26 August 1960.

79. Jenkins, *A Good Man*, 202; "U.S. Wins 1960 Olympics," *Converse 1960 Basketball Yearbook*, 39th ed. (Malden MA: Converse Rubber Company, 1960), 2 (Amateur Athletic Library, Los Angeles CA); Newell interview.

80. West interview; "U.S. Wins 1960 Olympics," 2.

81. Jenkins, *A Good Man*, 201, 202.

82. Ryan, "They're Baaack."

83. *Chicago Daily Tribune*, 30 August 1960.

84. Maraniss, *Rome 1960*, 234.

85. Robertson, *The Big O*, 128.

86. West interview.

87. Maraniss, *Rome 1960*, 236.

88. Dischinger interview.

89. Dischinger interview.

90. Robertson, *The Big O*, 128; Newell interview; Dischinger interview; Maraniss, *Rome 1960*, 238.

91. Maraniss, *Rome 1960*, 237.

92. *New York Times*, 4 September 1960; "U.S. Wins 1960 Olympics," 2; Newell interview.

93. Qtd. in Bingham, "Bucket Brigade of '60," 73.

94. Robertson, *The Big O*, 129.

95. West interview; Libby and West, *Mr. Clutch*, 69; Jenkins, *A Good Man*, 206; Newell interview.

96. Qtd. in Ryan, "They're Baaack."

97. *New York Times*, 9 September 1960.

98. *New York Times*, 9 September 1960; "Basketball," *The Games of the XVII Olympiad Rome: The Official Reports of the Organizing Committee* (1960, 629–60 (accessed online 11 September 2009).

99. Jenkins, *A Good Man*, 205.

100. *Washington Post*, 11 September 1960.

101. West, *Mr. Clutch*, 69; "U.S. Wins 1960 Olympics," 2.

102. Maraniss, *Rome 1960*, 366.

103. Dischinger interview.

6. TEAMWORK, TELEVISION, AND THE COLD WAR IN TOKYO

1. *New York Times*, 6 April 1964.

2. *Chicago Tribune*, 13 October 1964; "A Reek of Cement in Fuji's Shadow," *Time*, 11 September 1964, http://www.time.com/time/magazine/article/0,9171,830645,00.html (accessed 7 October 2006); "Tokyo—Getting Prepared," *1964 U.S. Olympic Team Trials*, Official Program, 21 (Amateur Athletic Library, Los Angeles CA).

3. Allen Guttmann and Lee Thompson, *Japanese Sports: A History* (Honolulu: University of Hawaii Press, 2001), 163.

4. Mansel G. Blackford, *The Rise of Modern Business in Great Britain, the United States, and Japan* (Chapel Hill: University of North Carolina Press, 1998), 176, 177. In less than a decade, Japan's prosperity and its dynamic marketplace, along with the successes of Hong Kong, Singapore, Taiwan, and South Korea, a group Friedman has referred to as the "East Asia Tigers," had not gone unnoticed by other Asian countries, particularly China—even though in 1964 China stilled reeled from the disastrous "Great Leap Forward," a planned-economy program that had been haplessly initiated by Mao, and had yet to even undergo the destructive Mao-led "Cultural Revolution." Milton Friedman, *Capitalism and Freedom* [1962] (Chicago: University of Chicago Press, 2002), ix.

5. "The Fresh Start," *Time*, 10 July 1964; "Reek of Cement"; "Tokyo—Getting Prepared," 18.

6. "Tokyo—Getting Prepared."

7. J. B. Strasser and Laurie Becklund, *Swoosh: The Unauthorized Story of Nike and the Men Who Played There* (New York: HarperCollins, 1993), 17.

8. William J. Baker, *Sports in the Western World* (Urbana: University of Illinois Press, 1988), 272.

9. Baker, *Sports in the Western World*.

10. The tradition of relying on private funds for the Olympic movement was well entrenched, and it remained intact despite the push for funding. John Grombach's 1960 article in the *American Mercury*, alluded to in the last chapter, reflected the argument in favor of relying on the private market for Olympic funding. John V. Grombach, "The Cold War in International Athletics," *The American Mercury*, June 1960, 39–40.

11. *Chicago Daily Tribune*, 26 December 1960.

12. Nicholas Rodis, "The State Department's Athletes Give a New Look to Foreign Policy," *The Amateur Athlete*, no. 8 (August 1964): 18, 23 (Amateur Athletic Union [AAU] Archives, Orlando FL).

13. Public Information Office, "News From Springfield College," Press release from Springfield College, Springfield MA, 20 May 1963 (Edward J. and Gena G. Hickox Library, Basketball Hall of Fame, Springfield MA, hereafter referred to as the Hickox Library).

14. Larry Brown, telephone interview by author, 13 August 2007, Chicago IL, handwritten notes.

15. John Paul Bischoff, *Mr. Iba: Basketball's Aggie Iron Duke* (Oklahoma: Oklahoma Heritage Association, 1980), 13–16. The Kurland quotes appear on pages 115 and 118.

16. Qtd. in Bischoff, *Mr. Iba*, 118.

17. Much criticism of the 1972 team's inability to score has been leveled at Iba, both by the media and some of the players. But the performance of Iba's previous Olympic squads suggests such claims are overemphasized. It seems that a collective lack of offensive skills on the part of the 1972 roster, as much as Iba's tactics, contributed to its struggles to score.

18. G. Russell Lyons, "The Best Is None Too Good—Selection of the 1964 Olympic Team," *1964 U.S. Olympic Team Trials*, Official Program, 24A (Amateur Athletic Library, Los Angeles CA).

19. Letter from Walter Byers, Executive Director NCAA, to Robert Ray, Everett D. Barnes, and the NCAA Olympic Basketball Committee, 4 March 1964 (Hickox Library). Committee members Leon Williams and Robert Brown, both from NCAA schools, tried to gain a fourth NCAA team. The committee voted against the measure, even though by that time, as *Sports Illustrated* put it, "everyone knows the best nonprofessional basketball in the country is played by the 20 or so top big-college teams." "Once Again to Nowhere," *Sports Illustrated*, 22 April 1963, 8.

20. At the trials, the official ball of the U.S. Olympic team, the Last Bilt basketball, was used. Hoping to eliminate the problem of adjusting to different, substandard international balls that had plagued U.S. teams in the past, the basketball committee pushed to have the 1964 Last Bilt basketball adopted by Japan as the official ball of the Games. Japan agreed, but during the Olympic trials, it shifted its position and announced that Japanese basketballs would be used in Tokyo. Minutes of the U.S. Olympic Basketball Committee Meeting, 4 April 1964, Hotel Whitman, Jamaica NY (Hickox Library).

21. "Key Rules for International Basketball," *1964 U.S. Olympic Team Trials*, 24C (Amateur Athletic Library, Los Angeles CA).

22. "Yugoslav Coach Visits USA," *Converse 1964 Basketball Yearbook*, 43rd ed. (Malden MA: Converse Rubber Company, 1964), 49 (University of Notre Dame Archives, South Bend IN).

23. The AAU's Wilson, at six feet eight, was considered one of the greatest players to come out of Chicago's scholastic Public League. He had helped carry on the winning tradition at Cincinnati, started by Oscar Robertson, by leading the Bearcats to the national title in 1962. *Chicago Tribune*, 6 April 1964.

24. Adolph H. Grundman, *The Golden Age of Amateur Basketball: The AAU Tournament, 1921–1968* (Lincoln: University of Nebraska Press, 2004), 223.

25. John Bach, "George Wilson Helps USA Basketball Stay Perfect in '64," *UC Magazine*, January 2009, http://www.magazine.uc.edu/0109/wilson.htm (accessed 14 April 2009).

26. Tom C. Brody, "Who Says You Can't Win 'em All?" *Sports Illustrated*, 13 April 1964, 104.

27. Barnes did not play on the 1966 Texas Western national championship that boasted the first all-black starting five to win the title, but he did play a pivotal role in building the program to make such a run. As a senior, Barnes averaged 29.2 points and 19.2 rebounds per game and was selected first in the NBA draft by the New York Knicks. In his rookie campaign Barnes averaged 15.5 points. The media picked Willis Reed as rookie of the year, but NBA players voted for Barnes. *Jonesboro Sun*, 22 September 2002.

28. *Chicago Tribune*, 4 May 1963.

29. Brown interview; Grundman, *Golden Age of Amateur Basketball*, 200.

30. Grundman, *Golden Age of Amateur Basketball*, 223; Brown interview.

31. *Chicago Tribune*, 6 April 1964; Grundman, *Golden Age of Amateur Basketball*, 224.

32. Brown interview.

33. "Sensing His Moment: Changed by his parents' deaths and his wife's illness, careful Bill Bradley takes the risky step that he's always avoided," *People Weekly*, 31 January 2000, 17; *Washington Post*, 21 December 1964.

34. *Washington Post*, 21 December 1964.

35. Bill Bradley, *Time Present, Time Past: A Memoir* (New York: Vintage Books, 1996), 59–60.

36. *Chicago Tribune*, 7 May 1965.

37. The trip involved a U.S. team sponsored by the State Department but under the direction of the AAU. Minutes of the U.S. Olympic Basketball Committee Meeting, 4 April 1964, Jamaica NY (Hickox Library). The U.S. Olympic Basketball Committee leader and high-ranking AAU member G. Russell Lyons had penned a bulletin a few weeks before the April 1964 Olympic trials declaring that he planned to turn the upcoming trip to the Soviet Union into an unofficial warm-up for the Olympic tournament. In the bulletin Lyons stated, "My recent conversation with the Soviet sports leaders . . . as well as other reports out of Europe, gave me the information that the rest of the world actually believes they have caught up with the United States in basketball. They expect either Russia, Poland, Yugoslavia, or Brazil to beat us during the Olympic Games."

To meet the challenge, Lyons suggested that the team headed to the Soviet Union include "the best 10 or 12 players from the Olympic basketball trials who are available." G. Russell Lyons, "Recommendation for Appointment of the U.S. Olympic Basketball Team Head Coach," bulletin to all members of the U.S. Olympic Basketball Committee (Hickox Library).

But the AAU's proposed starting date for the Soviet trip fell just before the end of most college semesters. Since most of its players could not miss this crucial class time, the NCAA disagreed vehemently with the AAU's plan to use the trip as a kind of Olympic warm-up. Prodded by the increasing influence of its NCAA members, in the end, the basketball committee made it clear that the Soviet trip would not influence the selection process for the Olympic team. The whole episode showed the amateur bodies' struggles to unify their efforts to export basketball. *Washington Post*, 23 April 1964.

38. *Washington Post*, 22 April 1964.

39. Walter Bingham, "The Bucket Brigade of '60 (Special Advertising Section)," *Sports Illustrated*, 29 August 1988, 74.

40. "Wither, Oh Wither?" *Time*, 27 January 1961, 52.

41. After the 1970 World Championships and then after the 1980 Moscow Games, Gomelsky was removed from the national team for not winning the championship and because the Soviet government suspected that he intended to defect. However, the "Silver Fox" triumphantly wrestled back the reins of the national team after the 1984 Los Angeles Games, leading the Soviets to their second Olympic basketball gold medal four years later in Seoul. International Jewish Sports Hall of Fame, http://www.jewishsports.net/BioPages/AlexanderGomelsky.htm (accessed 20 July 2005); "Carl Schreck, 'Papa' of Soviet Basketball Dies at Age 77," MoscowTimes.com, 17 August 2005, http://www.themoscowtimes.com/stories/2005/08/17/003.html (accessed 27 August 2007).

42. *Washington Post*, 23 April 1964. Pressure to maintain U.S. basketball supremacy had ratcheted up a year earlier when, in the run-up to the Pan-Am Games, speculation from prognosticators that the United States faced imminent defeat grew quite strong. However, the U.S. squad, led by the future Olympians Lucious Jackson and Jerry Shipp, along with Willis Reed, won the 1963 Pan-Am championship with a 57–51 victory over Argentina in the final (*Washington Post*, 3 May 1963).

43. In 1951 Indonesia and other "emerging nations" in Asia, namely, Afghanistan, Burma, Ceylon, India, Pakistan, the Philippines, and Thailand, had organized a federation that led to the first Asian Games in New Delhi. Relatively successful, the Asian Games took place again in 1954, this time in Manila, and then in 1958 in Tokyo. Baker, *History of Western Sports*, 274.

44. Baker, *History of Western Sports*, 88.

45. *Asahi Evening News*, 24 October 1964 (Hickox Library).

46. Baker, *History of Western Sports*, 90.

47. *New York Times*, 11 October 1964.

48. Jack Olsen, "The Doves and Gongs of Tokyo," *Sports Illustrated*, 22 October 1964, 35.

49. *New York Times*, 11 October 1964.

50. "It'll Be an Automated Olympics," *Amateur Athlete*, no. 8 (August 1964): 20 (AAU Archives, Orlando FL). In addition, Japan's brand-new monorail, which it dubbed the "world's longest," had opened in time for the Olympics. At a cost of $54.4 million, the monorail stretched nine miles and carried passengers at speeds of up to 65 mph, allowing visitors to get from the airport to downtown Tokyo in fifteen minutes. *Chicago Tribune*, 17 September 1964.

51. *Washington Post*, 10 July 1962.

52. *Chicago Tribune*, 15 July 1964.

53. Dave Brady, *Washington Post*, 24 May 1964.

54. *Washington Post*, 23 July 1964.

55. *Washington Post*, 23 July 1964.

56. In 1960 CBS enjoyed broadcasting rights only in North America. Television rights income for other areas of the world, notably in Europe, brought the total income from television rights for the IOC to $1.178 million. In 1964 NBC enjoyed nearly exclusive coverage throughout the entire world, except for the Caribbean, which contributed $78,000, bringing the IOC's total income from the sale of television rights in 1964 to $1.578 million. Miquel de Moragas Spa, Nancy K. Rivenburgh, and James F. Larson, *Television in the Olympics: International Research Project* (London: John Libbey, 1995), 19.

57. Brown interview.

58. *New York Times*, 11 October 1964.

59. Chuck O'Donnell, "Mel Counts: With the United States Playing the 'Underdog' Role, the Squad Came Together to Keep an Olympic Winning Streak Alive," *Basketball Digest*, 1 November 2004, 22.

60. Arthur Daley, *New York Times*, 12 October 1964.

61. *Basketball Digest*, 12 October 1964.

62. O'Donnell, "Mel Counts," 22; Brown interview.

63. *New York Times*, 14 October 1964.

64. "Yugoslav Coach Visits USA," *Converse 1964 Basketball Yearbook*, 43rd ed. (Malden MA: Converse Rubber Company, 1964), 21 (University of Notre Dame Archives, South Bend IN).

65. Bob Ryan, *Boston Globe*, 21 October 1988.

66. Shipp and Bradley led the United States with 22 and 18 points, respectively.

67. Bach, "George Wilson Helps USA Basketball"; *Washington Post*, 17 October 1964.

68. *Asahi Evening News*, 18 October 1964 (Hickox Library).

69. *Asahi Evening News*, 18 October 1964 (Hickox Library).

70. *New York Times*, 22 October 1964.

71. The Williams quote is from the *Chicago Tribune*, 17 October 1964. The Rossini quote appeared in Jack Underwood, "An Exuberant Finish in Tokyo," *Sports Illustrated*, 2 November 1964, 30.

72. R. Protokollid Taru, "Raagivad koigile," *Edasi*, 30 October 1964, 4. Gomelsky is quoted in Underwood, "Exuberant Finish in Tokyo," 29–30.

73. Underwood, "Exuberant Finish in Tokyo," 29–30; *New York Times*, 24 October 1964; Brown interview, 13 August 2007.

74. Underwood, "Exuberant Finish in Tokyo," 30.

75. Underwood, "Exuberant Finish in Tokyo," 30; Brown interview; O'Donnell, "Mel Counts," 22.

76. Taru, "Raagivad koigile," 4; "Nagu ikka-ainult hobemedalid," *Kehakultuur*, no. 23 (1964): 718–20.

77. *Chicago Tribune*, 24 October 1964.

78. Brown interview.

79. Brown interview.

7. SATELLITES, CABLE, AND SHOES IN MEXICO CITY

1. Miquel de Moragas Spa, Nancy K. Rivenburgh, James F. Larson, *Television in the Olympics* (London: John Libbey, 1995), 19.

2. *New York Times*, 6 October 1968.

3. Roone Arledge, "The Biggest Live Remote Telecast in TV History," *Amateur Athlete*, no. 10 (October 1968): 16–17 (Amateur Athletic Union [AAU] Archives, Orlando FL).

4. *Washington Post*, 23 June 1967; *Washington Post*, 25 July 1969.

5. "The Golden Age of Sport," *Time*, 2 June 1967, http://www.time.com/time/maga zine (accessed 7 October 2006).

6. J. B. Strasser and Laurie Becklund, *Swoosh: The Unauthorized Story of Nike and the Men Who Played There* (New York: HarperCollins, 1993), 83.

7. As a result of the Puma versus Adidas rivalry, an estimated two hundred athletes accepted more than $100,000 in payoffs in Mexico City, which put many of them under suspicion. Strasser and Becklund, *Swoosh*, 82–83.

8. Strasser and Becklund, *Swoosh*, 82.

9. Converse advertisement, *Sports Illustrated*, 30 September 1968, 4.

10. Spencer Haywood, *The Rise, The Fall, The Recovery* (New York: Amistad Press, 1992), 16.

11. Haywood, *The Rise, The Fall, The Recovery*, 16.

12. Haywood, *The Rise, The Fall, The Recovery*, 5.

13. Bill Hosket, interview by author, 7 July 2008, Portage IN, tape recording.

14. *Chicago Tribune*, 7 March 1968.

15. *Chicago Tribune*, 26 March 1968.

16. *Washington Post*, 1 April 1968.

17. *Washington Post*, 6 April 1968.

18. *Washington Post*, 6 April 1968.

19. Terry Pluto, "Out of Their League: Former Stars of the American Basketball Association," *The Sporting News*, 8 January 1996, available from http://www.highbeam.com/library/docfree.asp?DOCID=1G1:17989468&num=4&ctrlInfo=Round18%3AProd%3ASR%3AResult&ao=&FreePremium=BOTH (accessed 14 February 2006).

20. Larry Brown, telephone interview by author, 13 August 2007, Chicago IL, handwritten notes.

21. Walter LaFeber, *America, Russia, and the Cold War, 1945–2000* (Boston: McGraw Hill, 2002), 270.

22. In November 1967 the boycott movement gained further backing in Los Angeles, where Edwards broached the matter with Reverend Martin Luther King Jr. and Floyd McCissick, head of CORE, both of whom voiced support for the cause. By February 1968, however, an *Ebony* poll suggested that only 1 percent of black athletes agreed with the boycott proposal, while 28 percent were "undecided" and "a massive 71 per cent reject

the idea outright." In March 1968 Edwards declared that Lew Alcindor could be counted among those "prepared to sacrifice his personal opportunity at the Olympics in order to win some recognition for the plight of the race." And, in a *Saturday Evening Post* article, Edwards defended the boycott by recalling that during his childhood in East Saint Louis, Illinois, his family "drank boiled ditch water." Edwards also decried that in East Saint Louis, trade union jobs remained off-limits to blacks. Harry Edwards, "Why Negroes Should Boycott Whitey's Olympics," *Saturday Evening Post,* 9 March 1968, 6–8.

23. Kareem Abdul-Jabbar, *Giant Steps* (New York: Bantam Books, 1983), 171, 170–71.

24. Like Russell, Abdul-Jabbar commented on a number of political and social issues. His autobiography covers a remarkable breadth of topics. In one two-page section, he touches on Vietnam, public confusion about Islam and Black Muslims in the 1960s, the respect for Jews that his Muslim mentor held, the gaudy wealth of Arab princes, and the tactics of major oil companies and other international corporations. Abdul-Jabbar, *Giant Steps,* 178–79. In 2004 he published a nonfiction book, *Brothers in Arms,* about an all-black tank battalion in World War II.

25. "The Angry Black Athlete," *Newsweek,* 15 July 1968, 56.

26. Abdul-Jabbar, *Giant Steps,* 170–71.

27. Qtd. in "Angry Black Athlete," 56.

28. Qtd. in "Angry Black Athlete," 56.

29. Edwards, "Why Negroes Should Boycott Whitey's Olympics," 6–8.

30. "Ebony Poll of Athletes Indicates Mexico City Sports Spectacular," *Ebony,* 27 February 1968, 113.

31. Qtd. in "Angry Black Athlete," 56.

32. Milton Katz, *Breaking Through: John B. McClendon, Basketball Legend and Civil Rights Pioneer* (Fayetteville: University of Arkansas Press, 2007), 165–66.

33. Curry Kirkpatrick, "The Team That Went over the Hill: The Olympic Trials Were Chiefly Distinguished by the Absence of 20 of Our Best College Players," *Sports Illustrated,* 15 April 1968, 91. Ironically, Scott, who went on to lead the ACC in scoring his senior year and had a fine pro career, became known to some as a "black militant" at North Carolina, according to Barry Jacobs, for associating with members of the Black Student Movement. Barry Jacobs, *Across the Line: Profiles in Basketball Courage: Tales of the First Black Players in the ACC and SEC* (Guilford: Lyons Press, 2008), 120–21.

34. "University Arena—Site of 1968 Olympic Trials," *Olympic Pictorial: 1968 U.S. Olympic Team Trials,* program for the 1968 Olympic Trials, 29G (Edward J. and Gena G. Hickox Library, Basketball Hall of Fame, Springfield MA, hereafter referred to as the Hickox Library).

35. Haywood, *The Rise, The Fall, The Recovery,* 105; Kirkpatrick, "The Team That Went over the Hill," 91.

36. Haywood, *The Rise, The Fall, The Recovery,* 95, 96.

37. Haywood, *The Rise, The Fall, The Recovery,* 16.

38. Haywood, *The Rise, The Fall, The Recovery,* 1.

39. Haywood, *The Rise, The Fall, The Recovery,* 16.

40. Haywood, *The Rise, The Fall, The Recovery*, 95, 96; Jayda Evans, "Spencer Haywood Timeline," *Seattle Times*, 25 February 2007, http://seattletimes.nwsource.com/htmlsports/2003588112_haywoodtimeline25.html (accessed 11 April 2008); Adolph H. Grundman, *The Golden Age of Amateur Basketball: The AAU Tournament, 1921–1968* (Lincoln: University of Nebraska Press, 2004), 237.

41. Haywood, *The Rise, The Fall, The Recovery*, 95, 96.

42. No players from the NCAA champion UCLA Bruins attended. NCAA Executive Director Byers said he had inquired about the availability of Wooden's star players Alcindor, Mike Warren, and Lucius Allen but that UCLA athletic director J. D. Morgan had cited scholastic reasons for their absences. When questioned by the press, UCLA public information official Vic Kelley stated that any conjecture that their absence was related to the "Negro boycott of the Olympics would be pure speculation." *Chicago Tribune*, 28 February 1968.

43. *Chicago Tribune*, 31 March 1968.

44. *Washington Post*, 13 March 1968.

45. Kirkpatrick, "The Team That Went over the Hill," 91.

46. This and the preceding quotes are from the Hosket interview.

47. Bill Gutman, *Pistol Pete Maravich: The Making of a Basketball Superstar* (New York: Grosset & Dunlap, 1972), 75, 76.

48. Hosket interview.

49. Kirkpatrick, "The Team That Went over the Hill," 92.

50. *Washington Post*, 6 April 1968.

51. Kirkpatrick, "The Team That Went over the Hill," 92.

52. Hosket interview; "Games of the XIXth Olympiad—1968," http://www.usabasketball.com/news.php?news_page=moly_1968 (accessed 21 July 2008).

53. Fowler had played on the NABL's Goodyear Wingfoots that season with the prospect of landing a spot on the Olympic team in mind. The previous summer, he had captained the undefeated, gold medal–winning U.S. Pan-American team in Winnipeg, Canada, which gave him an advantage with selectors. Though an unselfish player and strong leader, had he not benefited from a selection process that still chose players from the AAU, Fowler would not likely have been on the Olympic team. By then, it was clear that NABL ball had lost out to professional avenues. Fowler admitted as much to the *Amateur Athlete*, saying, "If you can't cut it with the pros, our setup is great." Bill Nichols, "Cal Fowler Dribbles toward Mexico City," *The Amateur Athlete*, no. 2 (February 1968): 14 (Amateur Athletic Union [AAU] Archives, Orlando FL). Robert Bradley et al., "History of the Amateur Athletic Union," *The Association for Professional Basketball Research*, http://www.apbr.org/aau.html (accessed 11 April 2008).

54. *Washington Post*, 18 April 1968; Bob Knight and Bob Hammel, *Knight: My Story* (New York: Thomas Dunne Books, 2003), 91, at http://books.google.com/ (accessed 18 July 2007).

55. *Washington Post*, 8 April 1968.

56. As a young man, McClendon attended Kansas University when Dr. Naismith was there and worked as a student basketball assistant for "Phog" Allen (blacks were

not allowed to play at Kansas then). Later, he spent many years as the head coach at North Carolina College and the Hampton Institute; he also worked at a couple of other all-black colleges, compiling 523 wins and only 165 losses. A two-time Olympic assistant, he was the first African American to coach in the ABA and also coached Cleveland State University. His coaching style is summed up by the titles of the two books he penned on the sport: *Fast Break Basketball* and *The Fast Break Game*.

57. *Washington Post*, 20 June 1968.

58. Haywood, *The Rise, The Fall, The Recovery*, 108.

59. *Washington Post*, 24 June 1968.

60. Haywood, *The Rise, The Fall, The Recovery*, 108, 109.

61. *Washington Post*, 30 June 1968.

62. Still, the attendance figures in the Soviet Union, overall, paled in comparison to those in the United States. Robert Edelman, *Serious Fun: A History of Spectator Sports in the USSR* (New York: Oxford University Press, 1993), 160, 164.

63. A. Tobi, "Olumpiakorvpalli stardi eel," *Kehakultuur*, no. 19 (1968): 584–86.

64. *Washington Post*, 1 September 1968.

65. *Washington Post*, 1 October 1968.

66. *Washington Post*, 1 October 1968; "Seventh Straight," *Time*, 1 November 1968, 56; "Basketball," *The Amateur Athlete*, no. 10 (October 1968): 22 (AAU Archives, Orlando FL).

67. Quotes from this and the previous paragraph are from the Hosket interview.

68. Bob Ottum, "Grim Countdown to the Games," *Sports Illustrated*, 14 October 1968, 38, 37; "The Scene a la Mexicono," *Time*, 18 October 1968, http://www.time.com/time/magazine (accessed 7 October 2006). In the two months leading up to the Games, *Time* estimated that the unrest had claimed around one hundred total deaths. "The Scene a la Mexicono."

69. Allen Guttmann, *The Olympics: A History of the Modern Games* (Urbana: University of Illinois Press, 2002), 128, 129. Problems in Africa had festered for months leading up to the Mexico City Games. On 15 February 1968, the IOC announced its decision to accept South Africa into the Olympics. Two days later, Ethiopia and Algeria announced their intention to boycott as a result. Within weeks, the remaining thirty nations in the Organization of African Unity followed suit.

70. *New York Times*, 13 October 1968.

71. Ottum, "Grim Countdown to the Games," 37.

72. Steve Cady of the *New York Times* reported that "perhaps the greatest show of spontaneous feeling" during the opening ceremonies came when the Mexican crowd, aware of Czechoslovakia's recent plight in standing up to the Soviet Union, met the Czech delegation with "wild cheers" of "Che-os." *New York Times*, 13 October 1968.

73. *New York Times*, 13 October 1968.

74. *New York Times*, 16 October 1968.

75. Bob Ryan, "Late, Great Cosic Worthy Hall Pick," *Boston Globe*, 7 May 1996, available from http://www.highbeam.com/doc/1P2-8371725.html (accessed 4 August 2008).

76. JoJo White led the team with twenty-four points, army captain Michael Silliman

scored fourteen, and Calvin Fowler of the AAU's Goodyear Wingfoots tallied thirteen. *Boston Globe*, 17 October 1968.

77. *Boston Globe*, 21 October 1968; Hosket interview.

78. *New York Times*, 24 October 1968. The comments about JoJo White in the previous paragraph are also from this article.

79. Associated Press, "United States Hoop Ace Ailing for Olympic Finale," 26 October 1968 (Hickox Library); *Chicago Tribune*, 26 October 1968.

80. Hosket's comments are from the author's interview with him. The comments on Haywood are from "Mexico '68: End in Triumph," *Sports Illustrated* vol. 29, 4 November 1968, 20–27. Coach Zeravica's first comment in the paragraph is from "Mexico '68" and the second is from the *New York Times*, 27 October 1968. The Chicago *Tribune*'s description of the action is from 26 October 1968.

81. "Seventh Straight," *Time*, 1 November 1968, 56; "Mexico '68," 20–27.

82. Associated Press, "Olympic Vets Pin 'Best Ever' Tag on Haywood," 27 October 1968 (Hickox Library).

83. "Learning New Moves," *The Detroit News*, 8 April 1991 (Hickox Library); Milton S. Katz, *Breaking Through: John B. McClendon, Basketball Legend and Civil Rights Pioneer* (Fayetteville: University of Arkansas Press, 2007), 170–72, 175.

84. Leonard Lewin, "Remembers Haywood," *New York Post*, 16 August 1972 (Hickox Library); Libby and Haywood, *Stand Up For Something*, 1, 10.

85. *Sunday Oregonian*, 30 September 1990. In 1988 Haywood, thanks in no small part to the efforts of Kareem Abdul-Jabbar, was given his 1988 championship ring, and in 1992 he received half of his share of the 1980 playoff money. Haywood, *The Rise, The Fall, The Recovery*, 273.

86. *The Sunday Oregonian*, 30 September 1990.

87. "The Olympics: Passionless Games," *Time*, 22 November 1968, 50.

8. MAYHEM IN MUNICH

1. *New York Times*, 27 August 1972.

2. Christopher Young, "Kaiser Franz and the Communist Bowl: Cultural Memory and Munich's Olympic Stadium," *American Behavioral Scientist* 46 (2003): 1480–81, http://abs.sagepub.com/cgi/content/abstract/46/11/1476 (accessed 17 February 2009); "Spitz," *Time*, 11 September 1972, http://www.time.com/time/magazine (accessed 7 October 2006).

3. Red Smith, article title *New York Times*, 27 August 1972.

4. Syncom was purchased by Boeing in 2000 and became Boeing Satellite Systems.

5. Miquel de Moragas Spa, Nancy K. Rivenburgh, and James F. Larson, *Television in the Olympics* (London: John Libbey, 1995), 19.

6. Roone Arledge, *Roone: A Memoir* (New York: HarperCollins, 2003), 122–23.

7. David Wharton, Associated Press, "Eye on the Storm: Events in Munich Forever Changed Games, and How TV Presents Them," *Los Angeles Times*, http://apse.dallas news.com/contest/2002/writing/over250/over250.enterprise.second1a.html (accessed 28 October 2005).

8. Richard Espy, *The Politics of the Olympic Games* (Los Angeles: University of California Press, 1979), 3.

9. James Mann, *About Face: A History of America's Curious Relationship with China, From Nixon to Clinton* (New York: Vintage Books, 2000), 29.

10. Brook Larmer, "The Center of the World," *Foreign Policy*, September/October 2005, 66–68.

11. *Washington Post*, 14 December 1968, 21 May 1969, 3 March 1971. In May of 1969 the Madison Square Garden Center and Manhattan Cable Television (MTC) announced a package of 125 sporting events, including basketball.

12. When the "Clydes" made a resurgence in the early 1990s, Butterfly, the front man for the legendary hip-hop group Digable Planets, told the *New York Times*, "Hip-hoppers dug the shoes because they came in mad flavors . . . The Puma Clyde is the ultimate icon of hip-hop culture." *New York Times*, 21 February 1993.

13. Angela Taylor, *New York Times*, 2 September 1972; *Washington Post*, 2 January 1972; "The Athlete as Peacock," *Time*, 4 January 1971, http://www.time.com/time/magazine (accessed 7 October 2006).

14. Benjamin G. Rader, *American Sports: From the Age of Folk Games to the Age of Televised Sports* (New Jersey: Prentice Hall, 2004), 293.

15. *Washington Post*, 6 May 1970.

16. Among the players whose uncertainty frustrated Iba was Kermit Washington of American University because he was a center. (He did end up attending the trials, though he did not make the team.) Iba told reporters, "I really think we'll be okay with guards and forwards, but I don't know if we'll have a top quality center." *Washington Post*, 24 March 1972.

17. *Washington Post*, 22 July 1972.

18. Bill Walton and Gene Wojciechowski, *Nothing But Net: Just Give Me the Ball and Get Out of My Way* (New York: Hyperion, 1994), 46–48.

19. Walton maintained that, if Olympic officials "had some foresight and had been willing to work with the players, I would have been there." Walton, *Nothing But Net*, 50–51.

20. Walton, *Nothing But Net*, 43.

21. Christopher Clark Elzey, "Munich 1972: Sport, Politics, and Tragedy" (PhD diss., Purdue University, 2004), 255.

22. Terry Pluto's *Loose Balls* offers a fine treatment of the ABA. Terry Pluto, *Loose Balls: The Short, Wild Life of the American Basketball Association* (New York: Simon and Schuster, 1990), 317.

23. The *New York Times* called the signing, worth an estimated $1.5 million over five years, a "coup" for the ABA. McGuire was not caught completely off-guard by the decision; he had said earlier that he would not blame Chones for turning pro "because I've looked in my icebox and I've looked in his." *New York Times*, 19 February 1972.

24. *Washington Post*, 24 March 1972, 22 June 1972.

25. "Anyone for Pallacanestro?" *Time*, 28 February 1969, http://www.time.com/time/magazine (accessed 7 October 2006); Ian Thomsen, "Russian Revolution," *Sports Illustrated*, 28 April 2008, 61.

26. An example of a basketball-sponsoring firm is Eldorado, an ice cream company that sponsored a team in Bologna, Italy. "Anyone for Pallacanestro?" *Time,* http://www.time.com/time/magazine (accessed 7 October 2006).

27. *Washington Post,* 21 March 1972.

28. *Washington Post,* 21 March 1972.

29. Elzey, "Munich 1972," 258; Neil Attner, *Washington Post,* 25 June 1972.

30. *Washington Post,* 22 June 1972.

31. *Washington Post,* 25 June 1972.

32. *Washington Post,* 22 June 1972.

33. *Washington Post,* 22 June 1972.

34. Elzey, "Munich 1972," 260.

35. *Washington Post,* 24 June 1972, 9 July 1975.

36. The unknown coach's comments appeared in the *Washington Post,* 25 June 1972; those of Attner are from the *Washington Post,* 24 June 1972.

37. *Washington Post,* 26 June 1972.

38. *New York Times,* 28 August 1972. After the Games, Henderson played collegiate basketball at the University of Hawaii.

39. *Washington Post,* 26 June 1972.

40. *Chicago Tribune,* 26 August 1972; Gary Smith, "A Few Pieces of Silver: 1972 Silver-medal Winning U.S. Basketball Team," *Sports Illustrated,* 15 June 1992, available from http://www.highbeam.com/library/doc3.asp?DOCID=1G1:12244782&num=3&ctrlI nfo=Round18%3AProd%3ASR%3AResult&ao=&FreePremium=BOTH (accessed 28 October 2005).

41. On McMillen as "establishment player," see *Washington Post,* 12 July 1972. The official's statement appears in the *Washington Post,* 26 June 1972.

42. Dan Raley, "Where Are They Now? Swen Nater, Former College and NBA Player," *Seattle Post-Intelligencer,* 9 January 2008, http://www.seattlepi.nwsource.com/basket ball/346598_where09.html (accessed 17 February 2009).

43. Nater's comments appear in the *Washington Post,* 22 July 1972; Bach's statement is qtd. in Elzey, "Munich 1972," 259.

44. *Washington Post,* 22 July 1972.

45. *Washington Post,* 19 July 1972.

46. *Washington Post,* 15 August 1972.

47. *Washington Post,* 30 July 1972, 11 August 1972, and 16 August 1972. Beard's comments are qtd. in Elzey, "Munich 1972," 260.

48. *Washington Post,* 28 August 1972.

49. *Chicago Tribune,* 28 August 1972.

50. *New York Times,* 28 August 1972.

51. *New York Times,* 30 August 1972.

52. All statements in the paragraph are from the *Chicago Tribune,* 31 August 1972.

53. *New York Times,* 3 September 1972; *Chicago Tribune,* 4 September 1972.

54. *New York Times,* 4 September 1972. In the Soviet Union's final test before the semifinal medal round, it squeaked by Yugoslavia 74–67. The six-feet-eight, sharpshooting

Belov played a crucial role again. It was a big win, as Yugoslavia, powered by the crafty big man Chosich Kalshimir, had upset the Soviets in Mexico City. The Soviets came into the game with some confidence, though, as they had won two of their last three meetings with Yugoslavia before Munich. *Washington Post*, 20 August 1972.

55. *Washington Post*, 20 August 1972; Elzey, "Munich 1972," 262.

56. *Washington Post*, 20 August 1972.

57. *New York Times*, 6 September 1972.

58. Allen Guttmann, *The Games Must Go On: Avery Brundage and the Olympic Movement* (New York: Columbia University Press, 1984), 254. Brundage received negative press for the way he handled the attack, largely because the Games continued so hastily and because he equated the terrorist attack with what he called the other "savage attack" on the Olympics, the threatened boycott of the Munich Olympics by many African nations on account of the Rhodesian government's treatment of its black citizens. "Dampening the Olympic Torch," *Time*, 18 September 1972, http://www.time.com/time/magazine (accessed 7 October 2006).

59. *New York Times*, 7 September 1972.

60. *Chicago Tribune*, 9 September 1972.

61. *New York Times*, 10 September 1972.

62. *Chicago Tribune*, 10 September 1972.

63. David Wharton, "Second-Hand Smoke: Thirty years have done little to cool the still-smoldering United States–Soviet Olympic basketball controversy, and American players are still doing a slow burn about the chaotic ending to the gold-medal game in Munich," *Los Angeles Times*, http://apse.dallasnews.com/contest/2002/writing/over250/over250.enterprise.second16a.html (accessed 28 October 2005).

64. The comments of Haskins and Ratleff appear in Wharton, "Second-Hand Smoke."

65. Elzey, "Munich 1972," 262–63; "Aleksandr 'Sascha' Gomelsky," International Jewish Sports Hall of Fame, http://www.jewishsports.net/BioPages/AlexanderGomelsky.htm (accessed 26 April 2008).

66. Smith, "A Few Pieces of Silver."

67. *New York Times*, 10 September 1972.

68. Brokhin, *Big Red Machine*, 133.

69. Brokhin, *Big Red Machine*, 134.

70. Elzey, "Munich 1972," 272.

71. Elzey, "Munich 1972," 288.

72. Wharton, "Second-Hand Smoke."

73. *New York Times*, 10 September 1972; Play-by-play broadcast, 1972 Olympic basketball final, "Confusion reigns," Munich, West Germany, September 11, 1972, http://www.historychannel.com/speeches/archive/speech_373.html (accessed 1 November 2005).

74. Smith, "A Few Pieces of Silver."

75. Wharton, "Second-Hand Smoke."

76. Wharton, "Second-Hand Smoke."

77. Elzey, "Munich 1972," 273.

78. Neil Amdur, *New York Times*, 10 September 1972; *Chicago Tribune*, 10 September 1972.

79. *New York Times*, 10 September 1972.

80. Forbes qtd. in Smith, "A Few Pieces of Silver"; the Iba quote is from the *New York Times*, 10 September 1972.

81. Elzey, "Munich 1972," 284.

82. *Washington Post*, 11 September 1972.

83. Smith, "A Few Pieces of Silver."

84. Wharton, "Second-Hand Smoke."

85. Hendrick Smith, *New York Times*, 25 October 1973; "Sports, Socialist Style," *Time*, 5 November 1973, http://www.time.com/time/magazine (accessed 7 October 2006).

86. *New York Times*, 25 October 1973.

87. *New York Times*, 25 October 1973.

88. Smith, "A Few Pieces of Silver." Bantom's comments from before the Games also appear in this article.

9. SPEED AND POLITICS IN MONTREAL AND MOSCOW

1. J. B. Strasser and Laurie Becklund, *Swoosh: The Unauthorized Story of Nike and the Men Who Played There* (New York: HarperCollins, 1993), 204.

2. Dean Smith, *A Coach's Life: My 40 Years in College Basketball* (New York: Random House, 2002), 170.

3. Dantley also said that he had broached the prospect of wearing Adidas shoes at the Games beforehand and was even directed to get a doctor's order to do so, which he apparently did. He also noted that early in his professional career he got out of a Nike contract that paid him better than an Adidas one because he thought Adidas shoes fit better. Adrian Dantley, telephone interview by author, 7 August 2007, Ogden Dunes IN handwritten notes.

4. *New York Times*, 12 May 1973; Ralph Wiley, ESPN.com Page 2 columnist, http://proxy.espn.go.com/page2/s/wiley/010607.html (accessed 14 September 2005).

5. Smith, *A Coach's Life*, 169.

6. *Chicago Tribune*, 1 August 1976.

7. *Chicago Tribune*, 14 February 1973.

8. *Washington Post*, 24 February 1973.

9. *Washington Post*, 24 February 1973.

10. *Washington Post*, 30 April 1973.

11. The cold war historian LaFeber notes, however, that as the two moved toward a more belligerent stance, seeds were planted that helped set the stage for the Soviet demise. Specifically, LaFeber points to Kissinger's work on the 1975 Helsinki agreements. The Helsinki agreements did elicit an agreement from the Soviet Union to follow a more liberal human rights policy. Later, a top Soviet diplomat asserted that the Helsinki accords "gradually became a manifesto of the dissident and liberal movement, a development totally beyond the imagination of the Soviet leadership." Walter LaFeber, *America, Russia, and the Cold War, 1945–2000* (Boston: McGraw Hill, 2002), 296–97.

12. Smith, *A Coach's Life*, 24.

13. Dantley interview.

14. *Chicago Tribune*, 6 June 1976.

15. *Chicago Tribune*, 8 July 1976.

16. Tree Rollins of Clemson, Ralph Dollinger of UCLA, Glenn Sudhop of North Carolina State, James Edwards of the University of Washington, and Jack Sikma of Illinois Wesleyan were the seven-footers at the trials.

17. *New York Times*, 6 June 1976.

18. *Washington Post*, 8 June 1976.

19. *Chicago Tribune*, 6 June 1976.

20. Smith, *A Coach's Life*, 167.

21. Robert Markus, *Chicago Tribune*, 7 June 1976.

22. Smith, *A Coach's Life*, 165.

23. *Chicago Tribune*, 27 June 1976.

24. Dantley interview.

25. Dantley interview.

26. *Washington Post*, 8 June 1976.

27. *Washington Post*, 8 June 1976.

28. *Washington Post*, 8 June 1976.

29. *Chicago Tribune*, 20 June 1976.

30. *Chicago Tribune*, 27 June 1976.

31. *Chicago Tribune*, 25 June 1976.

32. *Chicago Tribune*, 27 June 1976.

33. "Quebec's Big Owe Stadium Debt Is Over," CBCNews.ca, 19 December 2006, http://www.cbc.ca/canada/montreal/story/2006/12/19/qc-olympicstadium.html (accessed 4 August 2008).

34. Robert Barney, interview by author, 30 July 2008, Portage IN, tape recording.

35. "Ready to Raise the Torch," *Time*, 21 June 1976, http://www.time.com/time/magazine (accessed 7 October 2006).

36. "The Billion-Dollar Olympics," *Forbes*, 15 April 1976, 47–49.

37. "Quebec's Big Owe Stadium Debt Is Over."

38. Soviet Minister of Sport Sergei Pavlov argued that the "secret second ballot was not inspired by interests of sport and strengthening Olympic ideals." Other officials suggested Olympic bias against socialist bids. Meanwhile, Los Angeles mayor Sam Yorty, though disappointed that his city had lost, said he was glad the Games remained in the "free world." Richard Espy, *The Politics of the Olympic Games* (Los Angeles: University of California Press, 1979), 132.

39. Espy, *Politics of the Olympic Games*, 132.

40. *New York Times*, 18 July 1976.

41. *New York Times*, 21 July 1976.

42. *New York Times*, 18 July 1976.

43. *New York Times*, 20 July 1976.

44. *New York Times*, 18 July 1976.

45. David B. Kanin, "The Olympic Movement: Organized Sport in the International System," *Intellect* 104 (April 1976): 496, 497, 498.

46. *New York Times*, 15 October 1970.

47. *New York Times*, 16 March 1974.

48. "The Widest World of Sports," *Time*, 9 August 1976, http://www.time.com/time/magazine (accessed 7 October 2006); "Brought to You By . . . ," *Time*, 19 July 1976, http://www.time.com/time/magazine (accessed 7 October 2006).

49. "The Widest World of Sports"; "Brought to You By . . ."

50. *New York Times*, 18 July 1976.

51. *New York Times*, 18 July 1976.

52. Bill Hosket, interview by author, 7 July 2008, Portage IN, tape recording.

53. *Chicago Tribune*, 21 July 1976; Dantley interview.

54. *Chicago Tribune*, 2 September 1976.

55. *New York Times*, 22 July 1976.

56. The United States held a comfortable seventeen-point lead in the final minutes before Czechoslovakia tallied the game's final twelve points in relatively harmless fashion. *Washington Post*, 23 July 1976.

57. *New York Times*, 26 July 1976; *Washington Post*, 27 July 1976.

58. Donohue's comments are from the *New York Times*, 26 July 1976; Dantley's are from his interview with the author.

59. *Washington Post*, 27 July 1976.

60. *New York Times*, 28 July 1976; *Washington Post*, 28 July 1976; Dantley interview.

61. The point guard Phil Ford continued his masterful management of the squad, tallying twelve assists. *New York Times*, 28 July 1976.

62. Kenneth Denlinger, *Washington Post*, 28 July 1976.

63. Red Smith, *New York Times*, 25 July 1976.

64. Technically, the decision to boycott was made by secret ballot among USOC members. Some athletes fought the action, arguing that, among other things, the USOC had violated the 1978 Amateur Sports Act. But the courts ruled against them. The U.S. team sent to the Spartakiad finished fifth, but the crowd enjoyed the squad's "brilliant improvisations," according to *Time*. "Losing and Learning in Moscow," *Time*, 13 August 1979, http://www.time.com/time/magazine (accessed 7 October 2006).

65. "Olympics: To Go or Not to Go," *Time*, 28 January 1980, 15.

66. Peter Reddaway, a lecturer in political science at the London School of Economics and an expert on political dissent in the Soviet Union, stated, "The present purge is basically a pre-Olympic exercise, and well illustrates the inseparability of sports and politics in the Soviet Union." "Olympics and Human Brotherhood," *National Review*, 21 March 1980, 332.

67. "Olympics: To Go or Not to Go," 15; *New York Times*, 21 July 1976.

68. "Olympics: To Go or Not to Go," 15.

69. Hosket interview.

70. Qtd. in Jim Terhune, *Tales from the 1980 Louisville Cardinals* (Sports Publishing, 2004), 12.

71. "Olympics: To Go or Not to Go," 16.

72. Richard Pound, *Inside the Olympics: A Behind-the-Scenes Look at the Politics, the Scandals, and the Glory of the Games* (Canada: Wiley, 2006), 179.

73. "Cheers, Jeers in Moscow," *Time*, 4 August 1980, http://www.time.com/time/magazine (accessed 7 October 2006).

74. Though a thirteen-member committee headlined by Dean Smith was technically responsible for choosing the team, Gavitt held considerable sway. *Washington Post*, 29 December 1979.

75. *Washington Post*, 24 May 1980; *Chicago Tribune*, 24 June 1980.

76. The U.S. team won 97–84 behind Michael Brooks's eighteen points, Aguirre's fifteen, and Buck Williams's twelve. *Washington Post*, 17 June 1980. Brooks ended the summer leading the undefeated U.S. squad in scoring with a 13.2 average, followed by Bowie's 11.5, and Aguirre's 11.3. Bowie also led the team in rebounding and blocked shots, and Thomas led the way in assists (USA Basketball).

77. Qtd. in *Boston Globe*, 7 May 1996.

78. *New York Times*, 30 July 1980.

79. *Chicago Tribune*, 1 July 1984.

10. AIR JORDAN AND THE GENERAL IN ATLANTA

1. David Halberstam, *Playing for Keeps: Michael Jordan and the World He Made* (New York: Random House, 1999), 9.

2. Walter LaFeber, *Michael Jordan and the New Global Capitalism* (New York: W. W. Norton, 1999), 27.

3. "Unfortunately, the Bulls won't get a shot at him in the June 19 NBA draft, in which they have the third pick," Logan reported. The Bulls had lost fourteen of their last fifteen games the previous season, but their lone win late in the year kept them from a shot at that first pick. *Chicago Tribune*, 28 April 1984.

4. By the time of the June draft just seven weeks later, Jordan had demonstrated his undeniable brilliance in exhibition games. George Raveling, the 1984 assistant Olympic men's basketball coach, did his best to alert people: "Michael Jordan has the potential to be in a class with Oscar Robertson and Jerry West," he told reporters before the draft. *Chicago Tribune*, 17 June 1984.

5. *New York Times*, 5 August 1984.

6. Bob Knight, *Knight: My Story* (New York: St. Martin's Press, 2002), 215; Bruce Jenkins, *A Good Man: The Pete Newell Story* (Berkeley: Frog, 1999), 228; Pete Newell, interview by author, 23 June 2008, Ogden Dunes IN, tape recording.

7. Critics pointed to Knight's issues in Puerto Rico to argue that he was not the right person to represent the United States. *New York Times*, 30 December 1979.

8. Pete Axthelm, "Not a Knight for Diplomacy," *Newsweek*, 7 May 1984, 86.

9. Knight, *Knight: My Story*, 215.

10. *Washington Post*, 3 August 1984.

11. Axthelm, "Not a Knight for Diplomacy," 86.

12. *Chicago Tribune*, 10 July 1984.

13. *Washington Post*, 25 April 1981.

14. *Washington Post*, 12 January 1981.

15. *Washington Post*, 17 May 1973.

16. *Washington Post*, 3 March 1985.

17. *Washington Post*, 21 March 1983.

18. As part of an incentives package for success, the Chinese government offered every Olympic winner "close to $1,300 in such consumer goods as TV sets and tape recorders." As *Time*'s Janice Castro noted, "That is the equivalent of four years' income for the average citizen." Janice Castro, "Making of an Asian Contender," *Time*, 20 August 1984, http://www.time.com/time/magazine (accessed 7 October 2006).

19. Roger Rosenblatt, "Why We Play These Games," *Time*, 30 July 1984, http://www.time.com/time/magazine (accessed 7 October 2006).

20. Brook Larmer, "The Center of the World," *Foreign Policy*, September/October 2005, 69.

21. Brook Larmer, *Operation Yao Ming: The Chinese Sports Empire, American Big Business, and the Making of an NBA Superstar* (New York: Gotham Books, 2005), 3–4.

22. *Chicago Tribune*, 8 May 1984.

23. Australia's Rupert Murdoch anted up $10.6 million for the Australian broadcast rights, or $1.91 per television set, the priciest ratio of any nation. *Chicago Tribune*, 1 August 1984.

24. Roone Arledge, *Roone: A Memoir* (New York: HarperCollins, 2003), 290–91.

25. Tom Callahan, "Eve of a New Olympics," *Time*, 17 October 1983, http://www.time.com/time/magazine (accessed 7 October 2006).

26. Two-thirds of the television money networks shelled out for broadcast rights went to the organizing committee (in this case the LAOOC) and one-third to the IOC. *Chicago Tribune*, 16 April 1984.

27. *Chicago Tribune*, 14 August 1984.

28. *Chicago Tribune*, 17 August 1984.

29. Rajiv Desai, *Chicago Tribune*, 16 August 1984.

30. In the first half of 1984, advertising spent by computer companies totaled $104.4 million, compared to $78.2 million the year before. *Chicago Tribune*, 17 August 1984.

31. *Chicago Tribune*, 30 September 1984.

32. Walter LaFeber, *America, Russia, and the Cold War, 1945–2000* (Boston: McGraw Hill, 2002), 332–33.

33. LaFeber, *Michael Jordan*, 58–59.

34. *Daily News*, 25 July 2004.

35. Richard Pound, *Inside the Olympics: A Behind-the-Scenes Look at the Politics, the Scandals, and the Glory of the Games* (Canada: Wiley, 2004), 144–46, 168–71, 195.

36. Knight, *My Story*, 216.

37. Axthelm, "Not a Knight for Diplomacy," 86.

38. *Chicago Tribune*, 16 April 1984.

39. *Chicago Tribune*, 24 April 1984 and 20 April 1984.

40. *Chicago Tribune*, 21 April 1984.

41. *Washington Post,* 22 April 1984.

42. John Feinstein, *Washington Post,* 19 April 1984.

43. The formerly unheralded Terry Porter of the University of Wisconsin–Stevens Point was probably the most unlikely player to advance to the "final four," but chicken pox forced him to leave the trials. Dwayne "Pearl" Washington of Syracuse, Georgia Tech's Mark Price, and Villanova's Ed Pinckney led the list of those who did not make the first round of cuts. *Washington Post,* 22 April 1984.

44. Knight, *My Story,* 216.

45. *Chicago Tribune,* 10 July 1984.

46. Bill Hosket, interview by author, 7 July 2008, Portage IN, tape recording.

47. Knight, *My Story,* 120.

48. *Chicago Tribune,* 10 July 1984.

49. *Washington Post,* 11 July 1984.

50. *Washington Post,* 11 July 1984.

51. Allen Guttmann, *Games and Empires: Modern Sports and Cultural Imperialism* (New York: Columbia University Press, 1994), 184–87.

52. LaFeber, *Michael Jordan,* 48.

53. E. M. Swift, "From Corned Beef to Caviar; NBA commissioner David Stern, the son of a New York deli owner, took a downwardly mobile U.S. basketball league and turned it into a megarich international entertainment and marketing company," *Sports Illustrated,* 3 June 1991, available from http://www.highbeam.com/library/doc3.asp?docid=1CS1:58687 (accessed 14 March 2006).

54. Swift, "From Corned Beef to Caviar."

55. Qtd. in Filip Bondy, *Tip-Off: How the 1984 NBA Draft Changed Basketball Forever,* Advance Reading Copy (Cambridge: De Capo Press, 2007), 95.

56. Knight, *My Story,* 232.

57. Robert Fachet, *Washington Post,* 24 July 1984.

58. Bondy, *Tip-Off,* 87.

59. *Washington Post,* 24 July 1984.

60. Michael Wilbon, *Washington Post,* 24 July 1984.

61. *Washington Post,* 24 July 1984.

62. *Washington Post,* 24 July 1984.

63. Smith recognized the risk that Barkley's reputation might work against him at the trials. Trying to defend him (though how effectively is in question), Smith explained, "He was never a bad kid—just a kid who wouldn't work . . . Earlier, Charles and I had some very hard times." At the same time, he claimed Barkley's body fat was just 13 percent. *Washington Post,* 24 July 1984.

64. Bondy, *Tip-Off,* 88, 90.

65. Knight, *My Story,* 233.

66. Bundy, *Tip-Off,* 95.

67. "Olympics Hostage to Big Power Politics," *U.S. News & World Report,* 21 May 1984, 25.

68. *Sports Illustrated,* 16 July 1984, 57.

69. "Olympics Hostage to Big Power Politics," 24.

70. Arledge, *Roone*, 290.

71. Tom Callahan, "Eve of a New Olympics," *Time*, 17 October 1983, http://www.time .com/time/magazine (accessed 7 October 2006).

72. *Chicago Tribune*, 28 July 1984.

73. *New York Times*, 28 July 1984.

74. Kenny Moore, "Hey, Russia, It's a Heck of a Party," *Sports Illustrated*, 6 August 1984, 26.

75. Arledge, *Roone*, 291.

76. Moore, "Hey Russia," 34.

77. Frank Deford, "Cheer, Cheer, Cheer, for the Home Team," *Sports Illustrated*, 13 August 1984, http://vault.sportsillustrated.cnn.com/vault/article/magazine/MAG112402/ index.htm (accessed 17 March 2009).

78. Describing the action, *Chicago Tribune*'s Michael Ventri wrote that the U.S. fast break "caused photographers to increase their shutter speeds" *Chicago Tribune*, 30 July 1984.

79. *Chicago Tribune*, 30 July 1984.

80. *New York Times*, 6 August 1984.

81. *New York Times*, 6 August 1984.

82. *New York Times*, 1 August 1984 and 2 August 1984.

83. *New York Times*, 4 August 1984.

84. *New York Times*, 4 August 1984.

85. *Washington Post*, 5 August 1984.

86. Michael Moran, *New York Times*, 5 August 1984.

87. Roger Rosenblatt, "Why We Play These Games," *Time*, 30 July 1984, http://www .time.com/time/magazine (accessed 7 October 2006).

88. *Chicago Tribune*, 7 August 1984.

89. Qtd. in Bundy, *Tip-Off*, 99.

90. In the preliminary round the United States had won by an average of 39.2 points, but they beat West Germany only by 11, 78–67. But the score suggested a closer affair than it really was. *Chicago Tribune*, 7 August 1984.

91. Jordan played spectacularly too, scoring nineteen first-half points and finishing with seven rebounds and six blocked shots. Sam Perkins tallied eleven rebounds and Tisdale eight rebounds. Alford, playing another strong all-around floor game, had seven rebounds and five assists. *New York Times*, 9 August 1984.

92. *Chicago Tribune*, 9 August 1984.

93. *New York Times*, 12 August 1984.

94. *Washington Post*, 24 July 1984.

95. *Washington Post*, 3 August 1984.

96. *New York Times*, 5 August 1984.

97. Bob Verdi, *Chicago Tribune*, 12 August 1984.

98. Larmer, "Center of the World," 71.

99. Roy S. Johnson, "The Jordan Effect," *Fortune*, 22 June 1998, available from http://

www.highbeam.com/library/doc3.asp?DOCID=1G1:21053976&num=6&ctrlInfo=Ro
und19%3AProd%3ASR%3AResult&ao=&FreePremium=BOTH (accessed 14 March
2006).

100. Scott Bedbury, *A New Brand World: 8 Principles for Achieving Brand Leadership in the 21st Century* (New York: Penguin Books, 2002), 91–93.

101. *New York Times*, 16 June 1974.

102. Strasser and Becklund, *Swoosh*, 215–16.

103. Strasser and Becklund, *Swoosh*, 215–16.

104. Strasser and Becklund, *Swoosh*, 215–16, 191. Nike's Pro Club upped the ante for everybody involved in the basketball market. By 1977, according to Strasser and Becklund, Adidas would pay a player anywhere from $3,000 to $10,000 a year just to wear its shoes and from $40,000 to $100,000 for an official endorsement relationship. Converse felt the pressure. In the early 1970s, Adidas managed to remove Converse from the top spot in the American basketball shoe market, prompting Converse to sign the ABA's Julius "Dr. J" Erving. Reflecting the advancing quality of the basketball shoe, Converse's tagline for the shoes it outfitted Erving with read "lim-o-zeens for the feet." Strasser and Becklund, *Swoosh*, 189.

105. Tom Vanderbilt, *The Sneaker Book: Anatomy of an Industry and an Icon* (New York: New Press, 1998), 27.

106. Vanderbilt, *The Sneaker Book*, 29–31; Strasser and Becklund, *Swoosh*, 432.

107. Strasser and Becklund, *Swoosh*, 435.

108. *Washington Post*, 30 September 1984.

109. Bedbury, *A New Brand World*, 91–93.

110. Vanderbilt, *The Sneaker Book*, 51–54.

111. Jim Impoco and Warren Cohen, "Nike Goes to the Full-court Press," *U.S. News & World Report*, 19 April 1993, available from http://www.highbeam.com/library/doc3.asp?docid=1CS1:58717 (accessed 14 March 2006).

112. Vanderbilt, *The Sneaker Book*, 27.

11. ODDITIES IN SEOUL OPEN THE LANE FOR THE DREAM TEAM

1. "Our executive board suggested to our full congress in July that all basketball players—NBA, CBA, all of them—should be allowed into our world championship and the Olympics. It went to a vote: 31 opposed, 27 in favor, 14 abstentions. So it is shelved until after 1988, but we will introduce it again, and by 1992 the new rule will exist, I think. All pros will be welcome," Stankovic said. *Chicago Tribune*, 24 July 1987.

2. Lee Griggs, Kumiko Makihara, and Ellie McGrath, "Final," *Time*, 10 October 1988, http://www.time.com/time/magazine (accessed 7 October 2006).

3. Russ Granik, interview by author, 13 June 2008, Chicago IL, tape recording.

4. *Chicago Tribune*, 24 July 1987.

5. Granik interview.

6. *Chicago Tribune*, 24 July 1987.

7. Scott Wolff, "Hoops But No Scoops," *Sports Illustrated*, 30 May 1988, 36.

8. Wolff, "Hoops But No Scoops," 35–36.

9. Wolff, "Hoops But No Scoops," 35–36.

10. Tom Vanderbilt, *The Sneaker Book: Anatomy of an Industry and an Icon* (New York: New Press, 1988), 25, 26.

11. Curry Kirkpatrick, "The Old Soft Shoe; With Some Fancy Footwork, Sneaker Salesman Sonny Vaccaro Has Become a Power in College Basketball," *Sports Illustrated*, 16 November 1988, available from http://www.highbeam.com/library/doc3 .asp?docid=1CS1:58703 (accessed 15 March 2006).

12. *Washington Post*, 8 February 1988.

13. Kirkpatrick, "The Old Soft Shoe."

14. *Washington Post*, 8 February 1988.

15. *Chicago Tribune*, 18 May 1986. Information on Mary Fenlon from *Washington Post*, 11 June 1999; and the USA Basketball Web site.

16. *Chicago Tribune*, 23 July 1987.

17. *Washington Post*, 1 August 1986.

18. Shortly before the trials, the *New York Times*'s William Rhoden wrote an article on the subtleties of selecting a national team by contrasting the decision-making process of Bobby Knight, who chose players in 1984 that he thought could adapt to his persona and style, with that of Louisville's Denny Crum, who, for the 1987 Pan-Am Games, emphasized versatility and athleticism. Given that Knight won at the LA Games and Crum lost at the Pan-Am Games, Rhoden seemed to side with Knight, but he rightly argued that deciding the team was an especially tough job for Thompson because the level of international play continued to improve. *New York Times*, 1 May 1988.

19. *Chicago Tribune*, 15 May 1988.

20. Peter Alfano, *New York Times*, 8 August 1988.

21. Tom Callahan, "Newly at a Loss for Worlds," *Time*, 28 September 1987, http:// www.time.com/time/magazine (accessed 7 October 2006).

22. *Chicago Tribune*, 8 May 1988.

23. *Washington Post*, 9 June 1988.

24. Walter LaFeber, *America, Russia, and the Cold War, 1945–2000* (Boston: McGraw Hill, 2002), 332–33.

25. *Chicago Tribune*, 8 May 1988.

26. LaFeber, *America, Russia, and the Cold War*, 340.

27. *Chicago Tribune*, 24 July 1987.

28. Jack McCallum, "Tomorrow the World: NBA Will Be International by the End of the Century," *Sports Illustrated*, 7 November 1988, available from http://www.highbeam .com/library/doc3.asp?docid=1CS1:58686 (accessed 20 March 2006).

29. *Chicago Tribune*, 8 May 1988.

30. *Chicago Tribune*, 6 August 1987.

31. Alexander Wolff, "Team United States Seeks Revenge, At Last, for the 1972 Loss to the USSR," *Sports Illustrated*, 26 September 1988, 63.

32. *Chicago Tribune*, 23 July 1987.

33. *Chicago Tribune*, 23 July 1987.

34. *Chicago Tribune*, 27 May 1988.

35. *Washington Post*, 23 July 1987.

36. *Chicago Tribune*, 23 May 1988.

37. Curry Kirkpatrick, "Back to Olympian Heights: Struggling United States Star David Robinson Finally Reigned in Spain," *Sports Illustrated*, 4 July 1988, 73–75.

38. Qtd. in Kirkpatrick, "Back to Olympian Heights," 73–75.

39. *Chicago Tribune*, 27 May 1988.

40. Qtd. in Kirkpatrick, "Back to Olympian Heights," 73–75.

41. *Chicago Tribune*, 6 July 1988.

42. *Chicago Tribune*, 27 May 1988.

43. Ian Thomsen, "Russian Revolution," *Sports Illustrated*, 28 April 2008, 61.

44. *Moscow News*, 12 March 1993.

45. Tiit Sokk, interview by author, 2 April 2003, Tallinn, Estonia, handwritten notes.

46. Thomsen, "Russian Revolution," 61.

47. Sokk interview.

48. Sokk interview.

49. *Boston Globe*, 31 July 1992.

50. Adrian Wojnarowski, "In New Russia, Basketball Is Progressive," *Yahoo! Sports*, 12 August 2008, http://sports.yahoo.com/olympics/beijing/basketball/news?slug=aw-blatt081208&prov=yhoo&type=lgns (accessed 30 August 2008).

51. LaFeber, *America, Russia, and the Cold War*, 334.

52. Jack McCallum, "So Near, So Far," *Sports Illustrated*, 17 October 1988, 46.

53. McCallum, "So Near, So Far," 46.

54. *New York Times*, 7 August 1985.

55. McCallum, "So Near, So Far," 46–48.

56. McCallum, "So Near, So Far," 46.

57. McCallum, "So Near, So Far," 48.

58. Jack McCallum, "Rare Birds Sighted," *Sports Illustrated*, 8 August 1988, 22, 24, 29.

59. McCallum, "Rare Birds Sighted," 22, 24, 29.

60. McCallum, "Rare Birds Sighted," 22, 24, 29.

61. Skip Myslenski, *Chicago Tribune*, 15 August 1988.

62. *Chicago Tribune*, 22 August 1988.

63. *Chicago Tribune*, 15 May 1988.

64. *Chicago Tribune*, 21 August 1988.

65. *Washington Post*, 1 August 1986.

66. J. D. Reed, "A Symbol of Pride and Concern; Tear Gas Clouds the Olympics, But the Games Will Probably Go On," *Time*, 29 June 1987, available from http://www.time.com/time/magazine/article/0,9171,964778,00.html (accessed 8 March 2006).

67. James F. Larson and Heung-Soo Park, *Global Television and the Politics of Seoul Olympics* (Boulder: Westview Press, 1993), 20.

68. Peter Petri and Carl Shapiro, "China and the Lessons of the 1988 Olympics,"

Bridge News Knight Ridder/Tribune Business News, 10 July 2001, available from http://www.highbeam.com/library/doc3.asp?docid=1G1:76438797&refid=ip_hf (accessed 10 January 2005).

69. Petri and Shapiro, "China and the Lessons of the 1988 Olympics."

70. Not wanting to be overshadowed, North Korea had spent years trying to get part of Seoul's Olympic action, arguing that it deserved 50 percent of the Olympics. But those assertions went largely unheeded, though they did get to host ping-pong and soccer. This reflected the liberal-leaning bent of the IOC.

71. Larson and Park, *Global Television*, 25.

72. Larson and Park, *Global Television*, 21.

73. Larson and Park, *Global Television*, 22.

74. Nye recognizes that some parts of American culture are found unattractive elsewhere but asserts that, taken as a whole, "American popular culture, embodied in products and communications, has widespread appeal." Nye also argues that countries that gain a soft power advantage in the information age will be those "whose dominant culture and ideas are closer to prevailing global norms (which now emphasizes liberalism, pluralism, and autonomy)," nations with the "most access to multiple channels of communication," and those "whose credibility is enhanced by their domestic and international performance." Joseph S. Nye Jr., *Power in the Global Information Age: From Realism to Globalization* (New York: Routledge, 2004), 78, 90; and Joseph S. Nye Jr., *Soft Power: The Means to Success in World Politics* (New York: Public Affairs, 2004), 69–72.

75. Roone Arledge, *Roone: A Memoir* (New York: HarperCollins, 2003), 302–3. For the 1988 Games, IOC member and television-deal negotiator Richard Pound implemented new methods to "level" the bidding playing field. According to Pound, ABC's Arledge was "unhappy" with the changes and thought ABC should get special treatment because of its long-standing relationship with the Games. Richard Pound, *Inside the Olympics: A Behind-the-Scenes Look at the Politics, the Scandals, and the Glory of the Games* (Canada: Wiley, 2006), 173.

76. Jack Kroll and Pamela Abramson, "The Toughest Job in TV: NBC Starts Out with Low Ratings and Endless Ads," *Newsweek* 3 October 1988, 72; Meri-Jo Borzilleri, "Ebersol Increased Olympics' Popularity," *The Gazette*, 30 November 2004, http://olympics.gazette.com/fullstory.php?id=4070 (accessed 5 March 2006).

77. Larson and Park, *Global Television*, 6. With satellites and fiber optics reaching more homes throughout the world, and the Olympic movement's membership rivaling that of the United Nations, the cost of broadcasting the Games continued to escalate. William Taaffe, "The Big Three Aren't Sold on Seoul: United States Networks Refused to Meet Price for 1988 Olympics TV Rights," *Sports Illustrated*, 23 September 1985, available from http://www.highbeam.com/library/doc3.asp?docid=1G1:3946711&refid=ip_hf (accessed 16 January 2005); William A. Henry III, "No Time for the Poetry," *Time*, 3 October 1988, http://www.time.com/time/magazine (accessed 7 October 2006).

78. *Chicago Tribune*, 18 September 1988.

79. Qtd. in Jim Savage, *The Force: David Robinson, the NBA's Newest Sky-High Sensation* (New York: Dell, 1992), 169–70.

80. *Chicago Tribune*, 20 September 1988.

81. Wolff, "Team USA Seeks Revenge," 70.

82. Wolff, "Team USA Seeks Revenge."

83. *Chicago Tribune*, 19 September 1988.

84. *Chicago Tribune*, 27 September 1988.

85. *Washington Post*, 18 November 1987.

86. *Chicago Tribune*, 28 September 1988.

87. *New York Times*, 30 September 1988.

88. *New York Times*, 28 September 1988; Alfred E. Senn, *Power, Politics, and the Olympic Games: A History of the Power Brokers, Events, and Controversies That Shaped the Games* (Champaign: Human Kinetics, 1999), 231.

89. *New York Times*, 30 September 1988.

90. *Boston Globe*, 31 July 1992.

91. *Boston Globe*, 31 July 1992.

92. Lenny Wilkens and Terry Pluto, *Unguarded: My Forty Years Surviving in the NBA* (New York: Simon and Schuster, 2001), 253.

93. Savage, *The Force*, 245–48.

94. Initially, the association had balked at the prospect, fearing that allowing NBA players to participate would put them in the uncomfortable position of declining an invitation. *Chicago Tribune*, 24 July 1987.

95. *Chicago Tribune*, 24 July 1987.

96. In 1986 the USOC came out against the idea. They feared people would be reluctant to support the Olympic movement with contributions if wealthy professionals participated, and they feared that their junior and collegiate-level programs would weaken. The USOC president Robert H. Helmick argued that each individual sporting body should have the right to define professionalism. *Chicago Tribune*, 19 March 1986.

97. "Carl Schreck, 'Papa' of Soviet Basketball Gomelsky Dies at Age 77," MoscowTimes.com, 17 August 2005, http://www.themoscowtimes.com/stories/2005/08/17/003.html (accessed 27 August 2007).

98. Tom Callahan, "Illusions Lost and Regained," *Time*, 10 October 1988, http://www.time.com/time/magazine (accessed 7 October 2006).

12. BASKETBALL BEDLAM IN BARCELONA

1. Alan Greenberg, "U.S. Team: All-Stars to All-World," *Hartford Courant*, 26 July 1992.

2. *Hartford Courant*, 26 July 1992.

3. *New York Times*, 26 July 1992.

4. Burns and Krimsky are quoted in Jack McCallum, "USA, Inc.," *Sports Illustrated*, 22 July 1992, 124.

5. *Washington Post*, 15 May 1996.

6. McCallum, "USA, Inc.," 124.

7. David Halberstam, *Playing for Keeps: Michael Jordan and the World He Made* (New York: Broadway Books, 1999), 17.

8. Larry Bird, *Drive: The Story of My Life* (New York: Bantam Books, 1989), 11, 17.

9. Bird, *Drive*, 3, 4, 6.

10. Bird, *Drive*, 43–44.

11. Bird, *Drive*, 44–46.

12. Earvin Johnson, *Earvin "Magic" Johnson: My Life* (New York: Fawcett Books, 1992), 3.

13. Johnson, *My Life*, 3, 8.

14. Johnson, *My Life*, 3, 12.

15. Johnson, *My Life*, 15.

16. *New York Times*, 10 August 1992.

17. *New York Times*, 10 August 1992.

18. Halberstam, *Playing for Keeps*, 11, 12.

19. David L. Andrews ed., *Michael Jordan, Inc.: Corporate Sport, Media Culture, and Late Modern America* (Albany: State University of New York Press, 2001), xv.

20. Halberstam, *Playing for Keeps*, 295.

21. Donald Katz, *Just Do It: The Nike Spirit in the Corporate World* (New York: Random House, 1994), 7–8. Later, Jordan's designer cohort Tinker Hatfield, who is credited with sketching the Jumpman logo, would attain similar status.

22. Tom Vanderbilt, *The Sneaker Book: Anatomy of an Industry and an Icon* (New York: New Press, 1998), 33.

23. Katz, *Just Do It*, 7–8.

24. Bill Saporito, "Can Nike Get Unstuck?" *Time*, 30 March 1998, http://www.time.com/time/magazine (accessed 7 October 2006).

25. Robert Goldman and Stephen Papson, *Nike Culture: The Sign of the Swoosh* (London: Sage Publications, 1998), 102.

26. Eric Michael Dyson, *The Eric Michael Dyson Reader* (New York: Basic Civitas Books, 2004), 402, 411, 414.

27. Dyson, *Dyson Reader*, 467–68.

28. Vanderbilt, *The Sneaker Book*, 31.

29. Jim Savage, *The Force*, 249.

30. Goldman and Papson, *Nike Culture*, 102.

31. Vanderbilt, *The Sneaker Book*, 41.

32. Goldman and Papson have studied how Nike turns the relationship between class and race into visual pop culture in its television ads, arguing that while some Nike ads acknowledge the existence of inequality and alienation, they do not name the source of such problems. As a result, Nike "simultaneously acknowledges and denies unequal social and economic realities that influence probabilities for both success and suffering." This enables them to provide a "realist" voice and advocate sport as a "vehicle for spiritually transcending race and class divides." This ultimately enables Nike to retell a "mythology of sport that has grown dear to our society." Goldman and Papson, *Nike Culture*, 94.

33. James B. Twitchell, *20 Ads That Shook the World: The Century's Most Groundbreaking Advertising and How It Changed Us All* (New York: Crown Publishers, 2000), 202, 210.

34. Dan Wieden, transcript of speech given in 1999, quoted in the blog Welcome to Optimism, http://wklondon.typepad.com/welcome_to_optimism/2005/02/words _from_wied.html (accessed 27 August 2007).

35. *Oregonian*, 10 August 1992.

36. Dyson, *Dyson Reader*, 461. Dyson has also maintained that the "culture of sport has physically captured and athletically articulated the mores, folkways, and dominant visions of American society, and at its best has been conceived as a means of symbolically embracing and equitably pursuing the just, the good, the true, and the beautiful." Dyson sees Jordan as helping to explain "productive and disenabling forms of knowledge, desire, interest, consumption, and culture in three spheres: the culture of athletics, the expression of elements of African American culture," and "the market forces and processes of commodification expressed by, and produced in, advanced capitalism." Dyson, *Dyson Reader*, 467–68.

37. Kay Schaffer and Sidonie Smith, *The Olympics at the Millennium: Power, Politics, and the Games* (New Brunswick: Rutgers University Press, 2000), 70–71; *USA Today*, 1 October 1998.

38. E. M. Swift, "Reach Out and Touch Someone; Some Black Superstars Cash in Big on an Ability to Shed Their Racial Identity," *Sports Illustrated*, 5 August 1991, available from http://www.highbeam.com/library/doc3.asp?docid=1CS1:51224 (accessed 14 February 2006).

39. Swift, "Reach Out and Touch Someone."

40. Jack McCallum, "Life after Death: Magic Johnson has pulled off one of the great comebacks in sports history, and it's got nothing to do with basketball," *Sports Illustrated*, 20 August 2001, available from http://www.highbeam.com/library/doc3 .asp?docid=1CS1:63061 (accessed 7 February 2006); Marc Hequet, "Urban Magic," *Retail Traffic*, 1 September 2004, available from http://www.highbeam.com/library/ doc3.asp?docid=1CS1:64809 (accessed 20 February 2006).

41. Hequet, "Urban Magic."

42. Chuck Daly with Joe Falls, *Daly Life: "Every Step a Struggle": Memoirs of a World-Champion Coach* (Grand Rapids: Masters Press, 1990), 29–30, 32–33, 35–36.

43. Chuck Daly with Alex Sachare, *America's Dream Team: The Quest for Olympic Gold* (Kansas City: Turner, 1992), 37, 39, 41, 43–44, 49.

44. Daly and Sachare, *America's Dream Team*, 41.

45. Daly and Sachare, *America's Dream Team*, 37, 39, 41, 43–44.

46. Daly and Sachare, *America's Dream Team*, 43.

47. Russ Granik, interview by author, 13 June 2008, Chicago IL, tape recording.

48. On Stockton, see Cameron Stauth, *The Golden Boys: The Unauthorized Inside Look at the U.S. Olympic Basketball Team* (New York: Pocket Books, 1992), 170, 172. On the "freeze out," see the *Chicago Tribune*, 8 February 2003. Granik's comments are from the author's interview with him.

49. Joshua Levine, "Slam Dunk," *Forbes*, 20 July 1996, 96; Granik interview.

50. Levine, "Slam Dunk," 96.

51. On criticism of the "high-class living," see *New York Times*, 25 July 1992. Johnson's comments are from Johnson, *My Life*, 352; Bird's are from the *Boston Globe*, 10 August 1992.

52. *New York Times,* 26 July 1992.

53. Paul A. Witteman Badalona, "Basketball Look for the Silver Lining," *Time,* 10 August 1992, http://www.time.com/time/magazine (accessed 7 October 2006).

54. Malcolm Gray, "A Glitch in the Big Red Machine," *Maclean's,* 27 July 1992, 63.

55. *St. Louis Dispatch,* 6 August 1992.

56. *Boston Globe,* 31 July 1992.

57. Mike Krzyzewski, with Jamie K. Spatola, *The Gold Standard: Building a World Class Team* (New York: Business Plus, 2009), 17; "Basketball; Olympics Are Opened to Serbian Players," *New York Times,* 30 November 1994.

58. *New York Times,* 27 July 1992.

59. Jack McCallum, "Wild Bull of Las Ramblas," *Sports Illustrated,* 10 August 1992, 88–91.

60. The Kukoc and Radja quotes are from the *Baltimore Sun,* 28 July 1992; Pippen's statement is from the *New York Times,* 28 July 1992.

61. *New York Times,* 30 July 1992.

62. Granik interview.

63. J. B. Strasser and Laurie Becklund, *Swoosh: The Unauthorized Story of Nike and the Men Who Played There* (HarperCollins: New York, 1993), 209–10.

64. Randy Shaw, *Nike, Clean Air, and the New National Activism* (Berkeley: University of California Press, 1999), 13–14.

65. By that time, the Central Intelligence Agency (CIA) had put General Suharto—a former Indonesian trade minister who utilized totalitarian tactics to control the populace—into power.

66. Ironically, the goods these multinationals produced were endorsed by American cultural icons, like Michael Jordan, who were supposed to represent opportunity, individuality, success, and freedom, commodities not offered to most Indonesians.

67. Bob Garfield, "Best of Show; and Apparel/Accessories: Nike; 'Freestyle,' Wieden & Kennedy, Portland, Ore.," *Advertising Age,* 6 May 2002, available from http://www.highbeam.com/doc/1G1-85673767.html (accessed 10 August 2007).

68. Jeff Ballinger, "Nike's Profit Jumps on the Backs of Asian Workers," *Harper's Magazine,* August 1992, 46–47; Randy Shaw, *Reclaiming America: Nike, Clean Air, and the New National Activism* (Berkeley: University of California Press, 1999), 14, 19.

69. Dan Clawson, *The Next Upsurge: Labor and the New Social Movement* (Ithaca: Cornell University Press, 2003), 173–74.

70. Laura P. Hartman, Denis G. Arnold, and Richard E. Wokutch, eds., *Rising above Sweatshops: Innovative Approaches to Global Labor Challenges* (Westport: Preager, 2003), 142–59.

71. *Financial Times,* 17 April 2005.

72. The Daly quote is from the *Financial Times,* 17 April 2005. The Jordan statistics are from the *Seattle Times,* 29 July 1992, and the Bird stats are from the *New York Times,* 30 July 1992.

73. On Souza and Schmidt's comments, see the *New York Times,* 1 August 1992; the Dream Team's responses appear in the *Los Angeles Times,* 1 August 1992.

74. *New York Times*, 31 July 1992, 1 August 1992.

75. *New York Times*, 30 July 1992.

76. Hannah Beech, "Wang Zhizhi's Fast Break," *TimeAsia*, 11 November 2002, http://www.time.com/time/asia/covers/1101021118?zhizhi.html (accessed 7 September 2008); "Wang Zhizhi rejoins Chinese National Team after Public Apology," *Xinhua People's Daily Online*, 1 May 2006, http://english.peopledaily.com.cn/200605/01/print 20060501_262399.html (accessed 7 September 2008); *Toronto Globe and Mail*, 19 August 2004.

77. *St. Louis Dispatch*, 5 August 1992.

78. *New York Times*, 9 August 1992.

79. Katz, *Just Do It*, 30; *Moscow News*, 9 August 1992.

80. Jack McCallum, "Dreamy: The United States Men's Basketball Team Was As Good As Promised. But Will Such Talent Ever Come Together Again? Dream On," *Sports Illustrated*, 17 August 1992, 17.

81. *New York Times*, 25 July 1992.

82. Fred Bruning, "Sweet Dreams of Desert Storm," *MacLean's*, 3 August 1992, 9.

83. Carl Mollins, "Whose Games Are They?" *MacLean's*, 3 February 1992, 59.

84. Rob Morse, *Seattle Post-Intelligencer*, 3 August 1992; Stephen King, *New York Times*, 9 August 1992. The Castro quote is from the *Houston Chronicle*, 12 August 1992.

85. Bill Walton, *New York Times*, 26 July 1992.

86. Harvey Araton, *New York Times*, 25 July 1992.

87. Johnson, *My Life*, 354. The Schmidt quote appears in the *Boston Globe*, 10 August 1992. The Gomelsky statement is from the *New York Times*, 9 August 1992.

88. *New York Times*, 9 August 1992.

89. Charles Barkley, *I May Be Wrong But I Doubt It* (New York: Random House, 2002), 189; Johnson, *My Life*, 354.

90. Frederick Klein, *Wall Street Journal*, 24 December 1992.

91. Qtd. in Bob Ryan, *Boston Globe*, 10 August 1992.

92. Miquel de Moragas Spa, Nancy K. Rivenburgh, and James F. Larson (in cooperation with researchers from twenty-five nations), *Television in the Olympics* (London: John Libbey, 1995), 218.

93. George Vescey, *New York Times*, 9 August 1992.

94. Larry Brown, telephone interview by author, 13 August 2007, Chicago IL, handwritten notes.

95. Walter LaFeber, *Michael Jordan and the New Global Capitalism* (New York: W. W. Norton & Company, 1999), 19.

13. GAP CLOSED IN ATHENS

1. Qtd. in Phil Taylor, "Slam Dunk," *Sports Illustrated*, 12 August 1996, 49–50, 52–53.

2. *New York Times*, 8 August 1992.

3. *The Milwaukee Journal Sentinel*, 27 June 1996.

4. *Washington Post*, 25 April 1995.

5. *New York Times*, 2 October 1998; *Los Angeles Sentinel*, 10 January 2001; *The Record* (Bergen County, New Jersey), 4 February 1994; *Washington Post*, 17 December 1994; Keith

Chappell, "Lenny Wilkens: The winningest basketball coach of all time," *Ebony*, 1 April 1999, available from http://www.highbeam.com/DocPrint.aspx?DocId=1G1:54216340 (accessed 6 September 2008).

6. *Washington Post*, 12 April 1996; Lenny Wilkens and Terry Pluto, *Unguarded: My Forty Years Surviving in the* NBA (New York: Simon and Schuster, 2001), 258.

7. Jack McCallum and Richard O'Brien, "The Thrill Is Gone," *Sports Illustrated*, 29 July 1996, 25–26. The *Chicago Tribune's* Bob Greene wrote a piece titled "The Nicest Dream Would Be for Somebody to Beat Them." He claimed, "One thing is even more than the concept of capitalism—and that thing is the triumph of the underdog." *Chicago Tribune*, 17 July 1996.

8. Charles Barkley, *I May Be Wrong But I Doubt It* (New York: Random House, 2003), 187; Phil Taylor, "Slam Dunk," *Sports Illustrated*, 12 August 1996, 49–50, 52–53.

9. O'Neal also wrote at that time: "I would never play for Pat Riley." (He won an NBA championship with Riley in 2005.) Shaquille O'Neal, *Shaq Talks Back* (MacMillan, 2002), 177–78.

10. Gary Smith, "It's Greek to U.S.," *Sports Illustrated*, 29 July 1996, 33–38.

11. Smith, "It's Greek to U.S."

12. Terry Armour, *Chicago Tribune*, 7 July 1996.

13. *Los Angeles Times*, 19 July 1996.

14. *Washington Post*, 15 May 1996.

15. *New York Times*, 5 August 1996.

16. Taylor, "Slam Dunk," 49–50, 52–53.

17. Lisa Jones Townsel, "Shaquille O'Neal: Superstar Pays Tribute to His Supermom," *Ebony*, 1 May 1996, available from http://www.highbeam.com/doc/1G1–18205132.html (accessed 9 August 2008).

18. "*Sports Illustrated* Scrapbook: Shaquille O'Neal," http://sportsillustrated.cnn.com/basketball/nba/features/shaq/timeline/1/ (accessed 9 August 2008).

19. Townsel, "Shaquille O'Neal."

20. Mark Starr, "The $16 Million Man," *Newsweek*, 1 May 1995, available from http://www.highbeam.com/doc/1G1-16868730.html (accessed 6 August 2008).

21. *Daily News*, 29 November 2001.

22. Robert Jablon, "Shaq Adds MBA to His Three NBA Titles," AP *Online*, 25 June 2005, available from http://www.highbeam.com/doc/1P1-110453558.html (accessed 31 December 2006).

23. "Basketball Star Shaquille O'Neal Becomes Police Officer," *New Zealand Herald*, 10 December 2005, (accessed 31 December 2006).

24. Rick Kissell, "Olympics Take Gold," *Variety*, 9 October 2000. All told, NBC generated $690 million from its top fifty advertisers, which paid an average of $500,000 for thirty seconds of ad time during primetime. *Los Angeles Times*, 19 July 1996.

25. Jim Impoco, "Live from Atlanta: TV Broadcast of the 1996 Olympics," *U.S. News & World Report*, 15 July 1996.

26. *New York Times*, 28 July 1996.

27. Mobile phones had also started to make a sizable imprint. *Sports Illustrated*'s Gary Smith noted their seemingly ubiquitous use in Atlanta, and mobile phone technology came to provide yet another outlet for video content. By 2005, streamlining sports highlights through cell phones, utilizing technology such as Verizon's V CAST 3G broadband multimedia services, became a popular feature of cell phones. "Verizon Wireless Vaults over the Bar with V CAST; Customers Embracing V CAST On-Demand Video and 3D Games," PR *Newswire*, 14 March 2005, available from http://www.highbeam.com/library/doc3.asp?DOCID=1G1:130208610&num=3&ctrlInfo=Round20%3AProd%3AS R%3AResult&ao=&FreePremium=BOTH (accessed 10 March 2008). The technology's ability to accommodate wireless signals proved particularly important in places where cable Internet connections were limited, especially in China. *Rocky Mountain News*, 21 February 2005.

28. Daniel Stickberger, *Wall Street Journal*, 15 February 1994.

29. Angolan coach Vlademiro Romero had studied instructional tapes of his idol Bobby Knight. *Wall Street Journal*, 12 July 1996.

30. Michael Moran, *New York Times*, 25 July 1996.

31. *New York Times*, 27 July 1996; Phil Taylor, "Slam Dunk," *Sports Illustrated*, 12 August 1996, 49–50, 52–53.

32. Wilkens and Pluto, *Unguarded*, 259–60.

33. *New York Times*, 31 July 1996; Ralph Routon, "Not Even the Dream Team Can Upstage Oscar Schmidt (originated from the *Colorado Springs Gazette-Telegraph*)," *Knight Ridder/Tribune News Service*, 31 July 1996, available from http://www.highbeam.com/doc/1G1-18557129.html (accessed 10 August 2008).

34. *New York Times*, 4 August 1996.

35. In the other semifinal, Yugoslavia beat Lithuania 66–58 behind a strong performance by Vlade Divac. *New York Times*, 2 August 1996.

36. *New York Times*, 4 August 1996.

37. Barkley, *I May Be Wrong But I Doubt It*, 187.

38. Frederick Klein, *Wall Street Journal*, 1 August 1996.

39. *South Florida Sun-Sentinel*, 30 October 2006.

40. Taylor, "Slam Dunk," 49–50, 52–53; *Los Angeles Sentinel*, 10 January 2001.

41. Michael Clough, *Los Angeles Times*, 4 August 1996.

42. *Los Angeles Times*, 4 August 1996.

43. *Financial Times*, 6 October 2006.

44. Gene Keady, interview by author, Summer 2004, handwritten notes.

45. For instance, *Sports Illustrated*'s Jere Longman complimented Sydney for outshining Atlanta's shortcomings in technological and transportation shortcomings and avoiding its excess commercialism. Samaranch apparently concurred. He proclaimed that Sydney had "presented to the world the best Olympic Games ever." *New York Times*, 2 October 2000.

46. Kay Schaffer and Sidonie Smith, *The Olympics at the Millennium: Power, Politics, and the Games* (New Brunswick: Rutgers University Press, 2000), 2.

47. "The Sydney 2000," *Sydney Marketing Review*, 21 May 2001, http://72.14.203.104/ search?q=cache:l97H2IbSLuIJ:www.olympic.org/common/asp/download_report .asp%3Ffile%3Den_report_249.pdf%26id%3D249+total+number+of+Olympic+telev ision+viewers+in+2000&hl=en&gl=us&ct=clnk&cd=1&client=firefox-a (accessed 26 December 2006).

48. In 1960 the broadcasting rights went for just over $300,000. *New York Times*, 5 August 1996. By 2000, INTELSAT operated nineteen satellites that were capable of broadcasting images, sound, and data to over 200 countries and territories across the globe. "Telstra Reaches Agreement with NBC to Provide Sydney 2000 Olympic Games Transmission via INTELSAT," PR *Newswire*, 13 April 1999, available from http://www .highbeam.com/library/doc3.asp?DOCID=1G1:54363200&num=16&ctrlInfo=Round 19%3AProd%3ASR%3AResult&ao=&FreePremium=BOTH (accessed 10 September 2008).

49. Special Advertising Section, "Viewer's Guide," *Sports Illustrated*, 18 September 2000. A "unique viewer" constitutes anyone who watches at least six minutes of action over the seventeen days. *Washington Post*, 27 September 2000.

50. In Sydney NBC struggled to capitalize on the Internet attention the Games attracted, but nonetheless, Web traffic bustled. From NBC's Olympic site to olympic.com to ABC-News.com to CNNSI.com, Internet sites saw surges in web visits for their Olympic related coverage. The numbers showed, as Kathleen Nelson of the *St. Louis Post-Dispatch* noted, that in the early 1990s, when NBC had garnered the rights to broadcast the Olympics through 2008 for $3.5 billion, both NBC and the IOC "failed to foresee the leaps in internet technology." *St. Louis Post-Dispatch*, 26 September 2000; "IBM Features Local Heroes from around the World in Ad Campaign for the Sydney 2000 Olympic Games," *Business Wire*, 11 September 2000, available from http://www.highbeam.com/library/docfree.as p?DOCID=1G1:65127325&num=19&ctrlInfo=Round19%3AProd%3ASR%3AResult&a o=&FreePremium=BOTH (accessed 10 September 2008).

51. *Washington Post*, 18 September 2000; Phil Taylor, "Still Dreaming," *Sports Illustrated*, 25 September 2000, 58.

52. The *Financial Times* even pointed to a boom in the number of psychiatrists working in China as an indication of increased individualism there. *Financial Times*, 28 April 2001.

53. "Reebok Launches Largest Global Integrated Marketing and Advertising Campaign in Nearly a Decade: 'I Am What I Am,'" Reebok press release, 7 February 2005, http:// www.reebok.com/useng/ir/press/2005/I_am_what_I_am.htm (accessed 5 January 2007). Ironically enough, in response to a question about being compared to Yao Ming, the Milwaukee Bucks' 2007 first-round pick Yi Jianlian, only the second Chinese player ever to be chosen in the first round, told an interviewer he was not planning to become the next anyone because "I am what I am." Zhao Rui, "Yi: Stop Comparing Me with Yao," *China Daily*, 29 June 2007, http://www.chinadaily.com.cn/sports/2007-06/29/ content_905691.htm (accessed 20 July 2007).

54. "Dunk Described as One of the Best Ever," ESPN.com, 25 September 2000, http://espn.go.com/oly/summer00/news/2000/0925/775681.html (accessed 11 August 2008).

55. *Washington Post,* 29 September 2000.

56. *New York Times,* 30 September 2000. Jasikevicius did sign with the Indiana Pacers in 2005, and the forward Darius Songalia started his NBA career in 2003.

57. *New York Times,* 30 September 2000.

58. Keady interview.

59. *Financial Times,* 16 November 2002; *New York Times,* 30 September 2000.

60. *New York Times,* 1 October 2000; *Washington Post,* 2 October 2000.

61. *New York Times,* 1 October 2000.

62. *Financial Times,* 6 September 2002.

63. *Financial Times,* 16 November 2002. By 2003–4 the NBA boasted seventy-three international players from thirty-four countries. "2003–04 Season Delivers Big for NBA; Double-digit Increases in Merchandise Sales, TV Ratings . . . ," *AllBusiness via Business Wire,* 20 April 2004, http://www.allbusiness.com/marketing-advertising/market-research-analysis-market/5646414-1.html (accessed 11 August 2008).

64. *Financial Times,* 16 November 2002.

65. Tim Noonan Fukuoka, "America's Pro Basketball Teams Are Jumping at the Prospect of Signing a Few of China's Highly Skilled—And Very Tall—Players," *Asia Time,* 20 September 1999.

66. *Financial Times,* 28 April 2001.

67. *Financial Times,* 3 February 2001.

68. *Financial Times,* 3 February 2001.

69. According to ESPN.com's Chris Sheridan, strict FIBA rules disallowing roster changes after a certain date, except in cases of clear injury, prevented Brown from removing Marbury from the team. Chris Sheridan, "Team USA Update: Going Small Could Cause Big Problem," ESPN.com, 20 June 2008, http://sports.espn.go.com/espn/print?id=3454537&type=Columnist&imagesPrint=off (accessed 29 August 2008).

70. *Financial Times,* 1 August 2004.

71. Robert Andrew Powell, "Olympics; Tardiness Disrupts a Perfect First Week," *New York Times,* 1 August 2004, http://query.nytimes.com/gst/fullpage.html?res=9C0CE1DB1F3DF932A3575BC0A9629C8B63&sec=&spon=&pagewanted=1 (accessed 22 August 2008).

72. John MacAloon, "The Revival of the Olympic Games," *Proceedings of the International Olympic Academy,* 1984, pp. 169–82, http://www.ioa.leeds.ac.uk/1980s/84169.htm (accessed 13 August 2008).

73. Karolos Grohmann, "Oly: IOC Gives Athens All-clear for August Games," *AAP Sports News* (Australia)," 12 May 2004, available from http://www.highbeam.com/doc/1P1-94497178.html (accessed 13 August 2008).

74. *Washington Post,* 12 August 2004. Coral Davenport, "A Post-Olympic Hurdle for Greece: The Whopping Bill," *Christian Science Monitor,* 1 September 2004, available from http://www.highbeam.com/doc/1G1-121457184.html (accessed 13 August 2008).

75. *Financial Times,* 17 August 2004.

76. *Financial Times,* 6 September 2002.

77. *Washington Post,* 22 August 2004.

78. Many question Jianlian's true age, and he was evasive enough on the matter to further fuel speculation. Even Yao joked, "He's not 16. He's 17." *Financial Times*, 2 August 2004.

79. Wang Jingyu, "Yao 'Hurt' by His National Teammates," *Xinhua News Agency*, 16 August 2004, available from http://www.highbeam.com/library/doc3.asp?DOCID=1G1:120718534&num=14&ctrlInfo=Round19%3AProd%3ASR%3AResult&ao=&FreePremium=BOTH (accessed 23 January 2006).

80. Jingyu, "Yao 'Hurt' By His National Teammates."

81. *Toronto Globe and Mail*, 19 August 2004.

82. *Financial Times*, 26 August 2004.

83. *New York Times*, 29 August 2004.

84. Wang Jingyu and Shan Lei, "Era of U.S. Dream Team Terminated in Athens," *Xinhuanet*, 29 August 2004, http://news.xinhuanet.com/english/2004-08/29/content_1914985.htm (accessed 28 December 2006).

85. *Washington Post*, 28 August 2004.

86. Ian O'Connor, "Iverson's a Winner for Not Making Excuses for Losses," *USA Today*, 27 August 2004, http://www.usatoday.com/sports/columnist/oconnor/2004-08-27-oconnor-iverson x.htm (accessed 22 August 2008); Dan Wetzel, "China Offers Warm Embrace for U.S. Team," *YahooSports*, 10 August 2008, http://sports.yahoo.com/olympics/beijing/basketball/news?slug=dw-menshoops081008&prov=yhoo&type=lgns (accessed 22 August 2008).

87. O'Connor, "Iverson's a Winner"; Wetzel, "China Offers Warm Embrace."

88. *Washington Post*, 28 August 2004.

89. Adrian Wojnarowski, "A.I. Gets It Right: It's an Honor to Be Here," ESPN.com, http://sports.espn.go.com/oly/summer04/basketball/columns/story?id=1870490 (accessed 11 August 2008); *New York Times*, 29 August 2004.

90. *Oregonian*, 9 November 2006.

14. RECLAMATION IN BEIJING

1. *New York Times*, 14 August 2008. Sales figures for the jerseys are from a thousand China-based Adidas stores. Tim Lemke, "Kobe Big in China," *Washington Times*, 12 August 2008, http://washingtontimes.com/weblogs/sportsbiz/2008/Aug/12/kobe-big-china/ (accessed 16 August 2008); Alan Paul, "What the Redeem Team Means for the NBA in China," *Slam*, 25 August 2008, http://slamonline.com/online/2008/08/what-the-redeem-team-means-for-the-nba-in-china/ (accessed 26 August 2008).

2. "Rock-star Treatment Greets NBA Players," *Toronto Star*, 9 August 2008, http://olympics.thestar.com/2008/article/475300 (accessed 2 September 2008).

3. Associated Press, "2008 Host China Has Mixed History of Sports," 27 February 2006, http://www.msnbc.com/id/11592789/from/ET (accessed 7 December 2006).

4. By February 2006 the IOC program had twelve worldwide sponsors—Johnson & Johnson, Coca-Cola, Atos Origin, General Electric, Kodak, Lenovo, Manulife, McDonalds, Omega, Panasonic, Samsung, and Visa—which had invested a total of $866 million (the money is divided between the IOC, national Olympic committees, and international sports federations). Those figures do not include the more than a billion dollars UPS,

Volkswagen, and Adidas had invested in the Beijing Organizing Olympic Committee for title sponsorships. *Boston Globe,* 25 February 2006.

5. Thomas L. Friedman, *The World Is Flat: A Brief History of the Twenty-First Century* (New York: Farrar, Straus and Giroux, 2005), 250–51.

6. *Cincinnati Post,* 24 August 2002.

7. Jim Litke, "Colangelo the Basketball Sheriff," AP Online, 15 March 2006, available from http://www.highbeam.com/doc/1P1-119918428.html (accessed 11 August 2008).

8. Litke, "Colangelo the Basketball Sheriff."

9. *Washington Post,* 1 September 2007; Mike Krzyzewski, with Jamie K. Spatola, *The Gold Standard: Building a World Class Team* (New York: Business Plus), 5.

10. Krzyzewski, *Gold Standard,* 2, 16.

11. Dave Zirin, "Troops and Hoops," *The Nation,* 20 August 2006, http://www.thenation.com/doc/20060828/troops_and_hoops (accessed 31 December 2006).

12. *Houston Chronicle,* 4 August 2006; *Miami Herald,* 4 August 2006; "Greece Oust USA in Massive Upset," 1 September 2006, http://news.bbc.co.uk/sport2/hi/other_sports/basketball/5302000.stm (accessed 6 September 2008); Ivan Carter and Micheal Lee, "Wizards Insider: Spanoulis Isn't Eager to Make NBA Return," WashingtonPost.com, http://voices.washingtonpost.com/wizardsinsider/2008/08/spanoulis_isnt_eager_to_make_n.html (accessed 15 August 2008).

13. Darren Rovell, "Wade Adds Gatorade to Already High-Profile Portfolio," ESPN.com, 3 October 2005, http://sports.espn.go.com/ESPN (accessed 10 December 2006); *The Plain Dealer,* 13 August 2006; *Miami Herald,* 4 August 2006.

14. "Statistics," NBA.com, http://www.nba.com/statistics/player/3PointS.jsp?league=00&season=22005&conf=OVERALL&position=0&splitType=9&splitScope=GAME&qualified=Y&yearsExp=-1&splitDD= (accessed 22 August 2008). Michael Redd shot just under 40 percent from the three-point line during the 2005–6 season, and Gilbert Arenas shot a higher percentage than Wade, Anthony, and James from the NBA three-point line in the two seasons before the World Championships in Japan. Bowen ranked rather high in three-point percentage. Among other NBA players who could probably have helped with shooting had they been on the team were Raja Bell, Jason Terry, Brent Barry, Ben Gordon, and Rashard Lewis.

15. Krzyzewski, *Gold Standard,* 97.

16. Charles F. Gardner, "Redd's Olympian Feat: Guard Lands One of 12 Spots for U.S. Men's Basketball," JournalSentinel.com, 19 June 2008, http://www.jsonline.com/story/index.aspx?id=764112 (accessed 22 August 2008); Alexander Wolff, "The Redeem Team: After failing to win a major basketball competition in eight years, the U.S. has taken a new (and distinctly foreign) approach," *Sports Illustrated,* 28 July 2008, http://vault.sportsillustrated.cnn.com/vault/article/magazine/MAG1142296/index.htm (accessed 10 September 2008). On Redd's drive straight from practice to interview, see Krzyzewski, *Gold Standard,* 9.

17. "Kobe Says Europe a Possibility," Yahoo! Sports, 9 August 2008, http://sports.yahoo.com/olympics/beijing/basketball/news?slug=aw-kobeuropenewsero80908&p

rov=yahoo&type=lgns (accessed 26 August 2008); *Washington Post*, 14 August 2008; Lemke, "Kobe Big in China."

18. J. A. Adande, "With NBA Salaries Capped, Superstars Like Kobe Eye European Riches," ESPN.com, http://sports.espn.go.com/nba/columns/story?columnist=adande_ja&page=eurodraw-080809 (accessed 15 August 2008).

19. Chris Sheridan, "Dispelling Two Myths on Eve of US-Argentina Semifinal," ESPN .com, 21 August 2008, http://sports.espn.go.com/oly/summer08/basketball/columns/story?columnist=sheridan_chris&page=Myths-080821 (accessed 22 August 2008).

20. "Reebok Launches Largest Global Integrated Marketing and Advertising Campaign in Nearly a Decade: 'I Am What I Am,'" Reebok press release, 7 February 2005, http://www .reebok.com/useng/ir/press/2005/I_am_what_I_am.htm (accessed 5 January 2007).

21. Brook Larmer, *Operation Yao Ming: The Chinese Sports Empire, American Big Business, and the Making of an NBA Superstar* (New York: Gotham Books, 2005), xii.

22. Bay Fang, "Spending Spree: They're young. They have money to burn. And the race is on to win them as customers," *U.S. News & World Report*, 1 May 2006, 44, 48.

23. Fang, "Spending Spree," 50.

24. Huang Ying, "Kobe Bryant to Coach Beijing Street Basketball Matches," *People's Daily*, 22 June 2001, http://english.people.com.cn/english/200106/22/eng20010622_73268.html (accessed 5 May 2006).

25. Tom Walsh, "Wynnewood, Pa., Basketball Apparel Retailer AND 1 Scores Big Time," *Knight Ridder/Tribune Business News*, 26 August 1996, originally appeared in the *Philadelphia Inquirer* and available from http://www.highbeam.com/doc/1G1-18613834 .html (accessed 31 December 2006); "AND 1 Announces 2005 Mix Tape Tour: The World's Best Streetballers Return as a Part of Summer's Hottest Basketball Tour," *Business Wire*, 3 May 2005, available from http://www.highbeam.com/doc/1G1-132090139.html (accessed 31 December 2006).

26. Liu Jie, "'Prince's' Sporting Goods Group Goes Public in Hong Kong," *China Daily*, 16 June 2004, available from http://www.highbeam.com/DocPrint .aspx?DocId=1P2:8817755 (accessed 27 August 2008); Normandy Madden, "Spotlight," *Advertising Age*, 13 February 2006, available from http://www.highbeam.com/DocPrint. aspx?DocId=1G1:142116207 (accessed 27 August 2008); Normandy Madden, "Chinese Sportswear Brand Anta Aims to Become Next Nike," *Advertising Age*, 7 May 2007, available from http://www.highbeam.com/DocPrint.aspx?DocId=1G1:163167263 (accessed 27 August 2008).

27. Andrew Bagnato, Associated Press, "'Redeem Team' Dunks Past China in Olympic Basketball," *New York Sun*, 10 August 2008, http://www.nysun.com/sports/redeem-team-dunks-past-china-in-olympic-basketball/83539/ (accessed 26 August 2008); Pat Forde, "In Historic Game, U.S. Dominance Trumps Hoops Diplomacy," ESPN .com, 10 August 2008, http://sports.espn.go.com/espn/print?id=3528438&type=story (accessed 26 August 2008); Associated Press, "USA Beats China in Olympic Opener; Bush Joins US Basketball Huddle," *HuffingtonPost*, 10 August 2008, http://www.huffingtonpost.com/2008/08/10/usa-beats-china-in-olympi_n_118006.html (accessed 26 August 2008).

28. Becky Cheung, "184 Million Chinese Viewers Tuned into the Team China versus USA Dream Team Basketball Game," CSM *Media Research*, 11 August 2008, http://www.tnsglobal.com/_assets/files/TNS_Market_Research_Reveals_184_million_chinese_basketball.pdf (accessed 15 August 2008); David Owen, "Chinese Grow Close to US in Sport of Giants," FT.com, 10 August 2008, http://us.ft.com/ftgateway/superpage.ft?news_id=ft0081020082127434874 (accessed 15 August 2008); Mike Reynolds, "Super Bowl XLII Tackles Record 97.5 Million Viewers: Giants-Pats Most-Watched Super Bowl, Trails Only M*A*S*H Finale," *Multichannel News*, 4 February 2008, http://www.multichannel.com/article/CA6528715.html (accessed 15 August 2008).

29. Don Lee, "LA Stadium Owner AEG Is Playing to Win in Foreign Arena: China," *Los Angeles Times*, 23 August 2008, http://www.latimes.com/business/la-fi-chinasports23-2008aug23,0,7296423.story (accessed 26 August 2008); Associated Press, "NBA Hopes to Capitalize on Basketball's Popularity in China," 19 August 2008, http://sports.espn.go.com/espn/print?id=3542013&type=story (accessed 26 August 2008); Marc J. Spears, "Worlds Collide," *Boston Globe*, 10 August 2008, http://www.boston.com/sports/articles/2008/08/10/worlds_collide/?page=1 (accessed 26 August 2008); "BWCSC, NBA China and AEG Form Strategic Partnership to Operate the Beijing Olympic Basketball Arena," NBA.com, 31 January 2008, http://www.nba.com/global/nba_china_bwcsc_partner.html (accessed 26 August 2008).

30. Lee, "LA Stadium Owner AEG."

31. *Washington Post*, 21 April 2008; Peter Ford, "Games Spur Little Progress on Human Rights," *Christian Science Monitor*, 5 August 2008, http://features.csmonitor.com/olympics08/2008/08/05/games-spur-little-progress-on-rights/ (accessed 15 August 2008).

32. *International Herald Tribune*, 7 August 2007; "Political Prisoner He Depu Writes to IOC President Jacques Rogge," *Human Rights Watch in China*, 6 August 2008, http://www.hrichina.org/public/contents/press?revision%5fid=68830&item%5fid=68030 (accessed 15 August 2008; Depu letter translated by *Human Rights in China*); *Washington Post*, 21 April 2008; Ford, "Games Spur Little Progress on Human Rights."

33. In 1996 that record was rated the worst possible by the Freedom House. In fact, China rated lower than such countries as Algeria and Lebanon that year. http://freedomhouse.org/template.cfm?page=15&year=2005 (accessed 14 June 2009).

34. Tsan-Kvo Chang, Jian Wang, and Yanru Chen, *China's Window on the World: TV News, Social Knowledge, and International Spectacles*, Hampton Press Communication Series (Cresskill NJ: Hampton Press, 2002), 83, 101.

35. Simon Montlake, "China Reins in Reach of Foreign News," *Christian Science Monitor*, 13 September 2006.

36. *Wall Street Journal*, 11 December 2006.

37. Rick Reilly, "The Life of Reilly," ESPN *The Magazine*, 25 August 2008, http://sports.espn.go.com/espnmag/story?id=3542649; David Sarno, "Hundreds of Websites Still Censored at Beijing Olympics," *Los Angeles Times*, 5 August 2008, http://latimesblogs.latimes.com/webscout/2008/08/hundreds-of-web.html (accessed 20 August 2008); Benjamin Kang Lim and Karolos Grohmann, Reuters, "Hu Stands by Games Pledges,

Web Curbs Lifted," 1 August 2008, http://www.reuters.com/article/GCA-Olympics/i dUSL131393420080801?pageNumberBrandChannel=0 (accessed 20 August 2008).

38. *Financial Times*, 25 August 2008.

39. The former vice president of Beijing Remnin's University wrote a 2008 essay that expounded on the "virtues of Swedish-style social democracy" in an "influential" Chinese magazine. In response, China's *People's Daily* newspaper offered a tempered rebuke. The episode prompted the publisher of the article that trumpeted Swedish-style government, Du Daozheng, to note that the incident marked the first time since the Tiananmen Square crackdown on democratic protests that "such a complicated and important theoretical issue was discussed fairly and calmly." Qtd. in Richard McGregor, "China Opens Up to Redefine Democracy," *Financial Times*, 13 June 2007, http://www.ft.com/cms/s/0/af9 dd842-194b-11dc-a961-000b5df10621.html (accessed 16 August 2008).

40. *Financial Times*, 5 March 2007.

41. *Wall Street Journal Asia*, 6 August 2008.

42. Reuters, "UK's Brown to Raise Human Rights with China," 20 August 2008, http://www.reuters.com/article/worldNews/idUSLK40835620080820 (accessed 25 August 2008).

43. The analyst James Mann was among those who seemed to argue that no change within China would result from the United States' present "engagement" course. In fact, he suggested that not altering the strategy could pose geopolitical problems for the United States down the road. Johns Hopkins University's David M. Lampton was among those who thought "engagement" was in the United States' best interests, even though China might be "a rare case of a capitalist state in which the middle class grows but political rights lag far behind." *Los Angeles Times*, 25 February 2007; David M. Lampton, James Mann, "What's Your China Fantasy?" *Foreign Policy* (Web exclusive), May 2007, http://www.foreignpolicy.com/story/cms.php?story_id=3837 (accessed 29 August 2008).

44. *Financial Times World Media Abstracts*, 9 September 2002.

45. Lindsey, "Joey Cheek's Visa to China Revoked," *Team Darfur*, 6 August 2008, http://teamdarfur.org/node/573 (accessed 30 August 2008); Dan Wetzel, "Will Kobe, LeBron Pass on Darfur?" Yahoo! Sports, 7 August 2008, http://sports.yahoo.com/olympics/beijing/basketball/news?slug=dw-darfur080708&prov=yhoo&type=lgns (accessed 30 August 2008).

46. Andrew England, "Hu Urges Sudan to Act on Darfur Crisis," *Financial Times*, 2 February 2007, http://www.ft.com/cms/s/0/a981d188-b2e0-11db-99ca-0000779e2340 .html (accessed 30 August 2008).

47. Tim Reynolds, Associated Press, "Wade Comes Back to Miami, Olympic Gold in Tow," Yahoo! Sports, 25 August 2008, http://sports.yahoo.com/olympics/beijing/basketball/news?slug=ap-bko-wadecomeshome&prov=ap&type=lgns (accessed 31 August 2008).

48. Throughout their coverage of the Games, Doug Collins (the father of Chris Collins, a member of the 2008 U.S. men's Olympic basketball support/scout team) and Mike Breen provided keen insight about Olympic basketball, and that insight has been drawn on in this text.

49. Chris Sheridan, "Team USA Update: Going Small Could Cause Big Problems," ESPN.com, 30 June 2008, http://sports.espn.go.com/espn/print?id=3454537&type=Columnist&imagesPrint=off (accessed 28 August 2008).

50. Brent Hunsberger, "Road to Redemption through Nike," Playbook & Profits Blog, *The Oregonian*, 2 July 2008, http://blog.oregonlive.com/playbooksandprofits/2008/07/road_to_redemption_through_nik.html; "Nike and USA Basketball to Unveil New Look for Team USA to Thousands of Fans," Nike, Inc., press release via Yahoo! Finance, 30 June 2008, http://www.nikebiz.com/media/pr/2008/06130_USAB.html (accessed 14 March 2009); Darren Rovell, "USA Basketball Team Photo: Artistic or Logo Conspiracy?" CNBC SportsBIZ, 3 July 2008, http://www.cnbc.com/id/25513177 (accessed 1 September 2008). The flywire description was provided for a shoe used by the U.S. track-and-field team in Beijing. Reuben Lee, "Super-light Nike Flywire Shoes to Make Olympic Debut," cnet, 24 July 2008, http://news.cnet.com/8301-17938_105-9998061-1.html (accessed 31 August 2008); "United We Rise: Nike Debuts New Team USA Basketball Creative," Nike, Inc., press release, *Wall Street Journal*, 5 August 2008, http://wsj.com/article/PR-CO-20080805-902196.html?mod=wsjcrmain (accessed 31 August 2008); *Washington Post*, 30 June 2008; "NBA Feet-USAB Olympic Gold Medal Game," *sneakernews*, 25 August 2008, http://sneakernews.com/2008/08/25/nba-feet-usab-olympic-gold-medal-game/ (accessed 31 August 2008); Tommy Craggs, "Dunks, Mom, and Apple Pie: The Marketing Genius of USA Basketball's 'Redeem Team,'" *Slate*, 22 August 2008, http://www.slate.com/id/2198323/ (accessed 31 August 2008).

51. *Financial Times*, 13 September 2003.

52. The "Kasky ruling" that the *Financial Times* was referring to involved a case brought against Nike regarding a public relations campaign. In its response, Nike cited the first amendment in an effort to protect itself from being sued for a public relations campaign. Nike technically won the case but became more transparent in its aftermath. *Financial Times*, 13 April 2005. Increasing transparency did not mean that everything would suddenly function ideally at Nike's suppliers. Nike admitted, "Despite anecdotal instances of success, we remain profoundly challenged to understand how to systematically measure the impact of our own interventions." Furthermore, Nike admitted that some workers might not open up about unfair conditions and that determining exactly what transpires at their more than 800 offices, though they receive visits by Nike monitors as well as from the Fair Labor Association, is "at times an overwhelming and incomplete body of work." Still, Jones emphasized that the company had reaped benefits from its new openness. In 2006 Nike showed that it was serious about it its policy of holding suppliers responsible for violating Nike's labor codes when it cancelled orders from a Pakistan-based producer for violating them. "We are developing new sources with factories committed to upholding our standards and treating workers fairly," Nike CEO and president Mark Parker asserted. Paul Garwood, Associated Press, "Ball Maker: Nike Move Could Cost Jobs," 21 November 2006, http://biz.yahoo.com/ap/061121/nike_soccer_balls.html? (accessed 7 December 2006). Nike's actions indicated that the company truly thought a more open and ethical labor policy served its best interests.

53. *Financial Times*, 20 April 2005; Jagdish Bhagwati, *In Defense of Globalization* (New York: Oxford University Press, 2004), 23.

54. *Financial Times*, 11 May 2001. The tactics of a group such as the private-based, non-profit National Labor Committee (NLC) show that certain business and ethical standards are now expected from the mainly liberal capitalist international sporting community. The NLC openly admits to using highly visible targets, such as Nike or individual sporting stars, to engender support for its cause. Charles Kernaghan, the executive director of the NLC, said in 2001, "Imagine if just one player stood up, like Latrell Sprewell or Shaquille O'Neal, and said I don't want my name on an NBA jersey made under these conditions. That would have an enormous impact on the big retailers."

55. *Chicago Tribune*, 9 August 2008.

56. Adrian Wojnarowski, "In New Russia, Basketball Is Progressive," Yahoo! Sports, 12 August 2008, http://sports.yahoo.com/olympics/beijing/basketball/news?slug=aw-blatto81208&prov=yhoo&type=lgns (accessed 30 August 2008).

57. Chris Sheridan, "Team USA's Flaws Exposed in Ugly Win over Australia," ESPN .com, 6 August 2008, http://sports.espn.go.com/espn/print?id=3520292&type=Columnist&imagesPrint=off (accessed 29 August 2008); "Official Basketball Box Score," USA Basketball, 5 August 2008, http://www.usabasketball.com/seniormen/2008/08_msnt_exh_05_box.pdf (accessed 29 August 2008).

58. "NBA Players to be Flag-bearers," *Sporting News*, 8 August 2008, http://today .sportingnews.com/sportingnewstoday/20080808/?pg=29 (accessed 9 April 2009); Krzyzewski, *Gold Standard*, 27.

59. "Olympics LED Screen to Reappear during Paralympics Ceremony," 29 August 2008, http://chinadaily.com.cn/olympics/2008-08/29/content_6981864.htm (accessed 29 August 2008); *Washington Post*, 9 August 2008.

60. The Reuters report is quoted in the *Washington Post*, 9, 13, 16 August 2008. Reilly's comments are from Reilly, "Life of Reilly." On the criticism of Chinese government tactics, see the *Washington Post*, 15 August 2008. The comments of the Beijing Organizing Committee and Games spokesman appear in "Organizing Committee Executive Vice President Slams Media," http://www.earthtimes.org/articles/show/227447,organizing-committee-executive-vice-president-slams-media.html (accessed 22 August 2008).

61. *Washington Post*, 14 August 2008.

62. Many of the statistics in this chapter come from the USA Basketball home page. "USA Soars Past Greece 92–69, Secures Quarterfinal Berth," USA Basketball, 14 August 2008, http://www.usabasketball.com/news_archive.php?news_page=08_moly_03&page=msnt (accessed 14 March 2009).

63. Chris Sheridan, "After Dismantling Spain, Team USA Stands at Gold-worthy Level," ESPN.com, 16 August 2008, http://sports.espn.go.com/oly/summer08/basketball/columns/story?columnist=Sheridan_Chris&page=USA-Spain-080816 (accessed 30 August 2008).

64. Julia Boorstin, "The Olympics Final Gold Goes to NBC," CNBC, 26 August 2008, http://www.cnbc.com/id/26406944 (accessed 1 September 2008); *Financial Times*, 25 August 2008.

65. *New York Times*, 22 August 2008.

66. "USA Dominates Germany 106–57, Advances to Quarterfinals Undefeated," USA Basketball, 18 August 2008, http://www.usabasketball.com/news.php?news_page=08_moly_05 (accessed 1 September 2008).

67. "USA Dominates Germany."

68. "Rock-star Treatment"; Melody K. Hoffman, "Mom Rejoices after Son Dwyane Wade Buys Her a Church," Jet 23 June 2008, available from http://www.highbeam.com/doc/1G1-180662712.html; "From the Olympics: U.S. Redeem Team Duo Adds Perspective to Redemption," Baptist Press, via Townhall.com, 26 August 2008, http://townhall.com/news/religion/2008/08/26from_the_olympics_us_redeem_team_due_adds_perspective_to_redemption (accessed 3 September 2008); Washington Post, 14 August 2008.

69. Quotes from Wojnarowski here and in the preceding paragraph are from Adrian Wojnarowski, "Team USA Lets Verdict Speak for Itself," Yahoo! Sports, 20 August 2008, http://sports.yahoo.com/olympics/beijing/basketball/news/?slug=aw-usaaustralia08 2008&prov=yhoo&type=lgns (accessed 1 September 2008).

70. Wojnarowski, "Team USA Lets Verdict Speak for Itself."

71. Chris Sheridan, "Team USA Has a Shot at Gold after Winning Weird One," ESPN.com, 22 Au7gust 2008, http://sports.espn.go.com/oly/summer08/basketball/columns/story?columnist=sheridan_chris&page=US-Argentina-080822 (accessed 1 September 2008).

72. Sheridan, "Team USA Has a Shot at Gold."

73. "Official Basketball Box Score," USA Basketball, 24 August 2008, http://www.usabasketball.com/seniormen/2008/MOLY-Box%20Scores/USAB.pdf (accessed 1 September 2008); Associated Press, "US Hoops Back on Top, Beats Spain for Gold Medal," Yahoo! Sports, 24 August 2008, http://sports.yahoo.com/olympics/beijing/basketball/news?slug=ap-bko-spain-us (accessed 1 September 2008); Washington Post, 25 August 2008; Reynolds, "Wade Comes Back to Miami."

74. Krzyzewski, Gold Standard, 205.

75. Washington Post, 25 August 2008.

76. David Barboza, "China's Promise Excites the Sports Stars," New York Times, 26 August 2008, http://www.nytimes.com/2008/08/27star.html?partner=rssnyt&emc=rss (accessed 1 September 2008); Reynolds, "Wade Comes Back to Miami."

77. Pete Thamel, "After Sitting in 2004, Ready to Stand and Deliver," New York Times, 28 July 2008, http://www.nytimes.com/2008/07/28/sports/olympics/28hoops.html?pagewantd=print (accessed 1 September 2008).

78. "Did the Redeem Team Really Come Through?" ESPN.com, 27 August 2008, http://sports.espn.go.com/espn/print?id=3553868&type=Story&imagesPrint=off (accessed 1 September 2008).

79. "PR No25—The FIBA Central Board Approves Historic Rule Changes," FIBA.com, 26 April 2008, http://www.fiba.com/pages/eng/fc/newslateNews/p/newsid/24352/arti.html (accessed 7 September 2008).

80. "James Outdistances Bryant in Winning Kia MVP Award," NBA.com Press Release, 4 May 2009, http://www.nba.com/2009/news/05/04/mvp.release.20090504/index.html (accessed 12 June 2009); "The 15 Best International Players of the 2008–09 NBA Sea-

son," *Interbasket.net*, 1 April 2009, http://www.interbasket.net/news/1676/2009/04/01/best-international-nba-players-200809/ (accessed 12 June 2009).

81. *Washington Post*, 8 June 2008.

82. Mike Reynolds, "TNT, ESPN Close 2009 NBA Playoffs with Record Ratings," *Multichannel News*, 3 June 2009, http://www.multichannel.com/article/277997-TNT_ESPN_Close_2009_NBA_Playoffs_With_Record_Ratings.php (accessed 12 June 2009); *Financial Times*, 7 June 2009.

83. "Olympians Could Return for Worlds," *Associated Press*, http://sports.espn.go.com/oly/olybb/news/story?id=4187292 (accessed 12 June 2009).

INDEX

Page numbers in italic indicate illustrations.

AAU. *See* Amateur Athletic Union (AAU)

ABA. *See* American Basketball Association (ABA)

ABC, 174–75, 194; and the Los Angeles Games (1984), 263–64, 265, 274, 277; and the Montreal Games (1976), 245–46; and the Munich Games (1972), 203–4, 220. *See also* television viewership

Abdul-Jabbar, Kareem (Lew Alcindor), 192, 284, 446n24, 447n42, 449n85; and boycott of Mexico City Games (1968), 177, 180–81, 198, 445n22

Abdur-Rahim, Shareef, 364; and statistics, *383*

Adams, K. S. ("Boots"), 72, 422n64

Adidas, 173, 284, 295, 392, 453n3; and endorsements, 176, 233–34, 445n7, 460n104; and sales, 393; and the Unified Team, 333. *See also* shoe companies

Adorno, Ruben, 170

advertising, 58–59, 103, 354; and African American players, 101, 205; during the Atlanta Games (1996), 469n24; during the Beijing Games (2008), 289; and China, 392, 408; and computer companies, 264–65, 457n30; and Converse, 176; global, 261–62, 263, 408; during the Montreal Games (1976), 245; and Nike, xviii–xix, 283–85, 291, 320, 324, 402, 465n32. *See also* endorsements

African American coaches, 101, 139, 183, 237, 293, 352–53, 447n56

African American players, 41–42, 70, 426n46; and the AAU, 42, 43, 46, 70; and advertising, 101, 205, 327; and boycotts, 178, 180–83, 445n22; and college basketball, 42–43, 45, 70–71, 96–98, 442n27; and racism, 44, 45–47, 100–102, 127–29, 132, 231, 433n39; on U.S. team rosters, 100, 105, 120, 160, 352

Aguirre, Mark, 254, 268, 456n76; and statistics, *256*

Ain, Barney, 23

Air Jordans, 285, 287, 326. *See also* Nike

Akhtaev, Vrais, 91, *92*, 93, 94

Alcindor, Lew. *See* Abdul-Jabbar, Kareem (Lew Alcindor)

Alford, Steve, 267, 270, 271, 278, 279–80, 281; and statistics, *286*, 459n91

Allen, Forrest ("Phog"), 14, 38–39, 236, 422n64, 447n56; and African American players, 70–71; and the Berlin Games (1936), 18–19; feuds of, with the AAU, 67–68, 69; and the Helsinki Games (1952), 69, 74, 78, 80, 87; rivalry of, with Hank Iba, 156

Allen, Lucius, 192, 284, 447n42

Allen, Ray, 363–64, 367, 369, 379; and statistics, *383*

All-Union Ministry of Physical Culture and Sports (Sports Ministry), 63, 91, 304. *See also* Soviet Union

Amateur Athletic Union (AAU): and African American players, 42, 43, 46, 70; and amateur classification, 43, 47–48, 72, 94–96, 124–25; and membership in FIBA, 6; and Phog Allen, 67–68, 69; and qualifying tournaments, 8, 35–36, 37–38, 66, 68–69, 102–3, 104, 126, 158–59, 188, 207; rivalry of, with the NCAA, 19, 124–25, 137, 150, 154, 157, 235, 437n20; and rule changes, xvi, 2, 4, 27–28, 31. *See also* industrial league teams; National Basketball Association (NBA); National Collegiate Athletic Association (NCAA); National Industrial Basketball League (NIBL)

amateur classification, xvi, 43, 47–48, 72, 94–96, 124–25, 175–76, 178, 206–7, 238; and European players, 237; and NBA players, 178, 206–7, 288–90, 317, 344–45, 351–52, 413, 464n93, 464n96

American Basketball Association (ABA), 179–80, 188, 206, 208–9. *See also* National Basketball Association (NBA)

American Basketball Association of the United States of America (ABA/USA), 125, 236, 259, 289, 290, 293. *See also* National Collegiate Athletic Association (NCAA)

American Broadcasting Company (ABC). *See* ABC

American Olympic Association (AOA), 8, 72, 419n16. *See also* U.S. Olympic Committee (USOC)

American Olympic Committee (AOC), 7, 18. *See also* U.S. Olympic Committee (USOC)

Anderson, Willie, 300; and statistics, 316

Andrews, David, 323

Andreyev, Vladimir, 191

Angolan Olympic team, 335, 336, 358, 377, 405–6, 470n29

Anthony, Carmelo, 374, 386, 388, 389, 400, 402, 409, 410; and statistics, 384, 415

Antsey, Chris, 404

Arabadjian, Artenik, 226

Araton, Harvey, 335, 345

Arenas, Gilbert, 474n14

Argentine Olympic team, xviii, 94; and the Athens Games (2004), 378–79; and the Atlanta Games (1996), 351, 358; and the Beijing Games (2008), 409–10; and the Helsinki Games (1952), 75, 78, 84, 85; and the London Games (1948), 54–55, 58, 75, 78, 84, 85, 94

Arledge, Roone, 175, 203–4, 246, 251, 274, 275, 309, 463n75

Armstrong, Tate, 237; and statistics, 255

Arnette, Jay, 135, 138; and statistics, 149

Asian Games, 164, 443n43

Athens Games (2004): basketball tournament at the, 374–75, 376, 377, 378–79; facilities at the, 375–76; nations participating in the, 375; selection of, as host city, 375. *See also* U.S. Olympic Basketball team (2004)

Atlanta Games (1996): attendance, 358; basketball tournament at the, 350–51, 358–61, 470n35; bombing at the, 359; and corporatism, 354–55; nations participating in the, 357; number of athletes participating in the, 357; and television viewership, 357. *See also* U.S. Olympic Basketball team (1996)

Atlanta Hawks, 245, 303–5

attendance: at the Atlanta Games (1996), 358; at the Beijing Games (2008), 394, 406; at the Berlin Games (1936), 2; at Chinese basketball games, 4; and college basketball, 9, 261; and European basketball championships, 13, 91, 139; at exhibition games, 51, 72, 123, 139, 162, 235, 268, 305; at Harlem

Globetrotter games, 73, 100; at the Helsinki Games (1952), 80; at the London Games (1948), 55; at the Los Angeles Games (1984), 277; at the Melbourne Games (1956), 108, 111, 113; at the Mexico City Games (1968), 194, 197; at the Munich Games (1972), 202, 217, 220; at qualifying tournaments, 37, 68, 267–68; at the Rome Games (1960), 141, 143, 145; at the Spartakiad, 91; at the Sydney Games (2000), 366; at the Tokyo Games (1964), 165

Attner, Neil, 211–12

Attner, Paul, 240–41

Auerbach, Red, 102, 169, 179, 187, 236, 248

Augmon, Stacey, 299, 300; and statistics, 316

Australia, 364. *See also* Australian Olympic team; Sydney Games (2000)

Australian Olympic team, 167, 278, 314, 359, 376; in the Beijing Games (2008), 404, 409

Bach, John, 186–87, 210, 215

Baker, Justin ("Sam"), 423n106

Baker, Vin, 364; and statistics, 383

Baker, William J., 33–34, 53, 61–62, 83, 89

Balter, Sam, xiii, xiv, 2, 11, 15, 22, 23, 24, 25, 27; and boycott of Berlin Games (1936), 6–7; and statistics, 26

Bantom, Mike, 213, 219, 226, 231–32; and statistics, 232

Barcelona Games (1992), xv; basketball tournament at the, 333–34, 335, 336–37, 340, 341–43; nations participating in the, 319; Opening Ceremonies of the, 333; and television viewership, 347. *See also* U.S. Olympic Basketball team (1992)

Barker, Cliff, 37; and statistics, 59

Barkley, Charles ("Round Mound of Rebound"), 258, 261, 266, 267, 271–73, 305, 329, 371, 458n63; and the Atlanta Games (1996), 350, 352, 354, 359, 360, 361, 382; and the Barcelona Games (1992), 328, 335–36, 340, 341, 342–43, 346, 348; and Nike, 320, 327, 337; and statistics, 348, 382

Barksdale, Don, xiv, 40, 41–42, 43–47, 44, 57, 70, 96, 426n50; and statistics, 59

Barnes, Jim ("Bad News"), 158, 159, 162, 442n27; and statistics, 172

Barrett, Michael, 188, 189; and statistics, 200

Barry, Brent, 474n14

Barry, Rick, 160

Bashkin, Sergey, 218, 224

Basilio, Norma Enrique, 194

Basketball Federation of the United States of America (BFUSA), 155, 206

basketballs, 2, 33, 73, 77–78, 141–42, 441n20; Berg balls, 2, 24; stitchless, 23, 78

Battier, Shane, 271, 389

Baylor, Elgin, 106, 240

Beard, Ralph, 37, 51; and statistics, 59

Beck, Lew, 40; and statistics, 59

Bedbury, Scott, xviii, 283

Bee, Clair, 6, 9, 420n18, 420n28

Beijing Games (2008): attendance, 394, 406; basketball tournament at the, 394–95, 405–11; broadcast rights to the, 407; and commercialism, 391–94, 402; facilities at the, 385, 395; and human rights, 396–98, 476n33, 477n39; Opening Ceremonies of the, 404–5; and scheduling, xix; selection of, as host city, 386, 396–98; and television viewership, xiv, 395, 407–8. *See also* China; U.S. Olympic Basketball team (2008)

Bell, Raja, 401, 474n14

Bellamy, Walter, 135, 138, 146; and statistics, 149

Belov, Alexander, 218–19, 222, 226, 312, 451n54

Belov, Sergei, 218, 220, 249

Benson, Kent, 237, 239

Berg balls, 2, 24. *See also* basketballs

Berlin Games (1936), 203; attendance, 2,
21; basketball tournament at the, 1–2,
21–24, 25–26, 423n78; boycott of the,
6, 7, 9, 13–14; facilities at the, 1, 3, 21,
23–24, 419n14; and Nazi politics, 4–7;
number of athletes participating in
the, 21; Opening Ceremonies of the,
21; selection of, as host city, 419n16;
and television viewership, 21; and
weather conditions, 23–24, 25. *See also*
U.S. Olympic Basketball team (1936)

Bettman, Gary, 289

Bias, Len, 266

Bibby, Mike, 379

Billups, Chauncey, 400

Bing, Dave, 240

Bingham, J. Lyman, 9, 35, 47

Bird, Larry, xiv, 129, 268, 289, 295, 387;
and the Barcelona Games (1992), 317,
320, 321–22, 332, 340, 341, 346; and
popularity of the NBA, 253, 261, 270;
and statistics, *348*

Bishop, Ralph, 14, 15; and statistics, *26*

Blab, Uwe, 279

Blackman, Rolando, 254; and statistics,
256

Blatt, David, 404

Bodiroga, Dejan, 359

Bogut, Andrew, 404

Bonham, Ron, 159

Bontemps, Ronald, 69, 429n31; and
statistics, *88*

Boozer, Robert ("Bob"), 135; and
statistics, *149*

Boozer, Carlos, 374, 400; and statistics,
384, 415

Boryla, Vince, 30–31, 40–41, 45, 51, 54;
and statistics, *59*

Bosh, Chris, 400, 406; and statistics, *415*

Boston Celtics, 101, 102, 117, 179, 270

Boushka, Dick, 105; and statistics, *117*

Bowen, Bruce, 389, 474n14

Bowie, Sam, 254, 266, 456n76; and
statistics, *256*

boycotts, 419n13; and African Americans,
178, 180–83; Berlin Games (1936),
6, 7, 9; Helsinki Games (1952), 75;
Los Angeles Games (1984), 264,
273–75; Melbourne Games (1956),
109, 111; Mexico City Games (1968),
178, 180–83, 194, 445n22, 448n69;
Montreal Games (1976), 242–44;
Moscow Games (1980), 251–54,
455n64; and the NAIB championship,
42–43; Tokyo Games (1964), 165; and
Universal Pictures, 7, 13–14

Bradley, Bill, 151, 158, 159, 160–62, 168, 171;
and statistics, *172*

Brand, Elton, 379

Brazil, 210, 293. *See also* Brazilian
Olympic team

Brazilian Olympic team, 106, 107, 278,
310; at the Athens Games (2004),
359; at the Barcelona Games (1992),
340–41; at the Berlin Games (1936),
21; at the Helsinki Games (1952), 74,
78, 84; at the London Games (1948),
58; at the Melbourne Games (1956),
113; at the Mexico City Games (1968),
196, *197*; at the Munich Games (1972),
217–18; at the Rome Games (1960),
142, 146, *147*, 148; at the Tokyo Games
(1964), 169

Breen, Mike, 477n48

Bressler, Marvin, 327

Brewer, Jim, 213, 214, 218, 226, 235; and
statistics, *232*

Brezhnev, Leonid, 200–201

broadcast rights, 120, 167, 174, 203, 245,
253, 263–64, 265, 308, 365, 407, 457n23,
457n26, 471n48, 471n50. *See also*
television viewership

Brokhin, Yuri, 66, 223, 229–30

Brooks, Michael, 254, 456n76; and statistics, 256

Brown, Dale, 356

Brown, John, 213, 216

Brown, Larry, xv, 162, 173, 212, 216, 241; and the ABA, 179; as coach, 254, 349, 363, 374–75, 376, 379; and statistics, 172; and the Tokyo Games (1964), 156, 159, 160, 167, 168, 171, 172

Brown, Robert, 441n19

Brown, Sip, 237

Browning, Omar ("Bud"), 41, 46, 48, 51, 56, 57

Browning, William, 30, 31

Brundage, Avery, 5–6, 7, 75–76, 83, 124, 143, 166, 193, 419n13; and amateur status, 48, 72, 94–95, 102, 178, 238; and boycotts, 109, 111, 165, 182, 194; and the Munich tournament attack, 213, 452n58; and Phog Allen, 19. See also International Olympic Committee (IOC)

Bruning, Fred, 344

Bryant, Kobe, 357, 379–80, 399, 400, 413; and the Beijing Games (2008), 386, 389, 390, 395, 400, 406, 409, 410–11; and statistics, 415

Buchan Bakers, 102–3, 104, 105. See also industrial league teams

Buckner, Quinn, 237, 238, 239, 241; and statistics, 255

Bulgarian Olympic team, 77, 113

Burleson, Tom, 214; and statistics, 232

Bush, George W., 373, 394

Busmel, Robert, 57

Butautas, Stepas, 85, 431n87

Byers, Walter, 157, 447n42

cable television, 205, 244–45, 261, 450n11. See also television viewership

Cage, Michael, 266

Cain, Carl, 100, 105; and statistics, 117

Calderon, Jose, 407, 410

Caldwell, Joe, 158, 159, 171; and statistics, 172

Canadian Olympic team, 168, 249, 277, 280, 310; and the Berlin Games (1936), 1, 21, 23, 25

Carpenter, Gordon ("Shorty"), 40, 47, 54; and statistics, 59

Carr, Antoine, 266

Carr, Austin, 240, 284

Carr, Kenny, 237, 239; and statistics, 255

Carter, Jimmy, 252–53

Carter, Vince, 363, 367–68, 369, 379; and statistics, 383

Caterpillar Cats, 67, 68–69, 70, 126. See also industrial league teams

CBS, 33, 73, 120–21, 167, 269, 283, 444n56. See also television viewership

Centennial Park bombing, 359. See also Atlanta Games (1996)

Chamberlain, Wilt, 71, 106, 125, 131

Chandler, Tyson, 400–401

Chapman, Rex, 293, 298–99

Checketts, Dave, 269–70

Chilean Olympic team, 74, 84

China, 50, 75–76, 141, 165, 242–43, 379, 477n43; and human rights, 396–98, 476n33, 477n39; and the NBA, 372–73; popularity of basketball in, xix, 4, 263; selection of, for 2008 Olympics, 386; and sports, 262–63, 276, 307, 341–42, 391–93, 395–96, 457n18; and "table tennis democracy," 204, 243. See also Beijing Games (2008); Chinese Olympic team

Chinese Olympic team, 31; and the Athens Games (2004), 377–78; and the Atlanta Games (1996), 358–59; and the Barcelona Games (1992), 342; and the Beijing Games (2008), 394–95, 405, 407; and the Berlin Games (1936), 21–22; and the Los Angeles Games (1984), 276; and the Sydney Games (2000), 365–66

Chomicius, Valdemaras, 314, 334

Chones, Jim, 208–9, 450n23

Chuck Taylor All-Star shoes, 24–25, 33, 59, 73, 103–4, 115–16, 152, 167, 173, 176, 233–34, 283–84. *See also* Converse

City College of New York, 96–97

Clawson, John, 188, 192; and statistics, 200

Clifton, Nat ("Sweetwater"), 70

Clough, Michael, 362–63

coaching staff, xv; Athens Games (2004), 374–75; Atlanta Games (1996), 352–53; Barcelona Games (1992), 329–30; Beijing Games (2008), 387–88, 410–11; Berlin Games (1936), 16–19, 26–27; Helsinki Games (1952), 69, 74; London Games (1948), 41, 44–45, 46, 51, 55, 56; Los Angeles Games (1984), 258–61, 265–66, 270–73, 281; Melbourne Games (1956), 106, 434n59; Mexico City Games (1968), 183–84, 186, 187, 188–89, 192, 197–98; Montreal Games (1976), 236–37, 240–41, 248; Moscow Games (1980), 253–54; Munich Games (1972), 206–7, 209, 211–12, 214, 215, 216–17, 221, 226–27; Rome Games (1960), 123, 126–27, 136–38, 140, 142, 144; Seoul Games (1988), 290–93, 294, 295, 296–97, 305–6, 309–11, 315; Sydney Games (2000), 363; Tokyo Games (1964), 155–57, 160, 167–68

Coimbra, Herlander, 335

Colangelo, Jerry, 266, 387, 388, 389–90, 402, 414

cold war, 33–34, 61–65, 89, 91, 121–22, 153–55, 274, 453n11; and China, 75–76; and the Helsinki Games (1952), 63–66, 80–82, 85–86, 87–88; and the Melbourne Games (1956), 108–9, 111, 115; and the Montreal Games (1976), 234–36, 242; and the Munich Games (1972), 230–32; and the Rome Games (1960), 143–45, 153; and satellites, 119, 121, 244–45, 265; and the Seoul Games (1988), 294, 302–3; and television, 121; and the Tokyo Games (1964), 163–64. *See also* Soviet Union

Coles, Vernell ("Bimbo"), 299, 300, 305; and statistics, 316

college basketball: and attendance, 9, 261; popularity of, 19, 39, 68, 206, 253, 261, 268, 421n30; and racism, 42–43, 45, 70–71, 96–98; and rule changes, 4; and speed of play, 2. *See also* National Collegiate Athletic Association (NCAA)

Collins, Doug, 235, 400, 477n48; and the Munich Games (1972), 212, 213, 214, 216, 218, 221, 222–24, 232; and statistics, 232

Columbia Broadcasting System (CBS). *See* CBS

Converse, 58–59, 73, 291, 343, 434n50, 460n104; basketballs produced by, 23, 33; Chuck Taylor All-Star shoes, 24–25, 33, 59, 73, 103–4, 115–16, 152, 167, 173, 176, 233–34, 283–84. *See also* shoe companies

Cooper, Chuck, 70

Corbin, Tyrone, 266

corporate sponsorship, 4, 394, 451n26, 473n4; and the Beijing Games (2008), 386; and boycotts, 7, 13–14; and the Los Angeles Games (1984), 265; and Olympic fundraising, 73, 274. *See also* advertising; industrial league teams; shoe companies

Cosic, Kresimir, 194–95, 251, 254, 311, 314

Coubertin, Pierre de, xvi, 375

Counts, Melvin, 159, 167, 168, 171, 237; and statistics, 172

court dimensions, 31, 158, 241, 257, 369, 412, 435n66. *See also* rules, basketball

Cousy, Bob, 90, 235–36

Crispus Attucks High School, 128–29, 438n36

Croatian Olympic team: and the Atlanta Games (1996), 358; and the Barcelona Games (1992), 333, 334, 335, 336–37, 340, 343

Crum, Denny, 293, 461n18

Cuba, 153, 228, 236. *See also* Cuban Olympic team

Cuban Olympic team, 59, 217, 220

cultural currency: American, 32, 33, 49–50, 154–55, 308, 463n74, 466n36; and basketball, xvii, 16, 172–73, 392; and the cold war, 64, 230; and shoes, 25, 59, 104, 325, 450n12, 465n32; and telecommunications, 204–5

Cunningham, Billy, 160

Czechoslovakia, 193. *See also* Czechoslovakian Olympic team

Czechoslovakian Olympic team, 22, 54, 106, 248, 448n72, 455n56; and the Helsinki Games (1952), 75, 78; and the Munich Games (1972), 216, 217

Daley, Arthur J., 16, 26, 61, 80–81, 83, 139, 141, 168

Dalipagic, Drazen, 248

Daly, Chuck, xv, 319, 323, 329–30, 340, 344, 377, 414

Danilovic, Predrag, 335

Dantley, Adrian, 236, 237, 238, 239–40, 241, 246, 247, 249; and shoes, 233–34, 453n3; and statistics, 240, 251, 255

D'Antoni, Mike, xviii

Danzig, Allison, 63, 76, 80, 104, 115

Darling, Chuck, 104, 105, 107, 110, 116; and statistics, 117

Davies, Richard ("Dick"), 159, 162; and statistics, 172

Davis, Baron, 371

Davis, Ken, 213, 214

Davis, Walt, 96

Davis, Walt (1976 team), 237; and statistics, 255

Dawkins, Johnny, 267

Dee, Donald, 188, 194; and statistics, 200

Dee, Johnny, 96

defenses: half-court pressure, 86; help-side, 127; press, 114, 127; stout, 23; swinging gate, 156; zone, 25, 381. *See also* offenses

Deng Xiaoping, 262–63

Denver Chicago Truckers, 95–96, 123. *See also* industrial league teams

Diaz-Miguel, Antonio, 281, 283, 309

DiGregorio, Ernie, 235–36, 311

Dischinger, Terry, 126, 135, 138, 142, 143, 144, 148, 437n26; and statistics, 149

Divac, Vlade, 195, 311, 335, 345, 359, 360, 361, 369

Djordjevic, Sasha, 359

Donoher, Don, 266

Donohue, Jack, 249, 277, 280

Drake, Bruce, 106, 329, 434n59

Dream Team. *See* U.S. Olympic Basketball team (1992)

Dream Team II. *See* U.S. Olympic Basketball team (1996)

Dream Team III. *See* U.S. Olympic Basketball team (2000)

Drexler, Clyde, 328, 331; and statistics, 348

Dumars, Joe, 330

Duncan, Tim, 374, 378; and statistics, 384

dunk shot, 16, 38

Dyson, Michael Eric, 325, 326, 466n36

Ebersol, Dick, 308–9, 357

Edelman, Robert, 66, 91, 229

Edeshenko, Ivan, 225, 226

Edwards, Harry, 180, 183, 231, 257, 445n22

Edy, Jack, 43

Egyptian Olympic team, 55, 56, 59, 141, 217, 248

Eisenhower, Dwight D., 89–90, 100

Elliott, Sean, 293

Ellis, Monta, 401

Ellison, Pervis, 293

Elmore, Len, 207

Embry, Wayne, 266

endorsements, 205–6, 392; and David Robinson, 315, 317; and Jerry Lucas, 132; and Magic Johnson, 327–28, 343; and Michael Jordan, 283, 285, 287, 291, 323, 324, 326–27; and shoes, 234, 251, 283–85, 324–26; and Spencer Haywood, 176. *See also* advertising; salaries; shoe companies

Erving, Julius, 205, 207, 208, 216, 460n104

ESPN, 253, 265, 268, 401, 414

Estonia, 64–65, 190, 301; Olympic team of, 22, 169

European basketball championships, 66; of 1939, 13, 65; of 1947, 64; of 1952, 64, 66, 78, 428n23; of 1953, 91; of 1967, 190; of 1973, 230, 231; attendance at, 13, 91, 139

Evans, William, 105; and statistics, 117

Ewing, Patrick, 329; and the Barcelona Games (1992), 329, 346; and the Los Angeles Games (1984), 258, 267, 268–69, 270, 280; and popularity of the NBA, 261; and statistics, 286, 348

exhibition games, 235–36; in 1936, 14, 27; in 1948, 35, 45–47, 50–51; in 1952, 72; in 1956, 102, 106; in 1960, 123, 124, 138–39; in 1964, 162, 442n37; in 1968, 189–90; in 1972, 216; in 1976, 241; in 1980, 254, 456n76; in 1984, 268–69; in 1988, 298–99, 305–6; in 2008, 404; and fundraising, 14, 19, 35, 47, 72, 74, 124, 268; in the Soviet Union, 162, 189–90, 245, 304–5, 442n37; and television viewership, 216, 245. *See also* qualifying tournaments

Falkenstein, Max, 70

fast break basketball. *See* speed of play

Fengdi, Fang, 263

Fenlon, Mary, 293

Fernandez, Ruby, 407, 410, 411

Ferry, Danny, 293, 298, 299

FIBA. *See* International Basketball Federation (FIBA)

FIBA Americas tournament, 389

Fidler, Fred, 434n57

Finland, 75, 76–77, 81, 189, 264, 430n62, 430n64. *See also* Helsinki Games (1952)

Fleming, Vern, 267, 270; and statistics, 286

Forbes, James, 216, 226–27; and statistics, 232

Ford, Gilbert, 105; and statistics, 117

Ford, Phil, 237, 241, 246, 311, 455n61; and statistics, 255

Fortenberry, Joe, xiii, xvii, 15–16, 20, 23, 25, 71; and statistics, 26

Fotsis, Antonis, 388

fouling rules, 31, 87, 140, 157–58, 210, 255. *See also* rules, basketball

Fowler, Calvin, 188, 192, 447n53, 448n76; and statistics, 200

Frank, Stanley, 47–48, 51

Frazier, Walt ("Clyde"), 205–6, 234

Freiberger, Marcus, 69, 79; and statistics, 88

French Olympic team: and the Berlin Games (1936), 22; and the Helsinki Games (1952), 74; and the London Games (1948), 31, 57, 60; and the Los Angeles Games (1984), 277–78; and the Melbourne Games (1956), 113, 114–15; and the Moscow Games (1980), 252; and the Sydney Games (2000), 366, 369

Frontera, Jaime, 170

fundraising, 72–74, 154, 179, 264, 265, 274, 441n10; from exhibition games, 14, 19, 35, 47, 72, 74, 124, 268; from qualifying tournaments, 9, 103, 126, 420n29

Fuqua, Richard, 211

Gallardo, Arturo, 259

gambling, 36–37

Games of the New Emerging Forces (GANEFO), 164–65

Garastas, Vladas, 334

Garnett, Kevin, 363, 366, 369, 370; and statistics, 383

Gasol, Marc, 406, 410

Gasol, Pau, 347, 369, 378, 406, 410, 411

Gavitt, Dave, 194–95, 253, 254, 267, 456n74

Georgia, 66, 190

Germany, 141, 340, 346, 408. *See also* Berlin Games (1936)

Giancarlo, Primo, 219

Gibbons, John, and statistics, 26

Ginobli, Manu, xviii, xix, 347, 378, 405, 409, 414

Giudice, Ross, 99

Glasgow, Wayne, 69, 86; and statistics, *88*

Globe Oilers. *See* McPherson Globe Refiners (Oilers)

Globe Refiners. *See* McPherson Globe Refiners (Oilers)

Goebbels, Josef, 5

Gola, Tom, 68

Goldman, Robert, 325, 326, 465n32

Goldstein, Lloyd, 14–15, 421n48

Gomelsky, Alexander ("Silver Fox"), 222, 341, 346, 443n41; and the Mexico City Games (1968), 190, 191; and the Seoul Games (1988), 300–301, 310–11, 312, 313, 317; and the Tokyo Games (1964), 163, 170, 171. *See also* Soviet Olympic Basketball team

Goodrich, Gail, 160

Goodwill Games, 303

Gorbachev, Mikhail, 295, 300, 303

Gordon, Ben, 474n14

Gordon, Lancaster, 267, 271

Gottlieb, Eddie, 96

Goya, Gudina, 56

Granik, Russ, 289–90, 331, 337

Grayer, Jeff, 300; and statistics, *316*

Greek Olympic team, 376, 388, 389, 406

Green, A. C., 266

Gregory, George, 70

Greim, Willard N., 31, 77, 78, 85, 87, 125

Griffith, Darrell, 253, 254

Groza, Alex, 37, 39, 51, 54, 57; and statistics, 59

Grundman, Adolph H., 16, 43, 48, 69, 106

Grunfeld, Ernie, 237, 239; and statistics, 255

Guthridge, Bill, 237

Guttmann, Allen, 33, 193, 419n13

Halberstam, David, 323, 324, 417n6

Haldorson, Burdette, 105, 111, 116, 135; and statistics, *117, 149*

Hamilton, Richard, 374, 379

Hanzlik, Bill, 254; and statistics, *256*

Hardaway, Anfernee, 352, 353; and statistics, *382, 383*

Hardaway, Tim, 364, 366

Harlem Globetrotters, 73–74, 100, 125, 130

Harp, Dick, 236

Harris, Del, 377

Harris, Neil, 51, 55

Hartman, Laura P., 339–40

Haskins, Clem, 212

Haskins, Don, 155, 180, 221, 226

Havlicek, John ("Hondo"), 126, 133, 137, 258, 439n63

Hawkins, Hersey, 298, 299, 300, 310, 313; and statistics, *316*

Hayes, Elvin, 177, 178–79, 198, 284

Haywood, Spencer, 174, 177, 183–85, 188, 189–90, 198–200, 216, 222, 449n85; and endorsements, 176, 205, 284; and the Mexico City Games (1968), 192–93, 195, *196*, 197, 200; and statistics, *200*

Hazzard, Walt, 158, 159, 160, 168, 171; and statistics, *172*

Heathcote, George ("Jud"), 266

height, 30, 34, 38–39, 41, 66, 91, 93–94, 107; rules limiting, 20, 28, 142

Helsinki Games (1952): basketball tournament at the, 74–75, 77–78, 80, 82–83, 84–87; boycotts of the, 75; and the cold war, 63–66, 80–82, 85–86, 87–88; facilities at the, 77, 80, 81; nations participating in the, 61, 74, 76; number of athletes participating in the, 76; Opening Ceremonies of the, 76, 80, 430n61; selection of, as host city, 76–77. See also U.S. Olympic Basketball team (1952)

Henderson, Tom, 214, 216, 217–18, 235, 451n38; and statistics, 232

Hepp, Ferenc, 228

Hidalgo, Marie, 276–77

Hightower, Wayne, 209

Hill, Grant, 352, 353; and statistics, 382

Hitler, Adolf, 4–6, 15, 21, 27, 203

Hoag, Charles, 70; and statistics, 88

Hobson, Howard, 67–68, 74, 85

Hodges, Bill, 321–22

Holman, Nat, 2

Hosket, Bill, 177, 186–87, 188, 191, 192, 212, 247; and the Mexico City Games (1968), 194, 195, 197, 200; and statistics, 200; and the U.S. Olympic Basketball Committee, 247, 268

Hougland, William, 70, 73–74, 78, 86; and the Melbourne Games (1956), 90, 106, 116, 117; and statistics, 88, 117

Houston, Allan, 364, 369; and statistics, 383

Howard, Dwight, 400, 402, 408, 410, 413; and statistics, 415

Hubbard, Phil, 237, 238; and statistics, 255

Hungarian Olympic team, 77, 78, 142

Hwan, Chun Doo, 307–8

Iba, Henry ("Hank"), xv, 38–39, 236, 281; career statistics of, 155–56; and the Mexico City Games (1968), 183–84, 186, 187, 188–89, 191, 192, 197–98, 221; and the Munich Games (1972), 206–7,

209, 211–12, 214, 215, 216–17, 221, 226–27, 441n17; rivalry of, with Phog Allen, 156; and the Tokyo Games (1964), 155–57, 160, 167–68

Imhoff, Darrall, 135, 138; and statistics, 149

Indiana State Teachers' College (Indiana State), 42, 322

Indiana University, 258–59, 260

Indonesia, 164–65, 338, 339, 340, 399, 443n43, 467nn65–66

industrial league teams, 12, 418n11, 420nn23–24; Buchan Bakers, 102–3, 104, 105; Caterpillar Cats, 67, 68–69, 70, 126; Denver Chicago Truckers, 95–96, 123; McPherson Globe Refiners (Oilers), 7–8, 9–11, 14–15, 418n11, 420n24, 421n32; Oakland Bittners, 41, 42, 43, 58, 96; Phillips Oilers, 12, 15–16, 27, 35–36, 37–38, 39–40, 41, 45, 48, 58, 67, 68, 69, 71–72, 94–95, 96, 102–3, 104–5, 422n64. See also National Industrial Basketball League (NIBL)

Inman, Stu, 266

International Amateur Athletic Federation (IAAF), 83

international basketball: and American basketball, 27, 50, 51, 74, 117–18, 124–25, 151, 168–69, 172–73, 210, 249, 361–62, 413–14; development of, 12–13, 31, 119–20, 122–23, 148; popularity of, xix, 4, 33, 117–18, 139, 190; and standard of play, xviii, 2, 55, 58, 106–7, 112–13, 190, 201, 209–10, 229–30, 235–36, 246–47, 255, 269, 294, 315, 345–47, 349, 350–51, 361–63, 371, 381. See also International Basketball Federation (FIBA)

International Basketball Federation (FIBA), 6, 125, 155; and the Congress of Lyon, 20; and eligibility, 288–90, 317, 460n1; and the Helsinki Games (1952) boycott, 75; membership of the, 419n15, 435n66; and the Munich Games (1972), 208; origins of the,

417n2, 419n15; partnerships of the, xiv; and rule changes, xvii, 2, 4, 20, 27–28, 31–32, 59–60, 87, 107, 122–23, 140, 142, 157–58, 255, 257, 412–13. *See also* international basketball

International Basketball Federation (FIBB). *See* International Basketball Federation (FIBA)

International Olympic Committee (IOC), 83, 164, 417n9, 428n9, 473n4; and amateur status, 178; and commercialism, 355; and eligibility guidelines, 288–90; and fundraising, 264; and the gold medal controversy (1972), 229; and the Helsinki Games (1952) boycott, 75; and Olympic host cities, 5–6, 27, 30, 76, 193, 242, 251, 252, 307–8, 364–65, 373, 375, 396–98, 419n16, 454n38, 463n70; and television rights, 444n56, 457n26

Internet, 357, 365, 407–8, 471n50

IOC. *See* International Olympic Committee (IOC)

Irish, Ned, 27, 43

Isaacs, John, 16

Israel, 219, 426n70

Italian Olympic team, 366, 378; and the Los Angeles Games (1984), 278, 280; and the Melbourne Games (1956), 106–7; and the Mexico City Games (1968), 194, 195; and the Montreal Games (1976), 246–47; and the Moscow Games (1980), 254; and the Munich Games (1972), 219, and the Rome Games (1960), 142, 145–46

Italy, 106–7, 219. *See also* Italian Olympic team; Rome Games (1960)

Iverson, Allen, 366, 374, 375, 380–81

Jabbar, Kareem Abdul. *See* Abdul-Jabbar, Kareem (Lew Alcindor)

Jackson, Lucious, 159, 171, 443n42; and statistics, *172*

Jackson, Phil, 18, 134, 357

James, LeBron, 374, 375, 386, 388, 389, 394, 399–400, 402, 406, 409, 410–11, 413; and statistics, *384, 415*

Japan, 50, 150–52, 165–67, 244, 252, 440n4; and shoe companies, 152–53, 338. *See also* Japanese Olympic team; Tokyo Games (1964)

Japanese Olympic team, 31, 60, 142, 169, 218; and the Berlin Games (1936), 21–22; and the Melbourne Games (1956), 112–13

Jasikevicius, Sarunas, 366, 367, 376, 405, 472n56

Jeangerard, Robert, 105, 111; and statistics, *117*

Jefferson, Richard, 374, 380; and statistics, *384*

Jewish athletes, 5, 6–7

Jian, Ma, 342

Jianlian, Yi, 377, 471n53, 473n78

Jiminez, Carlos, 407, 411

Johnson, Earvin ("Magic"), xiv, 127, 199, 253, 261, 270, 289, 329; and the Barcelona Games (1992), 317, 320, 322–23, 332, 333, 340, 341, 343, 346, 348; and endorsements, 327–28, 344; and HIV/AIDS, 322; and statistics, *348*

Johnson, Francis, 15, 25, 421n32; and statistics, *26*

Johnson, Gene, 10, 16, 420n24

Johnson, Marques, 237

Jones, Bobby, 213, 214, 235; and statistics, 232

Jones, Damon, 394

Jones, Dwight, 213, 214, 216, 217, 220, 221, 226, 235; and statistics, 232

Jones, Jerry, 306

Jones, K. C., 98, 99, 100, 105, 107; and statistics, *117*

Jones, R. William, 20, 124, 155, 220, 224–25, 226, 228, 229, 312

Jones, Wallace ("Wah Wah"), 37, 54; and statistics, *59*

Jones, Wally, 159

Jordan, Michael, xiv, xv, 257–58, 261, 282, 289, 323, 326–27, 329, 387, 417n6, 456n4; and the Barcelona Games (1992), 317, 320, 323–24, 340, 343, 348; and the Chicago Bulls, 456n3; and the Los Angeles Games (1984), 267, 268, 270, 278–80, 281–83, 286; and Nike, xviii–xix, 283, 285, 287, 291, 320, 324, 326, 337; and statistics, 286, 348, 459n91

Joyce, Kevin, 213, 222, 226; and statistics, 232

Kaman, Chris, 408

Kanin, David B., 243–44

Kansas, University of. See University of Kansas

Kapono, Jason, 401

Katz, Donald, 324

Keady, Gene, 155, 266, 363, 368

Keller, John, 70; and statistics, 88

Kelley, Allen, 135; and statistics, 149

Kelley, Dean, 70

Kelley, Melvin, and statistics, 88

Kelly, John B., 49

Kemp, Shawn, 353

Kennedy, John F., 124, 150, 153–54

Kennedy, Walter, 178

Kenney, Robert, 68, 70, 77, 82, 86; and statistics, 88

Kentucky, University of. See University of Kentucky

Kerner, Ben, 72

Kerr, Steve, 298, 299

Keys, Barbara, 5, 27, 63, 417n9

Kidd, Jason, 364, 367, 369, 379, 400; and statistics, 383, 415

King, James, 188; and statistics, 200

Kirilenko, Andrei, 405

Kissinger, Henry, 204, 236, 394, 453n11

Klein, Frederick, 346–47, 361

Klein, Ralph, 279

Kleine, Joe, 267, 270; and statistics, 286

Knight, Bob ("The General"), xv, 237, 253, 439n63, 456n7; and the Los Angeles Games (1984), 258–61, 265–69, 270–73, 275, 276–77, 279–80, 281, 461n18

Knight, Phil, 152–53, 176, 284, 292, 338

Knowles, Carl, 25; and statistics, 26

Koide, Koh, 112–13

Kolowich, George J., 95–96

Koncak, Jon, 267, 270; and statistics, 286

Kondrashin, Vladimir, 190, 222, 223–24

Korean War, 70, 76, 131, 151. See also cold war

Korkia, Mikhail, 220

Korkija, Otar, 82, 84, 85, 86, 87, 428n23

Kovalenko, Sergei, 191

Krause, Jerry, 334, 336–37

Kristancic, Boris, 168–69

Krumminch, Ivan ("The Breadwinner"), 93, 94, 122, 123, 144, 168, 171; and the Melbourne Games (1956), xvii, 113, 114, 115, 116

Krussi (Kruus), Heino, 65

Krzyzewski, Mike, xv, 293–94, 334, 347; and the Beijing Games (2008), 387–88, 391, 401, 404, 410–11, 414

Kukoc, Toni, 195, 311, 345, 359; and the Barcelona Games (1992), 334, 335, 336, 343

Kullamit (Kullam), Ilmar, 65

Kupchak, Mitch, 237, 238, 246; and statistics, 255

Kurland, Bob, xvii, 38–39, 46, 49, 90, 96, 156; and the Helsinki Games (1952), 62, 66, 67, 69, 71, 77, 78, 79, 80, 82, 87, 88; and the London Games (1948), 40, 46, 49, 51, 55, 56, 57, 59; and statistics, 59, 88, 431n87

Kurtinaitis, Rimas, 313, 314

Laemmle, Carl, 7, 420n23

Laettner, Christian, 328, 331; and statistics, 348

LaFeber, Walter, xv, 257, 265, 269, 295, 303, 349, 453n11

LaGarde, Tom, 237, 238; and statistics, 255

Lamar, Dwight, 211

Lane, Lester, 135–36, 139–40; and statistics, 149

lanes, basketball court, xvii, 122–23, 241, 369, 412. *See also* court dimensions

Lardner, John, 48

Larmer, Brook, 204, 262, 392

Larson, James F., 307, 308

LaSalle Explorers, 68

Latvia, 13, 65, 93, 341

Lee, Butch, 247

Lee, Spike, 324, 325

Lewis, Rashard, 401, 474n14

Lewis, Troy, 298

Lienhard, William, 70; and statistics, 88

Li Ning (shoe company), 394

Lissov, Ivan, 64

Lister, Alton, 254; and statistics, 256

Lithuania, 11, 12–13, 190, 295, 301, 304, 314–15, 362–63, 404. *See also* Lithuanian Olympic team

Lithuanian Olympic team: and the Athens Games (2004), 13, 363, 376, 380; and the Atlanta Games (1996), 351, 358; and the Barcelona Games (1992), 13, 333–34, 341, 343; and the Helsinki Games (1952), 64–65; and the Sydney Games (2000), 366, 367–69

Lloyd, Earl, 70, 97

London Games (1948): basketball tournament at the, 54–57; facilities at the, 51, 53–54; nations participating in the, 53; number of athletes participating in the, 53; rule changes at the, 31–32; selection of, as host city, 30; and television viewership, 33, 58, 427n98. *See also* U.S. Olympic Basketball team (1948)

London Games (2012), 414

Long, Dallas, 143

Long Island University, 6, 9

Longman, Jere, 291, 470n45

Los Angeles Games (1932), 18, 21

Los Angeles Games (1984), 263, 274, 364; attendance, 277; basketball tournament at the, 276–80, 459n90; boycotts of the, 264, 273–75; broadcast rights to the, 263–64, 265, 457n23, 457n26; and China, 262–63; nations participating in the, 275; number of athletes participating in the, 275; Opening Ceremonies of the, 275–76; and television viewership, 264, 275. *See also* U.S. Olympic Basketball team (1984)

Los Angeles Lakers, 131, 199, 354, 356

Love, Bob, 241

Lovellette, Clyde, xvii, 70, 71–72, 77, 82, 83, 84–85, 86–87, 129, 162, 429nn37–38; benching of, during the Helsinki Games (1952), 78, 80; height of, 66, 71; and statistics, 88, 431n87; at the University of Kansas, 62, 67, 68

Lubin, Frank, 11–12, 14, 15, 23, 421n48; and Lithuanian basketball, 12–13, 65, 362; nicknames of, 11, 12; and statistics, 26

Lucas, Jerry, xiv, 120, 126, 131–35, 138, 144, 146, 258, 439n63; and endorsements, 132; and statistics, 149

Lucas, John, 237

Luisetti, Hank, 31

Lumpp, Ray, 40, 45, 54, 57; and statistics, 59

Lynch, R. G., 94–95

Lyons, G. Russell, 123, 159, 442n37

MacArthur, Douglas, 50, 76, 124, 150–51, 166

Macauley, Ed, 36, 424n17

Mahoney, Jeremiah T., 6

Majerle, Dan, 299, 300, 310

Malone, Karl, 328, 331, 348; and the Atlanta Games (1996), 352, 359, 361; and statistics, *348, 382*

Manhattan College, 42–43

Mann, James, 204, 477n43

Manning, Danny, 266, 293, 298, 300, 312, 313; and the Pan-Am Games, 293; and quitting rumors, 309, 310; and statistics, *316*

Maravich, Pete ("Pistol"), 177, 185–87

Marbury, Stephon, 374, 376, 378, 472n69; and statistics, *384*

Marciulionis, Sarunas, 301, 302–4, 317; and the Atlanta Games (1996), 358; and the Barcelona Games (1992), 334, 343; and the Seoul Games (1988), 313, 314–15

Marion, Shawn, 374, 380; and statistics, *384*

Martin, Bill, 36

Martin, Kenyon, 379

Mathias, Bob, 112

May, Scott, 233, 237, 238, 239, 241, 246; and statistics, *255*

Mays, Willie, 90, 182

McAdoo, Bob, 207, 210

McCabe, Frank, 69; and statistics, *88*

McCaffrey, Pete, 158, 159, 162; and statistics, *172*

McCallum, Jack, 303–4, 305, 328, 336, 353

McClendon, John B., 139, 199, 447n56; as Olympic assistant coach, 160, 162, 183, 184, 188–89

McCormick, Tim, 271

McCray, Rodney, 254; and statistics, *256*

McDonald's Open, 413

McDyess, Antonio, 364; and statistics, *383*

McGinnis, George, 207, 208

McGrady, Tracy, 379

McGregor, Jim, 106

McGuire, Al, 209, 247, 297, 450n23

McHale, Kevin, 268

McMillen, Tom, 210, 212–13, 214, 216, 222, 225, 226, 235; and statistics, 232

McPherson Globe Refiners (Oilers), 7–8, 9–11, 14–15, 418n11, 420n24, 421n32. *See also* industrial league teams

medal rounds: Athens Games (2004), 377, 378–79; Atlanta Games (1996), 359–61; Barcelona Games (1992), 342–44; Beijing Games (2008), 401, 409–11; Berlin Games (1936), 23–24, 25–26; Helsinki Games (1952), 84–85; London Games (1948), 56–57; Los Angeles Games (1984), 279–80; Melbourne Games (1956), 114–15; Mexico City Games (1968), 197–98; Montreal Games (1976), 249–51; Moscow Games (1980), 254–55; Munich Games (1972), 220–29; Rome Games (1960), 146–48; Seoul Games (1988), 312–14; Sydney Games (2000), 369; Tokyo Games (1964), 170–71

media: and the Beijing Games (2008), 397–98; and boycotts, 181; and individual stories, 204, 246, 309; and Jerry Lucas, 132–33; and the Melbourne Games (1956), 112; and qualifying tournaments, 290–91, 293; Russian, 81–82, 83. *See also* television viewership

Meir, Golda, 219

Melbourne Games (1956), 89–90, 99–100; attendance, 108, 111, 113; basketball tournament at the, 112–17; and boycotts, 109, 111; and the cold war, 108–9, 111, 115; facilities at the, 108; nations participating in the, 111; number of athletes participating in the, 111; Opening Ceremonies of the, 109, 111; predictions about the, 106–7; and television viewership, 111–12. *See also* U.S. Olympic Basketball team (1956)

Meneghin, Dino, 280

Merriweather, Joe C., 199

Mexican Olympic team, 74, 423n78; and the Berlin Games (1936), 3, 22, 23; and the London Games (1948), 31, 56, 58

Mexico City Games (1968): attendance, 194, 197; basketball tournament at the, 194–98; boycotts of the, 178, 180–83, 194, 445n22, 448n69; broadcast rights to the, 174; nations participating in the, 174, 194; number of athletes participating in the, 194; Opening Ceremonies of the, 194, 448n72; and political protests, 193, 448n68; and television viewership, 164–65, 194. *See also* U.S. Olympic Basketball team (1968)

Meyer, Ray, 241

Miglinieks, Igors, 333, 341

Mikan, George, 38, 39, 43, 90, 103

Miller, Mike, 389

Miller, Reggie, 352, 359; and statistics, 382

Mills, Patrick, 404

Milwaukee Hawks, 71, 72

Minashvili, Guran, 123

Ming, Yao. *See* Yao Ming

Missouri Valley (Industrial) League, 7. *See also* industrial league teams

Mollins, Carl, 344

Mollner, Art, 6–7, 15, 17, 20, 21, 26–27, 419n14; and statistics, 26

Montreal Games (1976): basketball tournament at the, 246–51, 455n56; and boycotts, 242–44; broadcast rights to the, 245; and the cold war, 234–36, 242; facilities at the, 242–43, 246; selection of, as host city, 454n38; and shoe companies, 234; and television viewership, 245–46. *See also* U.S. Olympic Basketball team (1976)

Moran, Mike, 309, 337

Moscow Games (1980): basketball tournament at the, 253, 254–55; boycotts of the, 251–54, 455n64; broadcast rights to the, 253; selection of, as host city, 242, 251. *See also* Soviet Union; U.S. Olympic Basketball team (1980)

Mount, Rick, 177, 185–86, 187

Mourning, Alonzo, 299, 364, 369, 371; and statistics, 383

Mullin, Chris: and the Barcelona Games (1992), 328, 348; and the Los Angeles Games (1984), 270, 278, 280, 286; and Nike, 320; and statistics, 286, 348

Mullins, Jeff, 158, 159, 170; and statistics, 172

Munich Games (1972): attendance, 202, 217, 220; basketball tournament at the, 216–29, 451n54; broadcast rights to the, 203; and the cold war, 230–32; facilities at the, 202; and gold medal final controversy, 220, 223–29; nations participating in the, 202; number of athletes participating in the, 202; Opening Ceremonies of the, 202–3; and television viewership, 203–5; terrorist attack at the, 203, 219, 452n58. *See also* U.S. Olympic Basketball team (1972)

Murphy, Calvin, 177, 185, 187

Murray, Jim, 199, 200, 253

Naismith, James, xv, xvi, 8

Naismith Memorial Basketball Hall of Fame, 98, 195, 292, 352, 387

Nash, Cotton, 158

Nash, Steve, xviii, xix

Nater, Swen, 212, 213, 214–16, 236

National Amateur Athletic Union Basketball League (NABL), 188, 207. *See also* National Industrial Basketball League (NIBL)

National Association of Basketball Coaches (NABC), 102, 124

National Association of Intercollegiate
Athletics (NAIA), 36, 126
National Association of International
Basketball (NAIB), 36, 42–43.
See also National Association of
Intercollegiate Athletics (NAIA)
National Basketball Association (NBA):
and African American coaches, 101;
and African American players, 42, 44,
97, 101; and amateur classification,
178, 206–7, 288–90, 317, 344–45,
351–52, 413, 464n93, 464n96; image
of the, 269–70, 283; and international
growth, 289, 295–96, 319, 363, 395–96,
413–14; international players in the,
xix, 231, 248, 269, 289, 294–95, 296,
303–4, 372, 471n53, 472n56, 472n63;
and merchandise sales, 319, 354–55,
386; and Olympic eligibility, 288–89,
344–45, 351–52, 413, 464n94, 464n96;
popularity of the, 124, 253; rivalry of
the, with the ABA, 179–80; and rule
changes, 381, 413; and salaries, 71,
95–96, 101, 162, 178, 205, 429n38; and
the shot clock, 87, 255; and television
viewership, 296. *See also* Amateur
Athletic Union (AAU); American
Basketball Association (ABA);
international basketball
National Broadcasting Company (NBC).
See NBC
National Collegiate Athletic Association
(NCAA), 6, 8–9, 102; and gambling,
37; and qualifying tournaments,
35, 36, 39, 102, 104–5, 126, 157, 206,
420n25; and racism, 42, 43, 70; rivalry
of, with the AAU, 19, 124–25, 137, 150,
154, 157, 235, 437n20; and television
viewership, 177, 206, 253, 268. *See
also* Amateur Athletic Union (AAU);
American Basketball Association of
the United States of America (ABA/
USA); college basketball

National Industrial Basketball League
(NIBL), 67, 71, 94, 95, 123, 124, 139,
207. *See also* Amateur Athletic Union
(AAU); industrial league teams
National Olympics Day, 89–90
Navarro, Juan, 407
Nazi party, 4–7. *See also* Berlin Games
(1936)
NBA. *See* National Basketball Association
(NBA)
NBC, 167, 253, 308–9, 357, 365, 407–8,
444n56, 469n24, 471n50. *See also*
television viewership
NCAA. *See* National Collegiate Athletic
Association (NCAA)
Needles, Jim ("Jimmy"), xv, 16–18, 22, 25,
26–27, 127
Nelson, Donn, 334, 341, 367, 368, 372, 376
Newell, Pete, xv, xvii, 28, 31, 154, 236,
266, 294, 369; and Bob Knight, 259;
defensive strategies of, 127, 144;
offensive strategies of, 17–18; and the
Rome Games (1960), 120, 122, 123,
126–27, 131, 136–40, 141–42, 143–44,
146, 148, 439n66
"New Order Olympics." *See* Barcelona
Games (1992)
Newton, C. M., 266, 330, 352
New York Knicks, 41, 43, 134, 161–62, 199
NIBL. *See* National Industrial Basketball
League (NIBL)
Nichols, Hank, 268
Niedler, Bill, 143
Nike, 50, 173, 176, 234, 283, 284, 292, 295,
315, 317, 326, 337, 392, 393; advertising
campaigns of, xviii–xix, 283–85, 291,
320, 324, 402, 465n32; Air Jordans,
285, 287, 326; and the Dream Team
(1992), 320, 337; and innovation, 285,
287, 325, 401–2; and Japan, 152–53;
and labor practices, 337–40, 398–99,
402–4, 467n66, 478n52, 479n54; and
the Nike Pro Club, 284, 460n104; and

the Redeem Team (2008), 401–2; and sales, 285, 287, 339, 393; summer basketball program of, 381. *See also* shoe companies

Nixon, Richard, 204

Nocioni, Andres, 378, 409

North Korea, 165, 463n70

Novosel, Mike, 249

Nowitzki, Dirk, xviii, xix, 347, 369, 404, 408, 414

Nye, Joseph, 308, 463n74

Oakland Bittners, 41, 42, 43, 58, 96. *See also* industrial league teams

O'Connor, Frank ("Bucky"), 434n59

Odom, Lamar, 374, 380–81; and statistics, 384

offenses: ball-control tactics, 84; Drake Shuffle, 106; false-motion, 18; figure-eight, 23, 25; four-corner, 18; motion, 260, 269, 369; reverse-action, 17–18, 127. *See also* defenses

Ohio State University, 126, 132–33

Okafor, Emeka, 374; and statistics, 384

Oklahoma A&M (Oklahoma State), 38, 39, 155, 156

Olajuwon, Hakeem, 258, 352, 355; and statistics, 382

Olderman, Murray, 96

Olympic movement, xiv, xvi, 5, 417n9. *See also specific Olympic host cities;* sports

O'Neal, Jermaine, 371, 379

O'Neal, Shaquille ("Shaq"), 328, 352, 354, 355–56, 394; and statistics, 355, 382

Onitsuka Company, 152–53. *See also* shoe companies

Organization of Petroleum Exporting Countries (OPEC), 236

Owens, Jesse, 27, 73, 182

Pachoutine, Evgueni, 367

Padilla, Ambrosie, 142

Pan-Am Games, 210–11, 212, 217, 241, 259, 293, 306, 443n42

Papson, Stephen, 325, 326, 465n32

Parish, Robert, 237, 268

Park, Heung-soo, 307, 308

Parker, Tony, 413

Paul, Chris, 386, 400, 401, 409, 413; and statistics, 415

Paulauskas, Modestas, 218–19

Pavlov, Sergei, 201, 454n38

Payne, Tom, 45

Payton, Gary, 352, 353, 364, 366, 369, 370; and statistics, 382, 383

Peng-san, Hang, 276

Peoria Caterpillar Cats. *See* Caterpillar Cats

Perkins, Sam, 266, 270, 275, 278, 280; and statistics, 286, 459n91

Perry, Hal, 98

Person, Chuck, 266

Peruvian Olympic team, 56, 168

Peterson, Dan, 301

Petri, Peter, 307

Petrov, Aleksandr, 173

Petrovic, Drazen, 280, 311–12, 334, 335, 336, 343

Phelps, Digger, 240

Phelps, Michael, 386, 408

Philippine Olympic team, 31, 59, 113, 142, 194; and the Berlin Games (1936), 3, 22, 23, 31, 59, 113, 142, 194

Phillips, Frank, 36

Phillips 66ers. *See* Phillips Oilers

Phillips Oilers, 12, 15, 35–36, 41, 45, 46, 58, 69, 71–72, 422n64; AAU championships won by the, 16; and amateur classification, 48, 94–95; and exhibition games, 27; and qualifying tournaments, 37–38, 39–40, 67, 68, 102–3, 104–5. *See also* industrial league teams

Pierce, Frank, 11, 12, 14, 16–17

Pierce, Paul, 371

Pinckney, Ed, 266, 458n43

Piper, Don, and statistics, 26

Pippen, Scottie, 329; and the Atlanta Games (1996), 352, 353, 354, 382; and the Barcelona Games (1992), 328, 336–37, 340, 348; and Nike, 320; and statistics, 348, 382

Pippin, Dan, 69, 77, 82; and statistics, 88

Pitts, R. C., 40, 54; and statistics, 59

Poland, 23, 228

pop culture. See cultural currency

Popovich, Gregg, 374, 387

Porter, Terry, 458n43

Pound, Richard, 120, 417n9, 463n75

Price, Mark, 458n43

Prince, Tayshaun, 400–401; and statistics, 415

Puerto Rican Olympic team: and the Athens Games (2004), 374, 375, 376; and the Barcelona Games (1992), 342–43; and the Mexico City Games (1968), 194, 195; and the Montreal Games (1976), 246–47; and the Munich Games (1972), 218; and the Rome Games (1960), 143; and the Seoul Games (1988), 312; and the Tokyo Games (1964), 168, 169–70

Puerto Rico, 259. See also Puerto Rican Olympic team

Puma, 173, 176, 205, 234, 284, 445n7, 450n12. See also shoe companies

Purnell, Oliver, 374

Putmaker, Arvo, 65

qualifying tournaments: in 1936, 8–11, 420n25; in 1948, 35–36, 37–38, 39–40; in 1952, 66–69, 429n24; in 1956, 102–3, 104–5; in 1960, 126; in 1964, 157, 158–59, 441n19; in 1968, 183–84, 185–87, 447n42; in 1972, 206–9, 212–14; in 1976, 237–38; in 1980, 254; in 1984, 266–68; in 1988, 290–91, 293, 297–99; and advertising, 103; and fundraising, 9, 103, 126, 420n29. See also exhibition games

racism, 44, 45–47, 100–102, 127–29, 132, 231, 433n39. See also African American players

Radja, Dino, 195, 334, 335, 336

Ragland, Jack, 15, 25l; and statistics, 26

Rand, Terry, 96

Ratleff, Ed, 213, 214, 216, 218, 221; and statistics, 232

Raveling, George, 266, 292–93, 298, 456n4

Ray, Cliff, 241

Reagan, Ronald, 274, 275, 294, 295, 308

Redd, Michael, 389–90, 400, 401, 408; and statistics, 415, 474n14

Reddick, J. J., 389

Redeem Team. See U.S. Olympic Basketball team (2008)

Reebok, 291, 295, 337, 366, 392, 393. See also shoe companies

Reed, Willis, 160, 266, 442n27, 443n42

Reid, J. R., 300, 310; and statistics, 316

Reid, Robert, 268

Reilly, Joseph A., 19, 422n54

Reinsdorf, Jerry, 336

Renick, Jesse ("Cab"), 40, 47; and statistics, 59

Reyes, Felipe, 407, 410

Rhoden, William, 461n18

Ri, Sohaku, 18

Rice, Glen, 298

Richardson, Nolan, 155

Richmond, Mitch, 293, 300, 352; and statistics, 316, 382

Rigaudeau, Antoine, 369

Righetto, Renato, 224, 228

Riley, Pat, 180

Rivers, David, 298

Robertson, Alvin, 270; and statistics, 286

Robertson, Oscar ("The Big O"), xiv, xvii, 191, 216; and racism, 127–29, 132;

and the Rome Games (1960), 120, 126, 135, 136, 137, 138, 141–42, 143, 144, 145, 146, *147*, 148, 149; and statistics, 127, *149*; at the University of Cincinnati, 130

Robeson, Paul, 70

Robinson, David: and the Atlanta Games (1996), 352; and the Barcelona Games (1992), 328–29, 348; and endorsements, 292, 315, 317, 320, 325, 327; and the Pan-Am Games, 293; and the Seoul Games (1988), 297–98, 299, 300, 305, 309, 310, 315, 316; and statistics, *316, 348, 382*

Robinson, Glenn, 129, 352

Robinson, Robert ("Jackie"), 36, 37, 40, 45–46, *52*, 53–55; at Baylor University, 29–30; meeting King George VI, 29, 424n1; and statistics, *59*

Rodgers, Guy, 97

Rodis, Nicholas, 154

Rodman, Dennis, 330

Rogge, Jacques, 396–97

Rollins, Kenny, 37, 54; and statistics, *59*

Rome Games (1960): attendance, 141, 143, 145; basketball tournament at the, 141–48; broadcast rights to the, 120, 167; and the cold war, 143–45, 153; facilities at the, 140–41, 143, 145; nations participating in the, 140; number of athletes participating in the, 140; Opening Ceremonies of the, 120, 140–41; and politics, 141; and television viewership, 119, 120, 121, 141. *See also* U.S. Olympic Basketball team (1960)

Rosenblatt, Roger, 279

Rossini, Lou, 170

Row, Dee, 254

Rubio, Ricky, 407

Ruby, Earl, 55, 56, 58

rules, basketball: at the Berlin Games (1936), 20; center-jump, 28; and changes, xvi–xvii, 2, 4, 20, 27–28, 31–32, 59–60, 87, 107, 122–23, 140, 142, 157–58, 180, 255, 257, 381, 412–13; and court dimensions, 31, 158, 241, 257, 369, 412, 435n66; and fouls, 31, 87, 140, 157–58, 210, 255; and height, 20, 28, 41; at the London Games (1948), 31–32, 51, 55, 59–60; at the Los Angeles Games (1984), 257; shot clock, 31, 87, 107, 140, 158, 255, 257, 420n18; substitutions, 2, 55, 57; ten-second, 28; three seconds in the lane, 2, 20, 28, 31, 60, 257, 420n18; timeouts, 158, 223–24; and the trapezoid-shaped lane, 122–23, 241, 369, 412

Rupp, Adolph, 37, 41, 46, 51, 56, 155, 168–69, 180, 185; and Don Barksdale, 44–45

Russell, Bill, xiv, *110*, 127–28, 433n33; and the African American boycott movement, 182; influence of, xvii, 90, 369; meeting President Eisenhower, 90, 100; and the Melbourne Games (1956), 99–100, 102, 103, 104–5, 107, 112, 113, 114, 115, 116–18; and racism, 100–102, 127–28, 433n39; and statistics, *117*; at the University of San Francisco, 97–99

Russia, 33, 50, 404; and the Sydney Games (2000), 366–67. *See also* Soviet Union

Sabonis, Aryvidas, 13, 303, 369; and the Atlanta Games (1996), 358; and the Barcelona Games (1992), 334; and the Seoul Games (1988), 293, 294–95, 296, 301, 312, 313, 314

salaries, 71, 95–96, 101, 162, 178, 205, 209, 429n38; and the AAU, 43, 71–72, 94. *See also* endorsements

Samaranch, Juan Antonio, 273–74, 277, 355, 470n45

San Francisco, University of. *See* University of San Francisco

Saperstein, Abe, 73, 100, 130

satellites, 166–67, 175, 203–4, 231, 246, 261–62, 365, 471n48; and the cold war, 119, 121, 244–45, 265. *See also* technological advances; television viewership

Saulters, Glynn, 188; and statistics, *200*

Schabinger, A. A., 8–9, 420n25

Schenkel, Chris, 222, 225–26

Schmidt, Oscar, 312, 340–41, 345–46, 359

Schmidt, Willard, 15, 16, 20; and statistics, *26*

Schrempf, Detlef, 279, 340

Schwartz, Harry, 63–64

Scola, Luis, 409

scoring, xvii, 84, 157, 255, 260; at the Barcelona Games (1992), 340, 343; at the London Games (1948), 30; at the Los Angeles Games (1984), 278; at the Melbourne Games (1956), 106, 113, 117; at the Montreal Games (1976), 246–47; at the Munich Games (1972), 221–22, 441n17; at the Rome Games (1960), 146–47, 148; at the Tokyo Games (1964), 169

Scott, Charlie, 183, 187–88, 189–90, 446n33; and statistics, *200*

Semashko, Nikolai, 162–63

Seoul Games (1988): basketball tournament at the, 309–14; broadcast rights to the, 308; and the cold war, 294, 302–3; facilities at the, 306; Opening Ceremonies of the, 308; scheduling of the, 297; selection of, as host city, 306–8; and television viewership, 308–9, 463n77. *See also* U.S. Olympic Basketball team (1988)

Shapiro, Carl, 307

Sharmukhamedov, Alshan, 224

Sheppard, Steve, 237; and statistics, *255*

Sheridan, Chris, 391, 401, 404, 407, 409, 472n69

Shipp, Jerry, 159, 162, 443n42; and statistics, *172*

shoe companies, xvii, 143, 152–53, 175–76, 251, 392–94; Adidas, 152, 173, 176, 233–34, 284, 295, 333, 392, 393, 445n7, 453n3, 460n104; and controversies, 337, 343; Converse, 24–25, 33, 58–59, 73, 103–4, 115–16, 152, 167, 173, 176, 233–34, 283–84, 291, 343, 434n50, 460n104; and endorsements, 175–76, 205, 284–85, 287, 324–26, 343, 460n104; and labor practices, 337–40, 398–99, 402–4, 466n66, 478n52, 479n54; Puma, 173, 176, 205, 234, 284, 445n7, 450n12; and qualifying tournaments, 291, 292; Reebok, 291, 295, 337, 366, 392, 393; sales of, 103. *See also* Nike

shot clock, 31, 87, 107, 140, 158, 255, 420n18. *See also* rules, basketball

Shy, Carl, and statistics, *26*

Silas, Paul, 158, 284

Silliman, Michael, 188, 195, 448n76; and statistics, *200*

Skansi, Peter, 333

slam dunks. *See* dunk shot

Smith, Adrian, 135, 138, 139–40; and statistics, *149*

Smith, Charles D., 300; and statistics, *316*

Smith, Charles E., IV, 300, 305, 309, 310; and statistics, *316*

Smith, Dean, xv, 18, 253, 260, 387, 456n74; and the Montreal Games (1976), 233, 236–37, 238, 239, 240–41, 246, 248, 249

Smith, Kenny, 266

Smith, Red, 4, 203, 251

Smith, Sonny, 272, 273, 458n63

Smith, Steve, 364; and statistics, *383*

Soares, Togo, 217

Sokk, Tiit, 301–2, 313

Songalia, Darius, 368, 472n56

South Korea, 169, 306–8, 338, 463n70

Souza, Marcel, 312, 341, 346

Soviet Olympic Basketball team: of 1952, 64–66, 75, 77, 80, 82–83, 84, 85–87, 428n23; of 1956, 104, 107, 111, 113–16,

118; of 1960, 123–24, 142–45, 148, 162–63; of 1964, 162, 163, 168, 169, 170–72; of 1968, 190, 191, 197; of 1972, 218–19, 220–29, 230–31, 451n54; of 1976, 246–47, 248, 249; of 1980, 254; of 1988, 293, 295, 296, 300, 301–2, 311, 312–14, *314*; and Lithuanian players, 13, 64–65, 295, 314–15, 333–34. *See also* Soviet Union; Unified Team (1992)

Soviet Union, 33–34, 121–23, 294–95, 302–3; and Afghanistan, 252; and the All-Union Ministry of Physical Culture and Sports, 63; basketball stadiums in, 190; and boycott of Los Angeles Games (1984), 264, 273–75; and Czechoslovakia, 193; exhibition games in the, 162, 189–90, 245, 304–5, 442n37; and exhibition games in the United States, 235–36; joining the IOC, 428n9; and Olympic participation, xvi–xvii, 60, 61–65, 80–81, 87–88, 153, 200–201; and the Spartakiad, 90–91, 93, 251–52; and the Suez Canal crisis, 109. *See also* Russia; Soviet Olympic Basketball team

Spain, Ken, 188, 189, 191, 194; and statistics, *200*

Spalding, 33, 59, 73, 78, 103

Spandarian, Stepan, 122, 124, 144, 162–63

Spanish Olympic team, 21, 109, 140, 194; and the Athens Games (2004), 377, 378; and the Beijing Games (2008), 401, 406–7, 410–11; and the Los Angeles Games (1984), 278–79, *280*; and the Munich Games (1972), 218; and the Seoul Games (1988), 309

Spanoulis, Vasileios, 388

Spartakiad, 90–91, 93, 251–52

speed of play, xviii, 2, 119–20, 148–49, 255, 418n3; and college basketball, 2; and fast-break tactics, 10, 28, 99, 236; and rule changes, xvi, 2, 4, 28, 59–60, 87, 107, 140, 157–58, 257; and Soviet

Olympic teams, 114, 116, 122, 123, 144–45, 168, 201, 222, 249; and U.S. Olympic teams, 30, 106, 116, 139, 145, 201, 211, 248, 249, 276, 381, 407, 459

sports: and China, 262, 276, 341–42, 391–93, 395–96, 457n18; and the cold war, 33–34, 76, 121, 143–45, 153–55, 163–64, 230, 243–44; Nazi attitudes toward, 4–5, 27; Soviet attitudes toward, 34, 61, 62–64, 65, 81–82, 83, 87, 90–91, 153, 154, 162, 200–201, 300–301, 428n5, 428n13, 431n89, 455n66; and technological advances, 175, 244–45, 261

Sports Ministry. *See* All-Union Ministry of Physical Culture and Sports (Sports Ministry)

Squires, La Vannes, 70, 429n36

Stalin, Joseph, xvi, 34, 61, 63, 65, 89

Stankovic, Borislav ("Boris"), 224, 288–90, 317, 319–20, 460n1

Staubo, Jan, 193

Stein, Bill, 297

Steinbrenner, George, 333

Stern, David, 270, 305, 317, 351, 369, 371, 379; and international basketball, 289, 295–96, 319, 363. *See also* National Basketball Association (NBA)

Stockton, John, 267; and the Atlanta Games (1996), 352, 382; and the Barcelona Games (1992), 328, 331, 340, 348; and Nike, 320; and statistics, *348*, *382*

Stonkous, Stassis, 93, 94, 114

Stoudemire, Amar'e, 374, 375, 400; and statistics, *384*

Suez Canal crisis, 109. *See also* cold war

Sullivan, Bloomer, 69

Summers, W. K., 227

Sutton, Eddie, 155

Swanson, Duane, and statistics, *26*

Swift, E. M., 270, 326–27

Sydney Games (2000), 470n45;

Sydney Games (*cont.*)
attendance, 366; basketball tournament at the, 363, 365–69; broadcast rights to the, 365; nations participating in the, 365; number of athletes participating in the, 365; selection of, as host city, 364–65; and television viewership, 365, 471n49. *See also* U.S. Olympic Basketball team (2000)

Taiwan, 75, 141, 165, 242–43, 262, 338
Takez, Bozhidar, 144
Tarakanov, Sergei, 302
Tax, Jeremiah, 127, 132, 138
Taylor, Chuck, 24. *See also* Chuck Taylor All-Star shoes
Taylor, Emmet, 182
technological advances, 418n14; and American businesses, 357–58; and the Atlanta Games (1996), 357–58; and the cold war, 119, 121; and the Internet, 357, 365, 407–8, 471n50; and leisure time, 32, 175; and the London Games (1948), 30; and the Mexico City Games (1968), 175; and mobile phones, 470n27; and the Munich Games (1972), 203; and personal computers, 264–65; and the Rome Games (1960), 119; and satellites, 119, 121, 166–67, 175, 203–4, 231, 244–45, 246, 261–62, 265, 365, 471n48; and the Tokyo Games (1964), 166–67
television viewership, xiv, xvii, 21; Atlanta Games (1996), 357; Barcelona Games (1992), 347; Beijing Games (2008), xiv, 395, 407–8; Berlin Games (1936), 21; and the cold war, 121; and exhibition games, 216, 245; London Games (1948), 33, 58, 427n98; Los Angeles Games (1984), 264, 275; Melbourne Games (1956), 111–12; Mexico City Games (1968), 164–65,

194; Montreal Games (1976), 245–46; Munich Games (1972), 203–5; and the NBA, 296; and the NCAA, 177, 206, 253, 268; Rome Games (1960), 119, 120, 121, 141; Seoul Games (1988), 308–9, 463n77; Sydney Games (2000), 365, 471n49; Tokyo Games (1964), 166–67. *See also* broadcast rights; media
terrorism attack, Palestinian, 203, 219, 452n58. *See also* Munich Games (1972)
Terry, Jason, 474n14
The-chu, Mu ("Mr. Mu"), 276
Thomas, Isiah, 254, 268, 330, 331, 456n76; and statistics, 256
Thompson, David, 207
Thompson, John, xv, 237, 269, 317; and the Seoul Games (1988), 290–93, 294, 295, 296–97, 305–6, 309–11, 315
Thorn, Rod, 271, 330, 331
three-point shot, 179–80
timeouts, 158, 223–24. *See also* rules, basketball
Tisdale, Wayman, 266, 269, 270, 459n91; and statistics, 286
Tkachenko, Vladimir, 249
Tokyo Games (1964): attendance, 165; basketball tournament at the, 167–72; boycotts of the, 165, 182; broadcast rights to the, 167; and the cold war, 163–64; facilities at the, 151–52, 443n50; nations participating in the, 165; number of athletes participating in the, 165; Opening Ceremonies of the, 165, 166, 167; and politics, 163–66; and the shoe industry, 153; and television viewership, 166–67. *See also* U.S. Olympic Basketball team (1964)
Tomjanovich, Rudy, xv, 284, 363
Tomsic, Ron, 105, 107, 111, 114, 115; and statistics 117
Tournament of Americas, 331–32, 340–41
Trade Union Games, 62

tryouts. *See* qualifying tournaments

Tucker, Gerald, 93–94, 106, 107, 112, 113, 114–15, 116

Turner, Jeff, 270; and statistics, 286

Turner, Ted, 231, 245, 303–5

Turpin, Melvin, 266

UCLA, 10, 42, 177, 181, 182, 447n42

Ueberroth, Heidi, 395

Ueberroth, Peter, 265, 274

Unified Team (1992), 333, 334, 341, 342, 343. *See also* Soviet Olympic Basketball team

United States Olympic Association (USOA), 35, 47, 69

Universal Pictures team, 7–8, 9–12, 13–15, 16–17, 26–27, 418n11, 420n23

University of Kansas, 67–68, 69–71, 429n24

University of Kentucky, 36, 37, 39, 40, 45, 180, 185

University of San Francisco, 97–99, 102, 127

Unseld, Wes, 45, 177

Uruguayan Olympic team, 107, 168; and the Helsinki Games (1952), 74, 78, 80, 84, 85; and the London Games (1948), 56; and the Los Angeles Games (1984), 277; and the Melbourne Games (1956), 115; and the Rome Games (1960), 142

USA Basketball, 268, 319, 320, 330–31, 332, 353, 354–55, 358, 379, 381, 386, 390, 402. *See also* U.S. Olympic Basketball Committee

U.S. Armed Forces, 103, 105, 188, 207

USOC. *See* U.S. Olympic Committee (USOC)

U.S. Olympic Basketball Committee, 34–35, 51, 67–68, 105, 155, 208, 253, 268, 330, 387; and fundraising, 9, 74, 154; and qualifying tournaments, 9, 103, 126; and racial issues, 101–2,

180; and rule changes, 28. *See also* qualifying tournaments; USA Basketball

U.S. Olympic Basketball team (1936): and boycott, 6–7, 13–14; coaching staff of the, 16–19, 26–27; and fundraising, 14; gold medal won by, 1, 26–27; and the Olympic basketball tournament, 21, 22–24, 25–26; and qualifying trials, 8–11, 420n25; roster of the, 11–12, 14–16; shoes worn by the, 24–25; sponsorship of the, 7, 26; and statistics, 26; and travel arrangements, 19–20. *See also* Berlin Games (1936)

U.S. Olympic Basketball team (1948), 49, 57; and African American players, 41–42, 44, 45–47; and aggressive play, 55–56; coaching staff of the, 41, 44–45, 46, 51, 56; and exhibition games, 45–47, 50–51; gold medal won by, 57–58; height of the, 30, 34; and the Olympic basketball tournament, 54–57; and qualifying trials, 35–36, 37–38, 39–40; roster of the, 40–42, 44–45, 54; shoes worn by the, 59; speed of the, 30; and statistics, 59; and travel arrangements, 48–49, 50–51. *See also* London Games (1948)

U.S. Olympic Basketball team (1952): coaching staff of the, 69, 74; and exhibition games, 72; gold medal won by, 86; and the Olympic basketball tournament, 74, 77–78, 80, 82–83, 84–87; and qualifying trials, 66–69, 429n24; roster of the, 62, 69–70, 71–72; shoes worn by the, 73; and statistics, 88; and travel arrangements, 74. *See also* Helsinki Games (1952)

U.S. Olympic Basketball team (1956): and African American players, 100, 105; coaching staff of the, 106, 434n59; and exhibition games, 102, 106; giving shoes to the Soviet team, 104, 115–16;

U.S. Olympic Basketball team (1956) (*cont.*)
gold medal won by, 116–17; and the Olympic basketball tournament, 112–17; predictions about the, 106–7; and qualifying trials, 102–3, 104–5; reputation of the, 116–17, 436n101; roster of the, 99–100, 105–6, 107, 434n57; shoes worn by the, 104; and statistics, 117. *See also* Melbourne Games (1956)

U.S. Olympic Basketball team (1960): coaching staff of the, 123, 126–27, 136–38, 140, 142, 144; and exhibition games, 138–39; gold medal won by, 146, 148; and the Olympic basketball tournament, 141–48; and qualifying trials, 126; reputation of the, 148; roster of the, 130–38, 439n66; and statistics, 149; training of the, 136, 139–40. *See also* Rome Games (1960)

U.S. Olympic Basketball team (1964): coaching staff of the, 155–57, 160, 167–68; and exhibition games, 162, 442n37; gold medal won by, 171; and the Olympic basketball tournament, 167–72; predictions about the, 167, 170; and qualifying trials, 157, 158–59, 441n19; reputation of the, 160, 163; roster of the, 159–62; and statistics, 172. *See also* Tokyo Games (1964)

U.S. Olympic Basketball team (1968): coaching staff of the, 183–84, 186, 187, 188–89, 192, 197–98; and exhibition games, 189–90; gold medal won by, 198; and the Olympic basketball tournament, 194–98; predictions about the, 177, 191–92; and qualifying trials, 183–84, 185–87, 447n42; roster of the, 177, 185–88, 192–93; and statistics, 200; training of the, 188–89, 192–93. *See also* Mexico City Games (1968)

U.S. Olympic Basketball team (1972), 225; coaching staff of the, 206–7, 209, 211–12, 214, 215, 216–17, 221, 226–27; concerns about the, 209–11, 216, 217, 441n17; and exhibition games, 216; and the Olympic basketball tournament, 216–18, 219–28; and qualifying trials, 206–9, 212–14; roster of the, 206, 213–16, 235–36, 450n16; silver medal won by the, 228–29; and statistics, 221–22, 232; training of the, 215–16. *See also* Munich Games (1972)

U.S. Olympic Basketball team (1976): coaching staff of the, 236–37, 240–41, 248; concerns about the, 239; and exhibition games, 241; gold medal won by the, 251; and the Olympic basketball tournament, 246–51, 455n56; predictions about the, 240–41, 246; and qualifying trials, 237–38; roster of the, 237–41; and statistics, 255. *See also* Montreal Games (1976)

U.S. Olympic Basketball team (1980): coaching staff of the, 253–54; and exhibition games, 254, 456n76; and qualifying trials, 254; roster of the, 254, 456n74; and statistics, 256. *See also* Moscow Games (1980)

U.S. Olympic Basketball team (1984): coaching staff of the, 258–61, 265–66, 270–73, 281; and exhibition games, 268–69; gold medal won by the, 280–81; and the Olympic basketball tournament, 276–80, 459n90; predictions about the, 260; and qualifying trials, 266–68; roster of the, 261, 266–69, 270–73; and statistics, 286. *See also* Los Angeles Games (1984)

U.S. Olympic Basketball team (1988): bronze medal won by the, 314; coaching staff of the, 290–93, 294, 295, 296–97, 305–6, 309–11, 315; concerns about the, 305, 306; and exhibition games, 298–99, 305–6; legacy of the, 289, 317; and the Olympic basketball tournament, 309–13; and qualifying trials, 290–91, 293, 297–99; roster of the, 297, 299–300; and statistics, 300, 316; training of the, 305. *See also* Seoul Games (1988)

U.S. Olympic Basketball team (1992), 329; coaching staff of the, 329–30; criticisms of the, 344–46; gold medal won by the, 343–44; and the Olympic basketball tournament, 335, 336–37, 340, 341, 342–43; popularity of the, xv, xvii–xviii, 318–20, 332–33, 336, 346–47; and promotional partners, 320, 332; and Reebok and Nike controversy, 337, 343; roster of the, 320–24, 328–29, 330–31, 335–36; and statistics, 343, 347, 348; and the "Tournament of Americas," 331–32, 340–41; training of the, 332. *See also* Barcelona Games (1992)

U.S. Olympic Basketball team (1996): and charitable work, 355; coaching staff of the, 352–53; criticisms of the, 350–51, 353–54, 358; gold medal won by the, 361; and the Olympic basketball tournament, 350–51, 358–61; roster of the, 352, 353, 355–57; and statistics, 351, 361, 382. *See also* Atlanta Games (1996)

U.S. Olympic Basketball team (2000): coaching staff of the, 363; criticisms of the, 364, 367–68; gold medal won by, 369; and the Olympic basketball tournament, 365–69; roster of the, 363–64; and statistics, 351, 383. *See also* Sydney Games (2000)

U.S. Olympic Basketball team (2004): bronze medal won by the, 374, 380; coaching staff of the, 374–75; concerns about the, 371, 374–75; and the Olympic basketball tournament, 374–75, 376, 377, 378–79; roster of the, 373–75, 379–80; and statistics, 351, 384; training of the, 379. *See also* Athens Games (2004)

U.S. Olympic Basketball team (2008), 385–86; coaching staff of the, 387–88, 410–11; criticisms of the, 388, 401, 404, 411–12; and exhibition games, 404; gold medal won by the, 411; and human rights, 399–400; image of the, 386–87; and international contract possibilities, 390; and Nike, 401–2; and the Olympic basketball tournament, 394–95, 405–11; popularity of the, 386, 408; roster of the, 386, 387–90, 400–401; and statistics, 404, 406, 415; and travel arrangements, 404. *See also* Beijing Games (2008)

U.S. Olympic Committee (USOC), 6, 7, 8, 72, 74, 154, 351–52, 419n16, 464n96. *See also* International Olympic Committee (IOC); USA Basketball

Vaccaro, Sonny, 291–93
Valdmanis, Maidon, 123
Valentine, Darnell, 254; and statistics, 256
Valjtin, Albert, 143
Vaughn, Hank, 160, 162, 163, 188–89
Vetra, Gundars, 333
Vinogradov, Georg, 22
Voljov, Genidin, 144
Volnov, Gennardi, 162, 218
Votchkarez, Arkadi, 93, 94, 114
Vranes, Danny, 254; and statistics, 256

Wade, Dwyane, xiv–xv, 374, 413; and the Beijing Games (2008), 386, 387–88, 400, 408, 409, 410–11, 415; and endorsements, 389, 392; and statistics, 384, 415
Walker, Clarence, 426n46

Walker, Leroy, 351
Walker, Wally, 237
Wall, Bill, 290–91, 293
Wallace, Ben, 371, 379
Walsh, James, 105; and statistics, 117
Walsh, Patrick J., 6
Walton, Bill, 207–8, 215, 236, 345, 450n19
Warren, Mike, 192, 447n42
Washington, Dwayne ("Pearl"), 458n43
Washington, Kermit, 213, 450n16
Weber, Roger, 144
Weimar Republic, 5
Weinberg, Larry, 295
Weis, Frederic, 367
Weisman, Michael, 308–9
Wells, Clifford, 104, 434n50
Welp, Christian, 279
West, Jerry ("Zeke from Cabin
    Creek"), 126, 130–31, 259, 387; and
    endorsements, 205; and the Rome
    Games (1960), 120, 135, 138, 140, 143,
    144, 145, 148; and statistics, 142, 146,
    149
West German Olympic team, 252, 279–
    80, 459n90
Westphal, Paul, 209, 210
Wheatley, William, and statistics, 26
White, Joseph ("JoJo"), 183, 188, 195, 197,
    198, 222; and statistics, 200, 448n76
Wieden & Kennedy, 283, 315, 326, 339. See
    also Nike
Wilke, Lou, 34–35, 47, 50–51, 95
Wilkens, Lenny, xv, 137, 315, 352–53, 359,
    362
Wilkerson, Bob, 239
Williams, Charles ("Buck"), 254, 271,
    456n76; and statistics, 256
Williams, Deron, 400, 401; and statistics,
    415
Williams, Howard ("Howie"), 68, 69,
    429n31; and statistics, 88
Williams, Leon, 170, 441n19
Williams, Roy, 374

Wilson, Charles, 185
Wilson, George, 158, 159, 169, 442n23;
    and statistics, 172
Wokutch, Richard E., 339–40
Wolff, Scott, 290–91, 296, 310–11
Womble, Warren, 69, 74, 77, 78, 80, 84;
    and the Rome Games (1960), 126, 127
Wood, Al, 254; and statistics, 256
Wood, Leon, 267, 270, 272, 278, 283; and
    statistics, 286
Wooden, John, xv, 42, 129, 158, 186, 260,
    352; and integration, 182, 426n46
Woolpert, Phil, 98–99, 434n59
World Championships, 122, 190, 207–8,
    209, 222, 271, 353, 371, 387–89, 390
World Games, 188
World University Games, 293
World War II, 28, 29–30, 32, 53, 76
Worrel, Johnny, 22

Yao Ming, 76, 263, 342, 372, 386, 404,
    414; and the Athens Games (2004),
    377–78; and endorsements, 392; and
    the Sydney Games (2000), 365–66
Yao Zhiyuan, 263
YMCA, 8, 22, 35, 67
Yoshinaga, Sayuri, 151–52
Yugoslavian Olympic team, 142, 189,
    210, 334–35, 451n54; and the Atlanta
    Games (1996), 359–61; and the Los
    Angeles Games (1984), 278, 280;
    and the Mexico City Games (1968),
    194–95, 197–98; and the Montreal
    Games (1976), 247, 248, 249–51; and
    the Moscow Games (1980), 254–55;
    and the Seoul Games (1988), 293–94,
    311–12, 314; and the Tokyo Games
    (1964), 168–69

Zeravica, Ranko, 197, 198, 255
Zhizhi, Wang, 342, 372–73
Zirin, David, 388
Zubkov, Viktor, 122, 123, 144